# FINANCIAL ACCOUNTING

## An International Introduction

**PEARSON**

We work with leading authors to develop the strongest educational materials in accounting, bringing cutting-edge thinking and best learning practice to a global market.

Under a range of well-known imprints, including Financial Times Prentice Hall, we craft high-quality print and electronic publications which help readers to understand and apply their content, whether studying or at work.

To find out more about the complete range of our publishing, please visit us on the World Wide Web at: **www.pearsoned.co.uk**

**Fourth edition**

# FINANCIAL ACCOUNTING
## An International Introduction

David Alexander and
Christopher Nobes

with an Appendix on Double-entry Bookkeeping
by Anne Ullathorne

**Financial Times
Prentice Hall
is an imprint of**

Harlow, England • London • New York • Boston • San Francisco • Toronto • Sydney • Singapore • Hong Kong
Tokyo • Seoul • Taipei • New Delhi • Cape Town • Madrid • Mexico City • Amsterdam • Munich • Paris • Milan

**Pearson Education Limited**

Edinburgh Gate
Harlow
Essex CM20 2JE
England

and Associated Companies throughout the world

*Visit us on the World Wide Web at:*
www.pearsoned.co.uk

———————————————

First published 2001
Second edition published 2004
Third edition published 2007
**Fourth edition published 2010**

© Pearson Education Limited 2001, 2010

ISBN: 978-0-273-72164-2

**British Library Cataloguing-in-Publication Data**
A catalogue record for this book is available from the British Library

**Library of Congress Cataloging-in-Publication Data**
Alexander, David, 1941–
   Financial accounting : an international introduction / David Alexander and Christopher Nobes ;
with an appendix on double-entry bookkeeping by Anne Ullathorne. – 4th ed.
      p. cm.
   ISBN 978-0-273-72164-2 (pbk.)
1. International business enterprises–Finance.   2. Accounting.   3. Financial statements.   I. Nobes,
Christopher.   II. Title.
   HF5686.I56A427 2010
   657–dc22

                                                                                    2010004228

10  9  8  7  6  5  4  3  2  1
14  13  12  11  10

Typeset in 9.5/12.5pt Stone Serif by 35
Printed and bound by Ashford Colour Press, Gosport

*The publisher's policy is to use paper manufactured from sustainable forests.*

# Contents

**Foreword to the first edition**                                    xi
**Preface**                                                          xiii
**Acknowledgements**                                                 xv
**Abbreviations**                                                    xvi


## Part 1 THE CONTEXT OF ACCOUNTING                                  1

### 1  Introduction                                                  3

Objectives                                                           3

1.1  Purposes and users of accounting                                4
1.2  Accounting regulation and the accountancy profession            7
1.3  Language                                                        9
1.4  Excitement in accounting                                        10
1.5  The path ahead                                                  10

Summary                                                              11
Exercises                                                            11

### 2  Some fundamentals                                             13

Objectives                                                           13

2.1  Introduction                                                    14
2.2  The balance sheet                                               14
2.3  The income statement                                            21
2.4  Two simple equations                                            27
2.5  How cash flows fit in                                           29

Summary                                                              30
Exercises                                                            30

### 3  Frameworks and concepts                                       34

Objectives                                                           34

3.1  Introduction                                                    35
3.2  Underlying concepts                                             37
3.3  The IASB's concepts                                             38
3.4  A hierarchy of concepts and some inconsistencies                42
3.5  Possible future developments                                    44

Summary                                                              44
References and research                                              45
Exercises                                                            45

### 4   The regulation of accounting    47

Objectives    47

4.1   Introduction: various ways to regulate accounting    48
4.2   Legal systems    48
4.3   Entities    50
4.4   Examples of regulation    53
4.5   The regulation of International Standards    58

Summary    59
References and research    59
Exercises    60

### 5   International differences and harmonization    61

Objectives    61

5.1   Introduction: the international nature of the development of accounting    62
5.2   Classification    63
5.3   Influences on differences    70
5.4   Harmonization in the European Union    80
5.5   The International Accounting Standards Board    85

Summary    89
References and research    90
Exercises    91

### 6   The contents of financial statements    93

Objectives    93

6.1   Introduction    94
6.2   Balance sheets (statements of financial position)    95
6.3   Comprehensive income    101
6.4   Statements of changes in equity    108
6.5   Cash flow statements    108
6.6   Notes to the financial statements    110
6.7   Other general disclosure requirements    110

Summary    113
References and research    114
Exercises    114

### 7   Financial statement analysis    115

Objectives    115

7.1   Introduction    116
7.2   Ratios and percentages    116
7.3   Profit ratios    119
7.4   Profitability ratios    122
7.5   Liquidity ratios    129
7.6   Interest cover    130

| | | |
|---|---|---:|
| 7.7 | Funds' management ratios | 131 |
| 7.8 | Introduction to investment ratios | 133 |
| 7.9 | Some general issues | 135 |
| | Summary | 136 |
| | Exercises | 137 |

## Part 2 FINANCIAL REPORTING ISSUES 143

### 8 Recognition and measurement of the elements of financial statements 145

| | | |
|---|---|---:|
| | Objectives | 145 |
| 8.1 | Introduction | 146 |
| 8.2 | Primacy of definitions | 146 |
| 8.3 | Hierarchy of decisions | 148 |
| 8.4 | Income recognition | 157 |
| | Summary | 160 |
| | References and research | 161 |
| | Exercises | 161 |

### 9 Tangible and intangible fixed assets 162

| | | |
|---|---|---:|
| | Objectives | 162 |
| 9.1 | Preamble: a tale of two companies | 163 |
| 9.2 | Introduction | 164 |
| 9.3 | The recognition of assets | 165 |
| 9.4 | Should leased assets be recognized? | 167 |
| 9.5 | Depreciation of cost | 170 |
| 9.6 | Impairment | 182 |
| 9.7 | Measurement based on revaluation | 185 |
| 9.8 | Investment properties | 188 |
| | Summary | 189 |
| | References and research | 190 |
| | Exercises | 190 |

### 10 Inventories 193

| | | |
|---|---|---:|
| | Objectives | 193 |
| 10.1 | Introduction | 194 |
| 10.2 | Counting inventory | 196 |
| 10.3 | Valuation of inventory at historical cost | 197 |
| 10.4 | Inventory flow | 198 |
| 10.5 | Other cost methods | 203 |
| 10.6 | Valuation of inventory using output values | 204 |
| 10.7 | Practice | 204 |
| 10.8 | Current replacement cost | 206 |

10.9   Construction contracts                                        206
10.10  Construction contracts in practice                            209

Summary                                                              211
References and research                                              211
Exercises                                                            211

**11  Financial assets, liabilities and equity**                    **214**
Objectives                                                           214

11.1   Introduction                                                  215
11.2   Cash and receivables                                          215
11.3   Investments                                                   218
11.4   Liabilities                                                   221
11.5   Equity                                                        226
11.6   Reserves and provisions                                       229
11.7   Comparisons of debt and equity                                232

Summary                                                              233
References and research                                              234
Exercises                                                            234

**12  Accounting and taxation**                                      **235**
Objectives                                                           235

12.1   Introduction                                                  236
12.2   International differences in the determination of taxable income  238
12.3   Tax rates and tax expense                                     240
12.4   Deferred tax                                                  241

Summary                                                              247
References and research                                              247
Exercises                                                            248

**13  Cash flow statements**                                         **249**
Objectives                                                           249

13.1   Introduction                                                  250
13.2   An outline of the IAS 7 approach                              251
13.3   Reporting cash flows from operating activities                253
13.4   The preparation of cash flow statements                       254
13.5   A real example                                                260

Summary                                                              260
References and research                                              260
Exercises                                                            262

**14  Group accounting**                                             **263**
Objectives                                                           263

14.1   Introduction: the group                                       264
14.2   Investments related to the group                              267

14.3  Accounting for the group    270
14.4  Uniting of interests    279
14.5  Proportional consolidation    280
14.6  The equity method    281
14.7  Conclusion on group relationships    283

Summary    284
References and research    284
Exercises    285

**15  Foreign currency translation**    **288**

Objectives    288

15.1  Introduction    289
15.2  Transactions    289
15.3  Translation of financial statements    292
15.4  A numerical illustration    294

Summary    295
References and research    296
Exercises    296

**16  Accounting for price changes**    **298**

Objectives    298

16.1  Introduction    299
16.2  Effects of price changes on accounting    299
16.3  European disagreement    305
16.4  General or specific adjustment    305
16.5  General price-level adjusted systems    310
16.6  Current value accounting    312
16.7  Mixed values – deprival value    316
16.8  Partial adjustments    319
16.9  Fair values    320

Summary    321
References and research    322
Exercises    322

**Part 3 ANALYSIS**    **327**

**17  Financial appraisal**    **329**

Objectives    329

17.1  Introduction    330
17.2  More on investment ratios    330
17.3  Interpreting the balance sheet    336
17.4  Valuation through expectations    339

17.5    Valuation through market values                                340
17.6    Accounting policies and financial appraisal                    341
Summary                                                                349
References and research                                                349
Exercises                                                             350

**18   International analysis                                          354**
Objectives                                                            354

18.1    Introduction                                                   355
18.2    Language                                                       355
18.3    Differences in financial culture                              359
18.4    Accounting differences                                        360
18.5    Help by multinationals                                        361
18.6    Increasing international harmonization                         361

Summary                                                                365
References and research                                                365
Exercises                                                             366
Annex: GlaxoSmithKline plc: Note on reconciliation from IFRS to US GAAP   367

**Appendices                                                           373**
**A  Double-entry bookkeeping                                          375**
**B  An outline of the content of International Financial**
    **Reporting Standards                                              420**
**C  An outline of the content of the EU's Fourth Directive**
    **on Company Law (as amended in 2001, 2003, etc.)                  431**
**D  Feedback on exercises                                            433**

**Glossary of terms                                                    451**
**Index                                                                469**

# Foreword to the first edition

For many years Professor Christopher Nobes and I have worked together as the two British representatives on the Board of the International Accounting Standards Committee. He and I have argued in many fora for the notion that there should be one single set of high quality worldwide standards so that a transaction occurring in Stuttgart, Sheffield, Seattle or Sydney should be treated in exactly the same way. That is not the case at present.

In a book recently published by Professor Christopher Nobes and David Cairns, 'The Convergence Handbook', they outlined the existing differences between British and International Accounting Standards. The intention of the book and the request by the UK's Accounting Standards Board for its production was to eliminate these differences. It is particularly important this should be done over the next five years as the European Commission has stated its intention that all consolidated statements of Listed Companies in the European Union should comply with International Accounting Standards by 2005. Clearly British Standards will have to change, although as British Standards themselves are of high quality it is very likely that some International Standards will also change.

To meet this challenge and to ensure that all countries have the same accounting standards, the International Accounting Standards Committee has been reconstituted with effect from 2001 to form a virtually full-time International Accounting Standards Board whose main mission is to seek convergence of accounting standards throughout the world.

This book by my friends, David Alexander and Christopher Nobes, is therefore particularly timely. It is based on a background in the European Union. It is written extremely clearly. (The real mark of a teacher is not to complicate but to simplify and the authors have certainly done that.) It is unusual in that it takes as its base not one country's standards but International Accounting Standards, which I firmly believe are going to be the worldwide requirements of the future.

The book will be of interest not only to the beginner but to those who wish to understand the thrust of International Accounting Standards. The authors make clear that accounting is still in many ways a primitive subject and is in a period of change, removing the most irrelevant aspects of the historical cost model and replacing them with accounting for fair values. Those coming into accounting now are going to see huge changes in the first few years of their careers as many of the ideas promulgated by academics many years ago become professional practice and as each country's national standards are changed to converge with the international consensus.

I enjoyed reading this book and I am sure that its many readers will also. I congratulate the authors for their foresight in producing such an excellent book and wish them well.

SIR DAVID TWEEDIE

January 2001                          *Chairman, International Accounting Standards Board*

# Preface

This is the fourth edition of our book that is designed as an introductory text in financial accounting. What sets it apart from many other books with that basic aim is that this book is not set in any one national context. Consequently, instead of references to national laws, standards or practices, the main reference point is International Financial Reporting Standards (IFRS).

Nevertheless, real entities operate in real countries even where they follow IFRS, and so such entities also operate within national laws, tax systems, financial cultures, etc. One of the backgrounds chosen in this book is the European Union (EU) and the wider European Economic Area (EEA). Where useful, we refer to the rules or practices of particular European countries or companies. However, we also take examples from elsewhere, e.g. Australia.

This book is intended for those with little or no previous knowledge of financial accounting. It might be particularly appropriate for the following types of financial accounting courses taught in English at the undergraduate or post-graduate (e.g. MBA) level:

- courses in any country in the EU (or EEA), given the increasing use of IFRS by companies including the compulsory use for listed companies' consolidated statements;
- courses outside the EU where IFRS are a relevant reference point, e.g. in Australia, New Zealand, Singapore and other parts of the (British) Commonwealth;
- courses in China or other countries where standards have been converged with IFRS;
- courses anywhere in the world with a mixture of students from several different countries.

Depending on the objectives of teachers and students, stress (or lack of it) might be placed on particular parts of this book. For example, it would be possible to precede or accompany a course based on this book with an extensive examination of double-entry bookkeeping, such that Appendix A is unnecessary. Or, on some courses, there might not be space or appetite for coverage of issues such as foreign currency translation (Chapter 15) or accounting for price changes (Chapter 16).

This edition is updated for the extensive changes of the three years since writing the third edition. In writing this book we have, of course, made use of our experience over many years of writing and teaching in an international context. Thus, in some places we have adapted and updated material that we have used elsewhere in more specialist books to which the intended readers of this text would not have easy access. We have tried to remove British biases, but we may not have been fully successful and we apologize to readers who can still detect some.

There are four appendices, which we hope readers will find useful during and after a course based on this book. Appendix A is a substantial treatment of double-entry bookkeeping. Appendices B and C summarize the requirements of IFRS and the EU Fourth Directive respectively. Appendix D provides outline feedback to the first two of each chapter's closing exercises. Feedback on the other exercises is given in an Instructor's Manual that is available electronically via the Companion Website at **www.pearsoned.co.uk/alexander**. The manual also contains other material to assist lecturers. This book ends with a glossary and an index.

In preparing the first edition, we were greatly assisted by comments from an apparently tireless team of reviewers, listed immediately hereafter. Certain reviewers have commented further this time. We are also grateful for much help from colleagues at Pearson. Despite all this help, there may be errors and omissions in our book, and for this we must be debited (in your books).

DAVID ALEXANDER
*University of Birmingham*

CHRISTOPHER NOBES
*Royal Holloway, University of London*

## Reviewers

This book has benefited very much from the advice and critical evaluation of the following reviewers, whose comments throughout the preparation of various editions are greatly appreciated:

Simon Pallett – University of Newcastle

Jim Hanly – Dublin Institute of Technology

Noreen Dawes – London Metropolitan University

Fredrik Ljungdahl – Jönköping International Business School

Deborah Lewis – Swansea University

Robert Major – University of Portsmouth

# Acknowledgements

We are grateful to the following for permission to reproduce copyright material:

**Figures**
Figure 5.2 adapted from A judgemental international classification of financial reporting practices, *Journal of Business Finance and Accounting*, Spring (Nobes, C. 1983); Figure 5.3 adapted from Towards a general model of the reasons for international differences in financial reporting, *Abacus*, Vol. 34, No. 2 (Nobes, C. 1998); Figures 6.1, 6.2, 12.1, 13.6 adapted from *Bayer Annual Report 2008*; Figures 7.5, 8.7 adapted from *Marks and Spencer plc Annual Report 2009*; Figure 8.5 from *CEPSA Consolidated Statement of Income for the Year Ended 31 December 1998*; Figures 18.1, 18.2 from *GlaxoSmithKline plc Annual Report 2005*.

**Tables**
Table 4.2 adapted from *Plan Comptable Général* (Conseil National de la Comptabilité); Table 5.2 from *The Accounting Review* (Nair and Frank 1980) © American Accounting Association; Table 5.14 adapted from *University of Reading Discussion Papers in Accounting, Finance and Banking* (Zambon, S. and Dick, W. 1998) No. 58; Tables 9.8, 10.13 adapted from *European Survey of Published Accounts 1991*, Routledge (FEE 1991); Table 14.6 adapted from extracts from published company financial statements, reproduced with the kind permission of Astrazeneca UK Ltd; Table 18.1 adapted from BT Group plc Annual Reports 1999 and 2008; Table 18.2 from *Comparative International Accounting*, Financial Times Prentice Hall (S.J. McLeay in C.W. Nobes and R.H. Parker (eds) 2008) Chapter 18; Table 18.3 after *Norsk Hydro Annual Reports, 1991, 1993, 2005*.

**Text**
Extracts on pages 148, 180, 218, 291 from BASF published parent financial statements and Annual Report of BASF 2008; extract on page 186 from ING 2008 statements; extract on page 341 from Bayer Annual Report 2005; Chapter 18 Annex from *GlaxoSmithKline plc Annual Report 2005*.

In some instances we have been unable to trace the owners of copyright material, and we would appreciate any information that would enable us to do so.

# Abbreviations

| | |
|---|---|
| ABC | activity-based costing |
| AE | anonymos etairia (public company, Greece – transliteration of Greek equivalent) |
| AG | *Aktiengesellschaft* (public company, Austria, Germany and Switzerland) |
| AktG | *Aktiengesetz* (German Stock Corporation Law) |
| AMF | *Autorité des Marchés Financiers* (France) |
| ApS | *anspartsselskab* (private company, Denmark) |
| ARC | Accounting Regulatory Committee (EU) |
| AS | *aktieselskab* (public company, Denmark) |
| | *aksjeselskap* (private company, Norway) |
| ASA | *almennaksjeselskap* (public company, Norway) |
| ASB | Accounting Standards Board (UK) |
| BV | *besloten vennootschap* (private company, Belgium and the Netherlands) |
| CESR | Committee of European Securities Regulators |
| COB | *Commission des Opérations de Bourse* (former Commission for Stock Exchange Operations, France) |
| CoCoA | continuously contemporary accounting |
| CONSOB | *Commissione Nazionale per le Società e la Borsa* (National Commission for Companies and the Stock Exchange, Italy) |
| CPP | current purchasing power |
| CRC | current replacement cost |
| CV | current value |
| DCF | discounted cash flow |
| DRSC | *Deutches Rechnungslegungs Standards Committee* (German Regulatory Standards Committee) |
| DV | deprival value |
| EBIT | earnings before interest and tax |
| EEA | European Economic Area |
| EFRAG | European Financial Reporting Advisory Group |
| EPE | etairia periorismenis efthynis (private company, Greece – transliteration of Greek equivalent) |
| EPS | earnings per share |

| | |
|---|---|
| EU | European Union |
| EV | economic value |
| FAR | *Föreningen Auktorisade Revisorer* (a national accountancy body, Sweden) |
| FASB | Financial Accounting Standards Board (USA) |
| FIFO | first in, first out |
| FRRP | Financial Reporting Review Panel (UK) |
| GAAP | generally accepted accounting principles |
| GmbH | *Gesellschaft mit beschränker Haftung* (private company, Austria, Germany and Switzerland) |
| GPLA | general price level adjusted |
| HC | historical cost |
| HGB | *Handelsgesetzbuch* (Commercial Code, Germany) |
| IAS | International Accounting Standard |
| IASB | International Accounting Standards Board |
| IASC | International Accounting Standards Committee |
| IASCF | International Accounting Standards Committee Foundation |
| IFAC | International Federation of Accountants |
| IFRIC | International Financial Reporting Interpretations Committee |
| IFRS | International Financial Reporting Standard(s) |
| IOSCO | International Organization of Securities Commissions |
| JV | joint venture |
| Lda | *sociedade por quotas* (private company, Portugal) |
| LIFO | last in, first out |
| Ltd | private limited company (United Kingdom) |
| NBV | net book value |
| NRV | net realizable value |
| NV | *naamloze vennootschap* (public company, Belgium and the Netherlands) |
| NYSE | New York Stock Exchange |
| OCI | other comprehensive income |
| Oy | *Osakeyhtiö-yksityinen* (private company, Finland) |
| Oyj | *Osakeyhtiö julkinen* (public company, Finland) |
| PE | price/earnings |
| PCG | *plan comptable général* (general accounting plan, France) |
| plc | public limited company (United Kingdom) |
| PPE | property, plant and equipment |
| RC | replacement cost |

| | |
|---|---|
| RJ | *Raad voor de Jaarverslaggeving* (Council for Annual Reporting, the Netherlands) |
| ROCE | return on capital employed |
| ROE | return on equity |
| ROOE | return on ordinary owners' equity |
| SA | *sociedade anónima* (public company, Portugal)<br>*sociedad anónima* (public company, Spain)<br>*société anonyme* (public company, Belgium, France and Luxembourg) |
| Sarl | *société à responsabilité limitée* (private limited company, Belgium, France and Luxembourg) |
| SEC | Securities and Exchange Commission (USA) |
| SIC | Standing Interpretations Committee (former IASC body) |
| SMEs | small and medium-sized entities |
| SOX | Sarbanes–Oxley Act (USA) |
| STRGL | statement of total recognized gains and losses |
| SpA | *società per azioni* (public company, Italy) |
| SRL | *società à responsabilità limitata* (private company, Italy)<br>*sociedad de responsabilidad limitada* (private company, Spain) |
| SRS | *Svenska Revisorssamfundet* (a Swedish accountancy body) |
| TFV | true and fair view |
| UK | United Kingdom |
| US | United States |

# Part 1

# THE CONTEXT OF ACCOUNTING

**1** Introduction

**2** Some fundamentals

**3** Frameworks and concepts

**4** The regulation of accounting

**5** International differences and harmonization

**6** The contents of financial statements

**7** Financial statement analysis

# Chapter 1

# Introduction

| Contents | | |
|---|---|---|
| 1.1 | Purposes and users of accounting | 4 |
| 1.2 | Accounting regulation and the accountancy profession | 7 |
| 1.3 | Language | 9 |
| 1.4 | Excitement in accounting | 10 |
| 1.5 | The path ahead | 10 |
| | Summary | 11 |
| | Exercises | 11 |

**Objectives**  After studying this chapter carefully, you should be able to:

- explain the scope and uses of accounting;
- outline the role of national and international regulators;
- give some examples of the usages of accounting terms in different varieties of English.

## 1.1  Purposes and users of accounting

There is no single authoritative and generally accepted definition of financial accounting, or of accounting in general. Accounting began as a practical activity in response to perceived needs, and for most of its development it has progressed in the same way, adapting to meet changes in the demands made on it. Where the needs differed in different countries or environments, accounting tended to develop in different ways as a response to a particular environment, essentially on the Darwinian principle: useful accounting survived. Because accounting developed in different ways, it is likely that definitions suggested in different surroundings will vary.

At a general level, accounting exists to provide a service. In the box below there are three definitions. These have all been taken from the same economic and cultural source (the United States) because that country has the longest history of attempting explicit definitions of this type. Note that each suggested definition seems broader than the previous one, and the third one does not restrict accounting to *financially* quantifiable information. Many would not accept this last point. As will be explored in this book, attitudes to accounting and its role differ substantially around the world and certainly between European countries.

---

**Some definitions of accounting**

Accounting is the art of recording, classifying and summarizing in a significant manner and in terms of money, transactions and events which are, in part at least, of a financial character, and interpreting the results thereof.

'Review and Resume', *Accounting Terminology Bulletin No. 1* (New York: American Institute of Certified Public Accountants, 1953), paragraph 5.

Accounting is the process of identifying, measuring and communicating economic information to permit informed judgements and decisions by users of the information.

American Accounting Association, *A Statement of Basic Accounting Theory* (Evanston, IL: American Accounting Association, 1966), p.1.

Accounting is a service activity. Its function is to provide quantitative information, primarily financial in nature, about economic entities that is intended to be useful in making economic decisions, in making resolved choices among alternative courses of action.

Accounting Principles Board, Statement No. 4, 'Basic Concepts and Accounting Principles Underlying Financial Statements or Business Enterprises' (New York: American Institute of Certified Public Accountants, 1970), paragraph 40.

---

If information is to be useful, then some obvious questions arise: useful to whom and for what purposes? A number of different types of people are likely to be dealing with business entities:

1. *Managers.* These are the people who have to take decisions, both day-to-day and strategically, about how the scarce resources within their control are to be used. They need information that will enable them to predict the likely outcomes of alternative courses of action. As part of this process, they need feedback on

the results of their previous decisions in order to extend successful aspects of the decisions, and to adapt and improve the unsuccessful aspects.

2. *Investors*. A large entity may have many investors who are not the managers of the entity. Some investors are owners (the shareholders); others provide long-term debt capital. These providers of capital are concerned with the risk inherent in, and return provided by, their investments. They need to determine whether they should buy, hold or sell their investments. Shareholders are also interested in information to assess the ability of the entity to pay them a return (known as a dividend). Potential investors have similar interests.

3. *Other lenders*. Lenders (such as banks) are interested in whether loans, and the interest attaching to them, will be paid when due.

4. *Employees*. Employees and their representative groups are interested in the profitability of their employers. They also want to assess the ability of the entity to continue to provide remuneration, retirement benefits and employment opportunities.

5. *Suppliers*. These want to be able to assess whether amounts owing will be paid when due. Suppliers are likely to be interested in an entity over a shorter period than lenders, unless they depend upon the entity as a major continuing customer.

6. *Customers*. Customers need information about the continuance of an entity, especially when they have a long-term involvement with the entity.

7. *Governments*. Governments and their agencies need information in order to regulate the activities of entities and to collect taxation, and as the basis for national income and similar statistics.

8. *Public*. Entities affect members of the public in a variety of ways; for example, entities pollute the atmosphere or despoil the countryside. Accounting statements (generally called 'financial statements') may give the public information about the trends and recent developments of the entity and the range of its activities.

This list leads to a very important distinction, namely that between *management accounting* and *financial accounting*. Management accounting is that branch of accounting concerned with the provision of information intended to be useful to management within the business. Financial accounting is the branch of accounting intended for users outside the business itself, i.e. groups 2–8 above. The above descriptions of these groups is closely based on a document called *Framework for the Preparation and Presentation of Financial Statements* of the International Accounting Standards Board (IASB), discussed further in Chapter 3.

It is clear from the previous paragraphs that the needs of users to whom financial accounting is addressed are very diverse, and so the same information will not necessarily be valid for all their purposes. Nevertheless, it is usually assumed that one set of financial statements in the public domain should be able to satisfy most needs. The IASB Framework (paragraph 10) goes on to assert that:

> While all of the information needs of these users cannot be met by financial statements, there are needs which are common to all users. As investors are providers of risk capital to the enterprise, the provision of financial statements that meet their needs will also meet most of the needs of other users that financial statements can satisfy.

This last sentence would earn a fail mark on any course in logic or philosophy, but the view is widely followed in practice; that is, financial reporting is seen by the IASB as largely designed to supply investors with useful information. Accepting, however, that the needs of different users are likely to be different and that different users may predominate in different countries, it is clear that different national environments (cultural, political and economic) are likely to lead to different accounting practices. Indeed, financial reporting to various users (as opposed to the mere recording of transactions, which is known as bookkeeping) reflects the biases and norms of the societies in which it is embedded. This relationship is developed later in Chapter 5.

| Activity 1.A | In what various ways can and should financial reporting (the end product of financial accounting) be different from reporting to management? Think about the different purposes of these two types of accounting, and how these purposes affect their operation. |
|---|---|

| Feedback | Management accounting can be carried out on the basis that no information need be kept secret for commercial reasons and that the preparers will have no incentive to disguise the truth. This is because the management is giving information to itself. So, the information does not need to be externally checked. It can be more detailed and more frequent than for financial reporting because there is no expense of external checking or publication. Also, the management will not want any biases, whereas some outside users may prefer a tendency to understate profits and values where there is uncertainty. Management may be happy for many estimates about the future to be made, which might be too subjective for external reporting. Indeed, some management accounting figures involve forecasting all the important figures for the *next* year, whereas financial reporting concentrates on the immediate past. |
|---|---|
| | Another point is that there do not need to be any rules imposed on management accounting, because management can trust itself. By contrast, financial reporting probably works best with some clear rules from outside the entity in order to control the management and help towards comparability of one entity with another. |

Having distinguished financial accounting from management accounting, there are some further possible confusions to address. The function of external *auditing* is quite separate from that of financial accounting. Auditing is a control mechanism designed to provide an external and independent check on the financial statements and reports published by those entities. Financial reports on the state of affairs and the past results of entities are prepared by accountants under the control of the managers of the entities, and then the validity of the statements is assessed by auditors. The wording used by auditors in their reports on financial statements varies considerably between countries, and the meaning and significance of the words that they use varies even more. There is inevitably some conflict between the necessity for an auditor to keep the management of the entity happy, and the necessity for provision of an expert and independent check. A study of auditing is outside the scope of this book, but the reader from any particular country should note that the role, objectives and effectiveness of the audit function in other countries may differ from those of his or her experience. For example, in Japan, the statutory auditors of most companies are not required to be either expert or independent; in contrast, in some other countries, statutory auditors have to comply with stringent technical and independence requirements.

Another set of distinctions which must be made clear are those between *finance*, *financial management* and *financial accounting*. Very broadly, finance is concerned with the optimal means of *raising* money, financial management is concerned with the optimal means of *using* it, and financial accounting is the reporting on the results from having used it. Finally, financial accounting must be carefully distinguished from bookkeeping. *Bookkeeping* underlies other types of accounting. It is about recording the data – about keeping records of money and financially related movements. It is financial accounting (and management accounting) that takes these raw data, and then chooses and presents them as appropriate for various purposes. It is financial accounting that acts as the *communicating* process to those outside the entity.

## 1.2  Accounting regulation and the accountancy profession

**Activity 1.B**   How should the provision of accounting information to users outside the entity be controlled? Think of as many regulators and ways of regulating as you can.

**Feedback**   Accounting could be regulated in many ways, for example by:

- the market
- the government, through ministries
- parliament, through laws or codes
- a stock exchange
- a governmental regulator of stock exchanges
- the accountancy profession
- a committee of members from large companies
- an independent foundation or trust.

Two extreme answers to the question of regulation can be envisaged. The first is that it should be determined purely by market forces. A potential supplier of finance will be more willing to supply it if a business gives relevant and reliable information about how and by whom the finance will be used. So, a business providing a good quality and quantity of financial information will obtain more and cheaper finance. Therefore, entities have their own market-induced incentive to provide accounting information that meets the needs of users. The second extreme answer is that the whole process should be regulated entirely by the 'state', and some legal or bureaucratic body should specify what is to be reported and should provide an enforcement mechanism.

Neither extreme is consistent with modern capitalist-based economies, but the balance adopted between the two varies quite sharply around the world. The points mentioned so far in this section only consider the market and the state, but there is a third important force to consider, namely the private sector, including the accountancy profession.

The profession is organized into associations under national jurisdictions. For example, the European Union requires two types of organization: qualifying bodies (which set exams and might set technical rules) and regulatory bodies (which are under government control and which supervise statutory audit). In some countries, such as the United Kingdom, various accountancy bodies are allowed to fulfil both roles, and many members of the profession do not work as auditors. In some other countries, such as France and Germany, the roles are fulfilled by separate bodies of 'accountants' and 'auditors', e.g. in France by *experts comptables* and *commissaires aux comptes* respectively. Professional bodies are responsible for monitoring the activities of their members and for standards of both general ethics and professional competence. However, in some countries the profession also takes on much of the role of *creating* the auditing rules under which its members will operate. In some countries (e.g. Australia, Denmark, the Netherlands, the United Kingdom and the United States), the rules that govern how entities perform their financial reporting are also set by professional bodies or by independent private-sector committees of accountants and others (as standard setters).

There is now widespread agreement within EU member states, and others elsewhere, of the need for carefully thought-out comprehensive regulation. This statement leaves open two important points of detail. The first is the extent to which comprehensive regulation needs to be flexible in detailed application, or (alternatively) to be precise but inflexible. The second is the relative position and importance of state regulation (e.g. Companies Acts or Commercial Codes) compared with private-sector regulation (e.g. accounting standards). As will be seen later (particularly in Chapter 4), differences in attitudes to both these questions can be significant in their effects on accounting practice in different jurisdictions.

The coordinating organization for the accountancy profession around the world is the International Federation of Accountants (IFAC). Its stated purpose is 'to develop and enhance a coordinated world-wide accountancy profession with harmonized standards'. International auditing standards are produced by IFAC's International Auditing and Assurance Standards Board. An important aspect of IFAC was its relationship with the IASB and its predecessor, the International Accounting Standards Committee (IASC). The latter was created in 1973 and, until 2001, all member bodies of IFAC were automatically members of IASC.

As discussed in more detail in Chapter 5, with effect from 2001 the International Accounting Standards Committee and the organisations surrounding it were completely restructured. The old IASC disappeared and was replaced by the IASC Foundation whose main operating arm is the International Accounting Standards Board (IASB). We generally refer to the IASB in this book, unless temporal specificity requires otherwise. The IASC's International Accounting Standards (IASs) were adopted by the IASB but new standards are called International Financial Reporting Standards (IFRSs). Taken together, IASs and IFRSs are generically called IFRSs.

The IASB is independent and has total autonomy in the setting of international standards. The objectives of the IASC Foundation are as follows:

(a) to develop, in the public interest, a single set of high quality, understandable and enforceable global accounting standards that require high quality, transparent and comparable information in financial statements and other financial reporting to help participants in the world's capital markets and other users to make economic decisions;

(b) to promote the use and rigorous application of those standards;

(c) in fulfilling (a) and (b), to take account of, as appropriate, the special needs of small and medium-sized entities and emerging economies; and

(d) to bring about convergence of national accounting standards and IFRS to high quality solutions.

The implications of diverse national backgrounds and attitudes, of diverse regulatory groupings, and of diverse attitudes to such factors as the role of law, professional independence and so on are a major underlying theme of this book.

## 1.3   Language

Many readers of this book will be trying not only to master a subject new to them but also doing so in a language that is not their first. One added difficulty is that there are several forms of the English language, particularly for accounting terms. UK terms and US terms are extensively different. Some examples are shown in the first two columns of Table 1.1. At this stage, you are not expected to understand all of these terms; they will be introduced later, as they are needed.

The International Accounting Standards Board operates and publishes its standards in English, although there are approved translations in several languages. The IASB uses a mixture of UK and US terms, as shown in the third column of Table 1.1. On the whole, this book uses IASB terms.

Table 1.1 **Some examples of UK, US and IASB terms**

| UK | US | IASB |
|---|---|---|
| Stock | Inventory | Inventory |
| Shares | Stock | Shares |
| Own shares | Treasury stock | Treasury shares |
| Debtors | Receivables | Receivables |
| Creditors | Payables | Payables |
| Finance lease | Capital lease | Finance lease |
| Turnover | Sales (or revenue) | Sales (or revenue) |
| Merger | Pooling of interests | Uniting of interests |
| Fixed assets | Non-current assets | Non-current assets |
| Profit and loss account | Income statement | Income statement |
| Associate | Equity accounted affiliate | Associate |

## 1.4 Excitement in accounting

Accounting is not universally regarded as an exciting and exhilarating area of activity or study, but it can be fascinating, in several ways:

- in itself, because it is an incomplete and rapidly evolving discipline and its study contains uncertainty and discovery;
- in application, because the theoretical ideas become intimately bound up with human attitude and human nature;
- in effects, because it has a major impact on financial decisions, share prices, etc.;
- in the international sphere, because of its integration with cultural, economic and political change.

At present, a further element exists that increases the interest of accounting. In the early years of this millennium there is enormous change in several factors connected with accounting. Business is increasingly being carried out electronically; old types of industry are giving way to new; markets have become global; accounting information can travel faster and more cheaply. In Europe in particular, closer cooperation is underway. A common currency (the euro) operates and expansion of the European Union continues.

The final reason – one that particularly relates to the authors – is that we are seeking to communicate the importance of accounting in a genuinely international rather than a national context. We hope that our work leads to greater understanding by readers (and between readers), whatever their background and starting point.

## 1.5 The path ahead

The structure of the remainder of this book is as follows. Part 1 continues by investigating the fundamental principles and conventions that form the basis of accounting thought and practice. Chapter 2 outlines the basic financial statements, and their relationships. There is also a substantial appendix to the book to introduce double-entry bookkeeping. Chapter 3 looks at the main conventions underlying accounting, and particularly at the framework of concepts used by the IASB. For the reader with no accounting background, it is essential to understand the thinking that underlies what accountants do; for the reader with previous accounting or possibly bookkeeping experience, the two chapters should still be regarded as essential reading, for they bring out the interrelationships between the various ideas and techniques. Depending on the nature of the students and the course, a study of the double-entry material in Appendix A might be suitable before, after or alongside Chapter 3.

Chapter 4 then looks at ways in which financial reporting *can* be regulated, and how it *is* regulated in several countries. Chapter 5 introduces the influences on, and the nature of, international differences in accounting. Chapter 6 outlines the normal contents of the annual reports of large commercial entities. The standards of the IASB are used as the main point of reference. Finally in Part 1, Chapter 7 introduces the topic of analysis: how to interpret financial statements and how to compare one entity with another.

Part 2 (comprising Chapters 8–16) explores the major topics of financial reporting in some detail. In many cases a variety of theoretical conclusions are possible, and a variety of different practices can be found in different countries. These are explored both for themselves and for their causes and implications. Again, the main context for the discussions is the standards of the IASB.

Finally, in Part 3 (Chapters 17 and 18) the techniques of analysing financial statements that were introduced in Part 1 are taken further, and the valuation of entities is examined. This Part can be seen as the culmination of what has gone before. Financial accounting is about communication, and study of the various influences on accounting in Part 1 and of the ways of tackling the problem issues in Part 2 should help in appreciating the real information content of accounting numbers – both what they mean and, just as importantly, what they do not mean.

## Summary

- Accounting is designed to give financial information to particular groups of users. Different users may need different information.

- This book is especially concerned with financial reporting by business entities to outside investors.

- Because the managers of an entity are often different people from the investors, the reports prepared by managers for those investors and other users need to be checked by auditors.

- The state and the accountancy profession may both play roles in the regulation of financial reporting.

- The International Accounting Standards Board (IASB) is an independent body that sets standards for financial reporting.

- The use of accounting terms differs considerably between UK, US and IASB practice.

## ? EXERCISES

*Feedback on the first two of these exercises is given in Appendix D.*

1.1 Is financial accounting really necessary?

1.2 At least eight different groups of users of accounting information can be distinguished, i.e.:
- Managers
- Investors
- Lenders
- Employees
- Suppliers and other creditors
- Customers
- Governments and their agencies
- Public

Suggest the information that each is likely to need from accounting statements and reports. Are there likely to be difficulties in satisfying the needs of all the groups you have considered with one common set of information?

1.3 Outline the relative benefits to users of financial reports of:

(a) information about the past;
(b) information about the present;
(c) information about the future.

1.4 Do you think that users know what to ask for from their accountant or financial adviser? Explain your answer.

1.5 In the context of your own national background, rank the seven 'external' user groups suggested in the text (i.e. omitting managers), in order of the priority that you think should be given to their needs. Explain your reasons.

1.6 If at all possible, compare your answer to Exercise 1.5 with the answers of students from different national backgrounds. Try to explore likely causes of any major differences that emerge, in terms of legal, economic and cultural environments.

# Chapter 2

# Some fundamentals

| Contents | | | |
|---|---|---|---|
| 2.1 | Introduction | | 14 |
| 2.2 | The balance sheet | | 14 |
| | 2.2.1 | Simple balance sheets | 15 |
| 2.3 | The income statement | | 21 |
| | 2.3.1 | Preparing the income statement | 22 |
| 2.4 | Two simple equations | | 27 |
| 2.5 | How cash flows fit in | | 29 |
| | Summary | | 30 |
| | Exercises | | 30 |

**Objectives**    After studying this chapter carefully, you should be able to:

■ describe the principles underlying the recording of financial data;

■ outline the form and properties of income statements and balance sheets;

■ explain the relationships between assets, liabilities, equity, revenue and expense;

■ prepare simple financial statements from details of transactions.

## 2.1 Introduction

The first chapter of this book looked at the role of accounting: what accounting is and why it exists. This chapter explores the basic ideas of financial accounting: the way accounting actually works, the logic behind the double-entry recording system, and the accounting statements of balance sheet and income statement. As suggested in Chapter 1, it is essential to understand the thinking that underlies accounting practice, but for this it is not necessary to master all the detailed techniques of bookkeeping. However, an introduction to the double-entry methodology will be needed for those who have not studied it before. Such an introduction is contained in Appendix A at the end of the book.

## 2.2 The balance sheet

A balance sheet is a document designed to show the state of affairs of an entity at a particular date. Students and practitioners of bookkeeping regard the balance sheet as the culmination of a long and complex recording process. If it does not balance, mistakes have definitely been made during the preparation process; they will have to be found. The public tends to regard the balance sheet, which contains lots of big numbers and yet apparently magically arrives at the same figure twice, as proof of both the complicated nature of accountancy and of the technical competence and reliability of the accountants and auditors involved.

However, reduced to its simplest, a balance sheet consists of two lists. The first is a list of the *resources* that are under the control of the entity – it is a list of *assets*. This English word derives from the Latin *ad satis* (to sufficient), in the sense that such items could be used to pay debts. One modern definition of 'asset' is that used by the International Accounting Standards Board (IASB):

> An asset is a resource controlled by the entity as a result of past events and from which future economic benefits are expected to flow to the entity.

The reference to a past event is so that accountants can identify the asset. It also helps them to attribute a monetary value to it.

The second list shows where the assets came from, i.e. the monetary amounts of the *sources* from which the entity obtained its present stock of *resources*. Since those sources will require repayment or recompense in some way, it follows that this second list can also be regarded as a list of *claims* against the resources. The entity will have to settle these claims at some time, and this second list can therefore be regarded as amounts due to others.

The first list could also be regarded as the ways in which those sources have been applied at this point in time, that is, as a list of *applications*. These terms can be summarized as in Table 2.1.

A balance sheet is often defined as a statement of financial position at a point in time. Indeed, the IASB in 2007 replaced the term 'balance sheet' with the term

Table 2.1 **The contents of a balance sheet**

| First list | Second list |
|---|---|
| Resources controlled | Sources |
| Assets | Where they came from |
| Applications | Claims |

'statement of financial position'. It is a list of sources, of where everything came from, and a list of resources, of everything valuable that the business controls. Since both lists relate to the same business at the same point in time, the totals of each list must be equal and the balance sheet must balance. It is defined and constructed so that it has to balance. It represents two ways of looking at the same situation.

## 2.2.1 Simple balance sheets

When a new business entity is created, the starting position is that there is no balance sheet because there is no entity. The new business will have to be owned by someone. This outside person or other body will put some cash (a resource) into the entity as *capital*. Capital is the source of the cash which the entity now owns. So, after this first transaction, we can prepare the balance sheet – our two lists of resources and claims – as in Table 2.2.

Table 2.2 **The balance sheet**

| Resources/Applications | Claims/Sources |
|---|---|
| Cash | Capital |

*Why it matters* — The separation of the entity from the owner is implied by showing the owner's contribution as a claim/source. Without this separation, the affairs of the owner and the business would become tangled up, so that the success of the entity would be unclear.

Notice that the cash is an asset, i.e. a resource, whereas the capital is a claim on the business by the owner. In a sense, the capital is 'owed' by the entity to the owner. Suppose that capital of €100,000 had been put in to begin the operation. This gives the balance sheet as in Table 2.3.

Table 2.3 **Balance sheet of a new entity**

| Resources (€) | | Claims (€) | |
|---|---|---|---|
| Cash | 100,000 | Capital | 100,000 |
| | 100,000 | | 100,000 |

Suppose the entity runs a retail shop that undertakes the following transactions after the initial input of capital of €100,000:

2. borrows €50,000 from the bank;
3. buys property for €50,000;
4. buys inventory (goods to be sold again) costing €45,000, paying cash;
5. sells one-third of the quantity of this inventory for €35,000, on credit (i.e. with the customer agreeing to pay later);
6. pays wages for the period, in cash, of €4,000;
7. €16,000 of the money due from the customer is received;
8. buys inventory costing €25,000, on credit (i.e. the entity pays later).

Transaction 2 creates an additional source, and therefore claim, of €50,000 in the form of a loan from the bank. In return, the business has an asset or resource of an extra €50,000 of cash.

**Activity 2.A**

All the transactions can be analysed in this way, as shown in Table 2.4. Look at Transactions 1 to 3 and make sure that you understand the changes in resources and claims (of matching size) for each.

Table 2.4 **An analysis of the transactions (in €000)**

| | Resources (€) | | | Claims (€) | |
|---|---|---|---|---|---|
| Transaction | Cash | Receivables | Other assets | Outsiders: liabilities | Owner: capital and profit |
| 1. Original capital | +100 | | | | +100 |
| 2. Borrowing | +50 | | | +50 | |
| 3. Buy property | −50 | | +50 | | |
| 4. Buy inventory for cash | −45 | | +45 | | |
| 5. Sell some inventory | | +35 | −15 | | +20 (i.e. 35 − 15) |
| 6. Pay wages | −4 | | | | −4 |
| 7. Customer pays | +16 | −16 | | | |
| 8. Buy inventory on credit | | | +25 | +25 | |
| TOTALS | +67 | +19 | +105 | +75 | +116 |

It is possible to prepare new balance sheets after each transaction. After Transaction 2, the balance sheet looks as in Table 2.5. The order of items in a balance sheet in many countries (e.g. those in the European Union) is traditionally that longer-term items are shown first.

Table 2.5 **Balance sheet after loan**

| Resources (€) | | Claims (€) | |
|---|---|---|---|
| Cash | 150,000 | Capital | 100,000 |
| | | Loan | 50,000 |
| | 150,000 | | 150,000 |

Transaction 3 involves using some of the cash to buy a long-term asset, a property from which to operate the business (see Table 2.6). One resource (part of the cash) is turned into another resource (property), so that the total resources and claims remain the same.

Table 2.6 **The balance sheet after buying property**

| Resources (€) | | Claims (€) | |
|---|---|---|---|
| Property | 50,000 | Capital | 100,000 |
| Cash | 100,000 | Loan | 50,000 |
| | 150,000 | | 150,000 |

**Activity 2.B** It is now time for you to try out a transaction to check that the topic is clear to you. Refer back to Transaction 4 in the earlier list. Which new resources or claims result from this transaction?

**Feedback** Like Transaction 3, Transaction 4 does not involve any new or additional resources, only a change in application of them: €45,000 which had previously been part of the store of cash has now been changed to a different application, i.e. inventory. Total resources and total claims remain constant (see Table 2.7).

Table 2.7 **The balance sheet after buying inventory**

| Resources (€) | | Claims (€) | |
|---|---|---|---|
| Property | 50,000 | Capital | 100,000 |
| Inventory | 45,000 | Loan | 50,000 |
| Cash | 55,000 | | |
| | 150,000 | | 150,000 |

Transaction 5 is rather more complicated. There are some easy aspects. First, one-third of the inventory has disappeared and so the inventory figure must be reduced from €45,000 to €30,000. Second, the customer has agreed to pay the entity €35,000. This does not mean that the entity has the cash; it does, however, have the *right* to receive the cash. This is an additional resource of the business, an additional asset. The business has something extra, namely the valuable and useful right to receive this cash. The €35,000 represents the receivable (or debtor; that is, the customer who has an obligation to pay and from whom the business has a right to receive the additional asset). The conclusion as regards Transaction 5 is that one resource has fallen by €15,000, and a new resource has appeared in the amount of €35,000. This means that total resources have risen by €20,000. However, we cannot have a resource without a claim. What is the origin of this increase in resources of €20,000?

In intuitive terms it should be fairly clear what has happened. The business has sold something for more than it had originally paid for it. It has turned an asset recorded as €15,000 (i.e. the cost of one-third of the physical amount of inventory) into an asset of €35,000 (i.e. the receivable) through its business operations. The business has made a profit. Numerically, in order to make the balance sheet balance, it is necessary to put this profit of €20,000 on to the opposite side of the balance sheet, i.e. as a claim (see Table 2.8). Would this make sense in logical as well as numerical terms?

Table 2.8 **The balance sheet after selling some inventory**

| Resources (€) | | Claims (€) | |
|---|---|---|---|
| Property | 50,000 | Capital | 100,000 |
| Inventory | 30,000 | Profit | 20,000 |
| Receivable | 35,000 | Loan | 50,000 |
| Cash | 55,000 | | |
| | 170,000 | | 170,000 |

The answer is 'yes', as can be seen by looking back at the second list in Table 2.1. Extra 'assets' have come from the profitable trading of the enterprise. The profits made by the business are made for the ultimate benefit of the owner, and therefore can be said to belong to the owner of the business. Since these profits have been made within the business and are still within the business, but belong to the owner, it follows that they can be regarded as claims against the business by the owner. The profit can be seen as an extra amount belonging to the owners. Finally, it was mentioned earlier that claims can also be seen as sources. What is the source of these extra resources? The answer is that the source is the successful result of the trading operation. Profits *are* a source. At its simplest, the profit can be measured as an increase in the assets.

So the balance sheet shown in Table 2.8 follows from this accounting. The extra resources of €20,000 are represented by extra sources of €20,000, namely the profit that is an additional ownership claim on the business. The profit change shown in the transition from Table 2.7 to Table 2.8 is not accompanied by a change in the amount of cash, because cash has not yet been received from the customer.

It should be obvious by now that each transaction has at least two effects on the financial position. This should also be clear from the analysis in Table 2.4. Note how Transaction 5 has been recorded there.

*Why it matters* *Without good records of the receivables (debtors) and loans and other payables (creditors), the business might forget to demand its money from debtors, and would not know whether a creditor's claim for money should be paid. Financial disaster would follow.*

Moving on to Transaction 6, what two numerical alterations are needed to the balance sheet in order to incorporate the new event?

First, the amount of cash that the entity controls as asset, resource or application goes down by €4,000. This sum of money has physically been paid out by the entity, so the amount remaining must be €4,000 less than it was before. Has this

€4,000 been applied by being turned into some other asset, some other resource available to the entity to do things with? The answer seems to be 'no'. The wages relate to the past, and therefore they represent the reward given by the entity for work, for labour hours that *have already been used*.

The wages represent services provided and already totally consumed by the business as part of the process of generating profit in the trading period, which we had previously recorded at €20,000. This needs to be taken into account in calculating the overall profit or gain made by the entity through the operations over this trading period. Thus €4,000 needs to be deducted from the profit figure of €20,000 in order to show the correct profit from the operations of the entity made for the benefit of the owner (see Table 2.9). The wages involved a reduction in assets (cash fell) and the recognition of a reduced claim by the owners (profits fell). This reduction in the measure of profit can also be called an *expense*.

Table 2.9 **The balance sheet after paying wages**

| Resources (€) | | Claims (€) | |
|---|---|---|---|
| Property | 50,000 | Capital | 100,000 |
| Inventory | 30,000 | Profit | 16,000 |
| Receivable | 35,000 | Loan | 50,000 |
| Cash | 51,000 | | |
| | 166,000 | | 166,000 |

Transaction 7 is straightforward. The starting position is that there was a receivable – an asset, an amount owed to the business – of €35,000. Some of this money is now received by the business. This tells us two things: first, the cash figure must increase by the amount of this cash received, i.e. by €16,000; second, the business is no longer owed the €16,000 because it has already received it. The receivable therefore needs to be reduced by €16,000 (see Table 2.10). In summary, we have an increase in the asset 'cash' and a decrease in the asset 'receivable', both by the same amount. Total applications remain the same, and therefore total sources remain the same too. The business has not borrowed money through this transaction and, equally clearly, there has been no effect on profit – all that has happened is that an earlier transaction has moved further towards completion.

Table 2.10 **The balance sheet after receipt from debtor**

| Resources (€) | | Claims (€) | |
|---|---|---|---|
| Property | 50,000 | Capital | 100,000 |
| Inventory | 30,000 | Profit | 16,000 |
| Receivable | 19,000 | Loan | 50,000 |
| Cash | 67,000 | | |
| | 166,000 | | 166,000 |

**Activity 2.C**

Look back to the earlier list of transactions to find the details of Transaction 8. In this final transaction of our example, the business buys more inventory for €25,000, and so the inventory figure in the balance sheet – the resource or asset of inventory – rises by €25,000. This has not yet been paid for and so there is no corresponding reduction in any of the other resources. The total of resources therefore rises by €25,000 – and so, of course, does the total claims. What is the particular claim on the business that increases by €25,000?

**Feedback**

The business owes the supplier some cash for the extra inventory and therefore there is an extra claim, known as a payable (or a creditor). This is shown in Table 2.11. Also, you can now check the analysis of all the transactions in Table 2.4 and the totals in that table.

Table 2.11 **The balance sheet after further purchase**

| Resources (€) | | Claims (€) | |
|---|---|---|---|
| Property | 50,000 | Capital | 100,000 |
| Inventory | 55,000 | Profit | 16,000 |
| Receivable | 19,000 | Loan | 50,000 |
| Cash | 67,000 | Payable | 25,000 |
| | 191,000 | | 191,000 |

The claims from third parties (outsiders other than the owner), such as the payable from Transaction 8 and the loan from Transaction 2, are obligations that can be called *liabilities*. This English word derives from the word 'liable', meaning tied or bound or obliged by law. The IASB defines a liability as:

> a present obligation of the entity arising from past events, the settlement of which is expected to result in an outflow from the entity of resources embodying economic benefits.

This definition portrays a liability as a negative version of an asset. Both definitions are taken further, particularly in Part 2 of this book. Claims by the owners are not called liabilities but owner's *equity* (or various similar expressions). This is because the entity generally has no legal obligation to pay particular amounts to the owners at any particular date. The English word 'equity' has a number of meanings, but in the accounting context it means the owner's stake in the entity. In Table 2.11, the equity is €116,000 (the sum of the first two items: the original capital plus the profit), whereas the liabilities to the third parties are €75,000 (the sum of the second two items).

The right-hand side of the balance sheet of Table 2.11 could be redrawn to show the two types of claims, as shown in Table 2.12. Notice how this fits in with the totals of the claims in Table 2.4.

**Table 2.12 The claims side of the balance sheet showing the two types**

| | | |
|---|---|---|
| *Equity:* | | |
| Capital | 100,000 | |
| Profit | 16,000 | |
| | | 116,000 |
| | | |
| *Liabilities:* | | |
| Loan | 50,000 | |
| Payable | 25,000 | |
| | | 75,000 |
| Total | | 191,000 |

This example has been explored at considerable length because it is useful to keep thinking in terms of resources and claims. Is a transaction changing one resource into another? Or is it getting more resources from somewhere and therefore increasing both lists, namely both sides of the balance sheet? And if total claims increase, is it through operating successfully and making a profit, or is it through borrowing money or simply not yet paying for resources acquired? Try Exercises 2.1 and 2.2 from the end of this chapter now in order to reinforce the lessons learned here.

## 2.3 The income statement

It has been shown that any transaction, event or adjustment can be recorded in a given balance sheet to produce a new and updated balance sheet. Also, provided that one follows the logic of the resources-and-claims idea, the new balance sheet must inevitably balance.

It would be possible to carry on this process in the same way for ever, producing an endless series of balance sheets after each transaction. This would not be very practicable. Instead, users of accounting information may wish to see balance sheets monthly, half-yearly or yearly. They may also require current information about the results of the operating activities of the business. In order to provide this, it is necessary to collect together and summarize those items that are part of the calculation of the profit figure for the particular period.

The transaction that led to profit in the example in Section 2.2 (the sale of inventory) was expressed as an increase in assets. The transaction that led to a reduction in the profit (the wages) was expressed as a fall in assets. The calculation of profit will generally consist of these positive and negative elements. When the business makes a sale, then the proceeds of the sale are a positive part of the profit calculation, which is referred to as a *revenue*. On the other hand, the operating process involves the consumption of some business resources, an *expense*, which is the negative part. In the example explored in detail earlier, there were two such items. First, the resource of inventory was used, and so the original cost of the used inventory was included as a negative component of the profit calculation. Second, some of the resource of cash was used to pay the wages that had necessarily been incurred in the process of the business operations. The cost of these wages is also a negative component of the profit calculation. The two components can be seen in the 'owner' column of Table 2.4.

The income statement (sometimes called the profit and loss account) reports on flows of revenues and expenses of a period, whereas a balance sheet reports on the financial position (i.e. the stock of resources and claims) at the balance sheet date. Figure 2.1 shows this diagrammatically. From time to time (at least yearly), the balance sheet is drawn up to show the financial position at that particular time. For example, in Figure 2.1, the balance sheet is drawn up at 31 December 20X7 and again at 31 December 20X8. During the year 20X8, assuming that the owners have not introduced or withdrawn capital, the explanation for the changing balance sheet is the operations of the company. Overall, the assets of the company will have grown in 20X8 if there is an excess of revenues over expenses. The balance of the assets over the liabilities is called the net assets. This profit can also be seen as the size of (and the cause of) the increase in equity in year 20X8.

Figure 2.1 **The balance sheet reports on stocks of things; the income statement reports on flows**

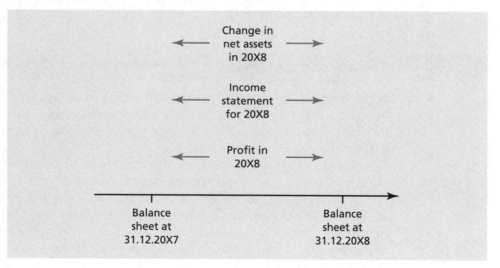

### 2.3.1 Preparing the income statement

The logic of the income statement in relation to the balance sheet can be explored by reworking the transactions we used earlier, and by segregating out the expenses and the revenues from the other aspects of the transactions.

First, let us examine all the resources. Some of these have been used up in the period under consideration; some continue to be valuable because they will provide benefits in the future. The resources that the entity had fall into two types:

- those used up in the period (expenses); and
- those remaining (assets).

The claims can be seen to fall into three types:

- those arising from operations in the period (revenues);
- those contributed by the owners (capital); and
- those due to outsiders (liabilities).

We can set up a simple layout for recording our transactions under this five-way split, as shown in Table 2.13. On the left, the assets and expenses are what has happened to the sources of the entity's finance. On the right, the sources are shown. The capital and the liabilities are shown together, because they are both outstanding claims at the balance sheet date.

Table 2.13 **Applications and sources**

| Applications | Sources |
| --- | --- |
| Assets | Capital and Liabilities |
| Expenses | Revenues |

**Activity 2.D**

Take a large sheet of paper and divide it into four, with the appropriate four headings (see Table 2.13). Then record the effects of the seven transactions from before (after the initial injection of capital):

2. borrows €50,000 from the bank;
3. buys property for €50,000;
4. buys inventory costing €45,000, paying cash;
5. sells one-third of the quantity of this inventory for €35,000, on credit (i.e. with the customer agreeing to pay later);
6. pays wages for the period, in cash, of €4,000;
7. €16,000 of the money owed by the customer is received;
8. buys inventory costing €25,000, on credit.

Record these transactions one at a time, as adjustments to the previous position, on the same sheet of paper. The starting position (stage 1 in our earlier list) will be a simple repeat of Table 2.3, as in Table 2.14.

Table 2.14 **The introduction of capital**

| Applications | | Sources | |
| --- | --- | --- | --- |
| Assets | | Capital and Liabilities | |
| Cash | 100,000 | Capital | 100,000 |
| Expenses | | Revenues | |
| | 0 | | 0 |
| | 100,000 | | 100,000 |

Transactions 2–4 are very straightforward, as they do not involve the creation of any profit and therefore do not give rise to the existence of any revenues or expenses. The position after incorporating Transactions 2, 3 and 4 is shown in Table 2.15.

Table 2.15 **The position after Transaction 4**

| Applications | | Sources | |
|---|---|---|---|
| *Assets* | | *Capital and Liabilities* | |
| Property | 50,000 | Capital | 100,000 |
| Inventory | 45,000 | Loan | 50,000 |
| Cash | 55,000 | | |
| | 150,000 | | 150,000 |
| *Expenses* | | *Revenues* | |
| | 0 | | 0 |
| | 150,000 | | 150,000 |

Compare this with Table 2.7. Totals have been put in on each of these tables, both for each of the four quarters and for each of the two sides. This is just to prove at each stage that the system is working properly both logically and numerically. There is no need for you to add the totals on your large sheet of paper and, indeed, since you are recording the adjustments cumulatively you would find it messy to do so. Your sheet of paper should at this point look like Table 2.16.

Table 2.16 **Working paper after Transaction 4**

| Applications | | Sources | |
|---|---|---|---|
| *Assets* | | *Capital and Liabilities* | |
| Property | 50,000 | Capital | 100,000 |
| Inventory | 45,000 | Loan | 50,000 |
| Cash | 55,000 | | |
| *Expenses* | | *Revenues* | |

Transaction 5 is more interesting. This gives rise to a revenue because some inventory has been sold for €35,000 and therefore puts a €35,000 sales figure into the revenues section of the table. As some of the resources have now been used, i.e. some of the assets have become expenses, an amount of €15,000 needs to be removed from the inventory asset and added to the expenses figure. We might call it the cost of goods sold. On the other hand, an extra resource has been created – an extra asset. The business is now owed €35,000, which it was not owed before, and this new item – this receivable of €35,000 – needs to be added to the assets section. When you have incorporated these adjustments on to your sheet of paper, in terms of pluses and minuses, you should arrive at the position shown in Table 2.17.

Table 2.17 **The position after Transaction 5**

| Applications | | Sources | |
|---|---|---|---|
| Assets | | Capital and Liabilities | |
| Property | 50,000 | Capital | 100,000 |
| Inventory | 30,000 | Loan | 50,000 |
| Receivable | 35,000 | | |
| Cash | 55,000 | | |
| | 170,000 | | 150,000 |
| Expenses | | Revenues | |
| Cost of goods sold | 15,000 | Sales | 35,000 |
| | 185,000 | | 185,000 |

Transaction 6 involves the payment of the wages bill for the period. Two points need to be recognized here: (a) the asset or resource of cash has gone down by €4,000; and (b) €4,000 of resources have been used in the operating process of the business, i.e. €4,000 has now become an expense. This €4,000 expense needs to be matched against the sales proceeds as part of the overall profit calculation for the operating period. This thinking leads to the position shown in Table 2.18.

Table 2.18 **After wages have been paid**

| Applications | | | Sources | |
|---|---|---|---|---|
| Assets | | | Capital and Liabilities | |
| Property | | 50,000 | Capital | 100,000 |
| Inventory | | 30,000 | Loan | 50,000 |
| Receivable | | 35,000 | | |
| Cash | | 51,000 | | |
| | | 166,000 | | 150,000 |
| Expenses | | | Revenues | |
| Cost of goods sold | 15,000 | | Sales | 35,000 |
| Wages | 4,000 | | | |
| | | 19,000 | | |
| | | 185,000 | | 185,000 |

The expenses (of €15,000 and €4,000) are shown indented to the left merely so that the total of assets (€166,000) and expenses (€19,000) can clearly be seen to be €185,000.

Neither Transaction 7 nor Transaction 8 involves the creation of any additional revenues or expenses. Transaction 7 increases the asset of cash and reduces the asset of receivables by the same amount. Cash is now being *received*, but it arises from an earlier revenue. The cash now received was earned at an earlier date and it is the act of earning, not the act of receiving, that determines the revenue. With Transaction 8 there is an additional source into the business, from the granting of credit to the business by the supplier. The application of this extra amount is the extra inventory. Incorporation of Transaction 7 and then Transaction 8 leads to the positions in Tables 2.19 and 2.20 respectively.

**Table 2.19 Incorporating Transaction 7**

| Applications | | | Sources | |
|---|---:|---:|---|---:|
| *Assets* | | | *Capital and Liabilities* | |
| Property | | 50,000 | Capital | 100,000 |
| Inventory | | 30,000 | Loan | 50,000 |
| Receivable | | 19,000 | | |
| Cash | | 67,000 | | |
| | | 166,000 | | 150,000 |
| *Expenses* | | | *Revenues* | |
| Cost of goods sold | 15,000 | | Sales | 35,000 |
| Wages | 4,000 | | | |
| | | 19,000 | | |
| | | 185,000 | | 185,000 |

When you work out all the pluses and minuses on your sheet of paper, you should arrive at the final position as shown in Table 2.20 – but what does it mean? The bottom half of Table 2.20, the revenues and expenses, is an income statement. It contains all the positive parts of the profit calculation (the revenues) and all the negative parts of the profit calculation (the expenses). One can extract the bottom half from Table 2.20 and present this as the detailed profit calculation – a detailed statement of the result of trading for the period. In total, the revenues are €35,000 and the expenses are €19,000. The profit is the difference between the two, i.e. €16,000.

**Table 2.20 After Transaction 8**

| Applications | | | Sources | |
|---|---:|---:|---|---:|
| *Assets* | | | *Capital and Liabilities* | |
| Property | | 50,000 | Capital | 100,000 |
| Inventory | | 55,000 | Loan | 50,000 |
| Receivable | | 19,000 | Payable | 25,000 |
| Cash | | 67,000 | | |
| | | 191,000 | | 175,000 |
| *Expenses* | | | *Revenues* | |
| Cost of goods sold | 15,000 | | Sales | 35,000 |
| Wages | 4,000 | | | |
| | | 19,000 | | |
| | | 210,000 | | 210,000 |

Table 2.20 may be interpreted in two ways. First, the profit (the excess of revenues over expenses) is clearly a *source*. Since at all times the sources into the business must equal the applications by the business, it follows that the income statement (the whole of the bottom half of Table 2.20) can be replaced by the single profit number of €16,000 on the sources side in the top half of the table. This half of the table is, of course, the balance sheet. Replacing the revenues and expenses parts of Table 2.20 by the single profit figure in the balance sheet as a

claim leads us exactly to Table 2.11 (check back for yourself). This profit, as shown earlier, represents an additional ownership claim on the business.

Second, one could look at Table 2.20 and think purely *numerically*. The bottom half, the income statement half, has an excess of €16,000 on the right-hand side. The top half, the balance sheet half, has an excess of €16,000 on the left-hand side. How can each part balance? The answer, in purely numerical terms, is that €16,000 can be put into the left-hand side of the bottom half, and be called profit. Then €16,000 can be put into the right-hand side of the top half, and be called profit. The bottom half can now be dropped away altogether (as it consists of an equal number of pluses and minuses), leaving a balance sheet that balances. The logical interrelationship can be summarized as follows:

$$\text{Applications} = \text{Sources}$$
$$\therefore \text{Assets} + \text{Expenses} = \text{Capital} + \text{Liabilities} + \text{Revenues}$$
$$\therefore \text{Assets} = \text{Capital} + \text{Liabilities} + \text{Revenues} - \text{Expenses}$$
$$\therefore \text{Assets} = \text{Capital} + \text{Liabilities} + \text{Profit}$$

## 2.4 Two simple equations

As explained above, at the end of the period the profit figure is recorded in the balance sheet to show the total claim that the owners now have on the entity. This claim is the owner's equity: the original capital plus the profit. Tables 2.11 and 2.12 showed the balance sheet in terms of assets, equity and liabilities.

This balance sheet structure could be expressed as 'the balance sheet equation':

**Assets = Owner's equity + Liabilities**

Re-arranged, this becomes:

**Owner's equity = Assets − Liabilities = Net assets**

That is, the claims of the owner at a point in time (e.g. point 1) are equal to the net assets of the entity. It will be useful to abbreviate this equation to:

$$OE_1 = A_1 - L_1$$

In this model, there are only two factors that can affect capital and cause it to change over time. These are, first, that the entity will operate and make a profit (or it could, of course, make a loss) and, second, that the owner will take some profit out of the business (by way of cash drawings) or the owner could invest extra capital into the business. Thus if profit for period 2 = $P_2$ and drawings = $D_2$, then the increase in capital is $P_2 - D_2$. So, if $OE_2$ is the owner's equity at the end of period 2, then:

$$OE_2 - OE_1 = P_2 - D_2$$

and

$$OE_1 + P_2 - D_2 = OE_2$$

This is our second simple equation.

We also know that $P_2$ equals the revenues ($R_2$) less the expenses ($E_2$) of the period:

$$P_2 = R_2 - E_2$$

The important point about these equations is the generality of their truth and application. To illustrate this generality, consider the classic schoolroom problem of the tank of water containing a given number of litres. A tap is pouring water in at the top at a given rate per hour, and water is leaking out of the bottom at a given rate per hour. Clearly (opening water) + (water in) − (water out) = (closing water). If we know any three of these items, we can find the fourth. Further, it does not matter how the water is measured, provided it is measured in the same way all the time; consistency must be applied.

The idea of using equations can be carried further by combining these equations, as follows (ignoring transactions with owners, such as drawings):

$$A_1 - L_1 = OE_1$$
$$\therefore A_1 - L_1 = OE_0 + P_1$$
$$\therefore A_1 - L_1 = OE_0 + R_1 - E_1$$
$$\therefore A_1 + E_1 = OE_0 + R_1 + L_1$$

This, of course, is a rephrasing of Tables 2.13 to 2.20, which showed assets and expenses on the left, and the other items on the right. The equation links together the five 'elements' of the financial statements. As explained in Appendix A, the items on the left (the applications) are called *debits* in the double-entry system, and the items on the right (the sources) are called *credits*.

<table>
<tr><td>*Why it matters*</td><td>■ *The self-balancing nature of the accounting system shows up certain types of errors very efficiently.*<br>■ *The equations are needed in computer systems that run the accounting of businesses.*</td></tr>
</table>

There is one further implication of all this, concerning the exact definitions of the five elements of the financial statements. The term 'equity' needs no separate definition because it rests on differences in the other four. However, there is a practical problem with the definitions of the other four elements, as will now be explained. Let us take the resources as in our examples. In principle, as explained before, there should be no contradiction here, because:

(a) Assets = the resources with remaining future benefits at the period end; and
(b) Expenses = the resources used up in the period.

It is time-consuming to have to measure both. Judgement is required in the measurement of either because there will be doubt about which category to put some resources into. Consequently, in practice, two solutions are available:

1. Expenses = resources used up in the period. Therefore
   Assets = the rest of the resources.
2. Assets = resources with remaining future benefits at the period end. Therefore
   Expenses = the rest of the resources.

Method 1 above, giving primacy to the definition of 'expense' (and 'revenue'), was the traditional way of doing accounting. It concentrates on transactions in a period. It leaves assets (and changes in their values) as a secondary consideration. However, from the 1970s onwards there have been moves towards Method 2, giving primacy to the definition of 'asset' (and 'liability'). This is now the IASB's approach when setting accounting standards. This major point affects many issues and will be taken further in later chapters.

## 2.5 How cash flows fit in

In order to understand the operations of an enterprise and to predict its future, it is useful to examine its flows of cash as well as its flows of profit. These two sets of flows are different. For example, in terms of the eight transactions of Section 2.2, the first four (receiving a capital input, borrowing money, and buying property and inventory) led to inflows and outflows of cash but no profits. The fifth transaction (selling the inventory for later payment by the customer) led to profit but no immediate cash flow.

As examined later in more detail (see Chapters 6 and 13), a statement of cash flows is drawn up for the accounting period. It shows how cash has come in and out in the period, as an explanation of the change in total cash in the balance sheet from the beginning to the end of the period.

A restatement of the earlier Figure 2.1 to include cash flows is shown as Figure 2.2. In terms of the earlier example, the first column of numbers in Table 2.4 shows all the transactions involving cash flows. They could be summarized in three types, as in Table 2.21.

Figure 2.2 **Flows during an example accounting period**

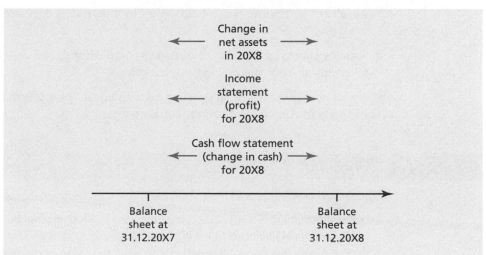

Table 2.21 **A summary of the cash flows in Table 2.4**

|  | €000 |
|---|---|
| Operating flows (inventory −45, wages −4, customers +16) | −33 |
| Investing flows (property −50) | −50 |
| Financing flows (owner +100, bank +50) | +150 |
| Cash change (starting from no cash) | +67 |

**Mastering the fundamentals**

*It is important that you are able to follow and to apply the logic behind the system outlined in this chapter. Self-assessment questions are available on the Companion Website. Appendix A at the end of the book contains a detailed introduction to double-entry bookkeeping. Some readers will already be familiar with the techniques involved, but nevertheless a revision of them might be useful. For any reader, some familiarity with double entry will be necessary. A number of numerical exercises are given at the end of this chapter, and there are suggested solutions and discussion of the adjustments required given in Appendix D at the end of the book. The exercises will be easier once the material in Appendix A has been mastered.*

## Summary

- A balance sheet is a periodic statement of the state of affairs or financial position of an entity. It contains a list of resources/applications and a list of claims/sources. The totals of the two lists are equal.

- Resources/applications are assets, and claims/sources are equity capital and liabilities. Transactions have equal-sized effects on both resources and claims. So the balance sheet balances.

- Making a profit leads to extra resources and increases the claims on the business from the owners.

- The income statement brings together all the revenues and expenses that cumulate to profit.

- Applications/resources can be used up in a period as expenses. What remains is assets.

- Sources/claims can be due to outsiders (liabilities) or can arise from this year's revenues or from the owners' contributions.

- Assets plus expenses equal opening owner's equity plus revenues plus liabilities. In terms of Appendix A, debits equal credits.

## ? EXERCISES

*Feedback on the first two of these exercises is given in Appendix D.*

2.1 The information in Table 2.22 relates to entity F, which started business on 1 January 20X7 when €150,000 was paid in as capital.

(a) Convert the above information into balance sheets at the end of the two years shown. What is then revealed as the missing item?

(b) What conclusion can you draw about the performance of F during 20X7 and 20X8?
(c) Would your conclusion be affected if you knew that the entity had paid €15,000 to the owner during 20X7?
(d) Does the figure for delivery vans at 31 December 20X8 surprise you? If so, why?

Table 2.22 **Financial statistics for F**

|  | 31 Dec. 20X7 (€) | 31 Dec. 20X8 (€) |
|---|---|---|
| Cash at bank | 19,000 | 36,000 |
| Inventory of goods | 32,000 | 29,000 |
| Shop | 135,000 | 135,000 |
| Wages owed to staff | 800 | 750 |
| Amounts owed to supplier | 26,500 | 21,250 |
| Amounts owed by customers | 35,000 | 34,000 |
| Loans | 50,000 | 50,000 |
| Cash | 500 | 2,000 |
| Delivery vans | 10,000 | 10,000 |

2.2 Company G has a hardware business. The balance sheet at the beginning of the financial year showed the position in Table 2.23.

Table 2.23 **Balance sheet for G**

|  |  | (a) | (b) | (c) | (d) | (e) | (f) | (g) |
|---|---|---|---|---|---|---|---|---|
| Shares | 50,000 | | | | | | | |
| Profit | 7,000 | | | | | | | |
| Payables | 12,000 | | | | | | | |
|  | 69,000 | | | | | | | |
| Premises | 20,000 | | | | | | | |
| Equipment | 9,000 | | | | | | | |
| Vehicle | 7,000 | | | | | | | |
| Inventory | 15,500 | | | | | | | |
| Receivables | 2,500 | | | | | | | |
| Bank | 14,700 | | | | | | | |
| Cash | 300 | | | | | | | |
|  | 69,000 | | | | | | | |

Show the adjustments, in the columns provided, for each of the following transactions:

(a) Goods were sold for €4,000 (cash sales €3,000, credit sales €1,000) which were included in the inventory at €2,800.
(b) An invoice for van expenses of €400 was received and paid immediately by cheque.
(c) Cheques of €8,000 were written and sent to creditors (payables). The €3,000 from cash sales was paid into the bank.
(d) The vehicle was sold at net book value for €7,000 cash, which was paid into the bank immediately.
(e) Cash €500 and cheques €2,000 were received from debtors (receivables).
(f) Office equipment (recorded in the books at €400) was sold for €700 cash.
(g) Company G then announced that it would pay €1,000 to the owners in one month's time, after the balance sheet for the year had been finalized.

### 2.3 Kings Cross Co.

| | € | | € |
|---|---|---|---|
| Land and buildings | 110,000 | Share capital | 150,000 |
| Machinery | 50,000 | Retained profits | 5,000 |
| Vehicles | 25,000 | Loans (10%) | 20,000 |
| Inventory at end of the year | 30,000 | Creditors | 50,000 |
| Debtors | 35,000 | | |
| Cash at bank | 10,000 | | |
| | 260,000 | | 225,000 |
| Cost of goods sold | 90,000 | Sales | 160,000 |
| Wages | 20,000 | | |
| Rent, insurance, sundry expenses | 15,000 | | |
| | 125,000 | | 160,000 |

The above information has been taken from the company's books as at 31 December 20X7, but the following have not yet been allowed for:

(a) Rent owing but not yet paid amounting to €1,000.
(b) Insurance paid includes €3,000 which relates to next year.
(c) Audit fees not yet included and not yet paid are €1,500.
(d) Machinery and vehicles are to be depreciated by 10%.
(e) Land and buildings have been revalued at €150,000.
(f) Interest on the loans has not yet been paid.

Record the appropriate adjustments on the quadrant and draw up the balance sheet and income statement.

### 2.4 Kings Happy Co.

| | € |
|---|---|
| Sales | 147,500 |
| Land and buildings | 60,000 |
| Plant and machinery | 40,000 |
| Purchases | 50,000 |
| Wages and salaries | 41,000 |
| Salesmen's commission | 6,000 |
| Vehicles | 30,000 |
| Share capital | 150,000 |
| Inventory at start of year | 20,000 |
| Debtors | 20,000 |
| Rent, insurances, sundry expenses | 8,500 |
| Cash discounts allowed | 1,500 |
| Shares in listed company | 40,000 |
| Cash at bank and in hand | 25,500 |
| Creditors | 37,000 |
| Retained profits | 6,000 |
| Dividends received from listed investment | 2,000 |

The above information has been taken from the company's books as at 31 December 20X7, but the following has not been allowed for:

(a) Inventory at the end of the year is €25,000.
(b) Audit fees owing amounted to €500.
(c) Machinery and vehicles are to be depreciated by 10% and 20% respectively.

Satisfy yourself that total sources equal total applications before making necessary adjustments for (a)–(c). Then draw up the balance sheet and income statement.

2.5 Kingsad Co.

|  | € |
| --- | --- |
| Land and buildings | 100,000 |
| Share capital | 100,000 |
| Plant and machinery | 50,000 |
| Retained profits at 1 January 20X7 | 46,000 |
| Purchases | 70,000 |
| Sales | 150,000 |
| Inventory at 1 January 20X7 | 30,000 |
| Wages and salaries | 40,000 |
| Sales returned by customers as unacceptable | 1,000 |
| General expenses | 10,000 |
| Debtors | 25,000 |
| Creditors | 30,000 |

This information has been taken from the company's books as at 31 December 20X7, but the information below has not been allowed for:

(a) Inventory at 31 December 20X7 is €20,000.
(b) Plant and machinery is to be depreciated by 10%.
(c) Land and buildings is to be revalued to €150,000.
(d) General expenses includes an insurance charge of €1,000 covering the period 1 July 20X7 to 30 June 20X8.
(e) A debtor for €1,000 has gone bankrupt.

Using the quadrant format, incorporate the additional information, and prepare the closing balance sheet and income statement.

# Chapter 3

# Frameworks and concepts

**Contents**  3.1  Introduction                                                    35
              3.2  Underlying concepts                                            37
                   3.2.1  Business entity                                          37
                   3.2.2  Accounting period                                        37
              3.3  The IASB's concepts                                             38
                   3.3.1  Overall objective                                        38
                   3.3.2  Underlying assumptions                                   38
                   3.3.3  Relevance                                                40
                   3.3.4  Reliability                                              41
              3.4  A hierarchy of concepts and some inconsistencies                42
              3.5  Possible future developments                                    44
                   Summary                                                         44
                   References and research                                         45
                   Exercises                                                       45

**Objectives**  After studying this chapter carefully, you should be able to:

- describe the links between the fundamentals of Chapter 2 and the financial reporting system used under IFRS;

- explain the main purposes of financial reporting under IFRS;

- outline some fundamental concepts underlying all financial reporting;

- define the concepts to be found in the IASB's Framework;

- explain the various levels of concepts, their interrelationship and some inconsistencies.

## 3.1 Introduction

Before you start reading this chapter, try to think of all the different types of people who might use balance sheets and income statements, and why. Draw up a list.

**Feedback** Financial statements might be used for various purposes by many users, including:

- managers of the enterprise (to assess performance, and to make financial decisions);
- the owners of an enterprise (to assess the performance of their investment and of the managers);
- potential investors who are thinking of becoming owners (to decide whether to invest);
- lenders, including the bank (to decide whether to lend);
- suppliers (to assess whether they will be paid);
- customers (to assess whether the company will continue);
- tax authorities (as a basis for the calculation of taxable profits);
- employees (to assess the stability and prospects of their employer);
- governments (for economic and social planning);
- competitors (to assess the strength of their competition).

Accounting has evolved over thousands of years without any clearly articulated purpose, or at least without any single purpose. Accounting has been used to record debts due from customers, calculate taxable income, calculate the split of profit among owners, help management to decide where to expand business, and so on. For different users and uses, different types and amounts and frequencies of accounting might be useful.

In the previous chapter, some fundamentals of accounting were examined, including the recording of transactions and the preparation of periodic financial statements. These fundamentals are relevant for any of the above purposes. However, this book is particularly concerned with financial reporting published by commercial entities for users who are external to the entity, particularly investors. Although there are several variations around the world, one general type of accounting has gradually come to be accepted internationally for this purpose, particularly for large commercial companies. This dominant type of accounting is that set out in International Financial Reporting Standards. The rules of this type of accounting are based on a published 'conceptual framework' of concepts which can be summarized as follows:

- the main users of financial statements are investors (existing and potential);
- the investors' main objective is to make economic decisions;
- this means that they need to predict an entity's future cash flows;
- so, financial reporting should provide understandable, relevant, reliable and comparable information for this purpose.

This Framework makes it clear that the primary purpose of financial reporting under this system is *not* to help management to make decisions, or to calculate taxable income, or to calculate what is legally and prudently distributable to the owners, or to check up on what the managers have done with the owners' money. All these uses for accounting are perfectly reasonable and some systems of accounting are particularly designed to achieve these purposes. In certain countries the bias is towards some of these uses, as explained in Chapter 5. For example, if the main purpose of accounting were to calculate prudently distributable income, great emphasis would be placed on never overstating any assets or income (see 'Prudence or conservatism' in section 3.3.4 below). Or, if the main purpose of accounting were to check up on the stewardship of managers, then some emphasis would be placed on recording assets at what had been paid for them. There are plenty of examples of such influences on current accounting practices. Even in IFRSs, many hints of other objectives of accounting can be detected, particularly the stewardship objective. Also, accounting information prepared specifically for one purpose could nevertheless be used for others. However, the main purpose of assisting economic decisions (see particularly paragraphs 10–14 of the IASB's Framework), as outlined above, is now assumed in the development of IFRSs.

Such a framework of ideas was first published in final form by the US standard setter (the Financial Accounting Standards Board, FASB) from the late 1970s, and was followed in most respects by the then International Accounting Standards Committee (IASC) in 1989. Several other English-speaking countries have very similar frameworks. In most countries other than these, there is no explicit detailed framework, particularly where accounting rules are largely confined to laws. This book will concentrate on the IASB's version of the conceptual framework.

**Why it matters**

- *Unless you decide on the intended users and uses of accounting it is unlikely that the accounting system will be designed to be useful.*
- *In most countries, there is no explicit framework. In many countries, other purposes than helping investors to make economic decisions seem to be the main focus of accounting. For these reasons, accounting is performed differently from place to place, and financial statements cannot be easily compared internationally.*

The IASB's and other frameworks also contain an examination of the five 'elements' of financial statements: assets, liabilities, equity, revenues and expenses. These were looked at in Chapter 2, where it was noted that primacy is given to the definitions of 'asset' and 'liability'.

**Activity 3.B**    Consider who is expected to make direct use of a conceptual framework.

**Feedback**    A framework is not itself an accounting standard, and its main purpose is to guide the standard setters when they are writing or revising accounting standards. However, it should also be used as general guidance by those preparing or auditing financial statements. Of more direct effect is International Accounting Standard No. 1 (IAS 1, *Presentation of Financial Statements*). This applies some of the Framework's ideas for use by accountants when preparing financial statements.

## 3.2 Underlying concepts

Before we get to the IASB's concepts, there are some other concepts that are so taken for granted that they are not mentioned in the IASB documents. These conventions include the following.

### 3.2.1 Business entity

This convention holds that an entity has an identity and existence distinct from its owners. To the accountant, whatever the legal position, the business and its owner(s) are considered completely separately. Thus the accountant can speak of the owner having claims against the entity. Think of the basic balance sheet, as in Table 3.1.

Table 3.1 **The basic balance sheet**

| Assets | Equity |
|--------|--------|
|        | Liabilities |
|        |        |
| Total  | Total  |

A properly prepared balance sheet can always be relied upon to balance. This is because equity is the balancing figure, as discussed in Chapter 2. The equity is the amount of wealth invested in the entity by the owner, or the amount of money obtained by the entity from the owner, or the amount the entity 'owes' the owner. None of these three statements could be made unless the accountant is treating the entity as separate from the owner. Another balance sheet could also be drawn up, namely for the owner as an individual. This would contain a record of the owner's investment in the entity, shown as one of the owner's personal assets.

### 3.2.2 Accounting period

This very simple convention recognizes that profit occurs over time, and we cannot usefully speak of profit until we define the length of the period. The maximum length normally used is one year. This does not, of course, preclude the preparation of statements for shorter periods as well. Increasingly, large businesses are reporting externally on a half-yearly or quarterly interim basis, and they may be reporting internally on a monthly basis.

*Why it matters*     *The activities of most businesses are designed to carry on indefinitely. However, users of accounting information need regular reports on progress. So, accountants have to make cut-offs at annual or more frequent intervals. Many accounting problems arise from trying to give an account of unfinished operations.*

## 3.3 The IASB's concepts

### 3.3.1 Overall objective

A large number of concepts, assumptions, etc. can be found in the IASB Framework and IAS 1, but they could be summarized as in Figure 3.1, although the IASB's documents do not list them so neatly into two columns. The overall objective is to give a fair presentation of the state of affairs and performance of a business, so that users of financial statements can make good decisions (IAS 1, paragraphs 5 and 10). In order to achieve this, it is important that the information presented is relevant and reliable. Most of the other concepts can be explained under those two headings. The Framework suggests that, in the IASB context, fair presentation could also be referred to as giving 'a true and fair view', which is the fundamental requirement in the European Union and a number of countries formerly under British influence (and Chapter 5 deals with this in more detail).

Figure 3.1 **IASB's concepts**

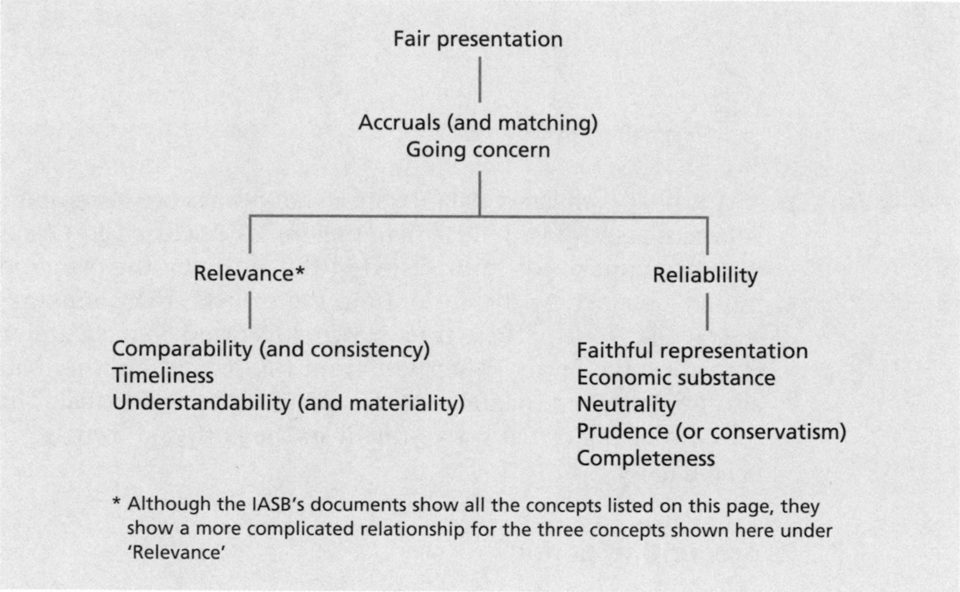

### 3.3.2 Underlying assumptions

#### Accruals, including matching

The essence of the accruals convention is that transactions should be recognized when they occur, not by reference to the date of the *receipt* or *payment* of cash. Also, the process of profit calculation consists of relating together (matching) the revenues with the expenses; it is not concerned with relating together cash receipts and cash payments. Both ways of calculating may be relevant for prediction of the future. The balance sheet and the income statement are based on the accruals convention, but the cash flow statement is not.

Let us take some simple examples of the application of the accruals basis to revenues and expenses. First, in some cases, cash receipts of last year may be revenues of this year. If a business rents out some premises and asks for rent in advance, there may be some rent paid to the business last year on behalf of this year. Also a social club may have received some of this year's subscriptions during last year. In cases like this, cash is received in the accounting year before the one in which it is recognized as revenue. At the time of its receipt there were the effects shown in Figure 3.2.

Figure 3.2 **Effects of accruals (1)**

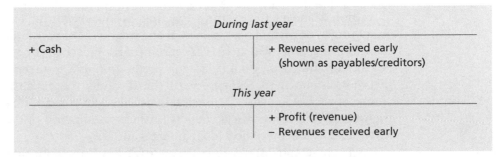

There may be examples of reverse situations to those above. That is, at the end of the year there may be rents not yet received that relate to the year, or credit sales not yet paid for by customers. When these amounts are received during the following year, the cash receipts of that later year will result from the revenues of this year. At the end of this year there will be cash due, as in Figure 3.3.

Figure 3.3 **Effects of accruals (2)**

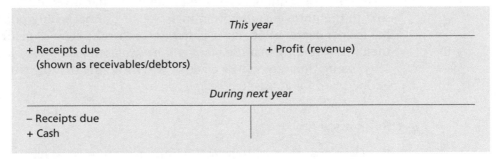

Similarly, payments of last year may be expenses of this year. Examples of this are rents or insurance premiums paid last year by a business to cover part of this year. This gives rise to effects as shown in Figure 3.4.

The reverse of this is where expenses of this year are not paid until next year. This gives rise to accrued expenses, shown as a credit balance in this year's balance sheet. These points are illustrated in a double-entry context in Appendix A.

Figure 3.4 **Effects of accruals (3)**

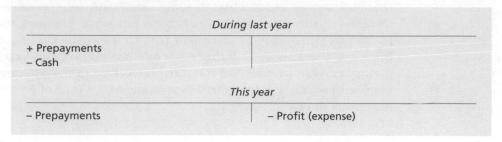

As noted above, the relating together of revenues and expenses is called 'matching'. For example, let us look at the treatment of the purchase of an asset, such as a machine, which lasts for more than one accounting period. It might be paid for immediately but be used in production to earn revenues for ten years. In order to match the expense with the revenue, the expense of the asset is charged over the ten years. This expense is called 'depreciation'; it is a charge for the wearing out of the asset. There is further examination of the recognition of revenue and of depreciation in Chapters 8 and 9.

IAS 1 (paragraph 26) describes the accruals basis of accounting, but notes that 'the application of the matching concept does not allow the recognition of items in the balance sheet which do not meet the definition of assets or liabilities'. This confirms the point made in Chapter 2 that the IASB Framework gives primacy to the definition of asset/liability rather than revenue/expense.

### Going concern

This important convention states that, in the absence of evidence to the contrary, it is assumed that the business will continue for the foreseeable future. This convention has a major influence on evaluating particular items in the balance sheet. The convention allows the assumption that inventory will eventually be sold in the normal course of business, i.e. at normal selling prices. It allows for the idea of depreciation. If the entity depreciates an item of plant over ten years, then it is assuming that the plant will have a useful life *to the entity* of ten years. This assumption can only be made by first assuming that the entity will continue in operation for at least ten years.

## 3.3.3 Relevance

It is clear that, in order to be useful, information must be relevant to its purpose, which is economic decision making. This requires predictions of future cash flows by the investors, which can be based partly on relevant past and present information in statements such as the balance sheet and income statement. Relevance is related to the following concepts.

### Comparability, including consistency

Financial information is unlikely to be relevant unless it can be compared across periods and across companies. This requires as much consistency as possible in the use of methods of measuring and presenting numbers; it requires also that any changes in these methods should be disclosed.

### Timeliness

Relevance is increased if information is up to date. This raises a common problem that there may be an inconsistency between concepts. For example, the need to ensure reliability of information may slow down its publication. The regulators of financial reporting in many countries set time limits for the publication of financial statements and require reporting more than once a year.

### Understandability, including materiality

Clearly, information cannot be relevant unless it can be understood. However, in a complex world, information may have to be complex to achieve a fair presentation. The rule-makers and preparers assume that the important users are educated and intelligent.

Connected with this is the concept of materiality, which implies that insignificant items should not be given the same emphasis as significant items. The insignificant items are by definition unlikely to influence decisions or provide useful information to decision-makers, but they may well cause complication and confusion to the user of financial statements. Immaterial items do not deserve separate disclosure and may not need to be accounted for strictly correctly. What is 'insignificant' in any particular context may be a highly subjective decision.

## 3.3.4 Reliability

For information to be useful, it must be possible for users to depend on it. The several concepts below are related to this, although some of them are also clearly related to relevance.

### Faithful representation

The readers of financial statements should not be misled by the contents of the statements. Transactions, assets and liabilities should be shown in such a way as to represent as well as possible what underlies them. For example, a balance sheet should not show an item under the heading 'assets' unless it meets the definition of an asset. This assumes that readers have a good grasp of the concepts used.

### Economic substance

This concept is related to faithful representation. It is sometimes expressed as showing the economic substance of transactions rather than their legal form. However, this is too simple. The exact economic substance will rest on the exact legal arrangements. The issue here is to see through any superficial legal or other arrangements to the real economic effects.

To take an example, suppose that an entity signs a lease that commits it to paying rentals to use a machine for the whole of the expected life of the machine. This is very similar to borrowing money and buying a machine, in the sense that the entity (under either arrangement) has control over the operational use of the asset and has an obligation to pay money. The legal form is that the entity does not own the machine or have any outstanding unpaid debt owing, but the economic substance is that it has an asset and a liability.

Similarly, if an entity sold a machine to a finance company and immediately leased it back for most of its life, the legal form is that there has been a sale but the substance is that the entity still has the asset.

### Neutrality

To be reliable, information needs to be free from bias, otherwise the prediction of the future will be warped.

### Prudence or conservatism

The most famous bias in accounting is prudence, or conservatism. There is still some room for this, despite the above requirement for neutrality.

Full-blown conservatism can still be found in some countries in order to protect certain users (including creditors) from the risk of making financial statements look too good, particularly given the excessive optimism of some businessmen. Recognizing that a number of estimates are involved in accounting, an accountant, according to this convention, should ensure the avoidance of overstatement by deliberately setting out to achieve a degree of understatement. This requires that similar items, some of which are positive and some of which are negative, should not be treated symmetrically.

In the IASB Framework, prudence is not supposed to be this overridingly strong. It is instead the exercise of a degree of caution in the context of uncertainty. In 2008, the IASB issued an exposure draft of parts of a revised Framework, in which prudence does not appear at all.

### Completeness

Information needs to be as complete as possible within the constraints of materiality. Any important omissions would cause the financial statements to be misleading. However, the regulators (the standard setters in the case of the IASB) should bear in mind that some demands for information may be too costly to an entity. The benefits of information should outweigh the costs of producing it.

*Why it matters*    *If you try to be neutral, you may overstate assets or profits, thereby misleading lenders and others about how strong the business is. If, instead, you try to be prudent, you will almost certainly understate assets and profits, so investors may make the wrong decisions by selling shares too soon or not buying enough. This is one of the many examples of the requirement for judgement in accounting. It is an art, not a mechanical numerical exercise. That makes it interesting.*

## 3.4   A hierarchy of concepts and some inconsistencies

There are several levels of concept. These could be summarized as:

- **Level A.** The ultimate purpose of accounting, according to the IASB: to give a fair presentation of information in order to help users to make economic decisions.

- **Level B.** A series of derivative concepts and conventions related to relevance and reliability.
- **Level C.** Detailed technical rules of how to recognize, measure and present assets, liabilities, equity, revenues, expenses, cash flows and various related disclosures. For example, a Level C rule would be that the valuation of land and buildings must be based on their original cost not on their current value.

One problem with Level B has already been noted when examining the various concepts. That is, there are inconsistencies. For example:

1. **Prudence and going concern.** The going concern convention assumes that the firm will 'keep going', e.g. that it will not be forced out of business by competition or bankruptcy. This may be a likely and rational assumption, but it is not necessarily prudent – indeed, in certain circumstances, such as the financial turmoil of 2008/9, it could be decidedly risky.
2. **Prudence and matching.** The matching convention, building on the going concern convention, allows us to carry forward assets into future periods on the grounds that they will be used profitably later. This clearly makes major assumptions about the future that may not be at all prudent. The tension between these two conventions is one of the major problems of accounting practice, and it underlies many of the more difficult issues discussed in Part 2 of this book.
3. **Prudence and neutrality.** Neutrality implies freedom from bias. However, prudence, quite explicitly, implies that the accountant *should* bias information in a certain direction.

| Activity 3.C | A more general problem than the inconsistency of various concepts is an overall tension between relevance and reliability. Consider the best way to arrive at a balance sheet value for assets, such as land and buildings. Which methods of valuation might be most relevant and which most reliable? |
| --- | --- |

| Feedback | Some form of current value (e.g. today's selling price or replacement cost) would provide more relevant information than the cost of several years ago. However, all these values are estimates, so original cost might be more reliably measured. |
| --- | --- |

Since the detailed rules at Level C are based on somewhat vague and potentially inconsistent concepts at Levels A and B, there is plenty of scope for different rules in different countries and at different times. Of course, this diversity is even more likely where different frameworks are in use or where there is no explicit framework. In many systems, including IFRS, some of the detailed rules were made before the frameworks were agreed upon. As a result, some IASB standards are not consistent with the IASB framework (e.g. see Section 9.4 on leasing).

In IFRSs, the Level A objective (fair presentation) is to be used for the following purposes:

- to guide standard setters when making Level C rules in individual accounting standards;

- to guide preparers and auditors of financial statements in interpreting the Level B concepts and the Level C rules;
- to guide preparers and auditors in the absence of a relevant Level C rule;
- to require preparers sometimes to make extra disclosures in order to achieve a fair presentation;
- in exceptional circumstances, to require preparers to depart from Level C rules in order to achieve a fair presentation.

The last of these (the 'override') is controversial. Philosophically, it makes sense to be able to override detailed rules in pursuit of the ultimate objective. However, given that that objective is vague, it might allow preparers to evade rules that they do not like. This issue is taken further in Chapter 5.

In member states of the EU and in some other European countries, laws are based on the EU Fourth Directive, which contains a similar Level A objective, somewhat similar Level B concepts, several Level C rules (including many options), and an override. Other national systems under former UK influence have, or have had, somewhat similar systems.

## 3.5 Possible future developments

We have pointed out that the IASB Framework was issued in 1989, and has not been revised. Since its issue there have been great changes to the requirements of particular IFRSs, and changes in the politics of financial reporting harmonization. In particular, the IASB and the US Financial Accounting Standards Board are now working closely together, and they are committed to providing a revised conceptual framework which is common to both bodies.

In 2008, an exposure draft was jointly issued by IASB and FASB, suggesting changes to those parts of the IASB Framework relating to the objective of financial reporting and to qualitative characteristics of decision-useful financial reporting information. For example, it is proposed that 'reliability', a key concept in 1989, should disappear as a separate concept, being subsumed within 'faithful representation' and (as noted earlier) that prudence should disappear altogether. It is too early, at the time of writing, to predict the eventual outcome as regards a new agreed and published Framework. Further discussion papers and exposure drafts will be issued. The whole debate and its progress should be followed, via the IASB's wedsite: **www.iasb.org**.

**Summary**

- This chapter has pointed out that the fundamentals of accounting could be applied in a number of ways, depending on the purposes of the accounting. This book is concerned with *external* financial reporting, not that for management, but even then various users and uses are possible. The type of accounting examined here is now the predominant sort used by most large companies in the world. Its main purpose can be seen in the IASB Framework: to enable investors to predict cash flows in order to make economic decisions.

- Present accounting (even that designed for investors) contains vestiges of other purposes, such as creditor-protection or accountability of management.

- Some underlying concepts are common to most reporting: separating the entity from the owner; recording two aspects of each transaction; and splitting up operations into regular periods.

- The IFRS system has several levels of concepts:
  - the overall objective of fair presentation;
  - a second level of concepts, which could be summarized as the need for relevance and reliability; and
  - a third level of detailed rules, which are generally found in individual accounting standards but are based on the IASB Framework.

- The first two levels are somewhat vague and contain inconsistencies. In particular, there is often a need to trade some reliability in order to gain some extra relevance, or vice versa.

- The overall objective should override the other levels of concepts and rules. This certainly applies to the standard setters, although it may be dangerous to allow individual companies to use such a vague excuse to break the rules.

## References and research

The most relevant IASB literature on the issues of this chapter is:

- the Framework
- IAS 1 (revised 2007): *Presentation of Financial Statements*

Some research papers of particular relevance are:

- D. Alexander, 'A benchmark for the adequacy of published financial statements', *Accounting and Business Research*, Vol. 29, No. 3, 1999.
- D. Alexander, 'The over-riding importance of internationalism: a reply to Nobes', *Accounting and Business Research*, Vol. 31, No. 2, 2001.
- L. Evans and C. Nobes, 'Some mysteries relating to the prudence principle in the Fourth Directive and in German and British Law', *European Accounting Review*, Vol. 5, No. 2, 1996.
- C. Nobes, 'Is true and fair of over-riding importance? A comment on Alexander's benchmark', *Accounting and Business Research*, Vol. 30, No. 4, 2000.

## ? EXERCISES

*Feedback on the first two of these exercises is given in Appendix D.*

3.1 (a) Which accounting conventions/concepts do you regard as most important in helping preparers and auditors of financial statements to do their work, and why?
    (b) Which accounting conventions do you regard as most useful from the viewpoint of the readers of financial statements, and why?
    (c) Explain any differences between your answers to (a) and (b) above.

3.2 'Substance over form is a recipe for failing to achieve comparability between accounting statements for different businesses.' Discuss.

3.3 What various purposes might there be for accounting? Which does the IASB focus particularly on?

3.4 Equity investors are major users of financial statements. Identify the general nature of the 'information needs' of this group of users. Describe the likely specific uses of company financial information by investors, and give examples of information that may be relevant to each of these uses.

3.5 'Neutrality is about freedom from bias. Prudence is a bias. It is not possible to embrace both conventions in one coherent framework.' Discuss.

3.6 To what extent is the search for relevance of financial information hampered by the need for reliability?

3.7 On 21 December 20X7, your client paid €10,000 for an advertising campaign. The advertisements will be heard on local radio stations between 1 January and 31 January 20X8. Your client believes that, as a result, sales will increase by 60 per cent in 20X8 (over 20X7 levels) and by 40 per cent in 20X9 (over 20X7 levels). There will be no further benefits.

Write a memorandum to your client explaining your views on how this item should be treated in the year-end financial statements for each of the three years. Your answer should include explicit reference to relevant traditional accounting conventions, and to the requirements of users of published financial statements.

# Chapter 4

# The regulation of accounting

**Contents**

| | | |
|---|---|---|
| 4.1 | Introduction: various ways to regulate accounting | 48 |
| 4.2 | Legal systems | 48 |
| 4.3 | Entities | 50 |
| 4.4 | Examples of regulation | 53 |
| | 4.4.1 Germany | 53 |
| | 4.4.2 France | 54 |
| | 4.4.3 The Netherlands | 54 |
| | 4.4.4 The United Kingdom | 56 |
| | 4.4.5 The United States | 56 |
| | 4.4.6 Australia | 57 |
| | 4.4.7 China | 57 |
| | 4.4.8 Some other countries | 57 |
| | 4.4.9 Generally accepted accounting principles (GAAP) | 57 |
| 4.5 | The regulation of International Standards | 58 |
| | Summary | 59 |
| | References and research | 59 |
| | Exercises | 60 |

**Objectives**

After studying the chapter carefully, you should be able to:

- describe the various sources from which accounting rules can come;

- outline the two main types of legal system to be found in much of the world, and how this affects accounting;

- explain the different ways in which entities might be legally organized;

- give examples of the ways in which the regulation of accounting is arranged in various countries.

## 4.1  Introduction: various ways to regulate accounting

This chapter is about how accounting can be regulated, about how it is regulated in particular countries, and about the different types of enterprises whose reporting is regulated.

The context here is mainly the regulation of the financial reports designed for those users who are outside the entity. On the whole, no regulation is appropriate for management accounting information. Entities choose what is most useful for themselves. Of course, the calculation of taxable profit for the tax authorities has to be regulated, but that is not considered in this book unless it directly affects financial reporting to other users, such as investors (see Chapter 12).

In most countries, it is not thought appropriate to regulate bookkeeping in any detail, although there are generally requirements that orderly books should be kept so that auditors and tax authorities could investigate them where this seems necessary to confirm the contents of financial reports. In a few countries, such as Belgium and France, bookkeeping is regulated in detail, as is noted below.

As explained briefly in Chapter 3, financial reporting could be regulated in a number of ways, including:

- legislation, such as Companies Acts and Commercial Codes;
- other rules issued by departments of government (such as a Ministry of Finance) or by committees operating under their control;
- rules of stock exchanges;
- rules from governmental regulators of stock exchanges;
- accounting guidelines or standards issued by committees of the accountancy profession;
- accounting guidelines or standards issued by independent private-sector bodies acting in the public interest.

The expression 'accounting standard' is used here to mean a document containing a series of instructions on a particular topic of financial reporting (e.g. how to value inventories), where the standard is written in the private (non-governmental) sector and is intended to be obeyed in full before an entity or an auditor can claim compliance with the system of rules of which the standards form part.

Section 4.2 looks at how legal systems differ around the world. Section 4.3 examines how the legal nature of entities can differ as they become larger and more complex. For financial reporting regulation, it is important to separate the creation of rules from their enforcement. For example, in the United States most accounting rules are to be found in accounting standards but the enforcement, for certain companies, comes from the stock exchange regulator. This example and others are examined in more detail in Section 4.4; and the regulation of IASB standards is considered in Section 4.5.

## 4.2  Legal systems

One of the reasons why accounting is regulated in different ways in different countries is that the whole nature of the legal system differs internationally.

Two main systems can be identified in the developed world: Roman codified law and common law. Most countries in continental Western Europe have a system of law that is based on the Roman *jus civile*, as compiled by Justinian in the sixth century AD and developed by European universities from the twelfth century. The word 'codified' may be associated with such a system; for example, commercial codes establish rules in detail for accounting and financial reporting. Both the nature of regulation and the type of detailed rules to be found in a country are affected. For example, in Germany, company accounting is to a large extent considered as a branch of company law. However, with the introduction of International Financial Reporting Standards for the consolidated financial statements of listed entities within the European Union, the relationship between financial reporting, at least at the consolidated level, and national legal systems is becoming less strong. These changes are discussed in Chapter 5.

In France, Belgium, Spain, Portugal and Greece, much of the detail of accounting rules is found in 'accounting plans' (e.g. the French *plan comptable général*), which are documents under the control of government committees. One feature of most accounting plans is a chart of accounts, which contains a detailed structure of account codes for use in the double-entry bookkeeping systems of entities. The chart covers the origination of entries and leads through to financial statements. Such uniform (or standardized) accounting was invented in Germany in the early years of the twentieth century, and it has been used in several Western European countries. For example, the chart within the French plan is compulsory for tax purposes for French entities. Charts have also been used extensively in Eastern Europe.

In Italy, Germany and several of the other countries already mentioned, commercial codes contain many legal instructions on accounting. In many such countries, the codes date back to Napoleon, who adopted and adapted the Roman legal system. Japan introduced a commercial legal system similar to that of Germany in the second half of the nineteenth century. China, too, has a similar system. Systems of commercial law in Nordic countries bear a relationship to the Roman legal system.

By contrast to these codified systems, many other countries use a version of the English legal system, which relies upon a limited amount of statute law. This is then interpreted by courts, which build up large amounts of case law to supplement the statutes. Such a 'common law' system was formed in England primarily after the Norman Conquest (1066) by judges acting on the king's behalf. The common law is less abstract than codified law; a common law rule seeks to provide an answer to a specific case rather than to formulate a general rule for the future. This common law system may be found in similar forms in many countries influenced by England. Thus, the federal law of the United States, the laws of Ireland, India, Australia, and so on are to a greater or lesser extent modelled on English common law. This naturally influences company law, which traditionally does not prescribe a large number of detailed all-embracing rules to cover the behaviour of companies and how they should publish their financial statements. To a large extent (at least up until the British Companies Act 1981), accounting within such a context is not dependent upon law but is an independent discipline.

Why it matters *The way in which accounting is regulated has a great effect on how it works. In Roman law countries, accounting tends to be in the control of governments and lawyers. In common law countries, accountants are more important in the setting and interpretation of accounting rules. This means that accounting rules can be changed more easily in common law countries, and are changed more often. In such countries, the rules are more likely to be designed to be commercially useful. However, in Roman law countries there can be more democratic control over accounting.*

**Activity 4.A**

For your own country, describe the balance between the regulatory influences on accounting. For example, how important are elements of law compared with guidance written by accountants?

**Feedback**

You should try to find out (or remember) whether in your country there are any of the following elements:

- Companies Acts;
- Commercial Code;
- accounting plans;
- mandatory accounting standards;
- professional guidelines;
- stock exchange requirements;
- requirements of a stock exchange regulator;
- other.

You may discover that some of these relate to only certain types of enterprises.

Having recorded your own answer, now read Sections 4.3 and 4.4 to see whether they would improve your answer.

## 4.3 Entities

This book has generally referred to business being conducted by 'entities', which is the word now used by the IASB. It is a word designed to cover all ways of organizing business operations. At one extreme, a business can be run by a single person with no other owners, and no organization which is legally separate from the person. This business might be called a 'sole trader'.

The sole trader has unlimited liability for the debts of the business and pays personal income tax on the profits. If the business is to be sold, then the trader must sell the separate assets and liabilities because there is no legal entity to sell. Nevertheless, the trader keeps the accounts for the business distinct from other personal activities, in accordance with the 'business entity' convention discussed in Chapter 3. Otherwise, the success of the business and the amount of tax to pay will be unclear.

As the business becomes larger, it may be useful to have some joint owners (partners) who can contribute skills and money. The business then becomes a partnership, which is formalized by a contract between the partners that specifies their rights and duties. In common law countries, such as the United States and

England (though not Scotland), a partnership does not have separate legal existence for most purposes. So, the partners are legally responsible for its assets and liabilities, and they pay tax on their share of the profits. Nevertheless, it is possible to set up a 'limited liability partnership' (LLP) and, for example, many accountancy firms have done so. The purpose of this is to seek to protect the partners from some part of the liabilities of the business if there are large legal cases. In Roman law countries, some forms of partnership do have separate legal status, although generally the partners still pay the business's tax.

The complete separation of owners from their business is achieved by setting up a company, usually with limited liability for the owners. The ownership of the company is denoted by shares, which can be transferred from one owner (a shareholder) to another without affecting the company's existence. A company is a separate legal entity from its owners. The company can buy and sell assets, and it pays tax on its own profit.

In many jurisdictions, including the whole of the EU, companies can be either private or public. The private company is not allowed to create a public market in its shares, so they have to be exchanged by private agreement between the owners and the company. Many small businesses are set up as private companies. Table 4.1 shows some designations of such companies in the EU.

Public companies are allowed to have their shares traded on markets. Some designations of public companies are also shown in Table 4.1. Public companies have to comply with some extra rules because they can offer shares to the public but these rules vary by country and are of no importance for your accounting studies at this stage. Figure 4.1 shows the four types of enterprise discussed so far. Size and complexity tend to increase towards the right.

**Table 4.1 Some EU (and EEA) company names**

| | Private | Public |
| --- | --- | --- |
| Belgium, France, Luxembourg | Société à responsabilité limitée (Sarl) | Société anonyme (SA) |
| Denmark | Anpartsselskab (ApS) | Aktieselskab (AS) |
| Finland | Osakeyhtiö-yksityinen (Oy) | Osakeyhtiö julkinen (Oyj) |
| Germany, Austria | Gesellschaft mit beschränkter Haftung (GmbH) | Aktiengesellschaft (AG) |
| Greece | Etairia periorismenis efthynis (EPE) | Anonymos etairia (AE) |
| Italy | Società a responsabilità limitata (SRL) | Società per azioni (SpA) |
| Netherlands, Belgium | Besloten vennootschap (BV) | Naamloze vennootschap (NV) |
| Norway | Aksjeselskap (AS) | Almennaksjeselskap (ASA) |
| Portugal | Sociedade por quotas (Lda) | Sociedade anónima (SA) |
| Spain | Sociedad de responsabilidad limitada (SRL) | Sociedad anónima (SA) |
| Sweden | Aktiebolag-privat | Aktiebolag-publikt |
| United Kingdom, Ireland | Private limited company (Ltd) | Public limited company (plc) |

Figure 4.1 **Four types of entity**

Sole trader ⟶ Partnership ⟶ Private company ⟶ Public company

The biggest form of market for shares is a stock exchange. Companies that are listed (quoted) on a stock exchange have extra rules to obey coming from stock exchanges, regulators of stock exchanges or other sources.

There are some linguistic problems here. First, the English word 'company' has no exact equivalent in some other languages. For example, the French *société* and the German *Gesellschaft* are broader terms also covering partnerships. Another problem is that the term 'public company' tends to be used, particularly in the United States, to mean *listed* company. It is true that only public limited companies in the UK (and their equivalents elsewhere in Europe) are *allowed* to be listed, but most such companies choose not to be. Figure 4.2 expresses some forms of entities in more detail than Figure 4.1.

Figure 4.2 **Entities in more detail**

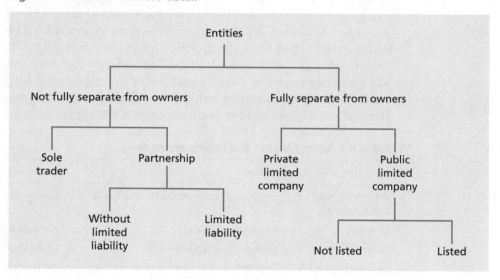

Activity 4.B For your own country, try to allocate legal designations (such as those in Table 4.1) to each of the types of entity identified in Figure 4.2.

Feedback Let us take the example of France. Some designations are clear:

- partnerships can come in several forms, such as 'snc' (*société en nom collectif*);
- private limited companies are designated as 'Sarl', and public companies as 'SA'.

As another example, in the UK:

- partnerships have no designation, except that the limited liability partnership would be labelled 'LLP';
- private companies have 'Ltd' after their names, and public have 'plc'.

As a business continues to increase in size and complexity, it may find it useful to arrange its affairs as a group of companies. This is particularly the case when it operates in more than one country, because it has to deal with different laws and taxes. Figure 4.3 illustrates a possible group. In this example, the Dutch Flower Company is a public limited company with many shareholders. It owns all the shares in private companies in the United Kingdom and Germany. The Dutch company can be called the parent and the other two companies are subsidiaries.

**Figure 4.3 An international group**

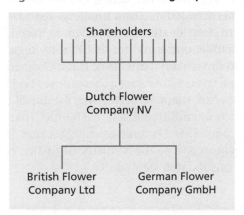

The managers of the parent control all the decisions of the three companies, which therefore act together as a group. For many purposes it is useful to look at the total operations of the three companies added together. Financial statements that do this are called group statements or consolidated statements. The process of preparing them is examined in detail in Chapter 14.

## 4.4 Examples of regulation

### 4.4.1 Germany

Except for financial reporting under IFRS, the basic source of accounting rules in Germany is the Commercial Code (*Handelsgesetzbuch*, abbreviated to HGB, and literally meaning the 'commercial law book'). The HGB is amended from time to time, most fundamentally in 1985 as a result of implementation of EU Directives (see Chapter 5). More recently, amendments have been more frequent, in order to keep pace with the implications of increasing international convergence. The HGB covers all types of enterprise in Germany, but limited companies have special rules and larger companies must be audited.

Because of the close links between tax and accounting in Germany (see Section 5.2), the rules of tax law and the decisions of tax courts are also important for financial reporting. For listed companies, there are some additional disclosure requirements in a special law.

Compliance with the rules is the responsibility of the management of an entity. Auditors will check certain features of compliance. The tax authorities will check matters of concern to them. However, the consolidated financial statements of groups are generally not relevant for tax, even though parents and certain subsidiaries can sometimes be treated together for tax purposes (see Section 12.2). Therefore, there may not be a fully effective enforcement mechanism, particularly for consolidated statements.

From 1998 in Germany, consolidated statements of listed companies were allowed to depart from the normal requirements of the HGB if they followed 'internationally recognized rules' instead. There were other conditions, but US rules and international standards were accepted. A number of large German companies took advantage of this permission. From financial years beginning in 2005, however, this nationally-inspired flexibility has been replaced by the EU-wide requirements relating to IFRS adoption. From 2007, IFRS regulations are compulsory for the consolidated financial statements of listed German companies, and those groups which changed to US GAAP for such purposes had to change again.

Also in 1998, a private-sector standard setter was established: the Deutsches Rechnungslegungs Standards Committee (DRSC). The fact that the German for 'standards committee' is 'Standards Committee' tells us that it is an imported concept. The DRSC can recommend to the Ministry of Justice rules designed for listed companies in their consolidated statements.

### 4.4.2 France

Except for companies using IFRS, the most detailed source of accounting instructions in France is the *plan comptable général* (PCG, general accounting plan). As explained in Section 4.2, the PCG is a large document within the control of a governmental committee. Part of the PCG is a chart of accounts that regulates how double entries should be made; another part specifies the formats that financial statements should follow. The tax system uses the output in PCG format, so that there is detailed enforcement.

An outline of the chart of accounts in the French PCG, as amended in 1999, is shown as Table 4.2. The table shows only two digits, whereas the full plan has detailed account codes down to four (and sometimes five) digits. The recording of each type of transaction can be specified in great detail, so that it can be standardized throughout France. For example, an increase in depreciation on plant and machinery is recorded as:

Debit:  Account 68112 (Depreciation expense on tangible fixed (non-current) assets)
Credit:  Account 2815 (Cumulative depreciation on plant and machinery).

France also has a Civil Code and several Companies Acts. All larger companies must be audited. For listed companies, there is a stock exchange regulator that exercises some enforcement powers.

### 4.4.3 The Netherlands

The Netherlands has a Civil Code but no history of great detail in its accounting regulations. Like the United Kingdom, the Netherlands implemented the relevant EU Directives by including many of the Directives' options. 'Guidelines'

**Table 4.2 Outline of French chart of accounts**

| Balance sheet | | | | | Operating | |
|---|---|---|---|---|---|---|
| Class 1 | Class 2 | Class 3 | Class 4 | Class 5 | Class 6 | Class 7 |
| *Owner equity, loans and similar liabilities* | *Fixed assets* | *Inventory and work in progress* | *Debtors and creditors* | *Financial* | *Charges* | *Income* |
| 10 Capital and reserves | 20 Intangible assets | 30 – | 40 Suppliers and related accounts | 50 Investment securities | 60 Purchases (except 603). 603: Change in stocks (supplies and goods for resale) | 70 Sales of manufactured goods, services, goods for resale |
| 11 Profit or loss carried forward | 21 Tangible assets | 31 Raw materials (and consumables) | 41 Customers and related accounts | 51 Banks and credit institutions | 61 External services | 71 Change in stocks of finished goods and work in progress |
| 12 Profit or loss for the financial year | 22 Assets in concession | 32 Other consumables | 42 Staff and related accounts | 52 – | 62 Other external services | 72 Own work capitalized |
| 13 Investment grants | 23 Assets in course of construction | 33 Work in progress (goods) | 43 Social security and other social agencies | 53 Cash in hand | 63 Taxes, levies and similar payments | 73 Net period income from long-term transactions |
| 14 Tax-regulated provisions | 24 – | 34 Work in progress (services) | 44 Government and other public authorities | 54 Expenditure authorizations and letters of credit | 64 Staff costs | 74 Operating grants |
| 15 Provision for liabilities and charges | 25 – | 35 Finished goods | 45 Group and associates | 55 – | 65 Other current operating charges | 75 Other current operating income |
| 16 Loans and similar liabilities | 26 Participating interests and related amounts owned | 36 – | 46 Sundry debtors and creditors | 56 – | 66 Financial charges | 76 Financial income |
| 17 Debts related to participating interests | 27 Other financial assets | 37 Goods for resale | 47 Provisional and suspense accounts | 57 – | 67 Extraordinary charges | 77 Extraordinary income |
| 18 Reciprocal branch and joint venture accounts | 28 Cumulative depreciation on fixed assets | 38 – | 48 Accruals | 58 Internal transfers | 68 Appropriations to depreciation and provisions | 78 Depreciation and provisions written back |
| 19 – | 29 Provisions for diminution in value of fixed assets | 39 Provisions for diminution in value of stocks and work in progress | 49 Provisions for doubtful debts | 59 Provisions for diminution in value of financial assets | 69 Employee profit share – income and similar taxes | 79 Charges transferred |

*Notes:* '–' = code not used.
*Source:* adapted and translated from the *plan comptable général*, Conseil National de la Comptabilité.

for financial reporting are prepared by a private-sector body: the Raad voor de Jaarverslaggeving (RJ; Council for Annual Reporting). The members of the RJ include preparers, users and auditors; and the auditing profession provides most of the technical support for the RJ. However, the guidelines cannot be enforced, and companies and auditors do not have to disclose non-compliance.

There is also an Enterprise Chamber of the High Court, which can hear cases concerning alleged poor financial reporting. However, it hears few cases and has not tried to enforce the guidelines.

This situation has in the past given Dutch companies considerable flexibility, but from 2007 (for most companies, from 2005) full IFRS is compulsory for consolidated financial statements of all Dutch-listed entities.

### 4.4.4 The United Kingdom

There have been Companies Acts in the UK since 1844, but the accounting content was not detailed until the relevant EU Directives were implemented in the 1980s. All companies are covered, and audits are required in all cases except small companies ('small' being defined).

There are also accounting standards, which are more detailed than the present Companies Act (of 2006) on many issues. The standards were set by a committee of the accountancy profession until 1990 but are now set by an independent private-sector body, the Accounting Standards Board. The overriding requirement of the Companies Act is that financial statements must give a true and fair view. This requirement is given more substance in the UK than elsewhere because the standard setters make requirements that remove some of the options in law and sometimes even contradict the detail of the law.

Enforcement of the rules (either national or IFRS) is achieved because companies and auditors can be taken to court (by the Financial Reporting Review Panel (FRRP), another private-sector body) for 'defective accounts', and legal opinion is that financial statements that break accounting standards are likely to be defective, although this would ultimately be subject to the court's interpretation of the implications of the true and fair override.

IFRSs are now compulsory for the consolidated financial statements of all listed companies. However, the national standard setter (the ASB) has moved many national standards towards IFRS, so differences between the two systems are often small.

### 4.4.5 The United States

There are no general Companies Acts or Codes in the United States, and so most companies have little regulation and no audit requirement although most details vary state by state. However, for listed companies there is the world's most active regulator: the Securities and Exchange Commission (SEC). The SEC was founded in 1934 as a reaction to the free-for-all in accounting that contributed to the Wall Street Crash of 1929. The SEC requires the use of 'generally accepted accounting principles' (GAAP) and also requires an audit. The SEC imposes serious penalties on auditors and companies that break the rules.

The SEC makes some of the content of GAAP but mostly chooses to rely upon the private sector to do this. Since 1973, the chosen body is the Financial Accounting Standards Board (FASB), which is a private-sector body set up to act in the public interest. The FASB is independent but is influenced by the fact that it can be overruled by the SEC.

### 4.4.6 Australia

Australia has for several decades developed a tradition of accounting standards, via the Australian Accounting Standards Board (AASB). Since 1998, the monitoring and enforcement of compliance with accounting standards by listed companies has been a function of the Australian Securities and Investments Commission (ASIC). The ASIC takes a proactive role, with its own surveillance programme. Like the FRRP in the UK the ASIC has the power to take companies to court and, unlike the FRRP up until the time of writing, has actually done so on a number of occasions, though more consensual procedures are in train.

For 2005 onwards, Australia has largely adopted IFRSs. This process is sometimes referred to as adoption, but minor adaptation would be a more accurate description because the AASB turns international standards into Australian ones.

### 4.4.7 China

Following decades of central planning following the introduction of communism, Western ideas have, especially since the early 1990s, had major influence on financial reporting in China. Several stock exchanges were opened, there is a professional body, the Chinese Institute of Certified Accountants (CICPA), and a large number of Chinese Accounting Standards, 33 at the time of writing, closely modelled on International Accounting Standards, have been issued.

Practical government influence remains strong by Western standards. For example, the CICPA is under the control of the Ministry of Finance, and its members audit the application of Chinese Accounting Standards which are issued by the Ministry of Finance. At the time of writing, all Chinese entities listed on local stock exchanges have more than 50 per cent of their equity owned by the government. Nevertheless, developments have been significant in recent years.

### 4.4.8 Some other countries

Many other countries are similar to one or more of the above. For example, the Nordic countries have Bookkeeping Acts and Companies Acts which have incorporated the EU Directives. They also have various forms of accounting standards, set by committees involving representatives of various bodies, such as the accountancy profession and stock exchanges.

### 4.4.9 Generally accepted accounting principles (GAAP)

The term 'GAAP' is of US origin but is commonly used to describe accounting requirements, and so the term 'Swedish GAAP' might also be used, for example.

In the United States, in the absence of company law, the term first meant the practices of large and respected companies, as recommended by textbooks and accepted by auditors. By the 1930s in the US, GAAP began to be codified, so that there is now also written (or promulgated) GAAP including accounting standards. The SEC requires companies registered with it to comply with GAAP.

In other countries, 'GAAP' is generally an unofficial term with no exact meaning, although there is a similar term, namely 'good accounting practice', in the laws of some countries, such as Denmark. For example, if one sees the term 'Swedish GAAP' it presumably includes Swedish law, Swedish accounting standards and the practices of respected companies and auditors.

## 4.5 The regulation of International Standards

The IASB and the content of its standards are examined in more detail in Chapter 5, but it is appropriate here to look briefly at regulation. IAS 1 requires that financial statements described as complying with International Financial Reporting Standards should comply with all requirements of all the IFRSs. If national rules require compliance with IFRSs, then domestic mechanisms can cover their enforcement. For example, in some countries (e.g. Malaysia), the national standard setter adopts IFRSs.

In the EU (and EEA), listed companies are required to use IFRSs for their consolidated statements. For unlisted companies and for unconsolidated statements, the position varies around Europe. IFRSs can either be compulsory, optional or not allowed. In 2009, IASB issued a separate 'IFRS for SMEs', i.e. for small and medium sized enterprises. It aims to provide in a simple document of 230 pages, plus some 100 plus pages of explanation and comment (compared with 3,000 pages for the full IFRS), a rigorous and common set of accounting standards for SMEs that is much simpler than the full IFRS. Its usage is entirely separate from full IFRS, and its usage or non-usage, and the role of such usage, is entirely a matter for individual jurisdictions. Where IFRSs or IFRS for SMEs are not used, the national systems continue. All this implies that such IFRS statements fall within the scope of national legal and enforcement systems. This means that the FRRP in the UK and the stock exchange regulator in France carry out the monitoring. In the EU, consolidated financial statements of listed entities are generally certified as being 'in accordance with IFRS as endorsed by the European Union'.

This book explains and examines financial reporting using IFRSs as the main regulatory reference but also bearing in mind the need for all EU companies (and those in other European Economic Area countries, such as Norway) to comply with EU rules.

*Why it matters*   *If national rules cannot be enforced, then the rule-makers are likely to set weak rules with many options in them. Even then, the rules might not be strictly complied with. The result will be a set of rules and financial statements that are not well regarded domestically or internationally.*

*The IASB's predecessor spent most of the 1990s improving its standards, as explained in the next chapter, but the IFRS system is presently somewhat undermined by a lack of consistent enforcement.*

## Summary

■ This chapter examines the various ways in which accounting (and particularly financial reporting) can be regulated, such as by legislation, stock exchange regulations or accounting standards.

■ Most countries of direct concern in this book can be neatly divided into two types with respect to the predominant legal system: codified law countries (Roman in origin) and common law countries (English in origin).

■ As entities become larger and more complex, they often move from a sole trader format to a partnership to a private limited company to a public limited company. Some of the last of these have their securities traded on stock exchanges.

■ Germany illustrates regulation by commercial code; France by accounting plan; the US by stock exchange regulator and private independent standard setter; the UK by Companies Act and private independent standard setter; and the Netherlands by civil code and by guidelines under the main influence of the accountancy profession.

■ International Financial Reporting Standards have no built-in regulatory mechanism of their own but can be imposed by national regulators.

## References and research

The IASB document particularly relevant to this chapter is IAS 1, *Presentation of Financial Statements*.

The following are examples of research papers in the English language that take the issues of this chapter further:

■ P. Brown and T. Tarca, '2005. Its here, ready or not: A review of the Australian financial reporting framework', *Australian Accounting Review*, July 2005.
■ B. Chaveau, 'The Spanish *Plan General de Contabilidad*: Agent of development and innovation?' *European Accounting Review*, Vol. 4, No. 1, 1995.
■ L. Evans, B. Eierle and A. Haller, 'The enforcer', *Accountancy*, January 2002.
■ K. Schipper, 'The introduction of international accounting standards in Europe: Implications for international convergence', *European Accounting Review*, Vol. 14, No. 1, 2005.
■ D. Street and S. Bryant, 'Disclosure level and compliance with IASs. A comparison of companies with and without US listings and filings', *International Journal of Accounting*, Vol. 35, No. 3, 2000.
■ D. Street and S. Gray, *Observance of International Accounting Standards: Factors explaining non-compliance*, Association of Chartered Certified Accountants, London, 2001.
■ D. Street, S. Gray and S. Bryant, 'Acceptance and observance of International Accounting Standards: An empirical study of companies claiming to comply with IASs', *International Journal of Accounting*, Vol. 34, No. 1, 1999.

## ? EXERCISES

*Feedback on the first two of these exercises is given in Appendix D.*

4.1 Do you think Roman law or common law provides a better context in which financial reporting can achieve its objectives? Explain the reasons for your choice.

4.2 What are the advantages and disadvantages of making accounting rules by law as opposed to private-sector standards?

4.3 Contrast the degree to which the state is involved in the regulation of accounting in Germany, the United Kingdom, the United States and (if not one of those three) your own country.

4.4 Who is supposed to obey accounting standards in the United States? Are they followed in practice?

4.5 Explain the various possible advantages that a number of sole traders might obtain by joining together as a partnership.

4.6 Explain the various advantages and disadvantages of moving to a corporate form of business instead of operating as a partnership.

# Chapter 5

# International differences and harmonization

**Contents**   5.1   Introduction: the international nature of the development of accounting          62
         5.2   Classification                                                                        63
                 5.2.1   Introduction                                                                63
                 5.2.2   Classifications using survey data                                           65
                 5.2.3   Nobes' classification                                                       65
                 5.2.4   An updated classification                                                   67
         5.3   Influences on differences                                                             70
                 5.3.1   Introduction                                                                70
                 5.3.2   Providers of finance                                                        71
                 5.3.3   Legal systems                                                               74
                 5.3.4   Taxation                                                                    75
                 5.3.5   The accountancy profession                                                  76
                 5.3.6   Synthesis                                                                   78
                 5.3.7   International influences                                                     79
         5.4   Harmonization in the European Union                                                   80
                 5.4.1   Introduction to harmonization                                               80
                 5.4.2   Relevant EU Directives                                                       80
                 5.4.3   The example of accounting 'principles'                                       82
                 5.4.4   The EU Regulation of 2002                                                    85
                 5.4.5   Expansion of the EU                                                          85
         5.5   The International Accounting Standards Board                                           85
                 5.5.1   Nature and purpose of the IASC/B                                             85
                 5.5.2   Influence of the IASB                                                        86
                 5.5.3   IFRS for SMEs                                                                89
                 Summary                                                                             89
                 References and research                                                             90
                 Exercises                                                                           91

**Objectives**   After studying this chapter carefully, you should be able to:

- outline the international nature of accounting developments;
- suggest the major causes of international differences in accounting;
- explain why it might be useful to group countries by accounting similarities;
- appraise some suggested international classifications of countries;
- distinguish between EU and international harmonization efforts;
- assess the success of these harmonization efforts.

## 5.1 Introduction: the international nature of the development of accounting

Different countries have contributed to the development of accounting over the centuries. When archaeologists uncover ancient remains in the Middle East, almost anything with writing or numbers on it is a form of accounting: expenses of wars or feasts or constructions; lists of taxes due or paid. It is now fairly well documented that the origins of written numbers and written words are closely associated with the need to keep account and to render account.

The Romans developed sophisticated forms of single-entry accounting from which, for example, farm profits could be calculated. Later, the increasing complexity of business in late-medieval northern Italy led to the emergence of the double-entry system. Later still, the existence of a wealthy merchant class and the need for large investment for major projects led to public subscription of share capital in seventeenth-century Holland. Next, the growing separation of ownership from management raised the need for audit in nineteenth-century Britain. Many European countries have contributed to the development of accounting: France led in the development of legal control over accounting; Scotland gave us the accountancy profession; Germany gave us standardized formats for financial statements.

From the late nineteenth century onwards, the United States has given us consolidation of financial statements (see Chapter 14), management accounting, capitalization of leases (see Chapter 9) and deferred tax accounting (see Chapter 12). The United Kingdom contributed the 'true and fair view' (see Section 5.4), which has been rounded out with the American 'substance over form'. In the late twentieth century, Japan contributed greatly to managerial accounting and control.

The common feature of all these international influences on accounting is that commercial developments have led to accounting advances. Not surprisingly, leading commercial nations in any period are the leading innovators in accounting. However, although international influences and similarities are clear, there are also great differences, particularly within Europe. An indication of the scale of international difference can be seen in those cases where companies publish two sets of accounting figures based on different rules – often domestic rules compared with US rules, published by foreign companies that were listed on US stock exchanges. Table 5.1 shows some interesting examples for earnings. Daimler-Benz was the first German company to provide this data, in 1993. The large differences (and the variation from year to year) between German and US profit figures were a surprise to many accountants and users of financial statements.

**Table 5.1 Reconciliations of earnings**

|  |  | *Domestic* | *US-Adjusted* | *Difference* |
|---|---|---|---|---|
| Daimler-Benz: | 1993 | DM615m | DM(1.839m) | −399% |
| (Germany) | 1994 | DM895m | DM1.052m | +18% |
|  | 1995 | DM(5.734m) | DM(5.729m) | +1% |
| British Airways: | 2003 | £72m | £(128m) | −278% |
| (UK) | 2006 | £451m | £148m | −67% |

*Source*: Authors' own work based on published company financial accounts.

The figures for British Airways, too, show that profits can need adjustment either up or down. The supply of these interesting reconciliations to US accounting dried up after 2006 because the US authorities accepted IFRS accounting without reconciliation from 2007.

The introduction of IFRS for consolidated statements in many countries in 2005 produced a large number of comparisons of the 2004 results, published under the previous national system in 2004, and republished as comparative figures under IFRS in 2005. A particularly interesting example is Fiat. The financial statements for the year ended 31 December 2005 contain a reconciliation between the consolidated balance sheet at 1 January 2004 (i.e. 31 December 2003), as published under Italian regulations, with what it would have been at 1 January 2004 under IFRS requirements as at 31 December 2005. This reconciliation is reproduced as Figure 5.1 (on page 64).

At this stage, do not concern yourself with the details. The point to emphasize is the sheer size of the figures in the 'reclassifications' and 'adjustment' columns. Notice for example that 'long-term financial payables' rose from just over 15 million euros under Italian GAAP to over 36 million euros under IFRS, an increase of some 240 per cent.

This chapter tries to put countries into groups based on similarities of accounting, and then investigates the causes of the international accounting differences. After that, the chapter contains an examination of the attempts in the EU and by the IASB to reduce the differences.

## 5.2 Classification

### 5.2.1 Introduction

Although no two countries have identical accounting practices, some countries seem to form pairs or larger groupings with reasonably similar influences on financial reporting, such as legal and tax systems. If this is so, it may be possible to establish a classification. Such an activity is a basic step in many disciplines; for instance, classification is one of the tools of a scientist – the Mendeleev table of elements and the Linnaean system of classification are fundamental to chemistry and biology. Classification should sharpen description and analysis. It should reveal underlying structures and enable prediction of the properties of an element based on its place in a classification.

One set of authors, while classifying legal systems, has supplied practical criteria for determining whether two systems are in the same group. Systems are said to be in the same group if 'someone educated in . . . one law will then be capable, without much difficulty, of handling [the other]' (David and Brierley, 1978). Also, the two systems must not be 'founded on opposed philosophical, political or economic principles'. The second criterion ensures that systems in the same group not only have similar superficial characteristics but also have similar fundamental structures and are likely to react to new circumstances in similar ways. Using these criteria a four-group legal classification was obtained: Romano-Germanic, common law, socialist and philosophical-religious.

## Figure 5.1 Effects of transition to IFRS on the consolidated balance sheet at 1 January 2004

| (in millions of euros) | Italian GAAP | Reclassifications | Adjustments | IAS/IFRS | |
|---|---|---|---|---|---|
| Intangible fixed assets: | 3,724 | – | 1,774 | 5,498 | Intangible assets |
| *Goodwill* | *2,402* | – | – | *2,402* | *Goodwill* |
| *Other intangible fixed assets* | *1,322* | – | *1,774* | *3,096* | *Other intangible assets* |
| Property, plant and equipment | 9,675 | (945) | 817 | 9,547 | Property, plant and equipment |
| *Property, plant and equipment* | *8,761* | *(31)* | – | – | |
| *Operating leases* | *914* | *(914)* | – | – | |
| | | 31 | – | 31 | Investment property |
| Financial fixed assets | 3,950 | 70 | (121) | 3,899 | Investment and other financial assets |
| Financial receivables held as fixed assets | 29 | (29) | – | – | |
| | | 914 | (50) | 864 | Leased assets |
| Deferred tax assets | 1,879 | – | 266 | 2,145 | Deferred tax assets |
| Total Non-Current assets | 19,257 | 41 | 2,686 | 21,984 | Non-current assets |
| Net inventories | 6,484 | – | 1,113 | 7,597 | Inventories |
| Trade receivables | 4,553 | (682) | 2,678 | 6,549 | Trade receivables |
| | | 12,890 | 7,937 | 20,827 | Receivables from financing activities |
| Other receivables | 3,081 | (148) | 541 | 3,474 | Other receivables |
| | | 407 | 10 | 417 | Accrued income and prepaid expenses |
| | | | | 2,129 | Current financial assets: |
| | | 32 | – | *32* | *Current equity investments* |
| | | 515 | 260 | *775* | *Current securities* |
| | | 430 | 892 | *1,322* | *Other financial assets* |
| Financial assets not held as fixed assets | 120 | (120) | – | – | |
| Financial lease contracts receivable | 1,797 | (1,797) | – | – | |
| Financial receivables | 10,750 | (10,750) | – | – | |
| Securities | 3,789 | (3,789) | – | – | |
| Cash | 3,211 | 3,214 | 420 | 6,845 | Cash and cash equivalents |
| Total Current assets | 33,785 | 202 | 13,851 | 47,838 | Current assets |
| Trade accruals and deferrals | 407 | (407) | – | – | |
| Financial accruals and deferrals | 386 | (386) | – | – | |
| | | | 21 | 21 | Assets held for sale |
| TOTAL ASSETS | 53,835 | (550) | 16,558 | 69,843 | TOTAL ASSETS |
| Stockholders' equity | 7,494 | | (934) | 6,560 | Stockholders' equity |
| | | | | 7,455 | Provisions: |
| Reserves for employee severance indemnities | 1,313 | 1,503 | 1,224 | *4,040* | *Employee benefits* |
| Reserves for risks and charges | 5,168 | (1,550) | (203) | *3,415* | *Other provisions* |
| Deferred income tax reserves | 211 | (211) | – | | |
| Long-term financial payables | 15,418 | 6,501 | 14,790 | 36,709 | Debt: |
| | | | | *10,581* | *Asset-backed financing* |
| | | | | *26,128* | *Other debt* |
| Total Non-current liabilities | 22,110 | 6,243 | | | |
| | | 568 | (223) | 345 | Other financial liabilities |
| Trade payables | 12,588 | – | (297) | 12,291 | Trade payables |
| Others payables | 2,742 | – | 1,948 | 4,690 | Other payables |
| Short-term financial payables | 6,616 | (6,616) | – | – | |
| Total Current liabilities | 21,946 | (6,048) | | | |
| | | 211 | 274 | 485 | Deferred tax liabilities |
| Trade accruals and deferrals | 1,329 | | (21) | 1,308 | Accrued expenses and deferred income |
| Financial accruals and deferrals | 956 | (956) | – | – | |
| | | | | – | Liabilities held for sale |
| TOTAL LIABILITIES AND STOCKHOLDERS' EQUITY | 53,835 | (550) | 16,558 | 69,843 | TOTAL STOCKHOLDERS' EQUITY AND LIABILITIES |

*Source*: Fiat Financial Statements, as at 31 December 2005.

In accounting, classification should facilitate a study of the logic of, and the difficulties facing, international harmonization. Classification should also assist in the training of accountants and auditors who operate internationally. Further, a developing country might be better able to understand the available types of financial reporting, and which one would be most appropriate for it, by seeing which other countries use particular systems. Also, it should be possible for a country to predict the problems that it is about to face and the solutions that might work by looking at other countries in its group.

## 5.2.2 Classifications using survey data

Some researchers have used surveys of accounting practices as data. Classification is achieved by the use of computer programs designed to put countries into groups by similarities of practices. For example, one set of researchers (Nair and Frank, 1980) divided financial reporting characteristics into those relating to measurement and those relating to disclosure. Table 5.2 represents a classification using measurement characteristics from 1973. As yet there was no hierarchy, but the overall results seemed very plausible and to fit well with the analysis in this chapter. The suggestion was that, in a worldwide context, much of continental Europe was seen as using the same system. However, the United Kingdom, Ireland and the Netherlands were noticeably different from that system.

Table 5.2 **Classification based on 1973 measurement practices**

| British Commonwealth model | Latin American model | Continental European model | United States model |
|---|---|---|---|
| Australia | Argentina | Belgium | Canada |
| Bahamas | Bolivia | France | Japan |
| Eire | Brazil | Germany | Mexico |
| Fiji | Chile | Italy | Panama |
| Jamaica | Columbia | Spain | Philippines |
| Kenya | Ethiopia | Sweden | United States |
| Netherlands | India | Switzerland | |
| New Zealand | Paraguay | Venezuela | |
| Pakistan | Peru | | |
| Singapore | Uruguay | | |
| South Africa | | | |
| Trinidad and Tobago | | | |
| United Kingdom | | | |
| Zimbabwe | | | |

*Source: The Accounting Review*, (Nair and Frank 1980) © American Accounting Association; full text of this article is available online at http://aaahq.org/ic/browse.htm

## 5.2.3 Nobes' classification

It would be possible to criticize the classifications discussed above for:

(a) lack of precision in the definition of what is to be classified;
(b) lack of a model with which to compare the statistical results;

## Figure 5.2 Groupings of some major countries in 1980

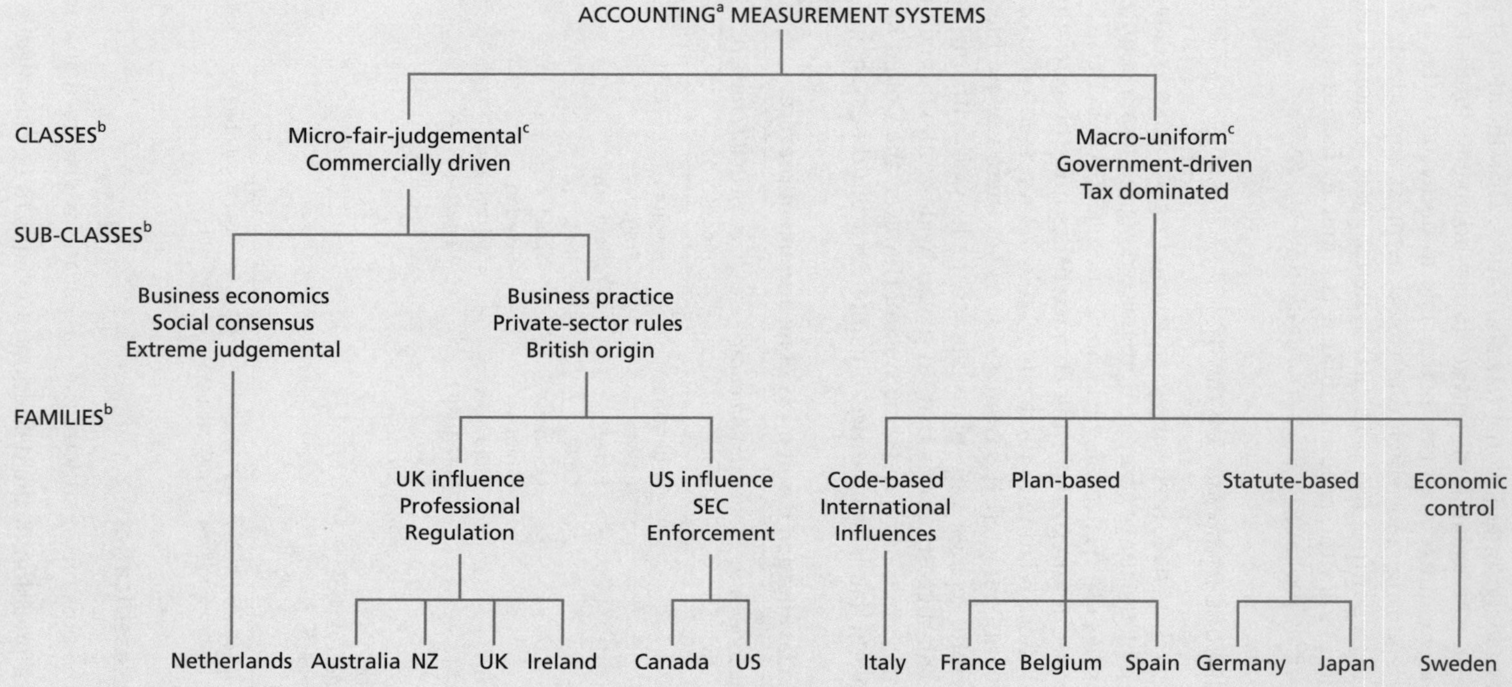

Notes:
a. This is an abbreviated term for corporate financial reporting.
b. These terms, while borrowed from biology, should be interpreted merely as loose labels.
c. The terms at these and other branching points are merely labels to be used as shorthand to try to capture some of the attributes of the members of the accounting systems below them. This classification has been prepared by a UK researcher and may contain usage of terms that will mislead those from other cultures.
Source: Adapted from Nobes (1983).

(c) lack of hierarchy that would add more subtlety to the portrayal of the size of differences between countries; and

(d) lack of judgement in the choice of 'important' discriminating features.

Can these problems be remedied? One of the authors of this book attempted to solve them in the following ways (see Nobes, 1983). The scope of the work was defined as the classification of some Western countries by the financial reporting practices of their *listed companies*, and it was carried out in the early 1980s. The reporting practices were those concerned with *measurement and valuation*. It is listed companies whose financial statements are generally available and whose practices can be most easily discovered. It is the international differences in reporting between such companies that are of main interest to shareholders, creditors, auditing firms, taxation authorities, management, and harmonizing agencies. Measurement and valuation practices were chosen because these determine the size of the figures for profit, capital, total assets, liquidity and so on. The result is shown in Figure 5.2.

This figure suggests that there were two main types of financial reporting 'system' in Europe at the time: the micro/professional and the macro/uniform. The first of these involved accountants in individual companies striving to present fair information to outside users, without detailed constraint of law or tax rules but with standards written by accountants. The macro/uniform type had accounting mainly as a servant of the state, particularly for taxation purposes.

The micro/professional side contained the Netherlands, the United Kingdom, Ireland, Denmark, the United States, Australia, New Zealand and Canada. The Netherlands had (and has) fewer rules than the other countries, and another distinguishing feature is that the influence of microeconomic theory led to use of replacement cost information to varying degrees. Denmark rearranged its accounting system after the Second World War and it now looks somewhat like the United Kingdom or the United States.

The macro/uniform side contained all other European countries and Japan. However, they were divided into subgroups. For example, accounting plans were (and are) the predominant source of detailed rules in France, Belgium, Spain and Greece. In Germany the commercial code was (and is) the major authority and there was (and is) much stricter observance of historical cost values. In Sweden, the predominant influence seems to have been the government as economic planner and tax collector.

Table 5.3 (on page 69) summarizes some of the typical differences between countries on a two-group basis. A number of the 'specific accounting features' are examined in Part 2 of this book.

### 5.2.4 An updated classification

The classification of Figure 5.2 was originally drawn up in the early 1980s, before the EU harmonization programme and before extensive globalization of capital markets. The fall of communism also meant that many more countries, such as China and Russia, have financial reporting systems that could be added to the 1983 classification. Some countries, such as Sweden (and Norway) have moved to the left of the chart since the early 1980s.

Figure 5.3 **Proposed scheme for classification**

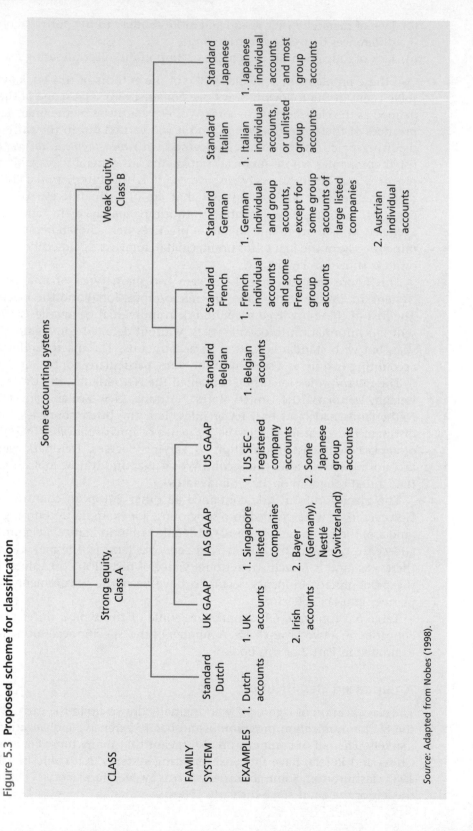

*Source: Adapted from Nobes (1998).*

**Table 5.3  A two-group classification (traditional practices[a])**

| Micro | Macro |
|---|---|
| *Background* | |
| 'English' common law | Roman law |
| Large, old, strong profession | Small, young, weak profession |
| Large stock exchange | Small stock exchange |
| *General accounting features* | |
| Fair | Legal |
| Shareholder-orientation | Creditor-orientation |
| Disclosure | Secrecy |
| Tax rules separate | Tax-dominated |
| Substance over form | Form over substance |
| Professional standards | Government rules |
| *Specific accounting features* | |
| Percentage-of-completion method | Completed-contract method |
| Depreciation over useful lives | Depreciation by tax rules |
| No legal reserves | Legal reserves |
| Finance leases capitalized | No lease capitalization |
| Funds flow statements | No funds flow statements |
| Earnings per share disclosed | No disclosures on earnings per share |
| No secret reserves | Secret reserves |
| No tax-induced provisions | Tax-induced provisions |
| Preliminary expenses expensed | Preliminary expenses capitalizable |
| Taking gains on unsettled foreign currency monetary items | Deferring gains on unsettled foreign currency monetary items |
| *Some examples of countries* | |
| Australia | Austria |
| Canada | Belgium |
| Denmark | Finland |
| Hong Kong | France |
| Ireland | Germany |
| Singapore | Greece |
| Netherlands | Italy |
| United Kingdom | Japan |
| United States | Sweden |

*Note:* [a] From the late 1980s in particular, accounting practices in several countries made significant shifts to the left.

A further complication is that, particularly from the early 1990s and in certain countries, large companies have chosen to follow internationally recognized practices rather than domestic practices. For example, by 2000 most of the largest 50 German companies were using US or IASB rules for their group accounting statements. In a sense, then, there have been several 'systems' being used in Germany. In 1998, Nobes published a revised classification to try to take account of some of these problems; this is shown in Figure 5.3. To repeat a point from earlier, the fact that the United Kingdom and the United States are both on the left of Table 5.3 does not imply that they are the same. For example, their regulatory systems are noticeably different. However, when compared to French or German accounting practices, UK and US practices look similar.

The use of two systems within a country is a major example of the fact that practices vary between companies within a country. This chapter has not examined in any detail the differences within a country. The widespread introduction from 2005 of IFRS for some entity financial statements, but in many countries not all, will cause further changes in national norms and attitudes as time goes on. It seems likely that different national versions of IFRS practice will emerge.

**Why it matters** *The purpose of Figures 5.2 and 5.3 is to organize countries into groups by similarities of financial reporting measurement practices. This means that a knowledge of one country enables inferences to be drawn about others. The 'distance' between two countries is suggested by how far back up the classification it is necessary to go to reach a common point. This should be useful for those accountants and auditors who have to deal with financial reports from several countries or who have to work in more than one country.*

*Such a classification can be borne in mind while studying the detailed accounting practices set out in Part 2.*

**Activity 5.A** If you were trying to predict what financial reporting practices would be found in various African countries, which non-accounting variables would you measure?

**Feedback** The activity asks you about African countries on the assumption that most readers of this book do not know much in detail about the accounting practices used in the continent of Africa. Consequently, you could try to use the model of this chapter to make predictions.

It is well known that most countries in Africa have been colonies of various European countries, often until at least the second half of the twentieth century. Consequently, it seems likely that languages, legal systems and other 'cultural' features will have been imported, voluntarily or otherwise. Some of these may influence accounting practices today.

Even more directly, the main elements of accounting systems may have been imported. This suggests that, at a first approximation, the identification of colonial influence may predict accounting differences in Africa. For example, you might expect various French accounting features in Senegal, but various British features in neighbouring Gambia.

This might overwhelm factors such as the strength of equity markets. So, some 'British' African countries have aspects of Anglo-American accounting even though they have no listed companies.

## 5.3 Influences on differences

### 5.3.1 Introduction

It is not possible to be sure that the factors discussed below cause the financial reporting differences, but relationships can be established and reasonable deductions about the directions of causality can be made. Factors that have been seen as affecting accounting development include colonial and other outside influences, the prevalent providers of finance, the nature of the legal system, the influence of taxation, and the strength of the accountancy profession.

On a worldwide scale, factors such as language, culture or geography have been referred to by researchers. To the extent that these also have some explanatory power, it seems more sensible to assume that this results from auto-correlation. For instance, the fact that Australian accounting bears a marked resemblance to accounting in New Zealand might be 'confirmed' by language and geographical factors. However, most of their similarities were probably not caused by these factors but by their historical connection with the United Kingdom, which passed on both accounting and language, and was colonizing most parts of Australasia in the same period.

If one wanted to encompass countries outside the developed Western world, it would be necessary to include factors concerning the state of development of their economy and the nature of their political economy. Of course, to some extent a precise definition of terms might make it clear that it is impossible to include some of these countries. For example, if our interest is in the financial reporting practices of corporations with shares listed on stock exchanges, those countries with few or no such corporations will have to be excluded. The four factors identified above (providers of finance, legal systems, taxation and the accountancy profession) are now considered in turn, after which international influences are examined in more detail.

### 5.3.2 Providers of finance

In some countries, a major source of corporate finance for two centuries has been the share capital and loan capital provided by large numbers of private investors. This has been the predominant mode of raising finance for large companies in the United States and the United Kingdom. Although it is increasingly the case that shares in these countries are held by institutional investors rather than by individual shareholders, this still contrasts with state, bank or family holdings (see below). Indeed, the increased importance of institutional investors is perhaps a reinforcement for the following hypothesis: 'In countries with a widespread ownership of companies by shareholders who do not have access to internal information, there will be a pressure for disclosure, audit and decision-useful information.' Institutional investors hold larger blocks of shares and may be better organized than private shareholders, and so they should increase this pressure.

By contrast, in France and Italy, capital provided by the state or by banks is very significant, as are family businesses. In Germany, the banks, in particular, are important owners of shares in companies as well as providers of debt finance. A majority of shares in some German public companies are owned directly, or controlled through proxies, by banks. In such countries the banks or the state will, in many cases, nominate directors and thus be able to obtain restricted information and to affect decisions. If it is the case that many companies in continental countries are dominated by banks, governments or families, the need for published information is much smaller because of this access to private information.

This also applies to the need for audit, because this is designed to check up on the managers in cases where the owners are 'outsiders'.

Evidence of the two-way characterization of countries may be found by looking at their numbers of listed companies. Table 5.4 shows the numbers, in early 2009, of domestic listed companies on stock exchanges where there are over 380 such companies and a market capitalization above $580 billion. Table 5.5 shows figures for the EU's eight largest economies in 1999, putting the size of the equity market in the context of the size of the economy, and the number of domestic listed companies in the context of the population. The comparison between the

### Table 5.4 Major stock exchanges, January 2009

| Country | Exchange | Domestic listed companies | Market capitalization of domestic equities ($bn) | Market capitalization as % of NYSE |
|---|---|---|---|---|
| Europe | | | | |
| – | Euronext | 1,013 | 1,863 | 20 |
| Germany | Deutsche Börse | 742 | 937 | 10 |
| Spain | BME | 3,517 | 871 | 9 |
| United Kingdom | London | 2,399 | 1,758 | 19 |
| The Americas | | | | |
| Brazil | São Paulo | 384 | 612 | 7 |
| Canada | Toronto | 3,747 | 998 | 11 |
| United States | NASDAQ | 2,602 | 2,204 | 24 |
| | New York | 2,910 | 9,363 | 100 |
| Asia-Pacific | | | | |
| China | Hong Kong | 1,252 | 1,238 | 13 |
| | Shanghai | 864 | 1,557 | 17 |
| India | Bombay | 4,925 | 613 | 7 |
| Japan | Tokyo | 2,373 | 2,923 | 31 |
| Australia | Australian | 1,918 | 587 | 6 |

Source: prepared using data from World Federation of Exchanges.

### Table 5.5 Measures of equity markets in Europe

| | Equity market capitalization/Gross domestic product | Domestic listed companies per million of population |
|---|---|---|
| United Kingdom | 1.86 | 41.2 |
| Netherlands | 1.44 | 13.7 |
| Sweden | 1.10 | 29.3 |
| Belgium | 0.87 | 15.2 |
| France | 0.61 | 13.4 |
| Spain | 0.59 | 11.9 |
| Italy | 0.48 | 4.2 |
| Germany | 0.44 | 9.0 |

Source: Prepared using Fact File 1999, London Stock Exchange; and Pocket World in Figures 1999, The Economist.

United Kingdom (with a large equity market) and Germany (with a much smaller equity market) is instructive.

**Activity 5.B**

Examine Tables 5.4 and 5.5. Try to put countries into groups with respect to the strength of their equity markets (in the context of a measure of the size of the country).

**Feedback**

A two-tier group categorization of all the countries in Table 5.5 and a few more from Table 5.4 might look as below, in Table 5.6. Incidentally, the country with the longest history of companies with publicly traded shares is the Netherlands. Although it has a fairly small stock exchange, many multinationals (such as Unilever, Philips, Royal Dutch) are listed on it. It seems reasonable, then, to place the Netherlands with the English-speaking world in a 'shareholder' group as opposed to a 'bank/state/family' group.

**Table 5.6 Countries classified by strength of equity markets**

| Stronger | Weaker |
| --- | --- |
| United States | France |
| United Kingdom | Spain |
| Netherlands | Germany |
| Sweden | Italy |
| Australia | Belgium |
| Hong Kong | Portugal |

Japan is not shown in Table 5.6 above because it is difficult to classify. It has a fairly important equity market, although not as important (in the context of the size of the economy) as that in the US or the UK. Furthermore, many Japanese companies own shares in each other, and so the total number of listed companies and market value is exaggerated when making an international comparison. Japanese accounting has both German and US features.

The characteristic of 'fairness' was mentioned above, as it has been in previous chapters. It is a concept related to the existence of a large number of outside owners who require unbiased information about the success of a business and its state of affairs. Although reasonable prudence will be expected, these shareholders are interested in comparing one year with another and one company with another. This entails judgement, which entails experts. This expertise is also required for checking financial statements by auditors. In countries such as the United Kingdom, the United States, Australasia and the Netherlands, this can, over many decades, result in a tendency to require accountants to work out their own technical rules. This is acceptable to governments because of the influence and expertise of the private sector, which is usually running ahead of the government (in its capacity as shareholder, protector of the public interest or collector of taxation). Thus 'generally accepted accounting principles' control accounting. To the extent that governments intervene, they impose disclosure, filing or measurement requirements, and these tend to follow best practice rather than create it.

In many continental European countries (such as France, Germany and Italy), the traditional scarcity of 'outsider' shareholders has meant that external financial reporting has been largely invented for the purposes of governments, as tax collectors or controllers of the economy. This has held back the development of flexibility, judgement, fairness or experimentation. However, it does lead to precision, uniformity and stability. It also seems likely that the greater importance of creditors in these countries leads to more prudent (conservative) accounting. This is because creditors are interested in whether, in the worst case, they are likely to get their money back, whereas shareholders may be interested in an unbiased estimate of future prospects.

Nevertheless, even in such countries as Germany, France or Italy, where there are comparatively few listed companies, governments have recognized the responsibility to require public or listed companies to publish detailed, audited, financial statements. There are laws to this effect in the majority of such countries, and the governments in France and Italy also set up bodies specifically to control the securities markets: in France the Commission des Opérations de Bourse (now the Autorité des Marchés Financiers – AMF), and in Italy the Commissione Nazionale per le Società e la Borsa (CONSOB). These bodies were to some extent modelled on the Securities and Exchange Commission (SEC) of the United States. They have been associated with important developments in financial reporting, generally in the direction of Anglo-American practice. This is not surprising, as these stock exchange bodies are taking the part otherwise played by private and institutional shareholders, who have, over a much longer period, helped to shape Anglo-American accounting systems.

### 5.3.3 Legal systems

Legal systems were considered in Section 4.2. It was suggested that many countries in the world can be put into one of two categories with respect to their main legal system: common law or Roman law. Table 5.7 illustrates the way in which some developed countries' legal systems fall into these two categories. The legal systems of the Nordic countries are more difficult to classify, as they do not fit neatly into either category. Notice how similar the list is to Table 5.6. There seems to be a relationship between financing system, legal system and accounting system, as noted later.

Table 5.7 **Legal systems: some examples**

| Common law | Codified Roman law |
| --- | --- |
| England and Wales | France |
| Ireland | Italy |
| United States | Germany |
| Canada | Spain |
| Australia | Netherlands |
| New Zealand | Portugal |
| Hong Kong | Japan (commercial) |

### 5.3.4 Taxation

Although it is possible to make groupings of tax systems in a number of ways, only some of them are of relevance to financial reporting (see Chapter 12). What is particularly relevant is the degree to which taxation regulations determine accounting measurements. For example, in Germany, the tax accounts (*Steuerbilanz*) should generally be the same as the commercial accounts (*Handelsbilanz*) as far as the financial statements of individual entities are concerned. There is even a word for this idea: the *Massgeblichkeitsprinzip* (principle of congruence or binding together). In Italy, a similar position prevailed until recently, described as *il binario unico* (the single-track approach).

By contrast, in the United Kingdom, the United States and the Netherlands, there can be many differences between tax numbers and financial reporting numbers. One obvious example of the areas affected by this difference is depreciation (which is discussed further in Chapter 9). In the United Kingdom, for example, the amount of depreciation charged in the published financial statements is determined according to custom established over the last century and influenced by the prevailing accounting standards. Convention and pragmatism, rather than exact rules or even the spirit of the standard, determine the method of depreciation, the estimates of the scrap value and the expected length of life.

The amount of depreciation for tax purposes in the United Kingdom is quite independent of these figures. It is determined by capital allowances, which are a formalized scheme of tax depreciation allowances designed to standardize the amounts allowed and to act as investment incentives, as designed by the government of the day. Because of the separation of the two schemes, there can be a complete lack of subjectivity in tax allowances but full room for judgement in determining the depreciation charges for financial reporting.

At the opposite extreme, in countries such as Germany the tax regulations lay down maximum depreciation rates to be used for particular assets. These are generally based on the expected useful lives of assets. However, accelerated depreciation allowances are available in some cases: for example, for industries producing energy-saving or anti-pollution products or for certain regions. Up until the reunification of Germany in 1990, large allowances applied in West Berlin or other areas bordering East Germany; they were later applied in the new German Länder in the east. If these allowances are to be claimed for tax purposes (which would normally be sensible), they must also be fully charged in the financial accounts. Thus, the charge against profit would be said by a UK accountant not to be 'fair', even though it could certainly be 'correct' or 'legal'. This influence is felt even in the details of the choice of method of depreciation, where a typical German note to a company's balance sheet might read: 'Plant and machinery are depreciated over a useful life of ten years on a declining-balance basis: straight-line depreciation is adopted as soon as this results in a higher charge' (e.g. the annual report of BASF for 2008).

With some variations, this *Massgeblichkeitsprinzip* operates in Germany, France, Belgium and Italy and many other countries. It is perhaps due partly to the pervasive influence of codification in law and partly to the predominance of taxation as a use of accounting. Nevertheless, by the late 1980s, there were clear moves away from this in some countries. For example, the Spanish accounting law of 1989 reduced the influence of tax and increased disclosures of the remaining tax effects. Similarly, in Nordic countries, the influence of taxation has been reducing. This has been clear since the early 1980s in Denmark and became important in Finland, Norway and Sweden in the 1990s. For consolidated statements under IFRS, the tax influences should be largely removed.

**Why it matters**   *Let us suppose that you would like to use the financial statements of a company for the purpose of assessing its performance, so that you can try to predict cash flows in order to make investment decisions. However, suppose also that the company operates in a country where a major purpose of accounting is the calculation of taxable income, using the government's rules for that purpose. These rules may not be designed to measure the performance of a year but to provide investment incentives for companies (e.g. by offering them large tax depreciation allowances) or to enable the statements to be checked easily by tax auditors. Disclosures designed to help the prediction of cash flows might be seen as irrelevant. Also, the company would usually be trying to make its income look as small as possible, in order to avoid or postpone tax.*

*In this case, the financial statements might not be very useful to you because they were being prepared to serve other purposes.*

When dealing with the financial statements of groups of companies (see Chapter 14), taxation influences can be reduced because taxable income is generally calculated for each legal entity rather than on a consolidated basis, as noted in Chapter 4. For example, France has substantially liberated consolidated accounts from tax rules.

## 5.3.5 The accountancy profession

The power, size and competence of the accountancy profession in a country may follow, to a large extent, from the various factors outlined above and from the type of financial reporting that they have helped to produce. For example, the lack of a substantial body of private shareholders and public companies in some countries means that the need for auditors is much smaller than it is in the United Kingdom or the United States. However, the nature of the profession also feeds back into the type of accounting that is practised and that could be practised. For example, a 1975 Decree in Italy (not brought into effect until the 1980s), requiring listed companies to have extended audits similar to those operated in the United Kingdom and the United States, could only be brought into effect initially because of the substantial presence of international audit firms.

The scale of the difference is illustrated in Table 5.8, which lists for several countries the main bodies whose members may audit the financial statements of companies (but see below for an explanation of the French and German situations). These remarkable figures (e.g. the small number of auditors in Germany) need some interpretation. For example, let us compare more carefully the German and the British figures. In Germany, there is a separate, though overlapping, profession of tax experts (*Steuerberater*), which is larger than the accountancy body. However, in the United Kingdom the accountants' figure is inflated by the inclusion of many who specialize in, or occasionally practise in, tax. Second,

Table 5.8 **Examples of accountancy bodies, age and size**

| Country | Body | Founding date[a] | Approx. number of members (thousands) 2008 |
|---|---|---|---|
| Australia | Australian Society of Certified Practising Accountants | 1952 (1886) | 122 |
| | Institute of Chartered Accountants in Australia | 1928 (1885) | 48 |
| Canada | Canadian Institute of Chartered Accountants | 1902 (1880) | 74 |
| China | Chinese Institute of Certified Public Accountants | 1988 | 140 |
| France | Ordre des Experts Comptables | 1942 | 19 |
| Germany | Institut der Wirtschaftsprüfer | 1932 | 13 |
| Japan | Japanese Institute of Certified Public Accountants | 1948 (1927) | 18 |
| Netherlands | Nederlands Instituut van Registeraccountants | 1967 (1895) | 14 |
| New Zealand | New Zealand Society of Accountants | 1909 (1894) | 30 |
| Sweden | Föreningen Auktoriserade Revisorer; Svenska Revisorsamfundet (FAR SRS) | 2006 (1899) | 5 |
| United Kingdom and Ireland | Institute of Chartered Accountants in England and Wales | 1880 (1870) | 132 |
| | Institute of Chartered Accountants of Scotland | 1951 (1854) | 18 |
| | Association of Chartered Certified Accountants | 1939 (1891) | 131 |
| | Institute of Chartered Accountants in Ireland | 1888 | 18 |
| United States | American Institute of Certified Public Accountants | 1887 | 339 |

Note: [a] Dates of earliest predecessor bodies in brackets.

a German accountant may only be a member of the *Institut* if he is in practice as an auditor, whereas at least half of the British figure represents members working in companies, government, education, and so on. Third, the training period is much longer in Germany than it is in the United Kingdom. It normally involves a four-year relevant degree course, six years' practical experience (four in the profession), and a professional examination consisting of oral and written tests plus a thesis. This tends to last until the aspiring accountant is 30–35 years old. Thus, many of the German 'students' would be counted as part of the qualified figure if they were in the British system. Fourth, in the 1980s, a second-tier body of *vereidigte Buchprüfer* (sworn bookcheckers) was established, whose members may audit certain private companies (GmbHs).

These four factors help to explain the differences; and some of them apply in other countries, e.g. there is a second-tier body of auditors in Denmark. However, there is still a very substantial residual difference, which results from the much larger number of companies to be audited and the different process of forming a judgement on the 'fair' view. The differences are diminishing as auditing is extended to many private companies in EU countries and as the United Kingdom introduces audit exemptions for smaller companies.

It is interesting to note a further division along Anglo-American versus Franco-German lines. In the Anglo-American countries, governments or government agencies require certain types of companies to be audited, and they put certain limits on who shall be auditors, with government departments having the final say. However, in general, membership of the private professional accountancy bodies is the method of qualifying as an auditor. On the other hand, in France and Germany there is a dual set of accountancy bodies. Those in Table 5.8 are private-sector professional bodies. However, in order to act as an auditor of companies, one must join a government-controlled auditing body (see Table 5.9). To a large extent the membership of the professional bodies overlaps with that of the auditing bodies, and membership of the professional bodies is part of the way of qualifying for membership of the auditing bodies. The Compagnie Nationale is responsible to the Ministry of Justice; the *Wirtschaftsprüferkammer* to the Federal Minister of Economics.

**Table 5.9 Accountancy and auditing bodies in France and Germany**

|         | Private professional body      | State auditing body                                    |
| ------- | ------------------------------ | ------------------------------------------------------ |
| France  | Ordre des Experts Comptables   | Compagnie Nationale des Commissaires aux Comptes       |
| Germany | Institut der Wirtschaftsprüfer | Wirtschaftsprüferkammer                                |

## 5.3.6 Synthesis

The above discussion of the factors relating to international accounting differences can be somewhat simplified, for some of the factors seem mainly to be influenced *by* accounting differences rather than the other way round. Such a case could be made for the last three of the above four factors, as now explained.

### Legal systems

Even in a Roman/codified law country, the regulation of accounting can be left up to accountants if commercial pressure demands this. For example, in the Netherlands, the Civil Code is not detailed and allows room for accountants to make rules, and in practice allows for some companies to follow US requirements. So, although the whole legal system is not strongly influenced by the nature of the accounting system, the regulation of accounting is.

### Tax systems

The existence of *Massgeblichkeit* or *il binario unico* is probably sensible in Germany and Italy respectively because, for the great mass of entities, the calculation of taxable income is the main purpose of accounting. Where there is a competing purpose for accounting (e.g. the provision of useful financial reports to millions of shareholders in thousands of listed companies), accounting has to be done twice. For example, as already discussed, there are separate rules for tax and financial reporting in the United Kingdom and the United States. The *Massgeblichkeitsprinzip* is not a cause of the main international accounting differences (the two groups in Figure 5.3 and Table 5.3); it is an *effect*.

Nevertheless, where tax strongly influences accounting, different national tax rules will result in different national accounting practices.

### The accountancy profession

The strength and size of the profession seems to be caused by the need for audit and by the room left for professional regulation by the legal system.

### Conclusion

If these three factors are largely influenced by accounting, the remaining potential independent variable is the financing system. It is suggested here that, apart from international influences (see below), this is the main explanatory variable for the most important international differences in financial reporting.

## 5.3.7 International influences

As noted at the beginning of this chapter, many nations have contributed to the development of accounting. In the case of some countries, ideas have been transferred wholesale. For example:

■ Several African countries that are members of the (British) Commonwealth have accounting systems closely based on that of the British Companies Acts of 1929 or 1948.

■ The French *plan comptable général* was introduced into France in the 1940s, based closely on a German precedent, and later into several former French colonies in Africa.

■ The Japanese accounting system consists largely of a commercial code borrowed from Germany in the late nineteenth century, overlaid with US-style securities laws imposed in the late 1940s.

By the end of the twentieth century, international influences had begun to affect accounting in all countries, sometimes overwhelmingly. The globalization of markets had led to an increased need for internationally comparable accounting information. Where several large multinational companies are based in comparatively small countries (e.g. the Netherlands and Sweden), international influences are likely to be particularly great.

Many large European companies responded to internationalization by volunteering to use one of two sets of internationally recognized rules: the United States' generally accepted accounting principles (GAAP) and the international standards of the IASB. In general – in Europe at least – this usage has been restricted to the consolidated financial statements prepared for groups headed by listed companies. As noted in Chapter 4, there are EU requirements in this area.

Another effect has been that national rule-makers have been trying to reduce differences between their national rules and the above international norms. At the extreme, certain countries have adopted IFRSs as part of their national rules. These issues were noted in Chapter 4 and are taken up again in Section 5.5.

## 5.4 Harmonization in the European Union

### 5.4.1 Introduction to harmonization

So far, this chapter has made it clear that there are major differences in the financial reporting practices of companies in different countries. This leads to great complications for those preparing, consolidating, auditing and interpreting published financial statements. Since the preparation of internal financial information often overlaps with the preparation of published information, the complications spread further. To combat this, several organizations throughout the world are involved in attempts to harmonize or standardize accounting.

'Harmonization' is a process of increasing the compatibility of accounting practices by setting bounds to their degree of variation. 'Standardization' appears to imply the imposition of a more rigid and narrow set of rules. However, within accounting these two words have almost become technical terms, and one cannot rely upon the normal difference in their meanings. Harmonization is a word that tends to be associated with the supranational legislation promulgated in the European Union, while standardization is a word often associated with the International Accounting Standards Board. In practice, the words are often used interchangeably. Convergence is a newer word, in this context, and means the gradual aligning of IFRS and US GAAP, followed by other jurisdictions aligning with the result of that.

It is necessary to distinguish between *de jure* harmonization (that of rules, standards, etc.) and *de facto* harmonization (that of corporate financial reporting practices). For any particular topic or set of countries, it is possible to have one of these two forms of harmonization without the other. For example, countries or companies may ignore the harmonized rules of standard setters or even law-makers. By contrast, market forces persuaded many listed companies in France or Switzerland to produce English-language financial reports that approximately followed Anglo-American practice.

The EU achieves its harmonizing objectives mainly through Directives (which must be incorporated into the laws of member states) and Regulations (which have direct effect). In the 1970s and 1980s attention was given to harmonizing national laws through Directives (see 5.4.2 and 5.4.3 below). During the 1990s, the EU began to take more notice of international standards, leading to a Regulation of 2002 requiring IFRSs for the consolidated statements of listed companies (see 5.4.4).

### 5.4.2 Relevant EU Directives

The relevant body of law for accounting is company law, and the concern of this section will be with the Directives on company law. These are listed in Table 5.10 with a brief description of their scope. The Fourth EU Directive will be discussed in more detail below, after an outline of the procedure for setting Directives. In addition to the Directives listed in Table 5.10, there are several others of relevance to accounting, e.g. the special versions of the Fourth Directive for banks and for insurance companies.

**Table 5.10 EU Directives most relevant to corporate accounting**

| Directives on company law | Draft dates | Date adopted | Topic |
| --- | --- | --- | --- |
| Second | 1970, 1972 | 1976 | Separation of public companies, minimum capital, distributions |
| Fourth | 1971, 1974 | 1978 | Formats and rules of accounting |
| Seventh | 1976, 1978 | 1983 | Consolidated accounting |
| Eighth | 1978 | 1984 | Qualifications and work of auditors |

The exact effects of any Directive on a particular country will depend upon the laws passed by national legislatures. For example, there are dozens of provisions in the Fourth Directive that begin with such expressions as 'member states may require or permit companies to . . .'

The Fourth Directive covers public and private companies. Its articles include those referring to valuation rules, formats of published financial statements, and disclosure requirements. It does not cover consolidation, which is left to the Seventh Directive (see Chapter 14). The Fourth Directive's first draft was published in 1971, before the United Kingdom, Ireland and Denmark (let alone the later entrants) had joined the EU (or its predecessors). This initial draft was heavily influenced by German company law, particularly the *Aktiengesetz* of 1965. Consequently, for example, valuation rules were to be conservative, and formats were to be prescribed in detail. Financial statements were to obey the provisions of the Directive.

The UK, Ireland and Denmark joined the then 'common market' in 1973. The influence of Anglo-Saxon thinking was such that a much amended draft of the Fourth Directive was issued in 1974. This introduced the concept of the 'true and fair view'. Another change by 1974 was that some flexibility of presentation had been introduced. This process continued and, by the promulgation of the finalized Directive, the 'true and fair view' was established as a predominant principle in the preparation of financial statements (Article 2, paragraphs 2–5). In addition, the four basic principles (accruals, prudence, consistency and going concern) were made clearer than they had been in the 1974 draft (Article 31).

More rearrangement and summarization of items in the financial statements was made possible (Article 4). There were also calls for more notes in the 1974 draft than the 1971 draft, and more in the final Directive than in the 1974 draft (Articles 43–46). Another concern of Anglo-Dutch accountants was with the effect of taxation on Franco-German accounts. The extra disclosures called for by the 1974 draft about the effect of taxation are included in the final Directive (Articles 30 and 35).

The fact that member states may permit or require a type of inflation accounting is treated in more detail than in the 1974 draft (Article 33). As a further accommodation of Anglo-Dutch opinion, a 'Contact Committee' of EU and national civil servants is provided for. This was intended to answer the criticism that the Directive gives rise to laws that are not flexible to changing circumstances and attitudes. The Committee looks at practical problems arising from the implementation of the Directive, and makes suggestions for amendments (Article 52).

For over twenty years, the Fourth Directive was not changed in any substantial way. However, in 2001, it was amended to allow financial instruments to be valued at fair value with gains and losses taken to income, as is required by the international standard (IAS 39). In 2003, further amendments removed other incompatibilities with IFRSs.

A feature of the Fourth Directive is that it allows member states to exempt some smaller private companies from audit and from some other requirements. In 2009, the EU Commission proposed that very small companies ('micro', i.e. those with 10 or fewer employees) could be exempted entirely.

The Second Directive concerns a number of matters connected with share capital and the differences between public and private companies. For example, the Directive requires all member states to have separate legal structures for public and private companies and to have separate names for the companies. Table 4.1 in the previous chapter shows some company names in the EU. As noted in that chapter, a 'public' company in this context is one that is legally allowed to have a market in its securities, although it does not *need* to have one. For example, many PLCs, SAs or AGs are not listed. It is important to note that 'public' in this sense means neither listed nor anything to do with government. The implementation of the Directive led to the creation of the BV in the Netherlands and to the invention of the label 'PLC' in the United Kingdom. The Second Directive also deals with the limits on distribution of profits to shareholders.

The Seventh Directive concerns consolidated accounting, a topic considered in Chapter 14. The Eighth Directive was watered down from its original draft, which might have greatly affected the training patterns and scope of work of accountants. However, its main effect now is to decide on who is allowed to audit financial statements in certain countries.

### 5.4.3 The example of accounting 'principles'

As an example of the evolution of the Fourth Directive's provisions, the requirements on accounting principles are examined here.

Anglo-Dutch financial reporting was traditionally free of legal constraints in the area of principles of valuation and measurement, whether from company law, tax law or accounting plan. However, this was far from the case in some other EU countries, especially Germany whose 1965 *Aktiengesetz* (AktG) was a major source of the Fourth Directive. There are three levels of principle in the AktG, in the Directive and in the resulting laws of member states. The first and vaguest level consists of a statement of the overriding purpose of the financial statements. In the AktG (paragraph 149), this overriding purpose was to obey the provisions of the law. By the final 1978 version of the Directive, the overriding purpose had become to give a true and fair view. The evolution of this may be seen in Table 5.11. Pressure from Anglo-Dutch countries had caused its insertion in the 1974 draft and its dominance in the Directive in special circumstances (see paragraph 5 of the final version of the Directive, as shown in Table 5.11). It should be noted that neither the 'true and fair' concept nor the 'special circumstances'

**Table 5.11 The development of 'true and fair' in the Fourth Directive**

**Stage 1: 1965 *Aktiengesetz* (paragraph 149)**

1. The annual financial statements shall conform to proper accounting principles. They shall be clear and well set out and give as sure a view of the company's financial position and its operating results as is possible pursuant to the valuation provisions.

**Stage 2: 1971 Draft (Art 2) of the Directive**

1. The annual accounts shall comprise the balance sheet, the profit and loss account and the notes on the accounts. These documents shall constitute a composite whole.
2. The annual accounts shall conform to the principles of regular and proper accounting.
3. They shall be drawn up clearly and, in the content of the provisions regarding the valuation of assets and liabilities and the layout of accounts, shall reflect as accurately as possible the company's assets, liabilities, financial position and results.

**Stage 3: 1974 Draft (Art 2)**

1. (As 1971 Draft)
2. The annual accounts shall give a true and fair view of the company's assets, liabilities, financial position and results.
3. They shall be drawn up clearly and in conformity with the provisions of this directive.

**Stage 4: 1978 Final (Art 2)**

1. (As 1971 Draft)
2. They shall be drawn up clearly and in accordance with the provisions of this Directive.
3. The annual accounts shall give a true and fair view of the company's assets, liabilities, financial position and profit or loss.
4. Where the application of the provisions of this Directive would not be sufficient to give a true and fair view within the meaning of paragraph 3, additional information must be given.
5. Where in exceptional cases the application of a provision of this Directive is incompatible with the obligation laid down in paragraph 3, that provision must be departed from in order to give a true and fair view within the meaning of paragraph 3. Any such departure must be disclosed in the notes on the accounts together with an explanation of the reasons for it and a statement of its effect on the assets, liabilities, financial position and profit or loss. The Member States may define the exceptional cases in question and lay down the relevant special rules.
6. The Member States may authorize or require the disclosure in the annual accounts of other information as well as that which must be disclosed in accordance with this Directive.

are defined. As mentioned in Chapter 3 of this book, the IASB's Framework suggests that 'fair presentation' is much the same as 'a true and fair view'. The implication is that, above all, the financial statements should be in accordance with the facts and not be misleading.

Implementation of the 'true and fair' concept has been interpreted in different ways in different countries, both linguistically and philosophically.

### Language

The expression 'true and fair view' (TFV) has found its way into the laws of the EU member states, in a variety of ways. The versions for the fifteen member states before the 2004 enlargement (plus Norway) are shown in Table 5.12. Four countries have an apparently dual concept (e.g. true *and* fair), whereas twelve have a unitary concept. Investigation (Parker and Nobes, 1991) in the United

Kingdom suggests that financial directors of large companies see TFV as unitary, whereas their auditors see it as dual: approximately, 'truth' is taken to mean that the financial statements are in accordance with the facts, and 'fairness' that they are not misleading (the two features mentioned above).

In most languages, but not Greek and Spanish, the indefinite article is used, leading to the conclusion that a number of different financial statements could all give a true and fair view of any particular state of affairs of profit or loss.

Table 5.12 **True and fair view**

| Country | TFV in home language(s) |
| --- | --- |
| UK (1947)<br>Ireland (1963) | a true and fair view |
| Netherlands (1970)<br>Belgium (1985) | een getrouw beeld |
| Denmark (1981) | et retvisende billede |
| France (1983)<br>Luxembourg (1984)<br>Belgium (1985) | une image fidèle (een getrouw beeld) |
| Germany (1985) | ein den tatsächlichen Verhältnissen entsprechendes Bild |
| Greece (1986) | tin pragmatiki ikona |
| Spain (1989) | la imagen fiel |
| Portugal (1989) | una imagem verdadeira e apropriada |
| Austria (1990) | ein möglichst getreues Bild |
| Italy (1991) | rappresentare in modo veritiero e corretto |
| Finland (1992) | oikeat ja riittävät tiedot |
| Sweden (1995) | en rättvisande bild |
| Norway (1998) | et rettvisende bilde |

### Philosophy

Accountants and lawyers in continental countries were, of course, aware of the forthcoming need to implement the TFV from at least the publication of the draft Directive of 1974. It was a topic of conversation at international meetings and even of specific European conferences in the 1970s and 1980s. The idea that law should be departed from as a result of the opinion of directors and auditors is hard to accept even for 'English' lawyers let alone for 'Roman' lawyers.

The national stances towards the implementation of the Directive may also be classified into several types, with the UK and Germany as extremes:

- UK: TFV is used by directors/auditors in interpreting the law and standards or where there is no law or standard, and sometimes to override the law or standards. TFV can also be used by standard setters to make rules that override details of the law.

- Germany: TFV may be used by directors/auditors to interpret government requirements or in cases where there are no requirements. The law cannot be departed from in order to give a TFV. Some hold the view that TFV relates only to notes to the financial statements.

### 5.4.4 The EU Regulation of 2002

By the early 1990s, it had become clear, even to the European Commission, that Directives were too cumbersome and slow to achieve further useful harmonization. The Fourth Directive, agreed in 1978, did not cover several topics and it had been too complicated to amend it often. Furthermore, global harmonization had become more relevant than regional harmonization.

It had also become clear that, for large European companies, voluntary harmonization might focus on US rules over which the European Commission and other Europeans have no influence. Consequently, from the middle of the 1990s, the European Commission began to support the increasingly important efforts of the International Accounting Standards Committee (later, the IASB). The EU also had in mind the creation of powerful harmonized European financial markets.

In 2000, the Commission proposed the compulsory use of IFRSs for the consolidated statements of listed companies for 2005 onwards. This was agreed by the European Parliament and the Council of Ministers in 2002, in the form of a Regulation.

This Regulation also allows member states to extend the use of IFRSs compulsorily or optionally to unlisted companies and unconsolidated statements. For any companies falling under the Regulation, the national laws and standards on accounting are overridden. For other companies, the national rules (including the national implementations of the Directives) are still in effect.

### 5.4.5 Expansion of the EU

Having reached a membership of fifteen countries in 1995, the EU remained at a constant size for nearly ten years. In 2004 a further ten countries joined: Cyprus, Czech Republic, Estonia, Hungary, Latvia, Lithuania, Malta, Poland, Slovakia and Slovenia. Romania and Bulgaria joined on 1 January 2007. It is noteworthy that all these new members except Malta and Cyprus are from the former 'Eastern bloc' of Soviet-controlled countries. All those joining in 2004 and afterwards are automatically subject to the 2005 Regulation referred to in Section 5.4.4. above.

This influx inevitably alters the balance of power, and affects attitudes to developments, in financial reporting. Implications are unclear at this stage, but there will undoubtedly be some.

## 5.5 The International Accounting Standards Board

### 5.5.1 Nature and purpose of the IASC/B

The IASB's predecessor, the International Accounting Standards Committee (IASC), was founded in 1973 and had a secretariat based in London. The original members were the accountancy bodies of nine countries: Australia, Canada, France, Germany, Japan, Mexico, the Netherlands, the United Kingdom (with Ireland) and the United States. By the millennium, there were over 140 member bodies from over 100 countries. Up until the end of 2000, the IASC was governed by a Board comprising representatives of 13 of the countries plus a few other relevant international organizations. From 2001, an independent Board of 14 or more (mostly full-time) members continues the IASC's work. The Board members are appointed by Trustees, drawn from the world's financial community, who represent the public interest.

It is the countries influenced by the Anglo-American tradition that are most familiar with setting accounting standards in the private sector. It is not surprising, then, that the working language of the IASB is English, that it is based in London, and that most standards are closely in line with, or compromise between, US and UK standards.

A list of IASB standards (collectively called IFRSs) is shown in Table 5.13. The process leading to the issue of an accounting standard includes the publication of an exposure draft prepared for public comment. A summary of the content of the IFRSs is given in Appendix B at the end of this book.

One particular issue concerning the content of IFRSs needs to be taken up here. IAS 1 (paragraph 15) requires above all else that financial statements must 'present fairly' the financial position, performance and cash flows of an enterprise. This is somewhat similar to the 'true and fair view' requirement examined earlier, and is also overriding – that is, in rare circumstances, if compliance with a requirement of a standard would be misleading it must be departed from. There must be full disclosures of any such departure, including the numerical effect.

## 5.5.2 Influence of the IASB

The importance of the IASB's work can be seen in three major areas:

- adoption of IFRSs as national rules;
- influence on national regulators;
- voluntary adoption of IFRSs by companies.

In several Asian and African countries of the (British) Commonwealth, IFRSs have been adopted exactly or approximately by national standard setters. This is a feature of a number of developing countries (e.g. Nigeria) and a number of now well-developed countries with a British colonial history (e.g. Singapore). Adoption of IFRSs (sometimes with local variants) is an inexpensive way of setting standards that avoids unnecessary or accidental international differences.

The second point, namely the influence on regulators, is connected. Even for countries whose standard setters thought of themselves as leaders rather than followers (e.g. the United States and the United Kingdom), the IASB acted as a focus for international collaboration. Several accounting standards were set jointly by the IASB and one or more national standard setters. Many other standard setters tried to avoid differences from IFRSs.

The third point, namely voluntary adoption by companies, was seen particularly in continental Europe. From the early 1990s onwards, many large European

Table 5.13 **IASB documents (as of 1 January 2010)**

*Framework for the preparation and presentation of financial statements (1989)*

| IAS | 1 | Presentation of financial statements |
|-----|-----|-----|
| IAS | 2 | Inventories |
| IAS | 7 | Statement of cash flows |
| IAS | 8 | Accounting policies, changes in accounting estimates and errors |
| IAS | 10 | Events after the reporting date |
| IAS | 11 | Construction contracts |
| IAS | 12 | Income taxes |
| IAS | 16 | Property, plant and equipment |
| IAS | 17 | Leases |
| IAS | 18 | Revenue |
| IAS | 19 | Employee benefits |
| IAS | 20 | Accounting for government grants and disclosure of government assistance |
| IAS | 21 | The effects of changes in foreign exchange rates |
| IAS | 23 | Borrowing costs |
| IAS | 24 | Related party disclosures |
| IAS | 26 | Accounting and reporting by retirement benefit plans |
| IAS | 27 | Consolidated and separate financial statements |
| IAS | 28 | Investments in associates |
| IAS | 29 | Financial reporting in hyperinflationary economies |
| IAS | 31 | Interests in joint ventures |
| IAS | 32 | Financial instruments: presentation |
| IAS | 33 | Earnings per share |
| IAS | 34 | Interim financial reporting |
| IAS | 36 | Impairment of assets |
| IAS | 37 | Provisions, contingent liabilities and contingent assets |
| IAS | 38 | Intangible assets |
| IAS | 39 | Financial instruments: recognition and measurement |
| IAS | 40 | Investment property |
| IAS | 41 | Agriculture |
| IFRS | 1 | First-time adoption of IFRS |
| IFRS | 2 | Share-based payment |
| IFRS | 3 | Business combinations |
| IFRS | 4 | Insurance contracts |
| IFRS | 5 | Non-current assets held for sale and discontinued operations |
| IFRS | 6 | Exploration for and evaluation of mineral resources |
| IFRS | 7 | Financial instruments: disclosures |
| IFRS | 8 | Operating segments |
| IFRS | 9 | Financial instruments |

IFRS for small and medium-sized entities

companies (notably in France, Germany and Switzerland) have volunteered to use IFRSs because they believe that international investors prefer financial statements prepared that way.

By 2000, most of the biggest Swiss groups (e.g. Nestlé, Roche and Novartis) were using IFRSs for their consolidated statements. As examples of developing practice, the position in France for large companies for 1996 is shown in Table 5.14. It can be seen that US and IASB rules were contending for the position of world standard, and that other national rules are likely to die out for the consolidated

Table 5.14 **Use of IASs in France, 1996**

| US GAAP | | | IAS | |
|---|---|---|---|---|
| 'Compatible' national set of accounts | | Supplementary set of accounts (20-F or full annual report) | 'Compatible' national set of accounts | |
| Fully | With exceptions | | Fully | With exceptions |
| Bull | Air Liquide | AB Productions | Bongrain | Aérospatiale |
| Chargeurs | Carrefour | Alcatel | Canal Plus | Béghin-Say |
| Dassault Systèmes | Danone | Alsthom | DMC | Cap Gémini |
| Elf | PSA | Axa-UAP | Essilor | Lafarge Coppée |
| Legrand | Technip | Bouygues | Moulinex | LVMH |
| Rhône-Poulenc | | Offshore | Saint Louis | Renault |
| SEB | | Business Objects | SEB | Saint-Gobain |
| | | Coflexip | Technip | |
| | | Dassault Systèmes | Thomson | |
| | | Elf | Usinor-Sacilor | |
| | | Flamel Technologies | Valéo | |
| | | Genset | | |
| | | Ilog | | |
| | | LVMH | | |
| | | Péchiney | | |
| | | Usinor-Sacilor | | |
| | | SCOR | | |
| | | Total | | |

*Source*: Adapted from S. Zambon and W. Dick, University of Reading Discussion Papers in Accounting, Finance and Banking, No. 58, 1998.

reporting of large listed companies. Of course, this is certainly the case for the EU for 2005 onwards.

From the late 1980s, the IASC had been in negotiation with the world's major stock market regulators through their international association called IOSCO (the International Organization of Securities Commissions). The objective was that IFRSs should become a global system accepted on all stock markets, particularly for foreign companies. IOSCO wanted improvements in IFRSs to be made, including the removal of options in standards and the coverage of several extra accounting topics. This process of improvement saw massive efforts by the IASC throughout the 1990s, was nearly completed with IAS 39 in 1998, and was fully completed with IAS 40 in 2000. In May 2000, IOSCO recommended acceptance of IFRSs to its members for financial reporting by foreign companies listed on the stock exchanges that they regulate. Many stock market regulators already accept IFRSs, and the US regulator (the SEC) is still considering the issue.

The EU's adoption of IFRS for the consolidated statements of listed companies for 2005 was followed by Australia for that year and by Canada for 2011. China and Japan have also been converging with IFRS. In 2008, the Securities and Exchange Commission of the United States announced that it was considering adopting IFRS from 2014 onwards.

In most cases (e.g. the EU and Australia), there are mechanisms to turn IFRS (and amendments to it) into local legal requirements. So, for example, the audit reports on EU listed companies financial statements still refer to national regulations and to 'IFRSs as adopted by the European Union'.

Although this means that, for many situations, national systems of regulation will become irrelevant, it does not mean that national attitudes towards the practical application of written regulations will become irrelevant. Where differences in such attitudes exist, implications may continue. Differences still exist between the US and general IASB philosophy on, for example, the extent to which regulation should be specific (rules) or more generic (principles). Also, companies from different countries can end up implementing IFRS in different ways, for example by choosing options within IFRS differently (Nobes, 2006).

In short, whilst the objective of moving standards more and more closely together is not in doubt, the achievement of that objective in the short term seems unlikely. Developments should be watched carefully.

### 5.5.3 IFRS for SMEs

In 2009, after six years of work, the IASB issued a special standard designed for those entities that are not publicly accountable, whatever their size. This means unlisted entities except for a few unlisted banks and insurance companies. SME-IFRS is much shorter and easier to read than full IFRS. It deletes some whole standards (e.g. segment reporting; see Chapter 6) and reduces disclosure requirements. It also contains some simplifications, for example expensing instead of capitalizing development costs (see Chapter 8) and amortizing instead of impairing goodwill (see Chapter 14).

Any permission or requirement to use SME-IFRS will depend on national regulations. It seems likely that some countries (e.g. the United Kingdom) will allow IFRS-private for unlisted entities, whereas others (e.g. France) will not because it would change profit and therefore taxable income.

**Summary**

- Today's financial reporting practices have developed over many centuries, with many countries contributing.

- Financial reporting practices can be classified into two main types of accounting system. However, for example, many large German companies voluntarily stopped using the traditional German accounting system for their group accounting.

- International differences seem to be connected to different purposes of accounting, particularly a contrast between use by investors for decision making and use for the legal purposes of creditor protection and the calculation of taxable income.

- In Europe, some countries (e.g. the United Kingdom) have large stock markets and large numbers of auditors. Other countries (e.g. Germany) have much smaller stock markets and numbers of auditors.

- Efforts to harmonize financial reporting within the EU were slow because of the need to reach agreement on the relevant EU Directives among the member states. This has also led to many options and omissions in the Directives. The spread of the requirement to give a true and fair view seems to be harmonization of form but not of substance. Also, the idea of harmonizing only within the EU is perhaps now out of date.

- EU progress has been made with some standardization of formats of financial statements and particularly with group accounting issues. The EU is now promoting the use of international standards.

- The IASC's attempts at harmonization were initially hampered by the problems of achieving international agreement and by the lack of enforcement mechanisms. However, with the support of stock market regulators and the spread of a global capital market, IFRSs are now extensively used. They are now compulsory in the EU and Australia for the consolidated statements of listed companies, and might become so in the United States.

 ## References and research

The following are examples of research papers in the English language which take the issues of this chapter further:

- D. Alexander, 'A European true and fair view?' *European Accounting Review*, Vol. 2, No. 1, 1993.
- D. Alexander and E. Jermakowicz, 'A True and Fair View of the Principles/Rules Debate', *Abacus*, Vol. 42, No. 2, 2006.
- R. Ball, 'International Financial Reporting Standards (IFRS): pros and cons for investors', *Accounting and Business Research*, special issue, 2006.
- J. Blake, H. Fortes, C. Gowthorpe and M. Paananen, 'Implementing the EU accounting directives in Sweden – practitioners' views', *International Journal of Accounting*, Vol. 34, No. 3, 1999.
- B. Colasse, 'The French notion of the *image fidèle*: The power of words', *European Accounting Review*, Vol. 6, No. 4, 1997.
- R. David and J.E.C. Brierley, *Major Legal Systems in the World Today* (London: Stevens, 1978).
- A. Haller, 'The relationship of financial and tax accounting in Germany: A major reason for accounting disharmony in Europe', *International Journal of Accounting*, Vol. 27, 1992, pp. 310–23.
- J.A. Lainez, J.I. Jarne and S. Callao, 'The Spanish accounting system and international accounting harmonization', *European Accounting Review*, Vol. 8, No. 1, 1999.
- M. Lamb, C.W. Nobes, and A.D. Roberts, 'International variations in the connections between tax and financial reporting', *Accounting and Business Research*, Summer, 1998.
- D. Mandl, 'The new Austrian Financial Reporting Act', *European Accounting Review*, Vol. 2, No. 2, 1993.
- G.G. Mueller, *International Accounting*, Part I (New York: Macmillan, 1967).
- R.D. Nair and W.G. Frank, 'The impact of disclosure and measurement practices on international accounting classifications', *Accounting Review*, July, 1980.
- C.W. Nobes, 'A judgemental international classification of financial reporting practices', *Journal of Business Finance and Accounting*, Spring, 1983.
- C.W. Nobes, 'Towards a general model of the reasons for international differences in financial reporting', *Abacus*, Vol. 34, No. 2, 1998.

■ C.W. Nobes, 'The survival of international differences under IFRS: Towards a research agenda', *Accounting and Business Research*, Vol. 36, No. 3, 2006.

■ D. Ordelheide, 'True and fair view: A European and a German perspective', *European Accounting Review*, Vol. 2, No. 1, 1993.

■ R.H. Parker, 'Harmonizing the notes in the UK and France: A case study in *de jure* harmonization', *European Accounting Review*, Vol. 5, No. 2, 1996.

■ R.H. Parker and C.W. Nobes, 'Auditors' view of true and fair', *Accounting and Business Research*, Autumn, 1991.

■ J.S.W. Tay and R.H. Parker, 'Measuring international harmonization and standardization', *Abacus*, Vol. 26, No. 1, 1990.

■ P. Thorell and G. Whittington, 'The harmonization of accounting within the EU: Problems, perspectives and strategies', *European Accounting Review*, Vol. 3, No. 2, 1994.

■ K. Van Hulle, 'The true and fair view override in the European accounting Directives', *European Accounting Review*, Vol. 6, No. 4, 1997.

■ G. Whittington, 'The adoption of international accounting standards in the European Union', *European Accounting Review*, Vol. 14, No. 1, 2005.

■ S. Zeff, 'Some obstacles to global financial reporting comparability and convergence at a high level of quality', *British Accounting Review*, Vol. 39, No. 4, 2007.

■ S.A. Zeff, W. Buijink and K. Camfferman, ' "True and fair" in the Netherlands: *inzicht* or *getrouw beeld*?' *European Accounting Review*, Vol. 8, No. 3, 1999.

## ? EXERCISES

*Feedback on the first two of these exercises is given in Appendix D.*

5.1 Explain how international differences in the ownership and financing of companies could lead to differences in financial reporting.

5.2 Explain for whom international differences in financial reporting are a problem. Describe any ways you know about in which those who face such problems are dealing with them.

5.3 Several factors have been suggested as related to financial reporting differences, i.e. legal systems, providers of finance, taxation, the accountancy profession, and accidents of history.

(a) Within your knowledge and experiences, which factors do you believe to be the most important, and why?

(b) To what extent do you think your views on (a) above have been influenced by your own national environment?

5.4 'International accounting classification systems are, by their very nature, simplistic.' Discuss.

5.5 By reference to any of the countries in Figures 5.2 or 5.3 with which you are familiar, comment on the apparent validity of the groupings. Make notes of points for and against the particular positions of the countries concerned. Be ready to update these notes as you read later chapters.

5.6 Do international differences in the rules for the calculation of taxable income cause accounting differences, or is the influence the other way round?

5.7 'The true and fair view requirement is now established in all European Union countries, and so the aim of financial reporting has been harmonized.' Discuss.

5.8 (a) Outline the objectives and achievements of the EU in the area of financial reporting.
   (b) Outline the objectives and achievements of the IASB and its predecessor in the area of financial reporting.
   (c) Do your answers to (a) and (b) suggest movement in the same direction: (i) in the 1980s, and (ii) now?

5.9 In which European countries have the standards of the IASB had the greatest influence?

5.10 Bearing in mind that Section 5.5.2 of this Chapter was written in 2009, rewrite it in the context of the time when you read this book.

# Chapter 6

# The contents of financial statements

**Contents**   6.1   Introduction                                                    94
6.2   Balance sheets (statements of financial position)                95
6.3   Comprehensive income                                          101
    6.3.1   Income statements                                    102
    6.3.2   Other comprehensive income                          104
6.4   Statements of changes in equity                                108
6.5   Cash flow statements                                          108
6.6   Notes to the financial statements                             110
6.7   Other general disclosure requirements                         110
    6.7.1   Segment reporting                                    110
    6.7.2   Discontinued operations                              111
    6.7.3   Earnings per share                                   112
    6.7.4   Interim financial reports                            112
Summary                                                             113
References and research                                             114
Exercises                                                           114

**Objectives**   Having thoroughly worked through this chapter you should be able to:

- outline the main component parts of published annual financial statements of corporations;

- describe and discuss the main requirements of IAS 1 as regards the contents of published financial statements;

- discuss the concept of comprehensive income, and demonstrate an understanding of the issues related to a single overall performance statement;

- outline the relationship of cash flow statements to other financial statements;

- outline and appraise disclosure requirements under IFRS in relation to segments, interim financial reports, earnings per share and discontinued operations;

- compare the above requirements with those in national jurisdictions within your experience.

## 6.1 Introduction

As has already been explored in Chapter 2, the two most fundamental components of a set of financial accounts are the balance sheet and the income statement. The balance sheet (or statement of financial position) presents a statement of the assets, liabilities and owner's equity, at the balance sheet date. It is prepared from the accounting records after the application of the conventions and practices discussed in Chapter 3.

The income statement has as its focus the financial performance of the reporting period, taking into account the revenues and expenses of the period. Until recently, the income statement did not include all income and expense items. For example, gains on the revaluation (but not sale) of assets meet the IASB's definition of income but are not yet realized in cash or promises of cash. So, traditionally they have not been recorded in the income statement. From the 1990s onwards, under IASB, UK or US rules, they have been recorded in a second type of income statement called various things, such as a statement of other comprehensive income.

One thing that the above statements do not do, as briefly explored in Section 2.5, is provide a focus on the cash position. To remedy this, a cash flow statement is widely regarded as an essential component. This statement seeks to highlight the movements of cash into and out of the business during the period under review.

*Why it matters*    *It is perfectly possible for a business operation to be profitable in the short term and still run out of money, because of delayed receipts or advance payments, or because of investment policies. It is, of course, also possible for a business to be making losses while still having large amounts of cash and, in the short term, positive annual cash flows. A cash flow statement is thus an essential part of the overall information package that is necessary for business appraisal.*

The typical annual financial report, particularly for listed companies, contains a number of additional sections. These are likely to include discussions by the company chairman and the management team of the activities and results of the business, and various graphs, photographs of relevance (or otherwise) to the business, and other material designed to ensure that the readers of the package receive the 'right' impression of the performance of the business and the management. It is unclear to what extent the company and its auditors are legally responsible for the validity and overall fairness of these voluntary sections. Formally, the auditors are required to give an opinion on the financial statements (including the notes) and to check that the directors' report is consistent with those statements. However, there is some evidence that many readers of financial statements give more attention to the voluntary material than to the detailed formal financial information. Logic would therefore suggest that it is the overall impression of the complete 'annual report' that needs to be true and fair.

The next four sections of this chapter look in some detail at the general disclosure requirements for the basic statements, with a particular focus on IAS 1. Sections 6.6 and 6.7 outline the other major requirements existing and emerging at the present time.

As discussed in Chapter 5, both IAS 1 and the EU Fourth Directive have a significant effect on the general contents of basic financial statements. Within Europe, the EU Fourth Directive is still relevant for those financial statements not prepared under the EU Regulation of 2002 (e.g. still relevant in many countries for all unconsolidated statements). Even where the Regulation is being followed, national practices under IFRS may reflect preferences formed by national implementations of the Directives. For non-EU countries, there is relevance in that several elements of the Fourth Directive have influenced IAS 1.

The approach we have followed here is to structure our coverage on IAS 1 (as revised in 2007), but to include detail from the Fourth Directive (as revised with effect from 2007 ) in the appropriate places. IAS 1 requires that financial statements that claim to follow IFRSs should be clearly distinguished from any other information that is included in the same published document. Figures, components and separate pages must be fully and clearly described. Financial statements should be presented at least annually, normally for a twelve-month period, and any exceptions (such as a change in reporting date following an acquisition by another entity) should be clearly explained.

## 6.2 Balance sheets (statements of financial position)

A number of items, if material, should be shown as separate totals on the face of the balance sheet. These are specified in IAS 1 as follows:

- property, plant and equipment
- investment property
- intangible assets
- financial assets (unless included under other headings below)
- investments accounted for using the equity method (see Chapter 14)
- biological assets
- inventories
- trade and other receivables
- cash and cash equivalents
- assets held for sale
- trade and other payables
- provisions
- financial liabilities (unless included under other headings)
- liabilities and assets for current tax
- deferred tax liabilities and assets
- liabilities of disposal groups held for sale
- non-controlling interests (see Chapter 14)
- issued capital and reserves attributable to the owners of the parent.

The above represents a minimum. Additional line items, headings and subtotals should also be included on the face of the balance sheet when any other IFRS requires it, or when such additional presentation is necessary in order to 'present fairly' the entity's financial position.

It is usual (and generally required by IAS 1 and by the Fourth Directive) for a balance sheet to present current and non-current assets, and current and non-current liabilities, as separate classifications on the face of the balance sheet. When an entity chooses not to make this analysis, assets and liabilities should still be presented broadly in order of their liquidity, although the IAS does not specify 'which way up' the liquidity analysis should go. For example, it is generally European practice for assets to end with cash (which is required by the Directive), whereas it is North American, Japanese and Australian practice to start with cash. Whichever method of presentation is adopted, an entity should disclose the amounts included in each item that are expected to be recovered or settled before, and after, twelve months.

IAS 1 states that an asset should be classified as current when it:

- is expected to be realized in, or is held for sale or consumption in, the normal course of the entity's operating cycle;
- is held primarily for trading purposes;
- is expected to be realized within twelve months of the balance sheet date; or
- is cash or a cash equivalent that is not restricted in its use.

This is a wide definition. By contrast European laws based on the Fourth Directive concentrate on the first of these criteria by defining fixed assets as those intended for continuing use in the business, and all other assets as current. Under European laws, a non-current asset remains non-current throughout its useful life to the entity, as it is not held primarily for trading purposes. It does not eventually become 'current' merely because its expected disposal is within less than twelve months. However, under IFRS 5 (based on US GAAP) when formerly non-current assets are held for sale, they are separated from non-current assets and valued like inventories (approximately speaking, at the lower of cost and market; see Section 6.5.2).

Where liabilities are classified, a comparable distinction is required. IAS 1 requires that a liability should be classified as a current liability when it:

- is expected to be settled in the normal course of the entity's operating cycle;
- it is held for trading; or
- is due to be settled within twelve months of the balance sheet date.

In the case of liabilities the 'current' portion of long-term interest-bearing liabilities is generally to be classified as current, unless refinance is arranged by the balance sheet date.

Figure 6.1 shows an IFRS balance sheet of Bayer AG, a German pharmaceutical company. The company has chosen a slightly different order of items compared to IAS 1's list. This is because of previous German practice (see below).

The Fourth Directive sets out considerably more detail in its specifications regarding balance sheets. It requires that member states should prescribe one or both of the layouts specified by its Articles 9 and 10. As noted earlier, this is relevant for EU companies not following IFRS. Article 9, reproduced in Table 6.1, gives a 'horizontal' format with the debits on one side and the credits on the other, following the general continental European tradition. Incidentally, the word

**Figure 6.1 Bayer Group consolidated balance sheet**

|  | 31 Dec. 2008 |
|---|---:|
| € million | |
| **Noncurrent assets** | |
| Goodwill | 8,647 |
| Other intangible assets | 13,951 |
| Property, plant and equipment | 9,492 |
| Investments in associates | 450 |
| Other financial assets | 1,197 |
| Other receivables | 458 |
| Deferred taxes | 1,156 |
| | 35,351 |
| **Current assets** | |
| Inventories | 6,681 |
| Trade accounts receivable | 5,953 |
| Other financial assets | 634 |
| Other receivables | 1,284 |
| Claims for income tax refunds | 506 |
| Cash and cash equivalents | 2,094 |
| Assets held for sale and discontinued operations | 8 |
| | 17,160 |
| **Total assets** | **52,511** |
| **Shareholder's equity** | |
| Capital stock of Bayer AG | 1,957 |
| Capital reserves of Bayer AG | 4,028 |
| Other reserves | 10,278 |
| | **16,263** |
| Equity attributable to non-controlling interest | 72 |
| **Stockholders' equity** | **16,340** |
| **Noncurrent liabilities** | |
| Provisions for pensions and other post-employment benefits | 6,347 |
| Other provisions | 1,351 |
| Financial liabilities | 10,614 |
| Other liabilities | 432 |
| Deferred taxes | 3,592 |
| | **22,336** |
| **Current liabilities** | |
| Other provisions | 3,163 |
| Financial liabilities | 6,256 |
| Trade accounts payable | 2,377 |
| Income tax liabilities | 65 |
| Other liabilities | 1,961 |
| Directly related to assets held for sale and discontinued operations | 13 |
| | **13,835** |
| **Total stockholders' equity and liabilities** | **52,511** |

*Source*: adapted from Bayer Annual Report 2008, p. 135.

'Liabilities' which heads the right-hand side (or lower half) of the balance sheet is a poor translation of the French '*passif*' or German '*passiv*' (see Chapter 11). Article 10, reproduced in Table 6.2, gives a 'vertical' format of the type more traditional in the UK. Companies are required to show the items in these tables in the order specified, except that the headings preceded by Arabic numbers may

### Table 6.1 **The EU Fourth Directive: horizontal balance sheet format**

*Assets*

**A. Subscribed capital unpaid**

**B. Formation expenses**

**C. Fixed assets**
    I  *Intangible assets*
        1.  Costs of research and development.
        2.  Concessions, patents, licences, trade marks and similar rights and assets.
        3.  Goodwill, to the extent that it was acquired for valuable consideration.
        4.  Payments on account.

    II  *Tangible assets*
        1.  Land and buildings.
        2.  Plant and machinery.
        3.  Other fixtures and fittings, tools and equipment.
        4.  Payments on account and tangible assets in course of construction.

    III  *Financial assets*
        1.  Shares in affiliated undertakings.
        2.  Loans in affiliated undertakings.
        3.  Participating interests.
        4.  Loans to undertakings with which the company is linked by virtue of participating interests.
        5.  Investments held as fixed assets.
        6.  Other loans.
        7.  Own shares.

**D. Current assets**
    I  *Stocks*
        1.  Raw materials and consumables.
        2.  Work in progress.
        3.  Finished goods and goods for resale.
        4.  Payments on account.

    II  *Debtors*
    (Amounts becoming due and payable after more than one year must be shown separately for each item.)
        1.  Trade debtors.
        2.  Amounts owed by affiliated undertakings.
        3.  Amounts owed by undertakings with which the company is linked by virtue of participating interests.
        4.  Other debtors.
        5.  Subscribed capital called but not paid.
        6.  Prepayments and accrued income.

    III  *Investments*
        1.  Shares in affiliated undertakings.
        2.  Own shares.
        3.  Other investments.

    IV  *Cash at bank and in hand*

**E. Prepayments and accrued income**

**F. Loss for the financial year**

Table 6.1 *Continued*

*Liabilities*

A. **Capital and reserves**
    I   *Subscribed capital*
    II  *Share premium account*
    III *Revaluation reserve*
    IV *Reserves*
        1.  Legal reserve.
        2.  Reserve for own shares.
        3.  Reserves provided for by the articles of association.
        4.  Other reserves.

    V  *Profit or loss brought forward*
    VI *Profit or loss for the financial year*

B. **Provisions**
    1.  Provisions for pensions and similar obligations.
    2.  Provisions for taxation.
    3.  Other provisions.

C. **Creditors**
(Amounts becoming due and payable within one year and amounts becoming due and payable after more than one year must be shown separately for each item and for the aggregate of these items.)
    1.  Debenture loans, showing convertible loans separately.
    2.  Amounts owed to credit institutions.
    3.  Payments received on account of orders in so far as they are now shown separately as deductions from stocks.
    4.  Trade creditors.
    5.  Bills of exchange payable.
    6.  Amounts owed to affiliated undertakings.
    7.  Amounts owed to undertakings with which the company is linked by virtue of participating interests.
    8.  Other creditors including tax and social security.
    9.  Accruals and deferred income.

D. **Accruals and deferred income**

E. **Profit for the financial year**

be combined or taken to the Notes. The chapters in Part 2 of this book explain the meaning of the various items.

In the European Union, companies that fall below a given size limit, which is updated as circumstances change, may be permitted by the laws of member states to produce abridged accounts. As far as the balance sheet is concerned, these would consist of only those items preceded by letters and roman numerals in Tables 6.1 and 6.2.

In some cases, more specific international standards provide precise requirements for presentation, as illustrated in a number of the chapters in Part 2 of this book. It should be remembered that such requirements do not apply to immaterial items. The fundamental requirement is to give a fair presentation, and the guiding factor should be not to mislead the careful reader of the financial statements.

## Table 6.2 The EU Fourth Directive: vertical balance sheet format

A. **Subscribed capital unpaid**

B. **Formation expenses**

C. **Fixed assets**

   I  *Intangible assets*
   1. Costs of research and development.
   2. Concessions, patents, licences, trade marks and similar rights and assets.
   3. Goodwill, to the extent that it was acquired for valuable consideration.
   4. Payments on account.

   II  *Tangible assets*
   1. Land and buildings.
   2. Plant and machinery.
   3. Other fixtures and fittings, tools and equipment.
   4. Payments on account and tangible assets in course of construction.

   III  *Financial assets*
   1. Shares in affiliated undertakings.
   2. Loans to affiliated undertakings.
   3. Participating interests.
   4. Loans to undertakings with which the company is linked by virtue of participating interests.
   5. Investments held as fixed assets.
   6. Other loans.
   7. Own shares.

D. **Current assets**

   I  *Stocks*
   1. Raw materials and consumables.
   2. Work in progress.
   3. Finished goods and goods for resale.
   4. Payments on account.

   II  *Debtors*
   (Amounts becoming due and payable after more than one year must be shown separately for each item.)
   1. Trade debtors.
   2. Amounts owed by affiliated undertakings.
   3. Amounts owed by undertakings with which the company is linked by virtue of participating interests.
   4. Other debtors.
   5. Subscribed capital called but not paid.
   6. Prepayments and accrued income.

   III  *Investments*
   1. Shares in affiliated undertakings.
   2. Own shares.
   3. Other investments.

   IV  *Cash at bank and in hand*

E. **Prepayments and accrued income**

F. **Creditors: amounts becoming due and payable within one year**
   1. Debenture loans, showing convertible loans separately.
   2. Amounts owed to credit institutions.

**Table 6.2 *Continued***

    3. Payments received on account of orders in so far as they are not shown separately as deductions from stocks.
    4. Trade creditors.
    5. Bills of exchange payable.
    6. Amounts owed to affiliated undertakings.
    7. Amounts owed to undertakings with which the company is linked by virtue of participating interests.
    8. Other creditors including tax and social security.
    9. Accrual and deferred income.

**G. Net current assets/liabilities**

**H. Total assets less current liabilities**

**I. Creditors: amounts becoming due and payable after more than one year**
    1. Debenture loans, showing convertible loans separately.
    2. Amounts owed to credit institutions.
    3. Payments received on account of orders in so far as they are now shown separately as deductions from stocks.
    4. Trade creditors.
    5. Bills of exchange payable.
    6. Amounts owed to affiliated undertakings.
    7. Amounts owed to undertakings with which the company is linked by virtue of participating interests.
    8. Other creditors including tax and social security.
    9. Accruals and deferred income.

**J. Provisions**
    1. Provisions for pensions and similar obligations.
    2. Provisions for taxation.
    3. Other provisions.

**K. Accruals and deferred income**

**L. Capital and reserves**
    I   *Subscribed capital*
    II  *Share premium account*
    III *Revaluation reserve*
    IV *Reserves*
        1. Legal reserve.
        2. Reserve for own shares.
        3. Reserves provided for by the articles of association.
        4. Other reserves.

    V  *Profit or loss brought forward*
    VI *Profit or loss for the financial year*

## 6.3 Comprehensive income

IAS 1 requires either a single statement of comprehensive income or two statements: an income statement and a statement of other comprehensive income (OCI). Most companies choose to present two statements because they regard the elements of OCI as volatile or beyond control. We assume below that two statements are presented.

### 6.3.1 Income statements

As with the balance sheet, IAS 1 requires certain disclosures on the face of the income statement, and other disclosures either on the face of the statement or in the Notes, at the discretion of the reporting entity.

As a minimum, the face of the income statement should include line items that present the following amounts:

- revenues
- finance costs
- share of the after-tax profits and losses of associates and joint ventures accounted for using the equity method (see Chapter 14)
- tax expense
- pre-tax gain or loss on discontinued operations and disposal of their assets/liabilities
- profit or loss
- the amounts of profit attributable to the parent and to non-controlling interests (see Chapter 14).

Additional line items, headings and subtotals should be presented on the face of the income statement when required by more specific IFRSs, or when such additions are necessary to present fairly the entity's financial performance. IAS 1 explicitly accepts that considerations of materiality and the nature of the entity's operations may require additions to, deletions from, or amendments of descriptions within the above list.

Beyond all the above, there is a requirement that an entity should present, either on the face of the income statement (which is 'encouraged' but not obligatory under IAS 1), or in the Notes to the income statement, an analysis using a classification based on either the nature of expenses or their function within the entity. The implications of this distinction between classification by nature and classification by function are conveniently illustrated by turning to the Fourth Directive's specifications for the income statement. The Directive requires that member states allow one or more of the four layouts given in its Articles 23 to 26.

These four layouts are necessary to accommodate the possibility of following either an analysis by nature or an analysis by function, combined with either a horizontal-type presentation or a vertical-type presentation. Table 6.3 classifies the expense items by nature showing, for example, staff costs as a single figure. Table 6.4 classifies by function. Thus, for example, staff costs as a total are not shown, being split up between the various functional heads related to staff activity, such as distribution and administration.

The formats in Tables 6.3 and 6.4 are vertical in style, treating the revenues (credits) as pluses and the expenses (debits) as minuses. However, the Directive allows a horizontal double-entry style of income statement, as illustrated in Chapter 2. Table 6.5 shows the horizontal version of the by-nature format, i.e. a rearrangement of Table 6.3. Although the Directive also allows a horizontal by-function format, this is not used in practice and is not illustrated here.

**Table 6.3  The EU Fourth Directive: vertical profit and loss account by nature**

| Item | Description |
|------|-------------|
| 1 | Net turnover. |
| 2 | Variation in stocks of finished goods and in work in progress. |
| 3 | Work performed by the undertaking for its own purposes and capitalized. |
| 4 | Other operating income. |
| 5 | (a) Raw materials and consumables. |
|   | (b) Other external charges. |
| 6 | Staff costs: |
|   | (a) wages and salaries; |
|   | (b) social security costs with a separate indication of those relating to pensions. |
| 7 | (a) Value adjustments in respect of formation expenses and of tangible and intangible fixed assets. |
|   | (b) Value adjustments in respect of current assets, to the extent that they exceed the amount of value adjustments which are normal in the undertaking concerned. |
| 8 | Other operating charges. |
| 9 | Income from participating interests, with a separate indication of that derived from affiliated undertakings. |
| 10 | Income from other investments and loans forming part of the fixed assets, with a separate indication of that derived from affiliated undertakings. |
| 11 | Other interest receivable and similar income with a separate indication of that derived from affiliated undertakings. |
| 12 | Value adjustments in respect of financial assets and of investments held as current assets. |
| 13 | Interest payable and similar charges, with a separate indication of those concerning affiliated undertakings. |
| 14 | Tax on profit or loss on ordinary activities. |
| 15 | Profit or loss on ordinary activities after taxation. |
| 16 | Extraordinary income. |
| 17 | Extraordinary charges. |
| 18 | Extraordinary profit or loss. |
| 19 | Tax on extraordinary profit or loss. |
| 20 | Other taxes not shown under the above items. |
| 21 | Profit or loss for the financial year. |

In the Directive's formats (and therefore in EU national laws) there are lines for 'extraordinary' items. These are defined, rather vaguely, as those outside ordinary activities. In France and Italy, such activities were taken to include the sale of fixed assets, but in the UK ordinary was defined so widely as to leave nothing as extraordinary. The revision to IAS 1 of 2003 abolished the concept of extraordinary.

**Activity 6.A**   Consider the relative advantages and usefulness of the Directive's four formats for the income statement.

**Feedback**   As regards the financial reports of large listed companies, there is no doubt that the vertical presentations are increasingly predominant. As between the by-nature and by-function classification, both methods have advantages. Showing expenses by nature

Table 6.4 **The EU Fourth Directive: vertical profit and loss account by function**

| Item | Description |
|------|-------------|
| 1 | Net turnover. |
| 2 | Cost of sales (including value adjustments). |
| 3 | Gross profit or loss. |
| 4 | Distribution costs (including value adjustments). |
| 5 | Administrative expenses (including value adjustments). |
| 6 | Other operating income. |
| 7 | Income from participating interests, with a separate indication of that derived from affiliated undertakings. |
| 8 | Income from other investments and loans forming part of the fixed assets, with a separate indication of that derived from affiliated undertakings. |
| 9 | Other interest receivable and similar income, with a separate indication of that derived from affiliated undertakings. |
| 10 | Value adjustments in respect of financial assets and of investments held as current assets. |
| 11 | Interest payable and similar charges, with a separate indication of those concerning affiliated undertakings. |
| 12 | Tax on profit or loss on ordinary activities. |
| 13 | Profit or loss on ordinary activities after taxation. |
| 14 | Extraordinary income. |
| 15 | Extraordinary charges. |
| 16 | Extraordinary profit or loss. |
| 17 | Tax on extraordinary profit or loss. |
| 18 | Other taxes not shown under the above items. |
| 19 | Profit or loss for the financial year. |

requires less analysis and less judgement but is arguably less informative. It fails to reveal the cost of sales, and therefore the gross profit, and it has the disadvantage that it might seem to imply (see Tables 6.3 or 6.5) that changes in inventory are an expense or a revenue in their own right, whereas they are an adjustment to purchases.

However, because information on the nature of expenses is regarded as useful in predicting future cash flows, IAS 1 and the Directive require additional disclosure on the nature of expenses, including depreciation and amortization expenses and staff costs, when the by-function classification is used. Table 6.6 shows the formats typically, but not universally, used in certain countries. Note that the different formats do not lead to differences in reported net income. Different formats do not imply different measurements.

Figure 6.2 shows the income statement of Bayer AG. This is in vertical form, by function.

## 6.3.2 Other comprehensive income

There has been considerable discussion in recent years over the issue of reporting total, or comprehensive, income. The difficulty began with the traditional view that only realized profits (see Chapter 3) should be included in the income statement, and therefore in reported 'earnings'. However, there are two problems here. First, the definition of 'realized' is unclear. Second, a wide variety of other

**Table 6.5 The EU Fourth Directive: horizontal profit and loss account by nature**

*Item    Description*

**A. Charges**

1    Reduction in stocks of finished goods and in work in progress.

2    (a) raw materials and consumables;
     (b) other external charges.

3    Staff costs:
     (a) wages and salaries;
     (b) social security costs with a separate indication of those relating to pensions.

4    (a) Value adjustments in respect of formation expenses and of tangible and intangible fixed assets.
     (b) Value adjustments in respect of current assets, to the extent that they exceed the amount of value adjustments which are normal in the undertaking concerned.

5    Other operating charges.

6    Value adjustments in respect of financial assets and of investments held as current assets.

7    Interest payable and similar charges, with a separate indication of those concerning affiliated undertakings.

8    Tax on profit or loss on ordinary activities.

9    Profit or loss on ordinary activities after taxation.

10   Extraordinary charges.

11   Tax on extraordinary profit or loss.

12   Other taxes not shown under the above items.

13   Profit or loss for the financial year.

**B. Income**

1    Net turnover.

2    Increase in stocks of finished goods and in work in progress.

3    Work performed by the undertaking for its own purposes and capitalized.

4    Other operating income.

5    Income from participating interests, with a separate indication of that derived from affiliated undertakings.

6    Income from other investments and loans forming part of the fixed assets, with a separate indication of that derived from affiliated undertakings.

7    Other interest receivable and similar income, with a separate indication of that derived from affiliated undertakings.

8    Profit or loss on ordinary activities after taxation.

9    Extraordinary income.

10   Profit or loss for the financial year.

**Table 6.6 Typical income statement formats by country**

| Vertical by nature | Vertical by function | Horizontal by nature |
|---|---|---|
| Finland | Denmark | Belgium |
| Germany (commonly) | Germany (IFRS) | France |
| Italy | Netherlands | Spain |
| Norway | Sweden | |
| | United Kingdom | |
| | United States | |

Figure 6.2 **Bayer Group consolidated statement of income**

| € million | 2008 |
|---|---:|
| **Net sales** | **32,918** |
| Cost of goods sold | (16,458) |
| **Gross profit** | **(16,462)** |
| Selling expenses | (8,105) |
| Research and development expenses | (2,653) |
| General administration expenses | (1,649) |
| Other operating income | 907 |
| Other operating expenses | (1,418) |
| **Operating result [EBIT]** | **3,544** |
| Equity-method loss | (62) |
| Non-operating income | 589 |
| Non-operating expenses | (1,715) |
| **Non-operating result** | **(1,188)** |
| **Income before income taxes** | **2,356** |
| Income taxes | **(636)** |
| **Income from continuing operations after taxes** | **1,720** |
| **Income from discontinued operations after taxes** | **4** |
| **Income after taxes** | **1,724** |
| of which attributable to minority interest | 5 |
| **of which attributable to Bayer AG stockholders (net income)** | 1,719 |
| Earnings per share € | |
| From continuing operations | |
| Basic | 2.22 |
| Diluted | 2.22 |

*Source*: adapted from Bayer Annual Report 2008, p. 134.

value changes affecting assets and liabilities may have taken place during the year, and fair presentation may require them to be reported. If so then this will inevitably affect owner's equity, which is the difference between assets and liabilities. Any event, other than a transfer of resources between the owners and the entity that alters the ownership claim on the business must in some sense represent a gain or a loss recognized in the year (see Section 2.4). These gains or losses are all part of 'comprehensive income'.

There has been a tendency in the past – perhaps shared by both preparers and users of financial statements – to focus attention on the income statement, and on the final net profit figure in particular. This probably had its origin in the view, perhaps valid from a creditor perspective, that only gains received in cash or near-cash are reliable. However, other recognized changes in assets and liabilities carry significant information content. It should also be remembered, as mentioned earlier in Part 1, that the IASB, explicitly in its Framework and generally in recent standards, puts emphasis on asset and liability definitions and measurement, rather than on revenue and expense definitions and measurement. So, for example, increases in assets are 'income'.

This thinking led to the idea of an additional reporting statement. A statement like this, called a statement of recognized gains and losses, was required in the United Kingdom from 1993. In IFRS, up to 2008, the equivalent was called a statement of recognized income and expense.

A statement of OCI begins with the balance from the income statement. After that, the most common items to be found in OCI are:

- gains and losses on translating items of foreign subsidiaries' financial statements into the group's presentation currency (see Chapter 15);
- revaluations of various assets, e.g. certain financial assets (see Chapter 11);
- actuarial gains and losses on pension plans (see Chapter 11).

**Activity 6.B**

Depending on your own particular circumstances, nationality and domicile, you may be interested in the interpretation of financial statements prepared under the laws, rules and norms of one or more national jurisdictions. You are in a much better position than the authors to investigate your 'local' scenario.

There are two respects in which you should explore the situation in relation to the general principles and the IFRS requirements that are described here. You have already been invited in Chapter 4 to consider the balance between legal, professional and other possible regulatory influences within your own environment. Now you can investigate local regulations and compare them with the international considerations discussed here. The optimal timing of this comparison will depend on your particular needs and study programme. If you have already studied a set of national regulations, then you should now compare the presentation and disclosure requirements contained therein regarding balance sheet and income statement with those outlined above. You should then ask yourself two questions:

1. What are the reasons for the differences?
2. Are the differences justified?

**Feedback**

Because of the nature of the task set, no detailed reply can be given here. The reasons for the differences will be essentially historical and contextual, and the earlier chapters of Part 1 should provide the necessary framework for your assessment. Whether or not you think the differences are justified is of course a more open question. It is likely in most cases that the differences can be rationalized by historical considerations, but that is not the same thing as saying that the differences will necessarily survive in a dynamic global economy. This task is designed for discussion among students, or between students and tutors.

*Why it matters*

*The argument in favour of a statement of comprehensive income is in essence the point that **all** information that has relevance to the determination of business wealth, and therefore to shareholder wealth, security for creditors, etc. should be made conveniently available to readers of the financial statements in a manner that does not emphasize one aspect rather than others. The often subjective separation of 'extraordinary' items in a way designed to minimize their apparent significance (when they are unfavourable!) was one example among many. Any such possibility* *of presentational bias increases the risk that the lazy or inexperienced reader will be misled. It also allows the directors deliberately to increase the chances of such a misleading outcome, by pushing favourable aspects of the overall results into the more visible parts of the overall reporting package, and less favourable aspects into those parts likely to be given less attention. It is also important, however, that a statement of comprehensive income does not try to present so much detail on one page that it becomes incomprehensible instead of comprehensive.*

## 6.4 Statements of changes in equity

Most of the changes in an entity's equity are caused by incomes and expenses of various sorts. However, there are some others:

- adjustments to the opening balance sheet caused by correcting errors or changing accounting practices;
- new capital contributed by the owners;
- distributions of cash (dividends) or other assets to the owners.

All these changes are shown in an entity's statement of changes in equity, which is required by IAS 1. Such a statement is also required in US GAAP, but in that accounting system it can also include the elements of OCI.

## 6.5 Cash flow statements

As already indicated, users of financial information need to know not only incomes and expenses as derived under the accruals convention, but also an entity's cash position and cash movements. To demonstrate the point in simple terms, look at Activity 6.C.

**Activity 6.C**    Consider the following two summarized statements about the same company for the same year, as set out in Tables 6.7 and 6.8.

Table 6.7 **Summarized income statement**

| | |
|---|---:|
| Sales | 250 |
| *less* cost of sales | (176) |
| | 74 |
| *less* other expenses | (44) |
| | 30 |
| *less* depreciation | (8) |
| | 22 |
| *less* taxation provided | (10) |
| Profit | 12 |

Table 6.8 **Summarized statement of cash flow**

| | |
|---|---:|
| Receipts from sales | 228 |
| *less* payments for goods for resale | (162) |
| | 66 |
| *less* payments for other expenses | (44) |
| | 22 |
| *less* capital expenditure | (46) |
| | (24) |
| *less* taxation paid | (4) |
| Net cash outflow | (28) |

Has the company had a successful year?

**Feedback** The first statement, the income statement, shows a successful year and positive results based on the accruals convention. The second statement is a summary of cash flows. This shows a reduction in the cash resources of the business even without the payment of any dividend. In any one year such a reduction may be sensible – even desirable – as part of the process of strategic development and the maximization of long-run returns. But of course in the long run such annual reductions cannot be allowed to continue, and an analyst or potential investor would need to monitor the cash situation and prospects carefully. The general point is that a report on the cash or liquid funds provides useful and important information that is different in focus and information content from the income statement.

The widespread publication of cash flow statements is relatively recent in some countries. There was no mention in the EU Directives of such statements. This may seem rather surprising, given the demonstrable importance of cash in the management of an entity. However, at the time of the creation of the Directives there was no general practice of any such thing in the major countries involved. The effect was that, when national governments came to enact national legislation derived from the Directives, there was usually still no mention of any such statement. Nevertheless, the rise of the cash flow statement as a necessary part of a comprehensive reporting package has been rapid. Something like it became a standard requirement in the UK in 1975, in international standards in 1977, and eventually in German law, for listed companies, in 1998. There have been a number of developments in the format – and, indeed, in the underlying principles – of such statements, and there have been two different versions of the International Accounting Standard for this, namely IAS 7.

The practices and regulatory influences involved are sufficiently important and complicated to require a chapter to themselves. We therefore defer a detailed consideration until Chapter 13.

## 6.6    Notes to the financial statements

The Notes to the financial statements are where the other compulsory information is shown. IAS 1 summarizes the functions of the Notes as being:

- to present information about the basis of preparation of the financial statements and the specific accounting policies used for significant transactions and events;
- to disclose any information required that is not included elsewhere;
- to provide additional information, which is not presented on the face of the financial statements but which is necessary to ensure a fair presentation.

Notes to the financial statements need to be presented systematically, with each item on the face of the balance sheet, income statement and cash flow statement cross-referenced to any related information in the Notes. It is usual to begin the Notes with a statement of compliance with the appropriate set of accounting principles. Each specific accounting policy that has been used, and the understanding of which is necessary for a proper understanding of the financial statements, is then described. The remainder of the Notes then give the required detailed disclosures, in the order corresponding to the item's appearance in the financial statements themselves.

## 6.7    Other general disclosure requirements

This is an introductory textbook, not a manual of requirements for statement preparation and disclosure. It is important, however, to give a flavour and overview of what you are likely to see in practice. It is also important to have some understanding of the overall picture so as to be able to consider its adequacy. This section looks briefly at IFRS requirements regarding segment reporting, discontinued operations, earnings per share, and interim financial reports.

### 6.7.1  Segment reporting

Many large companies are 'conglomerate' entities (i.e. they are involved in a number of distinct industries or types of business operation) or multinational corporations operating in several different countries or regions that have different economic and political characteristics. Understanding the past and potential performance of the entity as a whole requires an understanding of the separate component parts.

*Why it matters*    *Since the various parts of conglomerate and multinational companies are susceptible to different influences, it is quite likely that some components will be doing better than others, and that the risks – and potential – will be significantly different. It follows that it is not possible to appraise the position, progress and prospects of a whole entity without some separate information about the major components.*

*Consider, for example, the situation shown in Table 6.9. Company A and Company B have the same total sales figure of €100m. However, a fair presentation of the entity as a whole cannot be given without some detailed information about the component parts. For example, a belief that operations in the EU and United States will expand faster than those in Africa would make Company A seem preferable. However, a belief that software will expand faster than cotton would make Company B seem better.*

Table 6.9 **Segment reporting**

|  | Company A (€m) | Company B (€m) |
| --- | --- | --- |
| Total Sales: | 100 | 100 |
| EU | 40 | 20 |
| USA | 40 | 20 |
| Africa | 20 | 60 |
| Tobacco | 10 | 20 |
| Cotton | 70 | 10 |
| Petrol | 10 | 10 |
| Software | 10 | 60 |

The analysis outlined above has given rise to what is known as segment (or segmental) reporting. The present standard is IFRS 8, *Operating Segments*. It requires listed companies to report several items (e.g. sales) on a disaggregated basis, using the segments that are reporting internally to the company's chief operating officer. This might be done on a geographical basis, by line of business, or in a mixed way.

IFRS 8 requires that a segment of a company's operations should be reported separately if its revenue, results or assets are 10 per cent or more of the total. The reported segments should represent at least 75 per cent of the consolidated amounts. The items to be reported segmentally include profit, sales, assets, liabilities, interest, depreciation and tax.

## 6.7.2 Discontinued operations

Under IFRS 5, a 'discontinued operation' of an entity is a relatively large component that has been disposed of, or is to be disposed of within a year, completely or substantially. The effects of such discontinuation are likely to be significant, both in their own right and in changing the likely future results of the remaining parts of the entity. Fair presentation requires that the discontinued and continuing operations are distinguished from each other. This will improve the ability of investors, creditors and other users of statements to make projections of the entity's cash flows, earnings-generating capacity and financial position.

IFRS 5 focuses on how to present a discontinued operation in an entity's financial statements, and what information to disclose. As noted in Section 6.2, summary disclosures related to discontinued operations must be shown on the face of the balance sheet and the income statement. Note disclosure is required of the operations being discontinued and the segments in which they are reported. This will help the users of financial statements to predict the future figures after discontinuation.

### 6.7.3 Earnings per share

Earnings per share, known as EPS, is an important summary indicator of entity performance for investors and other users of financial statements. As the name suggests, it relates the total earnings of the entity, i.e. the profit attributable to the ordinary shareholders (before other comprehensive income (OCI)), to the number of shares issued. It can be used to calculate the Price/Earnings (PE) ratio, which provides a basis of comparison between listed entities and an indicator of market confidence. The PE ratio is calculated as market price per share divided by EPS or, more simply, as market price divided by earnings. High expectations of future performance lead to, and are indicated by, a higher share price and therefore a higher PE ratio.

IAS 33, *Earnings per Share*, requires EPS to be presented in two forms, namely 'basic' and 'diluted'. The basic EPS reports the EPS essentially as under current circumstances. The diluted EPS, on the other hand, calculates the ratio as if the dilutive effect of potential ordinary or common shares currently foreseeable had already taken place; i.e. it shows the position if a possible future increase in the number of shares has already happened. Earnings per share is discussed more fully in Chapter 17. Figure 6.2 (earlier) ends with Bayer's presentation of earnings per share.

### 6.7.4 Interim financial reports

Annual financial statements are something of a blunt instrument. They cover a long period, and do not appear until several months after the end of that period. This may fail to meet the criterion of timeliness described in Chapter 3. It is helpful to many users of financial statements to receive one or more progress reports at interim points through the year. This is a requirement for most stock exchanges, which are likely to have regulations on such interim statements. It is also, of course, good public relations to maintain an image of openness and transparency with one's lenders, customers and investors. The relevant standard here is IAS 34, which does not itself require the publication of interim financial reports but is available for regulators to impose or for companies to choose to follow. As examples, the US Securities and Exchange Commission requires all its registrants to produce quarterly reporting, and EU regulators require at least half-yearly reporting by listed companies.

IAS 34 sets out the minimum content of an interim financial report as including a condensed balance sheet, income statement, cash flow statement and statement of changes in equity, together with selected notes to the statements. The objective is to provide a report that updates the most recent annual financial statements by focusing on those items that are significant to an understanding of the changes in financial position and performance of the entity since its last year-end. Policies should be consistent with those used in the annual accounts. Measurements for interim purposes are generally made on a year-to-date basis. Seasonal or cyclical revenues or expenses should not be smoothed or averaged over the various interim periods, but reported as they occur.

**Activity 6.D**

We can now take Activity 6.B further. The next issue to consider is the extent to which the regulatory requirements, whatever they are and wherever they come from, are actually followed. You should attempt to obtain:

■ one or more sets of published financial statements prepared under your own national requirements;
■ one or more sets of financial statements prepared under IFRSs.

In each case, you should seek to build up a picture of the extent to which the disclosure and revealed measurement practices of those statements fully meet the relevant set of regulations. This will be a gradual process, which you should revisit as your reading and studying proceed; nevertheless, an introductory impression at this time would be interesting and useful.

**Feedback**

Inevitably, this one is largely up to you. But you should not be surprised if you discover examples of circumstances where the practices, whether local or international, do not appear to be fully consistent with the corresponding requirements.

**Summary**

■ This chapter discusses the content and format of published financial statements under IASB requirements. It encourages exploration of local national formats, and comparisons with the international requirements. In Europe, the EU Directives are an important source of regulation for non-IFRS reporting.

■ The basic contents of financial statements comprise balance sheet, income statement (and OCI), statement of changes in equity, cash flow statement and relevant notes.

■ Balance sheets require analysis by liquidity, usually distinguishing current and non-current (fixed) assets, current and long-term liabilities, and owners' equity. Horizontal and vertical formats are both found in practice.

■ Income statements can be horizontal or vertical in format, and analysed by function or by nature of expense. Horizontal by function is rare, but the other three possible combinations are used in various countries.

■ Cash flow statements provide useful information, different from that contained in an income statement. They are discussed further in Chapter 13.

■ Notes to the accounts contain a wide variety of supplementary information.

■ Various other disclosure requirements are common. Four are outlined here, relating to segment reporting, discontinued operations, earnings per share and interim financial reports.

## References and research

The IASB documents particularly relevant to this chapter are:

- IAS 1 (revised 2007)  *Presentation of Financial Statements*
- IAS 33 (2003)  *Earnings per Share*
- IAS 34 (1998)  *Interim Financial Reporting*
- IFRS 5 (2004)  *Non-current Assets Held for Sale and Discontinued Operations*
- IFRS 8 (2006)  *Operating Segments*

The Fourth Directive is also important in the EU and some other countries.

Discussion continues on possible changes or improvements to many of the disclosure issues covered in this chapter, both at international level and within some national regulatory systems. These debates should be followed, via discussion documents issued by the IASB, by national regulators, and in the professional accounting press. A discussion paper dealing with presentation was published in 2008.

The following may be of interest from a multinational perspective:

- M.L. Ettredge, K.S. Young, D.B. Smith and P.A. Zarowin, 'The impact of SFAS no. 131 business segment data on the market's ability to anticipate future earnings', *Accounting Review*, Vol. 80, No. 3, pp. 773–804, July 2005.
- O-K. Hope, W.B. Thomas, G. Winterbotham, 'The impact of nondisclosure of geographic segment earnings on earnings predictability', *Journal of Accounting, Auditing & Finance*, Vol. 21, No. 3, pp. 323–346, Summer 2006.
- J. Prather-Kinsey and G.K. Meek, 'The effect of revised IAS 14 on segment reporting by IAS companies', *European Accounting Review*, Vol. 13, No. 2, 2004.

## ? EXERCISES

*Feedback on the first two of these exercises is given in Appendix D.*

6.1 'The disclosure requirements of International Financial Reporting Standards are broadly sufficient to meet the needs of financial statement users.' Discuss.

6.2 Discuss the advantages and disadvantages of horizontal and vertical balance sheet formats.

6.3 Discuss the advantages and disadvantages of each of the four income statement formats allowed by the EU Fourth Directive, namely horizontal and vertical, and by function and by nature.

6.4 Is there a danger of having too much data in published financial statements?

6.5 Which disclosure formats are usually used in your own jurisdiction? Why is this so?

# Chapter 7

# Financial statement analysis

Contents

| 7.1 | Introduction | | 116 |
|---|---|---|---|
| 7.2 | Ratios and percentages | | 116 |
| 7.3 | Profit ratios | | 119 |
| | 7.3.1 | Gross profit margin | 119 |
| | 7.3.2 | Net profit margin | 120 |
| | 7.3.3 | Expenses to sales | 120 |
| | 7.3.4 | Net operating profit | 122 |
| 7.4 | Profitability ratios | | 122 |
| | 7.4.1 | Asset turnover ratios | 123 |
| | 7.4.2 | Non-financial resource ratios | 124 |
| | 7.4.3 | Return on equity (ROE) | 124 |
| | 7.4.4 | Return on capital employed (ROCE) | 125 |
| | 7.4.5 | Gearing and its implications | 126 |
| | 7.4.6 | Further analysis of ROE and ROCE | 127 |
| 7.5 | Liquidity ratios | | 129 |
| 7.6 | Interest cover | | 130 |
| 7.7 | Funds' management ratios | | 131 |
| | 7.7.1 | Debtors' collection | 131 |
| | 7.7.2 | Creditors' payment | 132 |
| | 7.7.3 | Inventory turnover | 132 |
| 7.8 | Introduction to investment ratios | | 133 |
| | 7.8.1 | Book value per share | 133 |
| | 7.8.2 | Market value per share | 133 |
| | 7.8.3 | Earnings per share | 133 |
| 7.9 | Some general issues | | 135 |
| | 7.9.1 | Industry-specific considerations | 135 |
| | 7.9.2 | Relationships between ratios | 135 |
| | 7.9.3 | Caveat | 136 |
| | Summary | | 136 |
| | Exercises | | 137 |

Objectives

After studying this chapter carefully, you should be able to:

- select appropriate information for different users;
- define, select and calculate a variety of common ratios, embracing profits, profitability, liquidity and the management of funds;
- explain the significance of calculated or given ratios;
- interrelate a variety of ratio figures and build up an overall picture;
- write reports discussing the implications of ratio calculations and original financial data for individual businesses covering one, two or more years, or for two or more businesses.

## 7.1 Introduction

The final essential element to consider in exploring the context of accounting is the usage and interpretation of financial statements. A vital part of the analysis of financial statements is to be fully aware of their weaknesses. Some of these are inherent in the tools of analysis used, but most of the important problems arise from the content and characteristics of the original data as prepared or published. The conventions and practices of accounting that have been covered in earlier chapters have to be thoroughly understood before effective financial analysis can be achieved. This chapter provides an introduction to interpretation and its techniques. A deeper exploration is deferred until Part 3, after several financial reporting issues have been examined more thoroughly.

In Chapter 1 we identified the users of accounting information and their differing needs. The following activity may provide useful revision.

| Activity 7.A | Identify the needs/objectives of the external users referred to in Activity 3.A, in more detail than in the feedback given in that activity. |
|---|---|

| Feedback | ■ *Investors/owners*  Is the money invested in the business making a suitable return for them or could it earn more if invested elsewhere? Is the business a safe investment; that is, is it likely to become insolvent/bankrupt? Should the investors invest more money in the business?
■ *Suppliers*  Is the business able to pay for the goods bought on credit? Will the business continue to be a recipient of the goods the supplier produces?
■ *Customers*  Is the business able to supply the goods that customers require and when they require them? Will the business continue in operation so that guarantees on goods purchased will be met?
■ *Lenders*  Is there adequate security for any loan made? Does the business make a sufficient profit and have enough cash available to make the necessary payments of interest and capital to the lender?
■ *Employees*  Does the business make sufficient profit and have enough cash available to make the necessary payments to the employees? Will the business continue in operation at its current level so that an employee has secure employment?
■ *Government*  What is the starting point for the calculation of taxable income?
■ *Public*  The majority of the public's needs in respect of employment, pollution, and health and safety are not as yet particularly well provided for in financial statements: can improvements in presentation be made? |
|---|---|

## 7.2 Ratios and percentages

A number, in isolation, is not a very helpful piece of information. For example, 'sales last year were 20 million Norwegian kroner': what information does this give? Without knowledge of the exchange rate between the home currency and Norwegian kroner, no comparison with home sales is possible. Without knowledge of the size of the Norwegian market for the products concerned, and without knowledge of the structure of that market in terms of size and number of competitors, no comparison with the general situation in Norway is possible. Without knowledge of sales figures for earlier years, and of the assets available and the expenses consumed to create those sales, no appraisal of progress, effectiveness or efficiency is possible.

Comparison is the key. A ratio is potentially a very powerful tool, but it is also a very simple one. A ratio is one number divided by another. If the total Norwegian market for the product is 400 million Norwegian kroner, then the ratio of sales by the company mentioned above to its total home market is 20 : 400 (or 1 : 20 or 5 per cent).

In many instances – perhaps only because of habit and experience – a percentage seems most helpful and easy to understand. One simple but effective application of this technique is the idea of *common size statements*. This involves reduction of the monetary figures in financial statements to percentages of relevant totals.

For effective comparison in practice, a number of years' results need to be taken together, preferably five or more. Note, however, that the more years that are considered, the greater the risk of changes in the accounting policies used over the period. Such changes will distort any trend considerations. They should be looked for and eliminated as far as possible, if necessary on a subjective basis.

A large number of ratios are looked at below. It should be stressed that there are no absolute 'rules' on how to define the ratios. The whole purpose of ratio analysis is to be *useful*, and so an individual analyst should adapt the techniques used to maximize their relevance to a specific situation encountered.

Figures 7.1, 7.2 and 7.3 give the summarized financial statements for a model retail company, Bread Co., for two successive years. These will be used as a basis of calculation and illustration throughout the chapter.

### Figure 7.1 Bread Co. income statements (€000)

|  | Year ended 31 Dec 20X1 | | Year ended 31 Dec 20X2 | |
| --- | --- | --- | --- | --- |
| Sales |  | 150 |  | 250 |
| Opening inventory | 8 |  | 12 |  |
| Purchases | 104 |  | 180 |  |
|  | 112 |  | 192 |  |
| Closing inventory | 12 |  | 16 |  |
| Cost of goods sold |  | 100 |  | 176 |
| Gross profit |  | 50 |  | 74 |
| Wages and salaries | 20 |  | 26 |  |
| Depreciation | 4 |  | 8 |  |
| Debenture interest | – |  | 2 |  |
| Other expenses | 14 |  | 16 |  |
|  |  | 38 |  | 52 |
| Net profit before tax |  | 12 |  | 22 |
| Taxation |  | 4 |  | 10 |
| Net profit after tax |  | 8 |  | 12 |

*Note*: During 20X2, Bread Co. paid out dividends of €6,000, being the dividends paid in relation to the year 20X1. The corresponding dividends paid in 20X3 in relation to 20X2 were also €6,000.

**Figure 7.2 Bread Co. balance sheets (€000): vertical presentation**

|  | At 31 Dec 20X1 | | At 31 Dec 20X2 | |
|---|---|---|---|---|
| Fixed (non-current) assets | | 72 | | 110 |
| Current assets | | | | |
| Inventory | 12 | | 16 | |
| Debtors (receivables) | 18 | | 40 | |
| Bank | 10 | | 4 | |
| | 40 | | 60 | |
| Creditors less than one year | | | | |
| Trade creditors (payables) | 10 | | 28 | |
| Taxation | 4 | | 10 | |
| Other creditors | 4 | | 6 | |
| | 18 | | 44 | |
| Net current assets (working capital) | | 22 | | 16 |
| Creditors greater than one year | | | | |
| 10 per cent debentures | | – | | 20 |
| Net assets | | 94 | | 106 |
| Financed by | | | | |
| Ordinary shares of €1 each | | 70 | | 76 |
| Retained profits | | 24 | | 30 |
| Shareholders' funds | | 94 | | 106 |

**Figure 7.3 Bread Co. balance sheets (€000): horizontal presentation**

**At 31 December 20X1**

| Fixed (non-current) assets | | 72 | Ordinary shares of €1 each | | 70 |
|---|---|---|---|---|---|
| | | | Retained profits | | 24 |
| Current assets | | | Shareholders' funds | | 94 |
| Inventory | 12 | | | | |
| Trade debtors (receivables) | 18 | | Creditors greater than one year | | – |
| Bank | 10 | | | | |
| | | 40 | Creditors less than one year | | |
| | | | Trade creditors (payables) | 10 | |
| | | | Taxation | 4 | |
| | | | Other creditors | 4 | |
| | | | | | 18 |
| | | 112 | | | 112 |

**At 31 December 20X2**

| Fixed (non-current) assets | | 110 | Ordinary shares of €1 each | | 76 |
|---|---|---|---|---|---|
| | | | Retained profits | | 30 |
| Current assets | | | | | |
| Inventory | 16 | | Creditors greater than one year | | |
| Trade debtors (receivables) | 40 | | 10 per cent debentures | | 20 |
| Bank | 4 | | | | |
| | | 60 | Creditors less than one year | | |
| | | | Trade creditors (payables) | 28 | |
| | | | Taxation | 10 | |
| | | | Other creditors | 6 | |
| | | | | | 44 |
| | | 170 | | | 170 |

## 7.3   Profit ratios

The income statement will be explored first, beginning with ratios constructed entirely from within the income statement itself.

### 7.3.1  Gross profit margin

The gross profit is the difference between the sales price and the cost of the goods sold. The gross profit margin is an indication of the extra inflow from an extra unit of sales. The formula is:

$$\text{Gross profit margin} = \frac{\text{gross profit}}{\text{sales}}$$

**Activity 7.B**    Calculate the gross profit margin for Bread Co. for 20X1 and 20X2.

**Feedback**    The values (from Figure 7.1) are as follows:

$$\text{Gross profit margin for 20X1} = \frac{50}{150} = 33.3 \text{ per cent}$$

$$\text{Gross profit margin for 20X2} = \frac{74}{250} = 29.6 \text{ per cent}$$

An alternative way to consider this aspect is to relate the gross profit to the figure for the cost of goods sold, thus giving the mark-up as a percentage of cost. This might well be the way that the business manager arrived at the selling price in the first place. The figures for mark-up would be as follows:

$$\text{Mark-up for 20X1} = \frac{50}{100} = 50 \text{ per cent}$$

$$\text{Mark-up for 20X2} = \frac{74}{176} = 42 \text{ per cent}$$

For Bread Co. the gross profit margin has fallen since the previous year. Some of the possible reasons for this are obvious. For instance, the selling price may have been deliberately lowered, or the cost of goods sold may have increased but a decision made not to increase selling prices correspondingly. Or the mix of sales may have altered, with an increase in the relative volume of low-margin goods. There might also be other less visible reasons, however. For example, note how the cost of goods sold, and therefore gross profit figures, are directly affected by the inventory figures. The fall in gross profit margin, if unexpected, could suggest an error in the calculation of one of the inventory figures, or that goods were being stolen from the business in 20X2.

The calculations for a manufacturing business would be more complicated because cost of sales means manufacturing cost. This will include a variety of separate items, including direct labour and materials, production overheads and possibly some arbitrary proportion of some of the more general overheads as well.

Full information enabling a proper split of the results between gross profit and net profit may be absent, and if it is available it is likely to be based on debatable assumptions covering cost behaviour and cost allocation.

An additional practical problem is that some companies in Europe use the alternative format for the income statement, illustrated in Table 6.5 (by-nature horizontal format). For a manufacturing company, this does not reveal the cost of goods sold and gross profit, but merely adds an increase in inventory to sales and then deducts all expenses including raw materials or finished products obtained from outside. Sometimes reasonable assumptions can be made to produce a useful approximation to gross profit, but sometimes such assumptions will be based on so much guesswork as to be self-defeating.

### 7.3.2 Net profit margin

The net profit is the difference between the sales and all the expenses. The net profit margin shows the net benefit to the business per unit of sales. The formula is:

$$\text{Net profit margin} = \frac{\text{net profit before tax}}{\text{sales}}$$

**Activity 7.C** Calculate the net profit margin for Bread Co. for 20X1 and 20X2 and comment briefly.

**Feedback** The figures are calculated thus:

$$\text{Net profit margin for 20X1} = \frac{12}{150} = 8.0 \text{ per cent}$$

$$\text{Net profit margin for 20X2} = \frac{22}{250} = 8.8 \text{ per cent}$$

These values show that the efficiency that Bread Co. demonstrates in turning sales into profit generation has slightly increased in 20X2 compared with 20X1.

The net profit margin will be affected by two major considerations, namely the gross profit margin and the size of the expenses. It may be useful, therefore, to compute an expenses-to-sales ratio as well, as set out below.

### 7.3.3 Expenses to sales

The expenses-to-sales ratio explains the movement between gross and net profit margins. The formula for this ratio is:

$$\text{Expenses-to-sales ratio} = \frac{\text{expenses}}{\text{sales}}$$

**Activity 7.D** Calculate the expenses-to-sales ratio for Bread Co. for 20X1 and 20X2 and comment on the picture revealed so far.

The figures can be calculated thus:

$$\text{Expenses-to-sales in 20X1} = \frac{38}{150} = 25.3 \text{ per cent}$$

$$\text{Expenses-to-sales in 20X2} = \frac{52}{250} = 20.8 \text{ per cent}$$

Bread Co. has successfully managed to increase sales quite substantially in 20X2 without a corresponding pro rata increase in the expenses of running the business.

It is interesting to put together the ratios that have been calculated so far. These are shown in Table 7.1.

Table 7.1 **Bread Co. profit ratios**

|  | 20X1 | 20X2 |
|---|---|---|
| Gross profit margin (%) | 33.3 | 29.6 |
| Expenses-to-sales (%) | 25.3 | 20.8 |
| Net profit margin (%) | 8.0 | 8.8 |

The reduction in gross profit margin in 20X2 has been more than compensated for by the reduction in the relative size of the expenses, leading to a slight improvement in the net profit margin.

These figures go part way towards the preparation of common-size income statements. A common-size income statement is usually prepared by expressing each item as a percentage of total sales. Furthermore, if this technique is applied to the income statements of two different businesses, two benefits emerge. First, any size differences are taken into account, so that the internal relationships can be compared on equal terms. Second, the internal relationships themselves are clarified and highlighted in a manner convenient to the eye and the mind.

The common-size statements for Bread Co. are shown complete in Figure 7.4, and give more detail of the way in which the success in controlling total expenses

Figure 7.4 **Bread Co. common-size income statements (all figures are percentages of sales)**

|  | Year ended 31 Dec 20X1 | | Year ended 31 Dec 20X2 | |
|---|---|---|---|---|
| Sales |  | 100 |  | 100 |
| Cost of sales |  | 66.7 |  | 70.4 |
| Gross profit |  | 33.3 |  | 29.6 |
| Wages and salaries | 13.3 |  | 10.4 |  |
| Depreciation | 2.7 |  | 3.2 |  |
| Debenture interest | – |  | 0.8 |  |
| Other expenses | 9.3 |  | 6.4 |  |
|  |  | 25.3 |  | 20.8 |
| Net profit before tax |  | 8.0 |  | 8.8 |

has been achieved. In effect, Figure 7.4 calculates each expense item separately as a percentage of sales. A similar technique can be used for balance sheets. Each item will be expressed as a percentage either of total assets or of total non-current (fixed) assets plus net current assets, depending on the balance sheet structure preferred.

### 7.3.4 Net operating profit

It should be noted that ratio preparation is a pragmatic business. It is, of course, possible to calculate a ratio that is 'wrong' in the sense of being defined or calculated in an illogical manner. Even so, once that hurdle has been overcome, it is still misleading to think of a limited list of 'right' ratios. For example, in the above discussion the debenture interest has been treated as just another expense. However, depending on the purpose of the analysis, it may be more helpful to view the debenture interest as different and separate from the other expenses, on the grounds that it is concerned with the financing structure rather than the operation of the business activities. This leads to the idea of calculating the percentage of net operating profit to sales, i.e. taking the profit before deduction of the debenture interest. Thus, we have:

$$\text{Net operating profit margin} = \frac{\text{net operating profit}}{\text{sales}} \times 100 \text{ per cent}$$

**Activity 7.E**  Calculate the net operating profit margin for Bread Co. for 20X1 and 20X2 and comment briefly.

**Feedback**  The values can be calculated thus:

$$\text{Net operating profit margin for 20X1} = \frac{12}{150} = 8.0 \text{ per cent}$$

$$\text{Net operating profit margin for 20X2} = \frac{(22 + 2)}{250} = 9.6 \text{ per cent}$$

This shows that, in terms of the costs of operating, as distinct from any costs of financing, the efficiency of Bread Co. clearly increased in 20X2.

**Why it matters**  *From a management perspective, the efficiency of operating (i.e. production and selling) activities is quite distinct from the question of the efficacy of the financing structure. The improvement of each of these two functions is independent of the other. It is likely to be helpful, therefore, to separate out the results for analysis purposes. Note, however, that net profit ratios and net operating profit ratios are not mutually exclusive alternatives. They both provide useful insights into the situation and progress of the business.*

## 7.4 Profitability ratios

It is not sufficient to analyse the income statement and the profit position in isolation. Business operation requires the use of scarce resources that are not cost-free and that need to be used as efficiently as possible. It is essential to analyse the results of the operations in relation to the resources being used by the business and controlled by the management of the business. This leads to a variety of relationships and ratios that need to be explored. Strictly speaking, when comparing an item from the income statement, which is a total of a year's activity, with an item from the balance sheet, the *average* balance sheet figure for the year is required. In practice, closing balance sheet figures are often taken as a reasonable approximation.

### 7.4.1 Asset turnover ratios

One approach to exploring the relationship between returns and resources is to consider some or all of the assets as recorded in the balance sheet. Possibilities include considering total assets, net assets (i.e. assets minus liabilities) or non-current assets alone. These could be related to, for example, sales, gross profit, net profit or net operating profit. Using net profit or net operating profit gives an indication of the rate of return being generated through the use of the assets.

Table 7.2 shows six such ratios calculated for Bread Co. for 20X1 and 20X2. Care has to be taken in applying ratios like these, for there are many influences on the asset figures used that are not related to business efficiency. For example, a business that buys additional inventory without paying for it, just before the balance sheet date, will show an increase in total assets but not an increase in net assets. Therefore, the net asset picture better reflects the economic reality. The figures used for non-current assets (which are incorporated into both the other asset figures as well) are notoriously susceptible to changes in depreciation, valuation or asset-replacement policies. Nevertheless, useful indications of trend can often be discovered from ratios like these, provided that the weaknesses and peculiarities behind the figures in each particular business are explored and understood – which, for the casual outsider, may not always be the case.

Table 7.2 **Bread Co.: some asset turnover ratios**

|  | 20X1 | 20X2 |
|---|---|---|
| $\dfrac{\text{sales}}{\text{fixed assets}}$ | $\dfrac{150}{72} = 2.1$ | $\dfrac{250}{110} = 2.3$ |
| $\dfrac{\text{sales}}{\text{net assets}}$ | $\dfrac{150}{94} = 1.6$ | $\dfrac{250}{106} = 2.4$ |
| $\dfrac{\text{sales}}{\text{total assets}}$ | $\dfrac{150}{112} = 1.3$ | $\dfrac{250}{170} = 1.5$ |
| $\dfrac{\text{net profit}}{\text{fixed assets}}$ | $\dfrac{12}{72} = 0.17$ | $\dfrac{22}{110} = 0.20$ |
| $\dfrac{\text{net profit}}{\text{net assets}}$ | $\dfrac{12}{94} = 0.13$ | $\dfrac{22}{106} = 0.21$ |
| $\dfrac{\text{net profit}}{\text{total assets}}$ | $\dfrac{12}{112} = 0.11$ | $\dfrac{22}{170} = 0.13$ |

**Activity 7.F**  Comment on the implications for the performance of Bread Co. of the information shown in Table 7.2.

**Feedback**  When looking at Table 7.2, it can be suggested that the efficiency of usage of net assets has increased significantly from 20X1 to 20X2, as sales to net assets and net profit to net assets have both risen sharply. The other four ratios presented have increased a little. It should also be noticed, however, that the net assets figure itself has not increased much, whereas fixed assets and total assets have both increased very substantially. The net assets, unlike either of the other two asset aggregates, have been held down by a sharp increase in liabilities.

### 7.4.2 Non-financial resource ratios

It is important to remember that much useful information about business activities is non-financial. This not only applies to information about some of the important outputs, such as chemical or noise pollution, but also to information about some of the inputs. Concentration on non-financial data may be especially useful in relation to a resource input that is particularly scarce or expensive. Sales per employee is a good example of this type of ratio, where sales could be expressed in money terms or in non-financial terms such as the number of units produced each year per employee. Another example is output or sales per square metre of retail space.

Whether non-financial ratios like these are useful will depend on the particular situation and available information. However, they may permit useful comparisons of different organizational structures and different trends of development.

### 7.4.3 Return on equity (ROE)

A further approach to investigating the relationship between returns and the resources employed to create them is to consider the sources of finance on the other side of the balance sheet. This is probably the most interesting approach, because it enables analysts to focus on various subsets of the total finance being provided, and to consider the return generated *for* that particular subset and its providers. Several different ratios are now considered.

Return on equity relates the return made *for* the shareholders with the finance made available *by* the shareholders. It can be calculated either before tax deductions or after them, and it may well be useful to do both. If the issue to be explored is the return potentially available for distribution to shareholders, then clearly the after-tax position has to be taken. On the other hand, if an investigation of the efficiency of management in organizing the operations of the business is required, or a comparison of ROE with rates of return on other sources of finance, then the deduction of tax is a distortion. In such cases, before-tax returns may be more useful. The formula for return on equity is:

$$\frac{\text{net profit}}{\text{share capital and reserves}}$$

**Activity 7.G**   Calculate the ROE for Bread Co. for 20X1 and 20X2, both before and after tax.

**Feedback**

$$\text{ROE before tax for 20X1} = \frac{12}{94} = 12.8 \text{ per cent}$$

$$\text{ROE before tax for 20X2} = \frac{22}{106} = 20.8 \text{ per cent}$$

$$\text{ROE after tax for 20X1} = \frac{8}{94} = 8.5 \text{ per cent}$$

$$\text{ROE after tax for 20X2} = \frac{12}{126} = 11.3 \text{ per cent}$$

The increase in ROE before tax is large, but the after-tax return is partly reduced by a larger-than-proportional tax charge.

### 7.4.4 Return on capital employed (ROCE)

In terms of assessing the efficient usage of the resources provided to the business, the ROCE is probably the most important single ratio. The capital employed is normally defined as the owners' equity plus the long-term borrowings of the business. It seeks to embrace all the long-term finance made available to the business. The ratio therefore investigates the efficiency of the business as a whole, rather than from the point of view of any particular subset of users, such as the owners.

Notice that the ROE compares the return made on the share capital and reserves with the amount of that share capital and reserves. However, in the case of the ROCE, the target is to compare:

(a) the return made on the total of the share capital, the reserves and the long term borrowings with
(b) the amount of that total.

That is, in contrast to the ROE, the denominator of the ROCE ratio is larger by the amount of a company's long-term borrowings. It therefore follows that the numerator of the ROCE will be larger than the numerator of the ROE by the amount of the return that relates to those borrowings, i.e. interest. This interest, being an expense of the business, has been deducted in arriving at net profit. So, in order to arrive at the correct 'return' figure relevant to the ROCE calculation, the interest on the long-term borrowings must be added back to the net profit figure. The formula for return on capital employed is:

$$\frac{\textbf{net profit before interest on long-term borrowings}}{\textbf{owners' equity plus long-term borrowings}}$$

Profit before tax is used because interest figures are given gross of any tax effect, and to take after-tax profit and then adjust for interest net of tax would require subjective adjustments to the tax charge. This figure is sometimes referred to as EBIT, which stands for earnings before interest and tax.

**Activity 7.H**    Calculate ROCE for Bread Co. for 20X1 and 20X2, compare the results with the ROE before-tax figures, and comment.

**Feedback**    The ROCE figures are as follows:

$$\text{ROCE for 20X1} = \frac{12}{94} = 12.8 \text{ per cent}$$

$$\text{ROCE for 20X2} = \frac{22 + 2}{106 + 20} = \frac{24}{126} = 19.0 \text{ per cent}$$

Table 7.3 summarizes the required figures.

**Table 7.3 ROE/ROCE comparison for Bread Co.**

|                  | 20X1  | 20X2  |
| ---------------- | ----- | ----- |
| ROE (before tax) | 12.8% | 20.8% |
| ROCE             | 12.8% | 19.0% |

In 20X1 the figures are identical, because there were no long-term borrowings. In 20X2 the return made by the business as a whole, considering all the long-term finance, was 19.0 per cent; yet the return to the shareholders, at 20.8 per cent, was more than this. The shareholders have arranged a company structure where they get more than their simple proportion of the ROCE increase. The reason for this should be clear: the providers of the remainder of the capital employed have accepted a fixed return, which is *less* than their simple proportion of the ROCE would be at present levels of profit: ROCE is 19.0 per cent, interest on debentures is 10.0 per cent. Therefore for that part of capital employed represented by the debentures, the difference of 19.0 per cent – 10.0 per cent = 9.0 per cent, is available for the owners, in addition to the 19.0 per cent that has been earned for them on their own proportion of the capital employed.

## 7.4.5 Gearing and its implications

The relationship between equity and long-term borrowings is known as the gearing (or leverage) of the financial structure. There are two common ways of calculating a gearing ratio:

(a) compare the debt (i.e. long-term borrowings) with the equity; or
(b) compare the debt with the capital employed (i.e. equity plus debt).

Formulae for the two gearing ratios are:

(a) $\text{Gearing} = \dfrac{\text{debt}}{\text{share capital plus reserves}} = \dfrac{\text{debt}}{\text{equity}}$

or

(b) $\text{Gearing} = \dfrac{\text{debt}}{\text{share capital plus reserves plus debt}} = \dfrac{\text{debt}}{\text{equity} + \text{debt}}$

For Bread Co. the figures are:

(a)  20X1: 0.0 per cent

$$20X2: \frac{20}{106} = 18.9 \text{ per cent}$$

(b)  20X1: 0.0 per cent

$$20X2: \frac{20}{126} = 15.9 \text{ per cent}$$

For this company, the shareholders might want to maximize the proportion of the total capital employed that is financed by debt rather than by themselves, as now explained. As shown in Table 7.3, with non-current debt of 20 (measured in €000), the ROCE for Bread Co. for 20X2 was 19 per cent and the ROE was 20.8 per cent.

If we were to increase the gearing ratio so that, for example, the same capital employed of 126 consisted instead of capital plus reserves of 66 and debentures (with 10 per cent interest) increased to 60, then the ratios for 20X2 would give the same ROCE but a much improved return to the equity investors, as follows:

$$\text{ROE} = \left( \frac{24 - 6}{126 - 60} \right) = \frac{18}{66} = 27.3 \text{ per cent}$$

There are limits to the feasibility of increasing the proportion of debt, however. Firstly, it is more risky to lend to a business that already has significant debt, and therefore increased interest rates would be needed to attract such lending – if, indeed, it could be attracted at all. Secondly, consider what happens to a highly geared structure when operating profits fall. Suppose that Bread Co. alters its capital structure (as above) to give owners' equity of 66 and 10 per cent debentures of 60, but then in 20X3 the level of operating profit falls back to that of 20X1, i.e. 12. This would lead to 20X3 ratios as follows:

$$\text{ROE for 20X3} = \left( \frac{12 - 6}{66} \right) = 9.1 \text{ per cent}$$

$$\text{ROCE for 20X3} = \frac{12}{126} = 9.5 \text{ per cent}$$

Now the gearing is working in the other direction, to magnify the fall suffered by the shareholders rather than to magnify the rise. The end result is that ROE is less than ROCE. Furthermore, with an operating profit of 12, the more the gearing ratio is increased, the greater the extent to which ROE is lower than ROCE. It is, of course, perfectly possible for ROCE to be positive and ROE to be negative at the same time. It should be remembered also that a company that cannot afford to pay dividends does not *have* to pay them. However, a company that cannot afford to pay interest still legally has to pay it. This can be the road to bankruptcy.

### 7.4.6 Further analysis of ROE and ROCE

In practice, life is much more complicated than for Bread Co. The text and case studies of this book are not designed to cover all possible complications that might be met, but to enable the diligent reader to work out how to deal with them. To begin this process, two complications are mentioned at this stage.

### What is long-term borrowing?

If a liability is defined as 'falling due within one year' or some similar phrase, the reality behind this may not be clear-cut. For example, consider the amounts set out in Table 7.4 as falling due within one year.

Table 7.4 **Example liabilities**

|                             | 20X1 | 20X2 |
|-----------------------------|------|------|
| Bank loans                  | 18   | 19   |
| Bank overdrafts             | 5    | 4    |
| Bills payable               | 20   | 10   |
| Trade payables              | 50   | 55   |
| Taxation                    | 32   | 34   |
| Dividends                   | 20   | 25   |
| Other payables and accruals | 18   | 20   |
|                             | 163  | 167  |

Does it look as though all of these items are genuine short-term liabilities arising from the trading and operating cycle? Or do some of them seem likely to be a continuing source of finance that happens to be legally constructed so as to be finite (but renewable) within one year? It seems likely that the bank loans and overdrafts, and possibly also the commercial bills payable, are being used to finance the activities of the business, rather than being an integral part of those activities.

If that view is taken, then these items might be included as long-term borrowing for the purposes of calculating capital employed. Further, the interest on those 'current' liabilities must then also be added back to net profit (or not deducted from operating profit) in arriving at the correct return figure for the ROCE ratio. This may involve a very careful analysis and division of the interest-payable amount between the various loans to which it relates.

### Different classes of owners

The above discussions also assume that all shareholders are identical. However, there may be several classes, and each class will then have its own viewpoint on the performance of the business. For example, suppose now that the share capital of Bread Co. (see Figures 7.2 and 7.3) had included 10,000 1 euro preference shares, each bearing a fixed 10 per cent dividend entitlement, the ordinary share capital then being 60,000 and 66,000 at the ends of 20X1 and 20X2 respectively. The ROE (and ROCE) will be the same as previously shown. ROE, taking before-tax figures to ease comparison, was:

$$20X1: \frac{12}{94} = 12.8 \text{ per cent}$$

$$20X2: \frac{22}{106} = 20.8 \text{ per cent}$$

However, it is also possible to calculate the return on ordinary owners' equity (ROOE). For this, the preference share capital must be deducted from the denominator, and the preference shareholders' dividend return must be deducted from the numerator. So, we have:

$$\text{ROOE in 20X1} = \left(\frac{12 - 1}{94 - 10}\right) = \frac{11}{84} = 13.1 \text{ per cent}$$

$$\text{ROOE in 20X2} = \left(\frac{22 - 1}{106 - 10}\right) = \frac{21}{96} = 21.9 \text{ per cent}$$

This leads to a more complete set of data, as shown in Table 7.5.

Table 7.5 **Returns ratios for Bread Co.**

|  | 20X1 | 20X2 |
| --- | --- | --- |
| ROCE (all capital employed) | 12.8% | 19.0% |
| ROE (all shareholders' equity) | 12.8% | 20.8% |
| ROOE (all ordinary owners' equity) | 13.1% | 21.9% |

The effect on the ordinary shareholders of adding a tranche of preference shareholders, with a lower dividend, is similar to the gearing effect on all shareholders together of adding a tranche of debentures with a lower interest rate.

*Why it matters*    *It is easy to be blinded by statistics. Consider the ROE of 20.8 per cent shown in Table 7.5. First of all, this is a numerically correct and logically valid figure. It reveals what the business has achieved after 'paying off' everyone involved except the owners (and except the tax authorities, since we have taken before-tax figures here). But it does not reveal the potential return to a potential shareholder. A potential shareholder would have to buy either an ordinary share, with 21.9 per cent generated for it in 20X2, or a preference share, with a dividend of 10 per cent. From this point of view, therefore, ROE is not revealing relevant information, whereas ROOE would be. Furthermore, the figure of 21.9 per cent is not, of course, the rate of return that a new shareholder would receive if buying a share today on the stock market. That rate of return would be dependent on the price actually paid for the share, and on future performance.*

## 7.5   Liquidity ratios

This section explores some ratios related to the liquidity (i.e. cash or near-cash position) and fund management of a business. A number of ratios can be calculated that compare short-term assets with short-term liabilities. Each ratio uses a different interpretation of just how short-term the assets or liabilities should be. The shorter the term considered, the more prudent, pessimistic or safe is the approach adopted. Each ratio in this section shows the extent to which the particular definition of 'short-term assets' chosen would allow (if the assets concerned turn into cash at their balance sheet value) the repayment of the short-term liabilities in existence at that date.

Three common ratios are:

1. Cash ratio $= \dfrac{\text{cash plus marketable securities}}{\text{current liabilities}}$

2. Acid test (or quick assets) ratio $= \dfrac{\text{current assets less inventory}}{\text{current liabilities}}$

3. Current (or working capital) ratio $= \dfrac{\text{current assets}}{\text{current liabilities}}$

| **Activity 7.1** | Calculate the above three ratios for Bread Co. for 20X1 and 20X2, using the data in Figures 7.2 and 7.3. |
| --- | --- |

| **Feedback** | 1. Cash ratio for 20X1 $= \dfrac{10}{18} = 0.55 : 1$ |
| --- | --- |

Cash ratio for 20X2 $= \dfrac{4}{44} = 0.09 : 1$

2. Acid-test ratio for 20X1 $= \dfrac{28}{18} = 1.6 : 1$

Acid-test ratio for 20X2 $= \dfrac{44}{44} = 1.0 : 1$

3. Current ratio for 20X1 $= \dfrac{40}{18} = 2.2 : 1$

Current ratio for 20X2 $= \dfrac{60}{44} = 1.4 : 1$

It is important to remember that these ratios take a static view. They assume that the relevant assets are all that will be available to settle the current liabilities, and that the assets will provide the cash amounts as recorded in the balance sheet (even though inventory is normally recorded at cost, i.e. below selling price). So, for example, the quick assets ratio assumes that all the debtors will pay, but excludes any cash sales from inventory.

The safety or acceptability of any particular ratio for any particular business is related to the everyday operations of the business. Each industry will have a typical operational and financial structure, which can be significantly different between different industries, and calculated ratios should be compared with competitor or general industry figures, or with past trends, to enable meaningful comparisons to be drawn.

## 7.6 Interest cover

Long-term liquidity is connected to gearing, as examined in Section 7.4. The balance sheet perspective discussed there can be supplemented by considering the *interest cover*. This is the number of times a business could pay its necessary interest charges out of the available operating profits of the current year. The formula for interest cover is:

$$\frac{\text{net profit before interest and tax}}{\text{interest charges}}$$

For Bread Co. the figures will be as follows:

$$\text{Interest cover in 20X1} = \frac{12}{0} \text{ (i.e. infinite value)}$$

$$\text{Interest cover in 20X2} = \left(\frac{22 + 2}{2}\right) = 12 \text{ times}$$

This figure is an indication of the risk, in the particular year, that Bread Co. might not be able to pay interest on its borrowings out of current operating income. The higher the interest cover, the greater the fall in profits that would have to occur before net profit (i.e. after charging interest) became negative. Note that for this ratio, *all* interest payable should be included, irrespective of whether it relates to long- or short-term borrowing.

## 7.7 Funds' management ratios

Insight into the liquidity implications of the operations of a business can be gained by examining some of the constituent elements of working capital, i.e. inventory, debtors and creditors. In each case the amount of the item is compared with the flow related to it. These ratios can be expressed in a number of ways, but probably the most easily understandable is to express the answer in days.

### 7.7.1 Debtors' collection

This ratio compares trade debtors (receivables) with sales. To calculate the average debtor collection period in days, the formula is:

$$\frac{\textbf{trade debtors}}{\textbf{sales}} \times 365$$

Arguably, cash sales should be excluded from the denominator, but information to enable this is unlikely to be available to an outside analyst. If necessary, total debtors will have to be used instead of trade debtors. Frequently, the amount is taken from the closing balance sheet, but a more theoretically valid ratio is obtained by using the average amount of each item over the trading cycle. A simple average of opening and closing balance sheet figures may well be a better approximation to the true average than taking just the closing balance sheet figure.

### 7.7.2 Creditors' payment

A similar ratio can be calculated for creditors (payables). To calculate the average creditor payment period, it is theoretically necessary to relate trade creditors with annual purchases. However, the purchases figure is often not available and then the cost of goods sold will have to be used as a surrogate. In some income statement formats, cost of sales is not shown either, and so the sales figure has to be used. It is worth noting that the 'error' introduced by taking a surrogate or proxy figure is common to all years, and therefore largely cancels out when trends over time are explored. Where cost of sales is available but the cost of purchases is not, the formula becomes:

$$\frac{\text{trade creditors}}{\text{cost of sales}} \times 365$$

### 7.7.3 Inventory turnover

The inventory turnover ratio indicates the average time that inventory remains in the business between purchase and sale. Since inventory is valued at cost, it should be compared with cost of goods sold (which is obviously at cost) rather than with sales (which are at selling price). Again, this assumes that the data are available. The formula for the ratio is:

$$\frac{\text{inventory}}{\text{cost of goods sold}} \times 365$$

**Activity 7.J**  Calculate debtors', creditors' and inventory ratios (in terms of days) for Bread Co. for 20X1 and 20X2.

**Feedback**  The figures can be summarized in tabular form, as shown in Table 7.6.

Table 7.6 **Inventory ratios for Bread Co.**

| Ratio | 20X1 | 20X2 |
|---|---|---|
| Debtors' collection | $\frac{18}{150} \times 365$ = 44 days | $\frac{40}{250} \times 365$ = 58 days |
| Creditors' payment | $\frac{10}{100} \times 365$ = 36.5 days | $\frac{28}{176} \times 365$ = 58 days |
| Inventory turnover | $\left(\frac{\frac{8+12}{2}}{100}\right) \times 365$ = 36.5 days | $\left(\frac{\frac{12+16}{2}}{176}\right) \times 365$ = 29 days |

Trends can be explored between 20X1 and 20X2 showing, for example, that customers seem to be taking longer to pay in 20X2. The ratios can also be related together. In 20X1, if purchases were made on day 1 then they were paid for (on average, of course) some 36 days later. Those purchases remained in store (or process) also for some 36 days, were then sold, and the sales were actually paid for 44 days after the sale. The outward cash flow therefore occurs on day 36, but the inward cash flow not until day 80.

## 7.8 Introduction to investment ratios

The profitability and finance ratios so far discussed investigate various relationships within financial statements. Investment ratios consider items inside and outside financial statements from the equity investor's perspective. The connection between an investor and a company is obviously through the medium of a share, and most investment ratios relate shares to some aspect of the financial statements. We give a brief introduction to investment ratios here. When Part 2 has been studied, your understanding of much of this data should have been considerably deepened, and more complexities can then be explored in Part 3.

### 7.8.1 Book value per share

The *book value* of an ordinary share is the value that would be attributable to each ordinary share if the assets and liabilities of the company were sold or settled at the figures shown in the published balance sheet (i.e. at the 'value in the books'). The book value of an ordinary share is therefore the net assets divided by the number of issued ordinary shares. For Bread Co. (see Figures 7.2 and 7.3) the figures are $\frac{94}{70}$ = €1.34 for 20X1 and $\frac{106}{76}$ = €1.39 for 20X2.

Since most figures in the balance sheet are not designed to show the value of the item in any market-orientated sense of value, this ratio – at least in isolation – is not particularly useful.

### 7.8.2 Market value per share

For a publicly quoted company the market value per share, i.e. the share price, is easily obtainable from reports of stock exchange transactions, e.g. from newspapers. For a private company, the value has to be estimated, because there is no regular market in such a company's shares.

### 7.8.3 Earnings per share

Earnings per share (EPS) is an important statistic that gives an idea of what the business has actually achieved during the year for the benefit of the shareholders, divided by the number of shares. If you buy one of these shares, what has been generated in the year that can be attributable to you? In a simple situation, the calculation of EPS is:

$$\frac{\text{earnings attributable to ordinary shareholders}}{\text{number of ordinary shares}}$$

**Activity 7.K**    Calculate EPS for Bread Co. for 20X1 and 20X2.

**Feedback**    The figures are as follows.

20X1    earnings attributable to shareholders = €8,000
number of shares (of €1 each) = 70,000

Therefore EPS $= \dfrac{8}{70} = $ €0.11

20X2    earnings attributable to shareholders = €12,000
number of shares (of €1 each) = 76,000

Therefore EPS $= \dfrac{12}{76} = $ €0.16

This rise in EPS obviously suggests an improved performance by Bread Co. from 20X1 to 20X2 when considered from the viewpoint of a shareholder.

**Real-world example**    IAS 33 requires listed companies to show EPS calculated in several different ways (see more detail in Chapter 17). Figure 7.5 shows the example of Marks and Spencer plc. The 'basic' EPS is the one outlined above. The 'adjusted' figures remove the effect of the exceptional items.

Figure 7.5 **Consolidated income statement, Marks and Spencer plc**

| | 52 weeks ended 28 March 2009 £m |
|---|---|
| **Revenue** | 9,062.1 |
| **Operating profit** | 870.7 |
| Finance income | 50.0 |
| Finance costs | (214.5) |
| **Profit on ordinary activities before taxation** | 706.2 |
| Analysed between: | |
| Before property disposals and exceptional items | 604.4 |
| Profit on property disposals | 6.4 |
| Exceptional costs | (135.9) |
| Exceptional pension credit | 231.3 |
| Income tax expense | (199.4) |
| **Profit for the year** | 506.8 |
| **Attributable to:** | |
| Equity shareholders of the Company | 508.0 |
| Minority interests | (1.2) |
| | 506.8 |
| Basic earnings per share | 32.3p |
| Diluted earnings per share | 32.3p |
| Non-GAAP measure: | |
| Adjusted profit before taxation (£m) | 604.4 |
| Adjusted basic earnings per share | 28.0p |
| Adjusted diluted earnings per share | 28.0p |

*Source*: Marks and Spencer plc Annual Report 2009, p. 38.

## 7.9 Some general issues

### 7.9.1 Industry-specific considerations

We have already made the point that it is vital to consider any particular set of financial statements in the context of what is normal or typical in the field of operations involved. The same figure for any chosen ratio may suggest danger in the context of one industry, but a high degree of safety or success in another. For a simple illustration of this point, try the following activity.

**Activity 7.L**

A sample of ratios for the same year for three firms, A, B and C is given in Table 7.7. The firms are in three different industries: one is a supermarket, one is in heavy engineering and one is a firm of accountants and auditors. Which do you think is which?

Table 7.7 **Ratios for A, B and C**

|  | A | B | C |
| --- | --- | --- | --- |
| Debtors' collection (days) | 1 | 35 | 55 |
| Inventory turnover (days) | 16 | 5 | 80 |
| Acid-test ratio | 0.1 : 1 | 0.3 : 1 | 1.1 : 1 |
| Current ratio | 1.0 : 1 | 0.4 : 1 | 2.3 : 1 |

**Feedback**

One can reasonably guess that A is the supermarket (fast debtors' turnover, significant inventory but not slow-moving), B is the accountants (rapid inventory turnover and a very low inventory), and C is in heavy engineering (slow-moving and apparently large inventory/work in progress).

### 7.9.2 Relationships between ratios

The relationship between the ratios can be charted. To take the example of return on capital employed, Figure 7.6 shows how it can be split up into components.

Figure 7.6 **Pyramid of ratios (levels 1–3)**

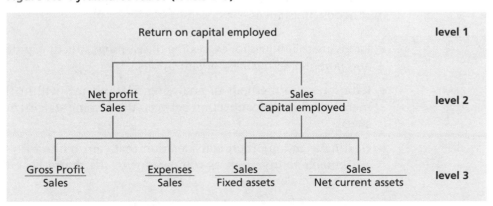

The result is a 'pyramid of ratios'. The pyramid can be extended to a further level by comparing, for example, the individual expenses to sales and by breaking down the fixed assets and net current assets into their constituent parts, as in Figure 7.7.

Figure 7.7 **Pyramid of ratios (level 4)**

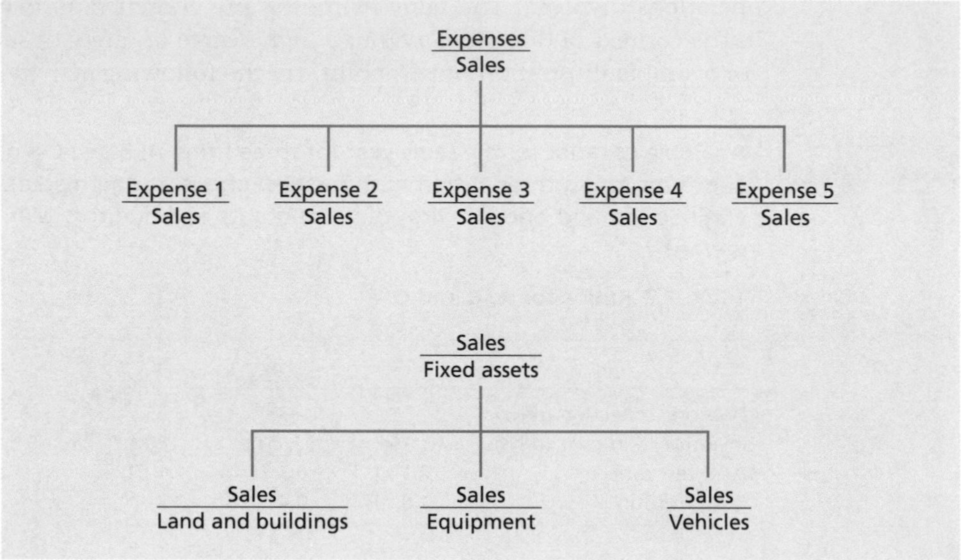

### 7.9.3 Caveat

There is a good deal more involved with interpretation than has been discussed in this chapter. We return to consider the whole area further in Part 3. Part 2 provides more detailed understanding of many of the accounting problems that affect the numbers used in financial statements. Such greater understanding should inform and affect the interpretation of the financial statements themselves.

Finally, it is important to remember that ratios are usually most informative when comparison is involved. A reasonable ratio in one industry, country or circumstance may be very different from what would be regarded as acceptable in other circumstances.

**Summary**

■ Ratios are techniques for expressing the earnings structure, profitability, liquidity and potential of business organizations.

■ Ratios are also methods of analysing relationships within the income statement and the interconnection between the income statement and the balance sheet.

■ Gearing is an important consideration that can significantly affect the return attributable to investors, as compared with the return generated by the business as a whole.

- Liquidity and funds management can also be assessed by various ratios.

- The interrelationship between various ratios is important, and an overall picture can be built up by considering such interconnections. No ratio is 'better' than the underlying data, but sometimes 'errors' can cancel out when considering trends rather than absolute numbers.

- The interrelationships between some of the important ratios can become clear if they are considered as components of more summarized ratios, forming what is often known as a pyramid of ratios.

## ? EXERCISES

*Feedback on the first two of these exercises is given in Appendix D.*

7.1 The simplified financial statements of two companies, P and Q, are shown below at Figure 7.8.

Figure 7.8 **Financial statements for P and Q**

|  | P | Q |
|---|---|---|
| **Income statement for 20X1** | | |
| Sales | 45,000 | 40,909 |
| *less* Cost of goods sold | (36,000) | (32,727) |
| Gross profit | 9,000 | 8,182 |
| *less* Depreciation | (3,500) | (2,917) |
| Other expenses | (1,500) | (1,364) |
| Net profit | 4,000 | 3,901 |
| **Balance sheet as at 31 December 20X1** | | |
| Equipment at cost | 35,000 | 29,167 |
| *less* Depreciation | (3,500) | (2,917) |
| | 31,500 | 26,250 |
| Inventory at cost | 10,500 | 10,000 |
| Net monetary current assets | 2,000 | 2,000 |
| *less* Long-term loan | (10,000) | (10,000) |
| | 34,000 | 28,250 |
| | | |
| Share capital | 25,000 | 25,000 |
| Retained profits | 4,000 | 3,901 |
| Other reserves | 5,000 | (651) |
| | 34,000 | 28,250 |

Assuming that interest is charged on the long-term loan at 10 per cent per annum, calculate the following ratios for 20X1 and comment on the results:

$$\frac{\text{gross profit}}{\text{turnover}}; \frac{\text{net operating profit}}{\text{turnover}}; \frac{\text{net profit}}{\text{owner's equity}}; \text{ROCE; gearing.}$$

7.2 The summarized balance sheets of company R at the end of two consecutive financial years were as shown in Figure 7.9.

Figure 7.9 **R's summarized balance sheets as at 31 March (€000)**

| 20X2 | | | | 20X3 | |
|---|---|---|---|---|---|
| | | *Fixed assets* (at written-down values) | | | |
| 50 | | Premises | 48 | | |
| 115 | | Plant and equipment | 196 | | |
| 42 | | Vehicles | 81 | | |
| | 207 | | | | 325 |
| | | *Current assets* | | | |
| 86 | | Inventory | 177 | | |
| 49 | | Debtors and prepayments | 62 | | |
| 53 | | Bank and cash | 30 | | |
| 188 | | | 269 | | |
| | | *Current liabilities* | | | |
| 72 | | Creditors and accruals | 132 | | |
| 20 | | Proposed dividends | 30 | | |
| 92 | | | 162 | | |
| | 96 | *Working capital* | | | 107 |
| | 303 | *Net assets* | | | 432 |
| | | *Financed by* | | | |
| 250 | | Ordinary share capital | 250 | | |
| 53 | | Reserves | 82 | | |
| | 303 | Shareholders' funds | | | 332 |
| | | Loan capital: 7 per cent debentures | | | 100 |
| | 303 | | | | 432 |

Sales were €541,000 and €675,000 for the years ended 31 March 20X2 and 20X3 respectively. Corresponding figures for cost of sales were €369,000 and €481,000 respectively. At 31 March 20X1, reserves had totalled €21,000. Ordinary share capital was the same throughout.

Calculate the following ratios for both years and comment briefly on the results:

(i)   Gross profit/Sales;
(ii)  Net profit/Sales;
(iii) Sales/Net/assets;
(iv)  Net profit/Net assets;
(v)   Current assets/Current liabilities;
(vi)  Quick assets/Current liabilities.

7.3 Mosca and Vespa are two sole traders with the financial statements (in euros) for the year ending 31 December as set out in Figure 7.10.

Figure 7.10 **Financial statements for Mosca and Vespa**

|  | Mosca | | Vespa | |
|---|---|---|---|---|
| **Income Statement** | | | | |
| Sales | | 144,000 | | 140,000 |
| Cost of goods sold | | 120,000 | | 120,000 |
| | | 24,000 | | 20,000 |
| Selling expenses | 7,000 | | 10,000 | |
| Administration expenses | 3,000 | | 6,000 | |
| | | 10,000 | | 16,000 |
| Net profit | | 14,000 | | 4,000 |
| **Balance Sheet** | | | | |
| Fixed assets | | 54,000 | | 30,000 |
| Current assets | | | | |
| Inventory | 20,000 | | 10,000 | |
| Debtors | 30,000 | | 50,000 | |
| Cash | 10,000 | | 5,000 | |
| | | 60,000 | | 65,000 |
| less Creditors | | 24,000 | | 5,000 |
| | | 90,000 | | 90,000 |
| Capital | | 90,000 | | 90,000 |

Using the information contained in the financial statements, and assuming opening and closing inventories are the same, calculate the following ratios and comment on the results of your analysis:

(i) return on capital employed;
(ii) gross profit margin;
(iii) current ratio;
(iv) inventory turnover period;
(v) debtors' collection period;
(vi) creditors' payment period.

7.4 The following information has been extracted from the recently published accounts of company D, as set out in Figure 7.11.

**Figure 7.11 Financial statements for company D as at 30 April**

**Balance sheets as at 30 April**

|  |  | 20X2 |  | 20X1 |
|---|---|---|---|---|
| Fixed assets |  | 1,850 |  | 1,430 |
| Current assets |  |  |  |  |
| Inventory | 640 |  | 490 |  |
| Debtors | 1,230 |  | 1,080 |  |
| Cash | 80 |  | 120 |  |
|  | 1,950 |  | 1,690 |  |
| Creditors due in less than 1 year |  |  |  |  |
| Bank overdraft | 110 |  | 80 |  |
| Creditors | 750 |  | 690 |  |
| Taxation | 30 |  | 20 |  |
| Dividends | 65 |  | 55 |  |
|  | 955 |  | 845 |  |
| Net current assets |  | 995 |  | 845 |
| Total assets less current liabilities |  | 2,845 |  | 2,275 |
| less Creditors due in more than 1 year |  |  |  |  |
| 10 per cent debentures |  | 800 |  | 600 |
|  |  | 2,045 |  | 1,675 |
| Share capital and reserves |  |  |  |  |
| Ordinary share capital |  | 800 |  | 800 |
| Reserves |  | 1,245 |  | 875 |
|  |  | 2,045 |  | 1,675 |

**Extracts from the income statements**

|  | 20X2 | 20X1 |
|---|---|---|
| Sales | 11,200 | 9,750 |
| Cost of goods sold | 8,460 | 6,825 |
| Net profit before tax | 465 | 320 |
| This is after charging: |  |  |
| Depreciation | 80 | 60 |
| Interest on bank overdraft | 15 | 9 |
| Audit fees | 12 | 10 |

The ratios set out in Table 7.8 are those calculated for D, based on its published accounts for the previous year, and also the latest industry average ratios.

*Required:*
(a) Calculate comparable ratios (to two decimal places where appropriate) for company D for the year ended 30 April 20X2. All calculations must be clearly shown.
(b) Analyse the performance of D, comparing the results against the previous year and against the industry average as supplied.

**Table 7.8 Financial ratios for company D**

|  | D as at 30 April 20X1 | Industry average |
|---|---|---|
| ROCE (capital employed = equity and debentures) | 16.70 per cent | 18.50 per cent |
| Profit/sales | 3.90 per cent | 4.73 per cent |
| Asset turnover | 4.29 | 3.91 |
| Current ratio | 2.00 | 1.90 |
| Quick ratio | 1.42 | 1.27 |
| Gross profit margin | 30.00 per cent | 35.23 per cent |
| Days debtors | 40 days | 52 days |
| Days creditors | 37 days | 49 days |
| Inventory turnover | 13.90 | 18.30 |
| Gearing | 26.37 per cent | 32.71 per cent |

7.5 Business A and Business B are both engaged in retailing but seem to take a different approach to this trade according to the information available. The information consists of a table of ratios, shown as Table 7.9.

**Table 7.9 Financial ratios for companies A and B**

| Ratio | Business A | Business B |
|---|---|---|
| Current ratio | 2 : 1 | 1.5 : 1 |
| Quick assets (acid-test) ratio | 1.7 : 1 | 0.7 : 1 |
| Return on capital employed (ROCE) | 20 per cent | 17 per cent |
| Return on owner's equity (ROE) | 30 per cent | 18 per cent |
| Debtors' collection | 63 days | 21 days |
| Creditors' payment | 50 days | 45 days |
| Gross profit percentage | 40 per cent | 15 per cent |
| Net profit percentage | 10 per cent | 10 per cent |
| Inventory turnover | 52 days | 25 days |

*Required:*
(a) Explain briefly how each ratio is calculated.
(b) Describe what this information indicates about the differences in approach between the two businesses. If one of them prides itself on personal service and one of them on competitive prices, which do you think is which, and why?

7.6 You are given in Figure 7.12, in summarized form, the financial statements of Non Co. for the years 20X1 and 20X2.

Figure 7.12 **Financial statements for Non Co. For 20X1 and 20X2**

|  |  | 20X2<br>Balance sheet<br>(€000) |  | 20X1<br>Balance sheet<br>(€000) |
|---|---|---|---|---|
| Machinery – cost | 11 |  | 10 |  |
| – depreciation | 5 |  | 4 |  |
|  |  | 6 |  | 6 |
| Building – cost | 90 |  | 50 |  |
| – depreciation | 11 |  | 10 |  |
|  |  | 79 |  | 40 |
| Investment at cost |  | 80 |  | 50 |
| Land |  | 63 |  | 43 |
| Inventory |  | 65 |  | 55 |
| Receivables |  | 50 |  | 40 |
| Bank |  | – |  | 3 |
|  |  | 343 |  | 237 |
| Ordinary shares of €1 each |  | 50 |  | 40 |
| Share premium |  | 14 |  | 12 |
| Revaluation reserve |  | 20 |  | – |
| Retained earnings |  | 25 |  | 25 |
| Debenture loan, 10% p.a. |  | 150 |  | 100 |
| Trade payables |  | 60 |  | 40 |
| Other creditors and accruals |  | 20 |  | 20 |
| Bank |  | 4 |  | – |
|  |  | 343 |  | 237 |

|  | 20X2<br>Income<br>statement | 20X1<br>Income<br>statement |
|---|---|---|
| Sales | 200 | 200 |
| Cost of goods sold | 120 | 100 |
| Gross profit | 80 | 100 |
| Expenses | 60 | 60 |
| Earnings | 20 | 40 |

Six months after each of the two year-ends, a dividend of €20,000 is paid in relation to the results of that year.

Prepare a table of ratios calculated for both years, showing your calculations, and comment on the position, progress and direction of Non Co. as far as the available evidence permits.

# Part 2

# FINANCIAL REPORTING ISSUES

**8** Recognition and measurement of the elements of financial statements

**9** Tangible and intangible fixed assets

**10** Inventories

**11** Financial assets, liabilities and equity

**12** Accounting and taxation

**13** Cash flow statements

**14** Group accounting

**15** Foreign currency translation

**16** Accounting for price changes

# Recognition and measurement of the elements of financial statements

**Contents**

| | | |
|---|---|---|
| 8.1 | Introduction | 146 |
| 8.2 | Primacy of definitions | 146 |
| 8.3 | Hierarchy of decisions | 148 |
| | 8.3.1 The first stage | 148 |
| | 8.3.2 Recognition | 148 |
| | 8.3.3 Measurement | 152 |
| 8.4 | Income recognition | 157 |
| | Summary | 160 |
| | References and research | 161 |
| | Exercises | 161 |

**Objectives**

After studying the chapter carefully, you should be able to:

- explain the effects of the primacy of the definition of 'asset' for the division of payments into assets and expenses;

- show the implications of the definition of 'liability' for recognition of liabilities;

- illustrate when an asset should be recognized in a balance sheet;

- explain the main issues concerning the initial and subsequent measurement of assets and liabilities;

- outline the main possible alternatives to historical cost measurement;

- outline the main principles for recognition of income.

## 8.1 Introduction

Part 2 of this book deals with recognition, measurement and presentation of the elements of financial statements: assets, liabilities, equity, revenues, expenses and cash flows. As in the rest of this book, the general context of the discussion is the standards of the IASB, with some reference to the regulations of particular countries and the practices of particular companies.

This chapter deals with some basic recognition and measurement issues. To take assets as the preliminary example, there are two basic issues:

- As pointed out in Section 2.4 of this book, it is helpful to establish a primacy of definitions based on either:
  - assets and liabilities; or
  - expenses and income.
- Then, assuming a primacy of assets and liabilities, and focusing to start with on assets, there is a hierarchy of decisions:
  - Is the item an asset?
  - If yes, should the asset be recognized in the balance sheet?
  - If again yes, how should it be measured?

These matters are introduced in this chapter and taken further for various types of assets and liabilities in Chapters 9–12. Income recognition is also outlined at the end of this chapter. The presentation of cash flow statements is examined in Chapter 13.

## 8.2 Primacy of definitions

The need to establish which definitions have primacy is examined first in the context of assets and expenses. When considering payments related to assets, decisions are frequently necessary about whether such payments should be added to the asset or should be treated as an expense. Examples of such payments are those for:

- repairs;
- decorating or redecorating;
- extensions;
- improvements;
- replacements of parts;
- future inevitable payments for dismantling, decommissioning or cleaning up.

All these items are 'applications' of resources in terms of the discussion of Chapter 2. They are all recorded as 'debits' in the double-entry system. Those costs that do not generate assets (and are not added to existing assets) are expenses. Figure 8.1 presents this in diagrammatic form.

To summarize Chapter 2 on this issue, accounting can work on one of two bases:

- *Method 1*
  - *Expenses* of 20X1 are the costs of any period that relate to 20X1; and therefore . . .
  - *Assets* at the end of 20X1 are any remaining costs.

Figure 8.1 **The relationship of payments, assets and expenses**

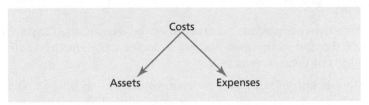

- ■ *Method 2*
  - – *Assets* at the end of 20X1 are resources controlled by the entity that are expected to give benefits; and therefore . . .
  - – *Expenses* of 20X1 are any remaining costs.

The IASB Framework gives primacy to the second way of defining the elements, by starting with an asset defined as follows (paragraph 49):

> a resource controlled by the entity as a result of past events and from which future economic benefits are expected to flow to the entity.

This has the effect of reducing the importance of the 'matching' concept, as discussed in Section 3.3.2. If an expense is postponed in order to match it against a future revenue, it would have to be stored in the balance sheet as an asset. However, this is not allowed under IFRS unless the amount meets the definition of an asset. This restriction on the items to be shown as assets does not come from a desire to be prudent but from a desire to comply with a coherent framework.

The IASB gives similar importance to the definition of 'liability' as it does to 'asset'. As noted in Chapter 2 (Framework, paragraph 49):

> a liability is a present obligation of the entity arising from past events, the settlement of which is expected to result in an outflow from the entity of resources . . .

An obligation is an unavoidable requirement to transfer resources to a third party. Many liabilities are clear legal obligations of exact amounts, such as accounts payable or loans from the bank. Some liabilities are of uncertain timing or amount. These are called 'provisions' (but see Chapter 11 for more discussion of the usage of this word). Depending on the nature of legal contracts, some of these provisions are also legally enforceable, such as provisions to pay pensions to retired employees or to repair machinery sold to customers that breaks down soon after sale. Some obligations are not based on precise laws or legal contracts but would probably be enforced by a court of law based on normal business practices or, at least, the entity would suffer so much commercial damage if it did not settle the obligation that it cannot reasonably avoid settling it.

However, outside of IFRS requirements, some companies might make provisions when there is no obligation. Let us take the example of provisions for repair expenses. The double entry for the creation of the liability is an expense. At a year end, it has been traditional German practice to charge the expected repair expenses of the first three months of the following year. This has a tax advantage in Germany because a (tax-deductible) expense can thereby be charged earlier. The large

German chemical company BASF provided an example (Annual Report of parent company, 2008):

> Maintenance provisions are established to cover omitted maintenance procedures as of the end of the year, and are expected to be incurred within the first three months of the following year.

The double entry for a repair provision would be as follows, at the end of 20X1:

Debit:    Repair expense of 20X1
Credit:   Provision for repair expense (to be carried out in 20X2).

Suppose that the definition of an expense is the traditional one as outlined above (Method 1), then it would be easy to argue that the German practice is right. The reason for the need for repair of a machine in early 20X2 was the wearing out of the machine in 20X1. So, the expense could be said to *relate* to 20X1, although this proportion is not completely clear.

However, let us now give primacy to the IASB's definition of 'liability'. In the above example of the repair, does the entity have an obligation to a third party at the balance sheet date to transfer resources? Probably not. If not, there is no liability at the end of 20X1; therefore, there can be no expense in 20X1; therefore the above double entry should not be made.

*Why it matters*    *This asset/liability approach seems to provide clearer answers to some accounting questions compared with the expense/revenue approach. The answers are often different for the two approaches, as will be noted several times in Part 2.*

## 8.3    Hierarchy of decisions

### 8.3.1  The first stage

Having decided upon the asset/liability approach, it is then necessary to apply a three-stage hierarchy of decisions. As noted briefly before, the IASB Framework, and most others, suggest that the first stage is to ask: 'Is there an asset/liability?' The definitions outlined above are useful for this purpose. However, not all assets and liabilities should be recognized, as now explained.

### 8.3.2  Recognition

The second stage in the hierarchy of decisions is to ask whether an asset or liability should be recognized in the balance sheet. For example, the value of some assets may be so difficult to measure that they should be omitted from balance sheets. The Framework (paragraph 83) gives recognition criteria for an asset as follows:

(a)  it is probable that any future economic benefit . . . will flow . . . to the enterprise; and

(b)  the item has a cost or value that can be measured with reliability.

Let us apply these ideas to various intangible items that can be found in some balance sheets. For example, the balance sheet of Costa Crociere SpA, an Italian company, for a year before IFRS adoption in 2005, is shown as Figure 8.2.

## Figure 8.2 Balance sheet of Costa Crociere SpA

| ASSETS | | LIABILITIES AND STOCKHOLDERS' EQUITY | |
|---|---|---|---|
| FIXED ASSETS | | STOCKHOLDERS' EQUITY | |
| Intangible assets | | Capital stock | 123,406,166,000 |
| Pre-operating and expansion costs | 430,788,400 | Additional paid-in capital | 100,019,657,500 |
| Research, development and publicity | 8,322,744,995 | Legal reserve | 9,957,183,361 |
| Goodwill | 17,504,906,718 | Other reserves | |
| Other | 7,728,844,063 | Merger surplus | – |
| | 33,987,284,176 | Reserve for grants received re article 55, Law 917/1986 | 16,626,003,837 |
| Tangible assets | | | 16,626,003,837 |
| Fleet | 1,545,376,990,994 | Cumulative translation adjustments | 4,146,160,964 |
| Furniture, office equipment and vehicles | 12,533,869,794 | Retained earnings | 272,122,576,707 |
| Land and buildings | 13,724,722,607 | Net income for the year | 61,230,802,224 |
| Advances to suppliers | 4,200,980 | | 587,508,550,593 |
| | 1,571,639,784,375 | Minority interests | 13,090,651 |
| Financial assets | | | 587,521,641,244 |
| Investments | | RESERVES FOR RISKS AND CHARGES | |
| ■ In subsidiary companies | 2,361,047,604 | Income taxes | – |
| ■ In associated companies | 9,585,321,141 | Other risks and charges | 9,685,481,239 |
| ■ In other companies | 441,359,551 | | 9,685,481,239 |
| | 12,387,728,296 | RESERVE FOR SEVERANCE INDEMNITY | 16,908,221,646 |
| Receivables due from | | RESERVE FOR GRANTS TO BE RECEIVED | |
| ■ Third parties, current | 810,299,509 | RE ARTICLE 55, LAW 917/1986 | 245,686,803,797 |
| ■ Third parties, non-current | 15,241,145,498 | PAYABLES | |
| | 16,051,445,007 | Bonds | 271,083,750,000 |
| | 28,439,173,303 | Banks | |
| TOTAL FIXED ASSETS | 1,634,066,241,854 | Advances | 1,334,387,305 |
| CURRENT ASSETS | | Secured loans | |
| Inventories | | ■ Current | 37,620,176,560 |
| Materials and consumables | 26,935,395,415 | ■ Non-current | 407,861,924,572 |
| Costs of uncompleted cruises | – | Unsecured loans | |
| Finished goods and goods for resale | 180,531,558 | ■ Current | 723,271,076 |
| Payments on account for goods | 181,248,671 | ■ Non-current | 1,808,177,702 |
| | 27,297,175,644 | | 449,347,937,215 |
| Receivables due from | | Other providers of finance, current | 4,543,000,000 |
| Customers | 115,202,164,925 | Advances received | 27,208,610,892 |
| Subsidiary companies | 597,461,385 | Suppliers, current | 128,837,650,343 |
| Third parties, current | 18,819,167,035 | Subsidiary companies | – |
| Advances to suppliers and agents | 13,635,070,629 | Parent company | 1,267,000,000 |
| | 148,253,863,974 | Tax authorities | 6,056,148,078 |
| Financial assets not held as fixed assets | | Social security authorities | 4,129,308,302 |
| Other securities | 3,811,127,944 | Other | 28,404,868,128 |
| Liquid funds | | | 920,878,272,958 |
| Bank deposits | 72,303,268,761 | ACCRUED EXPENSES AND DEFERRED INCOME | |
| Cash and cash equivalents | 14,333,697,020 | Accrued expenses | 25,688,281,827 |
| | 86,636,965,781 | Deferred income | 131,685,797,225 |
| TOTAL CURRENT ASSETS | 265,999,133,343 | | 157,374,079,052 |
| ACCRUED INCOME AND PREPAID EXPENSES | | | |
| Accrued income | 1,208,376,573 | | |
| Prepaid expenses | 36,780,748,166 | | |
| | 37,989,124,739 | TOTAL LIABILITIES AND STOCKHOLDERS' EQUITY | 1,938,054,499,936 |
| TOTAL ASSETS | 1,938,054,499,936 | | |

Guarantees and commitments are detailed in Notes to consolidated financial statements

*Source*: Published company financial statements.

It contains several items treated as intangible assets, including:

(a) pre-operating expenses (set-up costs of a business);
(b) research expenditure;
(c) development expenditure;
(d) publicity.

According to IAS 38 (*Intangible Assets*) the correct treatment for these items should be as follows:

(a) Pre-operating expenses are not an asset, because there is no resource with a future benefit (paragraph 69).
(b) Research expenditure can give rise to an asset but (if it is spent inside the entity) it is too difficult to demonstrate that the benefits are probable for the expenditure to be recognized in a balance sheet (paragraph 54).
(c) Development expenditure can give rise to an asset, which should be recognized if, and only if, certain criteria are met – such as there being a separately identifiable project that is technically feasible and commercially viable (paragraph 57).
(d) Publicity cannot be capitalized for the same reason as research cannot be (paragraph 69).

Consequently, Costa Crociere's treatment of pre-operating, publicity and research expenses would not be acceptable under IAS 38, but its treatment of development expenditure might be, depending on the detailed circumstances.

| Real-world examples | When Volkswagen adjusted from German accounting to IFRS, it discovered a new asset, 'development costs', of nearly €4 million. This alone increased its net assets by 41 per cent. This is shown in Figure 8.3. |

Figure 8.3 **Volkswagen 2001 (opening reconciliation)**

|  | €m |
| --- | --- |
| Equity (German law) 1.1.2000 | 9,811 |
| Capitalization of development costs | 3,982 |
| Amended useful lives and depreciation methods of tangible and intangible assets | 3,483 |
| Capitalization of overheads in inventories | 653 |
| Differing treatment of leasing contracts as lessor | 1,962 |
| Differing valuation of financial instruments | 897 |
| Effect of deferred taxes | −1,345 |
| Elimination of special items | 262 |
| Amended valuation of pension and similar obligations | −633 |
| Amended accounting treatment of provisions | 2,022 |
| Classification of minority interests not as part of equity | −197 |
| Other changes | 21 |
| Equity (IFRS) 1.1.2000 | 20,918 |

*Source*: Volkswagen Annual Report 2001.

Nokia, the Finnish telephone company, shows several intangible assets in its balance sheet, as in Figure 8.4.

Figure 8.4 **Nokia's intangible assets, 2008**

|  | €m | % of non-current assets |
|---|---|---|
| Development costs | 244 | 1 |
| Goodwill | 6,257 | 41 |
| Other intangible assets | 3,931 | 26 |

*Source*: Authors' own work based on published company financial statements.

Views differ around the world on these issues. Many companies in France, Italy and Spain follow Costa's practices for their unconsolidated statements. At the other extreme, under the rules of the United States, even development expenditure cannot be recognized as an asset unless it relates to software.

A more general European example of problems concerning the recognition of assets can be seen in the list of items shown under the heading 'Assets' in the EU Fourth Directive on company law, on which laws in EU countries (and in some others) are based. Table 8.1 shows the first two levels of headings in the English-language version of the balance sheet, from Article 9 of the Directive, as shown in more detail in Chapter 6. The right-hand side of the balance sheet (capital and liabilities) is dealt with in more detail in Chapter 11.

Table 8.1 **Balance sheet contents specified by the EU Fourth Directive**

| *Assets* | *Capital and Liabilities* |
|---|---|
| A   Subscribed capital unpaid[a] | A   Capital reserves |
|   |   I   Subscribed capital[a] |
| B   Formation expenses |   II   Share premium account |
|   |   III   Revaluation reserve |
| C   Fixed assets |   IV   Reserves |
|   I   Intangible assets |   V   Profit or loss brought forward |
|   II   Tangible assets |   VI   Profit or loss for the year |
|   III   Financial assets |   |
|   | B   Provisions for liabilities and charges |
| D   Current assets |   |
|   I   Stocks | C   Creditors |
|   II   Debtors |   |
|   III   Investments | D   Accruals and deferred income[d] |
|   IV   Cash |   |
|   | E   Profit for the year[c] |
| E   Prepayments and accrued income[b] |   |
|   |   |
| F   Loss for the year[c] |   |

*Notes*:
[a] Can be netted off, in which case the amount uncalled can be shown as an asset under A or D.II.
[b] Can be shown under D.II.
[c] Can be shown under reserves A.VI.
[d] Can be shown as creditors under C.

151

The left-hand side of Table 8.1 contains various options, reflecting previous (and present) practice in parts of Europe. Let us examine the problems:

1. *Subscribed capital unpaid* is amounts that a company could ask for from its shareholders, or amounts it has asked for but are as yet unpaid. The second of these seem to be assets (receivables), but the first are rather more contingent on future events. The company may never call in the money, which would mean that the company had no probable receipt, so no asset.
2. *Formation expenses* are discussed above as 'pre-operating expenses'. The EU Fourth Directive includes a potential heading for use in some countries for these doubtful assets.
3. *Loss for the year.* This clearly has a debit balance, and its presentation on the assets side would still enable the balance sheet to balance. However, the amount is equally clearly not an asset under the IASB's definition, and so it should be shown as a negative part of capital. The use of heading 'F' in Table 8.1 was normal French practice until 1984, Spanish practice until 1990, and so on.

**Why it matters** *The readers of a balance sheet will sometimes be interested in net assets or total assets to assess the strength of a company, using such ratios as those introduced in Chapter 7. They might be misled by phantom assets such as a former year's legal expenses of setting up the company, let alone by an asset called 'this year's loss'.*

### 8.3.3 Measurement

Once it has been decided that an asset or liability should be recognized, it is then necessary to measure its value before it can be put into a balance sheet. Under most systems of accounting that have been used in practice, initial recognition takes place at cost. If this were not the case, then the very act of purchasing an asset might lead to the recognition of a gain or loss.

Sometimes the cost of an asset is obvious, such as when a machine is bought in exchange for cash. However, even then, decisions have to be made about what to do with taxes on the purchase, delivery charges, and so on. The cost should include not only the invoice price of the asset but also all costs involved in getting the asset into a location and condition where it can be productive. So, this will include delivery charges, sales taxes and installation charges in the case of plant and machinery. For land and buildings, cost will include legal fees, architect's fees, clearing the land and so on, as well as the builder's bill and the cost of the land.

If a company has used its own labour or materials to construct an asset, these should also increase the cost of the asset rather than being treated as current expenses; that is, they are *capitalized*. It is also possible to capitalize the interest cost on money borrowed to create fixed assets. Indeed, this is required by both US GAAP and IFRS. Where labour or material is capitalized, certain formats of the income statement (described as 'by nature' in Chapter 6) show this item as revenue. This is because all the labour and materials used have been charged elsewhere in the income statement. However, the items capitalized do not relate to current operations, and so they are added back as though they were revenue (see Section 8.4), although they could more logically be seen as reductions in expenses. In the example of Figure 8.5 (CEPSA of Spain), the 4,079 million of capitalized expenses are a partial credit for the expenses shown on the debit side.

| Activity 8.A | As a digression from the discussion of the measurement of assets, it is worth checking that you can understand the format of the income statement shown in Figure 8.5. This is horizontal, by nature (see Chapter 6, Tables 6.5 and 6.6). Why, for example, did CEPSA show 'operating income' as a debit, and 'financial loss' and 'extraordinary loss' as credits? |

| Feedback | CEPSA was using a double-entry format and showing subtotals as it went down the page. The operating income (of 67,674) is the excess of the operating credits (1,172,175) over the operating debits (1,104,501). Strictly speaking, this is not very good double entry, because the debit balance of 67,674 for operating income is introduced as though it were an extra debit entry but not matched by a new credit entry of that size. Similarly, the financial loss of 12,684 is the excess of the four debit items of that sort over the three credit items; and the extraordinary loss of 7,925 is the excess of the four debit items of that sort over the four credit items. |

Expenditure on an asset after its initial recognition should sometimes also be added in. This includes inevitable future costs of dismantling or cleaning up. Any payments that make the asset better than it was originally are capitalized (added) to the asset. Any other payments are expenses. The principle in Figure 8.1 is being maintained here.

In general, repairs and maintenance are treated as current expenses, whereas improvements are capitalized. So, a new engine for a company vehicle will usually be treated as an expense, since it keeps the vehicle in running order rather than improving it, unless the engine is recorded as a separate asset. In contrast, the painting of advertising signs on the company's fleet of vans may well be treated as a capital item, if material in size. However, repainting the signs would be an expense.

Obviously, the accountant needs to consider whether the amounts relating to the improvements are material enough to capitalize them. He or she tends to treat as much as possible as expense, since this is the prudent and administratively more convenient method. If the inspector of taxes can be convinced that items are expenses, this will also speed up their tax deductibility, although this ought not to influence the accounting.

| Activity 8.B | There was a list of six payments at the beginning of Section 8.2, namely:<br><br>■ repairs;<br>■ decorating or redecorating;<br>■ extensions;<br>■ improvements;<br>■ replacement of parts;<br>■ future inevitable payments for dismantling, decommissioning or cleaning up.<br><br>Which of these should be added to the cost of an asset, and which should be treated as an immediate expense? |

**Figure 8.5 Consolidated statement of income for CEPSA***

| DEBIT | | CREDIT | |
|---|---|---|---|
| **Expenses:** | | **Revenues:** | |
| Procurements | 556,672 | Sales and services on ordinary activities | 868,148 |
| Personnel expenses | 53,225 | Excise tax hydrocarbons charged on sales | 292,392 |
| Period depreciation and amortization | 31,604 | Net Sales | 1,160,540 |
| Variation in operating provisions | 6,469 | Increase in finished products and work-in-process inventories | 3,693 |
| Other operating expenses: | | Capitalized expenses of Group in-house work on fixed asset | 4,079 |
| Excise tax on hydrocarbons | 292,529 | Other operating revenues | 3,863 |
| Other expenses | 163,972 | | **1,172,175** |
| | **1,104,501** | | |
| | | | |
| **Operating income** | **67,674** | | |
| | | | |
| Financial expenses | 14,604 | Revenues from shareholdings | 2 |
| Losses on short-term financial investments | 5 | Other financial revenues | 2,093 |
| Variation in financial investment provisions | 178 | Gains on short-term financial investments | 81 |
| Translation losses | 436 | Translation gains | – |
| | **15,223** | Exchange gains | 363 |
| | | | 2,539 |
| | | | |
| | | | **12,684** |
| | | | |
| | | **Financial loss** | **12,684** |
| | | | |
| **Amortization of goodwill in consolidation** | **383** | **Share in income of companies carried by the equity method** | **4,790** |
| **Income from ordinary activities** | **59,397** | | |
| Losses on fixed assets | 308 | Gains on fixed assets | 9,270 |
| Variation in intangible assets, tangible fixed assets and control portfolio provisions | 3,094 | Capital subsidies transferred to income for the year | 814 |
| Extraordinary expenses | 16,539 | Extraordinary revenues | 1,947 |
| Prior years' expenses | 376 | Prior years' revenues | 361 |
| | **20,317** | | |
| | | | **12,392** |
| | | **Extraordinary loss** | **7,925** |
| | | | |
| **Consolidated income before taxes** | **51,472** | | |
| Corporate income taxes | 13,058 | | |
| **Consolidated income for the year** | **38,414** | | |
| Income attributed to minority interests | 376 | | |
| Income attributed to the controlling company | 38,038 | | |

* As published by the company for the year before IFRS adoption in 2005.
*Source:* CEPSA Consolidated Statement of Income for Year Ended 31 December 1993.

**Feedback** Repairs would normally be expensed because they do not improve the asset beyond its original state. Decorating costs might be capitalizable if they were material in size and made an asset better than it ever had been. However, redecorating sounds like an expense. The cost of building extensions should normally be added to the asset being extended, or could create a separately identified asset. Improvements should probably be capitalized. Replacement of parts should be an expense unless the part is treated as a separate depreciable asset, so that replacement is treated as a disposal followed by a purchase. Future costs of dismantling, etc. should be discounted (see Chapter 11) and added to the cost of the asset.

The topic of depreciation was introduced briefly in Chapter 3 and will be considered at length in Chapter 9. For now, it should just be noted that the depreciation treatment of the new engine mentioned above will depend on the depreciation 'units' that the accountant works on. Normally, a whole vehicle will be a unit, and so a new engine will be a current expense. If the vehicle and the engine were separate units for depreciation, the new engine would be a capital item and the old engine would have been scrapped.

Some purchases are not made with cash but in exchange for the future payment of cash or for exchange with other assets. The general rule is that the current 'fair value' of the purchase consideration should be estimated as accurately as possible. The term *fair value* is of great importance in IFRSs. It means:

> the amount at which an asset could be exchanged, or a liability settled, between knowledgeable, willing parties in an arm's length transaction. [From IASB Glossary; an arm's length transaction is one where the parties are not related.]

After initial recognition, a major problem arises concerning whether to take account of subsequent changes in the value of an asset. For assets that are to be sold, the issue really becomes not whether, but *when*, to take account of changes in value, because eventually the current value is recognized at the point of sale in the calculation of profit. Conventional accounting in most countries continues to use cost as the basis for valuing most assets until the point of sale. The arguments in favour of this approach are substantial: cheapness and greater reliability.

Historical cost is an easier and cheaper method of valuation than most, because it uses information already recorded and does not require expensive estimations and the audit of them. In addition, for most assets the cost is more reliably determined than the fair value or other current valuation could be. It will be remembered that one of the key characteristics for external reporting, as examined in the IASB's Framework, is reliability. The Framework (paragraph 44) also suggests that regulators and preparers should be aware of the cost of the accounting, to ensure that it does not exceed the benefits to the users.

The problem is that the Framework's other key characteristic is relevance for economic decisions. It is difficult to see that the historical cost is the most relevant information for making decisions – which normally requires estimation of the future, particularly the prediction of cash flows.

**Activity 8.C**

Suppose that an entity buys an investment for €800 in June 20X1. It has a market value of €1,000 at the end of the accounting year, namely at 31 December 20X1. It is then sold for €950 in June 20X2.

In order to give useful information, should the balance sheet show cost or market value at the end of 20X1?

**Feedback**

It seems that the €800 cost is not a very useful predictor of cash flows at 31 December 20X1, particularly if the asset had been held for a longer period. Also, if only cost is recorded until sale, then a gain of €150 will be shown in 20X2 even though the asset has fallen in value in 20X2. The result of management's decision not to sell the asset early in 20X2 is not reflected in the 20X2 statements.

The main asset valuation bases that could be used instead of cost are:

- *fair value* (as defined above), which assumes that the business is neither buying nor selling;
- *replacement cost*, which takes account of the transaction costs of replacement;
- *net realizable value*, which is defined as expected sales receipts less any costs to finish and to sell;
- *value in use* (or *economic value*), which is the present value (i.e. discounted value) of the expected net cash flows from the asset.

It can easily be seen that, although these values may be more relevant than past values, they involve much more subjectivity than historical cost valuations. In practice, as will be shown, it is possible to introduce some conventions to narrow the range of choice. Also, some systems of accounting involve a choice of basis depending on circumstances. (This whole area is discussed in more detail in Chapter 16.) The alternatives mentioned in this section are summarized diagrammatically in Figure 8.6.

**Figure 8.6 Valuation methods**

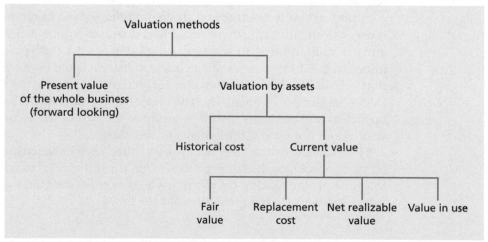

The choice of valuation method may also depend on who requires the valuation. Owners and prospective buyers will want the most realistic estimate of the worth of the business as a going concern. On the other hand, lenders may want a much more conservative valuation, based on the lowest likely valuation of the individual assets in the event that the business has to be closed down. Managers will, of course, also be interested in accounting information. They may be prepared to put up with more estimated numbers, because they can trust themselves to estimate fairly. However, this book is mainly concerned with information presented to outsiders – for example, in the form of published annual reports of companies. Consequently, there is a need for reliability and therefore a difficult trade-off between relevance and reliability.

In conventional accounting for most assets in most countries, the cheapness and reliability of historical cost has ensured its dominance, despite doubts about relevance. However, for certain assets – particularly those where there are active markets, such as some markets for shares – fair values are reliable. For such assets, there seems a strong argument for the use of fair values in financial reporting. In the case of IFRS, there has been a gradual move toward the use of fair values for various assets since the beginning of the 1990s.

**Why it matters** *A company owns two identical office blocks next door to each other in the centre of Stockholm. They are used as the company's head office. Office 1 was bought in 1980 for €1m and Office 2 was bought very recently for €4m. Under conventional accounting practice, Office 1 will be shown at less than €1m because it has worn out (depreciated) to some extent since 1980. The identical Office 2 will be shown at €4m. Is this a fair presentation? You can perhaps see, by this example, why the topic is important.*

Of course, even conventional accounting sometimes takes account of market values before the sale of assets. For example, in order to be prudent, inventories are usually valued at the lower of cost and net realizable value, and fixed assets are written down below cost if their value is impaired.

All the issues of this section are discussed again in the following chapters.

## 8.4 Income recognition

It has been agreed, in nearly all countries, that the recognition of income does not always need to await the receipt of cash; that is, the accruals convention is used. Consequently, the determination of the exact moment when income should be recognized becomes a major practical problem. Under EU laws, for example, the answer is expressed in terms of 'realization': income should be recognized in the income statement when it is realized. In practice, this does not help much because there is no clear way to define what is realized, if it does not mean 'received in cash'. One possibility is to define *realized* as having either received cash or a contractual right to cash. This allows income recognition before a customer pays a bill.

| Activity 8.D | An example may be useful here. Suppose that a manufacturing business produced a batch of output in the following way: |
|---|---|

| 12 January | Buy raw materials; store them |
| 19 February | Begin work on processing the materials |
| 3 April | Finished goods produced; store them |
| 10 May | Receive order for goods; order accepted |
| 17 May | Goods delivered; customer invoiced |
| 5 June | Customer pays invoice for goods |

It is clear that the eventual profit will be the difference between the final sales receipts and the various costs involved. However, at what point should the income be recognized? Is the profit earned gradually over the manufacturing process, or when a contract of sale is agreed, or when the goods are delivered, or when cash is finally paid?

| Feedback | The answer to the foregoing question for accountants is given by the *realization convention* – that is, profits that have not been realized are not recorded. In this case, the convention would require that income is not recognized until the goods are delivered. It must be admitted that 'realized' is a vague word. This postponement of the recognition of income conforms with the convention of prudence and with other aspects of reliability, because there is no reasonable certainty of income until the sale is made. |
|---|---|

In the above example, the sale is on credit rather than for cash, but the acquisition of a receivable is considered to be sufficiently reliable. The IASB and the FASB have been working for some years on a project to reform revenue recognition. A Discussion Paper was issued in 2008.

Sometimes the case is more complicated than in Activity 8.D. Suppose that a Dutch company has delivered goods to a US customer who will later pay an agreed amount of US dollars. If the US dollar rises by the balance sheet date, so that the Dutch company now has a contractual right to receive an amount worth more in euros, has the company made a further gain? It seems obvious that the company is better off, but is the gain realized? Even this relatively simple question is contentious, and is addressed further in Chapter 15.

The IASB's approach, as examined earlier in this chapter, is to give primacy to the definition of assets and liabilities, such that revenue is defined in the following way (Framework, paragraph 70):

> Income is increases in economic benefits during the accounting period in the form of inflows or enhancements of assets or decreases of liabilities that result in increases in equity, other than those relating to contributions from equity participants.

Confusingly, the Framework contrasts the word 'income' (rather than the word 'revenue') with the word 'expense'. The Framework uses the word 'revenue' to mean income from customers, but says that there is no important distinction between that and any other income (called gains).

The definition quoted above of income seems to suggest that special income recognition criteria are not necessary because any increase in an asset is an income. However, there are two sorts of problem here:

- practical problems for the recognition of revenue from the sale of goods and rendering of services; and
- major theoretical problems of when to recognize the gains on assets if they are revalued in the balance sheet.

The IASB addresses the first of the above two issues in IAS 18, *Revenue*, in approximately the same way as occurs already in most countries. In summary,

Figure 8.7 **Consolidated income statement, and consolidated statement of recognised income and expense, Marks and Spencer plc**

| Consolidated income statement | 52 weeks ended 28 March 2009 £m |
|---|---|
| **Revenue** | **9,062.1** |
| **Operating profit** | **870.7** |
| Finance income | 50.0 |
| Finance costs | (214.5) |
| **Profit on ordinary activities before taxation** | **706.2** |
| Analysed between: | |
| Before property disposals and exceptional items | 604.4 |
| Profit on property disposals | 6.4 |
| Exceptional costs | (135.9) |
| Exceptional pension credit | 231.3 |
| Income tax expense | (199.4) |
| **Profit for the year** | **506.8** |
| **Attributable to:** | |
| Equity shareholders of the Company | 508.0 |
| Minority interests | (1.2) |
| | 506.8 |
| | |
| **Profit for the year** | **506.8** |
| Foreign currency translation differences | 33.1 |
| Actuarial (losses)/gains on retirement benefit schemes | (927.1) |
| Cash flow and net investment hedges | |
| – fair value movements in equity | 304.8 |
| – recycled and reported in net profit | (206.8) |
| – amount recognised in inventories | (8.6) |
| Tax on items taken directly to equity | 225.8 |
| Net (losses)/gains not recognised in the income statement | (578.8) |
| **Total recognised income and expense for the year** | **(72.0)** |
| **Attributable to:** | |
| Equity shareholders of the Company | (70.8) |
| Minority interests | (1.2) |
| | (72.0) |

*Source*: Adapted from Marks and Spencer plc Financial Statements 2009.

revenue from the sale of goods is to be recognized when control and risks have passed to the customer. For services provided, recognition should occur when both the revenue and the stage of completion can be measured reliably. This is of particular relevance where there are long-term contracts (see Chapter 10).

The second issue (gains on unsold assets) is more of a problem. For example, where a company owns listed equities that rise in value, it was noted earlier that it might seem relevant and reliable to record the assets in the balance sheet at the higher values. Are such gains to be treated as income? The IASB concludes that sometimes they should indeed be (see Chapter 11).

However, when buildings are revalued (see Chapter 9), the resulting gains are not treated as income but go to a 'second income statement' unless the buildings are investment property. As noted in Chapter 6, two income statements are now to be found in some form under the rules of the IASB, the UK and the US. A British example is shown as Figure 8.7 from Marks and Spencer plc, the stores group. Some of the issues raised by Figure 8.7 are too complex for us to consider at this stage, but note that gains and losses appear in both statements. However, there is no clear rationale for the distinction between the gains in one statement and those in the other. In conclusion, a reform of the income statement is likely, such that there will be only one statement containing all 'income' as defined above (see Section 6.2).

**Why it matters**   *Does a company gain when its investments rise in value, although it has not sold them? The answer seems intuitively to be 'yes'. Should this gain be shown as income? If not, where should it be shown? The readers of financial statements try to use the profit figure to help them to make financial decisions. So, we need answers to these questions. Even if there are several plausible answers, it may be better to impose one of them, so that there is consistency between companies.*

*A further interesting complication is that revenues (such as sales) are recorded as gross receipts, whereas gains (such as those on selling fixed assets) are recorded net. So, the sale of inventory at a loss is still recorded as 'revenue'.*

**Summary**

- This chapter examines some fundamental issues relating to the recognition and measurement of the elements of financial statements. The implications of basing financial reporting on the definitions of 'asset' and 'liability' are explored. For example, expenses cannot be postponed unless they create an asset (as defined), and they cannot be anticipated unless they create a liability (as defined).

- The fact that something is an asset or a liability does not automatically lead to its inclusion in a balance sheet. It must still meet the recognition criteria: basically being reliably measurable.

- Measurement is initially made at cost, which includes a number of expenses related to the purchase and to subsequent improvement of the asset.

- There are various possibilities for subsequent revaluation. Many of these provide measurements that may be more relevant but less reliable.

- Income recognition depends in principle upon movements in assets and liabilities. However, on a day-to-day basis, practical rules are needed for the exact date of recognition. Also, not all increases in assets are presently treated as income.

### References and research

The main, relevant IASB documents for this chapter are:

- The Framework.
- IAS 18 (revised 1993), *Revenue.*

Notes on the research related to recognition and measurement of particular assets and liabilities are included in the following chapters.

## ? EXERCISES

*Feedback on the first two of these exercises is given in Appendix D.*

8.1 Explain, in a way that is understandable to a non-accountant, the following terms:
   (a) asset
   (b) liability
   (c) revenue
   (d) expense
   (e) equity

8.2 'The historical cost convention looks backwards but the going concern convention looks forwards.'
   (a) Does traditional financial accounting, using the historical cost convention, make the going concern convention (see Chapter 3) unnecessary? Explain your answer fully.
   (b) Which do you think a shareholder is likely to find more useful: a report on the past or an estimate of the future? Why?

8.3 Please arrange the following five symbols into an equation with no minus signs in it:
   $A_1$ = assets at end of period.
   $L_1$ = liabilities at end of period.
   $OE_0$ = owner's equity at beginning of period.
   $R_1$ = revenues and gains for the period.
   $E_1$ = expenses for the period.

8.4 Why is it necessary to define an expense in terms of changes in an asset (or vice versa) rather than defining the terms independently?

8.5 What general rule can be used to decide whether a payment leads to an expense or to an asset?

8.6 What disadvantages are there in measuring assets on the basis of historical cost?

8.7 What various alternatives to historical cost could be used for the valuation of assets? Which do you prefer?

# Chapter 9

# Tangible and intangible fixed assets

**Contents**

| | | |
|---|---|---|
| 9.1 | Preamble: a tale of two companies | 163 |
| 9.2 | Introduction | 164 |
| 9.3 | The recognition of assets | 165 |
| 9.4 | Should leased assets be recognized? | 167 |
| 9.5 | Depreciation of cost | 170 |
| | 9.5.1 The basic concept | 170 |
| | 9.5.2 What depreciation is *not* for | 173 |
| | 9.5.3 Allocation methods | 176 |
| | 9.5.4 Methods used in practice | 179 |
| | 9.5.5 Practical difficulties | 181 |
| 9.6 | Impairment | 182 |
| 9.7 | Measurement based on revaluation | 185 |
| | 9.7.1 An alternative to cost | 185 |
| | 9.7.2 Revaluation gains | 186 |
| | 9.7.3 Depreciation of revalued assets | 186 |
| | 9.7.4 Gains on sale | 187 |
| | 9.7.5 A mix of values | 188 |
| 9.8 | Investment properties | 188 |
| | Summary | 189 |
| | References and research | 190 |
| | Exercises | 190 |

**Objectives**

After studying this chapter carefully, you should be able to:

- explain the distinction between tangible and intangible assets, and why intangibles are becoming more important;

- outline the difference between fixed and current assets;

- decide which payments lead to fixed assets that should be recognized on a balance sheet;

- explain why IFRSs and some other accounting systems require certain leases to be capitalized by the lessee, and why perhaps it would be sensible to require this for all leases;

- choose between the methods available for depreciation of fixed assets;

- perform depreciation calculations using different methods;

- distinguish between depreciation and impairment;

- explain why and how assets can be revalued above cost;

- show how investment property might be distinguished from other property and accounted for differently.

## 9.1  Preamble: a tale of two companies

In 1994, the four largest companies in the world, as measured by sales value, were all Japanese, but the fifth-largest was the US company General Motors. By 1998, none of the top four were Japanese, and the largest in the world was General Motors. These international comparisons are difficult, partly because of large exchange rate movements. Therefore, let us concentrate for the moment on the United States.

In both 1994 and 1998, General Motors was the largest US company by sales, although it had fallen to third largest by 2004. Throughout the 1990s, General Motors was also nearly the largest in terms of assets, net assets and profits, but somewhat further down the list in terms of stock market value. It was a typical large US corporation: it used large tangible assets (machines and factories) to make other things you could touch (cars). You could say that it was a bit dull: of the 500 largest US Companies, it was below 300th in terms of its return to investors over ten years. These figures are shown in Table 9.1. Concentrate on the numbers in boxes. By the end of 2008, the bankruptcy of General Motors seemed very possible, and the audit report for 2008 referred to doubts about whether the company was a going concern.

Returning to 1994, a small computer software company called Microsoft was ranked 250th in sales and 262nd in assets. It looked successful because it was ranked 45th in profits, although it was too young to have a ten-year record.

Table 9.1 **A tale of two companies, in numbers**

| US rank by: | 1994/5 General Motors | Microsoft |
|---|---|---|
| Sales | 1 | 250 |
| Assets | 3 | 262 |
| Net Assets | 4 | 95 |
| Profits | 3 | 45 |
| Market value | 15 | 10 |
| Return to investors (10 years) | 375 | (too young) |
| **1998/9** | | |
| Sales | 1 | 109 |
| Assets | 12 | 126 |
| Net Assets | 28 | 24 |
| Profits | 29 | 11 |
| Market value | 42 | 1 |
| Return to investors (10 years) | 304 | 4 |
| **2004/5** | | |
| Sales | 3 | 41 |
| Assets | 10 | 51 |
| Net Assets | 28 | 8 |
| Profits | 46 | 12 |
| Market value | 156 | 3 |
| Return to investors (10 years) | 330 | 55 |

*Source*: Derived from *Fortune 500*, 1995, 1999 and 2005.

Despite its small size, an anticipation of success led the market to value this small young company at 10th in market value rank in the US.

By early 1999, Microsoft was the most valuable company in the United States (and the world), although it was still ranked only 109th in terms of sales and 126th in terms of assets. Microsoft uses a very small number of tangible assets, but a lot of unrecognized intangible assets, to make another intangible asset. By 2004, Microsoft had risen to 41st in terms of sales but had lost the top spot in terms of market value (Exxon Mobil and General Electric were above it).

*Why it matters*   *Accounting has grown up in a world where tangible items were the main fixed assets to account for, and cost was the main measurement basis. General Motors can be accounted for like that. However, Microsoft is all about intangibles and values. Most of the intangibles have no identifiable cost. Conventional accounting is not well suited to the changes whereby Microsoft became so rapidly more important than General Motors. If we do not want financial reporting to be left behind in a rapidly changing world, we will have to get better at accounting for intangibles and for values.*

## 9.2   Introduction

This chapter examines the recognition and measurement of tangible and intangible fixed assets. The term 'fixed assets' is not generally used in IFRSs. The same is true for US standards, but the term is found in European laws based on the EU Fourth Directive. The term 'non-current asset' is now used in IFRS instead. A *fixed asset* is one that is intended for continuing use in the business. This is a somewhat vague definition, which rests upon what the management of a company intends to do. However, this vagueness is difficult to avoid.

In IASB terms, tangible fixed assets are referred to as 'property, plant and equipment'. IAS 16 distinguishes them from tangible assets to be sold to customers (inventories) by noting that property, plant and equipment is:

(a) held for use in production or supply of goods or services;
(b) expected to be used during more than one period. [summary from paragraph 6]

The IASB refers in IAS 38 (paragraph 8) to an intangible asset as:

an identifiable non-monetary asset without physical substance.

The previous version of IAS 38 had a longer definition specifying in effect that all intangible assets are fixed. This is no longer the case, but the new IAS 38 explicitly states (para 3) that intangible assets held for sale in the ordinary course of business are treated as inventory under IAS 2 or IAS 11 (see Chapter 10). In practice most IASB intangibles are non-current.

There are no detailed lists of examples of fixed assets in IAS 16 or IAS 38, nor in the examples of balance sheets in IAS 1. However, the EU Fourth Directive, on which most European laws are based, contains the following list in its balance sheet formats (Articles 9 and 10):

**Fixed Assets**

I *Intangible assets*
1. Costs of research and development
2. Concessions, patents, licences, trade marks and similar rights and assets
3. Goodwill
4. Payments on account

II *Tangible assets*
1. Land and buildings
2. Plant and machinery
3. Other fixtures and fittings, tools and equipment
4. Payments on account and tangible assets in course of construction

**Activity 9.A**

Would the following items usually be fixed assets or current assets?

■ Motor vehicles.
■ Investments in shares of other companies.

If you answer 'fixed', could they ever be current? If you answer 'current', could they ever be fixed?

**Feedback**

An enterprise's motor vehicles would usually be fixed assets, even though they move! 'Fixed' refers to permanence of use in the business. Perhaps 'non-current' is a clearer term. However, if the enterprise was in the business of selling motor vehicles then those to be sold would be current assets.

An enterprise's investment in shares would often be fixed/non-current. This would certainly be the case for investment in subsidiary companies. However, it is possible to buy shares for the purposes of trading or for a temporary store of value. In these cases, the shares would be current assets. Investments are considered in more detail in Chapter 11.

## 9.3 The recognition of assets

As outlined briefly in Chapter 8, it is necessary first to identify whether items are assets and then to decide whether to recognize them in a balance sheet. It was explained that, under IFRS, certain items are not thought to be assets (e.g. the set-up costs of a company). Other items may be assets but are not to be recognized as such because it is not probable that benefits will flow or because the assets cannot be measured reliably. For example, IAS 38 specifically rules out the recognition of research costs.

Particular problems are also met with other intangible assets that are created by the company itself, such as brand names or customer lists. According to IAS 38 (paragraph 63) these cannot be capitalized (i.e. recognized as assets) unless they have been bought from somebody else, because otherwise a cost or value is difficult to determine. The same applies even more clearly to any increase in value of the company itself caused by loyalty of customers or increasing skills of staff. Such internally generated 'goodwill' cannot be capitalized by the company.

By contrast, some intangible assets are purchased separately and have a clear cost. For example, a company could buy the right to use a brand name in a particular country for a particular period. Sometimes they also have a clear market value. This might apply to taxi licences, milk quotas, airport landing rights, etc.; all these should be capitalized. As noted in Chapter 8, the same applies to certain development expenditure where it can be reliably identified and measured.

Sometimes, intangibles are purchased as part of a package of assets or of a whole company. Where the intangibles can be separately identified and valued, the accountants record as many of them as possible. The balance of the purchase cost in excess of the identified net assets is assumed to be an asset, called *goodwill*.

Let us take the example of a company (X) that buys all the shares of another company (Y) for €1m cash. Company X is buying some assets that form a going concern business from company Y; it is not buying that company. The following assets are bought, whose values can be estimated as:

| | |
|---|---|
| Land | €300,000 |
| Building | €150,000 |
| Machinery | €90,000 |
| Inventory | €70,000 |
| Receivables | €80,000 |
| Patent | €50,000 |
| Total | €740,000 |

Assuming that the company is not taking on any liabilities, it seems to be paying €260,000 too much for the assets. The excess is called goodwill. The split of the assets in the balance sheet of L'Oréal (the French cosmetics company) is shown as Table 9.2, illustrating the large proportion (33 per cent) of intangible assets. Goodwill is discussed again as part of group accounting in Chapter 14.

Table 9.2 **L'Oréal's assets as at 31 December 2008**

| | €m | % of total assets |
|---|---|---|
| Goodwill on consolidation | 5,533 | 24 |
| Other intangible assets | 2,038 | 9 |
| Tangible assets | 2,753 | 12 |
| Investments | 5,558 | 24 |
| Deferred tax assets | 427 | 2 |
| Current assets | 6,648 | 29 |
| Total assets | 22,957 | 100.0 |

*Source*: Authors' own work based on published company financial statements.

| Activity 9.B | In the above example of a company apparently paying €260,000 too much for the business, why would it be willing to do so? |
|---|---|

**Feedback** The company is willing to do this because it is buying the business as a going concern that already has other useful features, such as loyal customers for its existing products, access to this list of customers, and trained staff – in other words, the ability to make future profit.

As noted in Section 9.1, intangible assets are often important in the context of many rapidly growing companies. For *tangible* fixed assets, the problems of recognition are generally smaller than for the above intangible assets. This is because it is usually possible to physically identify tangible assets and to establish a cost or value. Although the standards of the IASB (and of most national laws) seem to be more restrictive for intangible assets than for tangible assets, this does not mean that intangible assets cannot be recognized. The sort of intangibles that might be included in an IFRS balance sheet are:

- software development costs;
- other development costs;
- purchased patents, licences, trademarks and brands;
- purchased goodwill.

## 9.4 Should leased assets be recognized?

A company may decide to acquire the use of fixed assets without buying them. There may be tax or liquidity advantages in doing this. For example, if an industrial company has little taxable income, it may not be able currently to use the tax depreciation allowances on the purchase of plant and machinery. However, if a financial company buys the assets and hires them to an industrial company, the financial company may be able to gain the tax allowances, thus enabling a lower rental charge.

In the case of certain long-term legal arrangements between the financial company (the lessor) and the industrial company (the lessee), the situation is very much as though the lessee had bought the plant. For example, the lessee may expect to keep the asset for the whole of its productive life, and there may be an option to purchase the plant at a future date at a low price from the lessor. In such cases, it can be argued that the commercial substance of the lessee's arrangements is that it has the asset and has contracted obligations that are liabilities. This, of course, is not the superficial legal form of the arrangements, because the lessor is still the owner even though the lessee has the exclusive legal right to use the asset.

For example, consider company A and company B. The first has borrowed €10m and bought machines with the money. Company B has borrowed no money, but has long-leased machines that would have cost €10m to buy. If company B accounts only for the legal form of the arrangement, its financial statements will look unfairly better than company A's (see the first two balance sheets of Figure 9.1). That is, B will seem to have a better profit in relation to assets used (because assets seem smaller) and will show smaller liabilities.

Accountants in the United States were the first to adjust for this problem by capitalizing certain leases – which in our example would mean adjusting company

Figure 9.1 **Capitalized leases**

| Company A | | Company B (form) | | Company B (substance) | |
|---|---|---|---|---|---|
| Fixed assets +10 | Loans +10 | | | Rights to fixed assets +10 | Lease obligations +10 |

B's balance sheet to the position on the right in Figure 9.1. By the 1980s, this had also become standard procedure in some other countries; for example, in the United Kingdom (SSAP 21) and the Netherlands (Guideline 1.05).

In countries with a more literal interpretation of legal requirements, such as Germany and Italy, either leases are not capitalized or the definition of capitalizable leases is such that leases are rarely capitalized in practice. By the late 1980s, many large French groups were capitalizing in their consolidated balance sheets but not in their individual company statements (because of legal and tax issues). The Spanish law of 1989, which implemented the EU Fourth Directive, required the capitalization of certain leases. Interestingly, although in most countries capitalized leases are included as tangible fixed assets, under Spanish law they are shown as intangibles. This recognizes the legal point that the company owns the *right* to the assets, not the assets themselves. In terms of the classification of accounting systems suggested in Figure 5.3 of this book, the 'strong equity' systems tend to exhibit capitalization and the 'weak equity' systems do not.

The above discussion concentrates on those leases that are recognized as assets and liabilities of the lessee. These are called 'finance leases' by the IASB and in the UK, and 'capital leases' in the US. For these leases, the lease payments to the lessor are treated as partly a reduction in lease liability and partly a finance expense. The expense is made to decline each year as the recorded lease liability itself declines. That is, the entries for the lease payments are:

Debit:    Finance charge
Debit:    Lease liability
Credit:   Cash

Also, the asset under a finance lease wears out, and so it is depreciated – as with any other asset – over its life (see Section 9.5). So, for finance leases, the lessee records expenses for both finance and depreciation but no rental charge.

The other leases that are not capitalized but are treated as rentals are called 'operating leases'. These are accounted for by recognizing the lease rental payments:

Debit:    Lease rental expense
Credit:   Cash

*Why it matters*    *For its 1998 group financial statements, the German national airline, Lufthansa, adopted the IFRS approach for the first time. Compared with its previous German accounting, this meant capitalizing a number of leases. The effects on the balance sheet of this particular change were to reduce net assets by DM722 million (14 per cent). This makes a large difference to the impression given by the balance sheet. For liabilities, the rise was unclear but would generally be much larger than the net effect (of assets minus liabilities). This will have a major effect on gearing ratios (see Chapter 7).*

*Incidentally, Lufthansa also largely removed its charter airline (Condor) from its balance sheet by a complex partial sale. This hid some of the leases, which would otherwise have made liabilities look even worse.*

An obvious question is: where exactly is the dividing line between finance leases and operating leases? IAS 17, *Leases*, defines a finance lease as (paragraph 4):

> a lease that transfers substantially all the risks and rewards incidental to ownership of an asset. Title may or may not eventually be transferred.

This is fairly vague, particularly for auditors and particularly as companies may wish to try to avoid capitalizing leases so that they do not have to show extra liabilities.

European laws (except tax laws) are generally silent on this issue, because the matter is not covered by the EU Fourth Directive. However, in the UK, SSAP 21 adds some precision about a finance lease (paragraph 15):

> [A finance lease] should be presumed . . . if at the inception of a lease the present value of the minimum lease payments . . . amounts to substantially all (normally 90 per cent or more) of the fair value of the leased asset.

The US standard (SFAS 13) contains something similar, plus other criteria, such as the lease lasting for 75 per cent or more of the useful life of the asset.

However, where do the 90 per cent and the 75 per cent come from? Why not 88 per cent and 77 per cent? Furthermore, why does the definition of a finance lease refer to risks and rewards, whereas the Framework's definitions of asset and liability (see Chapter 8) do not? It seems that, as the leasing standards were written before the Framework was fully established, they are not really consistent with it.

At the end of 1999, the IASC and several other standard setters issued proposals for dramatic reform of lease accounting. They concluded that, if the lessee has signed a contract to pay the lessor, there is always a liability. And, if the lessor has signed a contract giving control of the asset to the lessee for a period, the lessee always has an asset. In conclusion, all uncancellable leases should be treated as finance leases. This conclusion is an illustration of putting into effect the Framework's approach that starts with the consideration of assets and liabilities. However, the proposals were controversial and lacked detail. In 2009, the IASB and the FASB issued a more detailed, but similar, discussion paper.

Often, the capitalization of leases is used as an example of 'substance over form' (see Chapter 3). However, the notion of 'commercial substance over legal form' can now be seen as an unnecessary and misleading contrast. It is much simpler to rely on the definitions of asset and liability, which depend in each case on *legal* rights of control and *legal* obligations to pay money. The recognition of assets and liabilities requires one to identify the relevant legal rights, which are the source of the economic substance.

*If the IASB proposals to make all leases into finance leases are turned into standards, a large number of leases presently treated as rentals will appear on balance sheets as assets and liabilities. This will, for example, make ratios of debt to equity (gearing ratios; see Chapter 7) look much higher because liabilities will increase but the increase in assets will not directly affect gearing.*

## 9.5 Depreciation of cost

### 9.5.1 The basic concept

The topic of the measurement of those assets that have been recognized was introduced in Chapter 8. It was explained there that assets are initially recognized at cost. Subsequently, in most parts of the world the measurement of tangible and intangible assets continues to be based on cost, after taking account of expected wearing out (depreciation) and unexpected loss of value (impairment). This section examines depreciation; the next, impairment.

If a business buys goods or services (e.g. materials, electricity or labour) that are to be used up in the current year in the process of earning profit, they are charged to the income statement. The amount charged in the accounting year is not the amount paid in the year but the amount that relates to the year. This is a practical working out of the accruals convention, examined in Part 1.

A further result of the accruals convention relates to cases where a company buys goods of significant value that are *not* to be used up in the current year (non-current assets). In such cases the cost should be treated as a capital purchase, not as a current expense. The difference in effect can be seen on the balance sheets of Figure 9.2. The top half of the figure deals with the effect of a current expense (e.g. wages), and the bottom half deals with the purchase of a non-current asset (e.g. a machine).

In the case of an asset that does not wear out and has a potentially unlimited useful life, no expense should ever be charged for using it up. This generally applies to land. However, it would be unreasonable to charge nothing against

**Figure 9.2 Balance sheet representation of goods that are not used up in the current year**

(1) Expenses of 10,000:

| *Assets* | | *Capital and liabilities* | |
|---|---|---|---|
| Current assets: | −10,000 cash | Capital: | −10,000 profit |

(2) Capital purchase of 10,000:

| *Assets* | | *Capital and liabilities* | |
|---|---|---|---|
| Fixed assets: | +10,000 machine | | |
| Current assets: | −10,000 cash | | |

profit for the use of a machine that is being worn out. If the machine will last for ten years, the cost is spread over ten years rather than being charged totally to the year of purchase or not charged at all.

Activity 9.C What various reasons might there be for a non-current asset (such as a machine) gradually to become economically less useful?

Feedback An asset may be used up or become less useful for a variety of predictable reasons, which can be divided into two categories:

(a) *physical reasons*: deterioration or wearing out with use; the expiration of a lease or patent; the exhaustion of a mine;
(b) *economic reasons*: the obsolescence of the asset or the product that it makes; a change in company policy leading, for example, to the hiring of machines; expansion of the business, causing an asset to be inadequate in size or performance.

Just as it is reasonable to charge for the services provided, so it seems reasonable to consider that the fixed asset is used up because it has provided the services. Therefore, accountants allocate the cost to expense (in the income statement) over the life of the asset and recognize (in the balance sheet) that the asset is being used up. The 'life' in question is the *useful economic life* to the present owner, which takes into account the fact that a machine may become economically obsolete before it is physically worn out. The expense is labelled 'depreciation'.

IAS 16 (paragraph 6) confirms this notion:

*Depreciation* is the systematic allocation of the depreciable amount of an asset over its useful life.

*Depreciable amount* is the cost of an asset, or other amount substituted for cost, less its residual value.

So, depreciation aims to distribute the cost of assets, less salvage value (if any), over the estimated useful life of an asset in a systematic and rational manner. It is a process of allocation, not of valuation.

A slightly more detailed, but broadly consistent definition can be found in the UK's FRS 15:

*Depreciation*: The measure of the cost or revalued amount of the economic benefits of the tangible fixed asset that have been consumed during the period.

Consumption includes the wearing out, using up or other reduction in the useful economic life of a tangible fixed asset whether arising from use, effluxion of time or obsolescence through either changes in technology or demand for the goods and services produced by the asset.

The laws around Europe also contain instructions consistent with this, based on Article 35 of the EU's Fourth Directive.

As an example of depreciation, suppose that a €10,000 machine is estimated to last ten years and to be worthless at the end. An obvious and simple method of depreciation would be to allocate €1,000 of the cost as an expense for each of the ten years. For example:

| 1 January 20X2 | Purchase: | machine | +10,000 |
| | | cash | −10,000 |
| 31 December 20X2 | Depreciation recognized: | machine | −1,000 |
| | | profit | −1,000 |

So the machine stands at 10,000 – 1,000 = 9,000 in the balance sheet. This 9,000 is the amount of the cost not yet treated as an expense. It is called the *carrying value*, or sometimes the *net book value* (*NBV*) or the *written-down value* – although it is not, of course, a 'value' in any market sense. This method of depreciation is called the *straight-line* or *fixed instalment* or *constant charge method*. It is illustrated in Figure 9.3.

**Figure 9.3 Straight-line depreciation**

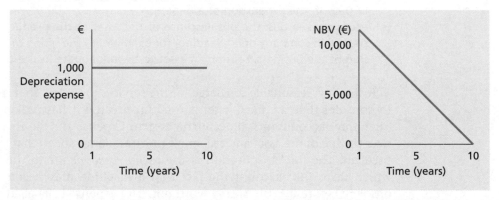

**Activity 9.D**

Suppose that, for another machine costing €10,000, a scrap value (residual value) of €3,000 was estimated and life was expected to be seven years. What would the annual depreciation charge be then?

**Feedback**

Again, it would be €1,000, as shown in Table 9.3. At the end of year 6 in the example of Table 9.3, the balance sheet or the notes would show:

| | € |
| --- | --- |
| Fixed asset: cost | 10,000 |
| Cumulative depreciation | 6,000 |
| | 4,000 |

**Table 9.3 Straight-line depreciation of net cost**

| End of year | Depreciation charge recognized | NBV |
| --- | --- | --- |
| 0 | – | 10,000 |
| 1 | 1,000 | 9,000 |
| 2 | 1,000 | 8,000 |
| 3 | 1,000 | 7,000 |
| 4 | 1,000 | 6,000 |
| 5 | 1,000 | 5,000 |
| 6 | 1,000 | 4,000 |
| 7 | 1,000 | 3,000 |

### 9.5.2 What depreciation is *not* for

Having examined the basic concept, it is useful now to make clear what depreciation is *not* for, under the three headings below. Many non-accountants misunderstand this.

**Not for valuation**

First, depreciation is not supposed to be a valuation technique. Although amounts of depreciation are deducted from the cost of non-fixed assets in order to show a net book value on a balance sheet, that NBV is not supposed to represent the amount for which the assets could be sold at the balance sheet date. The NBV is merely the cost that has so far not been allocated as an expense to the income statement.

In principle, of course, it would be possible to allocate depreciation on the basis of declining market values. However, this leads to all the problems of estimations – for example, the expense of annual valuations, the unreliability of the estimates and the difficulty of auditing them. Furthermore, some assets decline in value very rapidly and it is not clear that allocation of cost over useful lives should be based on that process. For example, specialized assets such as power stations or telephone exchanges may be effectively unmarketable immediately after they are bought, and motor cars lose a large proportion of value in their first month on the road. But even though they lose value rapidly, they do not generally become less useful to the business so rapidly.

Another approach would be that the value of an asset to a firm is not the market value but the discounted expected net cash inflows from the asset (the 'value in use' of Chapter 8). One needs to identify the net inflows of the company with and without the asset in order to measure the net contributions of the asset.

The net cash inflows of the asset will be called $R_1$ in year 1, $R_n$ in year $n$ and so on. It has been briefly mentioned in Chapter 8 that future flows need to be discounted in order to assess their present values. The present value of an asset ($PV_0$) can therefore be given by:

$$PV_0 = \frac{R_1}{1 + r} + \frac{R_2}{(1 + r)^2} + \ldots + \frac{R_n}{(1 + r)^n},$$

where $n$ is the life of the asset and $r$ is the appropriate discount rate. This rate may be the cost of capital or the rate of return on funds (see Chapter 17). The above equation can be restated as:

$$PV_0 = \sum_{t=1}^{t=n} \frac{R_t}{(1 + r)^t},$$

where $t$ is the year. One year later the asset's value ($PV_1$) will be given by:

$$PV_1 = \sum_{t=2}^{t=n} \frac{R_t}{(1 + r)^{t-1}},$$

and the depreciation for the year (measured by loss of value) will be $PV_0 - PV_1$.

There are, of course, great practical difficulties in isolating the net cash flows or cost savings of an asset after purchase. However, if it could be done it would lead to a justifiable current measure of the using up of the asset's value during the year, taking into account repairs and maintenance or deterioration in performance caused by lack of them. However, this would not be the allocation of cost, and would not fit with the conventional workings of accounting.

### Not for replacement

The second potential misunderstanding about depreciation is that it is a mechanism for providing funds for the replacement of the depreciating asset. The double entry for depreciation is:

Debit:    Depreciation expense
Credit:   Value adjustment (or allowance) for depreciation.

The credit entry is stored separately from the asset, so that the original cost and the accumulating depreciation allowance can be seen in the accounting records. In the balance sheet, it is usual to show the two amounts netted off, called the depreciated cost, the net book value or the written-down value. It is best to see the accumulating credit balance as a value adjustment or allowance against the asset. However, the amount is often called a 'provision', which is confusing because that word is also used to mean a type of liability (see Chapter 11).

The above double entry shows that there is no direct effect on cash or investments (except for any tax reduction; see below). Unless amounts of cash that are equivalent to the depreciation charges are put into a tin box or another easily accessible store (e.g. an investment fund), an amount equalling the cost will not be specifically available in liquid form at the end of the asset's life. Even if cash is available, the price of a replacement asset may have risen, and so the cash will be insufficient. Also, in many cases the company will not want to buy a similar asset but one that is technologically more advanced, bigger or concerned with the production of completely different goods.

Nevertheless, depreciation may help with replacement because it may help to maintain the original capital (in terms of historical money), because depreciation reduces profit available for distribution. So, less cash may be distributed, and this will build up in the company, perhaps converted into a variety of different assets such as receivables, inventory and even other non-current assets.

Let us look at an example of how charging depreciation may aid replacement in the extreme cases where either:

(a) no depreciation is charged (company A), or
(b) depreciation *is* charged, so both profit and dividends fall, and the assets that are consequently undistributed are kept as current assets (company B).

The two companies are assumed to be identical in other ways, and both distribute all their profits. They start by buying a non-current asset for €10,000, which will last for ten years and have no scrap value. There are also €10,000 of current assets. Figure 9.4 shows the situation after the first year. If this continues for another nine years, company A will have a worthless non-current asset and €10,000 of current assets, and will see that its capital is only €10,000. Company B will have a worthless non-current asset but €20,000 of current assets because it distributed €10,000 less 'profits' than company A did. So, B can purchase another

Figure 9.4 **The effect on assets of not charging depreciation**

| Company A | | | | Company B | | | |
|---|---|---|---|---|---|---|---|
| Gross profit | 5,000 | | | Gross profit | 5,000 | | |
| *less* Expenses | (3,000) | | | *less* Expenses | (3,000) | | |
| Net profit | 2,000 | distributed | | *less* Depreciation | (1,000) | | |
| | | | | Net profit | 1,000 | distributed | |
| *Balance sheet* | | | | *Balance sheet* | | | |
| Fixed assets | 10,000 | Capital | 20,000 | Fixed assets | 10,000 | Capital | 20,000 |
| | | Profit | 2,000 | *less* Depreciation | (1,000) | Profit | 1,000 |
| Current assets | 10,000 | *less* Distribution | (2,000) | Current assets | 11,000 | *less* Distribution | (1,000) |
| | 20,000 | | 20,000 | | 20,000 | | 20,000 |

non-current asset and continue business with its capital intact; A will have a serious financial problem. In essence, depreciation assists replacement by ensuring that profit is only measured or distributed after some form of maintenance of capital.

A well-run business has an overall cash plan for future months and years. Included in this is the expected need to replace assets. The assets that will be bought as replacements may be identical but more expensive, or they may be entirely different. It would be unusual, and probably commercially unwise, for a business to set aside amounts of money in liquid or time-matched investments in order to be prepared for the replacement of assets. These funds could be better used elsewhere in the business, and it is not until the time for replacement approaches that a good impression of the type and cost of replacement assets is obtainable.

### Not for tax purposes

A major international difference is that depreciation in some countries has been closely linked with taxation. At first sight, this might seem obvious for any country. However, in Anglo-Saxon countries and in Denmark and the Netherlands, there is a long tradition of having differences between tax depreciation and accounting depreciation. At the extreme, in the United Kingdom, the depreciation expenses charged in the profit and loss account (income statement) are not allowable at all as tax-deductible expenses for the calculation of taxable income. The tax calculations are done quite separately, and 'capital allowances', which amount to depreciation for tax purposes, are allowed instead. In the United States and a few continental European countries, the separation between tax depreciation and accounting depreciation is not so clear, but differences are common (leading to deferred taxation; see Chapter 12).

However, in most continental European countries, there is a close relationship between tax and accounting depreciation. Technically, in the majority of those countries, the tax figures should be based on the accounting figures rather than the other way round. For example, in Germany, the *Steuerbilanz* (tax statements) should be based on the *Handelsbilanz* (commercial statements); this is the authoritative principle or the *Massgeblichkeitsprinzip* (as mentioned in Chapter 5). In practice in these countries, since the tax rules will allow only certain maximum charges for tax purposes, the accounting depreciation charges are chosen to coincide with these maxima. So, the accounting figures end up being based on tax rules (the *umgekehrtes Massgeblichkeitsprinzip*, or reverse authoritative principle). These expenses are often larger than accountants might have chosen on grounds of fairness.

In many countries, governments offer accelerated tax depreciation in order to encourage investment in certain types of assets or certain regions. For example, this applies to the eastern *Länder* of Germany, to certain Greek islands and to the Highlands of Scotland. In Germany and countries like it (see Chapter 5), such accelerated depreciation must be recorded in the appropriate financial statements in order to be allowable for tax purposes.

However, under IFRS, it is clear that depreciation is an expense designed for financial reporting purposes rather than for tax calculations. If tax authorities wish to follow the accounting calculations, they may of course do so, but this should not, in principle, be allowed to affect how enterprises measure depreciation.

### 9.5.3 Allocation methods

**Activity 9.E**

The straight-line method of allocation was used earlier in the chapter for a basic illustration of depreciation. Referring to the earlier discussion of the definition of depreciation (see Section 9.5.1), one can see that straight-line allocation is 'systematic' – but is it 'rational'?

**Feedback**

In order to answer this question, it is necessary to recall why depreciation is being charged. Depreciation is a charge designed to recognize the loss of service that an asset has suffered in any year. As has been said, it is an example of the results of using the matching convention. Let us look at different types of assets with this in mind:

1. Leases, patents and some buildings can be said to require depreciation because of the passing of time. In this case, straight-line depreciation seems to be satisfactory.
2. Other assets have increasing repairs and maintenance. So, if straight-line depreciation is used, the total expense per year relating to an asset increases over its life. Therefore, if a reasonably constant total charge for an asset's services is to be charged in the income statement, a declining depreciation charge may be appropriate.
3. Some assets wear out in proportion to their use. Therefore, it may be appropriate to charge depreciation in line with this, at different amounts in different periods.

### Declining charge

For type-2 assets in Activity 9.E, it may be rational to have a declining depreciation charge. There are several ways of producing this systematically. The reducing balance method (or the constant percentage on reducing balance method) is one of them. With 20 per cent depreciation, this would give a situation as shown in Table 9.4. So, the net book value (written-down value) at the end of the third year will be 5,120 and the charge in the third year will be 1,280.

How many years would it take to write down the asset to zero? The answer, inconveniently, is that it would take an infinite number of years. However, if there

Table 9.4 **The reducing balance method**

|        |                         |        |
|--------|-------------------------|--------|
|        | Cost                    | 10,000 |
| Year 1 | *less* 20% depreciation | 2,000  |
|        | NBV                     | 8,000  |
| Year 2 | *less* 20% depreciation | 1,600  |
|        | NBV                     | 6,400  |
| Year 3 | *less* 20% depreciation | 1,280  |
|        | NBV                     | 5,120  |

is a scrap value, this problem does not arise. If there is no scrap value (residual value), a small figure to which the asset will be written down may be chosen. The residual at that point will be an extra depreciation charge for the final year.

To find the appropriate percentage to use for a given net cost and a given useful life, a formula may be used:

$$r = 1 - \sqrt[n]{\frac{S}{K}},$$

where $r$ is the depreciation rate, $n$ is the life of the asset, $S$ is the scrap value and $K$ is the gross cost. This formula may be simply derived, as in Table 9.5, which shows that, at the end of an asset's life, $S = K(1 - r)^n$, which thus gives the above equation.

Table 9.5 **The reducing balance formula**

| End of year | NBV                 | Standardized form of NBV |
|-------------|---------------------|--------------------------|
| 0           | $K$                 | $K(1 - r)^0$             |
| 1           | $K - Kr$            | $K(1 - r)^1$             |
| 2           | $(K - Kr) - (K - Kr)r$ | $K(1 - r)^2$          |
| 3           | etc.                | etc.                     |

As an example, let us use the asset costing 10,000, which will have a scrap value of 3,000 and a life of seven years. Applying the above formula, we obtain:

$$r = 1 - \sqrt[7]{\frac{3,000}{10,000}} = 0.158, \text{ or } 15.8 \text{ per cent.}$$

The detailed results of depreciation year by year for our example are tabulated in Table 9.6, repeating the straight-line results for comparison. It can be seen that more depreciation is charged in the earlier years using the reducing balance method. This helps to stabilize the total charge (of depreciation plus maintenance) for the contribution of the machine to earning profits.

Another way of producing systematically declining charges for depreciation is to use the sum of digits method. For this, one merely adds up the digits of the number of years of useful life. For example, for a useful life of six years the sum of digits is 21 (i.e. 6 + 5 + 4 + 3 + 2 + 1). The charge for year 1 will be 6/21, that for year 2 will be 5/21 and so on.

Table 9.6 **Depreciation methods contrasted**

| | Straight line | | Reducing balance | |
| Year | Charge | NBV | Charge | NBV |
|---|---|---|---|---|
| 0 | – | 10,000 | – | 10,000 |
| 1 | 1,000 | 9,000 | 1,580 | 8,420 |
| 2 | 1,000 | 8,000 | 1,330 | 7,090 |
| 3 | 1,000 | 7,000 | 1,120 | 5,970 |
| 4 | 1,000 | 6,000 | 940 | 5,030 |
| 5 | 1,000 | 5,000 | 790 | 4,240 |
| 6 | 1,000 | 4,000 | 670 | 3,570 |
| 7 | 1,000 | 3,000 | 570[a] | 3,000 |

[a] Adjusted for rounding differences.

Another method that can be used to obtain a declining charge is the double declining-balance method. Here, the straight-line depreciation rate is worked out and then doubled and applied on a reducing balance basis.

One of these three declining-charge methods might be appropriate for assets that are expected to have considerable repair and maintenance costs in later years. The total amount allocated will, of course, be the same in all these declining-charge methods and, for that matter, in the straight-line method. However, the amounts allocated to particular periods will vary with the method chosen.

It may be that the market value of most machines actually declines in a way that is more similar to the result of declining-charge depreciation than of straight-line depreciation. However, within the context of a historical cost system, this is not really an argument in favour of a declining-charge method, since the main aim is to get a fair yearly allocation of cost against profit over the whole life of the asset. Nevertheless, if the business is very uncertain about the useful life of the asset or the date of likely sale, there is an argument for rapid depreciation and for keeping the written-down value fairly close to the market value at all times rather than just at the estimated end of life. In these cases a declining-charge method may be more suitable.

### Usage

Assets that come to the end of their useful lives as a result mainly of wearing out through use may more rationally be depreciated on the basis of usage. According to the usage method, if the asset concerned is expected to produce 100,000 units or to run for 20,000 hours, the depreciation charge for the year will be that proportion of the original cost that the usage of the year bears to the total expected usage. For example, in the case of a machine costing €20,000 that is expected to produce 100,000 units, the usage may turn out to be as given in Table 9.7, leading to the annual depreciation charges shown (assuming zero residual value).

### The revaluation method

Some assets are difficult to depreciate by using any of the above methods (namely straight-line, declining charge and usage). These assets are such things as tools or crates, for which it may be unnecessary to keep item-by-item records. The assets

Table 9.7 **The usage method**

| Accounting year | Units produced | Depreciation charge (€) |
|---|---|---|
| 1 | 15,000 | 3,000 |
| 2 | 35,000 | 7,000 |
| 3 | 20,000 | 4,000 |
| 4 | 20,000 | 4,000 |
| 5 | 10,000 | 2,000 |
| | 100,000 | 20,000 |

may be capable of a long life, but in practice their lives are short because of damage, breakage, theft, loss and so on. In addition, their individual values are immaterial in the context of a whole company. Thus, it would be inefficient to record the purchase, the yearly depreciation charges, the disposal and adjustments to depreciation on disposal. In such instances, depreciation is charged using the revaluation method. This method involves valuing the set of similar assets at the beginning of the year, adding assets purchased and deducting a valuation of the set at the year end. This gives a measure of the using-up of the type of asset, which is charged to the profit and loss account as depreciation. The year-end valuation is recorded as a fixed asset in the balance sheet.

### 9.5.4 Methods used in practice

Straight-line depreciation is the most commonly used method in practice throughout Europe, particularly for buildings. Practice is not surveyed frequently, and Table 9.8 shows the most recently available widespread survey relating to the depreciation of plant and machinery. There seems to be no reason why the predominance of the straight-line method would have changed.

Table 9.8 **Depreciation of plant and machinery**

| | Bel | Den | Fra | Ger | Gre | Ire | Lux | Net | Swe | UK | Total |
|---|---|---|---|---|---|---|---|---|---|---|---|
| Sample size | 50 | 32 | 40 | 49 | 30 | 38 | 12 | 40 | 9 | 50 | 350 |
| Evidence of charge to the income statement for depreciation of plant and machinery | 45 | 32 | 32 | 46 | 30 | 33 | 11 | 32 | 9 | 47 | 317 |
| Basis for depreciation[a] Amortization | | | | | | | | | | | |
| Straight line | 30 | 29 | 28 | 36 | 30 | 29 | 11 | 30 | 9 | 47 | 279 |
| Reducing balance | 3 | 3 | 15 | 32 | – | 2 | 1 | – | – | – | 56 |
| Other | 4 | – | 1 | 6 | – | 2 | – | 2 | – | – | 15 |
| Other | – | 1 | 1 | 4 | – | – | – | – | – | – | 6 |
| Basis not disclosed | 8 | – | 2 | – | – | – | – | – | – | – | 10 |

[a] More than one answer possible.
*Source*: Adapted from FEE, *European Survey of Published Accounts 1991*, (London: Routledge, 1991).

Table 9.8 shows the importance of the reducing balance method for plant and machinery in Germany and France. This is due largely to the close connection of tax and accounting. In these countries the reducing balance method is allowed for both accounting and tax, but depreciation has to be charged as an accounting expense in order to be tax-deductible. Companies generally want to charge depreciation as fast as possible for tax purposes, and using a reducing balance achieves this faster than straight-line depreciation. This can even lead to inconsistent accounting policies over the life of an asset, as illustrated for Germany in the box below for 'moveable assets' (i.e. non-current assets other than land and buildings). This is an example of how tax policies can adversely affect financial reporting.

---

### Common German depreciation policy

**Property, plant and equipment:** They are stated at cost less scheduled depreciation over their estimated useful lives. Low-value assets are fully depreciated in the year of acquisition and are shown as disposals. . . .

Movable fixed assets are mostly depreciated by the declining balance method, with a change to straight-line depreciation when this results in higher depreciation amounts. Immovable fixed assets are predominantly depreciated using the straight-line method.

The weighted average periods of depreciation are as follows:

|                                              | 2008     | 2007     |
|----------------------------------------------|----------|----------|
| Buildings and structural installations       | 24 years | 23 years |
| Industrial plant and machinery               | 11       | 11       |
| Factory, office equipment and other facilities | 7      | 8        |

Write-downs are taken when an other than temporary impairment occurs and the carrying amount of an asset is not expected to be recoverable. Measurement of the write-down is based on the expected future cash flows from the use of the asset less costs for its removal. A write-down is made in the amount of the difference between the carrying amount and the discounted future cash flows.

*Source*: Extract from Annual Report of BASF, 2008 (parent company).

---

**Why it matters**  *Depreciation expenses are very much a matter of judgement. Preparers of financial statements may choose unreasonably rapid expensing (in order to reduce tax bills quickly) or unreasonably slow expensing (in order to make the assets and the profit look higher in early years). To take the example of unreasonably rapid expensing, this could make net assets significantly lower and, to start with, profits significantly lower. This would affect gearing and profit ratios, which might influence financial decisions.*

In principle, these points about France and Germany should not affect consolidated financial statements prepared under IFRS. If consolidated statements are irrelevant for tax purposes, and individual company financial statements are tax-driven and use national accounting regulations, there should be no influence by either one on the other. For example, in the consolidated IFRS statements of BASF, the company refers to a straight-line depreciation only, unlike the mixture reported in the box here. However, if both are prepared by the same set of accountants, based on the same underlying records, some influence of tax rules on IFRS practice may exist.

### 9.5.5 Practical difficulties

Assuming that depreciation is being calculated as an allocation of the historical cost of the asset, measurements or estimations will need to be made in the areas set out in this section.

#### Useful economic life

The causes of wearing out were mentioned earlier. IAS 16 gives some guidance on determining depreciable life (paragraph 57):

> The useful life of an asset is defined in terms of the asset's expected utility to the entity. The asset management policy of the entity may involve the disposal of assets after a specified time or after consumption of a certain proportion of the future economic benefits embodied in the asset. Therefore, the useful life of an asset may be shorter than its economic life.

This also makes it clear that 'useful life' relates to the use of the asset in the enterprise, not its total life, which may be longer.

The estimation of useful lives involves considerable judgement, which is likely to turn out to be wrong in any particular case. IAS 16 requires reviews of lives, followed by adjustments to depreciation to correct for errors in estimates. In practice, mis-estimation (or use of tax-based lives) often leads to the continued ownership and use by a business of fully depreciated assets. Strictly, the lack of any continued depreciation charge for them must mean that earlier charges were unfairly high and present charges (i.e. zero) are unfairly low.

Intangible assets generally wear out because of the passing of time rather than usage, so the word 'amortization' is used instead of depreciation. For certain intangible assets, the estimation of the life of an asset may be particularly difficult. Unless the intangible depends on a fixed-term legal right, it may be difficult to observe the wearing out of an intangible. Under most national laws a limit (e.g. 20 years) is often imposed. However, IAS 38 now requires (para 97) that the cost of an intangible asset with a finite useful life shall be allocated on a systematic basis over its useful life, but that (para 88) an intangible asset should be regarded as having an indefinite useful life when there is no foreseeable limit to the periods of expected future net cash flow generation. Note that indefinite is not the same as infinite. Intangible assets with an indefinite useful life (perhaps purchased brands for example) cannot, under IFRS, be depreciated. Instead, an impairment test, at least annually, is required (see Section 9.6 below).

As an example of the subjectivity inevitably involved, a typical accounting policy for research and development costs in 2010 is as follows.

> Research and development costs are expensed as they are incurred, except for certain development costs, which are capitalised when it is probable that a development project will generate future economic benefits, and certain criteria, including commercial and technical feasibility, have been met. Capitalised development costs, comprising direct

labour and related overhead, are amortised on a systematic basis over their expected useful lives between three and five years.

Capitalised development costs are subject to regular assessments of recoverability based on anticipated future revenues, including the impact of changes in technology. Unamortised capitalized development costs determined to be in excess of their recoverable amounts are expensed immediately.

### Residual value and disposal

As explained earlier for straight-line depreciation, if there is expected to be a residual value to an asset, the asset should gradually be written down to this rather than being written down to zero. That is, the *net* cost (i.e. cost less residual value) should be allocated over the useful life of the asset. In practice, estimates of residual value are difficult, and it is often assumed that there will be no residual value.

IAS 16 requires re-estimations of residual value at current prices, leading to the cessation of depreciation if price levels rise substantially, i.e. explicitly recognizing that the correctly calculated annual expense charge for depreciation could be zero.

### Mid-year purchases

What depreciation should be charged on an asset bought part way through an accounting year? There are two possibilities: either the appropriate proportion (perhaps by month) of one year's depreciation is charged in the years of acquisition and disposal, or a whole year's depreciation is charged for only those assets that are on hand at the end of the year. The first is theoretically preferable, but as long as the second method is used consistently, it should only lead to significant distortion when the business has few assets or has just acquired or disposed of a very valuable asset.

## 9.6 Impairment

As explained in the previous section, depreciation is designed to allocate the cost of a non-current (fixed) asset against income over the asset's life. However, negative events sometimes occur unexpectedly and these may make this systematic allocation inadequate. There is then a danger that the carrying value of the asset (usually the depreciated cost) may overstate what the asset is worth to the business or to anybody else.

**Activity 9.F**  What sort of events might happen to cause an impairment in the value of an asset below its depreciated cost?

**Feedback**  An asset may, for example, be physically damaged or may suffer rapid economic obsolescence.

European laws based on the EU Fourth Directive try to cope with this by requiring companies to take account of any 'permanent diminution in value' of a fixed asset. However, this is a vague concept and would tend to lead companies to have frequent diminutions in Germany (where they are tax-deductible) and rare diminutions in the UK (where they are not).

IAS 36 tries to impose standard practice in this area by providing a method of measuring the size of impairment. If there is any indication of impairment of an asset, the enterprise must compare the asset's carrying value with what it is worth to the business: its 'recoverable amount'. Normally, for a fixed asset, the recoverable amount is the future benefits from using it. These can be valued by discounting the expected future net cash flows. This 'value in use' or 'economic value' involves considerable estimation, as mentioned in Chapter 8. In practice, it may be impossible to make reasonable estimates for individual assets, and so impairment tests are carried out on groups of assets (called 'cash generating units') for which independent cash flows can be measured. The quotations in Section 9.5 both refer to this process of impairment.

One of the cash flows that will come from an asset is that from its eventual disposal. However, sometimes the asset is to be sold immediately, so that the recoverable amount is the expected net selling price, which is defined in much the same way as the net realizable value. Presumably, the enterprise will only sell a fixed asset if the expected net selling price exceeds the expected value in use.

Figure 9.5 summarizes the resulting valuation method for a non-current asset. On the left-hand branch is the usual carrying amount before any impairment: depreciated cost. Usually, this depreciated cost will end up being the balance sheet value because it is lower than the recoverable amount (on the right-hand branch), which is itself the higher of two values. Normally, a fixed asset is not to be sold immediately, and so the value in use is higher. Consequently, the rule usually boils down to: the lower of depreciated cost and value in use. Nevertheless, the net selling price may be easier to determine and, as long as it is above depreciated cost, there is no impairment required.

**Figure 9.5 Determining carrying values**

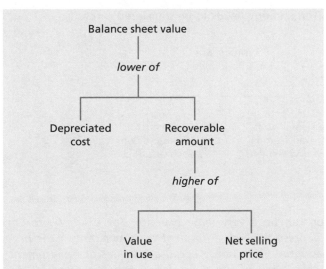

When there is an impairment, the difference between depreciated cost and the recoverable amount is an *impairment loss*, which is charged against income just as depreciation is.

Terminology

**Activity 9.G**  If you speak a Latin-based language (such as French, Spanish, Italian, Portuguese or Romanian), how would you translate the French term *dépréciation* into English? If you speak a Germanic language (such as German, Dutch or a Scandinavian language), how would you translate the German term *Abschreibung* into English?

**Feedback**  If you translated *dépréciation* as 'depreciation' or 'amortization', you would be making a common mistake. If you translated *Abschreibung* as 'depreciation', you would have missed half of its meaning. See the text below.

Having now examined depreciation and impairment, it is worth noting some potential international confusion in terminology. The English term 'depreciation' means the systematic allocation of cost over useful life, not 'loss of value'. The term 'amortization' has the same meaning, but tends to be used for intangible assets. By contrast, 'impairment' *is* about the loss of value.

The French term *amortissement* (and connected terms in other Latin languages) means depreciation/amortization. The '*mort*' part of the term refers to dying. However, the French term *dépréciation* does *not* mean depreciation but a loss of value or one-off write-down, of which an impairment is an example.

The German term *Abschreibung* (and connected terms in other Germanic languages) should not be translated as depreciation/amortization because it means any writing off of values, including both depreciation and impairment. The relationship between the terms is illustrated in Figure 9.6.

**Figure 9.6 Terminology needs to be translated carefully**

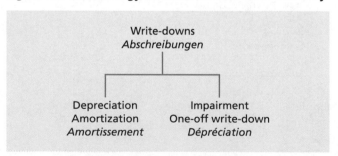

**Why it matters**  *Depreciation can be a very large expense. For example, for the Dutch company Heineken, depreciation was equivalent to 46 per cent of the pre-tax profits in 2002 (before it adopted IFRS), partly because it values at replacement cost. However, as usual, the calculation of the depreciation expense relies on estimates of life and*

*residual value. There are also choices about method. It would have been easy to re-estimate Heineken's depreciation upwards by 10 per cent, in which case its profit would have fallen by 5 per cent.*

## 9.7 Measurement based on revaluation

### 9.7.1 An alternative to cost

This chapter has been written in the context of majority practice with respect to the measurement of tangible and intangible assets: historical cost. However, Chapter 8 pointed out some disadvantages of this and some alternatives that might provide information of greater relevance.

The national accounting rules of several European countries, including the Netherlands, Denmark and the United Kingdom, allow revaluations above cost. In some countries, revaluations have occasionally been required by law; for example, in France in 1978, in Italy in 1991 and in Spain in 1996. Under the national rules of the United States and Germany, revaluation of tangible and intangible assets above cost is not allowed. Under IAS 16, both treatments are allowed (paras 29–31). There is similar permission in IAS 38 regarding some intangibles, provided certain conditions are fulfilled (paras 72–76).

In principle, the previous national practices of companies should not be relevant under IFRS. In practice, many national habits have been carried into IFRS, particularly the choice of options. For example, Dutch companies often revalued land and buildings before IFRS but German companies never did so. Under IFRS, German companies still use cost (or lower), whereas some Dutch companies revalue. ING, the Dutch bank, reports as follows in its 2008 statements:

**REAL ESTATE INVESTMENTS**
Real estate investments are stated at fair value at the balance sheet date. Changes in the carrying amount resulting from revaluations are recognised in the profit and loss account. On disposal the difference between the sale proceeds and book value is recognised in the profit and loss account.

**PROPERTY AND EQUIPMENT**
**Property in own use**
Land and buildings held for own use are stated at fair value at the balance sheet date. Increases in the carrying amount arising on revaluation of land and buildings held for own use are credited to the revaluation reserve in shareholders' equity. . . . Depreciation is recognised based on the fair value and the estimated useful life (in general 20–50 years). Depreciation is calculated on a straight-line basis.

The reason for allowing revaluation of various assets is that a current valuation probably provides more relevant information. However, the exact rationale is unclear, as can be illustrated by looking at three practical problems:

- where to put the revaluation gain;
- whether to depreciate revalued assets;
- how to measure the gain on sale.

### 9.7.2 Revaluation gains

Under IFRS requirements, the revaluation gains are not recorded in the income 'profit and loss' part of the income statement, perhaps because they are not 'realized' – although this concept is also unclear, as explained in Chapter 8. Instead, the gains are recorded as other comprehensive income (OCI) (see Chapters 6 and 8).

An example may be helpful. Suppose that a company buys land for €500,000 cash at the beginning of 20X7 and adopts the revaluation approach. By the end of 20X7, the fair value of the land is €800,000. The resulting effects on the financial statements will be worked out as in Figure 9.7.

### 9.7.3 Depreciation of revalued assets

Under IFRS requirements, the revaluation does not imply that any previous depreciation was unnecessary. In fact, an upwards valuation leads to the need to charge *more* depreciation because a more valuable asset is being worn out. This suggests that the revaluation is really being seen as an updating of the cost of the asset. This would also explain why the revaluation gain was not treated as income. However, perhaps the revaluation should then have been based on replacement cost rather than on fair value (see Section 8.3.3).

**Figure 9.7 Revaluation of land**

*Effects on balance sheet as at 31.12.20X7*

| Land: | Cost | +500,000 | Equity: Revaluation gain | +300,000 |
|---|---|---|---|---|
| | Revaluation | +300,000 | | |
| | Fair value | =800,000 | | |
| | Cash | −500,000 | | |

*Income statement for 20X7*

*Statement of changes in equity for 20X7*

| | Revaluation gain | +300,000 |
|---|---|---|

### 9.7.4 Gains on sale

Under IFRS requirements, the revalued amount of the asset is treated as its new cost. That is:

**Gain on sale = proceeds of sale – net book value**

To continue the example from before, suppose that the revalued land carried at €800,000 is sold in 20X8 for €600,000 cash, because the previous estimate of fair value was wrong or because the value has since fallen. The resulting effects on the financial statements are shown in Figure 9.8. Clearly, the land falls to zero in the balance sheet as it has been sold, and cash rises by €600,000. This means that a loss of €200,000 is recorded in the income statement. In conclusion, the land was bought for €500,000 and sold for €600,000, and the only gain ever recorded in income is a loss of €200,000!

This seems rather strange, because it is clear that there is a realized gain of €100,000 which never appears in income. The previously recorded revaluation gain of €300,000 was not recorded in income and is still not. A further conclusion is that the income statement is not a statement of realized gains and losses – and we are not sure what it is. This reinforces the need, mentioned in Chapter 8, to combine the income statement and OCI as 'comprehensive income'.

**Figure 9.8 Sale of revalued land**

| *Effects on balance sheet as at 31.12.20X8* | | | |
|---|---|---|---|
| Land: Book value | 800,000 −800,000 0 | Equity: Loss | −200,000 |
| Cash | +600,000 | | |
| *Income statement for 20X8* | | | |
| Loss | +200,000 | | |
| *Statement of changes in equity for 20X8* | | | |

### 9.7.5 A mix of values

It should be noted that there is an interesting mixture of valuation methods in this chapter, which could all end up in the same balance sheet for different assets:

- cost (for some land);
- revaluation, substituted for cost (for other land);
- depreciated cost (for most other fixed assets);
- depreciated revaluation (for some other fixed assets);
- value in use, i.e. discounted cash flows (for most impaired fixed assets);
- net selling price (for impaired fixed assets to be sold soon).

**Why it matters** *The various 'values' of fixed assets are added together on a balance sheet to show such totals as 'net assets' and 'total assets'. These are used to assess the company's position and its performance (see Chapter 7 and Part 3 of this book). If the 'values' are measured on several different bases, it is difficult to interpret the meaning of the totals.*

## 9.8 Investment properties

Under the national rules of most countries, properties held for rental or capital gain are treated in the same way as other properties. However, such 'investment properties' have been treated separately in the UK (under SSAP 19) and in a few other countries since the 1970s. These properties might be office blocks that the enterprise owns but does not occupy. The offices could be, for example, rented out under a five-year renewable contract.

The argument for a different treatment of such properties is that the really interesting fact about land and buildings in this category is their fair value, which can be determined with reasonable reliability because it depends upon the stream of rental income. It should be remembered that the objective for balance sheets is that they should be *relevant* and *reliable* (see Chapter 3). Since, in this case, the fair value is more relevant than cost and is reasonably reliable, it should be used in the balance sheet. Its use in the UK and elsewhere led to an option in IAS 40, *Investment Property*.

There are two further interesting features of the valuation option in IAS 40. First, since the properties are being held at fair value, the concept of depreciation makes no sense because depreciation is the allocation of cost. The revaluation at each balance sheet date takes account of the wearing-out that has occurred in the period. In effect, both depreciation and impairment are being subsumed into continual revaluations.

The second interesting feature of the valuation option in IAS 40 is that the gains and losses caused by constant revaluation are treated as part of the performance of the company and are taken to the 'profit and loss' part of the income statement.

It should be noted that there are therefore two major differences between the IAS 40 value option for investment property and the IAS 16 value option for other property. Under IAS 16, as explained earlier, properties can be revalued upwards but the gain does not go to income and the depreciation expense is still charged – indeed, charged at a higher level.

We can now add another valuation method to the list of those used under IFRS requirements for fixed assets, as shown earlier at the end of Section 9.7: investment properties can be valued at undepreciated revalued amounts even though they wear out, unlike land. This is a good illustration of the fact that conventional accounting under the IFRS regime and in any national system contains a 'mixed model' of costs and values. IFRS requires or allows more use of values than most systems, and it is moving further in that direction. The present position involves a mixture that is difficult to justify without knowing that we are on the move from one system to another and that we are trying to balance relevance against reliability.

## Summary

- This chapter concerns tangible fixed assets (property, plant and equipment) and intangible fixed assets. If such items meet the definition of 'asset', they should be recognized in the balance sheet if the benefits are probable and if the asset can be measured reliably. This cuts out goodwill, research, brands or customer lists if they were internally generated.

- If assets are bought individually or as part of a going concern, they should be recognized separately if possible.

- Assets do not have to be owned; control of the resources is what matters. Consequently, certain leased assets are treated as finance leases and capitalized. The present cut-off between finance and operating leases seems difficult to defend.

- The cost of assets with limited useful lives must be depreciated in a systematic and rational way against income over their lives. Depreciation is not designed as a technique for valuation or to help replacement or to calculate taxable income.

- Allocation methods include straight-line, reducing balance, sum of digits and usage. In practice, the straight-line method is the most common, except where reducing balance is used to accelerate tax deductions.

- There is considerable judgement needed in the estimation of useful lives and residual value.

- Sometimes assets suffer impairments of value that are not captured by systematic depreciation. When this occurs, the assets are usually written down to their value in use, based on discounted cash flows.

- Although most assets are valued at cost, revaluation is allowed in some countries and under the IFRS regime. The revaluations are treated as a new cost for the calculation of depreciation and any gain on sale.

- Investment properties can be treated on a valuation basis, with gains going to income and with no depreciation charges.

## References and research

This note refers to a few examples of English-language publications that are of relevance to the topics of this chapter. The IASB documents of greatest relevance are:

- IAS 16 (revised 2003), *Property, Plant and Equipment.*
- IAS 17 (revised 2003), *Leases.*
- IAS 36 (revised 2004), *Impairment of Assets.*
- IAS 38 (revised 2004), *Intangible Assets.*
- IAS 40 (2000), *Investment Property.*

Research on the issues of this chapter can be found in these articles:

- A. Burlaud, M. Messina and P. Walton, 'Depreciation: concepts and practices in France and the UK', *European Accounting Review*, Vol. 5, No. 2, 1996.
- S. Basu and G. Waymire, 'Has the importance of intangibles really grown? And if so, why?', *Accounting and Business Research*, Vol. 38, No. 3, 2008.
- L. Collins, 'Revaluation of assets in France: The interaction between professional practice, theory and political necessity', *European Accounting Review*, Vol. 3, No. 1, 1994.
- N. Garrod and I. Sieringhaus, 'European Union accounting harmonization: The case of leased assets in the United Kingdom and Germany', *European Accounting Review*, Vol. 4, No. 1, 1995.
- D.J. Skinner, 'Accounting for intangibles – a critical review of policy recommendations', *Accounting and Business Research*, Vol. 38, No. 3, 2008.

Because accounting for fixed assets is closely linked to tax rules in several countries, it will be helpful to look at a number of articles on the accounting–tax link in *European Accounting Review*, Vol. 5, Supplement, 1996.

## ? EXERCISES

*Feedback on the first two of these exercises is given in Appendix D.*

9.1 What are the essential criteria used to distinguish a fixed asset from other assets?

9.2 'What is relevant to investors is information about the future. Since this is not reliable, financial accountants give them irrelevant information instead.' Discuss.

9.3 Costa Co. uses three identical pieces of machinery in its factory. The cash price of these machines is €8,000 each and their estimated lives four years. These were all brought into use on the same date by the following means:

(a) machine 1 was rented from Brava Co. at a cost of €250 per month payable in advance and terminable at any time by either party;

(b) machine 2 was rented from Blanca Co. at a cost of eight half-yearly payments in advance at €1,500;

(c) machine 3 was rented from Sol Co. at a cost of six half-yearly payments in advance at €1,500.

Are the above machines rented by operating lease or by finance lease according to the current IASB rules?

9.4 For each of machines 1, 2 and 3 in Exercise 9.3, outline the effect on reported profits, and on the balance sheet, as included in the published financial statements.

9.5 'The idea of "substance over form" supports the recording of a finance lease as an asset, even though there is no legal ownership. This suggests that the idea of substance over form is a dangerous one.' Discuss.

9.6 Does research expenditure give rise to an asset? Explain your answer.

9.7 In Chapter 3 of this book, the following question was asked as Question 3.7:

> On 21 December 20X7, your client paid €10,000 for an advertising campaign. The advertisements will be heard on local radio stations between 1 January and 31 January 20X8. Your client believes that, as a result, sales will increase by 60 per cent in 20X8 (over 20X7 levels) and by 40 per cent in 20X9 (over 20X7 levels). There will be no further benefits.
>
> Write a memorandum to your client explaining your views on how this item should be treated in the year-end financial statements for the three years. Your answer should include explicit reference to relevant traditional accounting conventions, and to the requirements of users of published financial statements.

Now that we have investigated the relevant issues in more detail, what is your opinion of the answer? If you remember how you answered before, you may like to compare your answers.

9.8 A company borrows money at 10 per cent interest in order to finance the building of a new factory. Suggest arguments for and against the proposition that the interest costs should be capitalized and regarded as part of the 'cost' of the factory. Which set of arguments do you prefer?

9.9 Provide in your own words:

(a) an explanation of what depreciation is;

(b) an explanation of the net book value (NBV) of a partially depreciated fixed asset.

9.10 The payments set out in Table 9.9 have been made during the year in relation to a fixed asset bought at the beginning of the year:

Table 9.9 **Example fixed asset payments**

| Item | € | € |
|---|---|---|
| Cost as in supplier's list | 12,000 | |
| *Less* agreed discount | 1,000 | |
| | | 11,000 |
| Delivery charge | | 100 |
| Erection charge | | 200 |
| Maintenance charge | | 400 |
| Additional component to increase capacity | | 500 |
| Replacement parts | | 600 |

What cost figure should be used as the basis for the depreciation charge for the year, and why?

9.11 Outline three different depreciation methods, and appraise them in the context of the definition and objectives of depreciation.

9.12 The following actual and estimated figures are available:

| | |
|---|---|
| Cost | €12,000 |
| Useful life | 4 years |
| Scrap value | €2,000 |

Based on these figures, evaluate the following:

(a) Calculate annual depreciation under the straight-line method.

(b) Calculate the depreciation charge for each of the four years under the reducing balance method using a depreciation percentage of 40 per cent.

(c) If the estimated scrap value turns out to be correct and the asset is sold on the first day of year 5, list and contrast the effect on reported profit for each of the five years under each method.

9.13 Is depreciation either too subjective, or too arbitrary, to be useful?

# Chapter 10

# Inventories

**Contents**

| | | |
|---|---|---:|
| 10.1 | Introduction | 194 |
| 10.2 | Counting inventory | 196 |
| | 10.2.1 Periodic counts | 196 |
| | 10.2.2 Perpetual inventory | 196 |
| 10.3 | Valuation of inventory at historical cost | 197 |
| 10.4 | Inventory flow | 198 |
| | 10.4.1 Unit cost | 198 |
| | 10.4.2 First in, first out (FIFO) | 199 |
| | 10.4.3 Last in, first out (LIFO) | 200 |
| | 10.4.4 Weighted average | 200 |
| | 10.4.5 Base inventory | 201 |
| 10.5 | Other cost methods | 203 |
| | 10.5.1 Standard cost | 203 |
| | 10.5.2 Retail inventory and gross profit margin | 203 |
| 10.6 | Valuation of inventory using output values | 204 |
| 10.7 | Practice | 204 |
| 10.8 | Current replacement cost | 206 |
| 10.9 | Construction contracts | 206 |
| | 10.9.1 A worked example | 206 |
| 10.10 | Construction contracts in practice | 209 |
| | Summary | 211 |
| | References and research | 211 |
| | Exercises | 211 |

**Objectives**

After studying this chapter carefully, you should be able to:

- explain the nature of inventory, and outline methods of its physical quantification;

- define, calculate and appraise a variety of methods of valuing inventory under historical cost;

- outline regulatory requirements for inventory valuation;

- outline output value methods for inventory valuation;

- outline the problems of evaluating long-term construction contracts, and describe, simply illustrate and appraise the completed contract and percentage of completion methods of their evaluation.

## 10.1 Introduction

This chapter considers issues relating to the counting and valuation of inventories. Inventories are current assets, tangible in nature, that are, or will become, part of the product to be sold by an enterprise. As discussed in Part 1 of this book, conventional accounting is generally based on the recording of transactions and on revenue and expense calculation, rather than on valuations. Consequently, when calculating the depreciation of assets as analysed in the previous chapter, greater attention is paid to the meaning of the depreciation charge in the income statement than to the resulting effects on the written-down value of the depreciated asset in the balance sheet. The written-down value of a non-current asset is not supposed to represent the sale value of the asset at the balance sheet date.

Like depreciation, the valuation of inventory also directly affects the income statement and the balance sheet. As a current asset, and consistent also with the IASB emphasis on asset/liability definition and measurement rather than on expense/revenue, balance sheet considerations for inventory are important in their own right. Inventory valuation also affects the apparent liquidity of the company, the figure for inventory being included in a number of the ratios discussed in Chapter 7.

The valuation of inventory on hand at the end of an accounting period directly affects the profit figure. For example, for a retail company with no opening inventory, the gross profit, i.e. the margin on sales before charging operating expenses, might be:

|   | | |
|---|---|--:|
|   | Sales for the period | 1,000 |
| − | Purchases for the period | −800 |
| + | Closing inventory at the end of period | +50 |
| = | Gross profit | = 250 |

This can be rearranged as:

| | | |
|---|--:|--:|
| Sales for the period | | 1,000 |
| Purchases | (800) | |
| Closing inventory | 50 | |
| Cost of sales | | (750) |
| Gross profit | | 250 |

Purchases of materials in the period are all treated initially as expenses in this example. However, the materials are not all used up in the accounting period; so, in order to take account of the existence of closing inventory, it is necessary to make an adjustment that reduces the expenses. Although the total profit of all accounting periods is not affected by the valuation of inventory (because one year's closing inventory is the next year's opening inventory), the profit of any individual year *is* affected.

Since the concern is with finding a fair figure for profit for the year, there must be an attempt to match the charge for inventory used against the sales that relate to it. There are many ways of valuing the remaining inventory, some of which cause fairer charges for the inventory used than others. Any overvaluation of closing inventory by 1 euro leads to an overstatement of profit by 1 euro in the year in question. However, this would also make next year's opening inventory too large, and therefore next year's profit too small.

Table 10.1 gives summarized gross profit calculations for two years for the same enterprise.

Table 10.1 **Gross profit calculations**

|  | Year 1 |  | Year 2 |  |
|---|---|---|---|---|
| Sales (revenue) |  | 2,000 |  | 3,000 |
| Opening inventory | 800 |  | 950 |  |
| Purchases | 1,600 |  | 2,100 |  |
|  | 2,400 |  | 3,050 |  |
| less Closing inventory | 950 |  | 1,150 |  |
| Cost of sales (expense) |  | 1,450 |  | 1,900 |
| Gross profit |  | 550 |  | 1,100 |

After the end of year 2, it is discovered that an error was made in the inventory valuation at the end of year 1, and the figure of 950 is revised to 850. Redraft Table 10.1 and comment on the results.

The revised figures should be as shown in Table 10.2.

Table 10.2 **Revised gross profit calculations**

|  | Year 1 |  | Year 2 |  |
|---|---|---|---|---|
| Sales (revenue) |  | 2,000 |  | 3,000 |
| Opening inventory | 800 |  | 850 |  |
| Purchases | 1,600 |  | 2,100 |  |
|  | 2,400 |  | 2,950 |  |
| less Closing inventory | 850 |  | 1,150 |  |
| Cost of sales (expense) |  | 1,550 |  | 1,800 |
| Gross profit |  | 450 |  | 1,200 |

This demonstrates that the total result over the two years, i.e. 1,650 gross profit, is the same, whatever figure for year 1 closing inventory is used.

*Why it matters* *Activity 10.A does not imply that inventory valuation is unimportant. It affects ratios and interpretation of the year 1 position and results, as already stated. Furthermore, it affects the apparent trend of performance over the years. Table 10.1 suggested that gross profit had doubled between the years; Table 10.2 shows that it nearly trebled.*

Inventory is usually split into categories, typically:

- raw materials;
- work-in-progress;
- finished goods.

Table 10.3 **Comparative usage of 'stock'**

| United States | United Kingdom |
| --- | --- |
| Inventory | Stock |
| Work-in-process | Work-in-progress |
| Stock | Shares |
| Common stock | Ordinary shares |

A manufacturing business may have all three types, whereas a retail business may have only the last in the list.

A language point is worth making here. The word 'inventory' is used in North America and some other English-speaking areas of the world. It is also the word found in IASB statements. It is used in many translated annual reports of continental European companies, which tend to use a mid-Atlantic version of English. However, in law and standards in the United Kingdom and Ireland and some other English-speaking countries, the word 'stock' is used instead. This can lead to particular confusion, because 'stock' in US terminology means 'share'. A short comparative glossary for this point is shown as Table 10.3.

## 10.2 Counting inventory

Before *valuing* an inventory it is necessary to know how much there is. It is also useful to know what type of inventories there are. Consider a simple case where a business owns finished goods only, because it runs a wholesale warehouse. There are several ways of estimating the quantity of inventory on hand at a year end, and two of them are considered in this section.

### 10.2.1 Periodic counts

With *periodic counting*, warehouse staff, perhaps assisted by administrative staff, physically count and record all items of inventory on the premises. The auditors will probably wish to advise on procedures, attend the count and check the results for a few types of inventory. Adjustments have to be made for goods on the premises that do not belong to the firm and for goods off the premises that do. Also, there will be adjustments for inventory movements if the actual count is done on a day that is not the accounting year end, perhaps because a weekend is more convenient.

### 10.2.2 Perpetual inventory

When using the *perpetual inventory* method, a record is kept item by item of all inventory movements as they occur. Therefore, a figure for the amount of inventory of each type on hand at any moment should be easy to calculate. This is supplemented by occasional counts of selected items to see whether the inventory records are accurate. This avoids a massive and disruptive effort at the year end.

In practice, many inventory control systems are run by computers, which record sales and purchases and produce invoices and lists of debtors. They can also report current inventory figures, slow-moving lines, re-order possibilities, and so on. The running of a perpetual inventory is much easier in these circumstances.

Comparing these two methods, it is clear that perpetual inventory will discover pilferage more quickly and help in signalling that a re-order of inventory is necessary. Note that the periodic count gives a figure for usage during the year by residual, which obscures any pilferage and breakages. On the other hand, the perpetual inventory method counts up usage during the year but leaves closing inventory as a residual figure. The physical figures must always be those used for profit measurements, if available. The accounting records must be adjusted to the actual physical inventory in cases of discrepancy.

## 10.3 Valuation of inventory at historical cost

Like any other asset, inventory can in principle be valued either on an input value basis or an output value basis, as outlined in Chapter 8. The most common basis for the valuation of inventory is the input basis of historical cost, which we consider first. Once an entity has established the quantity of inventory, the key problem is how to evaluate the 'cost' of an item at each and every stage in the production process, how to determine the cost of items sold, and, therefore, the cost of items not yet sold (i.e. still in inventory). The first major difficulty is the appropriate allocation of overhead costs (i.e. indirect costs) to particular items or products. The principle is that the cost of inventories should comprise all costs of purchase, costs of conversion and other costs incurred in bringing the inventories to their present location and condition.

There are practical problems here. The inclusion of 'direct' items should present no difficulties, because figures can be related to particular inventory 'directly' by definition. But overhead allocation necessarily introduces assumptions and approximations: decisions have to be made about which overheads are 'attributable' to the present condition and location of an item of inventory. So, for any item of inventory that is not still in its original purchased state, it is a problem to determine the cost of a unit, or even of a batch. Methods in common use include job, process, batch and standard costing. For financial accounting purposes, cost should include the appropriate proportion of production overheads (as illustrated below). Other overheads (e.g. administration and selling) should *not* be included, according to the relevant International Accounting Standard (IAS 2), but may be included in some national systems.

Let us look at a simple example of overhead absorption:

| | | |
|---|---|---|
| Direct cost: | Labour | €3 per unit |
| | Materials | €2 per unit |
| Direct manufacturing overheads (specific supervisors and machines) | | €40,000 |
| Indirect manufacturing overheads (rent, factory managers, etc.) | | €60,000 |
| Administrative overheads of the rest of the company | | €80,000 |
| Selling overheads | | €20,000 |

If the year's production were 20,000 units and this type of production used one-third of the factory, the cost per unit for goods that had fully passed through production would be €8; that is:

| Direct costs | €5 | |
|---|---|---|
| Direct manufacturing overheads | €2 | (i.e. €40,000 ÷ 20,000) |
| Indirect manufacturing overheads | €1 | (i.e. €60,000 × one-third ÷ 20,000) |
| Other overheads | nil | |
| Total | €8 | |

This 'cost' of €8 is used for financial accounting purposes. For management accounting, other methods of calculating costs might be used, e.g. concentrating on direct costs only, or including all overheads. Activity-based costing (ABC) does not alter the principle of this issue concerning treatment of overheads, but it will tend to lead to a higher proportion of direct overheads and a lower proportion of indirect ones.

## 10.4 Inventory flow

A difficulty will arise when we have to determine the cost of particular remaining or sold units, when several identical items have been purchased or made at different times and therefore at different unit costs.

Consider the following transactions:

| Purchases: | January | 10 units at €25 each |
|---|---|---|
| | February | 15 units at €30 each |
| | April | 20 units at €35 each |
| Sales: | March | 15 units at €50 each |
| | May | 18 units at €60 each |

How do we calculate inventory, cost of sales, and gross profit? There are several ways of doing this, based on different assumptions as to which unit has been sold, or which unit is deemed to have been sold. Five possibilities are discussed below: unit cost, first in first out, last in first out, weighted average and base inventory.

### 10.4.1 Unit cost

Here, we can identify the actual physical units that have moved in or out. Each unit must be individually distinguishable, e.g. by serial number. In these circumstances – acknowledged as impractical in many cases – we simply add up the recorded costs of those units sold to give cost of sales, and of those units left to give inventory. This needs no detailed illustration. However, there are two problems with valuing using this assumption. First, many costs are overhead costs; that is, the costs are incurred for the processing of not only all these units but perhaps other types of units as well, and they are therefore difficult to allocate to individual types of inventory let alone to individual units. Second, reported profit can be manipulated by choosing which out of several similar units will be sold; if it were wished to defer some profit until next year, the most expensive units (perhaps the most recently produced ones) should be sold.

### 10.4.2 First in, first out (FIFO)

As implied in Section 10.4.1 above, in many cases it is inconvenient or impossible to identify the units being sold, and so some assumption is necessary. Under FIFO, it is assumed that the units moving out are the ones that have been in the longest (i.e. came in first). The units remaining will therefore be regarded as representing the latest units purchased.

**Activity 10.B**   Calculate the cost of sales and gross profit, based on a FIFO inventory cost assumption, from the data given at the start of Section 10.4 concerning purchases and sales from January to May. Assume that a perpetual inventory system is used, i.e. with continuous recalculation.

**Feedback**   Table 10.4 **Calculating cost of sales (FIFO method)**

| | | Inventory quantity | | Value | Cost of sales |
|---|---|---|---|---|---|
| January | + | 10 at €25 | = + | €250 | |
| February | + | 15 at €30 | = + | 450 | |
| February end total | | 25 | | 700 | |
| March | – | 10 at €25 (Jan.) | = – | 250 | |
| | – | 5 at €30 (Feb.) | = – | 150 | 400 |
| March end total | | 10 at €30 | = + | 300 | |
| April | + | 20 at €35 | = + | 700 | |
| April end total | | 30 | | 1,000 | |
| May | – | 10 at €30 (Feb.) | = – | 300 | |
| | – | 8 at €35 (Apr.) | = – | 280 | 580 |
| May end total | | 12 at €35 | | 420 | |
| | | | | | €980 |

The cost of sales (see Table 10.4) = €980. The value of sales is €750 + €1,080 = €1,830. Purchases amounts to € (250 + 450 + 700) = €1,400. This gives:

| | | |
|---|---|---|
| Sales | | €1,830 |
| Purchases | €1,400 | |
| Closing inventory | €420 | |
| Cost of sales | | €980 |
| Gross profit | | €850 |

**Feedback**   January purchase of base inventory 10 at €25 = €250.

**Table 10.7 Calculating the cost of sales (FIFO method) after base inventory**

|  | Inventory quantity |  | Value |  | Cost of sales |
|---|---|---|---|---|---|
| February | + | 15 at €30 | = + | €450 |  |
| March | – | 15 at €30 | = – | 450 | 450 |
| March end total |  | 0 |  | 0 |  |
| April | + | 20 at €35 | = + | 700 |  |
| April end total |  | 20 | = | 700 |  |
| May | – | 18 at €35 | = – | 630 | 630 |
| May end total |  | 2 at €35 | = + | 70 |  |
|  |  |  |  |  | €1,080 |

This gives:

| | | |
|---|---|---|
| Sales | | 1,830 |
| Purchases | 1,150 | |
| Closing inventory | 70 | |
| Cost of sales (Table 10.7) | | 1,080 |
| Gross profit | | €750 |

*Why it matters*   The summarized income statements, and closing inventory figures, from Activities 10.B to 10.E are given in columnar form in Table 10.8.

**Table 10.8 Summarized results of Activities 10.B to 10.E**

|  | FIFO € |  | LIFO € |  | Wt.av. € |  | Base inventory € |
|---|---|---|---|---|---|---|---|
| Sales |  | 1,830 |  | 1,830 |  | 1,830 |  | 1,830 |
| Purchases | 1,400 |  | 1,400 |  | 1,400 |  | 1,150 |  |
| Closing inventory | 420 |  | 320 |  | 392 |  | 70 |  |
| Cost of sales |  | 980 |  | 1,080 |  | 1,008 |  | 1,080 |
| Gross profit |  | 850 |  | 750 |  | 822 |  | 750 |

As can be seen from Table 10.8, the reported gross profit in our example firm, and therefore obviously the net profit, differs according to the cost assumption policy that has been chosen. The closing inventory figure (including both parts in the case of the base inventory method) also varies by a corresponding amount. These differences directly affect the reported impression of the year's activities. They also affect a number of ratios discussed in Chapter 7 and in Part 3.

It is important to remember that these differences arise solely because of changes in the accounting assumptions, and they do not reflect any differences in the underlying reality. All of these possible results are derived by a strict application of the historical cost principle.

*It should also be remembered, however, that last year's closing inventory is this year's opening inventory. In the second year, it is the difference between the opening inventory of year 2 and the closing inventory of year 2 that is deducted from sales to affect the gross profit. Consistent differences between differently calculated inventory figures will cancel out when year-end balance sheet figures are being compared.*

| Activity 10.F | The most commonly considered inventory cost assumptions are the FIFO, LIFO and weighted average methods. Which seems preferable? |
|---|---|

| Feedback | Inevitably, the response to this question is influenced by the chosen criteria. One rational criterion would be the suggestion that up-to-date historical costs are better than out-of-date historical costs. From a profit calculation perspective, LIFO matches more recent costs against current revenue levels, whereas FIFO matches older costs against current revenue levels. This sounds like an argument in favour of LIFO. From a balance sheet perspective, however, FIFO tends to leave the latest historical cost figures in the balance sheet, i.e. the closing inventory is more likely to be based on historical costs dated close to the balance sheet date under FIFO than under other methods. This sounds like an argument for FIFO. |
|---|---|

Weighted average is essentially a compromise between FIFO and LIFO. It is therefore less 'better' in one sense, and less 'worse' in another.

An alternative criterion might be the prudence convention. One might wish to argue that the preferred basis is that which gives a more conservative outcome. In times of rising cost levels, this would generally suggest LIFO, as Table 10.8 demonstrates, whereas in times of falling cost levels it would suggest the use of FIFO. As earlier chapters have indicated, different countries have traditionally had different views on the relative importance of matching and prudence. Of course, if tax bills are based on the method chosen for financial reporting, then LIFO would be preferred if prices are rising.

## 10.5 Other cost methods

### 10.5.1 Standard cost

For the purposes of cost accounting, a business may have established a series of standard costs for its inventories at various levels of completion. These costs may be used for inventory valuation. Further reference to standard costs is left to books on cost accounting.

### 10.5.2 Retail inventory and gross profit margin

These methods are used to overcome the practical problems in large shops of counting and valuing great numbers of different items. By using these methods, the inventory is counted on a periodic rather than a perpetual basis, and its value at selling prices is worked out. To find a value using any of the other methods discussed so far would be extremely difficult. Clearly, though, to value inventory at selling prices would be to take profit before sale. In order to avoid this, ratios of cost to price are worked out item by item or class by class; and these are applied to the inventories to reduce them to cost. Since current prices and current costs will be used, there will be a result similar to FIFO. This is called the *retail inventory method*.

An alternative method uses a gross profit margin, which is worked out using experience of prior years. Here, the valuation is even quicker, because the inventory cost is worked out by taking the goods bought *plus* opening inventory at cost, *less* the goods sold at selling price reduced to cost by application of the gross profit margin. So, no count is made. Consequently, this method should only be used as a check on other methods or when no other method is possible (e.g. to value inventory destroyed in a warehouse fire).

## 10.6 Valuation of inventory using output values

The use of output values would rely on the proposition that the value of the inventory to the firm is the future receipts that will arise from it. There are several ways that this output value could be measured:

1. *Discounted money receipts* can be used when there is a definite amount and time of receipt. This will seldom be the case except for contracts of supply.
2. *Current selling prices* may be used when there is a definite price and no significant selling costs or delays. For example, inventories of gold may be valued in this way.
3. *Net realizable value* is the estimated current selling price in the ordinary course of business, less costs of completion and less costs to be incurred in marketing, distributing and selling but without deduction for general administration or profit.

There seem to be grounds for using net realizable value when sales prices and other costs are known, particularly for inventories in an advanced state of completion. It can be argued that, if 90 per cent of the work has been done, then to take all the profit before sale is better ('fairer') than taking none. However, conventional accounting is not disposed towards a consistent use of this valuation method, because profit would then be taken before the inventory was sold.

## 10.7 Practice

The usual policy followed for the valuation of inventory is to measure it at the lower of historical cost and net realizable value. Cost, as discussed earlier, comprises all costs necessarily incurred in bringing the inventories to their present location and condition. Net realizable value is the estimated selling price in the ordinary course of business, less any estimated costs of completion and estimated costs necessary to make the sale.

IAS 2, *Inventories*, was revised with effect for accounting periods beginning on or after 1 January 2005. An earlier restrictive statement that it 'applied to inventories measured on the historical cost basis' was removed. However, the revised version continues to require that inventories are recorded at the lower of cost and net realizable value on an item-by-item basis. So, for each separate item we need to determine both cost, under one of the methods discussed earlier, and net realizable value as defined above. The EU Fourth Directive requires the same, and therefore so do laws in countries within the European Union.

The significance of the 'separate items' point should be noted. Suppose there are three products, A, B and C, with values as shown in Table 10.9. The value for inventory in the accounts is €30, not the lower of €33 and €36. This is, of course, a classic example of the prudence convention.

Table 10.9 **Lower of cost and net realizable value (NRV)**

| Product | Cost (€) | NRV (€) | Lower (€) |
|---------|----------|---------|-----------|
| A | 10 | 12 | 10 |
| B | 11 | 15 | 11 |
| C | 12 | 9 | 9 |
| Total | 33 | 36 | 30 |

There has been considerable debate over the last two decades or so as to whether restrictions should be placed on the choice of the inventory cost assumption method made by enterprises. The EU Fourth Directive allows 'weighted average prices, the first in first out (FIFO) method, the last in first out (LIFO) method, or some similar method'. IAS 2 (as revised in 1993) had its 'benchmark' requirement, where specific identification is not applicable, as 'by using the first in first out or weighted average cost formulas' but accepted LIFO as an 'allowed alternative'. However, the latest version of IAS 2 forbids the use of LIFO and explicitly permits, where specific identification is not applicable, only the FIFO or weighted average cost formulae (para 25).

LIFO is not usually allowed under the national rules of several countries (e.g. France and the United Kingdom), but is allowed (and found) in Germany, Italy and the Netherlands, for example. Moreover, it is a common method in the United States. This is because it is allowed for tax purposes there and, as noted earlier, tends to show lower profits than FIFO or weighted average.

A typical policy for inventory valuation for 2010 is shown below. Notice the vagueness of the word 'appropriate'.

Inventories are stated at the lower of cost or net realisable value. Cost is determined on a first in first out (FIFO) basis. Net realisable value is the amount that can be realised from the sale of the inventory in the normal course of business after allowing for the costs of realisation.

In addition to the cost of materials and direct labour, an appropriate proportion of production overheads is included in the inventory values.

An allowance is recorded for excess inventory and obsolescence based on the lower of cost and net realisable value.

## 10.8 Current replacement cost

Historical cost is undoubtedly the most often used type of input valuation basis. However, an alternative possibility is to use the current input cost, rather than the historical input cost, for inventory and cost-of-sales purposes. This has the theoretical advantage of using up-to-date cost levels both in closing inventory and in cost of sales (and therefore in calculating gross profit). However, the use of current input costs – often known as current replacement cost accounting – raises its own difficulties in both theoretical and practical terms. The whole question of current replacement cost accounting is discussed in Chapter 16.

## 10.9 Construction contracts

It is in the nature of construction contracts that they last over a long period of time – often over more than one accounting period. The issue of determining the *total* profit on such a contract raises no new accounting problems beyond those discussed above in relation to inventory. However, there is one important and difficult additional issue.

This is the question of allocation of the total profit over the various accounting periods during which the construction takes place. If a contract extends over, say, three years, should the contribution to profits be 0 per cent, 0 per cent and 100 per cent respectively for the three years? Can we make profits on something before we have finished it? The realization convention (see Chapter 8) might seem to argue against doing so, and the prudence convention would certainly argue against it too. But what would give a 'fair presentation' of the results for each period? All the various users want regular information on business progress. Can we not argue that we can be 'reasonably certain', during the contract, of at least *some* profit – and if we can, then surely the matching principle is more important than slavishness to prudence.

Two alternative approaches have emerged over the years. These are the completed contract method, which delays profit recognition until the end, and the percentage of completion method, which in defined conditions requires allocation over the accounting periods concerned. The effects of these two methods are best shown by a comparative example.

### 10.9.1 A worked example

The data set out in Table 10.10 pertain to a long-term construction contract with a sales value of €2,000,000. From the figures, we must first compute the gross profit recorded under the percentage of completion method, assuming for simplicity that the degree of completion is determined based on costs incurred, and show the necessary accounting entries.

In doing so, we find that, at the end of the first year, the total expected profit, being total revenue minus total expected costs, is €2,000,000 – (€500,000 + €1,000,000) = €500,000. This expected profit is allocated over the three years as shown below, in proportion to the costs of each year.

Table 10.10 **Construction contract example: initial data**

|  | 20X1 | 20X2 | 20X3 |
|---|---|---|---|
| Costs incurred during the year | €500,000 | €700,000 | €300,000 |
| Year-ended estimated costs to complete | 1,000,000 | 300,000 | – |
| Billing during the year | 400,000 | 700,000 | 900,000 |
| Collections during the year | 200,000 | 500,000 | 1,200,000 |

The entries for both the completed contract method and the percentage of completion method for the three years are as set out in Table 10.11.

Table 10.11 **Profit allocation by comparative methods**

|  | Completed contract | | Percentage of completion | |
|---|---|---|---|---|
| **20X1** | | | | |
| Construction in progress | €500,000 | | €500,000 | |
| Cash or creditor | | €500,000 | | €500,000 |
| Accounts receivable | 400,000 | | 400,000 | |
| Advance billings | | 400,000 | | 400,000 |
| Cash | 200,000 | | 200,000 | |
| Accounts receivable | | 200,000 | | 200,000 |
| Construction in progress | no entry | | 166,667 | |
| Gross profit | | | | 166,667 |
| **20X2** | | | | |
| Construction in progress | €700,000 | | €700,000 | |
| Cash or liability | | €700,000 | | €700,000 |
| Accounts receivable | 700,000 | | 700,000 | |
| Advance billings | | 700,000 | | 700,000 |
| Cash | 500,000 | | 500,000 | |
| Accounts receivable | | 500,000 | | 500,000 |
| Construction in progress | no entry | | 233,333 | |
| Gross profit | | | | 233,333 |
| **20X3** | | | | |
| Construction in progress | €300,000 | | €300,000 | |
| Cash or liability | | €300,000 | | €300,000 |
| Accounts receivable | 900,000 | | 900,000 | |
| Advance billings | | 900,000 | | 900,000 |
| Cash | 1,200,000 | | 1,200,000 | |
| Accounts receivable | | 1,200,000 | | 1,200,000 |
| Construction in progress | no entry | | 100,000 | |
| Gross profit | | | | 100,000 |
| Advance billings | 2,000,000 | | 2,000,000 | |
| Construction in progress | | 1,500,000 | | 2,000,000 |
| Gross profit | | 500,000 | | – |

20X1: $\frac{€500,000}{€1,500,000} \times €500,000 = €166,667$

20X2: $\frac{€700,000}{€1,500,000} \times €500,000 = €233,333$

20X3: $\frac{€300,000}{€1,500,000} \times €500,000 = €100,000$

Total gross profit €500,000

At the end of each year during which the contract is in progress, the excess of the Construction in progress account over the Advance billings account is presented as a current asset. Ignoring the cash and accounts receivable figures, this leads to the figures shown in Table 10.12.

Table 10.12 **Summarized results for completed contract method and percentage of completion method**

| Year | Completed contract method | Percentage of completion method |
|---|---|---|
| *20X1* | | |
| Construction in progress | 500,000 | 666,667 |
| Advance billings | 400,000 | 400,000 |
| Net current asset | 100,000 | 266,667 |
| Reported profit for year | 0 | 166,667 |
| | | |
| *20X2* | | |
| Construction in progress | 1,200,000 | 1,600,000 |
| Advance billings | 1,100,000 | 1,100,000 |
| Net current asset | 100,000 | 500,000 |
| Reported profit for year | 0 | 233,333 |
| | | |
| *20X3* | | |
| Reported profit for year | 500,000 | 100,000 |

In the above example, the estimated gross profit of €500,000 was the actual gross profit on the contract. If changes in the estimated cost to complete the contract had been appropriate at the end of 20X1 and/or 20X2, or if the actual costs to complete had been determined to be different when the contract was completed in 20X3, those changes would have been incorporated into revised estimates during the contract period.

The presentation of this example has focused on the profit calculation. Inspection of Table 10.12 makes it clear that the difference in the resulting net current asset figure under the two methods is equal to the difference in the cumulative reported profit under the two methods (e.g. €400,000 in 20X2) – as, of course, it must be if the balance sheet is to balance.

Under the IASB emphasis on balance sheet (asset and liability) definition and measurement in its Framework, discussed in Chapter 3, this current asset figure requires active consideration. Is the reported current asset amount of €500,000 at the end of 20X2 under the percentage of completion method justified? Is it valid from a creditor perspective? Can it be reliably regarded as a resource with future economic benefits? These can be difficult questions in some circumstances, and it perhaps should not always be assumed, at least in the case of long-term construction contracts, that revenue/expense considerations and asset/liability considerations will lead to the same reported results.

Why it matters *The choice between completed contract and percentage of completion methods matters, in essence, for the same reasons that the validity of current inventory figures matters. That is, there is a direct effect on reported periodic earnings, and therefore on the trend of performance over the years, and also a direct effect on balance sheet figures, on balance sheet relativities, and on a variety of commonly calculated ratios. With long-term contracts, the choice may be very significant, because of possible large numerical differences and greater uncertainties arising from extended time periods.*

## 10.10 Construction contracts in practice

The EU Fourth Directive allows both the completed contract method and the percentage of completion method. Different countries tend to use this flexibility in particular ways. Table 10.13 illustrates that, at the national level in Europe, the completed contract method has historically tended to dominate in more prudent Germany, whereas the percentage of completion method has been normal in the Netherlands and the United Kingdom.

IAS 11 requires the percentage of completion method, once the construction activity is sufficiently advanced for the outcome of the contract to be 'estimated reliably'. IAS 11 specifies the processes required in considerable detail. International practice is gradually moving further in this direction, but it does not follow from this that local practices in those countries with a tradition of using the completed contract method are necessarily changing.

The four essential conditions for revenue recognition under the percentage of completion method are set out in IAS 11, for a fixed price contract, as follows:

(a) total contract revenue can be measured reliably, and
(b) it is probable that the economic benefits associated with the contract will flow to the enterprise, and
(c) both the contract costs to complete the contract and the stage of contract completion at the balance sheet date can be measured reliably, and
(d) the contract costs attributable to the contract can be clearly identified and measured reliably so that actual contract costs incurred can be compared with prior estimates.

Table 10.13 **Valuation basis of long-term contracts**

| | Bel | Den | Fra | Ger | Ire | Net | UK | Total |
|---|---|---|---|---|---|---|---|---|
| Sample size | 50 | 32 | 40 | 49 | 38 | 40 | 50 | 299 |
| Evidence of long-term contracts | 12 | 9 | 6 | 7 | 2 | 9 | 11 | 56 |
| Valuation basis used for long-term contracts: | | | | | | | | |
| Completed contract method | 1 | 3 | 3 | 6 | – | 1 | 2 | 16 |
| Percentage of completion method | 4 | 5 | 2 | – | 1 | 5 | 7 | 24 |
| Both | – | – | 1 | – | – | 1 | – | 2 |
| Other | 1 | – | – | – | – | 1 | – | 2 |
| Valuation basis not disclosed | 6 | 1 | – | 1 | 1 | 1 | 2 | 12 |

*Source*: Adapted from FEE, *European Survey of Published Accounts 1991*, (London: Routledge, 1991).

Figure 10.1 **Inventory valuation**

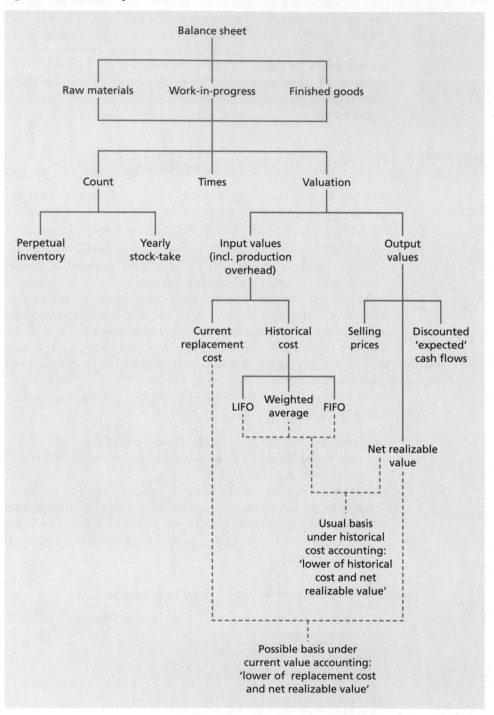

**Summary**  A diagrammatic summary of the various aspects of inventory valuation is given in Figure 10.1.

- Valuation of inventory involves establishing quantities, and a monetary amount for each unit. This amount is usually based on historical cost, reduced to net realizable value if this is lower.

- A number of different methods are commonly considered within the historical cost approach, producing different reported results for both inventory and gross profit. The preferable method depends on the criteria chosen as significant.

- Alternatives to historical costs are possible. Output values are not often regarded as desirable, but current replacement cost can be argued to have some economic and informational advantages, provided that certain assumptions about continuity are made.

- Long-term construction contracts, where production of the product is spread over two or more accounting periods, create additional problems as regards the calculation of periodic financial results. The practice of recognizing profits gradually related to the proportion of completion of the contract is becoming increasingly prevalent, but by no means universal. It is required by IAS 11.

## References and research

There are two important IASB documents that are relevant:

- IAS 2, Inventories.
- IAS 11, Construction Contracts.

The following papers extend relevant considerations in an international context:

- J. Forker and M. Greenwood, 'European harmonization and the true and fair view: The case of long-term contracts in the UK', *European Accounting Review*, Vol. 4, No. 1, 1995.
- D. Pfaff, 'On the allocation of overhead costs', *European Accounting Review*, Vol. 3, No. 1, 1994.

## ? EXERCISES

*Feedback on the first two of these exercises is given in Appendix D.*

10.1 'The production cost of inventory is always highly subjective and uncertain, because of the problem of overheads. Since the valuation of an inventory of manufactured items can never be reliable, accountants should concentrate on making it relevant.' Discuss.

10.2 V.O. Lynn commences business on 1 January buying and selling musical instruments. She sells two standard types, violas and cellos, and her transactions for the year are as set out in Table 10.14 (all prices are in euros):

Table 10.14 **Sale/purchase transactions for V.O. Lynn**

|  | Violas | | Cellos | |
|---|---|---|---|---|
|  | *Buy* | *Sell* | *Buy* | *Sell* |
| 1 January | 2 at 400 |  | 2 at 600 |  |
| 31 March |  | 1 at 600 |  |  |
| 30 April | 1 at 350 |  | 1 at 700 |  |
| 30 June |  | 1 at 600 |  | 1 at 1,000 |
| 31 July | 2 at 300 |  | 1 at 800 |  |
| 30 September |  | 3 at 500 |  | 2 at 1,100 |
| 30 November | 1 at 250 |  | 1 at 900 |  |

You are aware that the cost to V.O. Lynn of the instruments is changed on 1 April, 1 July and 1 October, and will not change again until 1 January following.

(a) Prepare a statement showing gross profit and closing inventory valuation, separately for each type of instrument, under each of the following assumptions:
   (i)   FIFO;
   (ii)  LIFO;
   (iii) weighted average (separately for each transaction);
   (iv)  replacement cost (assuming that this is equivalent to the most recent price).
(b) At a time of rising prices (i.e. using the cellos as an example), comment on the usefulness of each of the methods.

10.3 Marcus Co. has been in operation for three years. The purchases and sales information in Table 10.15 represents the company's activities for its first three years:

Table 10.15 **Sale/purchase transactions for Marcus Co.**

|  | *20X1* | *20X2* | *20X3* |
|---|---|---|---|
| Sales (unit) | 12,000 @ €50 | 20,000 @ €60 | 18,000 @ €65 |
| Purchases (units) | 4,000 @ €20 | 8,000 @ €35 | 7,000 @ €40 |
|  | 7,000 @ €20 | 4,000 @ €30 | 5,000 @ €35 |
|  | 8,000 @ €30 | 1,000 @ €40 | 8,000 @ €25 |

Prepare a schedule illustrating the number of units held at the end of each of the three years shown.

10.4 Using the information contained in Exercise 10.3 above, calculate the value of the year-end inventories using FIFO and LIFO. Also, prepare profit and loss accounts showing the gross profit under each of the valuation methods for all three years.

10.5 R and A are brothers. Recently, their aunt died leaving them €1,000 each. Initially, they intended setting up in partnership selling pils and lager. However, R felt that there was no future in the lager market, whereas A expected that lager sales would boom. After an argument, the brothers decided to set up their own separate businesses, R trading in pils and A in lager.

The following shows the transactions undertaken by R in their first trading period.

| Purchases | 260 pils at €1.25 each. |
|-----------|------------------------|
| Purchases | 100 pils at €1.50 each. |
| Purchases | 200 pils at €3.75 each. |
| Then, sales | 300 pils at €4 each. |

Whilst R was finding that prices were rising swiftly in the market for pils, A by shrewd buying was able to obtain a lower price per unit for each successive purchase he made. The transactions that A undertook in the trading period were:

| Purchases | 200 lager at €1.75 each. |
|-----------|--------------------------|
| Purchases | 200 lager at €1.70 each. |
| Purchases | 200 lager at €1.55 each. |
| Then, sales | 500 lager at €2 each. |

(a) At the end of the period both brothers wish to withdraw all their profits (all transactions were made in cash). How much will each brother be able to withdraw:
   (i) calculating profit on a FIFO basis;
   (ii) calculating profit on a LIFO basis?
(b) After withdrawing all profits in cash, what ability has each brother to replenish the stock of the goods he trades in? What assumptions do you need to make in answering this question?

10.6 A firm buys and sells a single commodity. During a particular accounting period it makes a number of purchases of the commodity at different prices. Explain how assumptions made regarding which units were sold will affect the firm's reported profit for the period.

10.7 What is meant by 'lower of cost and net realizable value'? What difficulties exist in the application of this rule?

10.8 'The four essential conditions of IAS 11 (see Section 10.10) provide entirely adequate safeguards for the use of the percentage of completion method in long-term contracts. When these requirements are met, failure to use the method leads to misleading financial statements.' Discuss.

# Chapter 11

# Financial assets, liabilities and equity

**Contents**

| | | |
|---|---|---:|
| 11.1 | Introduction | 215 |
| 11.2 | Cash and receivables | 215 |
| 11.3 | Investments | 218 |
| | 11.3.1 Types of investment | 218 |
| | 11.3.2 Valuation problems | 219 |
| | 11.3.3 Accounting for gains and losses | 220 |
| 11.4 | Liabilities | 221 |
| | 11.4.1 Definition | 221 |
| | 11.4.2 Creditors | 221 |
| | 11.4.3 Provisions | 223 |
| | 11.4.4 Contingent liabilities | 225 |
| 11.5 | Equity | 226 |
| | 11.5.1 Subscribed capital | 226 |
| | 11.5.2 Share premium | 227 |
| | 11.5.3 Revaluation reserve | 228 |
| | 11.5.4 Legal reserve | 228 |
| | 11.5.5 Profit and loss reserves | 228 |
| 11.6 | Reserves and provisions | 229 |
| 11.7 | Comparisons of debt and equity | 232 |
| | Summary | 233 |
| | References and research | 234 |
| | Exercises | 234 |

**Objectives**

After studying this chapter carefully, you should be able to:

- outline the nature, recognition and measurement of financial assets (cash, receivables and investments) and financial liabilities;

- tell when different types of investments should be valued in different ways, and when to record gains and losses;

- explain that there are two main types of liabilities (creditors and provisions) and outline the current practices relating to their recognition and measurement;

- list the components of an entity's residual equity;

- explain the differences in the meaning of accounting terms such as allowance, provision, fund and reserve;

- distinguish between debt and equity securities, while understanding that securities can have features of both.

## 11.1 Introduction

As explained earlier in this book, the items in a balance sheet can be summarized under the headings of three main elements: assets, liabilities and equity. Chapter 8 looked at the definition of assets and liabilities, and some ideas relating to their recognition. Chapters 9 and 10 concentrated on the recognition and measurement of a number of particular types of assets. This chapter includes coverage of the other main types of asset: financial assets, such as cash, receivables and investments.

The treatment of financial assets is closely linked to the treatment of financial liabilities, which are also examined in this chapter. The IASB has four important standards on financial assets and liabilities: IAS 32 (on presentation issues), IAS 39 (on recognition and measurement), IFRS 7 (on disclosures) and, issued as we go to press, IFRS 9, which updates and changes some aspects of IAS 39. As far as these standards are concerned, financial instruments are very widely defined – for example, financial assets include cash and receivables. This chapter also looks at other types of liability (e.g. provisions) and at equity: the residual interest in the net assets of the company. Equity itself is generally divided into various categories. As will be explained, some financial instruments contain elements of both liabilities and equity.

Since there is no standard format in IAS 1, it may be helpful to refer to the standard European balance sheet headings, as illustrated earlier in Table 8.1. For convenience, this is repeated here in a simplified form as Table 11.1.

This chapter deals with the financial assets (fixed and current investments, debtors and cash), and with all the items on the other side of a balance sheet.

Table 11.1 **Main headings in a balance sheet**

| Assets | Capital and Liabilities |
|---|---|
| Fixed assets | Equity |
|   Intangible assets |   Subscribed capital |
|   Tangible assets |   Share premium |
|   Investments |   Revaluation reserve |
| |   Legal reserve |
| Current assets |   Profit and loss reserves |
|   Inventories | |
|   Debtors | Provisions |
|   Investments | |
|   Cash | Creditors |

## 11.2 Cash and receivables

There are fewer problems of recognition and measurement with cash than with many other assets. If an entity controls some cash, there will clearly be a future benefit in the shape of things that can be bought. Again, apart from the problems of foreign currency (see Chapter 15) and inflation (see Chapter 16), the value of cash is generally its face value.

However, there are some difficulties of definition. For example, suppose that the entity deposits most of its spare cash with a bank in a 48-hour notice deposit account. Is that cash? The heading 'cash' in a balance sheet generally means 'cash at hand and in the bank'. Nevertheless, if money were deposited with the bank for a fixed one-year term in order to gain a higher level of interest, presumably the entity would have an investment rather than cash.

In other words, some dividing line has to be invented between 'cash' and 'investments'. In IFRSs, the heading in the balance sheet is 'cash and cash equivalents' which generally includes investments of up to three months maturity that are convertible to known amounts of cash. Such a meaning is also used in IFRS cash flow statements (see Chapter 13). However, alternative views could be taken. For example, for the purposes of cash flow statements under the UK standard, FRS 1, 'cash' means amounts on hand and deposits with up to 24 hours' notice.

**Real world example**

Practice differs from one company to another, even under IFRS. The current assets of Bayer and Nokia are shown as Figure 11.1. As can be seen, Bayer includes 'cash equivalents' with cash, but Nokia does not. So, the two 'cash' figures cannot be directly compared.

**Figure 11.1 Abbreviated versions of current assets, €millions, 31.12.2008**

| Bayer | |
|---|---|
| Inventories | 6.2 |
| Trade accounts receivable | 5.8 |
| Other financial assets | 0.3 |
| Other receivables | 1.5 |
| Claims for tax refunds | 0.2 |
| Cash and cash equivalents | 2.5 |
| Assets held for sale and discontinued operations | 0.1 |
| Total | 16.6 |
| | |
| **Nokia** | |
| Inventories | 2.5 |
| Accounts receivable | 9.5 |
| Prepaid expenses and accrued income | 4.5 |
| Current portion of long-term losses receivable | 0.1 |
| Other financial assets | 1.0 |
| Available-for-sale investments, liquid assets | 1.2 |
| Available-for-sale investments, cash equivalents | 3.9 |
| Bank and cash | 1.7 |
| Total | 24.4 |

*Source*: Authors' own work based on published financial accounts.

Generally, when amounts of money are due from persons or entities other than financial institutions, the amounts are called receivables (IAS 1 and US English) or debtors (UK English). As usual, it is necessary to check that there is an asset and that it should be recognized. Often this will be easy, because there may be a contractual right to receive a specified amount of cash on a particular date.

This will also give a good start to the process of measuring the asset. Generally, short-term receivables are valued at the amounts expected to be received, after making allowance for any clear or likely non-payment by the debtors. These allowances against (or impairments of) the value of receivables for possible bad debts can be split into specific and general categories. The first of these relates to identified debtors who are unlikely to pay because of bankruptcy or other reasons. The second (general allowances) are often calculated in terms of a percentage of the total receivables, based on the experience of previous years. Sometimes, these various allowances against the value of receivables are called 'provisions', or 'reserves'. This is unhelpful because those terms also have other meanings (see Chapter 8 and Section 11.4.3 below).

In most countries, the setting up or increase of specific allowances is a tax-deductible expense. By contrast, in several countries (e.g. Denmark, France, the UK and the US) a general allowance is not tax-deductible because it is too easy for the taxpayer to manipulate it. Nevertheless, in some of the countries where tax and financial reporting numbers are kept closely in line (e.g. Germany, Italy and Japan), general allowances are indeed tax-deductible, which may lead to deliberate inflation of them. The disclosures of Japanese companies before convergence with IFRS make this the most obvious, as in the box below.

---

**Allowances against receivables**

Allowance for doubtful receivables is provided at the maximum amount which could be charged to income under Japanese income tax regulations, as adjusted to correspond to receivables after eliminating intercompany balances.

*Source*: Matsushita published financial statements for 1999.

---

In cases where fixed amounts of money are to be received after a considerable period, it is necessary to ask whether the face value of these amounts represents a fair valuation. The market value of amounts to be received in one year's time would be less than their face value.

**Activity 11.A**

How much would an entity be willing to pay in order to gain the completely certain receipt of €100,000 in exactly five years' time? Assume that the current (and expected) rate of interest on government bonds is 5 per cent.

**Feedback**

A rational entity would be willing to pay noticeably less than €100,000 even if the expected receipt was not risky. The value could be obtained by discounting the sum at 5 per cent for five years. For one year, the discounted value (or net present value, NPV) would be:

$$€100,000 \times \frac{100}{105} = €95,238.$$

For five years, the NPV would be

$$€100,000 \times \left(\frac{100}{105}\right)^5 = €78,353.$$

IAS 39 (paragraph AG 64) requires that account should be taken of the time value of money for those receivables that are not short-term. This has not been the traditional practice in most countries. However, in Germany, there has been a long history of taking account of this in order to reduce the value of receivables (e.g. see box below). However, given that payables were not discounted, this discounting of receivables might be seen rather as an indication of prudence and a desire to reduce taxable income.

---

**Valuation of receivables**

Receivables are generally carried at their nominal value. Notes receivable and loans generating no or a low-interest income are discounted to their present values. Lower attributable values due to risks of collectability and transferability are covered by appropriate valuation allowances.

*Source*: BASF published parent financial statements for 2008.

---

## 11.3 Investments

### 11.3.1 Types of investment

The most common financial investments that many companies have, apart from deposits with banks, are holdings of the debt securities of other companies (e.g. debentures) or of the equity securities of other companies (e.g. ordinary shares). The nature of these securities is discussed in more detail later for the purposes of examining accounting for them by the entity that issues them. The securities become the investments of the entities or persons that acquire them.

Under EU national laws, investments are divided into 'fixed' and 'current' (as in Table 11.1) on the basis of whether or not they are intended by a company's directors for continuing use in the business. Then, fixed asset investments (or 'non-current investments') are usually valued at cost, less any impairment in value that takes account of the long term rather than the immediate market value (see Chapter 9). By contrast, current assets are valued at the lower of cost and net realizable value.

The problem with this conventional approach is that it rests on a vague distinction that cannot be easily checked by auditors or relied upon by users. Just how long is 'continuing'?

*Why it matters*    *Suppose that the fixed/current distinction is based on the intentions of directors, as above. Suppose also that a company has bought a large amount of investments early in the year. Because of a stock-market crash near the year end, the market value of the investments falls. If the directors want to make the financial statements look as good as possible, they will intend (or say they intend) to keep the investments. They can thereby avoid the use of any low net realizable value in the balance sheet and any resulting loss in the income statement. They would argue that the low value was unlikely to be permanent.*

*However, they may want to take account of the fallen market value, because the loss would be tax-deductible (e.g. in Germany) or because they want to show lower profits in order to avoid a claim for wage rises. If so, they can say that the investments are current assets.*

### 11.3.2 Valuation problems

It may seem unsatisfactory that identical pieces of paper can be valued in different ways by the same company, depending on the plans (or alleged plans) of a company's management. Admittedly, reference to the intentions of directors is the general basis for the determination of the fixed/current distinction. However, it is usually obvious in any particular entity whether materials are inventory or fixed assets. It is not obvious when looking at investments.

Returning to the 'Why it matters' problem above, it is not only losses that can be postponed or taken quickly. The same applies to gains. On this subject, try Activity 11.B.

**Activity 11.B**

Suppose that a company started with no investments but with cash of 100. It then buys some listed shares for 10. The result is shown in part A of Figure 11.2. Then, suppose that the investment does well so that its market value rises to 15. Has the company made a gain?

Figure 11.2 **Purchase, sale and repurchase of investments**

A. *Balance sheet effects after purchase*

| | |
|---|---|
| Investments | 0 |
| | + 10 |
| | 10 |
| Cash | 100 |
| | − 10 |
| | 90 |

B. *Balance sheet effects after sale and re-purchase*

| | | | |
|---|---|---|---|
| Investments | 10 | Profit | +5 |
| | − 10 | | |
| | + 15 | | |
| | 15 | | |
| Cash | 90 | | |
| | + 15 | | |
| | − 15 | | |
| | 90 | | |

**Feedback**

Under conventional accounting in most countries, the implied gain of 5 is neither realized nor recognized. However, supposing that a company *wants* to record a profit. All it has to do is to telephone the stockbroker and request a sale followed by an immediate repurchase. Ignoring any tax effects, the results will be as in part B of Figure 11.2. After this transaction, the company has the same investments and the same amount of cash as before, but the telephone call produced an increase in the recorded figure for the investments of 5 and the recognition of profit of 5. It would, of course, be possible to allow unrealized profits to build up for years and then to sell the investments (and buy them back) when a profit was needed to cover up a trading loss.

The real position is often even worse than that examined in Activity 11.B. Suppose that a company had a large number of investments, some with unrecognized gains and some with unrecognized losses. Then it would be possible to sell particular investments in order to achieve various amounts of gains or losses.

*Why it matters*  *The conclusion from this discussion is that financial reporting would be more relevant if there were continual use of current market values, irrespective of whether investments are sold. This would ensure the immediate reporting of all such gains and losses, independently of management action and possible manipulation. Of course, there would be major problems of cash flow for taxpayers if the tax system followed this approach and demanded tax on unsold investments – as has happened in many countries (e.g. France or Italy) – if the gains were included in the financial statements.*

Although current values may be more relevant, are they sufficiently reliable? This is the classic problem examined in Chapters 3 and 8. Fortunately, for some investments (e.g. listed shares), there is a market price published in most newspapers; this is both reliable and relevant. As explained below, in the case of some such investments, they are valued at current prices by banks and other financial institutions in several countries, and this is now required for companies in general by IAS 39 (paragraph 47).

However, for some investments it may be impossible to observe or to estimate a market price. Here, IAS 39 reverts to a cost basis. Furthermore, IAS 39 preserves some of the old idea of basing values on the intentions of the directors, in that those investments intended to be held to maturity are to be valued by relation to their cost. Equity investments do not have maturity dates, but most debt investments do. This means that fluctuations in value can remain unrecognized if directors state that their investments are intended to be held to maturity.

### 11.3.3 Accounting for gains and losses

When investments are revalued to fair value before they are sold, it is necessary to decide where to show the recognized gains and losses. The examination of revenue recognition in Section 8.4 suggested that gains should be taken to income when they can be reliably measured. The revaluations of investments under IAS 39 seem to fit this description, because the revaluation would not have been carried out if it could not have been measured reliably.

The conclusion in IAS 39 (paragraph 103) is that some revaluation gains and losses should be taken to profit and loss. Referring back to the example of Figure 11.2, under IAS 39 the investments would be revalued to 15 whether sold or not, and a gain of 5 would be recorded as profit whether there was a sale or not. Many company managers do not like to show gains and losses until there is a sale because this makes the profit figure more difficult to control. Their wishes were taken into account in IAS 39, in that gains and losses are shown in other comprehensive income (OCI) (see Chapters 6 and 8) if the investments were not for 'trading' but were merely 'available for sale'. This last category is a residual one, containing all the investments not classified as held to maturity or for trading.

Figure 11.3 summarizes the IFRS treatments of investments.

**Figure 11.3 IAS 39's treatment of financial assets**

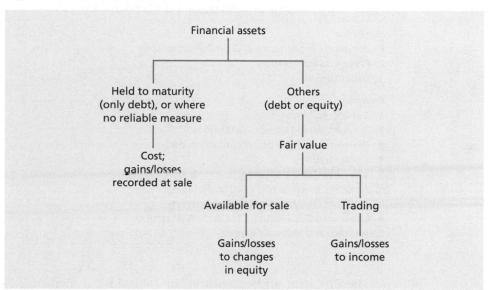

## 11.4 Liabilities

### 11.4.1 Definition

As mentioned in earlier chapters, the term 'liability' now has a precise definition in the IASB Framework, which is similar to that in the US, the UK and some other countries. As a reminder, the IASB definition is:

> A liability is a present obligation of the entity arising from past events, the settlement of which is expected to result in an outflow from the entity of resources embodying economic benefits.

This means that anything in the right-hand column of Table 11.1, excluding 'equity', needs to meet the definition of 'liability'.

### 11.4.2 Creditors

It will be simpler to start at the bottom of Table 11.1 with 'creditors'. The figures under 'creditors' are sums legally due to outsiders where their identity and the amount are clear. Consequently, there is generally no doubt that these items are liabilities or that they can be measured reliably enough to recognize them in the balance sheet. Examples are a bank loan or an unpaid invoice from a supplier. Table 11.2 adds detail to Table 11.1 by showing the standard headings for liabilities in one of the balance sheet formats of the EU Fourth Directive. There is no format in IAS. These items could be divided into 'non-current' and 'current' on the basis of whether they are to be repaid within one year. Such a distinction is generally required as explained in Chapter 6.

**Table 11.2 Headings of liabilities in the EU Fourth Directive**

*Provisions*
1. Provisions for pensions and similar obligations
2. Provisions for taxation
3. Other provisions

*Creditors*
1. Debenture loans
2. Amount owed to credit institutions
3. Payments received on account of orders
4. Trade creditors
5. Bills of exchange payable
6. Amounts owed to affiliated undertakings
7. Amounts owed to participating interests
8. Other creditors including tax and social security
9. Accruals and deferred income

The first item under 'creditors' in Table 11.2 is 'debenture loans'. These are amounts due at a fixed face value and a fixed date to creditors who have lent money to the company in the past. The piece of paper that acknowledges the debt can be passed from one person to another. In many cases, debentures can be traded on a stock exchange. Some debentures allow the holder to turn them into the company's shares under certain conditions. In this case, their substance is partly debt and partly equity. IAS 32 requires such instruments to be split into these elements.

The last item, 'accruals and deferred income', also needs some explanation further to that of Section 3.3.2. Accruals are a recognition that the business has used up services in the period but not paid for them. For example, suppose that a company pays for a service (e.g. the supply of electricity) once per year. The company's accounting year ends on 31 December 20X1. The electricity bill is measured for the year to 31 January 20X2. At the balance sheet date, there has been no bill for most of the year. However, the company has used electricity and will have to pay for it, and so an accurate estimate can be made (and recognized) of the relevant expense and the resulting liability.

When it comes to measuring the size of all these creditors, they are normally valued at their face values. If amounts are not to be paid in the near future, there is usually an interest payment to be made to the creditor. In the unlikely event of there being material amounts owing in the long term but with no interest to pay, it would be necessary, under IAS 39, to reduce the liability (to net present value) to take account of the time value of money.

### 11.4.3 Provisions

Provisions are defined by IAS 37 as being liabilities of uncertain timing or amount. A good example is the first entry in Table 11.2: provisions for pensions. Suppose that a company promises to pay a pension to an employee when she retires. The pension entitlement builds up as the employee works for the company for more and more years. The pension will be paid every year from retirement to death, and perhaps will be equal to half the final year's salary. Such an entitlement would be called a 'defined benefit pension'.

From the company's point of view, the pension is part of employee compensation; it is a current salary expense with a postponed payment date. Each year, the company should charge a pension salary expense and increase the liability to pay the pension later. The obligation to the employee meets the above definition of liability. However, the exact amount depends on many things, such as the final salary and how long the employee will live after retirement. Consequently, the company can only *estimate* the amount, and so the liability is called a *provision*.

It should be noted that this does *not* mean, in itself, that money or investments have been set aside to cover future payments to the pensioner. It might be a good idea to do this, but it requires the company to take deliberate action that is quite separate from accounting for the liability. If money is sent irrevocably from the company into the hands of financial managers who will invest it so as to pay pensioners, this activity is called *funding*. For the balance sheet, the value of any accumulated fund is set off against the accumulated obligation, because the fund can only be used to pay the pensioners, so this reduces the probable size of the company's liability. The balance sheet then shows the balance of the unfunded obligation as a provision.

It is vital not to confuse a provision with a fund. A provision is an obligation to pay money. A fund is a pile of assets (money or investments). Internationally, the scope for confusion is considerable; for example, the Italian for 'provision' is *fondo*; and the Italian for 'fund' is *fondo*. Other language points are considered at the end of this chapter.

Other examples of provisions are estimates of liabilities to pay tax bills or, in the case of a mining company, to pay for cleaning up the environment after extracting minerals from the earth. Also, a company should recognize a provision for its obligation for future repair costs on products as a result of warranties given at the time of sale.

It is obvious that a considerable degree of subjective estimation is likely to be involved here. A provision should generally be calculated on the basis of experience of the issue at hand, such as previous typical breakdown costs, or previously experienced cleanup costs, but further adjustments should be made to take account of known or likely changes in circumstances.

The particularly controversial issue in the area of provisions is the degree to which anticipated expenses and losses should be provided for. The Fourth Directive

(Article 20, as amended in 2003), on which laws in EU countries are based, states that 'provisions' covers:

1. liabilities likely to be incurred or certain to be incurred but of uncertain amount or timing; and
2. at the option of each country's law-maker, the heading can also cover charges to be incurred in the future but with origins before the balance sheet date.

This seems to allow the creation of provisions for trading losses, currency translation losses or repair expenses of an ensuing year, which are connected to actions of current or earlier years. As discussed in Section 8.2, such items generally do not meet the definition of a liability under IFRS requirements, and so they should not be provided for. Fortunately, the EU's item 2 in the above list is only an option, and item 1 is sufficiently vague to be capable of being interpreted in a way consistent with IAS 37, i.e. that there must be an obligation at the balance sheet date that will lead to a probable outflow of resources.

The IASB admitted in an exposure draft of 2005 that the definition of provision is not clear because few liabilities are of absolutely certain timing and amount. The proposal is to abandon the term, so that IAS 37 or its replacement would cover all liabilities that are not covered by other standards. However, the project intended to update and improve IAS 37 has met with many delays and difficulties.

| Activity 11.C | Suppose that a company has a 31 December 20X1 year end. It has had a very bad year, and its directors decide at a board meeting on 15 December 20X1 to close down half the factories and to lay off half the staff at the end of January 20X2. Detailed plans are made and minuted at the board meeting. However, in order to avoid an unhappy Christmas, the plans are kept secret until 7 January 20X2. When the financial statements for 20X1 are prepared in February 20X2, should the balance sheet record a provision for the large restructuring and redundancy costs? |
|---|---|

| Feedback | The traditional European (and prudent) answer to this question would be 'yes', and there would be no problem in fitting such a provision into the EU Fourth Directive's definition (as above). However, is there a liability at the balance sheet date? (Refer back to the definition of 'liability' at the beginning of this section.) There is expected to be a future outflow of resources, but the same could be said for next year's wages bill, which we would not expect to charge this year. Is there an obligation to a third party on 31 December 20X1? The answer, depending on the exact circumstances, seems to be 'no'. Therefore, no provision should be recognized under IFRS requirements or under other similar sets of rules, although the notes to the financial statements must explain the situation. |
|---|---|

| Why it matters | One of the objectives of the executives of a listed company is to make the earnings figure look as good as possible. However, that does not mean as high as possible, because they will be thinking about whether the earnings can be maintained at the high level in the future periods. Consequently, the executives will be trying to smooth the earnings gently upwards. It will help the executives if provisions can be made and reversed very easily because they are vaguely defined. IAS 37 attempts to control this by banning provisions until there is an obligation. |
|---|---|

| Activity 11.D | In the example discussed earlier in Activity 11.C, would an IFRS balance sheet give a fair presentation if it did not recognize a provision for the expenses of restructuring that had been decided upon by 31 December 20X1 and that were likely to be paid early in 20X2? |
|---|---|

| Feedback | In order to answer this question, it is necessary to remember that the financial statements are prepared using a series of conventions that users are expected to be familiar with. The definition of 'liability' under the IFRS regime is very similar to that used in the United States and the United Kingdom. It has been the same for well over a decade and is published in the Framework and various standards. Would it be fair to show an item under the heading 'liabilities' that clearly did not meet the definition? Probably not. |
|---|---|

Furthermore, it should be noted that, unless everyone sticks to this clear definition, it is very difficult to stop companies from distorting reported profits by choosing to make provisions in good years but not in bad years.

In order to inform the users, IFRS requires disclosures in the notes about any restructuring proposals when they have been announced or begun by the date that the financial statements have been authorized for issue.

When a provision is to be recognized, it becomes necessary to value it. By definition, there are estimates to make. The accountant must make the best possible estimates and be prepared to revise them at each balance sheet date in the light of better information. Provisions, such as those for pensions, may extend decades into the future. The fair valuation requires the use of discounting to take account of the time value of money.

IAS 37 (paragraph 36) requires a provision to be measured at the 'best estimate'. This does not mean the most likely outflow. It means the best estimate of what it would cost to be relieved of the liability by making a single payment at the balance sheet date. Consequently, an obligation that is 60% likely to lead to a payment of €10m, and 40% likely to lead to a payment of zero, should be valued at €6m, or less (because of discounting) if the payment would be delayed significantly into the future.

### 11.4.4 Contingent liabilities

Suppose that company X borrows €1 million from the bank but can only do so by persuading company Y to promise to pay the loan back to the bank in the unlikely event that company X cannot do so. Company Y has thereby guaranteed the loan. Is this guarantee a liability for company Y? In a sense, there is a legal obligation, but it is unlikely to be called upon. Where there are unlikely outflows caused by obligations or possible obligations, these are called *contingent liabilities* and should be disclosed in the notes to the financial statements.

One curious result of all the above is that a 60% chance of paying €10m is measured at €6m but a 40% chance is measured at zero, because it does not meet the recognition criterion of probable outflow.

In 2005, the IASB issued an exposure draft proposing to remove probability from the recognition criteria, so that the 40% obligation would be measured at

€4m, as it already would be if assumed as part of a business combination (see Chapter 14). But as indicated above, a coherent full replacement for IAS 37 has been a long time in the making.

## 11.5 Equity

As noted several times in this book, the total equity is just the residual difference between assets and liabilities. However, for various purposes it is helpful to identify components of equity. For example, it may be useful to know how much could legally be paid out to shareholders. Certain elements of equity, including share capital under most circumstances, cannot be distributed until the company is closed down. The five headings under 'equity' in Table 11.1 will now be examined.

### 11.5.1 Subscribed capital

All companies must have some ordinary shares (called 'common stock' in US English). These are the residual equity in the business after all other more specific claims have been considered. In simple terms, ordinary shareholders come last in the queue of claimants on the business resources, and they are entitled to everything 'left over'. A wide variety of other types of share may also exist for any particular business. Non-voting shares are those that do not allow the holders to vote at a company's annual general meeting. Companies may issue different classes of ordinary share where the precise rights of the different classes are defined by the company's constitution. In some countries, e.g. the Netherlands, a certain type of priority shares have dominating voting rights. Preference shares have preference over the ordinary shares as regards dividends, and usually also as regards the repayment of capital sums in the event of the company being closed down.

It must be remembered that a dividend is not receivable automatically as of right. Dividends are only receivable by shareholders if distributable profits are available in the company, and if the dividends are approved by the shareholders in general meeting. If only very limited scope for the payment of dividends exists, then the preference shareholders will come first in the queue for those limited dividends. Because preference shares are clearly safer than ordinary shares when things go badly, they can expect a lower return when things go well. Usually preference shares carry a known and fixed percentage entitlement to dividends (if dividends are available at all).

Preference shares may be cumulative, in which case any dividend 'entitlement' not declared in any particular year carries forward to the following year(s), and would need to be settled in the later year together with that year's preference entitlement before the ordinary shareholders could expect any dividend at all. In many jurisdictions, preference shares are no longer popular because it is usually beneficial from a tax point of view to raise loans (on which the interest payments are tax-deductible) rather than to create further preference shares.

Some types of share, particularly preference shares, may be redeemable. This means that they may be paid off and cancelled under terms defined in the original offer document. If a preference share thereby meets the definition of liability, IAS 32 requires it to be shown as a liability, and the dividend payment to be shown as an interest expense.

In most countries, shares have a *par value* (or *nominal value*) that distinguishes them from other types of share. This par value may have been the issue price of the type of share when it was first issued many years ago. The share capital figure in the balance sheet is the total number of shares multiplied by this par value.

Sometimes, shares may have been issued without calling immediately for full payment. This means that an amount of the potential share capital would be uncalled, or called but not yet paid. Such unreceived share capital is sometimes shown as an asset (see Chapter 9), leaving the share capital figure at the total par value.

In some jurisdictions, it is possible for companies to use cash in order to buy back their own shares from shareholders. This might be done in order to use the shares later to give to employees as 'share-based payments' instead of giving them salaries. While the shares are held, they are called 'treasury shares' by IAS 32 ('treasury stock' in US terms, or 'own shares' in UK law). Under IAS 32 such shares must not be shown as investments but as negative equity.

**Real world example**

The shareholders' equity section from Nokia's balance sheet is shown as Figure 11.4. Nokia has bought back so many of its shares (recorded at current prices) that the treasury shares exceed the share capital and share premium (recorded at original prices). So, it shows a negative share capital.

Figure 11.4 **Nokia's Shareholders' Funds (2008, €m)**

| | |
|---|---:|
| Share capital and premium | 688 |
| Treasury shares | −1,881 |
| Other reserves | 15,401 |
| Total capital and reserves | 14,208 |

*Source*: Authors' own work based on published company accounts.

### 11.5.2 Share premium

*Share premium* is called 'additional paid-in capital' or 'capital surplus' in US English. It is an amount paid to the company in excess of the par value when the company issued the existing shares to their original shareholders. For example, suppose that a million shares of nominal value €10 each are issued by a company in exchange for €30 million cash. The record of this will be:

| | |
|---|---|
| Debit: Bank | €30m |
| Credit: Share capital | €10m |
| Credit: Share premium | €20m |

For the purposes of interpreting a balance sheet, it is generally suitable to add the share premium to the share capital and to treat them identically.

*What is the significance of the difference between subscribed capital and share premium? Well, unusually for a 'Why it matters', it does not really matter for most purposes. This is really a legal point that does not affect analysis of a going concern company for most purposes. For the calculation of the ratios discussed in Chapter 7, the two elements can be added together as equity capital.*

### 11.5.3 Revaluation reserve

The third type of equity is the *revaluation reserve*. This represents the extra claims caused when assets are revalued without the gain being taken to profit and loss (e.g. under IAS 16). Depending on practice and legal restrictions, which vary widely in different countries (see Chapter 9), this reserve may be caused by *ad hoc* revaluation of certain assets, or may arise through a more rigorous and formal valuation policy. Under conventional accounting in most countries, these reserves are generally regarded as not available for distribution as long as the assets remain unsold.

### 11.5.4 Legal reserve

The heading *legal reserve* refers to undistributable reserves required to be set up by particular laws within a country. For example, French law requires certain companies to set aside 5 per cent of profits each year until the legal reserve equals 10 per cent of share capital. There are somewhat similar laws in most 'macro' countries (see Figure 5.2), such as Belgium, Germany, Italy, Japan and Spain. The purpose of the laws is to protect creditors by restricting the size of distributable profits and thereby inhibiting the company from paying cash out as dividends to shareholders.

Such legal reserves are not found in the United States, the United Kingdom, Denmark or the Netherlands. The requirement for legal reserves in Norway was removed in 1998, which is a symptom of the direction of change in accounting in that country in the 1990s.

There are some language difficulties here. The term 'legal reserve' is not used here to refer to all reserves that are undistributable by law, which would include revaluation reserves. Also, it is helpful not to call these amounts 'statutory reserves' because that raises a confusion between statute law and a company's own private rules, sometimes called its statutes.

### 11.5.5 Profit and loss reserves

*Profit and loss reserves* include undistributed profits not shown under other headings above. In a simple company with no legal reserves, this would be all of this year's and previous years' undistributed profits. This could be called 'retained earnings'.

It would be misleading to call this amount the 'distributable profit', which is an amount determined under the laws of each country. For example, if buildings are revalued upwards, depreciation expenses should rise (see Chapter 9). This would reduce profit and loss reserves. However, UK law, for example, requires distributable profit to be calculated ignoring this, so that the legally distributable profit does not depend on whether a company chooses to revalue or not. More importantly, when dealing with the consolidated financial statements of groups (see Chapter 14), the concept of distributable profit is meaningless in many countries because a group cannot distribute profit. This can only be done by an individual legal entity such as a parent company, although the overall group position will be considered when deciding on dividends.

| 11.6 | Reserves and provisions |
| --- | --- |

A major source of confusion surrounding the issues in this chapter is the international difference in the use of the words 'reserve' and 'provision'. In Section 11.2 it was pointed out that it would be helpful to refer to value adjustments against receivables as 'allowances' or 'impairments' rather than as provisions or reserves. In Section 11.4 it was stressed that provisions are obligations to pay money (liabilities), not funds of money (assets). From Sections 11.4 and 11.5 it should be clear that there is a vital distinction between a provision and a reserve. Setting up a provision for €1 million would involve:

| | |
| --- | --- |
| Debit: Expense | €1m |
| Credit: Liability | €1m |

Setting up a legal reserve, for example, would involve:

| | |
| --- | --- |
| Debit: Equity (retained earnings) | €1m |
| Credit: Equity (legal reserve) | €1m |

**Why it matters** *Setting up a provision in the manner described above makes profit worse by a million and net assets worse by a million, whereas setting up a legal reserve changes nothing of importance for interpreting the financial statements.*

**Activity 11.E** Examine the right-hand sides of the published balance sheets (of some years ago) of an Italian company (Costa Crociere, as seen before in Figure 8.2) and a French company (Total Oil). The relevant extracts are shown as Table 11.3. What is your opinion of the use of the word 'reserve'?

**Feedback** The translators have made a mistake here. They have used the English term 'reserve' to mean two vitally different things: reserves and provisions. This is despite the fact that the original Italian used *riserva* and *fondo*, and the French used *réserve* and *provision*. The text below will explain why the translators fell into this error.

The terminological confusion is largely caused because of a difference between UK and US usages. In the United Kingdom and under IFRS (in 2009), the distinction between 'reserve' and 'provision' is as used throughout this chapter and seen in Table 11.1. However, in the United States the words 'reserve' and 'provision' are, in practice, used interchangeably. For example, one could refer to a pension reserve or a pension provision. This is *not* confusing to Americans because they generally do not use the word reserve to mean a part of equity. Indeed:

229

**Table 11.3 Confusing use of the word 'reserve' on the right-hand side of balance sheets**

| *Costa Crociere (Italy)*[a] | *Total Oil (France)*[b] |
|---|---|
| STOCKHOLDERS' EQUITY | SHAREHOLDERS' EQUITY |
|   Capital stock |   Common shares |
|   Additional paid-in capital |   Paid-in surplus |
|   Legal reserve |   Revaluation reserves |
|   Other reserves |   Legal reserve |
|   Retained earnings |   Untaxed reserves |
|   Net income for the year |   General reserves |
| |   Retained earnings |
| RESERVES FOR RISKS AND CHARGES |   Income for the year |
|   Income taxes | |
|   Other risks and charges | CONTINGENCY RESERVES |
| |   Reserves for financial risks |
| RESERVE FOR SEVERANCE INDEMNITY |   Reserves for retirement benefits |
| |   Reserves for specific industry risks |
| RESERVE FOR GRANTS TO BE RECEIVED | |
| | DEBT |
| PAYABLES | |

[a] Abbreviated from Figure 8.2.
[b] Abbreviated from published report of Total Oil. These headings relate to the parent company for 1993. Subsequently, no parent accounts are available in English. The more recent consolidated statements contain the same confusion with the word 'reserve', but less plainly.

- there are no legal reserves in the US;
- revaluation reserves relating to available-for-sale investments (see Section 11.3) are shown as 'cumulative other comprehensive income';
- profit and loss account reserves are called 'retained earnings'.

The confusion arises when translators fail to spot this UK/US difference. To correct Table 11.3 would require the use of the word 'provision' for the items not shown within the 'equity' heading. This would be normal UK usage and IFRS usage. Table 11.4 summarizes the words used in several languages. The table does not take account of the unfortunate use of the word 'provision' to mean allowance or impairment. IFRS generally avoids the word 'reserve', except in the Implementation Guidance to IAS 1.

**Table 11.4 Words for 'provision' and 'reserve' in various languages**

| | | |
|---|---|---|
| UK English | *Provision* | *Reserve* |
| US English | *Provision/reserve* | *[Element of equity]* |
| IFRS | *Provision* | *Reserve* |
| French | *Provision* | *Réserve* |
| German | *Rückstellung* | *Rüucklage* |
| Italian | *Fondo* | *Riserva* |
| Danish | *Hensættelse* | *Reserve* |
| Dutch | *Voorziening* | *Reserve* |
| Norwegian | *Avsetning* | *Reserve* |
| Swedish | *Avsättning* | *Reserv* |

Another expression that is often found, particularly in prudent countries (e.g. Germany) and particularly relating to banks, is 'secret reserves' or 'hidden reserves'. These would arise because a company:

- failed to recognize an asset in its balance sheet; or
- deliberately measured an asset at an unreasonably low value; or
- set up unnecessarily high provisions.

These actions might have been taken in the name of prudence or, in some countries, in order to get tax deductions. They are illustrated in Activity 11.F below. In all three cases, net assets will consequently be understated and therefore equity will be understated. The amount of understatement could be called a secret reserve.

Of course, most systems of accounting contain some degree of secret reserve. For example, the IFRS regime does not recognize the internally generated asset 'research'; and it is normal to value assets at cost, which is usually below fair value.

**Activity 11.F**

Suppose that an entity's balance sheet looked as in Figure 11.5. Suppose also that you discover that the entity has not done its accounting correctly, because it should have:

- recognized an extra intangible fixed asset at a value of 3,
- not recognized a provision (because there was no obligation at the balance sheet date) of 2.

How would you correct the balance sheet? What difference will it make to a gearing ratio?

Figure 11.5 **A balance sheet containing secret reserves**

| | | | |
|---|---|---|---|
| Fixed assets | 10 | Share capital | 6 |
| | | Reserves | 4 |
| Current assets | 6 | | 10 |
| | | Provisions (long-term) | 3 |
| | | Loans (long-term) | 2 |
| | | Current liabilities | 1 |
| | 16 | | 16 |

**Feedback**

Before the corrections, the gearing ratio could be measured as:

$$\frac{\text{long-term liabilities}}{\text{equity}} = \frac{3+2}{10} = 50 \text{ per cent}$$

To correct the balance sheet, the following adjustments should be made:

- fixed assets + 3; reserves + 3;
- provisions – 2; reserves + 2.

So the total of equity will now be 15 not 10; and the total provisions will be 1 not 3. Consequently, the gearing ratio would become

$$\frac{1+2}{15} = 20 \text{ per cent}$$

Among other things, this would make the entity look much safer.

*Why it matters*    *A good time to spot secret reserves is when a company changes from one system of accounting to another. For example, in 1995 Germany's largest bank, the Deutsche Bank, disclosed for the first time financial statements under IFRS as well as under German accounting. The figures for equity were as set out in Table 11.5.*

**Table 11.5 Deutsche Bank equity (DM million)**

| Year | German HGB | IAS | % increase in quoted value |
|------|-----------|--------|----------------------------|
| 1994 | 21,198 | 25,875 | 22.1 |
| 1995 | 22,213 | 28,043 | 26.2 |

*Source:* Compiled by authors from Deutsche Bank's equity figures 1994 and 1995.

*So, the analysis of return on net assets or the comparison of debt to equity would have been greatly affected by the disclosure under IFRS of the reserves hidden under conventional German accounting.*

## 11.7   Comparisons of debt and equity

Companies raise finance in several ways. From outside, they can raise funds from their owners by issuing equity securities or from others by issuing debt securities. Loans can also come from a bank. Once in business, finance can come from retaining profits. For external capital raising, some distinctions are pointed out in Table 11.6.

**Table 11.6 External finance**

| | Debt | Ordinary shares |
|---|------|-----------------|
| Where from: | Non-owners | Owners |
| Payments out: | Interest | Dividend |
| Amount: | Fixed | Variable |
| Payment compulsory: | Yes | No |
| Expense: | Yes | No |
| Tax-deductible expense: | Yes | Not in most countries |

**Activity 11.G**

When preparing the annual report of a company for the year ended 31 December 20X1, the directors generally include information about the dividend that they propose to pay in 20X2 from the profits of 20X1. The Annual General Meeting of the shareholders, held perhaps in March 20X2, needs to vote in favour of the proposal. Under some rules (for example, those of Denmark, the Netherlands and the United Kingdom until 2004), companies include the proposed dividend as a current liability in the 20X1 balance sheet. In other countries (for example, France, Germany, Italy and the United States), companies do not recognize a liability in the 20X1 balance sheet. The size of the proposed dividend could be significant in the context of total current liabilities and in a comparison of the liquidity ratios of companies (see Chapter 7). Which is the better practice?

**Feedback** In favour of the recognition of a liability is the very high probability that there will be a cash outflow in the near future. That is useful information to analysts of financial statements. In favour of the lack of recognition is the simple point that there seems to be no legal obligation at the balance sheet date, and so there can be no liability. IAS 10, *Events after the Balance Sheet Date*, was revised in 1999 so as to ban recognition of a liability for proposed dividends on equity shares. Information on the proposed dividend can still be given in the notes or elsewhere in the annual report, and it can even be shown on the balance sheet by displaying a part of retained earnings (or profit and loss reserves) as a proposed distribution.

As mentioned before, another complication here is that some securities are superficially equity but actually debt, and some are hybrids: partly equity and partly debt. An example of the first case is where a preference share involves a guaranteed payment on redemption at a fixed date. This seems to meet the definition of a liability. Under IAS 32, the superficial form of an instrument should be overlooked in favour of its underlying substance.

For hybrid securities, a whole industry has grown up in recent years, creating various types. Variations on the theme are almost infinite, but the principle usually is that the security is issued in one form, with optional or guaranteed conversion at a later date into another form. For example, debentures may be issued with optional conversion rights into share capital at a predetermined price at some future date. As noted earlier, IFRS requires a convertible debenture to be split into part-debt and part-equity.

So far, most countries' national rules have not followed these modern IFRS ideas but have retained accounting based on the legal form.

**Summary**

- Even the definition of 'cash' is ambiguous because money in the bank is usually included, depending on the length of deposit.

- Receivables (or debtors) are valued at the amount realistically expected to be received. Allowances or impairments should therefore be made for bad debts. Such allowances are sometimes – confusingly – called provisions or reserves. Also, the time value of money may need to be taken into account by discounting the amounts receivable.

- Under EU laws, investments have traditionally been divided into 'fixed' and 'current'; but this rests on the intentions of directors, which can change and which are difficult to audit. Cost is usually the basis for valuation, although a lower market value is often taken into account.

- The current value of investments might seem more relevant information than cost and, in some cases, it is reliable. IFRS requirements have moved to market valuation for some investments, but this creates problematic dividing lines between types of investments.

- Liabilities can be divided into 'creditors' and 'provisions'. Both must meet the definition of liability, although provisions need more estimation in their measurement. In the past, and still in some countries, provisions are recorded even though they do not meet the IFRS definition of liability. This creates secret reserves.

- Equity is the residual of assets net of liabilities, but it can still be split into components. The two basic components are contributions from owners (share capital and share premium) and undistributed gains (various forms of reserves).

- Debt and equity securities are different in a number of ways, but it is possible to disguise one as the other and to create securities with features of both.

- It would be helpful to distinguish clearly between 'provision' (a liability of uncertain amount or timing) and 'reserve' (an element of equity caused by gains). Unfortunately, the words are sometimes used interchangeably, although not in IFRS or UK rules.

## References and research

The IASB documents of greatest relevance to the issues of this chapter are:

- IAS 1 (Revised at several dates), *Presentation of Financial Statements*.
- IAS 19 (Revised 2005), *Employee Benefits*.
- IAS 32 (Revised 2004), *Financial Instruments: Disclosure and Presentation*.
- IAS 37 (1998), *Provisions, Contingent Liabilities and Contingent Assets*.
- IAS 39 (Revised at several dates from 2003), *Financial Instruments: Recognition and Measurement*.
- IFRS 7 (2005) *Financial Instruments: Disclosures*.
- IFRS 9 (2009) *Financial Instruments*.

An English-language paper looking at one of the chapter's topics in a comparative international way is:

- D. Alexander, S. Archer, P. Delvaille and V. Taupin, 'Provisions and contingencies: An Anglo-French investigation', *European Accounting Review*, Vol. 5, No. 2, 1996.

## ? EXERCISES

*Feedback on the first two of these exercises is given in Appendix D.*

11.1 'All credit balances included in a balance sheet are either capital and reserves, or liabilities actual or estimated.' Discuss.

11.2 'The distinction between a prudent approach to the quantification of provisions on the one hand, and the creation of secret reserves on the other, will always be a matter for human attitude and whim.' Discuss.

11.3 If you owned some listed shares that had just doubled in value, would you say that you had gained and were better off than before?

11.4 'There is usually no problem with the valuation of receivables because it is clear how much is legally owed to an entity.' Discuss.

11.5 What is the definition of a fixed (or non-current) asset? Why is this difficult to use in the context of investments, and why does that matter?

11.6 What uses of the word 'reserve' might be found in practice in various parts of the world?

11.7 Distinguish between debt capital and equity capital, and suggest which is likely to be favoured by a company raising finance in a high-taxation environment.

11.8 How might a company seek to raise extra finance in ways other than issuing new debt or equity securities?

# Chapter 12

# Accounting and taxation

| Contents | 12.1 | Introduction | | 236 |
|---|---|---|---|---|
| | | 12.1.1 | Rationale for this chapter | 236 |
| | | 12.1.2 | Separate taxation for companies | 236 |
| | | 12.1.3 | International differences in taxes | 237 |
| | 12.2 | International differences in the determination of taxable income | | 238 |
| | | 12.2.1 | Introduction | 238 |
| | | 12.2.2 | Depreciation | 239 |
| | | 12.2.3 | Capital gains | 239 |
| | | 12.2.4 | Dividends received | 239 |
| | | 12.2.5 | Interest | 239 |
| | | 12.2.6 | Other taxes | 240 |
| | 12.3 | Tax rates and tax expense | | 240 |
| | 12.4 | Deferred tax | | 241 |
| | | Summary | | 247 |
| | | References and research | | 247 |
| | | Exercises | | 248 |

**Objectives**  After studying this chapter carefully, you should be able to:

- outline some of the main ways in which corporate taxation can differ internationally;
- explain the distinction between accounting profit and taxable income;
- discuss some major international differences in the tax base and give simple examples;
- outline the rationale for the recognition of deferred tax assets and liabilities in financial statements;
- calculate amounts of deferred tax for some basic examples.

## 12.1 Introduction

### 12.1.1 Rationale for this chapter

There are several related purposes of studying taxation. First, corporate taxation clearly has some significant effects on net profit figures and on other financial reporting matters. In particular, it has been shown earlier (e.g. in Chapter 5) that in some continental European countries the rules relating to the taxation of corporate income have a dominant effect on financial accounting measurement and valuation rules in an individual company. For example, there is a strong influence of tax rules on depreciation charges on individual company financial statements in Germany; and if asset values are changed on a balance sheet, this generally affects tax liabilities for individual companies in France. By contrast, neither of these two points is true for the United Kingdom.

A second major topic is how to account for the effects of the differences between the tax rules and the financial reporting rules. This is a major point under the national accounting rules in those countries where the tax and accounting practices are separated on a number of issues. Further, in any country, for those groups using IFRSs for the preparation of consolidated financial statements, there are likely to be substantial differences between tax and financial reporting. This leads to the topic of deferred tax, which is examined in the fourth section of this chapter.

Thirdly, an understanding of corporate taxation in different countries is a necessary introduction to a study of business finance and management accounting. However, it is often omitted from books on these subjects. Hence there is an introduction here.

### 12.1.2 Separate taxation for companies

In most countries, it has only been within the last hundred years that companies have begun to be treated differently from individuals for the purposes of taxation. However, the question of whether a business is a separate entity from its owner(s) has a long history in disciplines such as accounting, company law and economics. Italian accountants had decided by the thirteenth century that they wished to separate the business from its owners, so that the owners could see more clearly how the business was doing. Consequently, as examined in Chapter 2, balance sheets of businesses show amounts called 'capital' that represent amounts contributed by the owners. During the nineteenth century, various laws were enacted in European countries to the effect that companies have a legal existence independently from their owners, that these companies may sue and be sued in their own names, and that the owners are not liable for the debts of a company beyond their capital contributions. Economists have (in microeconomic theory) extended the separation of the owner from the business. When calculating the profit of the business to a sole trader, for example, economists would include as costs of the business the opportunity costs of the amounts that the owner could have earned with the invested time, the invested property and money if they had been invested outside the business instead.

As mentioned, it was not until the twentieth century that revenue law (i.e. taxation law) caught up with this separation and that companies began to be taxed in a different way from individuals. As is frequently the case with taxation, changes were associated with the need to finance warfare. In particular, the rearmament of nations before the two World Wars imposed a heavy burden on government finances, which was partly supported by the revenue from taxes on companies.

Another vital point – certainly in EU countries – is that tax is calculated on the basis of individual legal entities; it is not calculated on the basis of groups of companies, although in particular circumstances groups are allowed to pass losses or dividends around. This means that consolidated financial statements (as introduced in Chapter 4 and taken further in Chapter 14) are not generally relevant for the purposes of taxation.

This chapter is concerned with the taxation of corporate income, which is the major corporate tax in most countries. However, there are other taxes on corporations in Europe: on property, on share capital, on payroll numbers, and so on.

### 12.1.3 International differences in taxes

Three major types of difference between corporate income taxes concern tax bases, tax systems and tax rates.

The international differences in corporate income tax bases (or definitions of taxable income) are very great. Although in all countries there is some relationship between accounting income and taxable income, in several continental European countries (but not Denmark, the Netherlands or Norway, for example) the relationship is much closer than it is in the United Kingdom, the United States or Australia (see Chapter 5). Further, it has been pointed out throughout this book that the underlying measurement of accounting income itself varies substantially by country. These two points, which are of course linked, mean that companies with similar profits in different countries may have vastly different taxable incomes.

The second basic type of difference lies in tax systems. Once taxable income has been determined, its interaction with a tax system can vary, in particular with respect to the treatment of dividends. Corporations may have both retained and distributed income for tax purposes. If business income is taxed only at the corporate level and only when it is earned, then different shareholders will not pay different rates of personal income tax. If income is taxed only on distribution, taxation may be postponed indefinitely. On the other hand, if income is taxed both when it is earned and when it is distributed, this creates *economic double taxation*, which could be said to be inequitable and inefficient.

The third major international difference is in tax rates. There is a brief section on this later in the chapter.

These differences in tax bases, tax systems and tax rates could lead to several important economic effects: for example, on dividend policies, investment plans and capital-raising methods. Such matters are not dealt with here; and neither are the important issues of transfer pricing within groups and international double taxation that, in practice, help to determine taxable profits and tax liabilities.

Further international differences arise in the timing of the payment of taxes. For example, in some countries, corporate taxes are paid on a quarterly basis using estimates of taxable income for the year. In other countries, taxes are paid many months after the accounting year end – after the profit figures have been calculated and audited. In many continental countries taxes are not finally settled until a tax audit, which may be some years later.

In some countries, e.g. Italy and Germany, there are regional as well as national corporate income taxes. Both these taxes generally use a similar tax base, but the composite tax rate is, of course, higher.

The taxation of businesses is a very complex area, particularly when a business operates in more than one country. This chapter is only able to introduce some of the issues and therefore leaves out much of the complexity. One complication is that the legal types of businesses differ from country to country, as does the scope of particular business taxes. This chapter deals mainly with companies that can clearly be seen as separate from their owners for tax purposes.

## 12.2 International differences in the determination of taxable income

### 12.2.1 Introduction

The obvious way to classify corporate income taxation bases is by degrees of difference between accounting income and taxable income. As should be clear from Chapter 5, the influence of taxation on accounting varies internationally from the small in the United Kingdom to the dominant in Germany. Such is the importance of this difference for accounting that a simple classification of tax bases would look much like a simple classification of accounting systems (see Chapter 5). For example, a two-group classification in either case might put Denmark, the Netherlands, the United Kingdom and the United States in one group, and France, Germany and Japan in the other.

In the first of these groups, many adjustments to accounting profit are necessary in order to arrive at the tax base, namely taxable income. In the other group, the needs of taxation have been dominant in the evolution of accounting and auditing. Consequently, the tax base corresponds closely with accounting profit. As discussed in many places in this book, several of these continental European countries began in the late 1980s to de-couple accounting from tax rules. More recently, the impact of increasing globalization of the finance market and the rise in the influence of the IASB have accelerated this process, especially as regards consolidated financial statements. If a German company, for example, uses IFRSs for its consolidated financial reporting, this creates many significant differences between its financial reporting and the way that taxation works in Germany. However, even in Germany, tax and accounting began to move apart, particularly as a result of a law of 2008.

Some of the differences in tax bases are discussed below; in a few cases this summarizes the coverage of topics elsewhere in the book. There is a concentration here on four EU countries, but these should be taken as examples of how the calculation of taxable income can differ.

## 12.2.2 Depreciation

Naturally, in all the countries studied in this book the tax authorities take an interest in the amount of depreciation charged in the calculation of taxable income. This concern varies from fairly precise specification of the rates and methods to be used (as in most countries), to an interference only where charges are unreasonable (as in the Netherlands). As has been pointed out in earlier chapters, the vital difference for financial reporting is that tax depreciation must usually be kept the same as accounting depreciation in Franco-German countries, but not under Anglo-Dutch accounting.

For example, in the United Kingdom for large companies for 2009/10, machinery is depreciated at 25 per cent per annum on a reducing balance basis, and industrial buildings are depreciated at 4 per cent per annum on cost. There is a complete separation of this scheme of 'capital allowances' from the depreciation charged by companies against accounting profit. Unlike other countries, the United Kingdom does not give any depreciation tax allowance for most commercial buildings. By contrast, the quotation from the German company, BASF, in Chapter 9 illustrated some aspects of tax influence on depreciation.

## 12.2.3 Capital gains

Capital gains are increases in the value of fixed assets above their cost. They are taxed at the point of sale. The taxation of capital gains varies substantially by country. In the United Kingdom, the Netherlands and Germany, capital gains are added to taxable income in full. In France, short-term capital gains (defined as for periods less than two years) are fully taxed, but some types of long-term capital gains are taxed at a reduced rate. The degree to which taxation on a gain can be postponed by buying a replacement asset (known as *roll-over relief*) also varies internationally.

## 12.2.4 Dividends received

The degree to which the dividends received by a company must be included has an important effect on its taxable income. In Germany and the United Kingdom, domestic dividends are generally not taxed in the hands of a recipient company. In France and the Netherlands, dividend income is fully taxed unless there is a holding of at least 5 per cent.

## 12.2.5 Interest

Dividends paid are not tax-deductible in most systems, and of course nor are they considered to be expenses in the calculation of accounting profit. By contrast, interest payments are usually expenses for both accounting and tax purposes. Dividends are a share of post-tax profit paid to the owners of the company, whereas interest is a fixed payment that *must* be paid to outside lenders of money. Consequently, under most types of system, paying out €2,000 in interest is less expensive for the company in post-tax terms than paying out €2,000 in cash dividends, because the former payment reduces tax by €660 (assuming, for example, a corporation tax rate of 33 per cent). On the other hand, as shown below, €1,400 of cash dividends would be worth as much to an individual in some tax systems as €2,000 of gross interest. This is because, although both incomes are taxed, the dividends might receive a tax credit. The example shown in Table 12.1 assumes a corporation tax rate of 33 per cent, and a rate of withholding tax and tax credit based on an income tax rate of 30 per cent.

Table 12.1 **Comparing the effect of payments of dividends and interest on the tax: an example**

|  | Dividend payment € | Interest payment € |
|---|---|---|
| Net profit before interest and tax | 10,000 | 10,000 |
| *less* Interest (1,400 net, 600 income tax withheld at source) | – | 2,000 |
| Net profit before tax | 10,000 | 8,000 |
| *less* Tax at 33 per cent | 3,300 | 2,640 |
| Net profit after tax | 6,700 | 5,360 |
| Dividend[a] | 1,400 | – |
| Retained profit | 5,300 | 5,360 |

[a] Equivalent to €2,000 because of a tax credit of €600.

### 12.2.6 Other taxes

A very important complicating factor in determining overall tax burdens is the existence of other types of tax on companies and the degree of their deductibility for national corporate income tax purposes. In many countries there is some form of payroll tax or social security tax. In the United Kingdom there are local property 'rates'. In Germany there are regional income taxes, capital taxes and payroll taxes. In France there is a business licence tax. In general, these taxes are deductible in the calculation of national corporation tax. However, because of these taxes, the total tax burden is much higher than might be thought at first sight in countries such as Germany, where regional taxes are also important.

## 12.3 Tax rates and tax expense

Tax rates on corporate taxable income differ greatly around the world, and they change from year to year. There is a general trend in the world for tax rates to fall. As an example of how tax rates can differ, Table 12.2 shows the rates in the European Union for a particular period (2007/8), but already rates have fallen in some countries. The need to fund government expenditures during the 'credit crunch' of 2008/9 might change this.

The amount of corporate income tax payable by a company is calculated by multiplying the taxable income (see Section 12.2) by the tax rate. When the tax is paid, it will be recorded in the cash flow statement as a use of cash.

The calculation of the expense in the income statement is complicated by the issue of deferred taxation, which is dealt with in the next section. However, the *presentation* of tax expense in the income statement is straightforward and can be described here.

The tax expense is of sufficient importance that it is nearly always disclosed as a separate figure in an income statement. It is generally shown after other expenses and before dividends, although the exact location varies. This, and the effect of tax on the interpretation of financial statements, has been referred to in Chapter 7, and is looked at again in Part 3.

Particularly in countries where there is a strong separation of accounting from tax, the location of figures above or below the tax line in an income statement is not a reliable guide as to whether an item affects the actual tax bill.

Table 12.2 **EU corporation tax rates in 2007/8**

| Country | Tax rate per cent* |
|---|---|
| Austria | 25 |
| Belgium | 33 |
| Denmark | 28 |
| Finland | 26 |
| France | 34.43 |
| Germany | 26.38 |
| Greece | 25 |
| Ireland | 12.5 |
| Italy | 33 |
| Luxembourg | 22 |
| Netherlands | 29.6 |
| Portugal | 25 |
| Spain | 30 |
| Sweden | 28 |
| United Kingdom | 30 |

*Notes*
* Withholding taxes have been ignored throughout.

## 12.4 Deferred tax

Deferred tax is *not* amounts of tax bills that the tax authorities have allowed the taxpayer to postpone. Accounting for deferred tax is the recognition of the tax implied by the figures included in the financial statements. There are major international differences in accounting for deferred tax.

A simple example of deferred tax would occur in the context of a revaluation of fixed assets. Suppose that a Dutch company revalues a holding of land in the balance sheet from €3 million to €9 million. Suppose, also, that the Dutch corporate tax rate on capital gains is 35 per cent, but that the Dutch tax rules do not tax capital gains until disposal, which in this case is not intended by the company in the foreseeable future. No tax is payable as a result of revaluing, but accountants might think that the potential liability to tax of €2.1 million (i.e. €6 million revaluation × 35 per cent) relates to the period up to the balance sheet date. If so, they might account for the implicitly deferred tax, as in Table 12.3. Since the revaluation is not yet realized, there will be no current tax on the gain.

**Table 12.3 Deferred tax on revaluation**

*Balance sheet adjustments for Dutch company (€m)*

| | |
|---|---|
| Fixed asset: + 6.0 | Revaluation reserve: + 3.9 |
| | Deferred tax:      + 2.1 |

In the above example, the €6 million of revaluation that is not yet relevant for tax purposes is called a 'temporary difference' under IASB (or US) rules. Under IAS 12, entities should account for deferred tax on temporary differences. A temporary difference is the difference between the carrying value of an asset or liability for financial reporting purposes and its value as recorded in the tax records. In the above example of the Dutch land, the financial reporting carrying value was €9 million and the tax value was €3 million. So, the temporary difference was €6 million.

Under German rules, upward revaluation is not possible. In several other continental countries, revaluation is legal but would lead to current taxation. Consequently, under the national rules of many continental countries, deferred tax would not arise in such a case. However, if a German, French, etc. group is using IFRS rules in its consolidated statements, the issue could arise in these countries because accounting practices would depart from tax rules.

The most frequently cited cause of substantial amounts of deferred tax in Anglo-Saxon countries is depreciation. Depending on the industry sector, depreciation can be a large expense, and the tax rules can be substantially different from the accounting rules, as outlined in Section 12.2. Table 12.4 sets out a simple case, where there are 100 per cent tax depreciation allowances in the year of purchase of plant and machinery; a 50 per cent corporate income tax rate; the purchase for €10,000 of a machine that is expected to last for five years; and a country where tax and accounting are separated. The existence of 100 per cent tax depreciation is not fanciful. This applied for all plant and machinery in the United Kingdom

**Table 12.4 Depreciation and tax**

| Accounting records | | Tax calculations | | |
|---|---|---|---|---|
| Year | Depreciation | Year | Expense | Tax reduction |
| 1 | 2,000 | 1 | 10,000 | 5,000 |
| 2 | 2,000 | 2 | 0 | 0 |
| 3 | 2,000 | 3 | 0 | 0 |
| 4 | 2,000 | 4 | 0 | 0 |
| 5 | 2,000 | 5 | 0 | 0 |

from 1972 to 1984, to certain assets in West Berlin until the end of the 1980s, to capital investments in certain Greek islands, and on other occasions. The example would work, of course, with the less extreme tax allowances that are common in Europe.

In the example in Table 12.4, the accountants assume that the asset will have no residual value and will wear out evenly over time, irrespective of use. Consequently, for accounting purposes, they charge a depreciation expense of €2,000 per year. By contrast, the tax authorities allow an expense of €10,000 in the first year and, if the company takes this, no tax-deductible expense after that. Consequently, there is a reduction in the tax bill of €5,000 in year 1. This cash-flow advantage is designed to be the incentive to invest.

Supposing that the company in our example uses the new asset very inefficiently or does not use it at all in the first year, depreciation may still be charged because the asset is depreciating due to the passing of time. The net effect of the inefficient capital purchase on the post-tax accounting profit of year 1 appears to be that the profit *increases* by €3,000 (i.e. depreciation expense of €2,000, and tax reduction of €5,000). Of course, if the company uses the asset effectively, profit will increase by more than this, as the company should at least be able to earn enough by using the asset to cover the depreciation on it.

The above strange effect on profit is caused by deliberately charging the depreciation expense slowly but taking the tax reduction immediately. However, so far no account has been taken of deferred tax. In order to do so, under IAS 12, it is necessary to calculate the temporary difference. This, as explained earlier, is the difference between the financial reporting carrying value of the asset and its tax value. In the case of the depreciating machine at the end of year 1, the financial reporting carrying value is cost less depreciation €8,000, whereas the tax written-down value is zero because there is full depreciation for tax purposes. So, there is a temporary difference of €8,000 and (at the tax rate of 50 per cent) a deferred tax liability of €4,000.

The double entry to give effect to deferred tax accounting in this case would be a debit entry under 'Tax expense' of €4,000, and a credit entry under 'Deferred tax liability' of €4,000. Then the effect of buying the asset (and not using it) on the profit for year 1 would be a *decrease of* €1,000 (i.e. an extra depreciation expense of €2,000, an actual tax reduction of €5,000, but a deferred tax expense of €4,000). This is a more reasonable profit figure to present.

| Activity 12.A | A company commences trading in year 1, and purchases fixed assets in year 1 costing €20,000, in year 2 costing €8,000, in year 3 costing €10,000, in year 4 costing €12,000 and in year 5 costing €14,000. All fixed assets are depreciated for financial reporting purposes at 10 per cent per annum on cost. Tax depreciation of 25 per cent per annum on the reducing balance is available. The tax rate throughout is 30 per cent.

Complete the following table, to show the annual balance sheet figures for cumulative fixed assets in (a) the accounting records and (b) the tax records, and the temporary differences at each balance sheet date, in accordance with IAS 12. Year 1 is already done for you, as shown in Table 12.5. |

Table 12.5 **Deferred tax calculation (Year 1)**

| Year | 1 € | 2 € | 3 € | 4 € | 5 € |
|---|---|---|---|---|---|
| (a) *Accounting balances* | | | | | |
| Asset balance 1 January | – | | | | |
| Additions | 20,000 | | | | |
| Depreciation | 2,000 | | | | |
| Balance 31 December | 18,000 | | | | |
| (b) *Tax balances* | | | | | |
| Asset balance 1 January | – | | | | |
| Additions | 20,000 | | | | |
| Tax depreciation | 5,000 | | | | |
| Balance 31 December | 15,000 | | | | |
| Temporary differences | 3,000 | | | | |
| Deferred tax balance | 900 | | | | |

**Feedback**   The completed table should be as shown in Table 12.6. Taking year 2 as an example, the accounting depreciation is €2,800 (10 per cent of total cost of €28,000). The tax depreciation is €5,750 (25 per cent of net balance of €23,000). The temporary difference between accounting asset balance and tax asset balance is €5,950 (€23,200 – €17,250) and the deferred tax liability, provided in full under the liability basis as IAS 12 requires, is €1,785 (30 per cent × €5,950). In year 2 the deferred tax liability has therefore increased from €900 to €1,785, requiring an addition of €885 to the tax charge in the income statement for that year. The figures for the other years are calculated similarly.

Table 12.6 **Deferred tax calculation (Years 1–5)**

| Year | 1 € | 2 € | 3 € | 4 € | 5 € |
|---|---|---|---|---|---|
| (a) Accounting balances | | | | | |
| Asset balance 1 January | – | 18,000 | 23,200 | 29,400 | 36,400 |
| Additions | 20,000 | 8,000 | 10,000 | 12,000 | 14,000 |
| Depreciation | 2,000 | 2,800 | 3,800 | 5,000 | 6,400 |
| Balance 31 December | 18,000 | 23,200 | 29,400 | 36,400 | 44,000 |
| (b) *Tax balances* | | | | | |
| Asset balance 1 January | – | 15,000 | 17,250 | 20,437 | 24,328 |
| Additions | 20,000 | 8,000 | 10,000 | 12,000 | 14,000 |
| Tax depreciation | 5,000 | 5,750 | 6,813 | 8,109 | 9,582 |
| Balance 31 December | 15,000 | 17,250 | 20,437 | 24,328 | 28,746 |
| Temporary differences | 3,000 | 5,950 | 8,963 | 12,072 | 15,254 |
| Deferred tax balance | 900 | 1,785 | 2,690 | 3,622 | 4,576 |

We have now seen two examples of the possible causes of deferred tax: a revaluation of assets that is not taken into account by the tax system, and depreciation running at a faster rate for tax than for accounting. Other examples would include:

■ the capitalization of leases (under IAS 17), if the tax system still treats them as operating leases;
■ taking profits on long-term contracts as production proceeds (under IAS 11), if the tax system only counts profits at completion.

In order to account for deferred tax under IAS 12, it is necessary to look at the values of all the assets and liabilities in the balance sheet and compare them to the tax values that would apply. Large numbers of temporary differences and resulting deferred tax assets and liabilities can arise.

**Why it matters** *Particular care needs to be taken when carrying out ratio analysis, as discussed in Chapter 7, regarding the treatment of deferred taxation. The balance sheet figures – probably for liabilities, and possibly for assets – will be affected by deferred tax practices. After-tax earnings will also be affected, as Activity 12.A showed, and so will shareholders' equity. This affects a lot of ratios, such as earnings per share, gearing, and return on equity. As already suggested, it cannot be assumed that IAS 12 is being fully and consistently followed across countries and over past periods, although harmonization should increase in the future.*

Several causes of deferred tax liabilities were examined above. However, deferred tax assets are also possible. These can be caused, for example, by losses not yet allowed for tax or by provisions (e.g. pensions) not yet counted for tax purposes.

**Real-world example** Bayer's balance sheet, seen in earlier chapters but repeated here for convenience as Figure 12.1, shows four items related to tax. Under 'Non-current assets' there are deferred tax assets caused by such issues as losses and pensions. Under 'Current assets', there are actual claims against the tax authorities. Under 'Non-current liabilities', the deferred tax liabilities are shown including a large amount relating to intangibles that are not treated as assets under German tax practice, to create a large temporary difference. Lastly, under 'Current liabilities', there are amounts soon to be paid to the tax authorities.

Figure 12.1 **Bayer Group consolidated balance sheet**

|  | 31 Dec. 2008 |
|---|---:|
| € million | |
| **Noncurrent assets** | |
| Goodwill | 8,647 |
| Other intangible assets | 13,951 |
| Property, plant and equipment | 9,492 |
| Investments in associates | 450 |
| Other financial assets | 1,197 |
| Other receivables | 458 |
| Deferred taxes | 1,156 |
| | 35,351 |
| **Current assets** | |
| Inventories | 6,681 |
| Trade accounts receivable | 5,953 |
| Other financial assets | 634 |
| Other receivables | 1,284 |
| Claims for income tax refunds | 506 |
| Cash and cash equivalents | 2,094 |
| Assets held for sale and discontinued operations | 8 |
| | 17,160 |
| **Total current assets** | **52,511** |
| **Total assets** | |
| **Shareholder's equity** | |
| Capital stock of Bayer AG | 1,957 |
| Capital reserves of Bayer AG | 4,028 |
| Other reserves | 10,278 |
| | 16,263 |
| Equity attributable to non-coutrolling interest | 72 |
| **Stockholders' equity** | **16,340** |
| **Noncurrent liabilities** | |
| Provisions for pensions and other post-employment benefits | 6,347 |
| Other provisions | 1,351 |
| Financial liabilities | 10,614 |
| Other liabilities | 432 |
| Deferred taxes | 3,592 |
| | 22,336 |
| **Current liabilities** | |
| Other provisions | 3,163 |
| Financial liabilities | 6,256 |
| Trade accounts payable | 2,377 |
| Income tax liabilities | 65 |
| Other liabilities | 1,961 |
| Directly related to assets held for sale and discontinued operations | 13 |
| | 13,835 |
| **Total stockholders' equity and liabilities** | **52,511** |

*Source*: adapted from Bayer Annual Report 2008, p. 135.

**Summary**

- Corporate taxation is a major influence on some countries' financial accounting practices. A knowledge of corporate taxation is important for international business finance.

- Tax bases for corporate income tax differ in their treatment of depreciation, capital gains, losses, dividends received, certain expenses and many other matters. The importance of taxes other than national corporate income taxation also varies.

- Tax rates also vary greatly internationally, and alter frequently.

- Deferred taxation is a major accounting topic in those countries where there can be substantial differences between taxable income and accounting profit. It also becomes major where a company uses IFRSs for its consolidated statements and therefore moves its accounting away from that which would be used under national taxation rules. Practice varies within those countries, although IAS 12 is likely to have a harmonizing influence over the coming years.

## References and research

The relevant standard for the aspect of international accounting dealt with in this chapter is:

- IAS 12, *Income Taxes*.

The best starting point for a European exploration is a special edition of the *European Accounting Review*: Vol. 5, Supplement, 1996. Although now somewhat out of date, the main points are still relevant. The edition includes the following papers, all with further references.

- K. Artsberg, 'The link between commercial accounting and tax accounting in Sweden'.
- M. Christiansen, 'The relationship between accounting and taxation in Denmark'.
- A. Eilifsen, 'The relationship between accounting and taxation in Norway'.
- A. Frydlender and D. Pham, 'Relationships between accounting and taxation in France'.
- M.N. Hoogendoorn, 'Accounting and taxation in the Netherlands'.
- M.N. Hoogendoorn, 'Accounting and taxation in Europe – A comparative overview'.
- M. Järvenpääää, 'The relationship between taxation and financial accounting in Finland'.
- A. Jorissen and L. Maes, 'The principle of fiscal neutrality: The cornerstone of the relationship between financial reporting and taxation in Belgium'.
- M. Lamb, 'The relationship between accounting and taxation: The United Kingdom'.
- D. Pfaff and T. Schräoer, 'The relationship between financial and tax accounting in Germany – the authoritativeness and reverse authoritativeness principle'.
- F. Rocchi, 'Accounting and taxation in Italy'.

In addition, the following are recommended as further reading:

- S. James and C. Nobes, *The Economics of Taxation* (Birmingham: Fiscal Publications, 2009).
- M. Lamb, C. Nobes and A. Roberts 'International variations in the connections between tax and financial reporting', *Accounting and Business Research*, Summer 1998.

- C.W. Nobes and H.R. Schwencke, 'Modelling the links between tax and financial reporting: A longitudinal examination of Norway over 30 years up to IFRS adoption', *European Accounting Review*, Vol. 15 (1), 2006.

## ? EXERCISES

*Feedback on the first two of these exercises in given in Appendix D.*

12.1 In which countries does taxation tend to have a major influence on published company accounts? Discuss how this influence takes effect and what the position is regarding the treatment of taxation in *consolidated* accounts.

12.2 A company has a group of fixed assets that are summarized in its accounting records as shown in Table 12.7.

### Table 12.7 **Summarized fixed assets**

| Year | 1 | 2 | 3 | 4 |
|---|---|---|---|---|
| | € | € | € | € |
| (a) *Accounting balances* | | | | |
| Asset balance 1 January | 10,000 | 13,500 | 17,550 | 22,095 |
| Additions | 5,000 | 6,000 | 7,000 | – |
| Depreciation | 1,500 | 1,950 | 2,455 | 2,210 |
| Balance 31 December | 13,500 | 17,550 | 22,095 | 19,885 |

For tax purposes the asset balance brought forward on 1 January of year 1 is €7,000. Tax depreciation is available at the rate of 20 per cent per annum on the reducing balance basis. The tax rate is 30 per cent in years 1 and 2 but falls to 20 per cent in years 3 and 4.

Prepare a tabular summary of the tax balances relating to this group of assets over the four years of the example, calculate deferred tax balances for each of the four years, and show the effect of deferred tax on the income statement for years 2, 3 and 4.

12.3 In Activity 12.A, the balance on the deferred tax liability account is growing every year over the five-year period, and if tax conditions remain stable and annual investment continues to rise, then it will continue to grow. Could it be argued that, because the liability seems not to be leading to an outflow of resources, it fails to meet the IASB definition of a liability?

12.4 Explain the concept of a 'temporary difference' in the context of IASB rules. Why is it thought necessary to account for deferred tax on these differences?

# Chapter 13

# Cash flow statements

**Contents**    13.1  Introduction                                             250
                13.2  An outline of the IAS 7 approach                          251
                13.3  Reporting cash flows from operating activities            253
                13.4  The preparation of cash flow statements                  254
                13.5  A real example                                           260
                      Summary                                                  260
                      References and research                                  260
                      Exercises                                               262

**Objectives**   After studying this chapter carefully, you should be able to:

- explain the reasons for publishing cash flow statements;

- describe the main elements of a cash flow statement in accordance with IAS 7;

- explain and illustrate the direct and indirect methods for deriving cash flows from operating activities;

- prepare simple cash flow statements from given data, consistent with IAS 7;

- comment on the meaning of the numbers in simple cash flow statements.

## 13.1 Introduction

We briefly explored the idea of cash flow statements at the end of Chapter 2 and in Section 6.3. As a reminder, try the following activity.

**Activity 13.A**  Why are cash flow statements an important element in annual published financial statements, and how do the IASB's rules and national laws based on the EU Fourth Directive influence their content and presentation?

**Feedback**  The simple answer to why cash flow statements are important is that adequate liquidity and the availability of cash are vital to the successful operation of a business entity. The income statement and balance sheet do not provide adequate information about these factors, because the accrual basis of accounting is focused on revenues and expenses. Thus the matching principle relates earnings with consumption, not receipts with payments, and a business may be profitable but at the same time have severe cash shortages. Cash flow statements, which are not based on the accruals convention, focus on cash movements over the reporting period and therefore facilitate prediction of possible or likely cash movements in the future.

The EU Fourth Directive makes no mention of cash flow statements. This is a function of its origins, as discussed in Part 1 of this book, in an era before such statements were common. Thus, most national laws within the EU are also silent on this matter. The IASB, on the other hand, has issued IAS 7 (*Cash Flow Statements*). This, or national standards like it, are the basis for most practice internationally.

**Why it matters**  *It is important to remember that the traditional accounting process involves uncertainty. Not only is profit determination complex but it is also potentially misleading. In any accounting year, there will be a mixture of complete and incomplete transactions. Transactions are complete when they have led to a final cash settlement and these transactions cause few profit-measurement difficulties. Considerable problems arise, however, in dealing with the many incomplete transactions. For these, the profit can only be estimated by valuing assets and liabilities at the balance sheet date or by using the accruals concept, whereby revenue and costs are matched with one another so far as possible and dealt with in the income statement of the period to which they relate.*

*A statement that focuses on changes in cash and other liquid assets rather than on profits has two potential benefits. First, it provides different and additional information on movements and changes in net liquid assets, which assists appraisal of an entity's progress and prospects; and, second, it provides information that is generally more objective (though not necessarily more useful) than that contained in the income statement.*

**Activity 13.B**  Opinion has varied sharply in the last three decades on exactly what aspect of 'liquidity' should best be focused on in published financial statements. Consider the two balance sheet extracts from A Co., as shown in Table 13.1, which focus on working capital, i.e. on net current assets.

Table 13.1 **Balance sheet extracts for A Co.**

|  | 000s 31.12.X1 | 000s 31.12.X2 |
|---|---|---|
| Inventory | 4,600 | 4,300 |
| Accounts receivable | 1,300 | 2,600 |
| Cash and bank | 2,500 | 1,200 |
|  | 8,400 | 8,100 |
| Accounts payable | 7,900 | 6,500 |
| Working capital | 500 | 1,600 |

Identify the change in position.

**Feedback**   If we look solely at cash, we could state that A had experienced a decrease in cash of 1,300,000 over the year. On the other hand, looking at working capital (or net current assets) indicates an increase of 1,100,000 over the year. It is debatable which figure the users of financial statements should have regard to when taking decisions. If the company expects to have to pay its creditors quickly, then the decrease in cash might be alarming. Otherwise, assuming that the debtors will pay, the liquidity has improved.

Up to the end of the 1980s practice was generally focused on working capital, i.e. on the current assets and current liabilities. The original IAS 7, before a revision in 1992, reflected this preference, referring to funds flow rather than to cash flow. Now, however, the focus is much more closely on cash. More strictly, it is changes in both cash and cash equivalents, i.e. those items that are so liquid as to be 'nearly cash' (see below), that are analysed.

IAS 7 is uncompromising in that it applies to all entities. It requires that a cash flow statement is presented as an integral part of all sets of financial statements, unlike for example FRS 1 in the UK, which exempts small companies and parent's unconsolidated statements.

## 13.2   An outline of the IAS 7 approach

Statements prepared following IAS 7 distinguish cash flows under three headings: operating activities, investing activities and financing activities. The standard defines these as follows:

- *Operating activities* are the principal revenue-producing activities of the entity, and other activities that are not investing or financing activities.
- *Investing activities* are the acquisition and disposal of long-term assets and other investments not included in cash equivalents.
- *Financing activities* are activities that result in changes in the size and composition of the equity capital and borrowings of the entity.

The concept of cash equivalents requires further clarification:

Cash equivalents are held for the purpose of meeting short-term cash commitments rather than for investment or other purposes. For an investment to qualify as a cash equivalent it must be readily convertible to a known amount of cash and be subject to an insignificant risk of changes in value. Thus, an investment normally qualifies as a cash equivalent only when it has a short maturity of, say, three months or less from the date of acquisition (IAS 7, para. 7).

The last sentence of this quotation shows the IASC (the IASB's predecessor) desperately trying to write a 'principle' rather than a 'rule'. The result is a lack of clarity. This might mean that entities from other countries that report under IFRS may interpret the definition differently, in accordance with local cultures and characteristics. For example, bank borrowings are generally considered to be financing activities. However, in some cases, bank overdrafts that are repayable on demand form an integral part of an entity's cash management. In these circumstances, bank overdrafts are included as a component of cash and cash equivalents.

It should not be assumed that 'cash and cash equivalents' are interpreted identically in different countries. For example, in the United States the definition of cash equivalents is similar to that in IFRS (except that 'say, three months' becomes a 90-day limit), but under US GAAP the changes in the balances of overdrafts are classified as financing cash flows rather than being included within cash and cash equivalents. Under the UK standard, cash is defined as cash in hand and deposits receivable on demand (up to 24 hours' notice), less overdrafts repayable on demand. Cash equivalents are not included in the total to be reconciled to, but are dealt with under other headings.

Cash flows from operating activities are primarily derived from the principal revenue-producing activities of the entity. Therefore, they generally result from the transactions and other events that enter into the determination of net profit or loss. However, all cash flows from the sale of productive non-current assets, such as plant, are cash flows from investing activities.

It follows from the above, of course, that the nature of the business, i.e. of the principal revenue-producing activities, may differ significantly from one business to another, in which case the implications of apparently similar transactions may also differ. For example, an entity may hold securities and loans for dealing or trading purposes, in which case they are similar to inventory acquired specifically for resale. Therefore, cash flows arising from the purchase and sale of dealing or trading securities are classified as operating activities. Similarly, cash advances and loans made by financial institutions such as banks are usually classified as operating activities since they relate to the main revenue-producing activity of that entity.

The definitions of operating, investing and financing activities given earlier make it clear that any principal revenue-producing activity that is not a financing or investing activity, as defined, is automatically an operating activity.

Investing activities consist essentially of cash payments to acquire, and cash receipts from the eventual disposal of, property, plant and equipment and other long-term productive assets. Financing activities are those relating to the size of the equity capital, whether by capital inflow or capital repayment, or to borrowings (other than any short-term borrowings accepted as cash equivalents). Note that interest paid and dividends paid could be interpreted as either operating or as financing activities. Similarly, interest and dividends received could be treated as either operating or investing. Taxes paid are generally to be shown as operating flows.

## 13.3 Reporting cash flows from operating activities

Entities are allowed to use either of two methods to analyse and report cash flows from operating activities. These are:

(a) the direct method, whereby major classes of gross cash receipts and gross cash payments are disclosed; or
(b) the indirect method, whereby net profit or loss is adjusted for the effects of transactions of a non-cash nature, for any deferrals or accruals of past or future operating cash receipts or payments, and for items of income or expense associated with investing or financing cash flows.

IAS 7 encourages entities to report cash flows from operating activities using the direct method, but this is not a requirement. The indirect method takes reported net profit and removes non-cash items included in the calculation of that profit figure. The indirect method thus undoes the effects of the accrual basis. The direct method, in contrast, amounts to an analysis of the cash records. Therefore, the direct method provides information that may be useful in estimating future cash flows and that is not available under the indirect method.

The differences between the methods are best shown by example. Table 13.2 shows the typical headings that might be seen in a direct calculation of operating cash flows. Table 13.3 shows the headings for an indirect calculation.

**Table 13.2 Illustration of calculation of cash flow from operating activities by the direct method**

| Item | € |
| --- | --- |
| Cash received from customers | 144,750 |
| Cash paid to suppliers and employees | (137,600) |
| Cash dividend received from associate | 900 |
| Other operating cash receipts | 10,000 |
| Interest paid in cash | (5,200) |
| Taxes paid | (4,500) |
| Net cash from operating activities | 8,350 |

A comparison of the two tables makes it clear that the indirect method is at the same time more complicated for the reader, and less informative in terms of actual cash flows, than the direct method. As noted above, IAS 7 encourages – but does not require – the use of the direct method, and the same applies in US GAAP. However, the UK standard requires the indirect method, on the grounds that the benefits to users of the direct method are outweighed by the costs of preparing it, and that consistent practice is desirable. In practice, the indirect method seems generally widely used in IFRS or US practice, and the next section examines this method in more detail.

Table 13.3 **Illustration of calculation of cash flow from operating activities by the indirect method**

| Item | € | € |
|---|---:|---:|
| Net income | | 8,000 |
| Adjustments to reconcile net income to net cash provided by operating activities: | | |
| Depreciation and amortization | 8,600 | |
| Provisions for doubtful accounts receivable | 750 | |
| Provision for deferred income taxes | 1,000 | |
| Undistributed earnings of associate | (2,100) | |
| Gain on sale of equipment | (2,500) | |
| Payment received on instalment sale of product | 2,500 | |
| Changes in operating assets and liabilities: | | |
| Increase in accounts receivable | (7,750) | |
| Increase in inventory | (4,000) | |
| Increase in accounts payable | 3,850 | |
| Total adjustments to net income | | 350 |
| Net cash from operating activities | | 8,350 |

## 13.4 The preparation of cash flow statements

A cash flow statement prepared by the indirect method is in essence a reconciliation between the opening and closing cash and cash equivalents of the accounting period. A convenient way to begin is to determine the differences between opening and closing balance sheets. These differences can then be analysed and presented in the desired format, segregating the inflows from the outflows.

Table 13.4 shows summarized balance sheets for the years X1 and X2, and columns for difference, outflow and inflow.

**Activity 13.C**

Complete the blank columns in Table 13.4. Some of the items are more straightforward than others. Remember that depreciation is an expense, but not a cash movement. However, the depreciation for the year will have reduced the retained profits.

Table 13.4 **Balance sheet differences: (1) basic information**

| Item | X1 | X2 | Difference | Outflow | Inflow |
|---|---:|---:|---:|---|---|
| Fixed assets – cost | 94 | 140 | +46 | | |
| *less* depreciation | (22) | (30) | −8 | | |
| Inventory | 12 | 16 | +4 | | |
| Receivables | 18 | 40 | +22 | | |
| Cash | 10 | 4 | −6 | | |
| | 112 | 170 | | | |
| Share capital | 70 | 76 | +6 | | |
| Retained profits | 24 | 30 | +6 | | |
| Debentures | 0 | 20 | +20 | | |
| Payables | 18 | 44 | +26 | | |
| | 112 | 170 | | | |

**Feedback** The result should be as shown in Table 13.5.

Table 13.5 **Balance sheet differences: (2) inflows and outflows**

| Item | X1 | X2 | Difference | Outflow | Inflow |
|---|---|---|---|---|---|
| Fixed assets – cost | 94 | 140 | +46 | 46 | |
| *less* depreciation | (22) | (30) | −8 | | 8 |
| Inventory | 12 | 16 | +4 | 4 | |
| Receivables | 18 | 40 | +22 | 22 | |
| Cash | 10 | 4 | −6 | | 6 |
| | 112 | 170 | | | |
| Share capital | 70 | 76 | +6 | | 6 |
| Retained profits | 24 | 30 | +6 | | 6 |
| Debentures | 0 | 20 | +20 | | 20 |
| Payables | 18 | 44 | +26 | | 26 |
| | 112 | 170 | | 72 | 72 |

It is important that the logic of Table 13.5 is fully understood. Fixed assets have increased, i.e. money has been spent on buying new ones. This clearly represents a cash outflow. The argument concerning depreciation is rather more complicated. Depreciation is merely the allocation of cost over different accounting periods and, of itself, involves no cash flows at all. However, the depreciation charge for the year (of 8 in our example) will have been deducted from the profit for the year, and the net cash inflow from operating will therefore be understated by this non-cash-flow-related charge. It is in this sense that the depreciation charge for the year has the effect of increasing the calculated cash inflows.

As regards the inventory difference, the money tied up in closing inventory has increased by 4, and so an outflow of 4 has been necessary to finance this extra amount. With debtors, the entity is owed 22 more than before, i.e. it has received 22 less than a constant debtors figure would indicate – again having the effect of an outflow (strictly, perhaps, a negative inflow). The reduction in the cash balance of 6 is the balancing number.

The remaining items are fairly straightforward. Share capital has increased, by the sale of shares creating a cash inflow. Annual profits will in principle cause net cash inflows. The issue of debentures clearly creates a cash inflow of the amount borrowed. An increase in creditors, of 26, is equivalent to borrowing money of this amount, and so it represents a cause of cash increase.

Several simplifying assumptions have been made in this example. It is assumed that no fixed assets have been sold, and that there are no dividends or taxation paid. However, such issues could be dealt with using the logic of the previous paragraphs (see Activity 13.G later).

The next stage is to arrange the inflow and outflow figures in a more helpful way. This should be consistent with the layout headings of IAS 7, i.e.

- cash flows from operating activities;
- cash flows from investing activities;
- cash flows from financing activities;
- net change in cash or cash equivalents (simplified here to 'cash').

Figure 13.1 **Cash flow statement derived from Table 13.5**

| | | |
|---|---:|---:|
| Cash flows from operating activities: | | |
| net profit | | 6 |
| add back depreciation | | 8 |
| | | 14 |
| changes in current items: | | |
| increase in inventory | | (4) |
| increase in debtors | | (22) |
| increase in creditors | | 26 |
| net cash flow from operations | | 14 |
| Cash flows from investing activities: | | |
| purchase of fixed assets | | (46) |
| Cash flows from financing activities: | | |
| issue of share capital | 6 | |
| issue of debentures | 20 | |
| net cash flow from financing | | 26 |
| Net change in cash (14 − 46 + 26) | | (6) |
| Cash at beginning of year | | 10 |
| Cash at end of year | | 4 |
| Cash reduction | | (6) |

This leads to a statement as in Figure 13.1.

So the reduction in cash of 6 is made more understandable. A major cash outflow for fixed assets of 46 has been partly financed by new long-term money of 26, and partly by the effects of daily operations of 14, meaning that cash was reduced on balance by 6.

**Activity 13.D**

Assuming that the debentures were issued on 1 January of a particular year and that interest was paid on 31 December, redraft the 'net cash flow from operations' entry of the cash flow statement in Figure 13.1 using the direct method, given that the balance sheets are as shown in Table 13.5 and the income statements are as in Figure 13.2.

Figure 13.2 **Income statements (example)**

| | Year to 31 Dec X1 | | Year to 31 Dec X2 | |
|---|---:|---:|---:|---:|
| Sales | | 150 | | 250 |
| Opening inventory | 8 | | 12 | |
| Purchases | 104 | | 180 | |
| | 112 | | 192 | |
| Closing inventory | 12 | | 16 | |
| Cost of sales | | 100 | | 176 |
| Gross profit | | 50 | | 74 |
| Wages and salaries | 28 | | 42 | |
| Depreciation | 4 | | 8 | |
| Debenture interest | – | | 2 | |
| Other expenses | 14 | | 16 | |
| | | 46 | | 68 |
| Retained profit for the year | | 4 | | 6 |

**Feedback**  Net cash flow is as set out in Table 13.6.

Table 13.6 **Net cash flow (example)**

| | |
|---|---:|
| Cash receipts from sales in X2 (250 + 18 − 40) | 228 |
| Cash paid to suppliers and employers [(180 + 18 − 44) + 42 + 16] | (212) |
| Cash generated from operations | 16 |
| Cash interest paid | (2) |
| Net cash flow | 14 |

The figure for cash receipts and cash paid to suppliers are the income statement entries adjusted for the change in debtors and the change in creditors respectively.

Now try Activity 13.E for yourself.

**Activity 13.E**  The balance sheet of AN Co. for the year-ended 31 March 20X2 is as shown in Figure 13.3. Prepare the cash flow statement for the year ended 31 March 20X2 using the indirect method, given that no fixed assets were sold during the year, and given that the increase in debentures took place on 1 April 20X1.

Figure 13.3 **Balance sheets for AN Co.**

| | 20X1 (€000s) | 20X2 (€000s) |
|---|---:|---:|
| *Fixed assets* | 160 | 230 |
| *less* depreciation | 44 | 60 |
| | 116 | 170 |
| *Current assets* | | |
| Inventory | 20 | 25 |
| Debtors | 18 | 15 |
| Cash | 21 | 27 |
| | 59 | 67 |
| *Creditors payable within one year* | | |
| Creditors | 21 | 27 |
| Taxation | 12 | 16 |
| Dividend | 18 | 20 |
| | 51 | 63 |
| *Net current assets* | 8 | 4 |
| *Creditors payable after one year* | | |
| Debentures (10 per cent interest) | 30 | 32 |
| *Net assets* | 94 | 142 |
| *Represented by* | | |
| Ordinary share capital of €1 shares | 27 | 33 |
| Share premium account | 24 | 30 |
| Retained profits | 43 | 79 |
| | 94 | 142 |

**Feedback**  The cash flow statement derived from Figure 13.3 would look like that shown in Figure 13.4.

Figure 13.4 **Cash flow statement derived from Figure 13.3**

|  | €000 |
|---|---:|
| *Operating profit:* |  |
| Increase in retained profits | 36.0 |
| Add interest on loans | 3.2 |
| Taxation | 16.0 |
| Dividend | 20.0 |
|  | 75.2 |
| *Net cash inflow from operations is:* |  |
| Operating profit | 75.2 |
| Depreciation | 16.0 |
| Increase in inventory | (5.0) |
| Decrease in debtors | 3.0 |
| Increase in creditors | 6.0 |
| Interest paid | (3.2) |
| Taxes paid | (12.0) |
|  | 80.0 |
| We therefore have: |  |
| Cash inflow from operating activities | 80.0 |
| Cash flows from investing activities: |  |
| Purchase of fixed assets | (70.0) |
| Cash flows from financing activities: |  |
| Issue of new shares (6 + 6) | 12 |
| Dividends paid | (18) |
| Issue of new debentures | 2 |
|  | (4.0) |
| Net cash flows | 6.0 |
| Opening cash balance | 21.0 |
| Closing cash balance | 27.0 |
| Increase in cash | 6.0 |

**Activity 13.F** Comment on the implications for AN Co. of the statement prepared in Activity 13.E.

**Feedback** The broad picture is that cash inflows arise from operations (80) and from new long-term funding (12 + 2). Cash outflows arise from investment in fixed assets (70) and the payment of dividends (18). Most of the new long-term investment has therefore been financed out of the proceeds of day-to-day operations.

A common complication is that some fixed assets are likely to have been sold in the year, as in the next activity.

**Activity 13.G** All the information in Activity 13.E, as given in Figure 13.4, still stands except that, additionally, fixed assets originally costing €40,000, with accumulated depreciation of €15,000, have been sold during the year ended 31 March 20X2 for €26,000. Prepare a cash flow statement in the proper format that takes account of this additional information.

**Feedback** First of all we need to consider the effects of the new information. The amount spent on new fixed assets can be found:

Opening balance at cost + new cost – old cost = closing balance at cost.

Hence, in our example:

160,000 + new cost – 40,000 = 230,000,

and outflow on new fixed assets is therefore 110,000 to ensure a balance in the equation. Similarly for the depreciation figures in the balance sheet:

44,000 + annual charge – 15,000 = 60,000,

and so the annual charge is 31,000.

The resulting cash flow statement would look like that shown in Figure 13.5.

Figure 13.5 **Cash flow statement for Activity 13.G**

|  |  | €000 |
|---|---|---|
| *Operating profit:* |  |  |
| Increase in retained profits |  | 36.0 |
| Add interest on loans |  | 3.2 |
| Taxation |  | 16.0 |
| Dividend |  | 20.0 |
|  |  | 75.2 |
| *Net cash inflow:* |  |  |
| Operating profit |  | 75.2 |
| Depreciation |  | 31.0 |
| Profit on disposal |  | (1.0) |
| Increase in inventory |  | (5.0) |
| Decrease in debtors |  | 3.0 |
| Increase in creditors |  | 6.0 |
| Interest paid |  | (3.2) |
| Taxes paid |  | (12.0) |
|  |  | 94.0 |
| *Result* |  |  |
| Cash inflow from operating activities |  | 94 |
| Cash flows from investing activities: |  |  |
| Purchase of fixed assets | (110) |  |
| Disposal of fixed assets | 26 |  |
|  |  | (84) |
| Cash flows from financing activities: |  |  |
| Issue of new shares (6 + 6) | 12 |  |
| Dividends paid | (18) |  |
| Issue of new debentures | 2 |  |
|  |  | (4) |
| Net cash flows |  | 6 |
| Opening cash balance |  | 21 |
| Closing cash balance |  | 27 |
| Increase in cash |  | 6 |

It is important to interpret cash flow statements in the context of the particular entity, and taking a reasonably long-term view. Borrowing, which will tend to lead to negative figures in the cash flow statement, may be a good thing as long as an excessively high leverage ratio is avoided and as long as long-term profitability is enhanced. Some entities may be structured so as to provide much of their cash needs through a positive cash flow from operations. Different industries may have different typical cash flow structures. For example, large retailers – especially if they buy on credit and sell for cash – may have large positive operating cash flows. Capital-intensive industries may have a greater tendency to raise external finance.

## 13.5 A real example

In practice, and in the context of consolidated financial statements, published cash flow statements can be rather more complicated. We present in Figure 13.6 (on p. 261) the consolidated statement of cash flows for Bayer for the financial year ended 31 December 2008, prepared in accordance with IAS 7.

Study Figure 13.6 carefully. You should be able to explain the rationale behind the movements in Figure 13.6 in the same way as we have done it for you in relation to Table 13.5.

## Summary

- Cash flow statements provide a different focus from the income statement and balance sheet, giving important insights into cash and liquidity changes and trends.

- Cash flow statements are not always required by law; but they are virtually universal, for listed companies, and are required by national regulation in many countries. IAS 7 has had a major influence in this area.

- IAS 7 requires four major sections in a cash flow statement:
  - cash flows from operating activities;
  - cash flows from investing activities;
  - cash flows from financing activities;
  - net change in cash or cash equivalents.

- Cash flows from operating activities may be prepared using either the direct or the indirect method. In practice the indirect method generally predominates.

- Practice in the usage and interpretation of cash flow statements is required.

 ### References and research

The key reference is IAS 7, *Cash Flow Statements*.

Some specific suggestions for reading are as follows:

- G. Gebhardt and A. Heilmann, 'Compliance with German and International Accounting Standards in Germany: Evidence from cash flow statements', *The Economics and Politics of Accounting – International Perspectives on Trends, Policy and Practice* (C. Leuz, D. Pfaff and A. Hopwood, chapter 4.2), Oxford University Press, 2004.
- C. Yap, 'Users' perceptions of the need for cash flow statements – Australian evidence', *European Accounting Review*, Vol. 6, No. 4, 1997.

Figure 13.6 **Bayer Group consolidated statement of cash flows**

|  | 2008<br>€ million |
|---|---|
| Income from continuing operations after taxes | 1,720 |
| Income taxes | 636 |
| Non-operating result | 1,188 |
| Income taxes paid or accrued | (812) |
| Depreciation and amortization | 2,722 |
| Change in pension provisions | (292) |
| (Gains) losses on retirements of noncurrent assets | (75) |
| Non-cash effects of the remeasurement of acquired assets<br>   (inventory work-down) | 208 |
| **Gross cash flow** | **5,295** |
| Decrease (increase) in inventories | (692) |
| Decrease (increase) in trade accounts receivable | (134) |
| (Decrease) increase in trade accounts payable | (36) |
| Changes in other working capital, other non-cash items | (825) |
| **Net cash provided by (used in) operating activities (net cash flow),<br>   continuing operations** | **3,608** |
| Net cash provided by (used in) operating activities (net cash flow),<br>   discontinued operations | – |
| **Net cash provided by (used in) operating activities<br>   (net cash flow) (total)** | **3,608** |
| Cash outflows for additions to property, plant, equipment<br>   and intangible assets | (1,759) |
| Cash inflows from sales of property, plant, equipment and other assets | 167 |
| Cash inflows from (outflows for) divestitures | (41) |
| Cash inflows from (outflows for) noncurrent financial assets | (390) |
| Cash outflows for acquisitions less acquired cash | (1,617) |
| Interest and dividends received | 553 |
| Cash inflows from (outflows for) current financial assets | (2) |
| **Net cash provided by (used in) investing activities (total)** | **(3,089)** |
| Capital contributions | – |
| Dividend payments and withholding tax on dividends | (1,126) |
| Issuances of debt | 2,277 |
| Retirements of debt | (752) |
| Interest paid | (1,272) |
| **Net cash provided by (used in) financing activities (total)** | **(873)** |
| **Change in cash and cash equivalents due to business activities (total)** | **(354)** |
| **Cash and cash equivalents at beginning of year** | **2,531** |
| Change in cash and cash equivalents due to changes in scope of consolidation | 3 |
| Change in cash and cash equivalents due to exchange rate movements | (86) |
| **Cash and cash equivalents at end of year** | **2,094** |

*Source*: Adapted from Bayer Annual Report 2008, p. 132.

## ? EXERCISES

*Feedback on the first two of these exercises is given in Appendix D.*

13.1 'Expenses and revenues are subjective; cash flows are facts. Therefore cash flow statements cannot mislead.' Discuss.

13.2 Study Figure 13.6 in the chapter. Write a short report on Bayer's management of its cash flows over the period reported.

13.3 The balance sheet of Dot Co. for the year ended 31 December 20X2, together with comparative figures for the previous year, is shown in Figure 13.7 (all figures €000).

Figure 13.7 **Balance sheet for Dot Co.**

|  | | 20X1 | | 20X2 |
|---|---|---|---|---|
| *Fixed assets* | | 180 | | 270 |
| Less depreciation | | (56) | | (90) |
| | | 124 | | 180 |
| | | | | |
| *Current assets* | | | | |
| Inventory | 42 | | 50 | |
| Debtors | 33 | | 40 | |
| Cash | 11 | | – | |
| | | 86 | | 90 |
| | | | | |
| *Creditors payable within one year* | | | | |
| Trade and operating creditors | (24) | | (33) | |
| Taxation | (17) | | (19) | |
| Dividend | (26) | | (28) | |
| Bank overdraft | – | | (10) | |
| | | (67) | | (90) |
| *Net current assets* | | 19 | | – |
| Net assets | | 143 | | 180 |
| | | | | |
| *Represented by* | | | | |
| Ordinary share capital €1 shares | | 20 | | 25 |
| Share premium account | | 8 | | 10 |
| Retained profits | | 55 | | 65 |
| Shareholders' fund | | 83 | | 100 |
| Debentures (15 per cent interest) | | 60 | | 80 |
| Capital employed | | 143 | | 180 |

You are informed that there were no sales of fixed assets during 20X2, and that new shares and debentures issued in 20X2 were issued on 1 January.

Calculate operating profit and net cash flow from operations, and prepare a cash flow statement for the year 20X2, consistent with IAS 1, as far as the available information permits. Comment on the implications of the statement.

13.4 Repeat Exercise 13.3, but this time work on the assumption that fixed assets that had originally cost €30,000, with accumulated depreciation of €12,000, had been sold during the year ended 31 December 20X2 for €11,000.

# Chapter 14

# Group accounting

| Contents | | | |
|---|---|---|---|
| | 14.1 | Introduction: the group | 264 |
| | 14.2 | Investments related to the group | 267 |
| | 14.3 | Accounting for the group | 270 |
| | | 14.3.1 The parent's financial statements | 270 |
| | | 14.3.2 Consolidated balance sheets | 271 |
| | | 14.3.3 Subsequent treatment of goodwill | 275 |
| | | 14.3.4 Consolidated income statements | 276 |
| | | 14.3.5 Non-controlling interests | 276 |
| | | 14.3.6 Intercompany transactions | 277 |
| | 14.4 | Uniting of interests | 279 |
| | 14.5 | Proportional consolidation | 280 |
| | 14.6 | The equity method | 281 |
| | 14.7 | Conclusion on group relationships | 283 |
| | | Summary | 284 |
| | | References and research | 284 |
| | | Exercises | 285 |

**Objectives**  After careful study of this chapter, you should be able to:

- outline the idea of the group for financial reporting purposes;

- distinguish between the concepts of control, joint control and significant influence;

- explain why it may be useful to produce separate sets of financial statements for an investor and for its group;

- prepare simple consolidated balance sheets, taking account of minority interests and intercompany transactions;

- explain the different possible treatments of goodwill arising on consolidation;

- outline the proportional consolidation and equity methods.

## 14.1 Introduction: the group

As explained briefly in Chapter 4, the economic world is dominated by enterprises that are structured as groups, each comprising a large number of legally separate entities. The reasons for such complex structures include the following:

- the various entities in the group need to be legally separate because they operate in several countries under different laws;
- there are tax advantages in being separate or there would be tax disadvantages in combining formerly separate entities;
- the legal structures may partially reflect a hierarchical organizational structure or the way in which the group was put together over time.

So far in this book, the discussion has largely been set in the context of an individual legal entity. However, for the purpose of looking at the financial statements of nearly all the world's most important economic entities, which are groups, we must now change this approach. Since the components of a group act together as though they were a single economic entity, it makes sense for accountants to prepare financial statements for a group on this basis, which does not just mean adding all the figures of the group companies together, as will be explained. In many countries, financial statements are available both for the group and for the individual legal parts of it.

*Why it matters*    *Suppose that a company has several subsidiaries but that its shareholders or lenders look only at the unconsolidated financial statements of the company as a legal entity. As explained later, in many countries (e.g. France, Germany and the UK), the balance sheet would show the subsidiaries as investments (generally at cost), and the income statement would only show dividend income. If the parent sold some inventory to a subsidiary at an artificially high price, profits would be shown in the parent's income statement. If the subsidiaries borrowed large amounts of money for the group, this would not show up in the parent's balance sheet. In other words, the parent's statements give a misleading picture of the performance of the economic entity.*

Some possible relationships between an investor company and the entities in which it owns shares are shown in Figure 14.1. The circle in Figure 14.1 is the perimeter of the group for accounting purposes. The key question is: where should we draw the perimeter; what is in the group? This chapter considers that question, and then how to account for the group and things connected to it.

Since the group's financial statements are designed to present the group companies as if they were a single entity, the assets and liabilities in the group's balance sheet must meet the definition of asset and liability (see Chapter 8) from the group's point of view. For example, for an item to appear as an asset it must be controlled by the group. This implies that for an entity to be included in the group its financial and operating policies must be controlled by the investor company. IAS 27 (paragraph 4) defines a *subsidiary* as:

> an entity . . . that is controlled by another entity (known as the parent) . . . Control is the power to govern the financial and operating policies of an entity so as to obtain benefits from its activities.

**Figure 14.1  A group (1)**

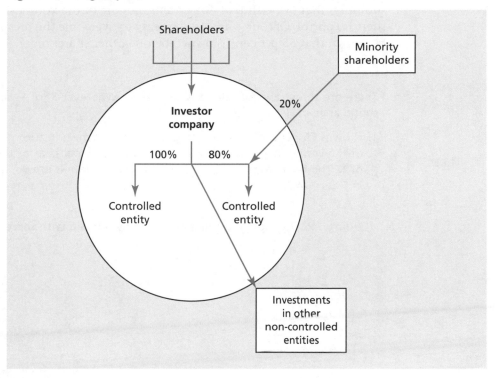

There is clearly a close connection between control and the ownership of voting shares. It is almost always the case that if company X owns more than half the voting shares of company Y, then X controls Y and so is the parent of Y. In some jurisdictions, the definition of a subsidiary rests on this ownership of shares (as in the United States).

*Why it matters*  *Groups might wish to hide their liabilities in order to present a better picture. If it is possible to set up controlled entities that are not consolidated, then the group can arrange for these entities to borrow money or sign a finance lease contract without it showing up as liabilities on the group balance sheet. This was one of the major features of the bad accounting by the US company, Enron, before it collapsed in 2001.*

However, IAS 27 and most European laws make it clear that all controlled entities are subsidiaries, and that control can exist with less than a majority of the voting shares, if somehow in practice there is power to appoint the majority of board directors or to control the majority of votes on the board. For example, if company X owns 48 per cent of voting shares of company Y and all the other shares are owned by thousands of small shareholders who do not use their votes, then company X will be able to control the board appointments of company Y.

In line with this, under the national law in France and Japan there is a presumption that ownership of 40 per cent or more of the voting shares means that there is control. Of course, it would be easy to overcome the presumption if it can be shown that 55 per cent is owned by one other shareholder.

**Activity 14.A**

There are three cases of relationships below. Wherever $S_1$ or $S_2$ appear, they are subsidiaries of H.

1. H owns 75 per cent of the voting shares of $S_1$, which in turn owns 40 per cent of the voting shares of X. H also owns directly 15 per cent of the voting shares of X. The relationships are easier to see if a diagram is drawn, and this is given in Figure 14.2.

Figure 14.2 **Example interrelationship of ownership with three companies**

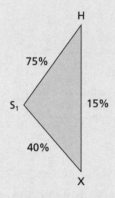

2. H owns 100 per cent of the voting shares of $S_1$, which in turn owns 30 per cent of X. H also owns 75 per cent of $S_2$, which in turn owns 25 per cent of X. This relationship is shown in Figure 14.3.

Figure 14.3 **Example interrelationship of ownership with four companies**

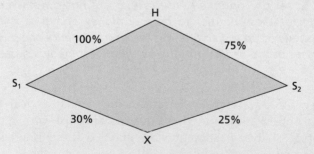

3. H owns 60 per cent of the voting shares of $S_1$, which in turn owns 20 per cent of the voting shares of X. H also owns directly 20 per cent of the voting shares of X. This relationship is shown in Figure 14.4.

Figure 14.4 **Example interrelationship of ownership with three companies**

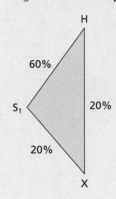

In which of these three cases is X also part of the group?

**Feedback**

1. $S_1$ is a subsidiary of H (75 per cent ownership); X is not a subsidiary of $S_1$ (assuming no dominant influence in practice). H directly owns:

$$[75\% \times (40\% \text{ of X})] + (15\% \text{ of X})$$
$$= 30\% + 15\%$$
$$= 45\%.$$

This might seem to imply no subsidiary relationship. However, H *controls* $S_1$ and thus controls (40% of X) plus 15 per cent. Therefore, X *is* a subsidiary of H.

2. $S_1$ and $S_2$ are subsidiaries of H. H directly owns:

$$(100\% \times 30\%) + (75\% \times 25\% \text{ of X})$$
$$= 30\% + 18.75\%$$
$$= 48.75\%.$$

However, H *controls* (30% + 25%) = 55% of X. Thus X is a subsidiary of H.

3. $S_1$ is a subsidiary of H.

H owns:     $(60\% \times 20\%) + (20\% \text{ of X}) = 32\%$ of X
H controls:  $20\% + (20\% \text{ of X}) = 40\%$

Thus X is *not* a subsidiary of H (assuming no control in practice).

## 14.2 Investments related to the group

In addition to the entities controlled by the group, there may be other investments outside the group, as shown in Figure 14.1. In more detail, these might be as shown in Figure 14.5.

The jointly controlled entity in Figure 14.5 may have one other shareholder owning the other half of the shares. There is more difficulty with applying the concept of control here. Such an entity is called a 'joint venture'. It occurs under IFRS where two or more venturers have a contract to control the venture by

**Figure 14.5 A group (2)**

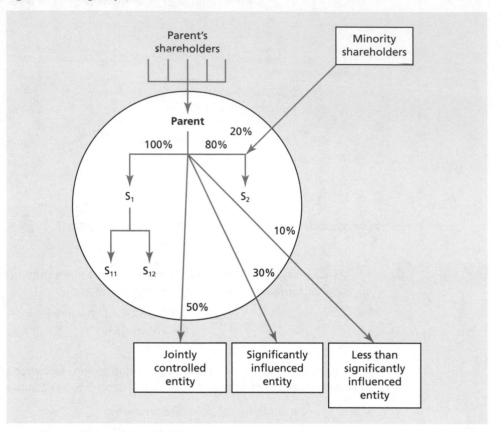

unanimous agreement. Under French rules, and as an option in IAS 31, *Joint Ventures*, joint venture entities are seen as partly within the group, not as in Figure 14.5. In the US and UK rules, they are seen as outside the group. In most countries, both views are allowed.

**Activity 14.B**   If a company owns 25 per cent of the shares in a joint venture (JV), does it control the assets of the JV? If not, does it control a quarter of the assets? Is the case different if the parent owns exactly one half?

**Feedback**   As noted earlier, control is defined by the IASB as power to control the operating and financial policies of an investee. At its most basic, the question becomes: could the investor go into the JV and do what it likes with the assets (or a proportion of the assets)? The answer is 'no' in both the 25 per cent and the 50 per cent case. Consequently, none of the assets of the JV is in the group. This seems to mean that proportional consolidation is inconsistent with the concept of 'control', on which group accounting is generally based. This will be discussed again later. The IASB has published a proposal to remove the option of proportional consolidation.

It is important to remember which entity we are accounting for. Whether it is the investor or the investor's group, there is no control. Taking the venturers together, there would be control, but we are not accounting for two or more venturers together.

The other investments identified in Figure 14.5 are clearly not part of the group because they are not controlled. However, one of these is included in a special category of entities over which an investor exercises 'significant influence' without control. This influence is generally presumed to exist when an investor has at least a 20 per cent holding in the voting shares of the other company. Evidence of significant influence would include the ability to appoint at least one director to the board of the associate. In the domestic rules of some countries, the presumption of significant influence starts at a lower threshold; for example, at 3 per cent for holdings in listed companies in Spain, and at 10 per cent for such holdings in Italy. Such investments are called 'associates' and are accounted for in a particular way, as described later.

Putting all these terms together, the group and its connected companies can be redrawn as in Figure 14.6. The parent has a series of subsidiaries, such as $S_1$ and $S_2$, which themselves can be parents of subsidiaries, such as $S_{11}$ and $S_{12}$. Not all subsidiaries are wholly owned by their parents. For example, $S_2$ is 80 per cent owned by the parent and 20 per cent owned by other shareholders who are said to have a *non-controlling interest* (or minority interest) in the group.

Figure 14.6 **A group (3)**

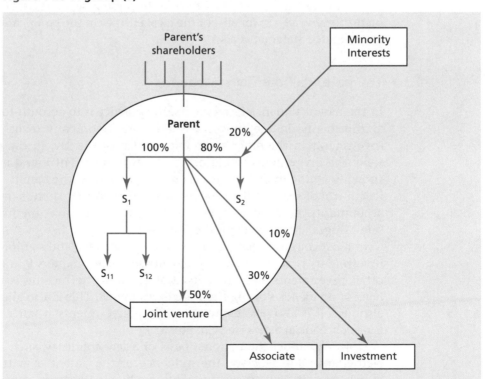

A typical policy statement for the year to 31 December 2010 reads as follows (the term 'equity method' being explained below).

> The consolidated financial statements include the accounts of Pubco's parent company ('Parent Company'), and each of those companies over which the Group exercises control. Control over an entity is presumed to exist when the Group owns, directly or indirectly through subsidiaries, over 50% of the voting rights of the entity, the Group has the power to govern the operating and financial policies of the entity through agreement or the Group has the power to appoint or remove the majority of the members of the board of the entity.
>
> The Group's share of profits and losses of associated companies is included in the consolidated profit and loss account in accordance with the equity method of accounting. An associated company is an entity over which the Group exercises significant influence. Significant influence is generally presumed to exist when the Group owns, directly or indirectly through subsidiaries, over 20% of the voting rights of the company.

Notice the clear statement that percentage of ownership is not the only criterion.

## 14.3 Accounting for the group

In the example of Figure 14.6, there are eight legally separate entities (the parent, four subsidiaries, one joint venture, one associate and one other investment). These can all borrow money and own buildings. They all pay tax and dividends. In most countries, it is thought useful to present separate sets of financial statements for several – or for all – of the legal entities in the group, and then to present consolidated statements also.

### 14.3.1 The parent's financial statements

In the parent's financial statements, the practice is to account for the direct legal arrangements. In the above case, the parent company owns and controls its investments in the other seven entities. Consequently, in the parent's balance sheet the investments would be shown as non-current investments rather than showing all the individual assets and liabilities that the parent controls through its control of some of the other entities. Also, in the parent's income statement, accountants show just a single line of 'income from investments' rather than the sales, wages, interest, etc. of the investees.

In most countries, the valuation of the controlled and significantly influenced investments is at cost (less any impairment; see Chapters 9 and 11), as it is for other investments and other fixed assets; and the income is measured at the level of dividends flowing from the investments. This is also allowed under IFRS, although it is also possible to show these investments at fair value as available-for-sale financial assets (see Chapter 11).

However, under the national basis of a few countries, such as Denmark, the Netherlands and Norway, the influence of the parent over the other entities is seen as sufficient to justify taking credit for its share of profit, not just for the dividends received. In a balance sheet, the parent then includes the excess of profit over dividends as an increase in value of the investment. This is called the *equity method*. It is important to learn about it for consolidated accounting in nearly all countries (and see section 14.6, where a fuller explanation is given).

Let us take an example. Suppose that a parent buys all of the shares of a company for €100 million. The double entry for this would be:

| Debit: | Investment | €100m |
| Credit: | Cash | €100m |

It is assumed for the moment that no goodwill is involved here – in other words, that the cost of the shares equals the value of the subsidiary's equity (net assets) at the date of acquisition.

Suppose that, in the first year, the new subsidiary makes a profit of €20 million and pays a dividend of one-quarter of that. The effects on the parent if the equity method were to be applied would be:

| Debit: | Cash | €5m |
| Debit: | Investment | €15m |
| Credit: | Income | €20m |

So the investment would now be shown at €115 million, which reflects the fact that the subsidiary's equity has grown by €15 million as a result of its undistributed profit.

This method is applied in investor company statements that follow national rules in Denmark, the Netherlands and Norway, not only to investments in subsidiaries but also to others that are at least 'significantly influenced', namely joint ventures and associates.

### 14.3.2 Consolidated balance sheets

In addition to the eight legal entities in Figure 14.6, there is also the economic entity of the group as a whole. For reasons mentioned in Section 14.1, it is now thought to be essential to show the position for the whole group as a single entity. This idea is taken to an extreme in the country at the extreme in terms of dominance of investors as users of financial statements, namely the United States. In the US, it is normal to present financial statements for the group only, and not to bother about publishing the statements of the lesser legal entities. An element of this can be found in some European countries, which exempt a subsidiary from having to publish financial statements if the parent company guarantees all the subsidiary's debts.

**Activity 14.C**

Let us now move on to the preparation of consolidated statements. Consider the situation shown in Table 14.1, in which Big Co. acquired the whole of the issued ordinary share capital of Little Co. at a price of €2.5 per share (i.e. €125,000 cash) as at 30 June, at which date their respective balance sheets were as shown.

▶

### Table 14.1 Balance sheets for Big Co. and Little Co.

|  | Big Co. (€) | Little Co. (€) |
|---|---|---|
| Land and buildings | 50,000 | 25,000 |
| Plant | 40,000 | 20,000 |
| Investment in Little Co. | 125,000 | – |
| Sundry other assets | 20,000 | 15,000 |
|  | 235,000 | 60,000 |
|  |  |  |
| €1 ordinary shares | 150,000 | 50,000 |
| Reserves | 85,000 | 10,000 |
|  | 235,000 | 60,000 |

As at this date, the estimated market values of Little Co. assets were different from those recorded in the balance sheet:

| Land and buildings | €30,000 |
|---|---|
| Plant | €22,000 |
| Sundry other assets | €15,000 |
| Total | €67,000 |

Think first about the statements of Big (the parent company) in isolation. If these statements were sent to the shareholders of Big, how useful would this information be?

**Feedback** In Big's balance sheet the shareholding in Little will simply appear as an investment at historical cost (unless it used the equity method). However, as with any other asset in a balance sheet, the use of historical cost would not normally give the shareholders of Big a good indication of the value of the subsidiary or of the underlying assets. In Big's income statement, the only reference to the subsidiary would be 'dividends received from Little' (assuming there were any) and, of course, this would give no indication of the subsidiary's profitability. The holding company's financial statements give no meaningful information about the whole group's activities.

Group statements are prepared by adding together (*consolidating*) the position and results for all the components of the group. The basic process of consolidation takes the balance sheet of Big Co. as the starting point. In order to show the group as a single entity, the 'Investment in Little' entry must be removed and replaced by the assets and liabilities of Little that it represents, and the remaining difference shown as 'Goodwill on consolidation'. So, the goodwill is what Big paid, less what is bought. This procedure means that the resulting group balance sheet shows no 'Investment in Little', because a group cannot own an investment in itself.

The above procedure leaves a crucial question unresolved, because two alternative values are available for the net assets (i.e. assets – liabilities) of Little Co.: (i) the figures taken from Little's own accounting records as shown in its balance sheet (largely based on historical cost), or (ii) the current market values or 'fair values'. It is clearly arithmetically possible to use either set of figures, as the goodwill arising on consolidation is simply a balancing number. It is now the practice in most countries, and required under IFRS 3, *Business Combinations*, to use the fair values rather than the book values. This whole procedure of accounting for the business combination of Big Co. and Little Co. is called acquisition accounting or the purchase method.

**Activity 14.D**  Redraw the balance sheet of Little Co. from Table 14.1 in order to show how it would be shown for the purposes of preparing the consolidated balance sheet.

**Feedback**  The current values shown in Activity 14.C would be used to replace those in Table 14.1. The result would be Table 14.2. The reserves now include a revaluation reserve of €7,000. In most countries, this redrawn balance sheet would not be the one published. It would only be used within the group as part of the process of preparing the consolidated statements.

**Table 14.2 Redrawn balance sheet of Little Co. (€)**

| | |
|---|---|
| Land and buildings | 30,000 |
| Plant | 22,000 |
| Sundry other assets | 15,000 |
| | 67,000 |
| | |
| €1 ordinary shares | 50,000 |
| Reserves | 17,000 |
| | 67,000 |

This use of revalued amounts in the consolidated statements does not mean that the consolidated balance sheet departs from the cost model: the fair value of the subsidiary's incoming assets is an estimate of what it would have cost to buy them individually at the date when the subsidiary was bought. The resulting consolidated balance sheet, starting from Table 14.1 but using the fair values as revised in Table 14.2, is shown in Table 14.3.

**Table 14.3 Big and Little consolidated balance sheet (€000s)**

| | | |
|---|---|---|
| Land and buildings | 80 | (50 + 30) |
| Plant | 62 | (40 + 22) |
| Sundry other assets | 35 | (20 + 15) |
| Goodwill on consolidation | 58 | (125 − 67) |
| | 235 | |
| | | |
| Ordinary share capital | 150 | (150 + 50 − 50) |
| Reserves | 85 | (85 + 17 − 17) |
| | 235 | |

As with any consolidation, only the holding company's share capital is shown as the capital of the group. The subsidiary's own share capital reflects internal financing within the group, and is simply a reflection of the investment in the subsidiary as shown in the assets of the holding company's individual balance sheet. In essence, these two items are 'netted off' as part of the 'goodwill on consolidation' calculation. The €50,000 + €17,000 of equity at the bottom of Table 14.2 is set off in the goodwill calculation.

The figure called 'goodwill on consolidation' can be thought of in a number of ways. The easiest way is to think of it simply as a number – as a difference created by the bookkeeping. This idea can be seen in the Italian expression for the number: *differenza da consolidimento*. Another way of looking at it is that the goodwill amount is a premium on top of the separate values of the net assets. This idea comes through in the French term: *écart d'acquisition*. In the above example, the goodwill is, as usual, what Big paid, less the net assets that it bought. Big bought 100 per cent of the ownership interest in Little, paying €125,000 for a collection of resources that appear to be worth only €67,000 even at current values. So, the goodwill is €58,000.

The next question to ask is whether the goodwill is an asset to be recognized in the group's balance sheet. Consider the IASB's definition of an asset (seen in earlier chapters):

An asset is a resource controlled by the entity as a result of past events and from which future economic events are expected to flow to the entity.

Such an item should be incorporated in the balance sheet if:

(a) it is probable that any future economic benefit associated with the item will flow to or from the entity; and

(b) the item has a cost or value that can be measured with reliability.

Why did Big pay €125,000? There are two possible reasons: first, the directors of Big are stupid or interested in expansion at any cost; second, the directors of Big believe the purchase to be worth at least €125,000. Ignoring the first possibility, it follows that:

(i)   the goodwill on consolidation results from a past transaction;

(ii)  Big believes that this goodwill on consolidation will probably lead to benefits in the future; and

(iii) the cost of the goodwill can be measured by subtracting the fair value of the identifiable net assets from the investment in shares.

The remaining issue in determining whether or not the goodwill is a recognizable asset is whether Big *controls* the resources. If the resources are seen as the loyal customers, trained staff, monopoly position, etc., it seems that these are *not* controlled because the customers and the staff could leave and the monopoly position could be worn away or legislated against. If the goodwill is the 'going concern' element, Big does seem to control that.

Anyway, most accounting systems, including IFRS, treat the goodwill as an asset that should be capitalized. In the domestic rules of some countries, such as Germany and the Netherlands, it is legally possible to write off goodwill against reserves immediately on acquisition, thereby never showing it as an asset.

### 14.3.3 Subsequent treatment of goodwill

As with other items shown as assets, goodwill presumably wears out. However, because it is not quite clear what the goodwill is, there are problems in assessing its useful economic life. Nevertheless, there seems to be a good argument that the elements of goodwill bought at the date of acquisition do wear out: eventually the customers die, the staff retire and fashions change. In a fast-moving industry, goodwill may have a short life.

The EU Fourth Directive (Articles 34.1 and 37.2) suggested a life of five years but allowed longer. Until 2005, UK and IAS standards imposed a rebuttable presumption of a limit of 20 years but longer periods could be used if a company could make a special case; but then an annual test of impairment had to be carried out (see Section 9.6). In order to eliminate charges based on an arbitrary length of life, the US standard setter (the FASB) changed its rule in 2001 to require annual impairment calculations instead of amortization. This approach is now followed by the IASB under IFRS 3, applicable from 1 January 2005. However, this can be criticized because it does not separate the initially purchased goodwill from that subsequently arising; so, as long as the cost of the initial goodwill is exceeded by the value of all the goodwill, no impairment is recognized. There is also a major practical problem here in annually measuring the 'value' of an asset as intangible as goodwill. This is done by assessing the value of the major components of the group to which the goodwill has been allocated.

One issue that is not relevant here is taxation. This is because goodwill on consolidation, and therefore amortization expenses related to it, occurs only in consolidated statements. Such statements are not relevant for taxation because tax works primarily on the basis of individual legal entities, such as a parent company. Consequently, the amortization or impairment of goodwill on consolidation is not relevant for tax.

**Why it matters**  *Using the example of Big Co. and Little Co., as in Table 14.3, four different treatments of goodwill can be illustrated:*

1. *Write off to reserves.*
2. *Amortize over 5 years.*
3. *Amortize over 20 years.*
4. *Impairment only.*

*Table 14.4 shows the position for the first three of these after two years, ignoring the effects of all other changes such as depreciating other assets, making profit, paying dividends. In Case 1, the initial goodwill of 58 has been amortized for two years at 20 per cent per year; in Case 2, the same has occurred at 5 per cent per year. Of course, the readers of the financial statements will also be interested in the group's profit figures. These will look best for Case 3 (because there is no amortization expense since goodwill is written off against reserves, and there is no asset to amortize) and worst for Case 1.*

*Case 4 (impairment only) might look even better because goodwill would remain at 58 (and reserves would be 85) unless the group suffered adverse conditions leading to an impairment.*

Table 14.4 **Big Co. and Little Co.: three different balance sheets after two years (€000)**

|  | Case 1 | Case 2 | Case 3 |
|---|---|---|---|
| Goodwill on consolidation | 34.8 | 52.2 | 0 |
| Land and buildings | 80 | 80 | 80 |
| Plant | 62 | 62 | 62 |
| Sundry other assets | 35 | 35 | 35 |
|  | 211.8 | 229.2 | 177 |
|  |  |  |  |
| Ordinary share capital | 150 | 150 | 150 |
| Reserves | 61.8 | 79.2 | 27 |
|  | 211.8 | 229.2 | 177 |

### 14.3.4 Consolidated income statements

As for the consolidated balance sheet, so for the consolidated income statement the idea is to present a picture of the group as though it were a single entity. For many items in the group's income statement, this is straightforward. For example, the consolidated wages expense is the total of the wages expenses of all the group enterprises. Similarly, the consolidated sales figure is the total of all the group's sales figures to outsiders. There is a complication in that some sales may be made to other members of the group. These need to be eliminated, as examined below in Subsection 14.3.6.

One expense that appears in the consolidated income statement but will not have appeared in the income statements of any component of the group is any amortization or impairment of goodwill arising on consolidation.

### 14.3.5 Non-controlling interests

It is now time to add an extra complication into the discussion of group accounting. Suppose that the holding company (or parent company) buys less than the whole of the shares in the subsidiary. This leaves a *non-controlling* set of shareholders (sometimes called 'minority interests') in the subsidiary who are not shareholders in the parent. In some countries, such as the United States up until 2010, consolidation is performed by taking the view of the parent company shareholders (the *parent company approach*). Although the consolidation process begins by adding together all the resources and results of the controlled entities, the proportion of the resources and results that is not actually owned by the parent (the minority interests) are then shown:

(a) in the income statement, as a reduction in net profits (or the reverse, if the subsidiary made a loss), to arrive at earnings attributable to the shareholders of the parent company;

(b) in the balance sheet, separately from shareholders' funds and liabilities.

The non-controlling interests shown as (b) above represent a claim on the group resources by those *outside* the controlling ownership interest, which is the interest of the owners of the parent.

However, according to the IASB's Framework, the minority interest must be equity because it does not fit the definition of a liability, because there is no obligation to pay share capital and reserves to the minority shareholders. Therefore, IAS 27 was amended in 2003 to require minority interests to be shown as part of group equity though separately from the parent shareholders' equity. The same applies in US GAAP from 2010.

In order to highlight one issue at a time, the example in Tables 14.1 to 14.3 had no minority interest, for the subsidiary was wholly owned. However, consider the companies H and S, as shown at 31 December 20X8 in Table 14.5. Suppose that H had purchased 80 per cent of the 8,000 shares of S for cash at 31 December 20X7 at a price of €1.50 per share, when the balance on S's reserves had stood at €2,000. At that date, then, the net assets and shareholders' funds (the equity) of S were €10,000 (i.e. €8,000 + €2,000). The purchase price was €9,600 (i.e. 80 per cent × €1.50 × 8,000 shares).

Table 14.5 **Balance sheets of H and S at 31 December 20X8**

|  | H | S |
|---|---|---|
| Plant and machinery | 60,000 | 5,000 |
| Investment in S | 9,600 | – |
| Sundry current assets | 35,000 | 6,000 |
|  | 104,600 | 11,000 |
| €1 ordinary shares | 40,000 | 8,000 |
| Reserves | 64,600 | 3,000 |
|  | 104,600 | 11,000 |

Since all of the assets of S (all of which are *controlled* by H) are being brought in, it is necessary to account for the minority's 20 per cent claim. The consolidated balance sheet as at 31 December 20X8 would be as shown in Figure 14.7. The non-controlling interest of €2,200 is calculated as in Note 3 but can also be seen to be equal to 20 per cent of the minority's initial stake, i.e. 20 per cent of (€8,000 + €2,000) = €2,000, plus 20 per cent of S's income since its purchase, i.e. 20 per cent of (€3,000 – 2,000) = €200.

In the consolidated income statement, the non-controlling share of profit is generally shown at the end in order to show separately the net profit attributable to the parent company shareholders. In the above example, €200 would be shown as the non-controlling share in the consolidated income statement for 20X8.

## 14.3.6 Intercompany transactions

It is likely that companies within a group will trade with each other and lend to each other. Remembering that H and S (holding and subsidiary companies) are separate legal entities, if H sells goods to S at above their cost, then H has made a profit. If S has not yet sold the goods to outsiders, then the total group has made no profit or loss, because the group, considered as an economic entity, has not done anything. In preparing consolidated accounts, therefore, the positions and

Figure 14.7 **Consolidated balance sheet of H and S at 31 December 20X8 (€)**

| | |
|---|---:|
| Goodwill on acquisition (Note 1) | 1,600 |
| Plant and machinery | 65,000 |
| Sundry current assets | 41,000 |
| | 107,600 |
| | |
| €1 ordinary shares | 40,000 |
| Reserves (Note 2) | 65,400 |
| Minority interests (Note 3) | 2,200 |
| | 107,600 |

*Notes*

1. There are two different ways of calculating goodwill when there are non-controlling interests. The following is the simpler one.

| | |
|---|---:|
| Cost of investment in S | 9,600 |
| *less* 80% of net assets of S (= shareholders' funds) | |
| at 31 December 20X7 80% × (8,000 + 2,000) | 8,000 |
| | 1,600 |

2. 

| | | |
|---|---:|---:|
| Reserves of H at 31 December 20X8 | 64,600 | |
| Reserves of S accruing to group since date of acquisition | | |
| (3,000 − 2,000) × 80% | 800 | |
| | | 65,400 |

3. 

| | | |
|---|---:|---:|
| Share capital at 31 December 20X8 of S relating to minorities | | |
| (20% × 8,000) | 1,600 | |
| Reserves at 31 December 20X8 of S relating to minorities | | |
| (20% × 3,000) | 600 | |
| | | 2,200 |

results of H and S cannot simply be added together. These sales and profits 'made' by H by selling to S must be removed from the consolidated results so as to leave only those profits that have been 'made' by the group as a whole by selling to outsiders. Intercompany loans between companies within the group structure must be similarly cancelled out, so as to present a picture of loans made by or to the group considered as a single economic entity.

If, for example, H owns 75 per cent of S, then it could be argued that 25 per cent of the profits have really been 'made' by the group, as 25 per cent of the sale from H to S related to the minority interest, which is by definition not part of the group. This logic would lead to the conclusion that only 75 per cent of the profit made between H and S would need to be removed on the consolidation. However, this practice is usually felt to be inappropriate, especially as H controls S and therefore controls the whole sale. IAS 27 (paragraph 25) requires the elimination of 100 per cent of such intercompany profits. This is also arithmetically easier for complex groups.

**Activity 14.E**

The financial year end of two companies *A* and *B* within the same group is 31 December. On 29 December, *A* despatched goods to *B* with an invoice value of €40,000 and charged *B*'s account accordingly. *B* does not receive either goods or invoice until 4 January. Prepare the consolidation adjustment in *B*'s books of account and note any other adjustment that may be required on consolidation.

**Feedback**

The following adjustment will bring the goods into *B*'s books as at 31 December:

|                          | Dr.      | Cr.      |
|--------------------------|----------|----------|
| Goods in transit         | €40,000  |          |
| Current account with *A* |          | €40,000  |

On consolidation the respective intercompany balances in the current accounts which are now of the same size will cancel out.

However, we must remember that this inventory of €40,000 in transit will contain an element of unrealized profit and this will need to be eliminated on consolidation.

## 14.4 Uniting of interests

The examples used so far are based on the concept of a takeover (or perhaps an agreed acquisition) of a small company by a larger one. However, it is possible for two enterprises to come together by agreement and on a more or less equal basis. In accounting terms this has been referred to as a *uniting of interests* (IFRS), *merger accounting* (UK) or *pooling of interests* (US). In such cases, two or more companies merge their previously separate businesses into one integrated unit and the combined new ownership's interests mirror the relative interests of the original entities. There is generally little or no cash involved because the combination is achieved by one of the companies issuing more shares and transferring them to the other company's shareholders. It should be noted that in several countries, e.g. the United Kingdom and the United States, these 'mergers' were usually achieved legally by a takeover. In other countries, a 'legal merger' (*fusion* in French or *fusione* in Italian) may occur.

Uniting of interests accounting is allowed under the EU Seventh Directive (Articles 19 and 20). The method assumes no purchase, and therefore there is no goodwill and no fair value exercise. The method was always rare in most European countries, although the DaimlerChrysler (German–US) combination was treated as a pooling under US accounting. Also, it was occasionally seen under UK accounting – for example, in the business combinations of BP (UK) with Amoco (US) and of Astra (Sweden) with Zeneca (UK).

In practice, it was possible for management to arrange for combinations to look like unitings/poolings in order to use the more flattering accounting. To stop this, the US standard setter (the FASB) abolished the method for any business combination from 1 July 2001. However, former poolings remain in place, so they continue to affect financial statements. The IASB also abolished the method by IFRS 3, effective from 1 January 2005.

Why it matters *Although fairly rare, the uniting of interests method was particularly found in very large business combinations and it can still have an enormous effect on the numbers. For example, the net assets (equal to the shareholders' funds) of the pharmaceutical company Astra-Zeneca are shown in Table 14.6 at the year ends before and after the merger that created it. As noted above, under UK accounting, it was treated as a merger. Under US accounting, it would have been treated as an acquisition, and so the assets (including goodwill) would have looked much larger.*

Table 14.6 **Astra-Zeneca's net assets for 1998 and 1999**

|      | UK published net assets (£m) | US adjusted net assets (£m) | Change |
|------|------|------|------|
| 1998 | 10,929 | 5,558 | −49% |
| 1999 | 10,302 | 33,375 | +227% |

*Source*: Extracts from published company financial statements.

## 14.5 Proportional consolidation

As mentioned earlier, entities other than subsidiaries can be connected to the group. Consider two companies, H and J. The former has acquired 50 per cent of the equity share capital of J for cash at 31 December at a price of €1.50 per share, and their respective balance sheets as at 31 December are as shown in Table 14.7. Suppose that another company owns the other half of J's shares and that J is a jointly controlled 'joint venture'.

Table 14.7 **Balance sheets of H and J**

|                          | H | J |
|--------------------------|------|------|
| Plant and machinery      | 50,000 | 4,000 |
| Investment in J          |  |  |
| (i.e. 8,000 shares × 50% × €1.50) | 6,000 | – |
| Sundry current assets    | 28,600 | 6,000 |
|                          | 84,600 | 10,000 |
| €1 Ordinary shares       | 40,000 | 8,000 |
| Reserves                 | 44,600 | 2,000 |
|                          | 84,600 | 10,000 |

It was mentioned in Section 14.2 that one way of dealing with this in the group financial statements is by proportional consolidation. Using this method we add together the various components of each company's balance sheet (assets and liabilities) on the basis of H's proportionate interest in J in order to arrive at the 'group' picture. The effect of this is to remove the 'Investment in J' from H's balance sheet and replace it with the proportion of all the individual items that it represents. The results are shown in Table 14.8. For simplicity, any subsidiaries of H are left out here.

Table 14.8 **Proportional consolidation of H and J**

| | | |
|---|---:|---|
| Goodwill on consolidation | 1,000 | {6,000 − [50% × (8,000 + 2,000)]} |
| Plant and machinery | 52,000 | [50,000 + (50% × 4,000)] |
| Sundry current assets | 31,600 | [28,600 + (50% × 6,000)] |
| | 84,600 | |
| | | |
| Ordinary share capital | 40,000 | |
| Reserves | 44,600 | |
| | 84,600 | |

## 14.6 The equity method

Earlier in this chapter it was noted that the equity method has several uses, including:

- to show the investments in subsidiaries in a parent's financial statements under the domestic rules of Denmark, the Netherlands and Norway (this also applying to investments in joint ventures and associates in those countries);
- to show investments in associates and some joint ventures in consolidated statements.

IAS 28 (paragraph 2) says:

> The *equity method* is a method of accounting whereby the investment is initially recognised at cost and adjusted thereafter for the post acquisition change in the investor's share of net assets of the investee. The profit or loss of the investor includes the investor's share of the profit or loss of the investee.

An illustration will be useful here. Suppose that company X had acquired 600 ordinary shares in company Y (which amounted to 30 per cent of the company) at a price of €1.50 per share on 31 December 20X7. Thus, the investment in the associate was €900 (600 shares at €1.50 each). At the original purchase date, the reserves of Y had been €800. The respective balance sheets of X and Y a year later (at 31 December 20X8) are shown in Table 14.9.

Table 14.9 **Balance sheets of X and Y**

| | X | Y |
|---|---:|---:|
| Fixed assets | 15,000 | 3,200 |
| Investment in Y | 900 | – |
| Net current assets | 1,000 | 1,800 |
| | 16,900 | 5,000 |
| | | |
| Share capital | 8,000 | 2,200 |
| Reserves | 8,900 | 2,800 |
| | 16,900 | 5,000 |

Suppose that X also has a subsidiary company and it is proposed to prepare consolidated statements for the X group for the year ended 31 December 20X8. In order to concentrate on the associate, one could draft the initial consolidated balance sheet of the group as at that date before inclusion of the income of the subsidiary, but inclusive of the associate's figures. The effects of the equity method are shown in Table 14.10. There is an assumption here that there is no goodwill involved in the purchase and that no dividends are paid by the associate.

Table 14.10 **Initial equity accounting of Y**

| | |
|---|---:|
| Fixed assets[a] | 15,000 |
| Investment in Y[b] | 1,500 |
| Net current assets[a] | 1,000 |
| | 17,500 |
| | |
| Share capital[a] | 8,000 |
| Reserves[c] | 9,500 |
| | 17,500 |

*Notes*
[a] Assets and share capital of X only, since Y is an associated company and will therefore be shown in the group balance sheet as an investment.

| | |
|---|---:|
| [b] cost | 900 |
| + share of post-acquisition reserves | |
| = 30% × 2,000 (i.e. 2,800 − 800) | 600 |
| | 1,500 |
| [c] Reserves of X | 8,900 |
| + group's share of post-acquisition | |
| reserves of Y (30% × 2,000) | 600 |
| | 9,500 |

This illustration demonstrates the effect of equity accounting for the results of an associate in a group's balance sheet. This method is often known as a *one-line consolidation*. The effect is that the assets (Investment in Y) and claims (Reserves) have both been increased by €600 (the group's share of the post-acquisition profits of the associate). However, the difference from proportional consolidation is that the proportion is added as one figure to the Investment, not as separate figures to the individual asset (and liability) accounts.

If, in the Table 14.10 example, dividends had been paid by the associate, then cash would have moved into the group and so the group cash figure would rise by the size of the dividend received. However, the net assets (= equity) of the associate would have fallen because it has paid out cash. So the 'investment in Y' would fall by the same amount as the cash rose.

Let us suppose that a total dividend of €1,000 was paid by Y to its various shareholders. X would receive 30 per cent of this, so that the double entry in its consolidated statements would be:

| | | |
|---|---|---:|
| Debit: | Cash | 300 |
| Credit: | Investment in associate | 300 |

The consolidated profit and loss account would be unaffected by the dividend because X's share of the total profit had already been recorded.

## 14.7  Conclusion on group relationships

As an investor company's influence over its various investees grows, so the degree of inclusion of their net assets and results in the investor's group financial statements increases. This is represented in Table 14.11. An investment without 'significant influence' is accounted for under the cost method. An investment with 'significant influence' (but no more) is accounted for under the equity method. A jointly controlled investment might be accounted for by proportional consolidation. An investment with control or *dominant influence* is fully consolidated. These distinctions, in a real business situation, will often contain elements of uncertainty. The 20 per cent threshold for 'significant influence' is, of course, arbitrary.

**Table 14.11 Degree of inclusion of investees in consolidated statements under IFRS**

| Investment | Balance sheet | Income statement |
| --- | --- | --- |
| 1. Less than significant influence (typically less than 20% of voting shares) | Investment treated as financial asset (see Chapter 11) | Dividends, and any revaluation gains and losses |
| 2. Significant influence: an associate (typically 20% or more of voting shares) | Investment measured by the equity method | Share of net income |
| 3. Joint control: a joint venture entity | Proportionate consolidation or equity method | Proportionate consolidation or share of net income |
| 4. Control but less than 100% ownership of voting shares: a subsidiary | Full consolidation; non-controlling interest shown | Full consolidation; non-controlling interest shown |
| 5. Control and 100% ownership of shares: a wholly-owned subsidiary | Full consolidation | Full consolidation |

*Why it matters*  Consolidated net assets would generally be the same whichever of methods 2 to 5 in Table 14.11 is applied to an investment; and the same goes for consolidated net income. However, many component figures will be different. For example, method 2 includes none of an investee's cash or sales in the group's financial statements; method 3 includes a proportion; and methods 4 and 5 include 100 per cent. This may have a major effect on the ratios calculated by investment analysts.

For example, under IAS 31, joint venture entities can be accounted for by methods 2 or 3. Under method 2 (equity accounting), none of the joint venture's cash or sales will appear in the cash, liabilities and sales lines of the consolidated balance sheet and income statement. Under method 3 (proportional consolidation), the group's proportion of cash, liabilities and sales will be included. If joint ventures are important to the group (as they often are in large international groups), this may have a major effect on many of the ratios introduced in Chapter 7. You may like to check which ones are affected.

**Summary**

- Most large economic enterprises operate as groups of legal entities, and so the accounting needs to present the state of affairs and performance of the group.

- A subsidiary is defined on the basis of control, although the exact definition varies internationally.

- There are other entities connected to the group by joint control or significant influence.

- A parent's unconsolidated financial statements generally show the cost of investments and the receipt of dividends from them, although domestic practices under Danish, Dutch and Norwegian rules is to use the equity method for some investments.

- Consolidated statements include the parent and its subsidiaries as though they were a single economic entity.

- Companies often pay more for subsidiaries than the value of the individual identifiable net assets. The difference is goodwill, which is treated as an asset in most countries.

- The amortization or impairment of goodwill varies greatly internationally, but an impairment-only approach is now required in IFRS.

- Non-controlling interests and intercompany transactions need to be accounted for.

- A rare but importantly different method of accounting for business combinations is uniting/merger/pooling accounting. Although not now allowed in IFRS or US GAAP, there are several old examples remaining in today's financial statements.

- In consolidated statements, associated enterprises and some joint ventures are accounted for by the equity method, although some sets of rules allow or encourage proportional consolidation for joint venture entities.

- Harmonization is more useful and easier if it concentrates on consolidated statements.

## References and research

The documents of the IASB of particular relevance to this chapter are:

- IFRS 3 (revised 2008), *Business Combinations*.
- IAS 27 (revised 2008), *Consolidated and Separate Financial Statements*.
- IAS 28 (revised 2003), *Investments in Associates*.
- IAS 31 (revised 2003), *Financial Reporting of Interests in Joint Ventures*.

Research in the English language on the topics of this chapter includes:

- P. Bircher, 'The adoption of consolidated accounting in Great Britain', *Accounting and Business Research*, Winter, 1988.
- F.D.S. Choi and C. Lee, 'Merger premia and national differences in accounting for goodwill', *Journal of International Financial Management and Accounting*, Vol. 3(3), 1991.
- G. Diggle and C.W. Nobes, 'European rule-making in accounting: The Seventh Directive as a case study', *Accounting and Business Research*, Autumn, 1994.

- L.T. Johnson and K.R. Petrone, 'Is goodwill an asset?' *Accounting Horizons*, September 1998.
- M. Lamb, 'When is a group a group? Convergence of concepts of "group" in European Union corporation tax', *European Accounting Review*, Vol. 4(1), 1995.
- A. Mora and W. Rees, 'The early adoption of consolidated accounting in Spain', *European Accounting Review*, Vol. 7, No. 4, 1998.
- C.W. Nobes, 'A political history of goodwill in the UK: An illustration of cyclical standard setting', *Abacus*, Vol. 28, No. 2, 1992.
- C.W. Nobes, 'An analysis of the international development of the equity method', *Abacus*, February 2002.
- C.W. Nobes and J. Norton, 'International variations in the accounting and tax treatments of goodwill, and the implications for research', *Journal of International Accounting, Auditing and Taxation*, Vol. 5, No. 2, 1996.

## ? EXERCISES

*Feedback on the first two of these exercises is given in Appendix D.*

14.1 Explain the concepts of:

(a) subsidiary;

(b) joint venture;

(c) associate;

(d) trade investment which is none of the above.

Outline and discuss the usual approaches to the accounting treatment in each case in consolidated statements.

14.2 A Co. owns 75 per cent of the shares in B Co., bought when the reserves of B were €200,000. The individual balance sheets of A and B as at 30.6.20X8 are given in Table 14.12. During the year, B has sold goods to A at a profit margin of 25 per cent on cost. €50,000 of these goods remain in A's closing inventory as at 30.6.20X8. Also B owes A €2,000 as at 30.6.20X8. Prepare the consolidated balance sheet as at 30.6.20X8.

Table 14.12 **Individual balance sheets as at 30.6.20X8**

| | A 000s | B 000s |
|---|---|---|
| *Assets* | | |
| Land and plant | 1,000 | 200 |
| Investment in B | 275 | – |
| Inventory | 600 | 400 |
| Debtors (receivables) | 200 | 40 |
| | 2,075 | 640 |
| *Liabilities* | | |
| Creditors (payables) | 30 | 16 |
| | 2,045 | 624 |
| *Represented by:* | | |
| Ordinary €1 shares | 1,000 | 100 |
| Reserves | 1,045 | 524 |
| | 2,045 | 624 |

**14.3** The balance sheets of A and B as at 31 December 20X7 are as shown in Figure 14.8. In addition:

(a) A had acquired 37,500 shares in B in 20X3 when there was a debit balance on the reserves of €3,000.

(b) B purchases goods from A, providing A with a gross profit on the invoice price of $33\frac{1}{3}$ per cent. On 31 December 20X7 the inventory of B still included an amount of €8,000, being goods purchased from A for €9,000.

Prepare the consolidated balance sheet of A and its subsidiary as at 31 December 20X7.

**Figure 14.8 Balance sheets for A and B as at 31 December 20X7**

|  | A 000s |  | B 000s |  |
|---|---|---|---|---|
| Land and buildings | 108 |  | 64 |  |
| less Depreciation | 20 | 88 | 32 | 32 |
| Plant and machinery | 65 |  | 43 |  |
| less Depreciation | 25 | 40 | 29 | 14 |
|  |  | 128 |  | 46 |
| Investment: shares in B |  | 35 |  | – |
| Inventory | 25 |  | 27 |  |
| Debtors | 48 |  | 21 |  |
| Bank | 22 |  | 6 |  |
|  | 95 |  | 54 |  |
| Creditors (current) | 112 | (17) | 34 | 20 |
|  |  | 146 |  | 66 |
| Ordinary €1 shares |  | 100 |  | 50 |
| Share premium |  | 10 |  | – |
| Reserves |  | 36 |  | 16 |
|  |  | 146 |  | 66 |

**14.4** Two companies, A and M have balance sheets as at 31 December 20XX as shown in Table 14.13.

**Table 14.13 Balance sheets for A and M as at 31 December 20XX**

|  | A | M |
|---|---|---|
| Plant and machinery | 6,000 | 7,000 |
| Net current assets | 5,000 | 2,000 |
|  | 11,000 | 9,000 |
| Ordinary shares (€1) | 9,000 | 6,000 |
| Reserves | 2,000 | 3,000 |
|  | 11,000 | 9,000 |

A acquired the whole of the share capital of M on the basis of a one-for-one share exchange as at the above date (not yet reflected in A's balance sheet), at which point the market (unit) values of their respective shares were €4 for both A and M. The fair values of M's tangible assets as at 31 December 20XX were:

| | |
|---|---|
| Plant and machinery | €8,000 |
| Net current assets | €2,500 |

Prepare consolidated balance sheets under both the acquisition and merger methods. Comment on the major differences that emerge.

14.5 (a) How would you define goodwill?
   (b) Three possible accounting treatments of goodwill are:
       (i)   retain goodwill as an asset to be amortized over its estimated useful life;
       (ii)  retain goodwill as an asset indefinitely, subjecting it to annual impairment tests;
       (iii) write off goodwill to reserves at the time of acquisition.

Discuss briefly the principles underlying each of these three approaches. Indicate your preferences.

# Chapter 15

# Foreign currency translation

Contents
15.1  Introduction                                          289
15.2  Transactions                                          289
15.3  Translation of financial statements                   292
       15.3.1  Current rate method                          292
       15.3.2  Mixed rate (temporal) method                 292
       15.3.3  The methods compared                         293
15.4  A numerical illustration                              294
       Summary                                              295
       References and research                              296
       Exercises                                            296

Objectives    After studying this chapter carefully, you should be able to:

■ distinguish between currency conversion, the translation of transactions, and the translation of financial statements;

■ explain and simply illustrate the accounting treatment of transactions expressed in foreign currencies;

■ discuss alternative views on the recognition of unsettled gains and losses arising from currency differences;

■ outline alternative methods for translating financial statements expressed in foreign currencies;

■ describe, illustrate and contrast the closing rate and temporal methods of translation;

■ state and appraise the basic IAS 21 requirements for translation of financial statements expressed in foreign currencies.

## 15.1 Introduction

Several linked issues need to be discussed under the heading of currency translation. First, a note on technical terms is necessary.

1. *Conversion* is the process of changing one currency into another, as typically conducted in a bank or *bureau de change*.
2. *Transactions translation* is the accounting activity whereby transactions in foreign currency are re-expressed in the currency of the enterprise's accounting records or financial statements. For example, sales to foreign customers or loans from foreign banks might be denominated as amounts of foreign currency. They will need to be translated into the home currency in order to be included in the accounting records of the enterprise.
3. *Translation of financial statements* is the accounting activity whereby financial statements are re-expressed in another currency. Typically, this means the translation of a foreign subsidiary's statements into the parent currency for the purpose of preparing consolidated financial statements for the group.

This chapter does not deal with point 1 above. It does deal with point 2. It only deals with point 3 for the main purpose of group accounting. For other purposes, e.g. assessment of an overseas company by an analyst, the users of foreign financial statements can choose their own methods of translation – usually the exchange rates ruling on the balance sheet date. The context of the discussion in this chapter is the IASB's standard in this area, IAS 21, *The Effects of Changes in Foreign Exchange Rates*.

Language can be a problem here. For example, accounting terms are sometimes not easily translated:

| English terms | French terms |
|---|---|
| Conversion | *Change* |
| Translation | *Conversion* |

Consequently, an inexpert translator may mislead the readers of an annual report that has been translated from one language to another.

## 15.2 Transactions

This section deals with the problems of a company that has no subsidiaries or parent but engages in foreign trading activities.

*Why it matters*  *Business is increasingly international, and whenever an enterprise has any dealings abroad it will be involved in foreign currencies. Since it must keep its accounting records and prepare accounting reports in its own 'home' currency, figures expressed in foreign money units need to be re-expressed in home units. If foreign currency exchange rates remain absolutely constant, i.e. if the value of one currency in terms of the other does not change, then no difficulties arise. However, this is generally not the case, as exchange rates can – and do – fluctuate considerably over relatively short periods. Clearly, the introduction of the euro in Europe has helped for some countries, but the problem remains for a company in euroland that ever has to deal with subsidiaries, lenders, customers or suppliers from outside the area. In practice, it is possible to reduce the risk of exposure to currency fluctuations by a policy of* **hedging,** *i.e. of creating asset and liability risks such that the effects of currency movements will tend to cancel out. This is a complicated area, beyond the scope of an introductory text.*

The easiest situation is where an overseas transaction is completed within an accounting period. Consider, for example, a Ruritanian company that keeps its accounts in the local currency, R, but sells goods to a Swiss company in May 20X1 for SF750,000. Payment is received in August 20X1. Assuming a 31 December year end, in May the company will record a debtor in its records of the Ruritanian equivalent of SF750,000 at the exchange rate in May 20X1 of R1 = SF3.5544, i.e. the transaction will be recorded at R211,006. Suppose that, when payment is received in August, the exchange rate has moved to 3.7081 so that the actual amount received is R202,260. The loss on exchange of R211,006 − R202,260 = R8,746 should be reported in the income statement. So the formal double entry in May will be:

| | | | |
|---|---|---|---|
| Debit: | Debtors | 211,006 | |
| Credit: | Sales | | 211,006 |

and in August:

| | | | |
|---|---|---|---|
| Debit: | Bank | 202,260 | |
| Debit: | Loss on exchange | 8,746 | |
| Credit: | Debtors | | 211,006 |

Any profit on exchange would be credited to the income statement.

Similarly if, in May 20X1, the Ruritanian company bought a fixed asset, such as a machine, for SF750,000, this would be translated and recorded into its accounts as a debit to the Machinery account of R211,006. The subsequent exchange rate change would not affect the recorded amount for the machine, but any gain or loss on settlement of the purchase price would be charged or credited to the income statement.

However, suppose that a sale or purchase transaction is not completed by the accounting year end, in the sense that a debtor or creditor is still outstanding. In this case, the debtor or creditor needs to be translated into the home currency so that it can be shown in the balance sheet, and a gain or loss might arise. Consider now a Ruritanian company that bought a machine from a Belgian company in November 20X1 for €11 million when the exchange rate was R1 = €62.09. At the accounting year end of 31 December 20X1, the payment for the machine had not been made. The machine would be recorded at R177,162, by use of the November rate. However, the creditor entry in the closing balance sheet would be recorded at the 31 December rate of R1 = €61.29, i.e. at R179,475. This would mean that a loss on exchange of R2,313 should be recognized in the income statement of 20X1. If the exchange rate continues to move in the same direction until the transaction is settled in January 20X2, then a further loss will be recognized, this time in the 20X2 income statement.

Controversy arises on the accounting treatment in cases like that in the previous paragraph but where exchange rates move such that a *gain* might be recognized at the 31 December 20X1 year end. Under IFRS rules, and consistent with the IASB Framework discussed in Chapter 3, fair presentation demands that unsettled gains should be recognized as well as unsettled losses. These gains could even be called 'realized' in the same way as are profits on credit sales where the customer has not yet paid. In some European countries (basically those on the right of Figure 5.3, e.g. Germany or France), the traditional accounting thinking holds that such a treatment is imprudent, and that gains should be recognized on settlement only.

In Germany, for example, it is normal in unconsolidated statements to translate foreign currency debtors or creditors at the higher of historical rate and closing rate for creditors, and at the lower of historical rate and closing rate for debtors. This recognizes losses but not gains. It also, on average, records lower debtors and higher creditors than would be recorded under IAS accounting. For example, BASF's 2008 annual report (of the parent company) noted:

> **Translation of foreign currency items:** The cost of assets acquired in foreign currencies and revenues from sales in foreign currencies are recorded at the exchange rate at the date of transaction.
>
> Short-term foreign currency receivables and liabilities are valued at the rate on the balance sheet date. Long-term foreign currency receivables are recorded at the rate prevailing on the acquisition date or at the lower rate on the balance sheet date. Long-term foreign currency liabilities are recorded at the rate prevailing on the acquisition date or at the higher rate on the balance sheet date.

In France, year-end rates are used but, in individual company practice, gains are stored in the balance sheet as deferred credits until they are settled.

The discussion so far has concerned transactions that are settled or are soon to be settled. Similar issues arise when there are long-term foreign currency items, such as a ten-year foreign currency loan. Suppose that a UK company borrowed $10,000 from a US bank in London for five years, from 20X1 to 20X5. At each year end, the loan must be shown in pounds sterling in the company's balance sheet. Under IFRS and in most countries (though not under normal German practice – see above), the year-end rate would be used. So, assuming the exchange rates shown below, the following translations would have occurred at the first two year ends:

| | | |
|---|---|---:|
| 31.12.X1 | $10,000 at £1 = $1: | £10,000 |
| 31.12.X2 | $10,000 at £1 = $1.50: | £6,667 |
| | Gain in 20X2 | £3,333 |

Because in our example the pound strengthened against the dollar during 20X2, a gain is implied. For short-term gains, companies in some countries (such as the Netherlands and the United Kingdom, and under IFRS) would recognize the gain in the 20X2 income statement. Others (such as those in France) would defer it. However, it seems a stretch of terminology to say that the £3,333 gain is 'realized' in 20X2, as it will not be settled until 20X5. However, IFRS is not concerned with realization, and IAS 21 demands that such a gain should be taken to income.

## 15.3 Translation of financial statements

This section concerns the translation of a foreign subsidiary's financial statements into the currency of the parent for the purposes of preparing consolidated statements. When translating any particular item, we can take two basic possible views: either we can use the exchange rate ruling when the item was created (historical rate), or we can use the exchange rate ruling when the item is being reported (current rate). Since we can apply this choice to each item one at a time, it is clear that many different combinations are possible. Two that are commonly used are outlined below.

### 15.3.1 Current rate method

This method of translation is based on the idea that the holding company has a net investment in the foreign operation, and that what is at risk from currency fluctuations is this net financial investment in the equity of the foreign enterprise. All assets and liabilities will be translated at the current rate (balance sheet date rate). Revenues and expenses are translated at the appropriate current rate, or (for simplicity) at the average rate for the year. Exchange differences will arise if the closing rate differs from the previous year's closing rate, or from the rate on the date when the transaction occurred. Under IFRS, such gains and losses are shown as other comprehensive income.

Another way of looking at this method is that it applies when the 'functional currency' of the foreign subsidiary is not the parent's currency but the currency of the subsidiary's country. Therefore, the amounts need to be translated into the parent's currency for consolidation, assuming the usual case that the group statements are presented in the parent's currency.

### 15.3.2 Mixed rate (temporal) method

This method is based on the idea that any foreign operations are simply a part of the group that is the reporting entity, where some of the individual assets and liabilities of the group just 'happen' to be abroad. In effect, therefore, the temporal method amounts to treating all the individual transactions and balances of the foreign subsidiary as though they were those of the parent. The valuation basis used to value the assets and liabilities determines the appropriate exchange rate. Those assets recorded on a historical cost basis would be translated at the historical rate – the rate ruling when the item was established. Assets recorded on a current value basis would be translated at the current rate. Revenues and expenses should be correspondingly translated at the rate ruling on the date when the amount shown in the accounts was established. For many items (assuming an even spread of trading), this might be at the average rate for the year. However, for depreciation of an asset held at historical cost, the appropriate exchange rate would be the historical rate. Gains and losses arising from translation differences go to the income statement under this method.

It is important to avoid the assumption that the temporal method automatically means using historical exchange rates. 'Temporal' means literally 'at the time', i.e. consistent with the underlying valuation basis. So the temporal method *does* mean using historical exchange rates *when applied to historical cost statements*, but using current exchange rates *when applied to current value accounts*.

In terms of 'functional currencies', this method is appropriate when the subsidiary's functional currency is the currency of the parent. If the subsidiary operates in a way that is dominated by its parent's currency, then it can be seen as conducting all its transactions in the parent's currency. This will have the same effect as using historical exchange rates for historical transactions.

### 15.3.3 The methods compared

The use of the current rate method is intuitively simpler. That is, it is normal to assume that the subsidiary's country's currency is the one most relevant for its operations. Indeed, this is the method generally used around the world for foreign-currency balance sheets.

IAS 21 says that an entity should identify its functional currency by considering the currency of its sales prices and its costs. In some cases, it may be clear that a subsidiary is a mere sales conduit of the parent and can charge prices linked to the parent's currency. However, the identification of functional currency will often require the balancing of several factors (discussed in paragraphs 9–14 of IAS 21).

**Activity 15.A**

SAP is a multinational operation, based in Germany and prepared its financial statements in accordance with US GAAP until forced to produce IFRS consolidated financial statements in 2007. Its accounting policy for foreign currencies in its 2005 financial statements was as follows:

> The assets and liabilities of foreign operations where the functional currency is not euros are translated into euros using period-end closing exchange rates, whereas items of income and expense are translated into euros using average exchange rates during the respective periods. The resulting foreign currency translation adjustments are included in Other comprehensive income/loss in the Consolidated Statements of Changes in Shareholders' Equity.
>
> Assets and liabilities that are denominated in foreign currencies other than the functional currency are translated at the period-end closing rate with resulting gains and losses reflected in Other non-operating income/expense, net in the Consolidated Statements of Income.

Which method was it using in which circumstances?

**Feedback**

Where the functional currency is not euros, the closing rate is being used, with gains and losses taken to equity. This is the current rate method. Where denomination is in a foreign currency other than the functional currency, gains or losses are taken to income, implying the temporal method. Since it is explicitly stated that the period-end closing rate is being used in these cases, rather than the mix of historical and current rates, the sentence is presumably referring to monetary balances rather than to foreign financial statements.

| 15.4 | **A numerical illustration** |
|------|------------------------------|

The current rate and temporal methods are illustrated below for a French parent with a subsidiary in a foreign country where the currency unit is T. Suppose that Home SA established a 100-per-cent-owned subsidiary, Away Ltd, on 1 January 20X1 by subscribing €25,000 of shares in cash when the exchange rate was T12 to €1. Away Ltd raised a long-term loan of T100,000 locally on 1 January 20X1 and immediately purchased equipment costing T350,000, which was expected to last ten years with no residual value. It was to be depreciated under the straight-line method.

Table 15.1 shows the financial statements of Away Ltd for 20X1, during which the relevant exchange rates were:

|  | T to € |
|--|--------|
| 1 January | 12.0 |
| Average for year | 11.0 |
| Average for period in which closing inventory acquired | 10.5 |
| 31 December | 10.0 |

The 'T' column in Table 15.1 shows the original balance sheet amount in the foreign currency. The '€ (current)' column shows translation using the closing rate method (i.e. assuming that the T is the subsidiary's functional currency).

**Table 15.1 Away Ltd's financial statements**

| Income statement for 20X1 | T | € (current) | € (temporal) |
|---------------------------|---|-------------|--------------|
| Sales | 450,000 | 40,909[a] | 40,909[a] |
| *Less* Cost of sales | (360,000) | (32,727) | (32,727) |
| Gross Profit | 90,000 | 8,182 | 8,182 |
| *Less* Depreciation | (35,000) | (3,182)[a] | (2,917)[b] |
| Other expenses | (15,000) | (1,364)[a] | (1,364)[a] |
| Net profit | 40,000 | 3,636 | 3,901 |

| Balance sheet as at 31 December 20X1 | | | |
|---------------------------|---|-------------|--------------|
| Equipment at cost | 350,000 | 35,000[d] | 29,167[b] |
| *Less* Depreciation | (35,000) | (3,500) | (2,917)[b] |
|  | 315,000 | 31,500 | 26,250 |
| Inventory at cost | 105,000 | 10,500 | 10,000[c] |
| Net monetary current assets | 20,000 | 2,000 | 2,000[d] |
| *Less* Long-term loan | (100,000) | (10,000) | (10,000)[d] |
|  | 340,000 | 34,000 | 28,250 |
| Share capital | 300,000 | 25,000[b] | 25,000[b] |
| Retained profits | 40,000 | 3,636 | 3,901 |
| Exchange differences | – | 5,364 | (651) |
|  | 340,000 | 34,000 | 28,250 |

Notes on exchange rate used:
[a] T11.0 to €1.0 (average rate).
[b] T12.0 to €1.0.
[c] T10.5 to €1.0.
[d] T10.0 to €1.0 (closing rate).

Note that, under any method, the share capital is translated at the historical rate. The exchange difference could be worked out in detail but is also the balancing figure in shareholders' funds. The '€ (temporal)' column shows the translation using the temporal method, involving the historical rate for certain items (i.e. assuming that the € is the subsidiary's functional currency). The profit figure in the balance sheet comes from the income statement. The exchange loss could be worked out in detail but, again, is also the balancing figure. Under IAS 21, the €651 exchange loss would be recorded in the income statement.

**Why it matters** *By the time that the subsidiary's translated statements from Table 15.1 are consolidated into the group statements, the translation method chosen may have a major effect on the financial statements and the interpretation of them. The exchange rate movements in Table 15.1 are fairly small, but still group profit would be affected by inclusion of the different figures, where:*

|  | € |
|---|---|
| Current rate profit | 3,636 |
| Temporal method profit | 3,901 |
| *Less* translation loss | (651) |
| | 3,250 |

*The difference between the current rate and temporal method could have a major effect on group earnings.*

*The apparent level of group gearing (see Chapter 7) will also be affected. One measure of gearing is made by a comparison of long-term debt with shareholders' funds. In this case, the subsidiary's figures (which will then affect the group financial statements) show:*

$$\text{Current rate gearing} = \frac{10,000}{34,000} = 29.4 \text{ per cent}$$

$$\text{Temporal method gearing} = \frac{10,000}{28,250} = 35.4 \text{ per cent}$$

*So, in this case, the temporal method will lead to the presentation of higher gearing figures, although it should be noted that different circumstances could lead to the opposite relationship. Remember that the underlying events are identical for both sets of figures.*

**Summary**

- There are several topic areas that might be considered under the heading of foreign currency translation, and there are some linguistic difficulties in making it internationally clear what topic one is discussing. This chapter deals with foreign currency transactions of individual companies and then with the translation of the financial statements of foreign subsidiaries.

- Transactions are generally translated at the rate of exchange ruling on the date of the transaction, and so asset purchases are generally frozen into home currency at the date of purchase. Outstanding debtors and creditors are translated in most countries at current rates, but in some countries at the worse of transaction and current rates, thereby not recognizing translation gains until settlement. In some countries where current rates are used, resulting gains are thereby recognized but postponed.

■ For translation of foreign subsidiaries' financial statements, the current rate (foreign currency functional) is the most popular internationally. Gains and losses that result from this process are taken to reserves. Nevertheless, the use of historical rates for certain items (parent's currency functional) may be found, and this can have a large effect on group financial statements.

## References and research

A key IASB reference is:

■ IAS 21 (revised 2003), *The Effects of Changes in Foreign Exchange Rates*.

Some further insight into the issues is given by the following two papers. Do not read one without also reading the other. The papers are:

■ P. Feige, 'How "uniform" is financial reporting in Germany? – The example of foreign currency translation', *European Accounting Review*, Vol. 6, No. 1, 1997.
■ C. Nobes and G. Mueller, 'How "uniform" is financial reporting in Germany?: Some replies', *European Accounting Review*, Vol. 6, No. 1, 1997.

## EXERCISES

*Feedback on the first two of these exercises is given in Appendix D.*

15.1 A loan is made to a company of $20,000, which is equal to €10,000 at the date of the loan during year 1. The loan is denominated in dollars. At the end of year 1 the loan is translated as €9,500, at the end of year 2 as €10,500 and during year 3 it is repaid, the proceeds being converted to €10,600. The company keeps accounts in euros.

(a) Show the accounting entries for each year, explaining your workings.
(b) State how, under the appropriate IFRSs, you would deal with the gains or losses on exchange for each year, at that time. Justify your answer.

15.2 Home Inc. (an American company) has a wholly owned subsidiary, S, which it acquired on 1.1.X0. The balance sheets of S as at 1.1.X0 and 31.12.X0 are as set out in Figure 15.1 in foreign currency (FC) units:

Figure 15.1 **Balance sheets for S as at 1.1.X0 and 31.12.X0**

|  |  | 1.1.X0 (FC units) |  | 31.12.X0 (FC units) |
|---|---|---|---|---|
| Fixed assets |  | 450 |  | 330 |
| Inventory | 240 |  | 360 |  |
| Debtors | 120 |  | 240 |  |
|  | 360 |  | 600 |  |
| Creditors | 210 | 150 | 240 | 360 |
|  |  | 600 |  | 690 |
| Ordinary share capital |  | 600 |  | 600 |
| Retained profits |  | – |  | 90 |
|  |  | 600 |  | 690 |

The income statement account for the year 31.12.X0 is as set out in Figure 15.2.

**Figure 15.2 Income statement for S on 31.12.X0 (FC units)**

| | | |
|---|---:|---:|
| Sales | | 1,500 |
| Cost of sales (240 + 1,200 − 360) | 1,080 | |
| Depreciation | 120 | 1,200 |
| Net profit | | 300 |
| Taxation | | 150 |
| | | 150 |
| Proposed dividend | | 60 |
| Retained profit | | 90 |

Translate the financial statements of S using both (a) the closing rate method and (b) temporal method, given the following:

> On 1 January 20X0, $1 = FC3.0
> On 30 June 20X0, $1 = FC2.5
> On 31 December 20X0, $1 = FC2.0

15.3 'The variety of possible methods of foreign currency translation, and the different ways of treating gains arising, show that adequate harmonization for international comparison purposes is a long way away.' Discuss.

15.4 The stated accounting policy treatment for foreign currency translation for SKF, a Swedish company, for 2002 was as follows:

**Translation of foreign financial statements**
The current rate method is used for translating the income statements and balance sheets into Swedish kronor as the majority of subsidiaries are considered independent. All balance sheet items in foreign subsidiaries have been translated in Swedish kronor based on the year-end exchange rates. Income statement items are translated at average exchange rates. The translation adjustments that arise as a result of the current rate method are transferred directly to shareholders' equity.

For the translation of financial statements of subsidiaries operating in highly inflationary economies, the Group applies the monetary/nonmonetary method (MNM-method). Monetary balance sheet items are translated at year-end exchange rates and non-monetary balance sheet items, as well as related income and expense items, are translated at rates in effect at the time of acquisition (historical rates). Other income and expense items are translated at average exchange rates. Translation differences that arise are included in the related lines in the income statement.

**Translation of items denominated in foreign currency**
Transactions in foreign currencies during the year have been translated at the exchange rate prevailing at the respective transaction date.

Accounts receivable and payable and other receivables/payables denominated in foreign currency have been translated at the exchange rates prevailing at the balance sheet date. Such exchange gains and losses are included in other operating income and other operating expense. Other foreign currency items have been included in financial income and expense net.

Write a brief memorandum, in non-technical language, explaining the meaning and significance of these policies.

# Chapter 16

# Accounting for price changes

| Contents | | |
|---|---|---|
| 16.1 | Introduction | 299 |
| 16.2 | Effects of price changes on accounting | 299 |
| 16.3 | European disagreement | 305 |
| 16.4 | General or specific adjustment | 305 |
| 16.5 | General price-level adjusted systems | 310 |
| | 16.5.1 A worked illustration | 310 |
| 16.6 | Current value accounting | 312 |
| | 16.6.1 Economic value | 313 |
| | 16.6.2 Net realizable value | 313 |
| | 16.6.3 Current replacement cost | 313 |
| | 16.6.4 A worked illustration | 314 |
| 16.7 | Mixed values – deprival value | 316 |
| 16.8 | Partial adjustments | 319 |
| | 16.8.1 Ad hoc government-controlled revaluations | 319 |
| | 16.8.2 Ad hoc revaluations by business management | 319 |
| | 16.8.3 LIFO inventory valuation | 320 |
| 16.9 | Fair values | 320 |
| | Summary | 321 |
| | References and research | 322 |
| | Exercises | 322 |

Objectives After studying this chapter carefully, you should be able to:

- explain the meaning of inflation;
- explain the significance of differences between historical cost profit and replacement cost profit;
- illustrate and discuss simple examples of different concepts of capital maintenance;
- prepare and discuss simple financial statements using general price-level adjustments;
- prepare and discuss simple financial statements using current replacement cost accounting;
- explain the implications of net realizable value, and of deprival value, as bases for the preparation of financial statements;
- outline the relevant regulations from IAS and EU sources, and the practice in certain countries.

## 16.1 Introduction

This chapter looks at some of the problems involved in adjusting accounting information for general and specific price changes. The chapter looks first at inflation, then at the reasons why inflation causes conventional profit figures to be unrealistic for some purposes, and then at the problems that follow from this lack of realism. After that, there is an examination of the possible adjustments to correct financial statements for general and specific price changes, and of actual accounting systems proposed in Europe and elsewhere to deal with the problems caused by changing prices.

Inflation is a general increase in prices that causes a fall in the purchasing power of money. The causes of inflation are widely discussed and disputed, but they are problems of economics rather than of accounting: the average of prices faced by one particular consumer will change at a different rate from the average faced by another. Again, there will be a difference between price changes faced by consumers and those faced by producers. However, one generally available measure of inflation is an *index of retail prices*.

Indices of retail prices are produced on a monthly basis by official statistical departments in most countries. There are many technical problems relating to the choice of items involved, their weighting and delays in the collection of information. For the input costs and output prices of a particular business, such a general index is not likely to be very informative; the costs of different raw materials and capital equipment may move up (and down) at very different rates. Therefore, some agencies also produce specific price indices that cover various raw materials, intermediate outputs and capital equipment. Some companies keep their own very specific price indices, and of course actual current costs can be discovered from invoices or price lists. It is obvious that specific price information is relevant to the planning and budgeting of a business; how to take account of it in the reporting of past financial results is not so clear.

*Why it matters* — *General inflation rates can be significantly different between countries at any time and, within one country, inflation rates may be very significant and may vary sharply in significance at different times. Ratio analysis over time, or comparison between entities in different countries with different inflationary conditions, will be significantly affected. The interpretation of such analysis must take full account of the implications, developed below, of these changes and differences.*

## 16.2 Effects of price changes on accounting

The effects of price changes are at their clearest when considering the valuation of assets in a conventional balance sheet. For example, land and buildings may be recorded and added together at a variety of values, including historical cost and subsequent valuations. Similar properties may be recorded and added together at very different values because they were bought at different times. For those users of a balance sheet who are expecting to gain information about the value of a business, such a balance sheet may be very misleading. Proposed solutions for this problem will be examined later.

The effects on profit measurement are more complicated. Normally, three main deficiencies are identified. In each case the problem concerns *matching* – one of the conventions introduced in Chapter 3 as an important rule in the calculation of profit by the comparison of revenues with expenses. The point here is that, unless adjustments are made to correct for changing prices, some expenses based on *past* costs will be matched against revenues based on *current* sales prices. It is worth exploring this whole issue in some detail.

<table>
<tr><td>**Activity 16.A**</td><td>On 1 January, Mr Jones starts off in a retail business with €100. His transactions are as follows:

2 January    Buys one bag, as inventory, for €40.
4 January    Sells one bag for €50.
6 January    Buys one bag for €44 (the replacement cost rose on 3 January).

Prepare balance sheets on 3 January and on 7 January, and an income statement for the intervening period, using conventional accounting practice.</td></tr>
</table>

**Feedback**    The required financial statements are set out in Figure 16.1.

**Figure 16.1 Financial statements for Jones (€)**

**Balance sheet 3 January**

| Inventory | 40 | Capital | 100 |
|---|---|---|---|
| Cash | 60 | | |
| | 100 | | 100 |

**Balance sheet 7 January**

| Inventory | 44 | Capital | 100 |
|---|---|---|---|
| Cash | 66 | Retained profit | 10 |
| | 110 | | 110 |

**Income statement so far**

| Sales | 50 |
|---|---|
| Cost of sales | 40 |
| | 10 |

So Jones has made a profit of €10. This, of course, is the usual accounting approach. But it is important to notice that there are really two stages in the progress from 1 January to 7 January. Between 1 January and 5 January, after the sale was made, Jones has turned €100 cash into €110 cash. On 5 January he actually has physically €110 cash and nothing else. Then between 5 January and 7 January he has changed €110 cash into €66 cash plus a bag. Since the second bag cost €44 and we are recording all our resources at original, or historical, cost it necessarily follows that we show total resources of €110 on both 5 January and 7 January. The 5 January balance sheet was as given in Figure 16.2.

Figure 16.2 **Balance sheet for Jones as at 5 January (€)**

| Balance sheet 5 January | | | |
|---|---|---|---|
| Cash | 110 | Capital | 110 |
| | 110 | | 110 |

Comparing this 5 January position with the 3 January and 7 January balance sheets confirms that:

1. a profit of €10 was made between 3 January and 5 January; and
2. no profit or loss at all was made between 5 January and 7 January.

Jones is running a business, of course. He has to live. So, on 8 January, he decides to withdraw the business profit for his own spending purposes. If he takes €10 out, then the business still has the same amount of capital as originally put in. This €10 must therefore be genuine gain, so that it can apparently be withdrawn from the business without reducing the resources of the business. So we can draw up our balance sheet, after the withdrawal, as given in Figure 16.3.

Figure 16.3 **Balance sheet for Jones as at 9 January (€)**

| Balance sheet 9 January | | | |
|---|---|---|---|
| Inventory | 44 | Capital | 100 |
| Cash | 56 | | |
| | 100 | | 100 |

**Activity 16.B**

Compare the physical possessions of Jones's business on 3 January with those on 9 January.

**Feedback**

In physical terms, the business possesses on 3 January one bag and €60 in cash. On 9 January it possesses one bag and €56 in cash.

By simple subtraction, using the figures in Activity 16.B, we can compare the physical position between 3 January and 9 January in terms both of bags and of euros. In terms of bags, we are comparing one bag with one bag; in terms of bags, the business is exactly the same size as it was before. In terms of euros, the business had 60 on 3 January and 56 on 9 January; the business has therefore got smaller by four euros.

Something must be wrong somewhere. The accountant has shown us that there is a 'gain' of €10 over and above the original €100 capital put in. Jones has therefore withdrawn the €10, and yet the result is *not* that the business is 'back where it started'. The result is that the business has *got smaller* by €4.

This suggests that either the physical comparison is wrong, or the income statement prepared in Activity 16.A is wrong. If the physical comparison is correct, then the 'gain' of €10 mentioned above is not genuine! Further thinking is needed. On 5 January we had, in physical terms, as we have already seen, a pile of 110 euros. We have also already seen that the profit of €10 was made by 5 January. It therefore follows that the accountant's statement at 5 January is identical with the actual physical position at that date. It is obvious that since the physical position and the accounting position were identical as at 5 January, the difference between the two positions must have occurred *after* 5 January. But only one event has happened after 5 January. This was the purchase of the second bag on 6 January. So the problem *must* be something to do with the accounting treatment of the second bag.

Question: Why did Jones have to buy a second bag for €44? The answer is: because the business is a going concern and he had sold the first bag (for €50). He would not have bought the second bag if he had not sold the first one. It seems, therefore, that the selling of the first bag and the buying of the second bag are really two parts of one complete action. If he had not sold the first bag and had not bought the second bag, he would clearly have ended up with the same amount of cash on 7 January as he had on 3 January, i.e. €60. If he sells the first bag for €50 and buys a second bag for €44, he will end up with €6 more cash on 7 January than he had on 3 January. So the result of selling the first bag and buying a second bag *as compared with doing neither*, is a gain of €6. We can show this as follows:

|  | € |
|---|---|
| Sales | 50 |
| Costs incurred as a direct result of making sale | 44 |
| Profit | 6 |

We are now suggesting a profit of €6, as compared with the earlier suggestion of €10. This will presumably reduce the maximum drawing payable by €10 – €6 = €4. And remember that we argued earlier that the difference between the original accountant's calculations and physical reality – the amount by which Jones's business had unintentionally 'got smaller' – was €4. We have produced an accounting calculation that now agrees with actual physical events.

The essential conclusion from the above is simple: it may be more informative if a cost of sales figure is measured as the *cost of the resulting replacement*, rather than as the cost of the item actually sold. This raises a difficulty. In order to be able to transfer this higher replacement figure out of the balance sheet and into the income calculation, the higher replacement figure must first be recorded in the balance sheet. The complete picture is most easily seen by a series of balance sheets, as set out in Figure 16.4.

We have solved a major problem. On the assumption that Jones wishes to carry on selling and buying bags, this is the correct answer. We have shown the

**Figure 16.4 Balance sheet for Jones at various dates**

### 1 January

| | | | |
|---|---|---|---|
| Cash | 100 | Capital | 100 |
| | 100 | | 100 |

### 3 January

| | | | |
|---|---|---|---|
| Bag | 40 | Capital | 100 |
| Cash | 60 | | |
| | 100 | | 100 |

### 3 January (restated on a replacement cost basis)

| | | | |
|---|---|---|---|
| 1st bag | 44 | Capital | 100 |
| Cash | 60 | Restatement gain | 4 |
| | 104 | | 104 |

### 5 January

| | | | |
|---|---|---|---|
| Cash | 110 | Capital | 100 |
| | | Restatement gain | 4 |
| | | Profit | 6 |
| | 110 | | 110 |

### 7 January

| | | | |
|---|---|---|---|
| 2nd bag | 44 | Capital | 100 |
| | | Restatement gain | 4 |
| Cash | 66 | Profit | 6 |
| | 110 | | 110 |

accountant how to produce a profit figure that actually makes physical sense, and one that Jones can actually believe. But we have created another difficulty. The statement from the accountant shows not only a profit of €6, but also a separate, different gain of €4. This gain of €4 occurred earlier than the profit. The gain was included in the balance sheet of 3 January and the profit did not appear until the sale on 4 January. We know that this 'gain' is not the same as profit – the whole point of all this is that the 'total' profit, i.e. the total increase in the capacity of the business to do things, is only €6. So if the 'gain' is not profit, what is it?

In the most simple of terms, it is the double entry for an increase in the recorded figure for an item of inventory.

*Why it matters*    *The above discussion and illustration make it clear that the effect of the replacement cost approach to inventory valuation is to split the historical cost profit into two distinct elements, namely the holding gain, and the gain through operating activities (known usually as the current operating profit). Thus we have:*

Historical cost profit = current operating profit + holding gain
[10]                 [6]                [4]

*It is clear that additional information is given by reporting the two elements separately. The holding gain, other things equal, must be kept in the business to maintain the volume of activity; the money that it represents has to be spent on the replacement item of inventory. Since the money has to be used internally, it perhaps should not be seen as available for distribution to owners and, since the holding gain has to be retained, it perhaps should not be seen as an increase in the real wealth of the business, considered as a going concern.*

*The use of historical costs fails to reveal this information, producing a reported profit that seems too high.*

The above discussion of replacement cost as applied to inventory suggests that one way of looking at the value of inventory is its replacement cost, because this is what the business would have to pay if it did not already own the inventory or if it were deprived of it. Similarly, the using up of inventory can be said to involve an expense that is equal to its replacement cost rather than its historical cost. This would suggest a *cost of sales adjustment* to historical cost profit, since the latter only allows for the historical cost of inventory used.

A similar problem concerns depreciation expenses, which may in some sense be inadequate because they are based on past costs (i.e. the historical cost of fixed assets). For example, one year's usage of a machine with no scrap value and a five-year life may more realistically be said to incur a charge of one-fifth of the replacement cost of the asset rather than one-fifth of its historical cost. This would suggest a *depreciation adjustment* to historical cost profit, since the latter only allows for the historical cost of fixed assets used up.

A third problem concerns gains and losses on monetary items. A company that borrows money in inflationary periods for long-term use is making a gain, in the sense that the money eventually paid back will be worth less in purchasing power terms. The same factor affects those short-term assets and liabilities that are fixed in money terms. If there is inflation, a 'gain' will be made on holding overdrafts and creditors, and a 'loss' will result from holding debtors and cash. Deciding upon the correct treatment of these long-term and short-term monetary items has given rise to the most controversy among the three problems discussed here.

It is widely argued that, if profit is used to measure the economic performance of a company, historical cost profit is greatly overstated because of the lack of depreciation and cost of sales adjustments; and unless this net overstatement of profit is recognized, the usefulness of accounting data for decision making will be seriously impaired. For example, decisions about what dividends to pay or what pay rises can be afforded may be seriously in error. Even if a company understands the problem, shareholders and employees may not, and they may press for dividend and wage payments based on historical cost results.

There is a similar problem with tax on the profits of businesses. As taxation is levied on taxable profit, which, in times of inflation and rising prices, is based on overstated historical cost accounting profit, the effective rate of tax on a more realistic measure of profit will surely be high. However, as shown in Chapter 12, there are substantial adjustments involved in the calculation of taxable profit in some countries.

Other problems – perhaps even more serious – concern the effects on the decision making of management. In decisions about prices, types of production, the assessment of the performance of managers, and so on, accounting information will be used. Correct decisions require relevant information, which includes adjustments for the effects of inflation and changing prices – although the dangers of an excessive sacrifice of reliability must be considered too.

## 16.3 European disagreement

Although the problems outlined in the last section are clear, there has been opposition from some countries to any adjustments to financial reporting that is designed to correct for price changes. The most obvious opposition to departures from historical cost has come from Germany, which suffered more than any other European country from hyperinflation during the 1920s. The German view was that accounting should not be adjusted away from reliable cost-based numbers. The purpose of accounting is connected to the distribution of profits, the protection of creditors and the calculation of taxes. These, it is claimed, will all be jeopardized by such tinkering. There was German opposition to inclusion in the EU Fourth Directive of optional departures from historical cost. These options were examined in Chapter 8. They have not been permitted under German national accounting regulations.

In many other European countries, either the accountancy profession or the government made moves in the 1970s and 1980s to adjust accounting for inflation, and most countries have taken some of the optional provisions in the EU Fourth Directive to enable revaluations (as discussed in Chapter 8). Full systems of inflation accounting have only been seriously proposed in Europe in countries where the government takes a hands-off approach to accounting and where tax numbers can be disconnected from accounting numbers. This is because price adjustment can be so complex and can have such large effects on accounting that full-scale, continuous use of it seems inappropriate as a legal requirement for all companies. Consequently, it is generally only in countries such as the United Kingdom and the Netherlands, or in countries suffering from hyperinflation, such as in parts of South America, that the systems discussed in the next section have been tried.

The IASB introduced a standard in this area, IAS 15, but this was for long optional and of little practical significance, and has long been withdrawn. A separate standard, IAS 29, deals with 'hyperinflationary' economies and requires adjustments for general inflation, as defined and discussed below, in such circumstances.

## 16.4 General or specific adjustment

The major divide between different systems of accounting for price changes is that existing between those systems that adjust primarily for the changes in prices of the specific assets owned by the business and those that adjust for a general price movement, namely inflation. The specific adjustments could be made by taking account of replacement costs, as examined in the previous section. By contrast, a system for general adjustment could be called *current purchasing power (CPP) accounting*. Those current value systems that do not include an adjustment for general price changes have been said by some not to be systems of *inflation accounting* at all because they do not take account of the falling value of money. The type of adjustments for depreciation and cost of sales depends upon which system is being used.

The underlying difference between the two systems concerns the concept of *capital maintenance*. In Chapter 2 of this book it was mentioned that one way of measuring profit for a year is to compare the net worth of a business at the beginning of the year with that at its end. Any increase will be the profit, assuming that no capital has been introduced or withdrawn. That is, profit is any excess left over after maintaining the capital of the business.

When there are specific and general price changes, the concept of capital maintenance involves several possible results. Consider a simple business that buys land for €10,000 with cash introduced by the owner. It may be represented as in Figure 16.5. After several years the business sells the land for €15,000. In the meantime the general price index has risen from 100 to 130, and the specific land index has risen from 100 to 145. The business intends to buy a very similar replacement for €14,000 in a more convenient location. What profit does the business make on the sale of the land? The answer depends upon which concept of capital maintenance is being used.

Figure 16.5 **Cash of €10,000 introduced and used to buy land**

|  | Balance sheet |  |  |
|---|---|---|---|
| Land | 10,000 | Capital | 10,000 |
|  | 10,000 |  | 10,000 |

The *historical cost* (HC) concept is that the original nominal money capital should be maintained.

**Activity 16.C**  Prepare the balance sheet of the business shown in Figure 16.5 after the sale of the land, under the HC concept.

**Feedback**  Immediately after the original land has been sold, the balance sheet will appear as shown in Figure 16.6, showing a profit of €5,000, which is the current sales revenue *less* the original historical cost.

Figure 16.6 **Balance sheet after sale of the land based on historical cost**

|  | HC balance sheet |  |  |
|---|---|---|---|
|  |  | Capital | 10,000 |
| Cash | 15,000 | Profit | 5,000 |
|  | 15,000 |  | 15,000 |

An alternative concept is that the business should maintain the general purchasing power of the original capital and treat any excess over this as profit.

**Activity 16.D**

Prepare the balance sheet of the business after the sale, on a general purchasing power maintenance (CPP) basis, that is by adjusting for the change in purchasing power of the monetary unit, as measured by the movements in the general price index.

**Feedback**

In this case, to maintain the real value of the capital to the owners will require €13,000 (i.e. €10,000 × 130/100). This will lead to a profit of €2,000, as shown in the restated balance sheet in Figure 16.7.

**Figure 16.7 Taking the general price index into account**

| | | | | |
|---|---|---|---|---|
| | | **CPP balance sheet** | | |
| | | Original capital | | 10,000 |
| | | Purchasing power adjustment | | 3,000 |
| | | CPP capital | | 13,000 |
| Cash | | 15,000 | Profit | 2,000 |
| | | 15,000 | | 15,000 |

A further possibility is to hold that the business only makes profit after it has maintained its physical capital intact. This is a *current value* (CV) concept. It need not mean that the exact original assets are maintained, but it does mean that there is the same productive potential.

**Activity 16.E**

Prepare the balance sheet of the business after the sale, on a physical capital maintenance basis, in other words by adjusting for cost movements as indicated by a specific property index.

**Feedback**

Since the capital figure in this case represents a single piece of land, it can be said that to maintain the physical capital will require a figure of €14,500 (i.e. €10,000 × 145/100). This will lead to a profit of €500, as shown in Figure 16.8. The 'specific adjustment' to capital may be called a *capital maintenance reserve*.

**Figure 16.8 Profit after physical capital is maintained**

| | | | | |
|---|---|---|---|---|
| | | **CV balance sheet** | | |
| | | Original capital | | 10,000 |
| | | Specific adjustment | | 4,500 |
| | | Current value capital | | 14,500 |
| Cash | | 15,000 | Profit | 500 |
| | | 15,000 | | 15,000 |

However, it should be noted that the specific land price index is only used as a proxy for more detailed information about the actual replacement cost (RC) of the business's asset. In this case the business has decided that it can maintain its productive potential by buying a replacement costing €14,000. When this transaction is completed, it is very clear that the physical capital has been maintained and that the profit on a current value basis should be regarded as €1,000. An alternative way of looking at this is that current 'expense' (replacement cost) has been compared to current sales revenue, as set out in Figure 16.9.

**Figure 16.9 Actual current value**

| CV balance sheet | | | |
|---|---|---|---|
| Property | 14,000 | Original capital | 10,000 |
| | | Specific adjustment | 4,000 |
| | | Current value capital | 14,000 |
| Cash | 1,000 | Profit | 1,000 |
| | 15,000 | | 15,000 |

These various possibilities are summarized in Table 16.1. There are arguments in favour of each of them. The historical cost concept is simple to use and avoids the need for subjective estimates. Also, for the purposes of strict accountability, there is an advantage in the sense that the accounting system deals only with actual amounts of money received or spent. This makes it reliable and easily verifiable.

**Table 16.1 Capital maintenance concepts: variation of results**

| Concept | Capital to be maintained | Profit |
|---|---|---|
| Historical cost | Historical cost capital | 5,000 |
| Current purchasing power | Capital adjusted by general index | 2,000 |
| Current value (approx.) | Capital adjusted by specific index | 500 |
| Current value (actual) | Capital adjusted by specific RC | 1,000 |

From the point of view of the owners it may be suggested that the effect of inflation on the spending power of their capital is more relevant than the specific price changes of the business's assets. This is because the shareholders wish to spend their returns on retail purchases and, arguably, the best indication of changes in their capacity to do this is given by the general inflation index. Under this assumption, a current purchasing power system would be preferred. However, it is more usual in accounting to use the *entity convention*, whereby the business is viewed as being quite separate from the shareholders. It is also a fundamental accounting concept that the business is usually assumed to be a going concern; it therefore does not intend to return to the owners the assets that represent the capital. Normally (as in this case), the business will intend to replace the original item with another of similar economically productive potential. Since the assets are not to be returned to the owners but to be replaced by assets performing a similar function, their specific current value is surely of greater relevance than their general purchasing power.

If this argument is followed, it will lead to the adoption of a current value approach. The use of the actual replacement cost is clearly more relevant than a specific index. However, obtaining the former information before the asset is sold may often be too difficult or too expensive to be practical. Furthermore, critics of current value systems have pointed out that, although there are obvious advantages of such systems irrespective of any general movement in prices, they do not take account of *inflation* as previously defined in terms of a general decline in the purchasing power of money. In order to meet this criticism it is possible to combine adjustments for both general and specific price changes. The original capital of the owners can be adjusted for inflation by using a general index. However, the need for the going concern to take account of specific price changes can also be recognized. This is done by ensuring that any part of current purchasing power 'profit' that relates to the specific increase in the value of assets is treated as an undistributable holding gain.

| Activity 16.F | Taking Figure 16.9 as the starting point, prepare a balance sheet taking account of general inflation as well as a need for physical capital maintenance – that is, by separating the effects of specific and general index changes. |
|---|---|

| Feedback | The balance sheet will be as shown in Figure 16.10. |
|---|---|

Figure 16.10 **Treating the 'profit' on property as an undistributable gain**

| Balance sheet | | | |
|---|---|---|---|
| Property | 14,000 | Original capital | 10,000 |
| | | Purchasing power adjustment | 3,000 |
| Cash | 1,000 | CPP capital | 13,000 |
| | | Undistributable reserve | 1,000 |
| | | | 14,000 |
| | | Distributable profit | 1,000 |
| | 15,000 | | 15,000 |

Such a system may be considered to be too complex for many users of financial statements. However, it has the obvious advantage of adjusting the assets for specific price changes and the capital for changes in purchasing power.

Once an approach to capital maintenance has been chosen, the detailed problems of adjusting the accounting system for price changes can be looked at. In practice, balance sheets and income statements are required yearly without the above simplifying assumption that the property has been sold. Thus, the assets as well as the capital must be adjusted for specific or general price changes. The adjustments to profit follow from this. For example, the type of adjustment for depreciation will depend upon whether a fixed asset is restated using a general or a specific index. If a current value approach is adopted, a fixed asset will be restated using a specific index, and depreciation for a year will be based on this restated amount. This is discussed in the next sections, where actual proposals for systems of accounting to replace or supplement historical cost are examined.

## 16.5 General price-level adjusted systems

General price-level adjusted (GPLA) accounting systems were being discussed as long ago as the 1920s and 1930s, particularly in Germany, the Netherlands and the United States. In the early 1970s, when interest in inflation accounting was very strong because of the high levels of inflation mentioned earlier, many accountancy bodies in the English-speaking world investigated such systems. In 1974 a provisional Standard (PSSAP 7) on the topic was issued by the UK accountancy bodies. In the United Kingdom, it was called current purchasing power (CPP) accounting, but it did not become standard practice because of the intervention of the government-sponsored Sandilands Committee in favour of current cost accounting (see Section 16.7). However, about 150 UK companies produced supplementary CPP information in their annual accounts. Now the place to look for more consistent and general use of GPLA systems is South America.

GPLA systems are based on historical cost accounts adjusted with general price index numbers. The basic task is to translate money of different periods into current money of uniform purchasing power. Current items in the balance sheet are already in end-of-year money, but fixed assets need to be analysed by age and adjusted accordingly, using the general price index.

The income statement adjustments are the three discussed earlier: depreciation, cost of sales and monetary items. In each case the general price index is used, so that all figures are adjusted for *inflation* rather than for specific price changes.

Work through the following illustration carefully.

### 16.5.1 A worked illustration

Mushroom Co. was established on 1 January 20X1. Its opening balance sheet (on this date) was as given in Table 16.2.

Table 16.2 **Mushroom's opening balance sheet at 1.1.X1**

|  | € |
| --- | --- |
| Land | 6,000 |
| Equipment | 4,000 |
| Inventory | 2,000 |
| Equity | 12,000 |

During 20X1, the following applies to Mushroom:

(a) it purchased extra inventory of €10,000;

(b) it sold inventory for €11,000 cash, which had a historical cost of €9,000;

(c) its closing inventory on 31 December 20X1 had a historical cost of €3,000 and was bought when the general price index averaged 115 (1.1.X1 = 100);

(d) the equipment it owns has an expected life of four years, and nil residual value; the straight-line method of depreciation is used;

(e)  the general price index stood at:
- – 100 on 1 January 20X1;
- – 110 on 30 June 20X1;
- – 120 on 31 December 20X1.

It can be assumed that purchases and receipts occur evenly throughout the year. There are no debtors or creditors.

*Required*: to calculate the CPP profit for 20X1 and prepare the CPP balance sheet as at 31 December 20X1. The solution is set out next.

### Solution

The CPP income statement is as shown in Figure 16.11 for the year.

**Figure 16.11 CPP income statement for Mushroom for 20X1**

|  |  | €(CPP) | €(CPP) |
|---|---|---|---|
| Sales | (11,000 × 120/110) |  | 12,000 |
| Opening inventory | (2,000 × 120/100) | 2,400 |  |
| *add* purchases | (10,000 × 120/110) | 10,909 |  |
|  |  | 13,309 |  |
| *less* closing inventory | (3,000 × 120/115) | 3,130 |  |
|  |  |  | 10,179 |
|  |  |  | 1,821 |
| *less* depreciation |  |  | 1,200 |
|  |  |  | 621 |
| Loss on holding monetary assets (cash)[a] |  |  | 91 |
| CPP profit |  |  | 530 |

[a] If cash accrues evenly over the year, the loss is €(1,000 × 120/110) − €1,000 = €91.

The CPP balance sheet for Mushroom as at 31 December 20X1 is as set out in Figure 16.12.

**Figure 16.12 CPP balance sheet for Mushroom at 31.12.X1**

|  |  | €(CPP) | €(CPP) |
|---|---|---|---|
| Land | (6,000 × 120/100) |  | 7,200 |
| Equipment | (4,000 × 120/100) | 4,800 |  |
| *less* depreciation | (1,000 × 120/100) | 1,200 |  |
|  |  |  | 3,600 |
| Inventory | (3,000 × 120/115) | 3,130 |  |
| Cash | (11,000 − 10,000) | 1,000 |  |
|  |  |  | 4,130 |
|  |  |  | 14,930 |
| Equity | 12,000 × 120/100 |  | 14,400 |
| CPP profit |  |  | 530 |
|  |  |  | 14,930 |

It is important to think carefully when comparing the position at 31 December 20X1, as reported under CPP, with the position 12 months earlier. The opening balance sheet was expressed in euros of 1 January spending power and the closing balance sheet is now expressed in euros of 31 December spending power. These different measuring units are not comparable and the original balance sheet will need to be re-expressed in 31 December 20X1 euros before a rational comparison can be drawn with the closing position.

| Activity 16.G | Prepare, side by side, summary balance sheets for Mushroom Co. for 1 January 20X1 and 31 December 20X1, both expressed in 31 December purchasing power units. |
| --- | --- |

| Feedback | The result is shown in Figure 16.13. |
| --- | --- |

**Figure 16.13 CPP balance sheets for Mushroom with adjusted opening comparatives**

| 1 January 20X1 | | Item | 31 December 20X1 | |
| --- | --- | --- | --- | --- |
| 6,000 × 120/100 | 7,200 | Land | | 7,200 |
| 4,000 × 120/100 | 4,800 | Equipment | 4,800 | |
| | – | *less* depreciation | 1,200 | |
| | | | | 3,600 |
| | 12,000 | | | 10,800 |
| 2,000 × 120/100 | 2,400 | Inventory | 3,130 | |
| | – | Cash | 1,000 | |
| | | | | 4,130 |
| | 14,400 | | | 14,930 |
| 12,000 × 120/100 | 14,400 | Equity | | 14,930 |

The work involved in producing GPLA accounts is relatively straightforward. There are fewer difficulties than those involved with the specific adjustments of CV systems, and GPLA accounts remain fairly objective. However, the major reason for the failure of GPLA accounting to be adopted in the English-speaking world is the serious doubt about whether the information that it provides is particularly relevant. Criticisms have been made about the difficulty – simply but amply illustrated in the Mushroom Co. example – of comprehending accounts not produced in 'physical money' terms but in constantly changing units, about the lack of relevance of adjusting fixed assets, depreciation and inventory by a general index, and about the inclusion of monetary gains in published profit figures.

## 16.6 Current value accounting

The current value of an asset can be considered to be based on one of the three concepts briefly introduced in Chapter 8: *economic value* (EV), *net realizable value* (NRV) and *current replacement cost* (CRC). It would be possible to establish complete accounting systems based on each of these concepts or, alternatively, to combine them – as, for example, in systems based on deprival value (see Section 16.7).

### 16.6.1 Economic value

A current value accounting system based on economic values would have a strong theoretical basis, because the theoretical value of an asset depends upon the discounted future net flows of money from it. However, there are serious practical problems in estimating such future flows and establishing suitable discount rates. Also, the attendant subjectivity would make an auditor's job very difficult and reduce the reliability of accounting information. In addition, if the individual assets and liabilities of a business were all to be separately valued using an economic value basis, there would be the theoretical problem that, because cash flows result from assets working in combination, the estimation of the flows resulting from one asset alone is perhaps not a sensible task.

For these reasons no country has seriously considered proposing a system of accounting based mainly on economic values. Nevertheless, EV has been included as a basis to be used in exceptional circumstances within systems such as current cost accounting. It is also used for calculations of the impairment of assets (see Chapter 9).

### 16.6.2 Net realizable value

Another possibility is to have a current value system based on net realizable values. An example of such a system is 'continuously contemporary accounting' (CoCoA), proposed by the Australian academic R.J. Chambers. Under such a system, assets are adjusted to NRV, and depreciation is measured as the fall in the NRV of a fixed asset over an accounting period.

This approach may well provide useful information for management when making decisions about the future of assets, for creditors and for banks. However, it is fairly complex and difficult to use. For example, it is not possible to rely on the use of index numbers in the calculation of second-hand values of many fixed assets or partially completed inventory; thus, individual values must be calculated. Also, major criticisms have been levelled at the subjectivity involved and the fact that most businesses have no intention of selling most of their fixed assets in the near future, which casts doubt on the relevance of NRVs. However, as an exceptional basis, NRV is included in the proposals for current cost accounting examined in the next section. Also, as examined in Chapters 9, 10 and 11, NRV is used as a safety net in the valuation of inventories and in impairment tests. For certain assets, particularly investments, IASB and other standard setters have moved towards the use of 'fair value' (a current market value that specifies neither buying nor selling), discussed briefly in 16.9 below.

### 16.6.3 Current replacement cost

A third basis for a current value system is current replacement cost. This has already been considered at some length as regards inventory. The values of fixed assets are their depreciated CRCs. The gross CRC may be determined by valuers, by suppliers' catalogues or by age analysis of fixed assets followed by the application of specific indices. Suppose that a company buys a machine for €10,000 on 1 January 20X0. The machine is expected to have a useful life of five years and no scrap value. It is to be depreciated at 20 per cent per year on a straight-line basis. After three years, on 31 December 20X2, a CRC balance sheet is drawn up. The specific index has risen over the three years from 100 to 140. Therefore the gross CRC, in the absence of more exact information, will be €14,000 (i.e. €10,000 × 140/100). The net CRC will be €5,600 (i.e. €14,000 less 60 per cent cumulative depreciation of €8,400). The value of inventory will also be based on CRC, although this may be difficult to determine in the case of partially worked or finished goods.

One of the problems with the CRC of any asset is the difficulty that there may be in finding the cost of an effective replacement. This is particularly obvious in the case of obsolete fixed assets. It is necessary to establish the concept of the 'modern equivalent asset', the current cost of which is adjusted for any improvements that it embodies compared with the asset that it replaces. When the CRCs have been established, the excesses over historical costs are reflected in an asset revaluation reserve.

As far as the income statement is concerned, there are two important adjustments. Depreciation is based on the current cost of fixed assets. It is generally proposed for simplicity that the end-of-year, rather than the average-for-the-year, CRC of a fixed asset should be used. The second adjustment would be to eliminate the stockholding gains from profit by increasing the value of inventory used by a cost-of-sales adjustment. This would be done by using a company's detailed records or a set of specific indices. It is generally thought that these holding gains should not be regarded as distributable because they are part of maintaining the operating capability. An adjustment for gains and losses on monetary items is not usually included in CRC systems, which concentrate on specific price changes of physical resources.

### 16.6.4 A worked illustration

Let us assume, for illustrative purposes, that C Co.'s balance sheet on 31 December, year 1, after one year's trading, is as set out in Figure 16.14.

Figure 16.14 **Balance sheet for C at 31 December, year 1**

| | € | € | | € |
|---|---|---|---|---|
| Land and buildings at cost | | 110,000 | Capital – €1 | 200,000 |
| Plant and equipment at cost | 40,000 | | Ordinary shares | |
| *less* Depreciation | 4,000 | 36,000 | Profit | 26,000 |
| | | 146,000 | | 226,000 |
| Inventory | 90,000 | | Creditors | 50,000 |
| Debtors | 90,000 | | Loan | 50,000 |
| | | 180,000 | | |
| | | 326,000 | | 326,000 |

Further parameters to the illustration are as follows:

(a) The capital and loan had been contributed in cash and the land and buildings, plant and equipment and opening inventory of €60,000 had been purchased on 1 January.

(b) Transactions took place evenly during the year. The situation may therefore be treated as if all opening balances were held from 1 January until 30 June, as if all transactions took place on 30 June, and as if all closing balances were held from 30 June until 31 December.

(c) Price indices were as follows:

|  | Plant | Inventory |
|---|---|---|
| 1 January | 100 | 100 |
| 30 June | 105 | 115 |
| 31 December | 110 | 130 |

(d) The land and buildings were professionally valued at 31 December of year 1 at €135,000.

*Required*: to prepare a closing balance sheet on CRC lines. The solution to the problem is set out next.

### Solution

The income statement and balance sheet for C for its first year of trading are as shown in Figure 16.15.

**Figure 16.15 CRC income statement and balance sheet for C for year 1's trading**

| Income statement |  | € | € |
|---|---|---|---|
| HC profit |  |  | 26,000 |
| *Less* Adjustments: |  |  |  |
| Depreciation | $\left(4,000 \times \dfrac{(110-100)}{100}\right)$ | 400 |  |
| Inventory | $\left(60,000 \times \dfrac{(115-100)}{100}\right)$ | 9,000 | 9,400 |
| Current operating profit |  |  | 16,600 |
| Holding gains: |  |  |  |
| Inventory: realized as above |  | 9,000 |  |
| unrealized | $\left(90,000 \times \dfrac{(130-115)}{115}\right)$ | 11,740 |  |
| Plant and equipment: realized as above |  | 400 |  |
| unrealized | $\left(40,000 \times \dfrac{(110-100)}{100}\right) - 400$ | 3,600 |  |
| Land and buildings: unrealized | $(135,000 - 110,000)$ | 25,000 |  |
| Total holding gains |  |  | 49,740 |

**Figure 16.15** *Continued*

| Balance sheet | | € | € |
|---|---|---:|---:|
| Fixed assets: | | | |
| Land and buildings | | | 135,000 |
| Plant and equipment | $\left(40,000 \times \dfrac{110}{100}\right)$ | 44,000 | |
| *less* depreciation | $\left(4,000 \times \dfrac{110}{100}\right)$ | 4,400 | 39,600 |
| Current assets: | | | 174,600 |
| Inventory | $\left(90,000 \times \dfrac{130}{115}\right)$ | 101,740 | |
| Debtors | | 90,000 | 191,740 |
| | | | 366,340 |
| Share capital | | | 200,000 |
| Holding gain reserve | | | 49,740 |
| Profit | | | 16,600 |
| | | | 266,340 |
| Loan | | | 50,000 |
| Creditors | | | 50,000 |
| | | | 366,340 |

### Concluding comment on CRC

The Netherlands was the leader in replacement cost theory and practice. In the early twentieth century, a leading Dutch accounting academic and practitioner, Th. Limperg, developed an extensive theory, based in microeconomics, that was influential in the teaching of accounting. Many companies, notably including Philips, used replacement cost accounting (or elements of it) at various times since the 1950s. Nevertheless, there have been no direct requirements for departures from historical cost, and this minority practice has further declined in recent years. The revaluation of property, plant and equipment allowed under IAS 16 is based on a sort of replacement cost concept. This is clear because gains are not taken to income, but depreciation expenses and gains on disposal are subsequently adjusted to be based on the new 'cost'.

Revaluations are rare under IAS 16 (perhaps because depreciation expense rises and gains on sales fall). However, the Dutch bank, ING, revalues both IAS 16 property and IAS 40 property in its 2008 financial statements.

## 16.7 Mixed values – deprival value

Assume that a business owns an asset. What is that asset 'worth' to the business? The deprival value (DV) approach says that the DV of an asset is the loss that the rational businessperson would suffer if he or she were deprived of the asset. This loss will depend on what the business person would rationally do if he or she lost (were deprived of) it.

**Activity 16.H**

A businesswoman is in possession of six assets, labelled A to F respectively. The various monetary evaluations of each asset by its owner are shown in Table 16.3.

The owner has signed a contract with an insurance agent under which she would be reimbursed, in the event of loss of any asset, by 'the amount of money a rationally acting person would actually have lost as a result of losing the asset'. Put yourself in the position of the rationally acting person, decide what action you would take in each circumstance, if you lost the asset, and then calculate the net effect on the monetary position.

Table 16.3 **Assets owned and valued under different bases**

| Asset | HC | CRC | NRV | EV |
|-------|-----|-----|-----|-----|
| A | 1 | 2 | 3 | 4 |
| B | 5 | 6 | 8 | 7 |
| C | 9 | 12 | 10 | 11 |
| D | 16 | 15 | 14 | 13 |
| E | 17 | 19 | 20 | 18 |
| F | 23 | 22 | 21 | 24 |

**Feedback**

In each situation the first question to ask is: 'Would the rationally acting businesswoman replace the asset or not?' She would replace it if the proceeds of either selling it (NRV) or using it (EV) are higher than the costs of replacing it. If it would be replaced, then the loss suffered is clearly the cost of replacement. Thus, in situations where a rationally acting person would replace the asset, the deprival value is CRC. If the businesswoman would not replace it, then the loss suffered is given by the value of the benefits that would have been derived from the asset but that she will now never receive. Being rational, the intention must be to act so as to derive the highest possible return, i.e. the higher of NRV and EV. Therefore, in situations where the rationally acting business-woman would not replace the asset if deprived of it, the deprival value is the higher of NRV and EV. This last element, the higher of NRV and EV, is known as the *recoverable amount*, and we have met it before in the context of impairment tests in Chapter 9.

So we can formally state that deprival value is the lower of CRC and recoverable amount, where recoverable amount is the higher of NRV and EV (see Figure 16.16).

Given three different concepts (CRC, NRV and EV), there are only six possible different rankings:

$$EV > NRV > CRC$$
$$NRV > EV > CRC$$
$$CRC > EV > NRV$$
$$CRC > NRV > EV$$
$$NRV > CRC > EV$$
$$EV > CRC > NRV$$

Our example contains all six of these alternatives. The DV in each situation is as shown in Table 16.4. Notice the irrelevance of the HC figures.

Figure 16.16 **Relationship between DV, CRC, NRV and EV**

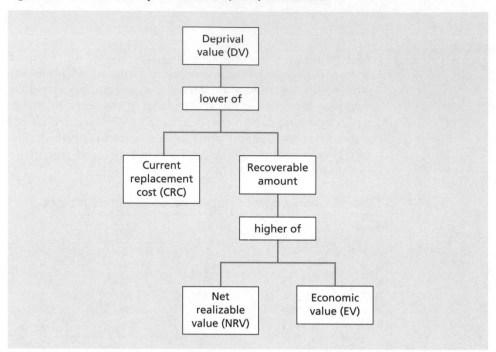

Table 16.4 **Deprival values for six assets**

| Asset | Deprival value | Reason |
|-------|---------------|--------|
| A | 2 | Cost of replacement |
| B | 6 | Cost of replacement |
| C | 11 | EV not to be received |
| D | 14 | NRV not to be received |
| E | 19 | Cost of replacement |
| F | 22 | Cost of replacement |

Because the deprival value arguably takes account of the intentions – or at least the logical actions – of the business concerned, it is often termed the *value to the business* of an asset.

What about capital maintenance? Profit is here being regarded as the excess after maintaining the value to the business of its assets. The value to the business is clearly seen to be related to actual operations (i.e. what the business would do). Following from this, we can say that the deprival value basis seeks to maintain the business's capacity to do things, usually expressed as the *operating capacity* or *operating capability*. We saw above that in four of the six possible rankings, deprival value equals RC. In the practical business situation, the chances of replacement cost being higher than both NRV and EV will generally be relatively small, and so the other two rankings will in practice not occur frequently. This means that in a practical business context, deprival value will equal RC much more frequently than four cases out of six.

The logic of deprival value seems intuitively attractive. It formed the basis of a practical attempt in preparing financial statements taking account of specific price changes in the UK in the early 1980s (called current cost accounting). However, the complexity is clearly considerable, both in terms of some loss of objectivity in the preparation and, perhaps more importantly, in terms of comprehension by the non-specialist reader of the resulting statements. It is worth noting, however, that the logic of deprival value forms the basis of the concept of impairment in IAS 36 (see Section 9.6, and in particular Figure 9.5).

Since the early 1990s, practical interest in such methods has fallen in most countries, as inflation rates have generally been low. However, this is not necessarily logical. It must be remembered that replacement cost, deprival value, and so on are concerned with the price changes of *specific* goods or commodities. If the price of a major raw material doubles or halves – as has happened in recent years with crude oil, or coffee, for example – the effects on relevant businesses, which will be unreported under historical cost accounting, might well be enormous.

## 16.8 Partial adjustments

There have been a number of attempts to make relatively simple adjustments to historical cost accounting. This section will examine three of them.

### 16.8.1 Ad hoc government-controlled revaluations

In France, Spain, Italy and Greece revaluations of fixed assets and inventories have occurred several times in the last few decades. Some examples are briefly noted here.

1. *France*. A revaluation of fixed assets and inventories was required, for companies with traded securities, in balance sheets at 31 December 1978. This used specific indices as published by the government for 31 December 1976 prices. The revaluation was tax-exempt, and subsequent depreciation charges were adjusted back to historical cost in order to avoid changing the tax calculations.
2. *Spain*. A revaluation was carried out in 1983. This was tax-exempt but had a subsequent beneficial tax effect in that it increased depreciation charges for the calculation of taxable income. Thus it aided the liquidity of Spanish companies in an inflationary period. In 1996 a further taxable revaluation was required.
3. *Italy*. Revaluations were required for certain companies in 1983, 1991 and other years. These had some tax effects.

### 16.8.2 Ad hoc revaluations by business management

In certain countries (such as the United Kingdom, Denmark and the Netherlands) some fixed assets have been revalued, largely at the discretion of the directors of companies. A few Dutch companies have used full systems of current value accounting, but generally revaluation in these countries involves only some companies, a selection of assets (particularly land and buildings), and is not necessarily performed annually. In the United Kingdom, from 1999, if assets are revalued they must be valued every year. These revaluations are mostly a rather messy partial attempt to update accounts for price changes.

### 16.8.3 LIFO inventory valuation

The last-in, first-out (LIFO) method of inventory valuation has been discussed in Chapter 10. It is a method that matches the most recent purchases against current sales and thus charges an approximately current cost for inventory used. A disadvantage is that the oldest purchases are deemed to remain in inventory, which leads to an unrealistically low balance sheet figure. Also, if inventory levels are reduced, some very old costs will enter the cost-of-sales calculation.

Nevertheless, the use of LIFO does approximately adjust the cost-of-sales figure for specific price changes, particularly if purchases are frequent. Thus, it reduces profit figures during inflationary periods. It is now used by many corporations in Germany and Italy and in the United States, mainly because it reduces profit for tax purposes. In some European countries it is not allowed for tax purposes, and is prohibited by law or by accounting standard. Under IFRS this method is no longer permitted, as discussed in Chapter 10.

## 16.9 Fair values

A significant recent trend is the increasing importance of the concept of *fair value*. This is defined by the IASB as 'the amount for which an asset could be exchanged, or a liability settled, between knowledgeable, willing parties in an arm's length transaction' – in effect, the market price in a theoretically perfect market. It is important to notice that fair value is not identical to net realizable value. Net realizable value is the expected sales proceeds reduced by any future transaction costs of the selling process. Fair value is the expected gross exchange value, without any reduction for transaction costs.

Fair value is referred to in a number of IASs, notably IAS 39 on financial instruments (see Chapter 11) and IAS 40 on investment properties (see Chapter 9). The importance of fair value seems likely to increase further on the international scene over the next few years, although this may well create tension and disagreement.

It is arguable that the use of fair value is likely in many situations to increase relevance for many users, though not necessarily for all. It is also arguable, however, that the use of fair value will reduce reliability as compared with historical costs. As discussed in Section 16.3, and more generally in Chapter 5, different country traditions will lead to different reactions to such a proposed change.

A number of standards attempt to create a hierarchy of calculation methods for fair value. These can be summarized as follows, in descending order.

1. current prices in an active market for similar assets in similar conditions;
2. current prices in an active market for different assets, adjusted to reflect those differences;

3. recent prices of similar assets on less active markets, with appropriate adjustments to reflect different market characteristics;

4. discounted cash flow projections based on 'reliable estimates' of future cash flows.

It is apparent that considerable subjectivity could be involved here. It is also apparent that the existence of reasonably mature and sophisticated markets in the resources concerned is assumed – an assumption less likely to be valid in developing economies than in advanced capitalist areas.

The European Accounting Directives have been amended to permit the usage of fair values, and there are strong signs that the IASB wishes to further increase the usage of this valuation basis over the next few years. Such proposals are meeting serious opposition, and the IASB has not yet fully established either the full theoretical implications or the practical operationalization of the fair value concept. Indeed the FASB has introduced a revised definition of fair value, and the implications for the IASB remain unclear at the time of writing. Follow the debate.

## Summary

- Inflation ran at a very high level in much of Europe in the mid-1970s, thus encouraging attempts to adjust historical cost accounting for general or specific price changes. Indices for both are available in many countries.

- The effects of price changes cause deficiencies in historical cost balance sheets and profit calculations. The effects on profit are more complex and may involve adjustments for depreciation, for cost of sales and for gains and losses on monetary items.

- Unless adjustments are made, users of accounts may be seriously misled about the value and profitability of a business and about what may be suitable levels of dividends, wages or prices. However, some countries oppose any departure from historical cost.

- Adjusted systems of accounting fall into two groups: those that adjust for general price changes and those that adjust for specific price changes. The underlying difference concerns the concept of capital maintenance. General adjustment aims to maintain the inflation-adjusted value of the owners' capital; specific adjustment aims to maintain the productive capacity of the business.

- The choice determines how assets are to be restated and, in each case, profit is what remains after the appropriate measure of capital has been maintained. It is possible to combine the two approaches, so that both inflation and specific price changes are taken into account.

- Current value systems could be based purely on economic values, on net realizable values or on current replacement costs. Deprival value is a system that uses all three bases, although mainly current replacement cost.

- In the absence of a standard method of adjusting accounts for changing prices, a number of partial adjustments were experimented with in Europe. These include government-controlled or ad hoc revaluations and the use of LIFO for calculating the cost of sales.

- Fair value has become an increasingly important concept internationally.

**References and research**

The relevant IASB standards are:

- IAS 15, *Information Reflecting the Effects of Changing Prices*, withdrawn some years ago.
- IAS 29, *Financial Reporting in Hyperinflationary Economies*.

There is a vast theoretical literature on the topics covered in this chapter. An excellent bibliography appears in:

- T. Lee, *Income and Value Measurement*, 3rd edition (New York: Van Nostrand Reinhold, 1985).

A paper of some practical interest is:

- H. Brink, 'A history of Philips' accounting policies on the basis of its annual reports', *European Accounting Review*, Vol. 1, No. 2, 1992.

See also, for itself and for the references therein:

- D. Tweedie and G. Whittington, 'The end of the current cost revolution', in T. Cooke and C. Nobes (eds), *The Development of Accounting in an International Context* (London: Routledge, 1997).

A good up-to-date survey, offering many avenues for further investigation, can be found in:

- P. Walton (ed.), *The Routledge Companion to Fair Values and Financial Reporting* (London: Routledge, 2007).

## ? EXERCISES

*Feedback on the first two of these exercises is given in Appendix D.*

16.1 P is a computer dealer. From the information in Table 16.5:

(a) compute the income statements and closing balance sheets for each of the years 20X0 and 20X1 under historical cost principles, assuming FIFO;

(b) construct the income statements and closing balance sheets for each of the years 20X0 and 20X1 under current replacement cost principles;

(c) comment briefly on the significance of a comparison of the results.

16.2 Duck Co. was formed on 1 January 20X0 with 10,000 issued €1 ordinary shares. The same day it obtained a 12 per cent loan of €8,000 and bought fixed assets for €9,000. During 20X0, the purchases and sales of widgets were as given in Table 16.6.
You are also told that:

(a) purchases and sales were all paid for in cash;

(b) the loan interest was paid early in 20X1;

(c) the buying price of widgets changed on 1 March, 1 June, 1 September and 1 December (when it was 100);

(d) the fixed assets are to be depreciated at 10 per cent per annum, and at 31 December 20X0 their replacement price was €12,600;

(e) general expenses during the year were €13,200.

Prepare a balance sheet as at 31 December 20X0, together with an income statement for the year to 31 December 20X0, on replacement cost lines. What are holding gains? In what circumstances are they distributable?

**Table 16.5 Transactions by P**

| Date | Event relating to trading in computers | Computers | Cash balance (€) |
|---|---|---|---|
| | | | *'Wealth'* |
| 1/1/X0 | Set up business with €10,000 in the bank | | 10,000 |
| 2/1/X0 | Buy six computers for €1,000 each | 6 | 4,000 |
| 1/5/X0 | Sell two computers for €1,500 each (replacement cost €1,100) | 4 | 7,000 |
| 1/9/X0 | Buy two computers for €1,200 each | 6 | 4,600 |
| 1/10/X0 | Pay annual rent of €600 | 6 | 4,000 |
| 31/12/X0 | Financial year end. Pay tax of €200 | 6 | 3,800 |
| 3/3/X1 | Sell two computers for €1,800 each (replacement cost €1,300 each) | 4 | 7,400 |
| 1/10/X1 | Pay annual rent of €700 | 4 | 6,700 |
| 1/11/X1 | Buy two computers for €1,400 each | 6 | 3,900 |
| 31/12/X1 | Financial year end. Pay tax of €450 | 6 | 3,450 |

**Table 16.6 Duck Co.'s widget transactions in 20X0**

| | Purchases | € | Sales | € |
|---|---|---|---|---|
| 3 January | 100 at €80 | 8,000 | | |
| 1 February | | | 60 at €120 | 7,200 |
| 1 April | 110 at €75 | 8,250 | | |
| 1 May | | | 90 at €120 | 10,800 |
| 1 July | 100 at €85 | 8,500 | | |
| 1 August | | | 130 at €120 | 15,600 |
| 1 October | 120 at €90 | 10,800 | | |
| 1 November | | | 110 at €130 | 14,300 |

16.3  From the historical cost accounts of Q Co., set out in Figure 16.17, prepare a set of CPP accounts for the year ended 31 December 20X8.

The movement on the retail price index can be taken as follows:

| | |
|---|---|
| 1 January 20X5 | 180 |
| 1 January 20X7 | 200 |
| Average for 20X7 | 210 |
| 31 October 20X7 | 215 |
| 31 December 20X7 | 220 |
| Average for 20X8 | 230 |
| 31 October 20X8 | 235 |
| 31 December 20X8 | 240 |

Assume all sales, purchases and expenses accrue evenly throughout the year.

16.4  Explain and demonstrate how replacement cost accounting affects reported profit compared with historical cost.

16.5  Is replacement cost more or less prudent than historical cost?

16.6  'Businesses should be required to publish their income statement on replacement cost lines and their balance sheet on net realizable value lines.' Discuss.

Figure 16.17 **HC accounts for Q for 20X8**

| Balance sheet | | 31.12.X7 €000 | | 31.12.X8 €000 |
|---|---|---|---|---|
| Fixed assets: | | | | |
| Cost (purchased 1.1.X5) | | 500 | | 500 |
| *less* depreciation | | 300 | | 400 |
| | | 200 | | 100 |
| Current assets: | | | | |
| Inventory (purchased 31 October) | 100 | | 150 | |
| Debtors | 200 | | 300 | |
| Bank | 150 | | 350 | |
| | 450 | | 800 | |
| *less* Current liabilities | | | | |
| Creditors | 300 | | 400 | |
| | | 150 | | 400 |
| | | 350 | | 500 |
| Share capital | | 100 | | 100 |
| Reserves | | 250 | | 400 |
| | | 350 | | 500 |

| Income statement for the year ended 31 December 20X8 | | |
|---|---|---|
| | | €000 |
| Sales | | 1,850 |
| Cost of goods sold: | | |
| Opening inventory | 100 | |
| Purchases | 1,350 | |
| | 1,450 | |
| *less* Closing inventory | 150 | |
| | | 1,300 |
| | | 550 |
| Gross profit | | |
| Expenses | 300 | |
| Depreciation | 100 | |
| | | 400 |
| Net profit | | 150 |

16.7  What do CPP adjustments do, and how do they do it?

16.8  Are general indices more or less useful in financial reporting than specific price changes?

16.9  Explain the meaning of capital maintenance.

16.10 Explain the meaning of deprival value. Is it an improvement on pure replacement cost accounting?

16.11 Ale Properties is a small family-owned company that only has equity share capital; it has no debt capital. Its net assets at 1 January 20X1 were €1,000, and on the

31 December 20X1 the net assets were €1,400. There have been no issues or withdrawals of share capital during the year. The general rate of inflation, as measured by the Retail Prices Index, is 10 per cent, whereas the specific rate of inflation for the type of goods sold by the company is 15 per cent.

Calculate three alternative measurements of profit for the company using:

(a) the money maintenance concept;
(b) the real capital maintenance concept;
(c) the maintenance of specific purchasing power.

16.12 'Historical cost accounting is simple and reliable. We should all use it as the basis of financial reporting.' Discuss.

16.13 Type 'fair value accounting' into Google or another suitable search engine. Attempt to make sense of, and summarize, what you discover.

# Part 3

# ANALYSIS

**17** Financial appraisal

**18** International analysis

# Chapter 17

# Financial appraisal

| Contents | | | |
|---|---|---|---|
| | 17.1 | Introduction | 330 |
| | 17.2 | More on investment ratios | 330 |
| | | 17.2.1 Non-recurring items | 330 |
| | | 17.2.2 Earnings per share (EPS) | 331 |
| | | 17.2.3 Dividend cover | 334 |
| | | 17.2.4 Dividend yield | 335 |
| | | 17.2.5 Price/earnings (P/E) ratio | 335 |
| | 17.3 | Interpreting the balance sheet | 336 |
| | 17.4 | Valuation through expectations | 339 |
| | 17.5 | Valuation through market values | 340 |
| | 17.6 | Accounting policies and financial appraisal | 341 |
| | | Summary | 349 |
| | | References and research | 349 |
| | | Exercises | 350 |

**Objectives**  After studying this chapter carefully, you should be able to:

- define, calculate, explain and interpret a variety of investment ratios, including the treatment of unusual items;

- discuss the usefulness of published balance sheets as a basis for entity valuation;

- outline the principles of entity valuation through expectations and market values;

- produce an overall financial appraisal for simple situations and comparisons, embracing the implications of differences in accounting policies and changes in accounting policies;

- explain the principles of basic and diluted earnings per share.

## 17.1 Introduction

Part 1 of this book explored the context of accounting, concluding in Chapter 7 with an introductory coverage of ratio analysis as a tool for helping to interpret the financial statements that the accounting process produces. Part 2 considered a number of accounting issues, as applications and extensions of the basic principles established in Part 1.

Part 3, without going beyond the level implied by an introductory text, explores some of the issues that emerge from a synthesis of the early chapters. Many of the 'Why it matters' paragraphs in Part 2 have pointed out that the choice of accounting policy, by affecting the numbers used in the financial statements, will affect the impression given by those statements and by the ratios calculated from them. To repeat: different accounting policies affect the *impression*, but not the underlying events. Proper financial statement appraisal attempts to get beyond the impression.

In this chapter, we develop some of the analysis of Chapter 7 a little further, and then begin to explore the practicalities of analysis and interpretation in the context of different accounting policies. Chapter 18 will begin to consider more explicitly the transnational scenario.

## 17.2 More on investment ratios

### 17.2.1 Non-recurring items

Chapter 7 (particularly Section 7.8) gave a brief introduction to investment ratios, used for analysis of financial statements from the equity investor's perspective. Now we develop this viewpoint. A number of ratios focus on the crucial figure of earnings, i.e. on the profits of the year available for the ordinary shareholders. Before investigating these ratios in detail, it is important to consider the concept of earnings more carefully. Perhaps the best way to highlight the issues is to ask why the earnings figure is of interest. In essence there are two possible answers:

(a) the analyst or shareholder may want a summary figure that expresses what has happened to the business as affects the owners;
(b) the analyst or shareholder may want to know what the recent past suggests is the maintainable earnings for the future.

*Why it matters*  *The essential difference between answers (a) and (b) above is that those items that are unlikely to recur, or unlikely to recur at a similar level of size or significance, would need to be excluded in order to provide information for purpose (b), but would need to be included for purpose (a). This issue has caused much debate and discussion over the last few decades in a number of jurisdictions. Of course, the main purpose in (b) is to predict future earnings and cash flows, but the idea that there are 'maintainable' earnings in a fast-changing world seems unlikely. Consequently, an earlier tendency to regard (b) as important has been significantly reversed, and the tendency now is to provide information largely focused on (a), i.e. providing a total picture of the results of the activities of the entity within the accounting period.*

It could be argued that, provided there is full and detailed disclosure of any unusual items, the precise layout and presentation of financial information makes no difference. This is not generally accepted in practice. First, many users of financial statements do not read the small print and, second, the scope for creative manipulation of results by preparers tends to be increased, the more items are excluded from the earnings figure.

International thinking is reflected in IAS 1, as revised in 2003 (and as retained in 2007). This abolished the concept of 'extraordinary items'. This removed the temptation for companies to present bad news as 'extraordinary' at the bottom of the income statement. However, an entity is required to disclose amounts of unusual items such as restructurings or disposal of non-current assets. By contrast, under most national rules, certain items are required to be shown in the income statement as extraordinary. A short list of such items applies under US GAAP. According to the EU Fourth Directive: 'Income and charges that arise otherwise than in the course of the company's ordinary activities must be shown under "Extraordinary income and extraordinary charges".' In France, Italy and Spain, the resulting concept is similar to 'non-trading' or 'non-recurring'. At the other extreme, in the United Kingdom, 'extraordinary' is very narrowly defined and intended to be so rare as never to occur in practice.

Another important issue in predicting the future is to know how much of the profit or the net assets will not be there next year because they are 'discontinued'. IFRS 5, which is similar to US GAAP, requires separate disclosure of the net amount of such items on the financial statements. With a disregard for grammar, the IASB includes in 'discontinued' those operations that are expected to discontinue in the following year. Companies might be tempted to put loss-making operations in such a category, so as to improve the impression of the future. Consequently, IFRS 5 has several paragraphs that try to control the use of the category.

**Real-world example**  Figures 17.1 and 17.2 show the income statement and assets of the Royal Bank of Scotland, a UK company that was much in the news in 2008, after it had to be rescued by the UK government in the financial crisis and after a disastrous take-over of the Dutch bank, ABN-AMRO.

## 17.2.2 Earnings per share (EPS)

'Earnings' is defined in IAS 33 as the net profit for ordinary shareholders, i.e. after any preference dividends. As explained in Chapter 6, a major issue to be resolved is the extent to which gains and losses outside of 'profit and loss' (e.g. certain revaluations, currency translation items and actuarial gains and losses) should in future be included in earnings. At present, these amounts of 'other comprehensive income' (OCI) are excluded from earnings. Many companies provide additional EPS disclosures using different definitions of earnings.

As well as a difficulty in deciding what to include in earnings for the purpose of EPS calculations, there may be two problems with the denominator (the number of shares) in the calculation, where there are:

Figure 17.1 **Royal Bank of Scotland's consolidated income statement for the year ended 31 December 2008**

| | 2008 £m |
|---|---:|
| Interest receivable | 49,522 |
| Interest payable | (30,847) |
| **Net interest income** | **18,675** |
| Fees and commissions receivable | 9,831 |
| Fees and commissions payable | (2,386) |
| (Loss)/income from trading activities | (8,477) |
| Other operating income (excluding insurance premium income) | 1,899 |
| Insurance net premium income | 6,326 |
| **Non-interest income** | **7,193** |
| **Total income** | **25,868** |
| Staff costs | 10,241 |
| Premises and equipment | 2,593 |
| Other administrative expenses | 5,464 |
| Depreciation and amortisation | 3,154 |
| Write-down of goodwill and other intangible assets | 32,581 |
| **Operating expenses** | **54,033** |
| **(Loss)/profit before other operating charges and impairment** | **(28,165)** |
| Insurance net claims | 4,430 |
| Impairment | 8,072 |
| **Operating (loss)/profit before tax** | **(40,667)** |
| Tax | (2,323) |
| **(Loss)/profit from continuing operations** | **(38,344)** |
| Profit/(loss) from discontinued operations, net of tax | 3,971 |
| **(Loss)/profit for the year** | **(34,373)** |
| **(Loss)/profit attributable to:** | |
| Minority interests | (10,832) |
| Other owners | 596 |
| Ordinary shareholders | (24,137) |
| | (34,373) |
| Per 25p ordinary share: | |
| Basic earnings | (145.7p) |
| Diluted earnings | (145.7p) |
| Dividends | 19.3p |

*Source*: Adapted from Royal Bank of Scotland's Annual Report for 2008, p. 174.

(a) changes in the equity share capital during the financial year;

(b) securities in existence, at the end of the accounting period, with no current claim on equity earnings but that may give rise to such a claim in the future.

Broadly speaking, the first problem is dealt with by calculating the average share capital outstanding during the year. The second problem is dealt with by calculating EPS twice:

(a) the earnings are related to the number of shares actually in issue at the balance sheet date (the basic EPS); and

Figure 17.2 **Extract from Royal Bank of Scotland's consolidated balance sheet at 31 December 2008**

|  | 2008 £m |
|---|---:|
| **Assets** | |
| Cash and balances at central banks | 12,400 |
| Loans and advances to banks | 138,197 |
| Loans and advances to customers | 874,722 |
| Debt securities subject to repurchase agreements | 80,576 |
| Other debt securities | 186,973 |
| Debt securities | 267,549 |
| Equity shares | 26,330 |
| Investments in Group undertakings | – |
| Settlement balances | 17,832 |
| Derivatives | 992,559 |
| Intangible assets | 20,049 |
| Property, plant and equipment | 18,949 |
| Deferred taxation | 7,082 |
| Prepayments, accrued income and other assets | 24,402 |
| Assets of disposal groups | 1,581 |
| **Total assets** | **2,401,652** |

*Source*: Adapted from Royal Bank of Scotland's Annual Report for 2008, p. 175.

(b) on the assumption that all the share conversions that would make EPS lower had happened (the diluted EPS).

IAS 33 requires that listed companies should disclose the basic and the diluted earnings per share, with equal prominence, on the face of the income statement, for all periods for which the income statement figures are given.

### A worked example

The number of ordinary shares of a company in issue is 2 million. In addition, there exists convertible loan stock of €500,000, bearing interest at 10 per cent. This may be converted by the lender into ordinary shares between 20X6 and 20X7 at the rate of one ordinary share for every €2 of loan stock. Assume that the corporate income tax rate is 40 per cent. Other parameters are given in Table 17.1.

The basic EPS for 20X2 will be:

$$\frac{\text{profit after tax, less preference dividends}}{\text{number of ordinary shares}} = \frac{€(700,000 - 50,000)}{2 \text{ million}} = \frac{€650,000}{2,000,000}$$

$$= €0.325 \text{ per share.}$$

To calculate the diluted EPS, there are two effects to consider. First, the share capital could increase by 250,000 shares (1 share for every €2 of the €500,000 loans). Second, the 'earnings' would then increase by the amount of interest on the loan, which would no longer be payable, less the extra tax payable as a result of the removal of

Table 17.1 **Example company figures**

|  |  | €000 |
|---|---|---|
| Profit before taxation, year to 31 December 20X2 |  | 1,000 |
| Taxation |  | 300 |
| Earnings |  | 700 |
| Preference dividend | 50 |  |
| Ordinary dividend | 100 | 150 |
| Retained profit for the year |  | 550 |

the interest expense. The interest at 10 per cent on €500,000 is €50,000, but the extra tax on this profit increase would be 40 per cent of €50,000, i.e. €20,000. Earnings would therefore increase by the net amount of interest saved less extra tax payable, i.e. by €50,000 − €20,000 = €30,000. The diluted EPS will be (after removing 000 from all figures):

$$\frac{€[(700 + 30) - 50]}{2,250} = \frac{€680}{2,250} = €0.302 \text{ per share.}$$

This latter figure will be the better indication of what a potential investor would be obtaining in the long run, on the assumptions that:

(a) the current earnings figure is a meaningful figure as regards future trends;
(b) those others who have *already been given* rights to convert into newly created additional ordinary shares do so.

**Real-world example**

In Figure 17.1 (earlier), the basic and diluted EPS numbers of the Royal Bank of Scotland are shown.

### 17.2.3 Dividend cover

The dividend cover is the number of times that a company could pay the intended dividend out of the available profits of the current year. This gives an indication of how secure the future dividend payments are likely to be. As before, alternative possibilities exist as to the inclusion or exclusion of unusual items in the calculation of the derived earnings figure.

The formula for dividend cover is:

$$\frac{\textbf{earnings}}{\textbf{total dividends on ordinary shares}}$$

The higher the ratio, the greater the coverage, or safety margin, of earnings over dividends. Note that it is perfectly possible for the dividend cover to be less than one, or to be negative. Directors often choose to maintain annual dividends in years when a poor result (even a loss) occurs, as a signal to the market of an expected upturn in performance. The dividend can be provided out of the retained profits from earlier years.

### 17.2.4 Dividend yield

The formula for dividend yield is:

$$\frac{\text{dividend per share}}{\text{market price per share}}$$

The ratio indicates the rate of return in terms of profit distribution that would be obtained by an investor who buys one share at the current market price. It can be compared with the ruling level of interest rates on investments, but of course it ignores those undistributed profits that are nevertheless attributable to the shareholders (i.e. the rest of earnings). It also ignores OCI. These other gains will help the expansion of the business and thus, if all goes well, lead to increased future dividend rates, and to eventual capital gains for the investor through a rising share price.

### 17.2.5 Price/earnings (P/E) ratio

The formula for the P/E ratio is:

$$\frac{\text{market price of one share}}{\text{EPS}}$$

The P/E ratio can be said to represent how much (in terms of the number of years' earnings) it is necessary to pay in order to acquire a share. It is potentially a highly volatile ratio, which will be affected both by changes in earnings per share (or in its definition), and by movements in the share price as quoted on a stock exchange.

P/E is widely regarded as important, and in some countries is published daily, for large quoted companies, in the financial pages of many newspapers. In Europe's most influential business newspaper, *The Financial Times*, the 'earnings' figure in the P/E ratio is not the one required by the accounting standards but uses a narrower definition (e.g. excluding goodwill impairment or amortization).

The P/E ratio represents the market's view of the strength or risk of the company, and of its expected further growth. A high P/E indicates that the market has a high opinion of the future prospects of the company. If company A has a P/E of 10, and company B has a P/E of 12, then 'the market' is willing to pay 12 times earnings to acquire a share in B, but only 10 times earnings to acquire a share in A. This must mean that future improvements in the performance of B are expected to be greater (or more likely) than is the case with A.

**Activity 17.A**

The information given in Table 17.2 relates to Snow Co. The market price per ordinary share is €1.75 at 31 December Year 1 and €1.82 at 31 December Year 2.

Calculate earnings per ordinary share and price/earnings ratios for each year, and comment briefly.

| Table 17.2 **Snow's statistics** | | |
|---|---|---|
| | *Year 1* | *Year 2* |
| €1 ordinary shares issued | 1,875,000 | 1,875,000 |
| €1 preference shares (8%) issued | 660,000 | 660,000 |
| Dividend on ordinary shares | €225,000 | €187,000 |
| Net profit after tax | €257,500 | €231,900 |

**Feedback**  EPS is defined as:

$$\frac{\text{net profit} - \text{preference dividends}}{\text{number of ordinary shares}}$$

For Year 1, this is:

$$\frac{€(257,500 - 52,800)}{1,875,000} = €0.109$$

For Year 2, it is:

$$\frac{€(231,900 - 52,800)}{1,875,000} = €0.096$$

The P/E ratio is defined as:

$$\frac{\text{market price per share}}{\text{EPS}}$$

For Year 1, this is:

$$\frac{€1.75}{€0.109} = 16.06$$

For Year 2, it is:

$$\frac{€1.82}{€0.096} = 18.96$$

These results show that, whilst earnings per ordinary share have fallen for Year 2, the price/earnings ratio has risen. This presumably suggests that investors at the end of Year 2 regard the future of Snow Co. in a more favourable light than was the case at the end of Year 1.

## 17.3 Interpreting the balance sheet

The balance sheet can be described as a statement of financial position at a point in time. It shows the resources of the business, as well as its sources of finance. Much time has been spent in earlier chapters in exploring how the figures in a balance sheet have been arrived at.

If the user wants a complete financial picture of the business, balance sheets suffer from several significant drawbacks:

1. *Absence of items.* In general, only those items acquired through external transactions will be recognized in a balance sheet. Resources created within the business (except for development assets) and resources that do not have clearly related costs, such as the collective experience of a project team or workforce, will not be included.

2. *Historical valuation of items.* Many resources are recorded in balance sheets at figures based on their original purchase price. Such historical book values may differ – often very substantially – from market values as at the date of the balance sheet. Chapter 11 examined the use of current values for some investments and Chapter 16 explored the issues more generally.

3. *Effect of accrual basis.* Given the interconnections between the income statement and the balance sheet, accountants have to choose between the alternative approaches of either:

   (a) calculating the figures for the income statement under defined procedures and formulae, and putting whatever number is left over in the balance sheet; or

   (b) calculating the figures in the balance sheet under defined procedures and formulae, and putting whatever number is left over in the income statement.

   Although there is increasing movement by standard setters toward the second approach, accountants still adopt the first approach for some items (depreciation, for example). The resulting balance sheet number is a residual, often of doubtful meaning.

4. *Flexibility of accounting policy.* The different and often conflicting implications of the common accounting conventions, and the significant degree of subjectivity involved in both choice of accounting policy and detailed application of accounting policy, lead to great flexibility of accounting numbers.

Notwithstanding all the above problems, a balance sheet is the nearest that accountants get to publishing a statement of business position and resources. It can be useful, provided that the bases on which it is prepared are understood. For most assets, it can be regarded as showing the lower of:

(a) the cost of the resource (or some proportion thereof in the case of a depreciated fixed asset);

(b) the benefit, i.e. the proceeds expected to be derived from using or selling the resource in the normal course of business.

The balance sheet figures can therefore be regarded as providing a prudent valuation for many of the recorded items, and therefore (remembering that there are also usually unrecorded resources) as a very conservative picture of the business as a whole. There is one important proviso to this statement, however: the phrase in (b) above, namely 'proceeds expected to be derived from the resource *in the normal course of business*'. This means that the figures generally follow the going concern convention and do not take account of the possibility of imminent closure of the business. Any such sudden closure would probably result in a break-up value for the business far smaller than implied by published financial statements. Doubts about whether companies were going concerns were a major worry for directors, auditors and investors in 2008/9. Note also that the above comments assume a historical-cost-based balance sheet, rather than one of the alternatives discussed in Chapter 16.

Within the limitations inherent in the above discussion, the balance sheet figures, usually known as book values, can be used as partial indicators of business size and financial strength. Net assets, at book value, could be calculated on per share basis, for example. Taking the Bread Co. balance sheets from Chapter 7 (repeated here as Figures 17.3 and 17.4), and remembering that the share capital consists of ordinary shares of €1 nominal value, net assets per share at book value would be:

$$\text{in 20X1: } \frac{€94}{70} = €1.34 \text{ per share}$$

$$\text{in 20X2: } \frac{€106}{76} = €1.39 \text{ per share}$$

The absolute figures may not mean very much, but the trend, particularly over a longer period, may be indicative of a company's underlying performance.

**Figure 17.3 Bread Co. balance sheets (€000): vertical presentation**

|  | At 31 Dec 20X1 | | At 31 Dec 20X2 | |
|---|---|---|---|---|
| *Non-current assets* | | 72 | | 110 |
| *Current assets* | | | | |
| Inventory | 12 | | 16 | |
| Debtors (receivables) | 18 | | 40 | |
| Bank | 10 | | 4 | |
| | 40 | | 60 | |
| *Creditors less than one year* | | | | |
| Trade creditors (payables) | 10 | | 28 | |
| Taxation | 4 | | 10 | |
| Other creditors | 4 | | 6 | |
| | 18 | | 44 | |
| Net current assets (working capital) | | 22 | | 16 |
| *Creditors greater than one year* | | | | |
| 10 per cent debentures | | – | | 20 |
| Net assets | | 94 | | 106 |
| *Financed by* | | | | |
| Ordinary shares of €1 each | | 70 | | 76 |
| Retained profits | | 24 | | 30 |
| Shareholders' funds | | 94 | | 106 |

Figure 17.4 **Bread Co. balance sheets (€000): horizontal presentation**

| | | | At 31 December 20X1 | | |
|---|---|---|---|---|---|
| *Non-current assets* | | 72 | Ordinary shares of €1 each | | 70 |
| | | | Retained profits | | 24 |
| *Current assets* | | | Shareholders' funds | | 94 |
| Inventory | 12 | | | | |
| Trade debtors (receivables) | 18 | | *Creditors greater than one year* | | – |
| Bank | 10 | | | | |
| | | 40 | *Creditors less than one year* | | |
| | | | Trade creditors (payables) | 10 | |
| | | | Taxation | 4 | |
| | | | Other creditors | 4 | |
| | | | | | 18 |
| | | 112 | | | 112 |

| | | | At 31 December 20X2 | | |
|---|---|---|---|---|---|
| *Non-current assets* | | 110 | Ordinary shares of €1 each | | 76 |
| | | | Retained profits | | 30 |
| *Current assets* | | | | | |
| Inventory | 16 | | *Creditors greater than one year* | | |
| Trade debtors (receivables) | 40 | | 10 per cent debentures | | 20 |
| Bank | 4 | | | | |
| | | 60 | *Creditors less than one year* | | |
| | | | Trade creditors (payables) | 28 | |
| | | | Taxation | 10 | |
| | | | Other creditors | 6 | |
| | | | | | 44 |
| | | 170 | | | 170 |

## 17.4 Valuation through expectations

The words 'value' and 'valuation' imply some element of future orientation. The value of something might be seen as the amount of benefit expected to be derived from it (not necessarily in money terms), or possibly the amount of sacrifice necessary in order to obtain it. Pursuing this, the value of a business can be related to the benefits that are expected to flow from ownership of the business, and the value of a share in a business can be related to the benefits that are expected to flow from ownership of the share.

It is generally agreed that the best theoretical approach to the valuation of a share in a business is to consider some defined future flows, and to discount the anticipated figures to give present value, i.e. to use the principles of discounted cash flow (DCF). Possible flows to use would include:

- the stream of expected future earnings;
- the stream of expected future cash flows of the business;
- the stream of expected future cash receipts by the investor (i.e. expected dividends and other cash receipts, e.g. proceeds of sale of shares).

In each case there is the problem, not only of predicting the size of the flows, but also of choosing a rational discount rate. The discount rate will embrace estimates of interest rates, the risk positions of the business concerned, and the attitude to risk of the individual investor. It will also be necessary to take account of estimates of market and economy developments, such as inflation rates and taxation policies.

In the long run, it can be suggested that the above three types of flow amount to the same thing. Earnings are cash flows adjusted and smoothed through accounting practices – in the long run, total earnings should equal total net cash flow. And, remembering that the stream of future dividends includes the 'final' distribution when the firm is liquidated, the total dividend stream should also equal the total net cash-flow stream. The timings of the flows may, of course, be very different, and for the individual shareholder it is the capital amount expected for the share when eventually sold on the stock market, rather than a final liquidation dividend, which usually represents the final item in the dividend stream.

The assumptions necessary for quantifying any of the three flows are obviously extremely subjective. Recognition of this leads to the third possible approach to valuation of a business, namely market values.

## 17.5 Valuation through market values

Suppose that you own ten shares in a company with one million issued shares, and the market value of one share as reported in the press of today's date is €6. This means that your ten shares have a value of €60, and also that 'the market' values the entire company at €6 million. Such statements assume that the market values parcels of shares of different sizes on a strictly pro rata basis – which is not the case, as a parcel large enough to give influence or control (see Chapter 14) is likely to command extra value. On the other hand, the sale of a large parcel of shares may depress the market price.

It can also be argued that the price of a share on a stock market is influenced by all kinds of factors that are extraneous to the particular business under consideration, such as general economic, political or exchange rate considerations. However, despite all these difficulties, the quoted market value in a stock market at a date does have one enormous advantage: it demonstrably exists. The market value *is* (allowing for transaction costs between buyer and seller) the money benefit to be derived from selling a share, and the money sacrifice necessary to acquire a share. It may or may not be a fact justified by rational appraisal and analysis, but it is still a fact.

It can be argued that, in a perfect world with perfect knowledge and foresight, the market value would exactly equal the value calculated by discounting expected flows. This would be consistent with the Efficient Markets Hypothesis in its 'strong' form, which assumes that market prices reflect both private and public information. More realistically, it can at least be suggested that active participants in public share markets will have taken account of all available published information. At a minimum, it can be suggested that the market value of quoted shares provides the one starting point that is objective for working out the worth of a business or of an investment in it. However, the market has taken account of the estimates of cash flows, and so this argument is somewhat circular.

A more detailed consideration of theories and techniques of entity valuation is beyond the scope of this introductory accounting text. But, a word of warning: many valuation techniques are based on financial data which are assumed to be factual and problem-free. By now, you know better.

## 17.6 Accounting policies and financial appraisal

Given that the market relies partly on accounting information to establish firm value, this leads back to ratio analysis, for which a number of limitations can be suggested, including:

- differences in accounting policies, from company to company or from year to year;
- the historical nature of accounting statements;
- changes in the value of money;
- hidden short-term fluctuations between financial statements;
- the absence of comparable data;
- differences in the environments of periods or firms being compared;
- other non-monetary factors, excluded from the financial statements completely.

Most of these difficulties can be adjusted for when undertaking real financial statement appraisal. Some of them can be analysed through an understanding of financial accounting practices, ideas and techniques, and adjustments can be made to improve comparability and the information content of figures and ratios by adjusting for differences in accounting policies. However, others of the above difficulties, particularly the later ones in the list, clearly involve both highly subjective and non-financial considerations. Adjustment for such matters will need to be qualitative rather than quantitative.

**Real-world example**

Bayer AG, which had been using IFRS for over a decade, explained in its 2005 Report the effect of a large number of policy changes. A large number of changes to IFRS came into force in 2005, which was the first year of IFRS reporting for most European groups. Here is an example:

In March 2004, in connection with the issuance of IFRS 3, the IASB revised IAS 36 (*Impairment of Assets*) and IAS 38 (*Intangible Assets*). The main revisions require goodwill and other indefinite-lived intangible assets to be tested for impairment annually, or more frequently if events or changes in circumstances indicate a possible impairment, prohibit reversal of impairment losses for goodwill, require an intangible asset to be treated as having an indefinite useful life when there is no foreseeable limit on the period over which the asset is expected to generate net cash inflows for the entity, and prohibit the amortization of such assets. The revised standards are effective for goodwill and other intangible assets acquired in business combinations for which the agreement date is on or after March 31, 2004 and for all other such assets for annual periods beginning on or after March 31, 2004. The new standard has been applied prospectively (i.e. the new recognition and valuation principles are applied only in the current statements and not for the preceding period). Had the new standard been applicable for the 2004 fiscal year, the absence of amortization of goodwill and other indefinite-lived intangible assets would have reduced operating expense by €185 million.

The adjustment for amortization would have been 10 per cent of the company's 2004 operating profit.

**Activity 17.B**  Identify as many examples as possible within IFRS where the choice of accounting policy could significantly affect the analysis and interpretation of published financial statements.

**Feedback**  There are many examples that could be chosen; we provide a selection, as follows:

- the policy on asset valuation – particularly regarding land and buildings, because historical cost may or may not be departed from – for this will affect profits (via depreciation charges) and balance sheet totals;
- depreciation policy, which will obviously affect profits and asset values;
- inventory valuations, which again will affect profits and asset values, and also liquidity ratios, through the cost flow assumptions made (FIFO or weighted average) and also the treatment of overhead costs;
- long-term contract assumptions, e.g. the policy on inclusion of activity in annual sales, and on treatment of possible future losses, and so on;
- the allocation between operating and finance leases, and the method of allocating finance charges relating to both lessee and lessor;
- policy in respect of the capitalization of development costs and any resulting amortization;
- whether to record actuarial gains and losses in the 'profit and loss' or in OCI;
- use of temporal or closing rate method (depending on the identification of a subsidiary's functional currency) for translation of foreign financial statements.

On a more general level, the judgements relating to conflicting accounting conventions and concepts will all affect the numbers. There may also be changes arising from the issue of new or revised accounting standards, which can cause major differences over time within the financial statements of any particular company or group.

It is important to understand the accounting implications of each of the possible different accounting policies outlined in the feedback above. If you do not, then you should go back to the relevant chapter in this book and revise your knowledge of the topic or topics concerned. Once you are happy that you fully understand the principles, then the way to make further progress is through practice, and working through artificial or real-life examples. The next three activities provide some essential practice. More examples are given in the exercises at the end of this chapter.

**Activity 17.C**  The information in Table 17.3 relates to companies X and Y for the year ended 31 December. The companies have identical balance sheets and operating profits for the year.

Each company is deemed to have obtained the use of an extra asset with a fair value of €100,000 on 1 January, in respect of which no entries have yet been made in the accounts. The use of the asset is obtained by means of a lease, with rentals, paid quarterly in advance, of €6,500. The term of the lease is five years and the useful life of the asset is eight years.

## Table 17.3 Financial figures for X and Y (initial)

| | X and Y<br>€000 |
|---|---|
| Fixed assets | 250 |
| Current assets | 70 |
| Current liabilities | (60) |
| | 260 |
| Long-term liabilities | (100) |
| | 160 |
| Share capital | 100 |
| Retained profits | 60 |
| | 160 |
| Operating profit for the year | 30 |

Identify the effects on the companies' operating profits and balance sheets and any relevant ratios if the lease is treated as an operating lease by company X but a finance lease by company Y. Assume that all rentals are paid when due. The relevant finance lease calculations show an obligation under a finance lease at 31 December of €84,370, of which €17,570 is due in less than one year.

**Feedback** The balance sheets and operating profit would become as shown in Table 17.4.

## Table 17.4 Financial figures for X and Y

| | X<br>€000 | Y<br>€000 |
|---|---|---|
| Fixed assets | 250 | 330[a] |
| Current assets | 44[b] | 44 |
| Current liabilities | (60) | (77.57)[c] |
| | 234 | 296.43 |
| Long-term liabilities | (100) | (166.8)[c] |
| | 134 | 129.63 |
| Share capital | 100 | 100 |
| Retained profits | 34 | 29.63 |
| | 134 | 129.63 |
| Operating profit for the year | 4[b] | (0.37)[d] |

Notes:
[a] Under a finance lease the asset is capitalized at fair value of €100,000 and depreciation calculated on a straight-line basis assuming no residual value over a five-year life. Therefore, the depreciation charge is €20,000, and the net book value of the asset at 31 December is €80,000.
[b] Cash adjusted for rental payments 4 × €6,500 = €26,000. So cash is €70,000 − €26,000 = €44,000. The rental payments are charged to operating profit assuming an operating lease. So, profit is €30,000 − €26,000 = €4,000.
[c] Current liabilities are €60,000 + €17,570 = €77,570. Long-term liabilities are €100,000 + €84,370 − €17,570 = €166,800. The interest charge is the balancing figure, i.e. interest charge = €84,370 − €(100,000 − 26,000) = €10,370.
[d] This is calculated thus:

| | €000s |
|---|---|
| Operating profit for the year | 30.00 |
| less Depreciation | (20.00) |
| less Interest charges | (10.37) |

Ratio calculations for X and Y are as set out in Table 17.5.

Table 17.5 **Financial ratios for X and Y**

| Ratio | X | Y |
|---|---|---|
| ROE (taking closing balance sheet figures) | $\dfrac{4}{134} = 2.98\%$ | loss |
| Liquidity: $\dfrac{\text{Current assets}}{\text{Current liabilities}}$ | $\dfrac{44}{60} = 73\%$ | $\dfrac{44}{77.57} = 57\%$ |
| Gearing: $\dfrac{\text{loans}}{\text{loans + equity}}$ | $\dfrac{100}{234} = 42.7\%$ | $\dfrac{166.8}{296.43} = 56.3\%$ |

If the lease is treated as an operating lease (as shown in company X's figures), then all these ratios give a stronger impression than if the lease is treated as a finance lease. When the latter applies (as with company Y), the ROE shows a loss, the liquidity ratio is decreased and the gearing ratio increased. Company Y might therefore be regarded less positively by the market than company X under this analysis. However, the only difference between them is the accounting treatment used for the leased asset.

**Activity 17.D**

Figure 17.5 gives summarized balance sheets for Eegrek Co. for the years 20X1 and 20X2. Figure 17.6 gives summarized income information for the same two years. Figure 17.7 gives a statement of cash flows for 20X2. The requirements are as follows:

Figure 17.5 **Balance sheets of Eegrek (€)**

| | 20X1 Balance sheet | | | 20X2 Balance sheet | | |
|---|---|---|---|---|---|---|
| | Cost | Depreciation | Net | Cost | Depreciation | Net |
| Building | 50,000 | 10,000 | 40,000 | 90,000 | 11,000 | 79,000 |
| Plant | 10,000 | 4,000 | 6,000 | 11,000 | 5,000 | 6,000 |
| | | | 46,000 | | | 85,000 |
| Land | | | 43,000 | | | 63,000 |
| Investments at cost | | | 50,000 | | | 80,000 |
| Inventory | | | 55,000 | | | 65,000 |
| Debtors (Receivables) | | | 40,000 | | | 50,000 |
| Bank | | | 3,000 | | | – |
| | | | 237,000 | | | 343,000 |
| Ordinary shares | | | 40,000 | | | 50,000 |
| Share premium | | | 12,000 | | | 14,000 |
| Revaluation reserve | | | – | | | 20,000 |
| Retained earnings | | | 25,000 | | | 25,000 |
| 10 per cent Debentures | | | 100,000 | | | 150,000 |
| Creditors (Payables) | | | 60,000 | | | 80,000 |
| Bank | | | – | | | 4,000 |
| | | | 237,000 | | | 343,000 |

## Figure 17.6 Income of Eegrek (€)

|  | 20X1 | 20X2 |
|---|---|---|
| Sales | 200,000 | 200,000 |
| Cost of sales | 100,000 | 120,000 |
|  | 100,000 | 80,000 |
| Expenses | 60,000 | 60,000 |
| Profit | 40,000 | 20,000 |
| Dividends | 20,000 | 20,000 |
|  | 20,000 | – |
| Balance of profit from before | 5,000 | 25,000 |
| Balance of unappropriated profit | 25,000 | 25,000 |

## Figure 17.7 Cash flow statement of Eegrek (€) for 20X2

| | | |
|---|---|---|
| Cash flows from operating activities | | |
| Cash receipts from customers | 190,000 | |
| Cash payments to suppliers | (110,000) | |
| | 80,000 | |
| Cash payments for operating expenses | (43,000) | |
| Interest paid | (15,000) | |
| | | 22,000 |
| Cash flows from investing activities | | |
| Purchase of investments | (30,000) | |
| Purchase of buildings | (40,000) | |
| Purchase of machinery | (1,000) | |
| | | (71,000) |
| Cash flows from financing activities | | |
| Proceeds from share issue | 12,000 | |
| Proceeds from debenture issue | 50,000 | |
| Dividends paid | (20,000) | 42,000 |
| Net reduction in cash and cash equivalents | | (7,000) |
| Cash and cash equivalents at beginning of year | | 3,000 |
| Cash and cash equivalents at end of year | | (4,000) |

(a) Calculate the following ratios for Eegrek for 20X1 and 20X2:

Return on capital employed (ROCE)
Return on equity (ROE)
Debtors' turnover (as a ratio, i.e. not converted to number of days)
Creditors' turnover (as a ratio, i.e. not converted to number of days)
Current ratio
Quick assets ratio
Gross profit percentage
Net profit percentage
Dividend cover
Gearing ratio

(b) Comment briefly on difficulties of comparing the two sets of ratios.
(c) Comment briefly on developments within the business over the two years.

**Feedback** Suggested financial ratio calculations (in response to requirement (a)) are shown in Table 17.6.

Table 17.6 **Financial ratios of Eegrek**

| Ratio | 20X1 | 20X2 |
|---|---|---|
| ROCE | $\dfrac{(40 + 10)}{177} = 28\%$ | $\dfrac{(20 + 15)}{259} = 14\%$ |
| ROE | $\dfrac{40}{77} = 52\%$ | $\dfrac{20}{109} = 18\%$ |
| Debtors' turnover | $\dfrac{200}{40} = 5$ times | $\dfrac{200}{50} = 4$ times |
| Creditors' turnover | $\dfrac{100}{60} = 1.7$ times | $\dfrac{120}{80} = 1.5$ times |
| Current ratio | $\dfrac{98}{60} = 1.6{:}1$ | $\dfrac{115}{84} = 1.4{:}1$ |
| Quick assets | $\dfrac{43}{60} = 0.7{:}1$ | $\dfrac{50}{84} = 0.6{:}1$ |
| Gross profit percentage | $\dfrac{100}{200} = 50\%$ | $\dfrac{80}{200} = 40\%$ |
| Net profit percentage | $\dfrac{40}{200} = 20\%$ | $\dfrac{20}{200} = 10\%$ |
| Dividend cover | $\dfrac{40}{20} = 2$ times | $\dfrac{20}{20} = 1$ time |
| Gearing ratio | $\dfrac{100}{177} = 56\%$ | $\dfrac{150}{259} = 58\%$ |

The land is shown at cost in year 20X1 but at a valuation €20,000 greater in 20X2. (It is clear that the increase in land from €43,000 to €63,000 represents revaluation, as a revaluation reserve of €20,000 has appeared.) Since the land is not depreciated, there is no effect on earnings, but there is an effect on reserves and therefore on ROCE and ROE, in each case increasing the denominator for 20X2 and reducing the ratio.

Note that there are probably dangers in the averaging assumptions made. The fixed assets shown in the balance sheet at the end of 20X1 may or may not be representative of the average fixed assets in use through 20X1. However, it is unlikely that the fixed assets shown in the balance sheet at the end of 20X2 are representative of the average fixed assets in use through that year. The 20X2 balance sheet figures would only be representative if all the additions shown in Figure 17.7 had occurred on 1 January 20X2, which is unlikely. Other general points could obviously be raised as well, such as uncertainty about rates of inflation, non-monetary unrecorded items, and so on.

Even allowing for the distortions mentioned above, developments in 20X2 appear adverse and potentially dangerous. Rapid expansion of the asset base has not led to extra earnings, and so Eegrek's profitability (ROCE and, especially, ROE) is very sharply reduced. The amount of dividend has been maintained (though not the rate, as there are more shares in 20X2) despite the worsening scenario. Is the firm at the worst point of the investment cycle – resources having been poured in, returns not yet begun – or is it overspending to no good purpose? The ratio analysis cannot answer these questions, but it can highlight the issues and dangers. Higher cost of goods sold but static sales is a discouraging sign.

**Activity 17.E**

You are presented with the draft statements for EU Co. as set out in Figure 17.8. You are required to:

**Figure 17.8 Financial statements for EU Co.**

### Income statement for the year ended 31 December

| | Notes | 20X2 €000 | 20X1 €000 |
|---|---|---|---|
| Sales | | 45,056 | 27,756 |
| Cost of goods sold | | (35,426) | (27,313) |
| Gross Profit | | 9,630 | 443 |
| Operating expenses | 1 | (8,613) | (9,314) |
| Operating profit/(loss) | | 1,017 | (8,871) |
| Investment income | | 16 | 340 |
| Interest payable | | (1,596) | (935) |
| Loss before taxation | | (563) | (9,466) |
| Taxation | | | |
| Loss for the financial year | | (563) | (9,466) |
| Accumulated deficit, brought forward | | (12,886) | (3,420) |
| Accumulated deficit, carried forward | | (13,449) | (12,886) |

### Balance sheet as at 31 December

| | Notes | 20X2 €000 | 20X1 €000 |
|---|---|---|---|
| *Non-current assets* | | | |
| Intangible assets | 2 | 17,700 | 18,700 |
| Tangible assets | | 9,608 | 7,186 |
| | | 27,308 | 25,886 |
| *Current assets* | | | |
| Inventory | | 374 | 161 |
| Receivables | | 10,287 | 5,387 |
| Cash at bank and in hand | | 4 | 38 |
| | | 10,665 | 5,586 |
| *Creditors: Amounts falling due within one year* | | | |
| Trade payables | | (5,498) | (3,809) |
| Other payables and accruals | | (2,968) | (2,360) |
| Bank overdraft | | (3,139) | (443) |
| | | (11,605) | (6,612) |
| *Net current liabilities* | | (940) | (1,026) |
| Total assets less current liabilities | | 26,368 | 24,860 |
| *Payables: Amounts falling due after more than one year* | | | |
| Bank loans – repayable 20X1 | | (12,923) | (10,856) |
| Net assets | | 13,445 | 14,004 |
| *Capital and reserves* | | | |
| Called-up share capital | | 132 | 131 |
| Share premium account | | 8,062 | 8,059 |
| Retained earnings | | 5,251 | 5,814 |
| Total capital and reserves | | 13,445 | 14,004 |

*Notes to the accounts*

1. *Operating expenses* include the launch costs of a new magazine, first published in September 20X2 and totalling €1.15 million.
2. The *intangible fixed assets* represent development costs capitalized by EU Co.

(a) prepare a table of ratios, showing your calculations in full, as the basis for financial analysis; state and explain any assumptions you make;

(b) write a report on the strengths and weaknesses of the company's position and progress, to the extent that the ratios, and the original information, indicate them;

(c) explain how you have dealt with the information in Notes 1 and 2 of Figure 17.8, and give reasons for your treatment.

**Feedback** (a) Taking the figures given at face value gives a set of ratios such as the following (money figures in €000s).

| | 20X2 | 20X1 |
|---|---|---|
| Gross profit | $\dfrac{9,630}{45,056} = 21.4\%$ | $\dfrac{443}{7,756} = 5.7\%$ |
| Net profit % | $\dfrac{(563)}{45,056} = (1.2\%)$ | $\dfrac{(9,466)}{7,756} = (122.0\%)$ |
| ROE | $\dfrac{(563)}{13,445} = (4.2\%)$ | $\dfrac{(9,466)}{14,004} = (67.6\%)$ |
| $\dfrac{CA}{CL}\%$ | $\dfrac{10,665}{11,605} = 91.9\%$ | $\dfrac{5,586}{6,612} = 84.5\%$ |
| ROCE | $\dfrac{(563) + 1,596}{13,445 + 12,923} = 3.92\%$ | $\dfrac{(9,466) + 935}{14,004 + 10,856} = (34.3\%)$ |
| Debtors' turnover | $\dfrac{10,287}{45,056} \times 365 = 83$ days | $\dfrac{5,387}{7,756} \times 365 = 254$ days |
| Creditors' turnover | $\dfrac{5,498}{35,426} \times 365 = 57$ days | $\dfrac{3,809}{27,313} \times 365 = 51$ days |
| Inventory turnover | $\dfrac{374}{35,426} \times 365 = 4$ days | $\dfrac{161}{27,313} \times 365 = 2$ days |
| Gearing | $\dfrac{12,923}{26,368} = 49\%$ | $\dfrac{10,856}{24,860} = 44\%$ |

The situation is obviously rather unusual. Analysts might make some alterations to these figures, such as:

- removing the intangible assets, thus making equity smaller (and removing the amortization charge of €1 million in 20X2, making earnings larger and turning earnings into a profit);
- treating the bank overdraft as long-term (strictly, the interest added back in the ROCE calculations includes the interest on the overdraft, which is incorrect if the overdraft is short-term).

(b) Very broadly, the situation was clearly disastrous in 20X1, and has been largely stabilized in 20X2. If 20X1 was the first full year of operation, as seems likely, and the trend of development continues, then the business may survive successfully. This is by no means certain. The lenders have very little security unless the intangible asset is saleable, and could probably demand repayment at any moment. However, it is most unlikely to impress a bank lender.

(c) No adjustments have been made above, but this is debatable. The launch expenses of €1.15 million *are* correctly treated as expenses. However, for trend analysis, they might be removed, as unlikely to recur in 20X3.

The last three activities are designed to show that, whilst practice at ratio calculation is necessary, ratios by themselves are never sufficient. Entities operate in a dynamic environment. The uniqueness and the variability of each situation must be digested before an intelligent appraisal can be made. In addition, the implications of accounting policies must be fully considered, and adjusted for numerically or allowed for qualitatively, in analysing any particular situation.

Real-world published financial statements will supply further examples.

**Summary**

■ Investment ratios focus on various aspects of actual or potential share ownership. Earnings per share (EPS) is a particularly important – but perhaps dangerously simplistic – statistic.

■ What is included and excluded in 'earnings' is a complex issue.

■ The valuation of businesses can be attempted via the balance sheet, through expectations, or from market values. All these methods suffer from difficulties and uncertainties.

■ A particularly important consideration is the implications of accounting policy choice or accounting policy change on the figures in, and the appropriate interpretation and analysis of, ratios. A number of examples have been explored. Ramifications and permutations of choice and change are effectively infinite.

■ It is important to develop an attitude of mind, when attempting an overall financial appraisal, not to seek a finite list of points to check or resolve.

 ### References and research

See:

■ T. Plenborg, 'A comparison of the information content of US and Danish earnings', *European Accounting Review*, Vol. 7, No. 1, 1998.

An interesting and perhaps representative insight into the difficulties of dealing with reporting differences in a non-national context is given in a research forum in *European Accounting Review*, Vol. 5, No. 2. The papers are as follows:

■ J-C. Scheid, 'Introduction'.
■ D. Alexander and S. Archer, 'Goodwill and the difference arising on first consolidation'.
■ D. Alexander, S. Archer, P. Delvaille and V. Taupin, 'Provisions and contingencies: An Anglo-French investigation'.
■ A. Burlaud, M. Messina and P. Walton, 'Depreciation: Concepts and practices in France and the UK'.

## ? EXERCISES

*Feedback on the first of these exercises is given in Appendix D.*

17.1 You are given summarized information about two firms in the same line of business, namely A and B, as shown in Figure 17.9.

Figure 17.9 **Financial statements for A and B**

| | | | | | | |
|---|---|---|---|---|---|---|
| **Balance sheets at 30 June** | | | | | | |
| | | *A* | | | *B* | |
| | €000 | €000 | €000 | €000 | €000 | €000 |
| Land | | | 80 | | | 260 |
| Buildings | | 120 | | | 200 | |
| *Less*: Depreciation | | 40 | 80 | | – | 200 |
| Plant | | 90 | | | 150 | |
| *Less*: Depreciation | | 70 | 20 | | 40 | 110 |
| | | | 180 | | | 570 |
| Stocks | | 80 | | | 100 | |
| Debtors | | 100 | | | 90 | |
| Bank | | – | | | 10 | |
| | | 180 | | | 200 | |
| Creditors | 110 | | | 120 | | |
| Bank | 50 | | | – | | |
| | | 160 | | | 120 | |
| | | | 20 | | | 80 |
| | | | 200 | | | 650 |
| Capital b/forward | | | 100 | | | 300 |
| Profit for year | | | 30 | | | 100 |
| | | | 130 | | | 400 |
| *Less*: Drawings | | | 30 | | | 40 |
| | | | 100 | | | 360 |
| Land revaluation | | | – | | | 160 |
| Loan (10 per cent p.a.) | | | 100 | | | 130 |
| | | | 200 | | | 650 |
| Sales | | | 1,000 | | | 3,000 |
| Cost of goods sold | | | 400 | | | 2,000 |

You are required to:

(a) produce a table of ratios calculated for both businesses;

(b) write a report briefly outlining the strengths and weaknesses of the two businesses, including comment on any major areas where simple use of the figures could be misleading.

17.2 Repeat Exercise 1.4 from Chapter 1. Do you think that users know what to ask for from their accountant or financial adviser?

17.3 Cross-sectional analysis (comparisons between different businesses over the same period) and trend analysis (comparisons between the same business over different periods) both suffer from significant limitations. What are the limitations of each form of analysis? How can they be overcome, and to what extent?

17.4 'Financial ratios are only as good as the accounting information from which they are calculated.' Discuss.

17.5 The details in Figure 17.10 relate to D Co. Using that information and appropriate ratios, prepare an analysed financial report on the above company.

Figure 17.10 **Financial statements for D**

**Summary Balance Sheet**

|  | 31.12.X1 Actual €000 | 31.12.X2 Budget €000 | 31.12.X2 Actual €000 |
|---|---|---|---|
| *Non-current assets* |  |  |  |
| Tangible assets | 957 | 1,530 | 1,620 |
| *Current assets* |  |  |  |
| Inventory | 205 | 290 | 325 |
| Debtors | 305 | 720 | 810 |
| Cash and bank balances | 175 | 70 | – |
|  | 685 | 1,080 | 1,135 |
| Creditors: Amounts due within one year |  |  |  |
| Trade creditors | 175 | 505 | 545 |
| Other creditors | 187 | 325 | 310 |
| Bank overdraft | – | – | 80 |
|  | 362 | 830 | 935 |
| Net current assets | 323 | 250 | 200 |
| Creditors: Amounts due in more than one year | – | 360 | 360 |
|  | 1,280 | 1,420 | 1,460 |
| *Capital and reserves* |  |  |  |
| Called-up share capital | 800 | 800 | 800 |
| Share premium account | 200 | 200 | 200 |
| Reserves | 280 | 420 | 460 |
|  | 1,280 | 1,420 | 1,460 |

**Income statements**

|  | 20X1 Actual €000 | 20X2 Budget €000 | 20X2 Actual €000 |
|---|---|---|---|
| Sales | 2,560 | 4,500 | 5,110 |
| Cost of sales | (1,700) | (3,150) | (3,580) |
| Gross profit | 860 | 1,350 | 1,530 |
| Admin. and distribution costs | (655) | (880) | (1,084) |
| Operating profit | 205 | 470 | 446 |
| Interest payable | – | (20) | (35) |
|  | 205 | 450 | 411 |
| Taxation | (95) | (200) | (185) |
|  | 110 | 250 | 226 |
| Extraordinary items | 9 | (2) | 3 |
|  | 119 | 248 | 229 |
| Dividends | (82) | (108) | (49) |
| Retained earnings | 37 | 140 | 180 |

The opening inventory value figures were €135,000 20X1 actual and €210,000 20X2 budget.

17.6 Set out in Figure 17.11 are summarized balance sheets and income statements for F Co. for 20X1 and 20X2.

You are required to:

(a) prepare a table of ratios, covering all aspects of interpretation as far as the information allows, for each of the two years.

(b) consider the following statement: 'The situation of the business has got worse, and anyone owning ordinary shares in F Co. would be advised to sell them as soon as possible.' Write a report explaining fully whether you agree or disagree, and why.

**Figure 17.11 Financial statements for F**

| Summarized balance sheets at year end (€m) | | | | | |
|---|---|---|---|---|---|
| | | *20X2* | | *20X1* | |
| *Non-current assets* | | | | | |
| Tangible – not yet in use | | 49 | | 41 | |
| – in use | | 295 | | 237 | |
| | | 344 | | 278 | |
| Investments | | 1 | | 1 | |
| Loan redemption fund | | 1 | | 1 | |
| | | | 346 | | 280 |
| *Current assets* | | | | | |
| Inventory | | 42 | | 41 | |
| Debtors – trade | 4 | | | 4 | |
| – other | 4 | | | 4 | |
| | | 8 | | 8 | |
| Bank | | 2 | | 5 | |
| Cash | | 2 | | 2 | |
| | | 54 | | 56 | |
| Creditors – due within one year | | | | | |
| – trade | 60 | | | 60 | |
| – other | 87 | | | 112 | |
| | | 147 | | 172 | |
| Net current liabilities | | | 93 | | 116 |
| Total assets *less* current liabilities | | | 253 | | 164 |
| Creditors – due between one and five years | | | 61 | | 1 |
| Provision for liabilities and charges | | | 4 | | 3 |
| Net assets | | | 188 | | 160 |
| Capital and reserves | | | | | |
| Ordinary shares of €0.1 each | | | 19 | | 19 |
| Preference shares of €1 each | | | 46 | | 46 |
| Share premium | | | 1 | | 1 |
| Profit and loss account | | | 122 | | 94 |
| | | | 188 | | 160 |

## Figure 17.11 *Continued*

| Summarized income statements for the year (€m) | 20X2 | | 20X1 | |
|---|---|---|---|---|
| Sales | | 910 | | 775 |
| Raw materials and consumables | | 730 | | 633 |
| | | 180 | | 142 |
| Staff costs | 77 | | 64 | |
| Depreciation of tangible fixed assets | 12 | | 10 | |
| Other operating charges | 38 | | 30 | |
| | | 127 | | 104 |
| | | 53 | | 38 |
| Other operating income | | 4 | | 3 |
| | | 57 | | 41 |
| Net interest payable | | 5 | | 4 |
| | | 52 | | 37 |
| Profit sharing – employees | | 2 | | 1 |
| | | 50 | | 36 |
| Taxation | | 17 | | 12 |
| | | 33 | | 24 |
| Preference dividends | | 2 | | 2 |
| | | 31 | | 22 |
| Ordinary dividends | | 3 | | 2 |
| | | 28 | | 20 |
| Net interest payable: | | | | |
| interest payable | | 12 | | 9 |
| interest receivable | | (1) | | (1) |
| interest capitalized | | (6) | | (4) |
| | | 5 | | 4 |

# Chapter 18

# International analysis

**Contents**

| | | |
|---|---|---|
| 18.1 | Introduction | 355 |
| 18.2 | Language | 355 |
| | 18.2.1 Introduction | 355 |
| | 18.2.2 Three examples of translation difficulties | 356 |
| 18.3 | Differences in financial culture | 359 |
| 18.4 | Accounting differences | 360 |
| 18.5 | Help by multinationals | 361 |
| 18.6 | Increasing international harmonization | 361 |
| | Summary | 365 |
| | References and research | 365 |
| | Exercises | 366 |
| | Annex: GlaxoSmithKline plc: Notes on reconciliation from IFRS to US GAAP | 367 |

**Objectives**

After studying this chapter carefully, you should be able to:

- understand the difficulties caused by problems when translating technical accounting terms in the context of financial statements;

- demonstrate an awareness of the implications of the existence of different financial cultures, and an awareness that what is typical in one environment may be abnormal in another;

- outline ways in which multinational entities can mitigate difficulties for the analyst;

- apply your knowledge and understanding to appraising performance of entities involving different sets of GAAP;

- adjust financial statements in appropriate ways towards benchmark policies to increase comparability, as a prelude to overall appraisal;

- demonstrate an awareness of the subjectivity that may be involved in financial statement preparation and appraisal.

## 18.1 Introduction

The analysis of financial statements is hard enough even when limited to reporting within one country. This is because of the complexity of the economic world and because of the incentives for some preparers of financial statements to mislead the users. When trying to compare companies internationally, the difficulties multiply, including differences under the following headings:

- language problems;
- differences in financial culture;
- valuation of assets;
- measurement of profits;
- availability of published accounting data;
- extent and type of audit;
- formats of financial statements;
- frequency of reports;
- quantity of data disclosed;
- different currencies;
- biases in the accounting data;
- user-friendliness of annual reports.

International comparative analysis might be made by many users of financial statements. These users include:

- brokers, investment analysts and journalists on behalf of shareholder investors;
- bankers and other creditors when deciding on lending;
- multinational companies when appraising existing or potential subsidiaries or competitors.

If analysts are unaware of the international differences, they will make the wrong investment decisions. If they try to make adjustments, this will be time-consuming and expensive. If they restrict themselves to their own home market, they will miss valuable opportunities for investment and the spreading of risk.

Several of the areas of difficulty listed above have been discussed earlier in this book. This chapter examines the first four and then addresses potential solutions for interpreters of financial statements.

## 18.2 Language

### 18.2.1 Introduction

Language is very obvious as a problem for international comparisons. This might be thought to be trivial in the sense that:

- many people can read more than one language;
- many large companies provide translations into English;
- experts can always be hired to translate (and they are a lot cheaper than accountants or financiers).

Indeed, compared to some of the other problems mentioned above, language *is* comparatively easy. Nevertheless, there are many pitfalls to be avoided.

**Activity 18.A**    Reappraise Table 1.1 from Chapter 1, which gives some examples showing how easy it is to be confused within the English language. Make a note of any additional English-language differences you have come across in later chapters.

**Feedback**    There are several differences in technical terms that you may have come across in this book or in your wider reading, such as leverage (US) for gearing (UK), or fiscal year (US) for financial year (UK). Two aspects are worthy of discussion here. The UK term 'fixed assets', which the IASB refers to as 'non-current assets', as does the US, includes 'Property, Plant and Equipment', which is the title of IAS 16. However, the word 'property' itself can have different meanings. In the UK its accounting meaning is restricted to land and buildings, but in the US it may have wider implications, to include tangible assets generally.

A second particular problem concerns the terms 'provision' and 'reserve'. In the UK, as the words are used in practice, a provision is an estimated liability *or* a reduction in the recorded value of an asset (as in 'provision for doubtful debts'). The IASB in its Glossary of Terms defines a provision as a liability of uncertain timing or amount, as FRS 12 does in the United Kingdom. This clearly excludes the second of the two meanings, i.e. the reduction in the recorded value of an asset. This should be called an impairment but 'provision' is still in common usage in the UK. In the UK and in IAS 1, a reserve is a part of shareholders' equity that arises from a gain. 'Reserve', in the US, is used much more loosely, to include estimated liabilities and adjustments against the value of assets (as in 'reserve for doubtful receivables'). Great care is needed in interpreting such terms. Further, the various usages suggested here may change over time.

The problem with the several types of English (UK, US and IASB) is, of course, not just that the language is different (the US version having largely evolved out of seventeenth-century UK English) but that a word that exists in both languages sometimes means something different. There is less scope for this sort of confusion when an American is translating from Japanese!

The importance of this problem is not confined to English-speaking countries. Many European companies produce translations, usually into approximately US English. However, these statements may have unreliable or misleading translations, partly because the work is often carried out by those who are not expert in accounting. At worst, the English version may be little more than a marketing document. Such translated statements are, of course, not the real statutory statements, nor do they have to obey UK or US rules, and so they may be extracts or manipulations of the original.

Some examples of translation problems now follow, in order to illustrate these points.

### 18.2.2 Two examples of translation difficulties

#### Example 1

The following is an extract from an English-version annual report of Total Oil:

Foreign currency balance sheets are converted into French francs on the basis of exchange rates at 31 December. The conversion is applied to fixed assets as well as to monetary assets and liabilities. Gains or losses on translation of their balance sheets at the end of the previous year are dealt with . . .

This extract shows the word 'conversion' being used interchangeably with 'translation' because the two accounting terms are the same in French (*conversion*). In English, the former means a physical act of exchange, whereas the latter (which would be correct here) means an accounting calculation.

### Example 2

When matters get complicated, a translation often becomes opaque or misleading. This extract is taken from the financial statements of the German company, AEG, of a few years ago. The note on consolidation techniques is very difficult to understand. It is shown below with our interpretation.

| *Published translation* | *Authors' suggestion* |
|---|---|
| Capital consolidation is performed using the 'book value method'. Under this method, the book values of the affiliated companies are netted against the underlying equity in these companies at the time of acquisition or initial consolidation. | Consolidation is performed using a version of fair value accounting. Under this method, the first stage is to compare the cost of the consolidated companies with the book value of the group's share of their net assets. Generally this is done at the date of acquisition, but for existing subsidiaries that have been consolidated for the first time this year, the year-end values are used. |
| Where the book values exceed underlying equity, the difference is allocated to the respective assets or liabilities according to their real value. A difference remaining after the allocation is shown as goodwill or disclosed as a reduction from the reserves. If the book values fall below the underlying equity, the difference is recorded as 'reserve arising from consolidation'. | Where cost exceeds net assets, the difference is allocated to the subsidiary's assets and liabilities up to and in proportion to their fair values. Any excess remaining is goodwill, which is either shown as an asset or written off against reserves. Where the initial exercise leads to a negative difference, this is shown as a 'reserve arising from consolidation'. |

These two examples are illustrations of the point that, although the language may be of good quality, the translation is often not done by accountants, perhaps because bilingual accountants are very expensive to hire. For example, there are no such terms in English as 'capital consolidation' or 'book value method' (second example). Of course, none of this should be read as implying a lack of gratitude for translations: it is a very rare US or UK company that bothers with translation at all, presumably because there is no commercial need to do so and because it would, therefore, not be obvious which language to choose.

We include as Table 18.1 an amended version of a glossary of UK and US accounting terms, as presented in the financial statements of BT Group plc, which is likely to be helpful. The items with asterisks were included in 1999 but excluded in 2008 because the 2008 UK report used IFRS terms instead of UK legal terms, which show fewer differences from US terms. However, the terms with asterisks are still used in UK GAAP reports (e.g. those of unlisted companies or of individual companies within listed groups).

### Table 18.1 UK and US accounting terms

| Term used in UK annual report | US equivalent or definition |
|---|---|
| Accounts | Financial statements |
| Associates | Equity investees |
| Capital allowances | Tax depreciation |
| Creditors | Accounts payable and accrued liabilities |
| Creditors: amounts falling due within one year* | Current liabilities |
| Creditors: amounts falling due after more than one year* | Long-term liabilities |
| Debtors: amounts falling due after more than one year* | Other non-current assets |
| Employee share schemes* | Employee stock benefit plans |
| Employment costs* | Payroll costs |
| Finance lease | Capital lease |
| Financial year | Fiscal year |
| Fixed asset investments* | Non-current investments |
| Freehold | Ownership with absolute rights in perpetuity |
| Interests in associates and joint ventures | Securities of equity investees |
| Loans to associates and joint ventures | Indebtedness of equity investees not current |
| Net asset value* | Book value |
| Operating profit* | Net operating income |
| Other debtors* | Other current assets |
| Own work capitalized | Costs of labour engaged in the construction of plant and equipment for internal use |
| Profit* | Income |
| Profit and loss account (statement)* | Income statement |
| Profit and loss account* (under 'capital and reserves' in balance sheet) | Retained earnings |
| Profit for the financial year* | Net income |
| Profit on sale of fixed assets* | Gain on disposal of non-current assets |
| Provision for doubtful debts | Allowance for bad and doubtful accounts receivable |
| Provisions | Long-term liabilities other than debt and specific accounts payable |
| Recognized gains and losses (statement)* | Comprehensive income |
| Redundancy charges* | Early release scheme expenses |
| Reserves | Shareholders' equity other than paid-up capital |
| Share premium account | Additional paid-in capital or paid-in surplus (not distributable) |
| Shareholders' funds* | Shareholders' equity |
| Statement of recognized income and expense | Comprehensive income |
| Stocks* | Inventories |
| Tangible fixed assets* | Property, plant and equipment |
| Trade debtors* | Accounts receivable (net) |
| Turnover* | Revenues |

*Source*: Adapted from BT Group plc Annual Reports, 1999 and 2008.

| 18.3 | **Differences in financial culture** |

It is not just accounting terms and accounting practices that must be disentangled before successful international comparison is possible. There are also different social, cultural and economic backgrounds that may continue to cause differences in ratios. Let us take two examples.

### Example 1

Because of the long history of debt finance in Germany, it is normal for German companies to have a high gearing ratio compared to US or UK norms. However, not only is this traditional but it is also safer in Germany because of the long-run nature of bank interests in German industry. Bankers might be expected to pump money *into* an ailing company rather than to try to be the first to 'pull the plug'.

So a high gearing ratio is both more normal and less dangerous in Germany. It has been shown in earlier chapters that accounting differences probably make German gearing ratios look higher as well.

### Example 2

Table 18.2 shows how the accounting treatment of supplementary employee remuneration influences the computation of the interesting total 'funds generated from operations' for three companies (one British, one French and one Italian).

We start in column 1 with the British company, which places cash equal to pension provisions with a financial institution so that the 'funds' leave the company. For a company operating in France, there is a statutory requirement that part of the company's profits be allocated for the benefit of employees, with reinvestment in external assets within two years. In the short term, we could consider that there is an element in Funds Generated from Operations (+FF800 in column 2 of the example), which relates to the allocation for the current period, while the only outflow is the cash placed in external investments (–FF700).

**Table 18.2 The impact of different remuneration schemes on funds generated from operations**

|  | UK (£) | France (FF) | Italy (Lire) |
|---|---|---|---|
| Earnings | 100 | 1,000 | 100,000 |
| *Add back* |  |  |  |
| Depreciation of fixed assets | 250 | 2,500 | 250,000 |
| Provision for employee pensions | 80 | – | – |
| *less* funds applied in the current year | (80) | – | – |
| Share of profits attributable to employees | – | 800 | – |
| *less* funds applied in the current year | – | (700) | – |
| Deferred employee remuneration | – | – | 80,000 |
| *less* funds applied in the current year |  |  | (30,000) |
| **Funds generated from operations** | 350 | 3,600 | 400,000 |

*Source*: S.J. McLeay, in C.W. Nobes and R.H. Parker (eds), *Comparative International Accounting* (Harlow: Financial Times Prentice Hall, 2008), Chapter 18.

Now compare these two approaches with the situation in Italy (column 3) where employees are entitled on leaving a company to one month's salary (at current rates of pay) for each year in service. There is no requirement for the company to place any funds in earmarked investments, although the appropriate provisions must be made. Thus, funds generated from operations includes the provision (+L80,000) net of the payment to retiring employees (–L30,000).

Of course, there are many ways of constructing a cash flow statement, and the example is perhaps contentious. However, it shows that, when we compare the funds generated by companies in different countries, part of the explanation of the variability in levels of self-financing lies in the different social systems within which the companies operate.

## 18.4 Accounting differences

Part 2 of this book has looked at a number of accounting issues that relate to measurement and valuation. There are many examples of potential differences in accounting treatments between entities, and in many cases national 'norms' tend to differ, reflecting the classification issues discussed in Part 1. As we saw in Chapters 7 and 17, these can have a distorting effect on ratio comparisons. Before we explore some of these in an international context, try the following revision activity.

**Activity 18.B** Go through Part 2 of this book, with particular attention to the 'Why it matters' paragraphs, and make a list of measurement and valuation, or accounting policy, differences that might be significant in the context of international comparison.

**Feedback** A suggested list of potentially important items is shown next, although you may have thought of some different ones. Some of these were relevant even *within* IFRS, in Chapter 17. We list the following:

- strict historical cost or revaluations for fixed assets;
- use of FIFO, LIFO or weighted average to determine inventory cost;
- use of percentage-of-completion or completed-contract method for long-term contracts;
- use of year-end rates or transaction rates for translation of foreign currency receivables and payables in an individual company's balance sheet;
- capitalization (or not) of interest on construction;
- capitalization of leases (or not);
- revaluation and depreciation (or not) of investment properties;
- basing bad debt impairments on tax rules (or not);
- basing depreciation charges on tax rules (or not);
- valuing current-asset marketable securities at fair value or at cost;
- recording actuarial gains and losses in 'profit and loss' (or not);
- proportional or equity consolidation for joint ventures;
- amortizing goodwill or impairing it;
- using the uniting of interests method (or not);
- using the current rate method or the temporal method for translation.

These differences may need to be dealt with in carrying out an effective analysis and comparison in an international context, as the remainder of this chapter begins to explore.

## 18.5 Help by multinationals

It is often cheaper for the preparer, rather than the user, of financial statements to do something about the problems of interpreting international differences. Companies wishing to raise money on the international markets may volunteer – or be forced, in the case of some stock exchange rules – to help the readers in one or more of the following ways:

1. Where possible, some companies choose accounting policies that are most in line with international practices; for example, many Swiss companies volunteer to consolidate, to capitalize leases or to follow IFRS completely, even though this is not required under Swiss law. At the extreme, some companies try to comply with two or more sets of rules simultaneously; for example, Royal Dutch/Shell complied for many years with both US and Dutch rules. Companies may also volunteer for an international audit even when this is not legally necessary.
2. Companies may provide versions of the annual report that translate only the language, although this may raise the problems discussed earlier. This is common for Japanese and European companies translating into English.
3. Some companies provide reports in another currency, e.g. US dollars, as well as in the local currency. These are sometimes called 'convenience statements', and a year-end translation rate is normally applied to all items. It is important to note that such convenience statements are currency translations, not GAAP-adjusted statements.
4. As part of 'convenience translations', some companies carry out 'limited restatement' of some accounting policies or formats of presentation, presumably as a supplement to domestic reports. It is quite normal for Japanese companies to restate towards US practices.
5. Companies provide reconciliation statements of net income or net assets from their domestic rules to another set. This was most obviously found in the case of companies obeying SEC rules, when a reconciliation to US GAAP was shown until 2007 as a supplementary statement (e.g. Nokia, British Airways).
6. Companies may publish a substantial reworking and retranslation of an annual report into another set of practices and terms. This amounts to producing secondary financial statements.

## 18.6 Increasing international harmonization

As discussed in Chapter 5, there is a significant trend towards increasing harmonization of accounting policies among large listed companies, and this trend seems certain to continue. First, the European Union's decision to require the use of IFRS for the consolidated statements of listed entities from 2005 greatly increased comparability. Secondly, the increasingly close cooperation between a number of standard setters and the IASB, discussed in Chapter 5, is leading to a reduction in the differences of principle between the different national and international systems.

An interesting example of increasing harmonization is Norsk Hydro, a large Norwegian company. Table 18.3 shows summary comparative figures for 1991, 1993 and 2006 as reported under US GAAP and Norwegian GAAP. The sharp increase in the similarity of the figures is very obvious, caused largely by new Norwegian regulations in 1992 and 1998. Incidentally, Norsk Hydro was allowed to continue with US GAAP rather than IFRS until (and including) 2006, under a special exemption of the EU's Regulation for companies previously using US GAAP.

Table 18.3 **Example of increasing GAAP harmonization: Norsk Hydro**

|  | 1991 (Nkr million) | | 1993 (Nkr million) | | 2006 (Nkr million) | |
| --- | --- | --- | --- | --- | --- | --- |
|  | US GAAP | Norwegian GAAP | US GAAP | Norwegian GAAP | US GAAP | Norwegian GAAP |
| Operating income | 925 | 610 | 4,037 | 4,599 | 52,224 | 50,679 |
| Net financial expense | (1,207) | (1,680) | (1,935) | (2,132) | (1,838) | (1,838) |
| Net income (loss) | (498) | (2,169) | 2,996 | 3,406 | 17,391 | 16,499 |
| Shareholders' equity | 19,156 | 6,056 | 22,735 | 19,307 | 96,496 | 95,389 |

*Source*: Norsk Hydro annual reports.

For most European, Australian and many other listed companies, IFRS is now required for consolidated statements. This provided vast amounts of data showing reconciliations from national practices to IFRS for 2004 figures in the 2005 reports (or, in the case of Norsk Hydro, from US GAAP to IFRS for 2006 figures in the 2007 report). You can access these 'transition' statements on company websites.

For 2005 and 2006, most large non-US companies that were listed on US exchanges provided reconciliations from IFRS to US GAAP. The reconciliation for GlaxoSmithKline (Europe's largest pharmaceutical company) for 2005 is summarized in Figures 18.1 and 18.2. This shows that large international differences remain. Many of them are due to permission under IFRS to retain previous practices for old items. So, even if current IFRS is similar to current US GAAP for a particular item (e.g. goodwill), large differences show up in these reconciliations.

| Activity 18.C | Study carefully the annex to this chapter, particularly the explanations of Glaxo's reconciliation of net income from IFRS to US GAAP. Then, explain in your own words the cause of the adjustments. |
| --- | --- |

Figure 18.1  **GlaxoSmithKline, 2005: IFRS to US (£m)**

| **Profit** | |
|---|---:|
| Under IFRS | 4,816 |
| Minority interests | (127) |
| | 4,689 |
| US GAAP adjustments: | |
| Amortization and impairment of intangible assets | (1,584) |
| Acquisition and disposal of product rights | (72) |
| Write-off in-process R&D acquired in business combinations | (26) |
| Capitalized interest | (1) |
| Investments | (2) |
| Pensions and post-retirement benefits | (127) |
| Stock-based compensation | 6 |
| Derivative instruments and hedging | (30) |
| Restructuring | 1 |
| Tax benefits on exercise of stock options | (47) |
| Deferred taxation | 585 |
| Other | (56) |
| Under US GAAP | 3,336 |

*Source*: GlaxoSmithKline plc Annual Report 2005.

Figure 18.2  **GlaxoSmithKline, 2005: IFRS to US (£m)**

| **Equity shareholders' funds** | |
|---|---:|
| Total equity under IFRS | 7,570 |
| Minority interests | (259) |
| Shareholders' equity under IFRS | 7,311 |
| US GAAP adjustments: | |
| Goodwill | 17,976 |
| Product rights | 12,065 |
| Pension intangible asset | 86 |
| Property, plant and equipment | 33 |
| Capitalized interest | 179 |
| Other investments | 576 |
| Pensions and other post-retirement benefits | 1,163 |
| Restructuring costs | 65 |
| Derivative instruments and hedging | (33) |
| Dividends | (568) |
| Deferred taxation | (4,531) |
| Other | (40) |
| Shareholders' equity under US GAAP | 34,282 |

*Source*: GlaxoSmithKline plc Annual Report 2005.

**Feedback**  This feedback is presented using the order of items in Figure 18.1.

  (i)  *Minority interests.* Such amounts are shown as deductions from income and equity under US GAAP.

  (ii)  *Amortization, goodwill.* The amount of goodwill (and therefore amortization of it) is larger under US GAAP. This is because the company is allowed to retain old 'poolings' under IFRS which were acquisitions under US GAAP. Under that treatment, no goodwill arose.

  (iii)  *Product rights and R&D.* This is part of the same point as above. Under US GAAP, these would be recorded and immediately expensed on an acquisition.

  (iv)  *Capitalized interest.* The company chooses not to capitalize under IFRS, but must do so under US GAAP. This increases assets. The amortization of past amounts slightly outweigh the cancellation of the year's expense.

  (v)  *Investments.* The company gives an explanation under the heading 'Marketable securities'.

  (vi)  *Pensions.* The company has chosen to recognize actuarial losses in full under IAS 19, but amortizes them under US GAAP.

  (vii)  *Stock-based compensation.* There is a complex technical point here.

  (viii)  *Restructuring.* Under US GAAP, certain restructuring costs (based on acquirer's intentions) are lost in the goodwill calculation rather than being charged in the income statement.

  (ix)  *Deferred tax.* This is largely the implied tax on the above adjustments.

**Activity 18.D**  What general conclusions could be drawn from Activity 18.C?

**Feedback**  We suggest three points. First, the issues can be complex, and very clear thinking needs to be combined with considerable knowledge and understanding of issues discussed in Parts 1 and 2 of this book. Second, the differences and effects can be both numerous and significant in effect, unlike the Norsk Hydro situation by 2006. Third, no general conclusions can be drawn about the direction of reconciling adjustments. Different companies and different years would show different sizes and different directions of adjustment to US GAAP.

Perhaps the real point to be emphasized is that there can be no general rules. When comparing one set of GAAP accounts to another, or when comparing two entities that report under different GAAP systems, the only safe approach is to look at every aspect of each accounting policy in each set of financial statements, and to make sensible reconciliations and adjustments. In principle, this is no different to the need in all analysis, even at the one-country level, to make full allowance for the accounting policies applied. In practice, the international scenario may make it more complicated, but the approach is the same.

To some extent, the life of some analysts has been made easier by:

- the adoption of IFRS in many countries;
- the convergence of IFRS and US GAAP;
- the gradual move of Japanese and Chinese accounting towards IFRS or US GAAP.

On the other hand, no analysts would have needed to look at Chinese or Russian statements before 1990, and few before 2000. There will be special social, cultural and regulatory issues to take account of in these countries.

**Summary**

- There are many reasons for analysts to try to carry out international comparative analysis. However, it has all the problems of domestic analysis plus several others.

- Language difficulties may be severe for some analysts and some countries, but translations do not solve all the problems. Differences in financial culture and presentation are also hard to adjust for.

- Multinational companies can make several types of adjustment to assist international analysis. However, it is nearly always necessary for the analyst to do further work before international comparisons of earnings, net assets, etc. are meaningful.

- The widespread use of IFRS has helped international analysis but not rendered it easy.

- There is no substitute for an individual, careful and intelligent assessment of each situation to be analysed or compared.

## References and research

The following are some research papers in the English language that explore issues relevant to this chapter:

- A. Alford, J. Jones, R. Leftwich and M. Zmijewski, 'The relative informativeness of accounting disclosures in different countries', *Journal of Accounting Research*, supplement, 1993.
- E. Amir, T. Harris and E. Venuti, 'A comparison of the value-relevance of US versus non-US GAAP accounting measures using Form 20-F reconciliations', *Journal of Accounting Research*, supplement, 1993.
- K.-H. Bae, H. Tan and M. Welker, 'International GAAP differences: the impact on foreign analysts', *Accounting Review*, Vol. 83, No. 3, 2008.
- R. Ball, 'International Financial Reporting Standards (IFRS): pros and cons for investors', *Accounting and Business Research*, Special Issue, 2006.
- M. Barth and G. Clinch, 'International accounting differences and their relation to share prices', *Contemporary Accounting Research*, No. 1, 1996.
- S. Gray, G. Meek and C. Roberts, 'International capital market pressures and voluntary annual report disclosures by US and UK multinationals', *Journal of International Financial Management and Accounting*, Vol. 6, No. 1, 1995.
- T. Harris, M. Lang and H. Möller, 'The value relevance of German accounting measures – an empirical analysis', *Journal of Accounting Research*, Autumn, 1994.
- P. Joos and M. Lang, 'The effects of accounting diversity: Evidence from the European Union', *Journal of Accounting Research*, Autumn, 1994.
- S. Miles and C. Nobes, 'The use of foreign accounting data in UK financial institutions', *Journal of Business Finance and Accounting*, April/May, 1998.
- P. Pope and W. Rees, 'International differences in GAAP and the pricing of earnings', *Journal of International Financial Management and Accounting*, No. 3, 1992.

- P. Weetman, E. Jones, C. Adams and S. Gray, 'Profit measurement and UK accounting standards: A case of increasing disharmony in relation to US GAAP and IASs', *Accounting and Business Research*, Summer, 1998.

## ? EXERCISES

*Feedback on this exercise is given in Appendix D.*

18.1 The best case study of all is probably the real-world situation. This allows you to:

- choose situations that are topical;
- choose countries about which you are both knowledgeable and interested;
- see just how difficult interpretation of financial statements in an international context can be.

Therefore:

1. obtain the published financial statements, in languages you read well, of two companies or groups of companies, from different countries, for the same year or, if possible, a series of years;
2. analyse the data in detail and produce a report on the companies' relative strengths and weaknesses. Your analysis will involve, among other things:

   (a) reading the information in full, several times;
   (b) carefully considering any language issues;
   (c) noting inconsistent accounting policies and different accounting treatments, and attempting to adjust for them to give greater comparability;
   (d) preparing ratios, as consistently as possible;
   (e) producing a report, which includes proper recognition of the weaknesses in the available information.

This exercise can of course be repeated, using different pairs of companies. Try using one under IFRS and one under national GAAP.

## ANNEX GlaxoSmithKline plc: Notes on reconciliation from IFRS to US GAAP

### Reconciliation to US accounting principles

The analyses and reconciliations presented in this Note represent the financial information prepared on the basis of US Generally Accepted Accounting Principles (US GAAP) rather than IFRS.

### Summary of material differences between IFRS and US GAAP

#### Acquisition of SmithKline Beecham

The Group has exercised the exemption available under IFRS 1 'First-time Adoption of IFRS' not to restate business combinations prior to the date of transition of the Group's reporting GAAP from UK Generally Accepted Accounting Principles (UK GAAP) to IFRS. Therefore the combination in 2000 of Glaxo Wellcome plc and SmithKline Beecham plc continues to be accounted for as a merger (pooling of interests) in accordance with UK GAAP at that time. Under US GAAP, this business combination did not qualify for pooling of interests accounting and Glaxo Wellcome was deemed to be the accounting acquirer in a purchase business combination.

Accordingly the net assets of SmithKline Beecham were recognised at fair value as at the date of acquisition. As a result of the fair value exercise, increases in the values of SmithKline Beecham's inventory, property, plant and equipment, intangible assets, investments and pension obligations were recognised and fair market values attributed to its internally-generated intangible assets, mainly product rights (inclusive of patents and trademarks) and in-process research and development, together with appropriate deferred taxation effects. The difference between the cost of acquisition and the fair value of the assets and liabilities of SmithKline Beecham is recorded as goodwill.

#### Capitalised interest

Under IFRS, the Group does not capitalise interest. US GAAP requires interest incurred as part of the cost of constructing a fixed asset to be capitalised and amortised over the life of the asset.

#### Goodwill

The Group has exercised the exemption available under IFRS 1 not to restate business combinations prior to the date of transition of the Group's reporting GAAP from UK GAAP to IFRS. Under UK GAAP, goodwill arising on acquisitions before 1998 accounted for under the purchase method was eliminated against equity, and under IFRS, on future disposal or closure of a business, any goodwill previously taken directly to equity under a former GAAP will not be charged against income. Under UK GAAP, goodwill arising on acquisitions from 1998 was capitalised and amortised over a period not exceeding 20 years. On the date of the Group's transition to IFRS, 1st January 2003, amortisation ceased in accordance with IFRS 3 'Business combinations'. The Group must instead identify and value its reporting units for the purpose of assessing, at least annually, potential impairment of goodwill allocated to each reporting unit. As permitted by the business combinations exemption available under IFRS 1, amortisation arising prior to 2003 was not reversed.

Under US GAAP, goodwill arising on acquisitions prior to 30th June 2001 was capitalised and amortised over a period not exceeding 40 years. In July 2001, the Financial Accounting Standards Board (FASB) issued Statement of Financial Accounting Standard (SFAS) 142, 'Goodwill and Other Intangible Assets'.

Like IFRS 3, SFAS 142 requires that goodwill must not be amortised and that annual impairment tests of goodwill must be undertaken. The implementation of SFAS 142 in 2002, a year earlier than the Group's transition to IFRS, results in goodwill balances acquired between 1998 and 2003 reflecting one year less of amortisation under US GAAP than under IFRS.

Under IFRS, costs to be incurred in integrating and restructuring the Wellcome, SmithKline Beecham and Block Drug businesses following the acquisitions in 1995, 2000 and 2001 respectively were charged to the income statement post acquisition. Similarly, integration and restructuring costs arising in respect of the acquisitions of Corixa and ID Biomedical in 2005 have been charged to the income statement under IFRS. Under US GAAP, certain of these costs are considered in the allocation of purchase consideration thereby affecting the goodwill arising on acquisition.

### In-process research & development (IPR&D)

Under IFRS, IPR&D projects acquired in a business combination are capitalised and remain on the balance sheet, subject to any impairment write-downs. Amortisation is charged over the assets' estimated useful lives from the point when the assets became available for use. Under US GAAP, such assets are recognised in the opening balance sheet but are then written off immediately to the income statement, as the technological feasibility of the IPR&D has not yet been established and it has no alternative future use. Under IFRS, deferred tax is provided for IPR&D assets acquired in a business combination. US GAAP does not provide for deferred tax on these assets, resulting in a reconciling adjustment to deferred tax and goodwill.

IPR&D acquired in transactions other than business combinations is discussed under Intangible assets below.

### Intangible assets

Under IFRS, certain intangible assets related to specific compounds or products which are purchased from a third party and are developed for commercial applications are capitalised but not subject to amortisation until regulatory approval is obtained. Under US GAAP, payments made in respect of these compounds or products which are still in development and have not yet received regulatory approval are charged directly to the income statement.

Under IFRS, intangible assets are amortised over their estimated useful economic life except in the case of certain acquired brands where the end of the useful economic life of the brand cannot be foreseen. Under US GAAP, until the implementation of SFAS 142 'Goodwill and Other Intangible Assets' in 2002, all intangible assets, including brands, were amortised over a finite life. On implementation of SFAS 142 in 2002, intangible assets deemed to have indefinite lives were no longer amortised. As a result of the difference in accounting treatment prior to the implementation of SFAS 142, the carrying values of indefinite lived brands are affected by amortisation charged before 2002 under US GAAP.

### Restructuring costs

Under IFRS, restructuring costs incurred following acquisitions were charged to the profit and loss account post acquisition. For US GAAP purposes, certain of these costs were recognised as liabilities upon acquisition in the opening balance sheet.

Other restructuring costs are recorded as a provision under IFRS when a restructuring plan has been announced. Under US GAAP, a provision may only be recognised when further criteria are met or the liability is incurred. Therefore adjustments have been made to eliminate provisions for restructuring costs that do not meet US GAAP requirements.

### Marketable securities

Marketable securities consist primarily of equity securities and certain other liquid investments, principally government bonds and short-term corporate debt instruments. Under SFAS 115 'Accounting for Certain Investments in Debt and Equity Securities', these securities are considered available for sale and are carried at fair value, with the unrealised gains and losses, net of tax, recorded as a separate component of shareholders' equity. Under IFRS, these are accounted for as available-for-sale financial assets in accordance with IAS 39 'Financial Instruments: Recognition and Measurement'.

The accounting treatment for marketable securities under US GAAP and IFRS is similar. However, differences do arise, principally as a result of the category of marketable securities as defined by SFAS 115 being smaller than the category of available-for-sale financial assets as defined by IAS 39. Investments which are not marketable securities under the SFAS 115 definition are accounted for at cost less impairments under US GAAP rather than at fair value.

The Group did not adopt IAS 39 until 1st January 2005, and, in accordance with the exemption available under IFRS 1, has presented financial instruments in the comparative periods in accordance with UK GAAP. Therefore in 2004 these securities are stated at the lower of cost and net realisable value.

Marketable securities are reviewed at least every six months for other than temporary impairment. For equity securities, the factors considered include:

- the investee's current financial performance and future prospects
- the general market condition of the geographic or industry area in which the investee operates
- the duration and extent to which the market value has been below cost.

Gross unrealised gains and losses on marketable securities were £36 million and £4 million, respectively, at 31st December 2005 (2004 – £60 million and £3 million, respectively). The fair value of marketable securities with unrealised losses at 31st December 2005 is £62 million (2004 – £21 million). All of these marketable securities have been in a continuous loss position for less than 12 months. Deferred tax provided against unrealised gains and losses at 31st December 2005 was £4 million (2004 – £16 million). Gains of £7 million were reclassified out of accumulated other comprehensive income into the income statement on disposals of equity investments during the year. The proceeds from sale of marketable securities under US GAAP were £19,416 million in the year ended 31st December 2005. The proceeds include the roll-over of liquid funds on short-term deposit. The gross gains and losses reflected in the consolidated income statement in respect of marketable securities were £7 million and £nil, respectively.

*Pensions and other post-retirement benefits*
The key difference between IFRS and US GAAP is the method of recognition of actuarial gains and losses. GSK has opted under IFRS to recognise actuarial gains and losses in the statement of recognised income and expense in the year in which they arise. Under US GAAP actuarial gains and losses are recognised using the 10% corridor approach and deferred actuarial gains and losses are amortised. Therefore the pension liability recognised under IFRS is greater than under US GAAP.

*Stock-based compensation*
Under IFRS 2 'Share-based Payment', share options are fair valued at their grant dates and the cost is charged to the income statement over the relevant vesting periods. Under US GAAP, the Group applies SFAS 123 'Accounting for Stock-Based Compensation' and related accounting interpretations in accounting for its option plans, which also require options to be fair valued at their grant date and included in the income statement over the vesting period of the options. Differences arise as a result of the application of differing measurement bases in respect of performance conditions attaching to share-based payments and in the treatment of lapsed grants.

*Derivative instruments*
SFAS 133 'Accounting for Derivative Instruments and Hedging Activities', as amended by SFAS 137 and SFAS 138 and as interpreted by the Derivatives Implementation Group, was adopted by the Group with effect from 1st January 2001. SFAS 133 establishes accounting and reporting standards for derivative instruments, including certain derivative instruments embedded in other contracts (collectively, referred to as derivatives) and for hedging activities. SFAS 133 requires that an entity recognise all derivatives as either assets or liabilities in the consolidated balance sheet and measure those instruments at fair value. Changes in fair value over the period are recorded in current earnings unless hedge accounting is obtained. SFAS 133 prescribes requirements for designation and documentation of hedging relationships and ongoing assessments of effectiveness in order to qualify for hedge accounting.

The Group also evaluates contracts for 'embedded' derivatives. In accordance with SFAS 133 requirements, if embedded derivatives are not clearly and closely related to the host contract, they are accounted for separately from the host contract as derivatives.

The key differences between IFRS under which the Group's financial statements are prepared and US GAAP, and in the Group's application of their respective requirements, are:

- certain derivatives which are designated by the Group as hedging instruments under IAS 39 are not designated as hedging instruments under SFAS 133. Accordingly, hedge accounting is not applied under US GAAP in respect of these arrangements
- the definition of derivatives within the scope of SFAS 133 excludes instruments for which there is no liquid market. This leads to certain items not being recognised on the balance sheet, although they are accounted for as derivatives under IFRS, most notably the call option over Theravance shares
- IAS 39 has an exemption from the requirement to recognise embedded foreign currency derivatives where the currency is commonly used in the economic environment of the host contract. SFAS 133 does not grant a similar exemption and so the Group identifies and separately accounts for more embedded derivatives under US GAAP than it does under IFRS.

The Group has exercised the exemption available under IFRS 1 to present financial instruments in the comparative periods in accordance with UK GAAP. Under UK GAAP, some derivative instruments used for hedges were not recognised on the balance sheet and the matching principle was used to match the gain or loss under these hedging contracts to the foreign currency transaction or profits to which they related. Gains and losses related to the fair value adjustments on these derivative instruments are therefore reconciling items. As in 2005, the Group did not designate any of its derivatives as qualifying hedge instruments under SFAS 133.

The fair value and book value of derivative instruments as at 31st December 2004 is disclosed in the 'Classification and fair value of financial assets and liabilities' table in Note 36.

*Valuation of derivative instruments*

The fair value of derivative instruments is sensitive to movements in the underlying market rates and variables. The Group monitors the fair value of derivative instruments on at least a quarterly basis. Derivatives, including interest rate swaps and cross-currency swaps, are valued using standard valuation models, counterparty valuations, or third party valuations. Standard valuation models used by the Group consider relevant discount rates, the market yield curve on the valuation date, forward currency exchange rates and counterparty risk. All significant rates and variables are obtained from market sources. All valuations are based on the remaining term to maturity of the instrument.

Foreign exchange contracts are valued using forward rates observed from quoted prices in the relevant markets when possible. The Group assumes parties to long-term contracts are economically viable but reserves the right to exercise early termination rights if economically beneficial when such rights exist in the contract.

*Dividends*

Under IFRS, GSK plc's quarterly dividends are recognised only on payment. Under US GAAP, the dividends are recognised in the financial statements when they are declared.

*Other*

The following adjustments are also included in the reconciliations:

- computer software – under IFRS, the Group capitalises costs incurred in acquiring and developing computer software for internal use where the software supports a significant business system and the expenditure leads to the creation of a durable asset. For US GAAP, the Group applies SOP 98-1, 'Accounting for the Costs of Computer Software Developed or Obtained for Internal Use', which restricts the categories of costs which can be capitalised.
- guarantor obligations – under US GAAP, the Group applies the FASB's Financial Interpretation No. 45 (FIN 45), 'Guarantor's Accounting and Disclosure Requirements for Guarantees, Including Indirect Guarantees of Indebtedness of Others'. This requires that the Group recognise certain guarantees issued, measured at fair value. Under IFRS, such guarantor obligations are recognised when further additional criteria are met or the liability is incurred.

- variable interest entities – under the FASB's Interpretation No. 46 Revised (FIN 46R), 'Consolidation of Variable Interest Entities', certain entities, known as Variable Interest Entities (VIEs), must be consolidated by the 'primary beneficiary' of the entity. The primary beneficiary is generally defined as having the majority of the risks and rewards arising from the VIE. Additionally, for VIEs in which a significant, but not majority, variable interest is held, certain disclosures are required. The Group has completed a review of potential VIEs and, as a consequence, has consolidated Theravance Inc. from May 2004 (see Note (c) on page 142). No other VIEs of which the Group is the primary beneficiary were identified.
- fixed asset and inventory impairments – reversals of impairments previously recorded against the carrying value of assets are permitted under IFRS in certain circumstances. US GAAP does not permit reversals of these impairments.
- various other small adjustments.

*Source*: GlaxoSmithKline plc Annual Report 2005, pp. 135–7.

# Appendices

**A**    Double-entry bookkeeping

**B**    An outline of the content of International Financial Reporting Standards

**C**    An outline of the content of the EU's Fourth Directive on Company Law (as amended in 2001, 2003, etc.)

**D**    Feedback on exercises

# Double-entry bookkeeping

Anne Ullathorne

This appendix explores the application and extension of ideas introduced in Chapters 2 and 3 of this book, focusing on practical aspects of double-entry bookkeeping. Most businesses now run their double-entry bookkeeping system with the aid of computer software, but it is still helpful to have a clear basic understanding of the way the system works, and when adjustments need to be made to financial statements. For example, at the balance sheet date, it is important to be aware of the effect of any such adjustment. The mechanics and terminology of simple bookkeeping principles will be used wherever necessary in later parts of the text.

If bookkeeping is new to you, then you should study this appendix carefully. If you have done a lot of bookkeeping before, then you should still read through it in order to ensure that you see fully how it relates to the presentation in the main body of the text.

This appendix is divided into five sections:

1. Rules of recording
2. Composition of financial statements
3. Accruals and prepayments
4. Depreciation, bad debts and other year-end adjustments
5. From trial balance to financial statements

## Rules of recording

Chapter 1 commenced with some definitions of accounting. The roles of recording, classifying and summarizing were identified as important. The double-entry system of recording, which is extensively practised throughout the world, manages this activity with great efficiency, as information is input whenever a transaction takes place, and is collated such that a summary of large amounts of information about diverse activities can be quickly produced in a clear format for decision-makers. Sections 2 and 3 of Chapter 2 describe the way in which the effect of any transaction may be recorded by using any of five categories: namely, applications of funds (being assets or expenses) and sources of funds (being liabilities, capital and revenues).

This has been further developed into the accounting equation whereby:

$$\text{Assets} - \text{Liabilities} = \text{Opening Owners' Equity} + (\text{Revenues} - \text{Expenses})$$

The following steps need to be understood as key elements in bookkeeping:

1. A **separate account is set up** in order to record all the information relating to one type of expense, revenue, asset, or liability. These accounts may develop in an

*ad hoc* fashion in a small business or may be summarized in a company manual, or a complex Chart of Accounts used nationally, as in France. They will include such items as:

- wages, power, rent (expenses)
- sales, interest received (revenues)
- buildings, tools, cash (assets)
- loans, payables (liabilities)

2. There is **flexibility in the system** as any number of accounts may be opened and they may be given any name, e.g. miscellaneous account or suspense account. This is to enable the system to be developed according to the needs of the particular business, and sometimes in the real world an account may be needed to 'hold' an item before it is allocated elsewhere. Originally these bookkeeping accounts (sometimes known as ledger accounts although the term is now old fashioned) were kept in handwritten books but may now be a column in a spreadsheet or a computer file. For each of these accounts, there may be an increase or decrease, and so, for convenience, a page may be divided into left and right side, giving the layout of a T (such as is shown in Figure A.1).

3. Every transaction that occurs has **two effects and therefore a 'double entry'** in the books of account. Consider the six example transactions shown in Table A.1.

Table A.1 **Sample transactions**

| Transaction | Value (€) | Effect A | Effect B |
|---|---|---|---|
| 1. Cash sale | 50 | +Cash | +Sales |
| 2. Credit sale to X | 80 | +Receivables | +Sales |
| 3. Loan raised from Y | 2,000 | +Cash | +Lenders |
| 4. Machine bought | 1,000 | +Assets | −Cash |
| 5. Electricity bill received | 100 | +Expenses | +Payables |
| 6. Electricity bill paid | 100 | −Payables | −Cash |

The effects are:

- for 1 and 3, the entity owns more cash;
- for 2, more cash is receivable;
- for 4, it controls more assets;
- for 5, it 'owes' less to its owners in profit (because of expenses);
- for 6, it owes less to outside creditors (payables).

For reasons discussed below, each of the Effects A is called a *debit* and each of Effects B is called a *credit*. And, at the end of a period during which accounts are run, the total of all debits equals the total of all credits. The system is self-balancing. There is no stigma attached to 'debit', nor congratulatory connotation attached to 'credit'; they are merely labels to describe two groupings of transactions. It can be seen that 'debit' is by no means synonymous with plus or with minus; it means an increase in resources or a decrease in claims.

The words 'debit' and 'credit' have their origins in early Italian accounting, which particularly concerned itself with amounts due to and from persons. The derivations of the words will be clear to those who are familiar with any Latin-based language.

'Debit' means *he ought* (to pay us); a debit on a person's account means that he must pay the business at some future date. Similarly, 'credit' means *he trusts* (us to pay him). From these basic entries all the others fall into place, as in Table A.2.

In practice, most accountants would not work out whether, for example, any particular transaction involved a debit to cash or a credit to cash but would know by reflex. Many might not be able easily to work out from first principles which entry should be made. The system is merely a convention that is fairly easily learned and works well.

### Table A.2 **The meaning of 'debit' and 'credit'**

| Debits | Credits |
|---|---|
| Increases in resources | Decreases in resources |
| Decreases in claims | Increases in claims |
| +Assets | −Assets |
| +Expenses | −Expenses |
| −Liabilities | +Liabilities |
| −Capital | +Capital |
| −Revenues | +Revenues |

4. The transactions over a period are recorded according to this method and there will come a point when a summary financial statement needs to be drawn up. Because of the system used, we find that the **balances** on the ledger accounts will be either a **debit**, representing assets held or expenses incurred, or a **credit** balance, representing income or liabilities or the ownership interest. The total of the debit balances will equal the total of the credit balances, because of the technique used. If this is not the case, it will be due to a breakdown or error in the recording.

*(When considering debit and credit balances, please note that the monthly statement issued to you by your bank is a copy of the ledger account held in the bank's books about its transactions with you. Consequently, when you deposit cash with the bank, the bank will record this as cash received (asset) and a liability to you. This credit balance in your name indicates that the bank has to repay its liability to you. If you were keeping your own books, the balance would be shown as a debit because the bank owes you the outstanding balance.)*

5. **At the end of the accounting period**, the balances on the revenue and expense accounts are transferred to the income statement and combined to calculate the profit for the period. The remaining balances, of assets, liabilities and capital, are carried forward to the next accounting period. They may be disclosed as a balance sheet.

## Worked example of sample transactions

We will now work through the six transactions in Table A.1:

1. A cash sale has been made and the increase of cash received is recorded as a debit entry, counterbalanced by the credit recorded under sales, a revenue account, which is effectively the source of the cash. Note that the descriptor indicates where the other entity is. The result is shown in Figure A.1.

Figure A.1 **Transaction 1**

| Cash account (€) | | | | Sales account (€) | | |
|---|---|---|---|---|---|---|
| Debits | | Credits | | Debits | | Credits |
| Sales | 50 | | | | | Cash | 50 |

2. For recording a credit sale, a new account is opened for receivables (this is usually in the individual names of the customers concerned to ensure that the business can arrange for the proper collection of amounts owed to it). The receivable account is debited and there is a corresponding entry in the sales account increasing the total of recorded sales to €130. Figure A.2 results.

Figure A.2 **Transaction 2**

| X (receivable) account (€) | | | Sales account (€) | | |
|---|---|---|---|---|---|
| Sales | 80 | | | Cash | 50 |
| | | | | X | 80 |

3. A loan from Y is recorded by debiting the cash account with the cash received and crediting a specific account for Y which will be set up for this purpose and which may be called Loan/Lender/Y account. This leads to Figure A.3.

Figure A.3 **Transaction 3**

| Cash account (€) | | | Y (lender) account (€) | | |
|---|---|---|---|---|---|
| Sales | 50 | | | Cash | 2,000 |
| Y | 2,000 | | | | |

4. The purchase of a machine for cash is recorded in Figure A.4.

Figure A.4 **Transaction 4**

| Non-current asset account (€) | | | Cash account (€) | | | |
|---|---|---|---|---|---|---|
| Cash | 1,000 | | Sales | 50 | Fixed assets | 1,000 |
| | | | Y | 2,000 | | |

5. The receipt of an electricity bill is recorded as an expense incurred (debit electricity expense) and an outstanding liability (credit Electricity company/ Payables/Creditors account). This gets us to Figure A.5.

Figure A.5 **Transaction 5**

| Electricity expenses account (€) | | | Creditors account (€) | | |
|---|---|---|---|---|---|
| Cash | 100 | | | Electricity | 100 |

**6.** The electricity liability is settled with cash at a later date (debit the liability account, credit cash). After that, Figure A.6 shows the position.

Figure A.6 **Transaction 6**

| Creditors account (€) | | | | Cash account (€) | | | |
|---|---|---|---|---|---|---|---|
| Cash | 100 | Electricity | 100 | Sales | 50 | Fixed assets | 1,000 |
| | | | | Y | 2,000 | Creditors | 100 |

Ensure that you are clear about the rationale for each of these recording entries and test the notion that all transactions of a business can be recorded in this way.

## The advantages of double entry

There are several important advantages to be gained from using a double-entry system. First, since there are clearly two effects from each transaction, it is useful to record them both. Before double entry, a cash sale would have been recorded only in the cash book, which contained all other transactions affecting cash. This meant that, in order to find a total of recorded sales, it was necessary to look through all cash transactions, picking out those relating to sales. For a large trader this would have been very laborious for even one day's sales, let alone one year's. So, double entry allows an easy totalling of sales, cash, electricity bills, wages, fixed assets, and so on. Without these totals, balance sheets and profit and loss accounts would be impossible to produce.

Totalling is made particularly easy because the accounts are two-sided, allowing positive and negative effects to be stored separately on the same account. This enables quick balancing of any accounts. For example, after the above six transactions, the total of cash in hand can be worked out to be €950 (i.e. €2,050 − €1,100). Table A.3 gives the balanced account.

Table A.3 **Cash account of example in Figure A.6 (€)**

| Sales | 50 | Non-current assets | 1,000 |
|---|---|---|---|
| Y | 2,000 | Creditors | 100 |
| | | Balance carried down | 950 |
| | 2,050 | | 2,050 |
| Balance brought down | 950 | | |

Double entry has been maintained by creating a brought-down debit of equal size to the balancing credit of €950. At the start of the next accounting period the cash account will already show €950, which is correct. Clearly, it will be a good idea to check the cash and the bank account to see whether there is in fact €950. If there is not, an investigation into shortages of cash or errors in the records should be carried out. The facts that all cash entries are on one account, that only cash entries are on it, and that the entries are separated into cash in (debit, left-hand side) and cash out (credit, right-hand side) aid quick totalling. The same applies to all accounts of whatever sort.

Another significant advantage is that it is known that the whole system should be self-balancing. That is, when all the debit balances are added together, they will equal all the credit balances. To ensure this, most bookkeeping software packages make it impossible for data to be entered on the system unless both entries are identified. There might still be errors of allocation to different accounts but nevertheless the figures, the total debits and credits, will still balance.

When the end-of-year balancing is made in a manual system, it is unusual for the accounts to balance straight away. This is due to inevitable errors of recording and analysing the entries in the accounts. Any lack of balance warns the accountant that errors should be searched for. Also, since each entry is cross-referenced to its equal and opposite entry, it is fairly easy to understand the origin of any entry.

The self-balancing process is checked by means of a trial balance. This is a two-column listing of all the debit and credit balances. Each column should total to the same amount. The trial balance after the six transactions is shown as Table A.4.

Table A.4 **Trial balance after six transactions (€)**

| Account | Debits | Credits |
| --- | --- | --- |
| X (receivable) | 80 | |
| Sales | | 130 |
| Cash | 950 | |
| Y (lender) | | 2,000 |
| Non-current asset | 1,000 | |
| Electricity expense | 100 | |
| Totals | 2,130 | 2,130 |

Accounting entries always carry a date in order to make it easier to understand them if they need to be checked in the future. For example, if Transaction 1 (the cash sale) occurred on 3 November 20X9, it might be recorded as in Figure A.7. (Note, however, that dates will only be used in accounts in this book when they are necessary for clarity.)

Figure A.7 **Transaction 1 (dated)**

| Cash account (€) | | Sales account (€) | |
| --- | --- | --- | --- |
| 3 Nov. X9 Sales 50 | | | 3 Nov. X9 Cash 50 |

Several of these factors make it more difficult fraudulently to manipulate items in the accounts. It has been mentioned that checking is fairly easy. It is helped by the fact that balancing is impossible if the totals of only one account are manipulated, and adjustments of more than one account may entail the alteration of a figure that is regularly checked (e.g. the cash balance).

## ? Practice questions

*A solution guide to these questions is given at the end of this appendix.*

**1. Athens Ltd**

Athens Ltd is a new hairdressing business into which the owner, Mr George, invests €40,000 on 1 January, when business commences. During the first week the following transactions occur:

1. Fittings are purchased for €22,000.
2. Wages are paid to staff – €8,000.
3. Cash takings from customers of €16,000 are banked.
4. The owner takes €4,000 out of the business for himself.
5. A stylist is persuaded to lend €5,000 to the business.
6. New hairdriers are purchased for €10,000 on credit (to be paid in two months' time).
7. The hair salon cuts and dresses hair for a number of the leading actors from a local film studio for a total price of €1,500, the bill to be paid by the studio during the next month.

*You are required to:*

(a) record the transactions in ledger accounts;
(b) calculate the final balance on each account at the end of the week;
(c) prepare a list of balances (trial balance);
(d) draw up a simple income statement and balance sheet as at 31 January, assuming no further transactions.

**2. Beijing Ltd**

Beijing Ltd runs a small hotel which commenced trading on 1 March. The following transactions occurred during the month of March:

| | |
|---|---|
| 1 March | Share capital of €50,000 was invested by the owners who also paid €5,000 for the first month's rent. |
| 2 March | Supplies were bought for the bar for €5,000 cheque payment and goods for the restaurant from Best Supplies Ltd for €1,500, for later payment. |
| 5 March | Weekend takings from customers amounted to €3,750. |
| 8 March | Wages paid of €1,600 and general expenses of €400. |
| 9 March | Takings from restaurant and bar sales of €7,100 were banked. |
| 10 March | A private party was held for I. Dance and an invoice sent for €5,200. |
| 15 March | Wages of €2,300 were paid. |
| 21 March | Clean Company's laundry bill for €700 was received. |
| 25 March | Best Supplies Ltd was paid but a further delivery of provisions costing €2,500 was received. |
| 28 March | Wages paid of €1,800. |
| 30 March | Takings from customers, €6,100, were banked. |

*You are required to:*

(a) record the transactions in the accounts;
(b) calculate the final balance on each account at the end of the month;
(c) prepare a trial balance;
(d) draw up a simple income statement and balance sheet as at 31 March.

## Composition of financial statements

At the end of the accounting period, the balances of the revenue and expense accounts are taken to the income statement, and combined to ascertain the profit or loss made during the period. This account is thus a part of the double-entry system, and the balance on it represents the increase, or decrease, in owners' equity for the period.

The revenue and expense accounts already met in Table A.1 are shown in Figure A.8 after year-end balancing and closing-off procedures have occurred (new entries have asterisks). Notice that the expense and revenue accounts have now been closed down by transferring their balances to the income statement. (Balances on the asset and liability ledger accounts are carried forward to begin the next period but will also be separately recorded in the balance sheet of the business at that particular date, as prepayments and accruals respectively. This is covered in more detail next.)

You should now be able to take a given list of ledger account balances (a trial balance) and produce from it an income statement and a balance sheet.

## Figure A.8 Revenue and expense accounts

```
                        Sales account (€)
        Income statement   *130 | Cash                50
                                | X                   80
                            130 |                    130

    Electricity expense account (€)          Income statement (€)
  Creditors      100 | Income    100*                    | Sales      130*
                     | statement            Electricity  100* |
                 100 |          100
```

## Worked example

Let us look at some more transactions specifically related to trading. For simplicity, consider the transactions of a new business called Ropa (Table A.5). Each of these entries will be recorded on the appropriate side of the appropriate account. The accounts specifically connected with trading will look like Figure A.9 (the other halves of the double entries being in other accounts, as noted in the table). If these were the only

## Table A.5 Transactions of Ropa

| Transaction (€) | Debit (€) | | Credit (€) | |
|---|---|---|---|---|
| 1. Purchase 3,000 worth of marble on credit from C | Purchases a/c | 3,000 | C (payable) a/c | 3,000 |
| 2. Sell 1,000 worth of marble for cash to D | Cash a/c | 1,000 | Sales a/c | 1,000 |
| 3. Purchase 2,000 worth of paint for cash from E | Purchases a/c | 2,000 | Cash a/c | 2,000 |
| 4. Sell 500 worth of paint on credit to F | F (receivable) a/c | 500 | Sales a/c | 500 |
| 5. Sell 800 worth of marble for cash to G | Cash a/c | 800 | Sales a/c | 800 |
| 6. Return of 100 worth of paint by F | Sales a/c | 100 | F (receivable) a/c | 100 |

Figure A.9 **Trading accounts**

| Purchases account (€) | | | | Sales account (€) | | | |
|---|---|---|---|---|---|---|---|
| 1. C | 3,000 | | | 6. F | 100 | 2. Cash | 1,000 |
| 3. Cash | 2,000 | | | | | 4. F | 500 |
| | | | | | | 5. Cash | 800 |

Figure A.10 **Balance transferred**

| Purchases account (€) | | | | Sales account (€) | | | |
|---|---|---|---|---|---|---|---|
| C | 3,000 | Trading a/c | 5,000 | F | 100 | Cash | 1,000 |
| Cash | 2,000 | | | Trading a/c | 2,200 | F | 500 |
| | | | | | | Cash | 800 |
| | 5,000 | | 5,000 | | 2,300 | | 2,300 |

| Trading account (€) | | | |
|---|---|---|---|
| Purchases | 5,000 | Sales | 2,200 |

Table A.6 **Trading account of Ropa for the period ending 31 December (€)**

| | | | |
|---|---|---|---|
| Purchases | 5,000 | Sales | 2,200 |
| *less* Closing inventory | 3,500 | | |
| | 1,500 | | |
| Gross profit c/d | 700 | | |
| | 2,200 | | 2,200 |
| | | Gross profit b/d | 700 |

trading entries in the accounting period, the trading account would be made up by closing down the above accounts and transferring the balances as shown in Figure A.10.

This does not seem to be a very healthy trading position, but it must be remembered that not all the purchases will have been turned into sales, because there is usually some closing inventory remaining at the end of an accounting period. If stock-taking shows that there is €3,500 worth of marble and paint left, the first part of the income statement will look like Table A.6. This shows how the income statement is traditionally viewed as two parts. The first part is known as the trading account, and shows the gross profit, which is the difference between the value of the sales and the cost of the goods (or services) actually sold. Notice that the double-entry system is being maintained. The gross profit entries balance each other. The closing inventory (and opening inventory) entries will be discussed later.

## The income statement

The rest of the income statement leads on from the trading account and contains all other revenues and expenses that are not raw trading transactions.

Suppose that the only extra transactions in this accounting period of Ropa are those shown in Table A.7. The revenue and expense account halves of these transactions

**Table A.7 Further transactions of Ropa**

| *Transactions* (€) | *Debit* (€) | | *Credit* (€) | |
|---|---|---|---|---|
| 7. Wages of 100 paid | Wages a/c | 100 | Cash a/c | 100 |
| 8. Rent for the period of 150 (not yet paid to the landlord) | Rent a/c | 150 | H (landlord) a/c | 150 |
| 9. Advertising bill for the period, paid 30 | Advertising a/c | 30 | Cash a/c | 30 |
| 10. Stationery bought for 20 | Stationery a/c | 20 | Cash a/c | 20 |
| 11. More wages paid, 80 | Wages a/c | 80 | Cash a/c | 80 |
| 12. Rent received from subletting part of the premises, 40 | Cash a/c | 40 | Rent received a/c | 40 |

will thus appear as Figure A.11 (the other halves being in the cash account and H account, as noted in the table). These accounts have been shown already closed off. The other halves of the double entry for each of the asterisked items are in the income statement in Table A.8.

As before, the double-entry system is strictly maintained. The rent received is not in the trading account because it does not result from its main trading activities. It is, of course, on the credit side, just like other revenues.

The order of the expense items is not very critical, although it seems sensible to start with the most important. Often, expenses are organized into groups (e.g. 'administrative', 'finance' and 'marketing'). Consistency from year to year will make comparisons easier. These issues are examined at greater length in Chapter 6. Note that the heading of the account includes the words 'for the period ending'. This emphasizes the fact that the income statement deals with flows over time. The wording is often 'for the year ending', 'for the quarter ending', and so on.

**Figure A.11 Revenue and expense accounts**

Wages account (€)

| | | | |
|---|---|---|---|
| 7. Cash | 100 | Income statement | *180 |
| 11. Cash | 80 | | |
| | 180 | | 180 |

Rent (expenses) account (€)

| | | | |
|---|---|---|---|
| 8. H | 150 | Income statement | *150 |
| | 150 | | 150 |

Advertising account (€)

| | | | |
|---|---|---|---|
| 9. Cash | 30 | Income statement | *30 |
| | 30 | | 30 |

Stationery account (€)

| | | | |
|---|---|---|---|
| 10. Cash | 20 | Income statement | *20 |
| | 20 | | 20 |

Rent (revenues) account (€)

| | | | |
|---|---|---|---|
| Income statement | *40 | 12. Cash | 40 |
| | 40 | | 40 |

* See Table A.8.

**Table A.8 Income statement of Ropa for the period ending 31 December (€)**

| | | | |
|---|---|---|---|
| Purchases | 5,000 | Sales | 2,200 |
| less Closing inventory | 3,500 | | |
| | 1,500 | | |
| Gross profit c/d | 700 | | |
| | 2,200 | | 2,200 |
| Wages | *180 | Gross profit b/d | 700 |
| Rent | *150 | Rent received | *40 |
| Advertising | *30 | | |
| Stationery | *20 | | |
| Total expenses | 380 | | |
| Net profit c/d | 360 | | |
| | 740 | | 740 |
| | | Net profit b/d | 360 |

* See Figure A.11.

## Inventory

During the period it is usual for no entries to be made in the inventory account. The business would be well advised to keep records of inventory movements and levels, but these will not be part of the double-entry system. The inventory account is only needed at the end of the accounting period, which is naturally the beginning of the next. Let us assume that a business has been left €2,000 of inventory from the previous year. Therefore, at the start of the year the inventory account appears as in Figure A.12.

**Figure A.12 Inventory account**

| Inventory account (€) | |
|---|---|
| Opening inventory | 2,000 |

At the end of the year, the inventory may be valued at €5,500. The accounting entries to record (a) the removal of the old inventory, and (b) the arrival of the new inventory figure are:

(a) trading a/c *debit* 2,000; inventory a/c *credit* 2,000; and
(b) inventory a/c *debit* 5,500; trading a/c *credit* 5,500.

This will give the asterisked entries of Figure A.13.

**Figure A.13 Inventory and trading accounts**

| Inventory account (€) | | | | Trading account (€) | | | |
|---|---|---|---|---|---|---|---|
| Opening | 2,000 | Trading a/c | *2,000 | Opening inventory | *2,000 | Closing inventory | *5,500 |
| | 2,000 | | 2,000 | | | | |
| Closing | *5,500 | | | | | | |

The normal presentation, as in the previous trading account, is different from this because it makes for better presentation to show the closing inventory as a negative figure on the left rather than as a positive figure on the right. It should be very clear by now that in all these manipulations we are adhering not to naturally occurring laws that have been discovered but to conventions that have been invented and adopted because they work well.

## The balance sheet (statement of financial position)

The observant reader may have noticed that the process of transferring various items of revenue and expense from their accounts to the income statement has left a number of accounts with balances remaining on them. These accounts are asset, liability or capital accounts (including the income statement, which now also has a balance remaining). The total of all the credit balances should still equal the total of all the debit balances because double entry has been maintained throughout, even in the income statement. When all the balances are collected together on a balance sheet (or sheet of balances), we have a picture of what is owned by and owed by the business at that moment in time.

The debit or credit balances on the asset, liability or capital accounts are *not being transferred* to the balance sheet; they are carried forward to the next period, as indeed are the real assets and liabilities that they represent. The balances are merely *recorded* on a balance sheet in order to show the financial position of the business at the end of the accounting period. That is, the balance sheet represents stocks, not flows. Therefore, it will have '*as at* December X3', for example, in its title.

## ? Practice questions

*A solution guide to these questions is given at the end of this appendix.*

### 3. Cadiz Ltd
The following is the trial balance of Cadiz Ltd as at 31 December:

|  | Debit €000 | Credit €000 |
|---|---|---|
| Accounts receivable | 450 | |
| Accounts payable | | 623 |
| Sales | | 5,750 |
| Light and heat | 570 | |
| Wages | 1,200 | |
| Rent | 800 | |
| Office expenses | 320 | |
| Capital at 1 January | | 1,350 |
| Inventory at 1 January | 250 | |
| Purchases | 2,160 | |
| Fixtures and fittings | 285 | |
| Cash | 2,188 | |
| Loan | | 500 |
| | 8,223 | 8,223 |

The inventory at 31 December is €380,000.

*You are required to* prepare an income statement for the year ended 31 December and a balance sheet as at that date.

### 4. Dublin Ltd

The following balances are taken from the books of Dublin Ltd at 31 December:

|  | €000 |
|---|---|
| Sales | 50,220 |
| Purchases | 18,750 |
| Rent and rates | 6,200 |
| Repairs | 3,116 |
| Wages | 4,520 |
| Fittings | 23,230 |
| Motor van | 8,050 |
| Van expenses | 2,134 |
| Office expenses | 3,610 |
| Capital at 1 January | 35,000 |
| Inventory at 1 January | 400 |
| Cash at bank | 6,000 |
| Accounts receivable | 6,200 |
| Accounts payable | 4,525 |
| Stationery | 350 |
| Power | 7,185 |

The inventory at 31 December is €500,000.

*You are required to* prepare an income statement for the year ended 31 December and a balance sheet as at that date.

## Accruals and prepayments

The IASB states in its Framework for the Preparation and Presentation of Financial Statements that financial statements inform users not only of past transactions involving the payment and receipt of cash but also of obligations to pay cash in the future and of resources that represent cash to be received in the future. As described in Chapter 3, the accruals basis of accounting recognizes transactions and other events when they occur (and not as cash, or its equivalent, is received or paid). A transaction may involve the recognition of a liability that will be satisfied by a transfer of cash at a future date but it will be recorded at the time of the initial transaction, without waiting for the flows of cash.

The requirement for periodic presentation of financial statements creates problems in recognizing outstanding assets and liabilities because most organizations do not complete and liquidate projects in one financial year. Costs incurred in any one period may be treated as either expenses used in the period or as an asset that is held for future benefit and consequently carried forward to the next accounting period. We have already considered the importance of identifying inventory that is carried forward as an asset to the next accounting period. Other expenses should be considered at the accounting date to ensure that the charge to an accounting period is only for those resources which are consumed during the period. Thus, accrued expenses (or accruals) are those costs which are applicable to the current accounting period but have not yet been recorded. Prepaid expenses or prepayments are those costs which have been recorded during the current period but which relate to consumption in a future accounting period. The double entry adjustments will be as follows:

- To accrue expenses: debit (increase) expense and credit (increase) payables.
- To recognize prepayment: debit (increase) receivables and credit (decrease) expense.

## Worked example

The following figures relate to one particular property for a calendar year.

1. Rent is paid half-yearly in arrears (€500 per half-year). Last payment was 30 September this year; next payment is due 31 March next year.
2. The telephone bill is paid quarterly. Next bill is expected 31 January next year (always about €120 per quarter).
3. Property taxes are paid half-yearly in advance (€200 per half-year). Last payment was 1 October this year; next payment is due 1 April next year.
4. The yearly insurance premium of €180 is paid on 1 November to cover 12 months from that date.

It has been explained that, in order to arrive at a profit figure, the payments *relating to* a period (i.e. the expenses), not the payments *made in* a period, are those that should be included. This is the accruals basis of accounting. Let us imagine that the business had started on 1 January with no balances outstanding. Without taking the above points into account, the total bills paid in the year for all the properties owned by the business was:

|  |  |  |  |
|---|---|---|---|
| Rent | 1,500 | Property tax | 1,000 |
| Telephone | 800 | Insurance | 500 |

The above four points imply that, at 31 December:

(a) rent is in arrears by €250;
(b) the telephone bill is in arrears by €80;
(c) property taxes are paid in advance by €100; and
(d) insurance is paid in advance by €150.

The expense accounts for the year, taking all this into account, will look like Figure A.14.

Thus, the actual charges in the income statement are increased by amounts owing that relate to the present accounting year and decreased by amounts paid on behalf of next year. Notice that next year's accounts have already been credited or debited with the appropriate amounts because of double entry. For example, when the €500 rent bill arrives and is paid at the end of March next year and debited to the rent account (the cash account being credited with €500 at the same time), the account will show a net charge of €250 (i.e. €500 – €250) so far. This is correct for one quarter (see Figure A.15).

## ? Practice questions

*A solution guide to these questions is given at the end of this appendix.*

### 5. Edinburgh Ltd
Electricity bills amounting to €4,500 were paid by Edinburgh Ltd during the year ended 31 December 20X7. All of these bills relate to the year ended 31 December 20X7. A bill of €1,500 was received in February 20X8 and covers the period from 1 November 20X7 to 31 January 20X8.

## Figure A.14 Expenses accounts

| Rent account | | | |
|---|---|---|---|
| Cash | 1,500 | Income statement | 1,750 |
| Accruals carried down | 250 | | |
| | 1,750 | | 1,750 |
| | | Accruals brought down | 250 |

| Telephone account | | | |
|---|---|---|---|
| Cash | 800 | Income statement | 880 |
| Accruals carried down | 80 | | |
| | 880 | | 880 |
| | | Accruals brought down | 80 |

| Property taxes account | | | |
|---|---|---|---|
| Cash | 1,000 | Prepayment carried down | 100 |
| | | Income statement | 900 |
| | 1,000 | | 1,000 |
| Prepayment brought down | 100 | | |

| Insurance account | | | |
|---|---|---|---|
| Cash | 500 | Prepayment carried down | 150 |
| | | Income statement | 350 |
| | 500 | | 500 |
| Prepayment brought down | 150 | | |

| Income statement | | | |
|---|---|---|---|
| Rent | 1,750 | Gross profit | x,xxx |
| Property tax | 900 | | |
| Telephone | 880 | | |
| Insurance | 350 | | |

## Figure A.15 The Rent account (next year)

| Rent account | | | |
|---|---|---|---|
| Cash | 500 | Accruals b/d | 250 |

What is the amount of electricity expense charged in the income statement for the year ended 31 December 20X7?

What figure would appear in the balance sheet at 31 December 20X7 relating to electricity and under what heading?

### 6. Florence Ltd

The financial year end for Florence Ltd is 31 December 20X7. Calculate the amount charged to the income statement and the balance outstanding (for the balance sheet) in respect of the following items:

(a) Motor expenses  Paid in year  €2,232
　　　　　　　　　　Owing at 31.12.X7  €310
(b) Insurance  Paid in year  €5,400
　　　　　　　Prepaid at 31.12.X6  €760
(c) Stationery  Paid in year  €2,200
　　　　　　　Owing at 31.12.X6  €150
　　　　　　　Owing at 31.12.X7  €520

(d) Rent                Paid in year          €5,760
Prepaid at 31.12.X6  €400
Prepaid at 31.12.X7  €280

### 7. Geneva Ltd

Geneva Ltd has a year end of 30 June for its financial statements. You are provided with the following information relating to rent payable.

| | |
|---|---|
| For the period 1 July X0 to 30 Sept X0 (paid in June X0) | €15,000 |
| For the six months to 31 Mar X1 (paid in December X0) | €30,000 |
| For the year to 31 Mar X2 (paid in June X1 to qualify for discount) | €72,000 |

*You are required to* calculate the amount which should be charged as an expense for the year ended 31 June 20X1 and the amount that is prepaid and carried forward as a current asset at that date.

## Depreciation, bad debts and other year-end adjustments

The accruals concept can be extended to encompass other adjustments to assets. For example, when balance sheet receivables (debtors) include debts about which there are suspicions (bad or doubtful debts) an adjusting entry can be made to the final balance.

For a bad debt, the entry would be: *debit* the bad debt expense account and *credit* the receivables account with the amount of the specific bad debt.

For doubtful debts, the entry would be similar: *debit* the bad debt expense account and *credit* an 'allowance for doubtful debts' account. The receivables would then be shown on the balance sheet net of the allowance (or impairment).

For the allocation of the cost of a fixed asset over its useful life, the entries will be to *debit* the depreciation expense in the income statement and *credit* the accumulated depreciation account with the calculated amount of depreciation to be charged. On the balance sheet, the net amount is shown as the 'net book value' or 'carrying amount'.

Chapter 9 of the text gives further detail about these calculations but it is important to be aware of the recording technique for such adjustments.

## ? Practice questions

*A solution guide to these questions is given at the end of this appendix.*

### 8. Hobart Ltd

Hobart Ltd purchases a truck on 1 July 20X7 for €200,000. The truck should last for 5 years and then could be sold for €40,000. The financial statements are made up to the year ended 31 December, with depreciation calculated monthly from the date of acquisition.

(a) Assuming straight-line depreciation, show the accounting entries relating to vehicles and depreciation of vehicles for 20X7 and 20X8, identifying the expense for depreciation and the balance sheet figure for vehicles.

(b) On 31 December 20X9 the truck is sold for €110,000. How is the income statement affected?

### 9. Kiev Ltd

Kiev Ltd purchases a machine on 1 January 20X0 for €240,000. Depreciation is charged at 10% on cost. On 30 June 20X4, the machine is sold for €120,000 and the proceeds used to buy a new vehicle for the chairman. Motor vehicles are depreciated at 25% on cost and all depreciation is calculated proportionately in the years of acquisition and disposal.

What are the entries in the income statement for the year ended 31 December 20X4?

## 10. Lhasa Ltd
The following income statement and balance sheet have been prepared for Lhasa Ltd:

### Income statement for the year ended 31 Dec 20X7

|  | €000 |
|---|---|
| Sales | 2,180 |
| Cost of sales | 600 |
| Gross profit | 1,580 |
| Selling and distribution expenses | 620 |
| Administrative expenses | 506 |
| Profit before interest | 454 |
| Interest | 4 |
| Profit for the year | 450 |
| Profit brought forward | 510 |
| Profit carried forward | 960 |

### Balance sheet as at 31 Dec 20X8

|  |  | €000 |
|---|---|---|
| **Non-current assets** |  |  |
| Plant and machinery |  | 1,600 |
| Vehicles |  | 500 |
|  |  | 2,100 |
| **Current assets** |  |  |
| Inventory | 300 |  |
| Accounts receivable | 100 |  |
| Bank | 80 |  |
|  | 480 |  |
| **Current liabilities** |  |  |
| Accounts payable | 200 |  |
| **Net current assets** |  | 280 |
|  |  | 2,380 |
| Long term loan (8%) |  | 100 |
|  |  | 2,280 |
| **Capital and reserves** |  |  |
| Share capital |  | 1,320 |
| Retained earnings |  | 960 |
|  |  | 2,280 |

After the accounts were prepared, the following information became available:

1. Interest payable on the long-term loan is paid half-yearly and interest for the second half-year has not been included in the accounts.
2. €5,000 of the long-term loan is to be repaid by 30 June 20X8.
3. Depreciation has not been charged on the motor vehicles. This class of assets is depreciated at 40% per annum using the reducing balance method.
4. A new machine has been purchased on credit, just before the year end, for €75,000 but this has not been included in the accounts. No depreciation is to be charged on this asset this year.

391

5. After reviewing the Accounts receivable balance, it was decided that bad debts of €4,000 should be written off.
6. An invoice for electricity for €12,000 for the quarter ended 31 December did not arrive until 23 January and has not been included.
7. Taxation is payable at 30% of the net profit before tax.

*You are required to:*
(a) list the adjustments required to record these events;
(b) prepare a balance sheet and income statement for Lhasa Ltd for the year ended 31 December 20X7 incorporating the new information given.

### 11. Mumbai Ltd
The trial balance of Mumbai Ltd at 31 December was as follows:

|  | €000 | €000 |
|---|---|---|
| Inventory at 1 January | 600 | |
| Purchases | 5,020 | |
| Cash at bank | 922 | |
| Premises at cost | 6,200 | |
| Insurance | 864 | |
| Light and heat | 1,226 | |
| Printing and stationery | 731 | |
| Professional fees | 860 | |
| Allowance for doubtful debts | | 10 |
| Accounts receivable | 812 | |
| Accounts payable | | 768 |
| Wages | 2,196 | |
| Bad debts | 21 | |
| Capital at 1 January | | 10,726 |
| Sales | | 9,642 |
| Office furniture | 1,040 | |
| Accumulated depreciation on furniture | | 220 |
| Rent | 874 | |
| | 21,366 | 21,366 |

The following information is applicable:

(a) Inventory on 31 December is €850,000.
(b) The cumulative allowance for doubtful debts is to be increased to €15,000.
(c) There is rent accrued of €300,000.
(d) Insurance of €125,100 had been paid in advance.
(e) Depreciation on office furniture is to be provided at 5% on cost.

*You are required to* prepare an income statement for the year ended 31 December and a balance sheet as at that date.

## From trial balance to financial statements

The majority of introductory accounting examinations require students to demonstrate their competence and ability to apply the standard year-end adjustments to a given trial balance and to produce an income statement and balance sheet in good format under time constraints. This exercise tries to simulate in a simple way what actually happens at the date of statement preparation for an organization. A logical procedure to deal with this task is as follows:

## 1. Check the composition of the trial balance

- It should balance, i.e. the total of debit balances should equal the total of credits. This should always be the case in a non-manual system of bookkeeping, as the software should not allow single entries. However, some of the entries made by a poorly instructed data input clerk may be nonsensical and lead to errors in allocation. In an examination question, there may be an imbalance and the difference is shown in a suspense account to be dealt with following the receipt of further information, or you may be guided to show the difference as owners' capital or shareholders' funds.
- Nevertheless, you should understand each item in the trial balance and know its position in the final statements, i.e. it is either an income statement item or a balance sheet item.

## 2. Adjust for all relevant additional information

- At every balance sheet date, there is additional information in respect of accruals and prepayments of various kinds and adjustments to balance sheet numbers. This is the case in the real world, and information has to be collected from other departments in the organization. In an examination question, though, the information will be given and you will only need to ensure that you record the appropriate adjustment by introducing a debit and a credit entry. Otherwise, of course, the statements will not balance. In the process of doing this, you should ensure that you can identify which items affect the balance sheet and which the income statement.

## 3. Completion of the financial statements

- In a real organization this will also usually be done electronically; however, practising this task manually ensures that you understand what is going on. You should prepare, on two separate sheets of paper, an income statement and a balance sheet. Ensure that these are headed clearly and in full so that any other person looking at your work will know exactly what has been done.
- Either work systematically down the income statement and then the balance sheet, taking the relevant values from the trial balance as you go, or prepare an outline of the financial statements and work systematically down the adjusted trial balance, making sure that each ledger account balance is included in the financial statements.
- Whichever method you chose, the key is to be systematic, because if your trial balance balanced and you completed the double entry of the adjustments, then your financial statements MUST balance! Practice is important for speed and accuracy and the finished article should look as neat and ordered as possible – this will also help your accuracy.

If the entity is a limited company then further entries are likely. Taxation estimated to be payable in relation to the year is shown as a deduction from profit in the income statement, and also as a liability in the balance sheet. Interest on debentures (which are loans with specified conditions) is an expense, and also a liability if not already paid. Note however that dividends, which are the payment to the owners of some of the profits generated for them, are an appropriation of profits, not a reduction in the calculation of the profit figure itself.

## A simple comprehensive example

First of all, here is a reminder of what a trial balance can and cannot do.

### The trial balance

*As we have already seen, at the end of an accounting year (or at any time during the year when a balance sheet or income statement is needed), the accounts in a manual system must be balanced. The balances are then listed with debits in one column and credits in another (this procedure being called extracting a trial balance), before the balances are transferred to the income statement or recorded on the balance sheet.* If the totals of the columns do not agree, this signifies an error (or errors) – for example:

1. *errors of posting*, where one part of the double entry is lost or recorded on the wrong side;
2. *arithmetic errors*, where the addition and balancing processes are inaccurate;
3. *omission of an account*, where the balance on an account is not recorded in the trial balance;
4. *misreading a balance*, where the wrong amount is transferred to the trial balance, or the correct balance written to the wrong column.

It is clear that these types of error should not arise in a computer system. A system should reject partial entries, which do not maintain the double-entry system, and all the calculations are automatic. However, a trial balance is still an essential step in the process of producing an income statement and balance sheet, as computer systems (and their operators) are not infallible. An imbalance must be immediately investigated as it indicates a breakdown of the accounting system.

It should be emphasized, however, that a trial balance which agrees is not necessarily correct. All that an agreed trial balance demonstrates is that errors of the type listed above are probably not present. We say 'probably' because it is always possible to have two or more such errors totalling equal but opposite amounts which are described as compensating errors. A moment's thought will make it obvious that other types of error will not be revealed by a trial balance, an entry on the correct side but posted to the wrong account being one example. Further, there might also be a completely omitted double entry.

Table A.9 contains a possible trial balance extracted from the books of the business of Great Dane on 31 December 20X9. Any errors revealed by imbalance have already been corrected in the trial balance.

At the end of the year there will be a variety of entries that are necessary before the accounts can be properly drawn up. In the case of Great Dane, the year-end entries might result from the following information:

1. 10% depreciation for the year should be provided on the cost of fixtures and fittings.
2. Rent has been paid in advance to the extent of €50.
3. Specific bad debts of €100 are to be written off.
4. An allowance for future bad debts of 10% of receivables is to be set up for the first time.
5. Closing inventory is valued at €5,000.

These entries can now be added to the previous trial balance of Table A.9. The result is shown as Table A.10, where the new entries have affected the asterisked balances. The adjustments that have been made are shown in the right-hand columns. The trial balance still works. The next stage is to transfer all the revenue and expense balances to an income statement by closing the accounts, using the double-entry method. As the balances are transferred, the record in the trial balance can be ticked off. (The

Table A.9 **Trial balance extracted from the books of Great Dane as at 31.12.20X9 (€)**

| Item | Debits | Credits |
|---|---|---|
| Capital | | 20,000 |
| Land | 10,000 | |
| Fixtures and fittings at cost | 4,500 | |
| Accumulated depreciation at 1.1.20X9 | | 900 |
| Opening inventory at 1.1.20X9 | 4,800 | |
| Purchases | 11,600 | |
| Sales | | 16,500 |
| Drawings by owner | 2,400 | |
| Receivables | 2,100 | |
| Payables | | 1,600 |
| Wages and salaries | 800 | |
| Lighting and heating | 100 | |
| Rent | 300 | |
| Miscellaneous expenses | 200 | |
| Cash and bank balances | 2,200 | |
| | 39,000 | 39,000 |

Table A.10 **Trial balance of Great Dane as at 31.12.20X9 after adjustments (€)**

| Item | Debits | Credits | Adjustments already made Debits | Credits |
|---|---|---|---|---|
| Capital | | 20,000 | | |
| Land | 10,000 | | | |
| Fixtures and fittings | 4,500 | | | |
| *Depreciation provision at 31.12.20X9 | | 1,350 | | +450 |
| ✔*Depreciation charge | 450 | | +450 | |
| ✔Opening inventory (in trading account) | 4,800 | | | |
| ✔*Closing inventory (in trading account) | | 5,000 | | +5,000 |
| *Closing inventory (in asset account) | 5,000 | | +5,000 | |
| ✔Purchases | 11,600 | | | |
| ✔Sales | | 16,500 | | |
| Drawings | 2,400 | | | |
| *Receivables | 2,000 | | −100 | |
| Payables | | 1,600 | | |
| ✔Wages and salaries | 800 | | | |
| ✔Lighting and heating | 100 | | | |
| ✔*Rent | 250 | | −50 | |
| ✔*Rent (opening balance for next year) | 50 | | +50 | |
| ✔*Bad debts | 300 | | {+100 +200 | |
| *Allowance for bad debts | | 200 | | +200 |
| ✔Miscellaneous expenses | 200 | | | |
| Cash and bank balance | 2,200 | | | |
| | 44,650 | 44,650 | +5,650 | +5,650 |

### Table A.11 Income statement of Great Dane for the year ending 31.12.20X9 (€)

| | | | |
|---|---:|---|---:|
| Opening inventory | 4,800 | Sales | 16,500 |
| Purchases | 11,600 | | |
| | 16,400 | | |
| *less* Closing inventory | 5,000 | | |
| | 11,400 | | |
| Gross profit carried down | 5,100 | | |
| | 16,500 | | 16,500 |
| Wages and salaries | 800 | Gross profit brought down | 5,100 |
| Lighting and heating | 100 | | |
| Rent | 250 | | |
| Depreciation | 450 | | |
| Bad debts | 300 | | |
| Miscellaneous expenses | 200 | | |
| | 2,100 | | |
| Net profit carried down | 3,000 | | |
| | 5,100 | | 5,100 |
| | | Net profit brought down | 3,000 |

revenue and expense balances have already been ticked in Table A.10.) In this case the account in Table A.11 will result, although in practice in many countries income statements are presented in a different way (see Chapter 6).

All the remaining unticked balances in the trial balance (Table A.10) will be asset, liability or capital balances. These can now be recorded on the balance sheet. As noted in Chapter 2, the balance sheet is not itself part of the double-entry system but a product from it; therefore, these unticked accounts are not closed down, nor are their balances transferred.

When all the balances in the trial balance have been used, the balance sheet in Table A.12 will result. Double entry has ensured that it balances.

### Table A.12 Balance sheet of Great Dane as at 31.12.20X9 (€)

| | Cost | Cumulative depreciation | Net book value | | |
|---|---:|---:|---:|---|---:|
| Fixed assets: | | | | Owner's equity: | |
| Land | 10,000 | | 10,000 | Capital (at 1.1.20X9) | 20,000 |
| | | | | Net profit for the year | 3,000 |
| | | | | | 23,000 |
| Fixtures and fittings | 4,500 | 1,350 | 3,150 | | |
| | 14,500 | 1,350 | 13,150 | | |
| | | | | *less* Drawings | 2,400 |
| | | | | Capital (at 31.12.20X9) | 20,600 |
| Current assets: | | | | Current liabilities: | |
| Inventory | | 5,000 | | Payables | 1,600 |
| Receivables | 2,000 | | | | |
| *less* Allowances | 200 | 1,800 | | | |
| Prepaid expenses | | 50 | | | |
| Cash at bank | | 2,200 | 9,050 | | |
| | | | 22,200 | | 22,200 |

## ? Practice questions

*A solution guide to these questions is given at the end of this appendix.*

### 12. Nairobi Ltd

Nairobi Ltd has an authorized share capital of 500,000 ordinary shares of €1.00 each. The following trial balance was extracted from the accounts as at 31 December 20X7:

|  | €000 | €000 |
|---|---|---|
| Issued share capital |  | 500 |
| Share premium account |  | 20 |
| Retained earnings at 1 January |  | 64 |
| 10% debentures |  | 100 |
| Allowance for doubtful debts |  | 3 |
| Trade receivables | 150 |  |
| Trade payables |  | 80 |
| Freehold buildings (cost) | 450 |  |
| Fixtures and fittings (cost) | 150 |  |
| Accumulated depreciation – freehold buildings |  | 10 |
| Accumulated depreciation – fixtures and fittings |  | 12 |
| Bank balance | 51 |  |
| Purchases | 660 |  |
| Sales |  | 1,218 |
| Audit fee | 16 |  |
| Wages and salaries | 220 |  |
| Discounts allowed and received | 18 | 16 |
| Carriage inwards | 6 |  |
| Rates and insurance | 5 |  |
| Debenture interest paid (half year to June X7) | 5 |  |
| Bad debts | 7 |  |
| Repairs | 17 |  |
| General expenses | 55 |  |
| Inventory 1 January 20X7 | 120 |  |
| Returns inwards | 12 |  |
| Returns outwards |  | 9 |
| Directors' remuneration | 90 |  |
|  | 2,032 | 2,032 |

The following matters are to be taken into account:

(i)   Inventory at 31 December 20X7 was €168,000.
(ii)  Wages and salaries outstanding at 31 December 20X7 were €7,000.
(iii) Rates and insurances paid in advance at 31 December 20X7 amounted to €1,000.
(iv)  Depreciation is to be provided on cost of fixed assets at the rate of 10% on fixtures and fittings and 2% on freehold buildings.
(v)   The allowance for bad debts is to be increased to €4,000.
(vi)  Provision is to be made for the second half year's debenture interest.
(vii) Taxation based on the profits for the year is estimated at €30,000.

*You are required to* prepare, for Nairobi Ltd, an income statement for the year ended 31 December 20X7, and a balance sheet as at that date.

13. Oslo Ltd

The trial balance of Oslo Ltd on 31 July 20X7 is given below:

|  | €000 | €000 |
|---|---|---|
| Ordinary €1 share capital | | 200,000 |
| 8% preference shares | | 100,000 |
| Share premium account | | 20,000 |
| Retained earnings at 1 Aug X6 | | 100,000 |
| 5% debenture stock | | 160,000 |
| Dividend paid | 8,000 | |
| Freehold buildings – cost | 320,000 | |
| Accumulated depreciation – buildings | | 108,800 |
| Motor vehicles – cost | 312,000 | |
| Accumulated depreciation – vehicles | | 56,000 |
| Equipment | 60,000 | |
| Accumulated depreciation – equipment | | 36,000 |
| Trade receivables and payables | 120,000 | 96,000 |
| Inventory at 1 August 20X6 | 165,000 | |
| Cash at bank | 48,400 | |
| Cash in hand | 10,400 | |
| Purchases | 850,000 | |
| Sales | | 1,244,000 |
| Bad debts | 6,000 | |
| Carriage inwards | 5,000 | |
| Carriage outwards | 7,000 | |
| Rent | 10,000 | |
| General administrative expenses | 80,000 | |
| Gas, electricity and water | 9,000 | |
| General selling expenses | 114,000 | |
| Total | 2,120,800 | 2,120,800 |

The following additional information is relevant:

1. Closing inventory is valued at €180,000.
2. An allowance for doubtful debts is to be made of 1% of the debtors figure.
3. Taxation on the current year's profits is estimated at €17,000.
4. Depreciation is to be provided at 2% of cost of freehold buildings, 20% of cost of motor vehicles and 10% of cost of equipment.
5. Lighting and heating of €500 is to be accrued and rent of €1,000 has been paid in advance.
6. Interest on debentures for the year ended 31 July 20X7 was paid on 6 August 20X7. No accrual has yet been made.
7. The final preference dividend of 4% is outstanding at 31 July X7.

*You are required to* prepare an income statement for the year ended 31 July 20X7 and a balance sheet as at that date.

## 14. Penang Ltd

The trial balance of Penang Ltd on 31 July 20X7 was as follows:

|  | €000 | €000 |
|---|---|---|
| Ordinary €1 share capital |  | 4,500 |
| Share premium account |  | 700 |
| 10% debentures |  | 1,500 |
| Retained earnings |  | 1,384 |
| Dividend paid | 175 |  |
| Buildings at cost | 5,500 |  |
| Equipment at cost | 420 |  |
| Vehicles at cost | 860 |  |
| Accumulated depreciation – buildings |  | 80 |
| Accumulated depreciation – equipment |  | 100 |
| Accumulated depreciation – vehicles |  | 198 |
| Bank balance at 31 July 20X7 | 709 |  |
| Inventory at 1 August 20X6 | 1,135 |  |
| Purchases | 2,695 |  |
| Sales |  | 4,910 |
| Carriage inwards | 81 |  |
| Debenture interest | 75 |  |
| Directors' remuneration | 315 |  |
| Discount allowed and received | 8 | 10 |
| General expenses | 28 |  |
| Motor expenses | 406 |  |
| Rates and insurance | 147 |  |
| Returns inwards and outwards | 20 | 15 |
| Salaries and wages | 312 |  |
| Trade receivables | 1,080 |  |
| Trade payables |  | 569 |
| Total | 13,966 | 13,966 |

The following additional information is available:

1. Inventory at 31 July 20X6 is valued at €1,361,000.
2. Depreciation for the year is to be charged using the straight line method as follows:

| Buildings | 2% |
|---|---|
| Equipment | 10% |
| Vehicles | 20% |

3. A half-year's debenture interest is to be accrued, as is the audit fee of €50,000.
4. Rates and insurance of €7,000 has been prepaid.
5. Taxation on the profits for the year is estimated at €80,000.

*You are required to* prepare an income statement for the year ended 31 July 20X7 and a balance sheet as at that date.

### 15. Shanghai Ltd

The trial balance of Shanghai Ltd on 31 March 20X7 is given below:

|  | €m | €m |
|---|---:|---:|
| Ordinary share capital | | 200 |
| Retained earnings | | 350 |
| 10% debentures | | 60 |
| Buildings at cost | 210 | |
| Plant and machinery at cost | 125 | |
| Motor vehicles at cost | 60 | |
| Accumulated depreciation – buildings | | 48 |
| Accumulated depreciation – plant | | 75 |
| Accumulated depreciation – vehicles | | 44 |
| Inventory at 1 April 20X6 | 128 | |
| Sales | | 1,300 |
| Purchases | 580 | |
| Bad debts | 17 | |
| Debenture interest | 3 | |
| Directors' remuneration | 115 | |
| Discounts allowed | 12 | |
| General expenses | 20 | |
| Heat and light | 34 | |
| Office expenses | 24 | |
| Rent | 27 | |
| Returns outwards | | 30 |
| Salaries and wages | 175 | |
| Allowance for doubtful debts | | 28 |
| Trade receivables | 750 | |
| Trade payables | | 160 |
| Bank | 15 | |
| Total | 2,295 | 2,295 |

The following information is also relevant:

1. Closing inventory is valued at €133m.
2. Electricity accrued is estimated to be €5m.
3. The last rent bill of €8m was paid in January 20X7 and was for the half-year to 30 June 20X7.
4. A staff bonus relating to the year ended 31 March 20X7 of €7m was paid in May 20X7.
5. Half-a-year's debenture interest is to be accrued.
6. Taxation for the year has been estimated at €83m.
7. Depreciation is to be charged on cost at the rate of:
   (i)   Buildings – 2% straight-line method.
   (ii)  Plant and machinery – 20% reducing balance method.
   (iii) Motor vehicles – 25% reducing balance method.
8. The company has been having problems with several debtors and it was decided that the allowance for doubtful debts is to be increased to 4% of outstanding debtors.

*You are required to* prepare an income statement for the year ended 31 March 20X7 and a balance sheet as at that date.

# Solution guide to appendix practice questions

## 1. Athens Ltd

### Cash at Bank

| | | | |
|---|---|---|---|
| Capital | 40,000 | Fittings | 22,000 |
| Sales | 16,000 | Wages | 8,000 |
| Loan | 5,000 | Drawings | 4,000 |
| | | Balance carried forward | 27,000 |
| | 61,000 | | 61,000 |
| Balance brought down | 27,000 | | |

### Sales account (€)

| | | | |
|---|---|---|---|
| | | Cash | 16,000 |
| Balance carried forward | 17,500 | Accounts receivable | 1,500 |
| | | | 17,500 |
| | 17,500 | Balance brought down | 17,500 |

### Wages expense account (€)

| | |
|---|---|
| Cash | 8,000 |

### Fittings (asset) account (€)

| | | | |
|---|---|---|---|
| Cash | 22,000 | | |
| A/cs payable | 10,000 | Balance carried forward | 32,000 |
| | 32,000 | | 32,000 |
| Balance brought down | 32,000 | | |

### Capital account (€)

| | | | |
|---|---|---|---|
| | | Cash | 40,000 |

### Drawings account (€)

| | |
|---|---|
| Cash | 4,000 |

### Loan account (€)

| | | | |
|---|---|---|---|
| | | Cash | 5,000 |

### Accounts Receivable

| | |
|---|---|
| Sales | 1,500 |

### Accounts payable

| | | | |
|---|---|---|---|
| | | Fittings | 10,000 |

## Athens: Trial balance at 31 January

| | Dr € | Cr € |
|---|---|---|
| Cash at bank | 27,000 | |
| Sales | | 17,500 |
| Wages | 8,000 | |
| Fittings | 32,000 | |
| Capital | | 40,000 |
| Drawings | 4,000 | |
| Loan | | 5,000 |
| Accounts receivable | 1,500 | |
| Accounts payable | | 10,000 |
| | 72,500 | 72,500 |

## Athens Ltd
### Income statement for the month of January

| | € |
|---|---|
| Sales (turnover) | 17,500 |
| Expenses | 8,000 |
| Profit | 9,500 |

### Balance sheet as at 31 January

| | | € |
|---|---|---|
| **Non-current assets** | | |
| Fittings | | 32,000 |
| **Current assets** | | |
| Accounts receivable | 1,500 | |
| Cash at bank | 27,000 | |
| | 28,500 | |
| **Current liabilities** | | |
| Accounts payable | 10,000 | |
| **Net current assets** | | 18,500 |
| **Non-current liabilities** | | |
| Borrowings | | 5,000 |
| | | 45,500 |
| **Equity** | | |
| Capital | | 40,000 |
| Add profit | | 9,500 |
| | | 49,500 |
| Less drawings | | −4,000 |
| | | 45,500 |

## 2. Beijing Ltd

### Cash at Bank

| | | | | | |
|---|---|---|---|---|---|
| 1 Mar | Capital | 50,000 | 2 Mar | Supplies | 5,000 |
| 5 Mar | Sales | 3,750 | 8 Mar | Wages | 1,600 |
| 9 Mar | Sales | 7,100 | 8 Mar | General expense | 400 |
| | | | 15 Mar | Wages | 2,300 |
| | | | 25 Mar | Best Supplies | 1,500 |
| 30 Mar | Sales | 6,100 | 28 Mar | Wages | 1,800 |
| | | | | Balance carried forward | 54,350 |
| | | 66,950 | | | 66,950 |
| | Balance brought down | 54,350 | | | |

### Sales account (€)

| | | | | |
|---|---|---|---|---|
| Balance carried forward | 22,150 | Cash | | 3,750 |
| | | Cash | | 7,100 |
| | | Accounts receivable | | 5,200 |
| | | Cash | | 6,100 |
| | 22,150 | | | 22,150 |
| | | Balance brought down | | 22,150 |

### Wages expense account (€)

| | | | | |
|---|---|---|---|---|
| Cash | 1,600 | | | |
| Cash | 2,300 | Balance carried down | | 5,700 |
| Cash | 1,800 | | | |
| | 5,700 | | | 5,700 |
| Balance brought down | 5,700 | | | |

### Supplies expense account (€)

| | | | | |
|---|---|---|---|---|
| Cash | 5,000 | | | |
| Best Supplies | 1,500 | Balance carried down | | 9,000 |
| Best Supplies | 2,500 | | | |
| | 9,000 | | | 9,000 |
| Balance brought down | 9,000 | | | |

### Capital account (€)

| | | | |
|---|---|---|---|
| Balance carried down | 55,000 | Cash | 50,000 |
| | | Rent | 5,000 |
| | | | 55,000 |
| | 55,000 | Balance brought down | 55,000 |

### Best Supplies account (€)

| | | | |
|---|---|---|---|
| Cash | 1,500 | Supplies | 1,500 |
| | | Supplies | 2,500 |

### Clean Co account (€)

| | | |
|---|---|---|
| | Laundry | 700 |

### General expenses

| | |
|---|---|
| Cash | 400 |

### Laundry expenses

| | |
|---|---|
| Clean Co | 700 |

### I Dance – Accounts Receivable

| | |
|---|---|
| Sales | 5,200 |

### Rent expense

| | |
|---|---|
| Capital | 5,000 |

## Beijing: Trial balance at 31 January

|  | Dr € | Cr € |
|---|---|---|
| Cash at bank | 54,350 |  |
| Sales |  | 22,150 |
| Wages | 5,700 |  |
| Supplies expense | 9,000 |  |
| Capital |  | 55,000 |
| Best Supplies |  | 2,500 |
| Clean Co. |  | 700 |
| I Dance | 5,200 |  |
| Rent | 5,000 |  |
| General expenses | 400 |  |
| Laundry expenses | 700 |  |
|  | 80,350 | 80,350 |

## Beijing Ltd
### Income statement for the month of March

|  | € | € |
|---|---|---|
| Sales (turnover) |  | 22,150 |
| Less |  |  |
| Rent | 5,000 |  |
| Provisions | 9,000 |  |
| Wages | 5,700 |  |
| General expenses | 400 |  |
| Laundry | 700 |  |
|  |  | 20,800 |
| Profit |  | 1,350 |

### Balance sheet as at 31 March

|  | € |
|---|---|
| **Current assets** |  |
| Accounts receivable | 5,200 |
| Cash at bank | 54,350 |
|  | 59,550 |
| **Current liabilities** |  |
| Accounts payable (2,500 + 700) | 3,200 |
| **Net current assets** | 56,350 |
| **Equity** |  |
| Capital | 55,000 |
| Add profit | 1,350 |
|  | 56,350 |

3. Cadiz Ltd

**Cadiz Ltd**
**Income statement for the year ended 31 December**

|  | €000 | €000 |
|---|---:|---:|
| Sales (turnover) |  | 5,750 |
| Less Cost of sales |  |  |
| Inventory 1 Jan | 250 |  |
| Purchases | 2,160 |  |
| Inventory 31 Dec | (380) |  |
|  |  | 2,030 |
| Gross profit |  | 3,720 |
| Light and heat | 570 |  |
| Wages | 1,200 |  |
| Rent | 800 |  |
| Office expenses | 320 |  |
|  |  | 2,890 |
| Net profit for the year |  | 830 |

**Cadiz Ltd**
**Balance sheet as at 31 December**

|  |  | €000 |
|---|---:|---:|
| **Non-current assets** |  |  |
| Fixtures and fittings |  | 285 |
| **Current assets** |  |  |
| Inventory | 380 |  |
| Accounts receivable | 450 |  |
| Cash at bank | 2,188 |  |
|  | 3,018 |  |
| **Current liabilities** |  |  |
| Accounts payable | 623 |  |
| **Net current assets** |  | 2,395 |
|  |  | 2,680 |
| **Non-current liabilities** |  |  |
| Borrowings |  | 500 |
|  |  | 2,180 |
| **Equity** |  |  |
| Capital |  | 1,350 |
| Add profit |  | 830 |
|  |  | 2,180 |

### 4. Dublin Ltd

**Dublin Ltd**
**Income statement for the year ended 31 December**

|  | €000 | €000 |
|---|---:|---:|
| Sales (turnover) | | 50,220 |
| Less Cost of sales: | | |
| Inventory 1 Jan | 400 | |
| Purchases | 18,750 | |
| Inventory 31 Dec | −500 | |
| | | 18,650 |
| Gross profit | | 31,570 |
| Less Expenses: | | |
| Office expenses | 3,610 | |
| Power | 7,185 | |
| Rent and rates | 6,200 | |
| Repairs | 3,116 | |
| Stationery | 350 | |
| Van expenses | 2,134 | |
| Wages | 4,520 | |
| | | 27,115 |
| Net profit for the year | | 4,455 |

**Dublin Ltd**
**Balance sheet as at 31 December**

|  |  | €000 |
|---|---:|---:|
| **Non-current assets** | | |
| Fixtures and fittings | | 23,230 |
| Motor van | | 8,050 |
| | | 31,280 |
| **Current assets** | | |
| Inventory | 500 | |
| Accounts receivable | 6,200 | |
| Cash at bank | 6,000 | |
| | 12,700 | |
| **Current liabilities** | | |
| Accounts payable | 4,525 | |
| | | 8,175 |
| **Net current assets** | | 39,455 |
| **Equity** | | |
| Capital | | 35,000 |
| Add profit | | 4,455 |
| | | 39,455 |

### 5. Edinburgh Ltd

|  |  |
|---|---:|
| Electricity bills paid during the year | 4,500 |
| Add: due for November and December | |
| = 2/3 × 1,500 | 1,000 |
| Expense for the year | 5,500 |
| | |
| Accrued expense as liability at year end | 1,000 |

### 6. Florence Ltd

| | Expense charged to income statement | Item outstanding on balance sheet | |
|---|---|---|---|
| (a) | 2,232 + 310 | 2,542 | 310 | Current liability |
| (b) | 5,400 − 760 | 4,640 | 760 | Current asset |
| (c) | 2,200 − 150 + 520 | 2,570 | 520 | Current liability |
| (d) | 5,760 + 400 − 280 | 5,880 | 280 | Current asset |

### 7. Geneva Ltd

Expense for year ended 31 June X1
$= 15,000 + 30,000 + (1/4 \times 72,000)$
$= 63,000$.

Current asset at 31 June X1
$= (3/4 \times 72,000)$
$= 54,000$.

### 8. Hobart Ltd

Depreciation charge
$=$ (Cost less residual value) / useful life
$= (200,000 − 40,000)$ / 5 years
$= 160,000$ / 5 years
$= 32,000$ per annum.

Recording entry will be:

*Debit* Depreciation expense (against income)
*Credit* Accumulated depreciation (against the cost of the asset)

| | Income Statement Depreciation exp. €000 | Balance sheet: Cost less accumulated depreciation €000 |
|---|---|---|
| Yr end 31 Dec X7 | 16 | 200 − 16 = 184 |
| Yr end 31 Dec X8 | 32 | 200 − 48 = 152 |
| Yr end 31 Dec X9 | 32 | 200 − 80 = 120 |
| Loss* on sale: 110 − 120 | 10 | 0 |

| * Loss on sale | Sale proceeds | €110,000 |
|---|---|---|
| | Less net book value | €120,000 |
| | | €10,000 |

### 9. Kiev Ltd

The machine is subject to a depreciation charge of €24,000 per annum, charged on a monthly basis.

■ Six months to 30 June 20X4, depreciation charge = 12,000

On 30th June 20X4, 4.5 years depreciation will have been charged = 108,000
Net book value will be 240,000 − 108,000 = 132,000
Sale proceeds of machine = 120,000

■ Loss on sale of machine = 12,000

On 31 December 20X4
■ Depreciation for six months on new vehicle = €120,000 × 25% × 6/12
= €15,000

Total charge for the year for fixed assets = €39,000

10. Lhasa Ltd

Adjustments should be recorded as follows:

| Detail | Debit € | Credit € |
|---|---|---|
| 1. Interest expense | 4,000 | |
|     Accrued expenses | | 4,000 |
| *Being the interest due for six months to 31 Dec X7* | | |
| 2. Long-term loan | 5,000 | |
|     Short-term loan (current liabilities) | | 5,000 |
| *Being the appropriate disclosure of the portion of the loan due for repayment in the next 12 months* | | |
| 3. Depreciation expense (selling and distribution) | 200,000 | |
|     Vehicles – accumulated depreciation | | 200,000 |
| *Being depreciation charged on vehicles* | | |
| 4. Plant and machinery | 75,000 | |
|     Accounts payable (current liabilities) | | 75,000 |
| *Being machine purchased on credit terms* | | |
| 5. Bad debts expense (selling and distribution) | 4,000 | |
|     Accounts receivable (current assets) | | 4,000 |
| *Being €4,000 bad debts written off* | | |
| 6. Power (cost of sales) | 12,000 | |
|     Accrued expenses (current liabilities) | | 12,000 |
| *Being the final quarter's cost of electricity* | | |
| 7. Taxation expense | 69,000 | |
|     Accrued expenses (current liabilities) | | 69,000 |
| *Being the taxation charge for the year (270 – 4 – 20 – 4 – 12 = 230 @ 30% = 69)* | | |

**Lhasa Ltd**
**Income statement for the year ended 31 Dec X7**

| | €000 |
|---|---|
| Sales | 2,180 |
| Cost of sales | 612 |
| Gross profit | 1,568 |
| Selling and distribution expense | 824 |
| Administrative expenses | 506 |
| Profit before interest | 238 |
| Interest | 8 |
| | 230 |
| Taxation | 69 |
| Profit for the year | 161 |

**Balance sheet as at 31 Dec X7**

|  |  | €000 |
|---|---|---|
| **Non-current assets** |  |  |
| Plant and machinery |  | 1,675 |
| Vehicles |  | 300 |
|  |  | 1,975 |
| **Current assets** |  |  |
| Inventory | 300 |  |
| Accounts receivable | 96 |  |
| Bank | 80 |  |
|  | 476 |  |
| **Current liabilities** |  |  |
| Accounts payable | 200 |  |
| Accrued expenses | 160 |  |
| Short-term loan | 5 |  |
|  | 365 |  |
| **Net current assets** |  | 111 |
|  |  | 2,086 |
| Long-term loan (8%) |  | 95 |
|  |  | 1,991 |
| **Capital and reserves** |  |  |
| Share capital |  | 1,320 |
| Retained earnings (510 + 161) |  | 671 |
|  |  | 1,991 |

## 11. Mumbai Ltd

Adjustments should be recorded as follows:

|  | Debit €000 | Credit €000 |
|---|---|---|
| 1. Closing inventory – current asset | 850 |  |
| Closing inventory from cost of sales |  | 850 |
| *Being inventory on hand at balance sheet date* |  |  |
| 2. Doubtful debt expense | 5 |  |
| Allowance for doubtful debts |  | 5 |
| *Being the adjustment required to give a balance of €15,000 on Allowance for Doubtful Debts account* |  |  |
| 3. Rent | 300 |  |
| Accrued expenses |  | 300 |
| *Being rent accrued at balance sheet date* |  |  |
| 4. Prepayments | 125 |  |
| Insurance |  | 125 |
| *Being insurance prepaid at balance sheet date* |  |  |
| 5. Depreciation expense | 52 |  |
| Furniture – accumulated depreciation |  | 52 |
| *Being depreciation charged on office furniture (1,040 × 5%)* |  |  |

**Mumbai Ltd**
**Income statement for the year ended 31 December**

|  | €000 | €000 |
|---|---|---|
| Sales |  | 9,642 |
| *Cost of sales* |  |  |
| Inventory at 1 January | 600 |  |
| Purchases | 5,020 |  |
| Inventory at 31 December | (850) |  |
|  |  | 4,770 |
| Gross profit |  | 4,872 |
| *Expenses* |  |  |
| Bad debts 21 + 5 | 26 |  |
| Insurance 864 − 125 | 739 |  |
| Light and heat | 1,226 |  |
| Printing and stationery | 731 |  |
| Professional fees | 860 |  |
| Wages | 2,196 |  |
| Rent 874 + 300 | 1,174 |  |
| Depreciation | 52 |  |
|  |  | 7,004 |
| Loss for the year |  | (2,132) |

**Mumbai Ltd**
**Balance sheet as at 31 December**

|  |  | €000 |
|---|---|---|
| **Non-current assets** |  |  |
| Premises |  | 6,200 |
| Furniture (1,040 − 272) |  | 768 |
|  |  | 6,968 |
| **Current assets** |  |  |
| Inventory | 850 |  |
| Accounts receivable (812 − 15) | 797 |  |
| Prepayments | 125 |  |
| Bank | 922 |  |
|  | 2,694 |  |
| **Current liabilities** |  |  |
| Accounts payable | 768 |  |
| Accrued expenses | 300 |  |
|  | 1,068 |  |
| **Net current assets** |  | 1,626 |
|  |  | 8,594 |
| **Capital and reserves** |  |  |
| Share capital |  | 10,726 |
| Retained earnings |  | (2,132) |
|  |  | 8,594 |

## 12. Nairobi Ltd

|  | Debit €000 | Credit €000 |
|---|---|---|
| 1. Closing inventory – current asset | 168 | |
|     Closing inventory from cost of sales | | 168 |
| *Being inventory on hand at balance sheet date* | | |
| 2. Wages and salaries | 7 | |
|     Accrued expenses | | 7 |
| *Being wages accrued at balance sheet date* | | |
| 3. Prepayments | 1 | |
|     Insurance | | 1 |
| *Being insurance prepaid at balance sheet date* | | |
| 4. Depreciation expense | 24 | |
|     Fixtures – accumulated depreciation | | 15 |
|     Buildings – accumulated depreciation | | 9 |
| *Being depreciation charged – 10% on fittings 150 and 2% on buildings 450* | | |
| 5. Doubtful debt expense | 1 | |
|     Allowance for doubtful debts | | 1 |
| *Being the adjustment required to give a balance of €4,000 on Allowance for Doubtful Debts account* | | |
| 6. Interest expense | 5 | |
|     Accrued expenses | | 5 |
| *Being second half-year's debenture interest accrued* | | |
| 7. Taxation expense | 30 | |
|     Accrued expenses | | 30 |
| *Being taxation accrued at balance sheet date* | | |

**Nairobi Ltd**
**Income statement for the year ended 31 Dec 20X7**

|  | €000 | €000 |
|---|---|---|
| Sales |  | 1,218 |
| Less returns inwards |  | 12 |
|  |  | 1,206 |
| *Cost of sales* |  |  |
| Opening inventory | 120 |  |
| Purchases | 660 |  |
| Add carriage in | 6 |  |
| Less returns out | −9 |  |
|  | 777 |  |
| Less closing inventory | 168 |  |
|  |  | 609 |
| Gross profit |  | 597 |
| Discounts received |  | 16 |
|  |  | 613 |
| **Expenses** |  |  |
| Audit fee | 16 |  |
| Repairs | 17 |  |
| Wages and salaries   220 + 7 | 227 |  |
| Discounts allowed | 18 |  |
| Insurance   5 − 1 | 4 |  |
| Bad debts   7 + 1 | 8 |  |
| General expenses | 55 |  |
| Directors' remuneration | 90 |  |
| Depreciation – buildings   2% × 450 | 9 |  |
| Depreciation – fixtures   10% × 150 | 15 |  |
|  |  | 459 |
| Profit before interest and tax |  | 154 |
| Interest (debentures 5 + 5) |  | 10 |
| Profit for the year before tax |  | 144 |
| Tax on profit for the year |  | 30 |
| Profit for the year |  | 114 |

**Nairobi Ltd**
**Balance sheet as at 31 Dec X7**

| | €000 | €000 | €000 |
|---|---|---|---|
| **Non-current assets** | Cost | Acc. Dep | |
| Land and buildings | 450 | 19 | 431 |
| Fixtures | 150 | 27 | 123 |
| | 600 | 46 | 554 |
| **Current assets** | | | |
| Inventory | | 168 | |
| Accounts receivable | 150 | | |
| Less allowance for doubtful debts | 4 | | |
| | | 146 | |
| Prepayments | | 1 | |
| Bank | | 51 | |
| | | 366 | |
| **Current liabilities** | | | |
| Trade payables | 80 | | |
| Accruals | 12 | | |
| Taxation | 30 | | |
| | | 122 | |
| Net current assets | | | 244 |
| Total assets less current liabilities | | | 798 |
| **Non-current liabilities** | | | |
| 10% debentures | | | 100 |
| | | | 698 |
| **Capital and reserves** | | | |
| Share capital | | | 500 |
| Share premium | | | 20 |
| Retained earnings (64 + 114) | | | 178 |
| | | | 698 |

13. Oslo Ltd

**Oslo Ltd**
**Income statement for the year ended 31 July 20X7**

|  | €000 | €000 |
|---|---|---|
| Sales |  | 1,244,000 |
| *Cost of sales* |  |  |
| Opening inventory | 165,000 |  |
| Purchases | 850,000 |  |
| Add carriage in | 5,000 |  |
| Less closing inventory | −180,000 |  |
|  |  | 840,000 |
| Gross profit |  | 404,000 |
| *Expenses* |  |  |
| Bad debts 6,000 + 1200 | 7,200 |  |
| Carriage out | 7,000 |  |
| Depreciation – buildings 2% × 320 | 6,400 |  |
| Depreciation – vehicles 20% × 312 | 62,400 |  |
| Depreciation – fixtures 10% × 60 | 6,000 |  |
| General administrative | 94,000 |  |
| General selling | 100,000 |  |
| Light and heat 9,000 + 500 | 9,500 |  |
| Rent 10,000 − 1,000 | 9,000 |  |
|  |  | 301,500 |
| Profit before interest and tax |  | 102,500 |
| Interest |  | 8,000 |
| Profit for the year before tax |  | 94,500 |
| Tax on profit for the year |  | 17,000 |
| Profit for the year |  | 77,500 |

**Oslo Ltd**
**Balance sheet as at 31 July 20X7**

|  | €000 | €000 | €000 |
|---|---|---|---|
| **Non-current assets** | Cost | Acc. Dep | |
| Land and buildings | 320,000 | 115,200 | 204,800 |
| Motor vehicles | 312,000 | 118,400 | 193,600 |
| Fixtures | 60,000 | 42,000 | 18,000 |
|  | 692,000 | 275,600 | 416,400 |
| **Current assets** | | | |
| Inventory | | 180,000 | |
| Trade receivables | 120,000 | | |
| Less allowance for doubtful debts | −1,200 | | |
|  | | 118,800 | |
| Prepayments | | 1,000 | |
| Cash in hand and at bank | | 58,800 | |
|  | | 358,600 | |
| **Current liabilities** | | | |
| Trade payables | 96,000 | | |
| Accruals | 12,500 | | |
| Taxation | 17,000 | | |
|  | | 125,500 | |
| Net current assets | | | 233,100 |
| Total assets less current liabilities | | | 649,500 |
| **Non-current liabilities** | | | |
| 5% debentures | | | 160,000 |
|  | | | 489,500 |
| **Capital and reserves** | | | |
| Share capital – preference | | | 100,000 |
| Share capital – ordinary | | | 200,000 |
| Share premium | | | 20,000 |
| Retained earnings (100,000 + 77,500 − 8,000) | | | 169,500 |
|  | | | 489,500 |

### 14. Penang Ltd

**Penang Ltd**
**Income statement for the year ended 31 July 20X7**

|  | €000 | €000 |
|---|---|---|
| Sales |  | 4,910 |
| Less returns inwards |  | −20 |
|  |  | 4,890 |
| *Cost of sales* |  |  |
| Opening inventory | 1,135 |  |
| Purchases | 2,695 |  |
| Add carriage in | 81 |  |
| Less returns outwards | −15 |  |
| Less closing inventory | −1,361 |  |
|  |  | 2,535 |
| Gross profit |  | 2,355 |
| Discounts received |  | 10 |
|  |  | 2,365 |
| *Expenses* |  |  |
| Audit fee (accrued) | 50 |  |
| Depreciation – buildings 2% × 5,500 | 110 |  |
| Depreciation – equipment 10% × 420 | 42 |  |
| Depreciation – vehicles 20% × 860 | 172 |  |
| Directors' remuneration | 315 |  |
| Discount allowed | 8 |  |
| General expense | 28 |  |
| Motor expense | 406 |  |
| Insurance 147 − 7 | 140 |  |
| Salaries and wages | 312 |  |
|  |  | 1,583 |
| Profit before interest and tax |  | 782 |
| Interest (75 + 75) |  | 150 |
| Profit for the year before tax |  | 632 |
| Tax on profit for the year |  | 80 |
| Profit for the year |  | 552 |

**Penang Ltd**
**Balance sheet as at 31 July 20X7**

| | €000 | €000 | €000 |
|---|---|---|---|
| **Non-current assets** | Cost | Acc. Dep | |
| Land and buildings | 5,500 | 190 | 5,310 |
| Equipment | 420 | 142 | 278 |
| Vehicles | 860 | 370 | 490 |
| | 6,780 | 702 | 6,078 |
| **Current assets** | | | |
| Inventory | | 1,361 | |
| Trade receivables | | 1,080 | |
| Prepayments | | 7 | |
| Cash at bank | | 709 | |
| | | 3,157 | |
| **Current liabilities** | | | |
| Trade payables | 569 | | |
| Accruals (75 + 50) | 125 | | |
| Taxation | 80 | | |
| | | 774 | |
| Net current assets | | | 2,383 |
| Total assets less current liabilities | | | 8,461 |
| **Non-current liabilities** | | | |
| 10% debentures | | | 1,500 |
| | | | 6,961 |
| **Capital and reserves** | | | |
| Share capital | | | 4,500 |
| Share premium | | | 700 |
| Retained earnings (1,384 + 552 − 175) | | | 1,761 |
| | | | 6,961 |

15. Shanghai Ltd

**Shanghai Ltd**
**Income statement for the year ended 31 Mar 20X7**

|  | €m | €m |
|---|---|---|
| Sales |  | 1,300 |
| *Cost of sales* |  |  |
| Opening inventory | 128 |  |
| Purchases | 580 |  |
| Less returns outwards | −30 |  |
| Less closing inventory | −133 |  |
|  |  | 545 |
| Gross profit |  | 755 |
| *Expenses* |  |  |
| Bad and doubtful debts (17 + 2) | 19 |  |
| Depreciation – buildings | 4 |  |
| Depreciation – plant | 10 |  |
| Depreciation – vehicles | 4 |  |
| Directors' remuneration | 115 |  |
| Discount allowed | 12 |  |
| General expense | 20 |  |
| Office expense | 24 |  |
| Power and light (34 + 5) | 39 |  |
| Rent (27 − 4) | 23 |  |
| Salaries and wages (175 + 7) | 182 |  |
|  |  | 452 |
| Profit before interest and tax |  | 303 |
| Interest (3 + 3) |  | 6 |
| Profit for the year before tax |  | 297 |
| Tax on profit for the year |  | 83 |
| Profit for the year |  | 214 |

**Shanghai Ltd**
**Balance sheet as at 31 Mar 20X7**

|  | €m | €m | €m |
|---|---|---|---|
| **Non-current assets** | Cost | Acc. Dep |  |
| Land and buildings | 210 | 52 | 158 |
| Equipment | 125 | 85 | 40 |
| Vehicles | 60 | 48 | 12 |
|  | 395 | 185 | 210 |
| **Current assets** |  |  |  |
| Inventory |  | 133 |  |
| Trade receivables (less provision) |  | 720 |  |
| Prepayments |  | 4 |  |
| Cash at bank |  | 15 |  |
|  |  | 872 |  |
| **Current liabilities** |  |  |  |
| Trade payables | 160 |  |  |
| Accruals | 15 |  |  |
| Taxation | 83 |  |  |
|  |  | 258 |  |
| Net current assets |  |  | 614 |
| Total assets less current liabilities |  |  | 824 |
| **Non-current liabilities** |  |  |  |
| 10% debentures |  |  | 60 |
|  |  |  | 764 |
| **Capital and reserves** |  |  |  |
| Share capital |  |  | 200 |
| Retained earnings (350 + 214) |  |  | 564 |
|  |  |  | 764 |

# An outline of the content of International Financial Reporting Standards

This appendix summarizes the content of IASs extant in late 2009.

## IAS 1 Presentation of Financial Statements

This standard was revised in 1997 and superseded the old IAS 1, IAS 5 and IAS 13. It was revised again several times up to 2007. The components of financial statements are the balance sheet, statement of comprehensive income, statement of changes in equity, cash flow statement, and notes (paragraph 10). Fair presentation is required and this may sometimes entail departure from an IFRS, which departure must then be disclosed including its numerical effect (paragraph 15).

The going concern assumption must be assessed for each set of financial statements, and departed from (in a disclosed way) when appropriate (paragraph 25). Offsetting is only allowed when specifically permitted by another standard (paragraph 32). Comparative information must be given relating to the previous period (paragraph 38).

The current/non-current distinction is preferred, but not presumed (paragraph 60). There are no required formats but there are lists of minimum contents of financial statements. There are also illustrations of formats in an appendix.

## IAS 2 Inventories

Inventories should be valued at the lower of cost and net realizable value (paragraph 9). Cost includes all costs to bring the inventories to their present condition and location (paragraph 10). Where specific cost is not appropriate, FIFO or weighted average is required.

## IAS 3 Replaced by IAS 27

## IAS 4 Withdrawn, because the content (on depreciation) is covered by asset standards (particularly IAS 16 and IAS 38).

## IAS 5 Replaced by IAS 1.

**IAS 6** Replaced by IAS 15.

## IAS 7 Cash Flow Statements

Cash flow statements are required (paragraph 1). They should classify cash flows into operating, investing and financial activities (paragraph 10). Cash and cash equivalents include short-term investments subject to insignificant risk of changes in value (paragraph 6).

Either the direct or indirect method is allowed (paragraph 18). Cash flows from taxes should be disclosed separately, within one of the three headings (paragraph 35).

## IAS 8 Accounting Policies, Changes in Accounting Estimates and Errors

Changes in policy should follow specific transitional provisions. If none, then they should be applied retrospectively, by adjusting the earliest presented opening balance of retained earnings (paragraph 19). The same applies to the correction of errors (paragraph 42).

**IAS 9** Replaced by IAS 38.

## IAS 10 Events after the Reporting Date

Events occurring after the reporting (balance sheet) date that provide additional information on conditions existing at that date should lead to adjustment of the financial statements (paragraph 8). However, disclosure should be made for other events, if necessary for proper evaluation (paragraph 21). Proposed dividends should not be accrued (paragraph 12).

## IAS 11 Construction Contracts

There is no reference to the length of a contract in its definition, but there is a requirement that the contract should be specifically negotiated (paragraph 3).

When the outcome of such a contract can be estimated reliably, revenues and costs should be estimated by stage of completion. Expected losses should be recognized (paragraph 22). The conditions for reliable estimation are (paragraph 23):

(a) revenue can be reliably measured;
(b) it is probable that the benefits will flow to the entity;
(c) future costs and stage of completion can be measured reliably; and
(d) costs can be identified and measured reliably.

If the outcome cannot be measured reliably, costs should be expensed and revenues should be recognized in line with recoverable costs (paragraph 32).

## IAS 12 Income Taxes

'Temporary differences' are differences between the carrying amount of an asset or liability and its tax base (paragraph 5). Deferred tax assets and liabilities should be recognized for temporary differences except when relating to goodwill (unless the amortization is tax-deductible) or certain transactions with no effect on tax or accounting profit (paragraphs 15 and 24). Deferred tax assets should not be accounted for unless sufficient future taxable income is probable (paragraphs 24 and 34). Certain deferred tax assets and liabilities relating to group companies should be recognized where the temporary differences will reverse (paragraphs 39 and 44).

Current and deferred tax assets and liabilities should use enacted or substantially enacted tax rates (paragraphs 46 and 47). Deferred tax assets and liabilities should not be discounted (paragraph 53).

Current and deferred taxes should be recognized as income or expense except to the extent that they relate to transactions not recognized in income or expense (paragraph 58).

## IAS 13 Replaced by IAS 1.

## IAS 14 Replaced by IFRS 8.

## IAS 15 Withdrawn.

## IAS 16 Property, Plant and Equipment

Property, plant and equipment (PPE) should be recognized when (i) it is probable that future benefits will flow from it, and (ii) its cost can be measured reliably (paragraph 7).

Initial measurement should be at cost (paragraph 15). Subsequently, cost or an up-to-date fair value by class of assets (paragraphs 30, 31 and 36). Revaluations should be credited to 'other comprehensive income' unless reversing a previous charge to profit and loss. Decreases in valuation should be charged to profit and loss unless reversing a previous credit to 'other comprehensive income' (paragraphs 39 and 40).

Gains or losses on retirement or disposal of an asset should be calculated by reference to the carrying amount (paragraph 71).

## IAS 17 Leases

Finance leases are those that transfer substantially all risks and rewards to the lessee (paragraph 4). Finance leases should be capitalized by lessees at the lower of the fair value and the present value of the minimum lease payments (paragraph 20).

Rental payments should be split into (i) a reduction of liability, and (ii) a finance charge designed to reduce in line with the liability (paragraph 25). Depreciation on leased assets should be calculated using useful life, unless there is no reasonable certainty of eventual ownership. In this latter case, the shorter of useful life and lease term should be used (paragraph 27).

Operating leases should be expensed on a systematic basis (paragraph 33).

For lessors, finance leases should be recorded as receivables (paragraph 36). Lease income should be recognized on the basis of a constant periodic rate of return (paragraph 39). The net investment method should be used (paragraph 39).

For sale and leaseback that results in a finance lease, any excess of proceeds over carrying amount should be deferred and amortized over the lease term (paragraph 59).

## IAS 18 Revenue

Revenue should be measured at fair value of consideration received or receivable (paragraph 9). Revenue should be recognized when (paragraph 14):

(a) significant risks and rewards are transferred to the buyer;
(b) managerial involvement and control have passed;
(c) revenue can be measured reliably;
(d) it is probable that benefits will flow to the entity; and
(e) costs of the transaction can be measured reliably.

For services, similar conditions apply by stage of completion when the outcome can be estimated reliably (paragraph 20).

## IAS 19 Employee Benefits

For defined contribution plans, the contributions of a period should be recognized as expenses (paragraph 44).

For defined benefit plans, the liability should be the total of the present value of the obligation, plus unrecognized actuarial gains, minus unrecognized past service costs, and minus the fair value of plan assets (paragraph 54). The income statement charge should be the total of current service cost, interest cost, expected return on assets, actuarial gains recognized, past service cost recognized, and the effect of curtailments and settlements (paragraph 61).

The actuarial valuation method is specified (one called the 'projected unit credit' method) (paragraph 64). The discount rate used should be based on the market yield on high-quality corporate bonds (paragraph 78).

Actuarial gains and losses can be taken directly to OCI or can be recognized on an amortization basis in income when they exceed 10 per cent of the obligation (or the fund, if greater). The amortization should be over the remaining working lives of employees in the plan (paragraph 93). Past service cost should be recognized over the period until the benefits are vested (paragraph 96).

## IAS 20 Government Grants

Grants should not be credited directly to reserves but should be recognized as income in a way matched with the related costs (paragraphs 7 and 12). Grants related to assets should be deducted from the cost or treated as deferred income (paragraph 24).

## IAS 21 The Effects of Changes in Foreign Exchange Rates

An entity should report in its functional currency, namely the currency of the primary economic environment in which it operates (paragraphs 8 and 9). A foreign currency transaction is initially recognized by applying the spot exchange rate at the date of the transaction (paragraph 21).

At the end of each subsequent period, monetary items are translated at the closing rate. Non-monetary items are translated at the date of the historical transaction, or the date of the fair value measurement if relevant (paragraph 23). Exchange differences are generally taken to profit or loss (paragraph 28).

Translation from the functional currency to a different presentation currency is permitted (paragraphs 38–43).

## IAS 22 Business Combinations

Replaced by IFRS 3.

## IAS 23 Borrowing Costs

Borrowing costs directly attributable to construction, etc. must be capitalized (paragraph 8). SIC Interpretation 2 requires entities to use the chosen treatment uniformly.

In cases of capitalization, where funds are specifically borrowed, the borrowing costs should be calculated after any investment income on temporary investment of the borrowings (paragraph 12). If funds are borrowed generally, then a capitalization rate should be used based on the weighted average of borrowing costs for general borrowings outstanding during the period. Borrowing costs capitalized should not exceed those incurred (paragraph 14).

Capitalization should commence when expenditures and borrowing costs are being incurred and activities are in progress to prepare the asset for use or sale (paragraph 17). Suspension should occur when active development is suspended for extended periods, and cessation should occur when substantially all activities are complete (paragraphs 20 and 22).

## IAS 24 Related Party Disclosures

Related parties are those able to control or exercise significant influence, although some exceptions are noted (paragraphs 9 and 11). Relationships and transactions should be disclosed (paragraphs 12 and 17).

## IAS 25 Replaced by IAS 39 and IAS 40.

## IAS 26 Reporting by Retirement Benefit Plans

This standard relates to accounting and reporting by retirement benefit plans themselves, not by employers. Separate rules are set out for defined benefit plans and defined contribution plans.

## IAS 27 Consolidated and Separate Financial Statements

A subsidiary is defined as one entity controlled by another entity (paragraph 4). Certain intermediate parent companies are exempted from preparing consolidated accounts (paragraph 8).

All subsidiaries must be included (paragraph 12).

The reporting dates of consolidated companies should be no more than three months different from the parent's (paragraph 23).

In parent financial statements, subsidiaries may be shown at cost or treated as available-for-sale investments (paragraph 38).

## IAS 28 Investments in Associates

An associate is an entity over which the investor has significant influence, i.e. the power to participate in financial and operating policy decisions (paragraph 2). This is a rebuttable presumption when there is a holding of 20 per cent or more in the voting rights (paragraph 6).

Associates should be accounted for by the equity method in consolidated accounts, unless held for disposal in the near future (paragraph 13). In parent company accounts, associates can be held at equity or as long-term investments (paragraph 35).

## IAS 29 Financial Reporting in Hyperinflationary Economies

Hyperinflation is indicated by several features, including cumulative inflation over three years of 100 per cent or more (paragraph 3).

Financial statements (including corresponding figures) should be presented in a measuring unit that is current at the balance sheet date (paragraph 8).

## IAS 30 Disclosures by Banks etc

Replaced by IFRS 7.

## IAS 31 Reporting Interests in Joint Ventures

A joint venture is a contractual arrangement subject to joint control (paragraph 3).

Jointly controlled *operations* should be recognized by including the assets controlled and the liabilities and expenses incurred by the venturer and its share of income (paragraph 15). Jointly controlled *assets* should be recognized on a proportional basis (paragraph 21).

In the consolidated financial statements, jointly controlled *entities* should be recognized (paragraphs 30 and 38). Using proportionate consolidation or the equity method.

However, interests held for resale should be treated in accordance with IFRS 5.

## IAS 32 Financial Instruments: Presentation

Financial instruments should be classified by issuers into liabilities and equity, which includes splitting compound instruments into these components (paragraphs 15 and 28).

Financial assets and liabilities can be set off when there is a legally enforceable right and an intention to do so (paragraph 42).

## IAS 33 Earnings per Share

The standard applies to entities with publicly traded shares (paragraph 2).

Basic earnings per share (EPS) should be calculated using (i) the net profit or loss attributable to ordinary shareholders, and (ii) the weighted average number of ordinary shares outstanding in the period (paragraph 10). The weighted average should be adjusted for all periods presented for events (e.g. bonus issues) that change the number of shares but not the resources (paragraph 19).

Diluted EPS should adjust earnings and shares for all dilutive potential ordinary shares (paragraph 31).

Presentation of basic and diluted EPS should be on the face of the statement of comprehensive income (paragraph 66).

## IAS 34 Interim Financial Reporting

This standard is not mandatory but might be imposed by stock exchange authorities, for example (paragraph 1).

The minimum contents of an interim report should be a condensed statement of financial position; statement of comprehensive income, presented as either (i) a condensed single statement or (ii) a condensed separate income statement and a condensed statement of comprehensive income; statement of changes in equity; statement of cash flows; and selected explanatory notes (paragraph 8). Minimum contents of the statements and the notes are specified (paragraphs 10 and 16). Prior period data should be presented (paragraph 20).

The frequency of reporting should not affect the annual results (paragraph 28). In most ways, the end of a period should be treated as the end of a year (paragraphs 28, 37 and 39).

## IAS 35 Discontinuing Operations

Replaced by IFRS 5.

## IAS 36 Impairment of Assets

Entities are required to check at each balance sheet date whether there are any indications of impairment; several examples are given (paragraphs 9 and 12). When there is an indication of impairment, an entity should calculate the asset's recoverable amount, which is the larger of its net selling price and its value in use. The latter is equivalent to the discounted expected net cash inflows, which should be calculated for the smallest group of assets (cash generating unit) for which the calculation is practicable (paragraph 66).

If the asset's recoverable amount is less than its carrying value, an impairment loss must be recognized (paragraph 59). Impairment losses should first be allocated to goodwill (paragraph 104). Impairment losses should be reversed under certain circumstances (paragraph 110).

## IAS 37 Provisions, Contingent Liabilities and Contingent Assets

A provision is defined as a liability of uncertain timing or amount. A liability requires there to be an obligation at the balance sheet date (paragraph 10). Provisions should be recognized unless a reliable estimate cannot be made or the possibility of outflow is unlikely (paragraph 14).

Contingent liabilities (where there is no obligation or where there is no reliable measure or no probability of outflow) should not be recognized as liabilities but disclosed, unless remote (paragraphs 10, 27 and 28). Contingent assets should not be recognized (paragraph 31).

## IAS 38 Intangible Assets

Intangible assets should be recognized where it is probable that benefits will flow to the entity and cost can be measured reliably (paragraph 21).

Internally generated goodwill must not be capitalized (paragraph 48). Research and many other internally generated intangibles cannot meet the above recognition criteria (paragraphs 63 and 68). Development expenditure might sometimes meet the criteria, and more detailed guidance is given on this (paragraph 57). Costs treated as expenses cannot subsequently be capitalized (paragraph 71).

Intangible assets for which there is an active market can be carried at fair value (paragraph 75).

Annual impairment tests are required for assets with no finite life (paragraph 108), but amortization is not permitted (paragraph 107).

## IAS 39 Financial Instruments: Recognition and Measurement

All financial assets and liabilities, including derivatives, should be recognized on the balance sheet unless covered by other IASs (paragraph 2).

Financial assets should be held at fair value except that the following should be held at cost:

(a)  loans and receivables originated by the entity and not held for trading;
(b)  held-to-maturity investments; and
(c)  assets whose fair value cannot be measured reliably (paragraph 46).

Financial liabilities should be held at cost, except that fair value should be used for those held for trading and for derivatives (paragraph 47).

There is an option to treat certain financial investments at fair value.

Gains and losses should be recognized in income, except that non-trading items are taken to equity (paragraph 55).

Hedge accounting is permitted under certain circumstances for derivatives and (only for foreign currency risks) for other financial instruments. The hedges must be designated and effective (paragraph 71).

## IAS 40 Investment Property

Investment property is held to earn rentals or for capital appreciation, rather than being owner-occupied (paragraph 5).

427

Initial measurement should be at cost, and there should be subsequent capitalization of expenditure that improves the originally assessed standard of performance (paragraphs 17 and 20). There should then be an entity-wide choice of the fair-value model or the cost model (paragraph 30). Under the first of these, gains and losses are taken to income (paragraph 35). If, under the fair value model, fair value of a particular property is not determinable at the beginning, then cost should be used (paragraph 53).

Transfers to owner-occupied property or inventory should take place at fair value (paragraph 60). Transfers to investment property should treat the initial change to fair value as a revaluation under IAS 16 (paragraph 61).

Under the cost model, fair value should be disclosed (paragraph 79).

## IAS 41 Agriculture

This standard covers all biological assets to the point of harvest (paragraphs 1 and 3). Such assets are measured at fair value less point-of-sale costs (paragraph 12). If fair value is not reliably determinable, then cost should be used (paragraph 30).

Agricultural produce is measured at harvest at fair value less point-of-sale costs, which then becomes the cost for inventory accounting (paragraph 13).

Gains and losses on changes in fair value should be taken to income when their conditions are met (paragraph 26).

## IFRS 1 First-time Adoption of International Financial Reporting Standards

This standard relates to entities that, for the first time, give an explicit and unreserved statement of compliance with IFRS (paragraph 3). An entity has to prepare an opening balance sheet for the earliest period presented that is in accordance with the standards ruling at the reporting date (paragraph 6). No other versions of standards are relevant. The transitional provisions of standards are not relevant. A series of exemptions are allowed, e.g. for business combinations (paragraph 18). A few retrospective applications are not allowed, e.g. related to hedge accounting (paragraph 13).

A reconciliation is required from accounting under the old rules to the opening IFRS balance sheet (paragraph 23).

## IFRS 2 Share-based Payments

Share-based payments should be recognized as an expense unless an asset is recognized. The payments can be settled in cash or in shares. The former give rise to liabilities; the latter to equity. The recognition should take place as the goods or services are received (paragraphs 7 and 8). Share-settled payments should be recognized at fair value: of the goods or services (for non-employees) or of the equity (for employees) (paragraph 10).

No adjustment should be made if shares or share options are forfeited or not exercised after vesting date (paragraph 23).

## IFRS 3 Business Combinations

All business combinations should be treated as purchases (paragraph 4). Goodwill is the difference between the fair value of the consideration given and the fair value of the subsidiary's assets, liabilities and contingent liabilities (paragraph 32). Any resulting contingent liabilities should continue to be recognized despite IAS 37 (paragraph 56).

Goodwill should be tested annually for impairment; negative goodwill should be recognized as income immediately (paragraph 54).

## IFRS 4 Insurance Contracts

This standard applies to insurance contracts whatever sort of company holds them (paragraph 2).

Insurers are temporarily exempted from the general requirements of IAS 8 on accounting policies. This is pending a full standard on insurance contracts (paragraph 13). Changes to policies are only allowed if the resulting information is more relevant (paragraph 22). A liability adequacy test is required (paragraph 15).

## IFRS 5 Non-current Assets Held for Sale and Discontinued Operations

Non-current assets should be classified as held for sale if expected to be sold within one year (paragraphs 6–8). They should be shown separately on the balance sheet at the lower of carrying value and fair value less costs to sell (paragraph 15).

A discontinued operation is a separate major line of business that has been disposed of or is classified as held for sale (paragraph 32). The statement of comprehensive income should show a single amount for all items related to discontinued operations (paragraph 33).

## IFRS 6 Exploration for and Evaluation of Mineral Resources

Pending a full standard on this subject, entities are exempted from certain requirements of IAS 8 on accounting policies (paragraph 7). Measurement of assets should follow IAS 16 (paragraph 12).

A special rule on impairment applies, which allows cash-generating units to be as large, but not larger than, a segment (paragraph 21).

## IFRS 7 Financial Instruments: Disclosures

All types of entities are required to make disclosures about financial instruments on a wide range of issues, including fair values (paragraph 25), credit risk (paragraph 36), liquidity risk (p. 39) and market risk (p. 40).

## IFRS 8 Operating Segments

Unusually, this standard applies only to entities whose debt or equity is publicly traded (paragraph 2).

The IFRS requires an entity to report financial and descriptive information about its reportable segments. Reportable segments are operating segments or aggregations of operating segments that meet specified criteria (paragraphs 5–10). Operating segments are components of an entity about which separate financial information is available that is evaluated regularly by the chief operating decision maker in deciding how to allocate resources and in assessing performance. Generally, financial information is required to be reported on the same basis as is used internally for evaluating operating segment performance and deciding how to allocate resources to operating segments.

## IFRS 9 Financial Instruments

On 12 November 2009, the IASB issued IFRS 9 *Financial Instruments*, as a first step in the eventual replacement of IAS 39. IFRS 9 introduces new requirements for classifying and measuring financial assets (note only assets) that must be applied from 1 January 2013, early adoption being permitted. IFRS 9 is expected to be 'expanded' before the end of 2010.

IFRS 9 divides all financial assets covered by IAS 39 into two classifications (instead of four), those measured at amortised cost and those measured at fair value. This note, added as we go to press, is likely to be out of date when you read it, and you should check for later developments regarding IFRS 9.

# Appendix C

# An outline of the content of the EU's Fourth Directive on Company Law (as amended in 2001, 2003, etc.)

Article 1 states that the Directive relates to public and private companies throughout the European Community, except that member states need not apply the provisions to banks, insurance companies and other financial institutions (for whom a special version of the Fourth Directive has been prepared). Article 2 defines the annual accounts to which it refers as the balance sheet, profit and loss account, and notes. Reference to cash flow or funds flow statements, which are standard in some countries (e.g. Spain and the United Kingdom), is omitted. The accounts 'shall be drawn up clearly and in accordance with the provisions' of the Directive, except that the need to present a 'true and fair view' may require extra information or may demand a departure from the provisions of the Directive. Such departures must be disclosed. The Directive is intended to establish minimum standards, and 'Member States may authorize or require' extra disclosure.

Articles 3–7 contain general provisions about the consistency and detail of the formats for financial statements. There is a specified order of items, and some items cannot be combined or omitted. Corresponding figures for the previous year must be shown. Articles 8–10 detail two formats for balance sheets, one or both of which may be allowed by member states. These Articles allow some combination and omission of immaterial items, but the outline and much detail will be standard. In 2003, an extra option was added: to present using a current/non-current basis.

Articles 11 and 12 allow member states to permit small companies to publish considerably abridged balance sheets. 'Small companies' are those falling below two of the following limits: employees, 50; and balance sheet total and turnover thresholds (specified in EC unit of account), which are raised from time to time. There is also the possibility of lesser reductions for 'medium-sized companies' (see Articles 27 and 47), whose size limits are also capable of being raised, and this happened in 1984 and 1990. Articles 13 and 14 concern details of disclosure. Articles 15–21 concern the definition and disclosure of assets and liabilities. It is useful that downward adjustments in value must be disclosed (Article 15(3)(a)); this might make clearer the comparatively conservative revaluations that are common in Franco-German systems.

Articles 22–26 specify four formats for profit and loss accounts, which member states may allow companies to choose between. Two of these classify expenses and revenues by nature, and the other two classify them by stage of production. There are two in each case because vertical or two-sided versions may be chosen. However, Article 27 allows member states to permit medium-sized companies to avoid disclosure of the items making up gross profit. In this case the limits are employees, 250, and thresholds for balance sheet total and turnover, which are double those for small companies. Articles 28–30 contain some definitions relating to the profit and loss accounts.

Articles 31 and 32 set out general rules of valuation. The normal principles of accounting (including the accruals convention) are promulgated. Article 33 is a fairly lengthy series of member-state options on accounting for inflation or for specific price changes. Whatever happens, member states must ensure that historical cost information is either shown or can be calculated using notes to the accounts. However, member states may permit or require supplementary or main accounts to be prepared on a replacement value, current purchasing power or other basis. Revaluation of assets would entail a balancing revaluation reserve; there are detailed requirements relating to this. In 2001 and 2003, member state options were added in order to allow fair values to be used for various assets and for gains and losses to be taken to income.

Articles 34–42 relate to detailed valuation and disclosure requirements for various balance sheet items. Again, the point about the disclosure of 'exceptional' value adjustments is made, this time with specific reference to taxation-induced writings down (Articles 35(1)(d) and 39(1)(e)). The periods over which research and development expenditure and goodwill are written off are regulated (Article 37).

Articles 43–46 concern the large number of disclosures that are obligatory in the annual report, including the notes to the accounts. 'Small companies' (as in Article 11) may be partially exempted. Articles 47–51 relate to the audit and publication of accounts. In general, procedures for these matters may remain as they were under different national laws. Member states may exempt 'small companies' from publishing profit and loss accounts (Article 47(2)(b)) and from audit (Article 51). This would mean that they would only produce unaudited abridged balance sheets. Article 47(3) allows members states to permit 'medium-sized companies' (as in Article 27) to abridge their balance sheets and notes. However, this abridgement is not as extensive as that for 'small companies', and both audits and profit and loss accounts are necessary.

Articles 52–62 deal with the implementation of the Directive and with transitional problems – particularly those relating to consolidation – that awaited the EU Seventh Directive. A 'Contact Committee' was to be set up to facilitate the application of the (Fourth, then also the Seventh) Directive and to advise on amendments or additions. Article 55 called for member states to pass the necessary laws within two years of the July 1978 notification, and then to bring these into force within a further 18 months. (As Table 5.12 shows, no country managed the first of these dates.)

# Appendix D

# Feedback on exercises

## Use of exercises

We have attempted to provide a wide variety of exercises without excessive volume or uninteresting repetition. There are different views on the advantages and disadvantages of giving suggested feedback on the exercises in the book. **Our policy is to give outline feedback here only to the first one or two exercises for each chapter.** Outline feedback on the remaining exercises is available for teachers elsewhere, as described in the Preface.

The exercises examine many of the points made in the chapters themselves, and provide an opportunity to develop the flexible and critical thinking that is so necessary for the understanding of accounting practice. Readers with a particular focus on interpreting financial statements, rather than preparing them, may sensibly omit some of the longer technical exercises.

It is clearly desirable to tackle an exercise thoroughly before looking at our own suggestions. Equally, the feedback given should be regarded as an input into the thinking and the discussion. It should never be regarded as automatically correct, and should never be used to stifle alternative viewpoints.

## Chapter 1

1.1 Theoretically, certainly. Financial accounting can provide useful information and therefore lead to more efficient and effective decision making by outside users. However, it is only justified in practice if:

(a) the information is actually useful;
(b) the information is actually used;
(c) the costs of producing and circulating the information do not exceed its benefits.

This may mean that financial reporting to outsiders is more likely to be justified for large companies with many shareholders than for small enterprises where there are only a few owners, who are also the managers.

1.2 Pointers towards the various likely information needs are given in the text (see Section 1.1), and significant differences of need or emphasis are suggested there. One solution would be just to provide more and more information, but this leads to acute problems of confusion and misunderstanding (as well as cost). Separate reports for different purposes? A general report ideal for nobody? Note that *managers* are usually considered separately, via management accounting, and that *tax authorities* may use a different set of rules from those for financial accounting.

## Chapter 2

2.1 (a) F's balance sheets (in euros) are as follows:

| | 31.12.X7 | 31.12.X8 |
|---|---|---|
| | € | € |
| Freehold shop | 135,000 | 135,000 |
| Delivery vans | 10,000 | 10,000 |
| Inventory of goods | 32,000 | 29,000 |
| Amounts owed by customers | 35,000 | 34,000 |
| Cash at bank | 19,000 | 36,000 |
| Cash | 500 | 2,000 |
| | 231,500 | 246,000 |
| **Capital** | **154,200** | **174,000** |
| Loans | 50,000 | 50,000 |
| Amounts owed to supplier | 26,500 | 21,250 |
| Wages owed to staff | 800 | 750 |
| | 231,500 | 246,000 |

The missing item was the **capital** at the relevant date.

(b) For 20X7, the opening capital was €150,000 and the closing capital was €154,200. The increase presumably represents the profit for the year of €4,200. Similarly, for 20X8, the profit would appear to be €174,000 − €154,200 = €19,800. Note that the capital figure is cumulative; its total increase from €150,000 to €174,000 represents the combined profits of the two years.

(c) If enterprise F paid €15,000 during 20X7 to the owner, the 31.12.X7 capital figure would be the net figure *after* deducting the dividend paid. This gives (in euros) for 20X7:

$$150,000 + \text{profit} - 15,000 = 154,200$$

The conclusion would therefore be that profits for the year 20X7 must have been €19,200.

(d) In several possible senses the delivery vans could be expected to be less good resources as they become older. It could be argued that some of the original new vans must have been used up during the operations of the two years. This might suggest that the assets figure, particularly for 20X8, is overstated, assuming that no new vans had been purchased. This would mean that the profit figure is also overstated. Think of possible ways of allowing for this, before the problem is considered more formally later.

2.2 Suggested adjustments are shown in the figure below. Alternative answers are not necessarily wrong. For example, consider item (g). Historically, practice here has differed sharply between different countries. In some countries, such as the United Kingdom, it has been normal practice to reduce retained profit by such intended future dividends, adding the figure to creditors, presumably on the grounds that the profit is not intended to be retained, and that a current liability exists by intention. However, it can be argued that company G has not yet done anything, merely indicated a future intention. If nothing has been done, and the formal process of 'declaring' the dividend has not yet happened, then no entries should be made, according to International Accounting Standards. In many countries, e.g. Germany, it has long been normal practice not to make any adjustment at all.

|  |  | (a) | (b) | (c) | (d) | (e) | (f) | (g) |
|---|---|---|---|---|---|---|---|---|
| Shares | 50,000 |  |  |  |  |  |  |  |
| Retained profit | 7,000 | +1,200 | −400 |  |  | +300 |  |  |
| Creditors | 12,000 |  |  | −8,000 |  |  |  |  |
|  | 69,000 |  |  |  |  |  |  |  |
| Premises | 20,000 |  |  |  |  |  |  |  |
| Equipment | 9,000 |  |  |  |  |  | −400 |  |
| Vehicle | 7,000 |  |  |  | −7,000 |  |  |  |
| Inventory | 15,500 | −2,800 |  |  |  |  |  |  |
| Debtors | 2,500 | +1,000 |  |  |  | −2,500 |  |  |
| Bank | 14,700 |  | −400 | −5,000 | +7,000 | +2,000 |  |  |
| Cash | 300 | +3,000 |  | −3,000 |  | +500 | +700 |  |
|  | 69,000 |  |  |  |  |  |  |  |

## Chapter 3

3.1  There is scope for wide differences of view, and considerable debate. For users, comparability seems vital because it relates to the basic decision-making purpose. Faithful representation also reaches the heart of the matter. We suspect that objectivity and prudence are likely to come higher up the 'importance' scale for accountants and auditors than they are up the 'useful' scale. This would lead to discussion of whether the user matters more or the producer matters more!

3.2  This is quite a complicated issue. Terms need to be defined, as in the text, and then explained in commonsense non-technical terms (not so easy). Perhaps the fundamental idea behind the problem here can be highlighted by posing another question: If a uniform accounting treatment is imposed for some particular transaction or type of contract based on its superficial legal form is this:

(a)  good, because uniformity automatically leads to comparability; or
(b)  bad, because the information given is likely to be irrelevant to the particular situations involved, and therefore the information cannot adequately allow comparison between those situations?

There is clearly scope for discussion here. One conclusion might be that if the substance of transactions is the same, then a uniform approach should be required. This suggests that preparers need mechanisms for identifying the substance.

## Chapter 4

4.1  There is scope for discussion here, and the background of those discussing the issue is likely to influence opinions. Note that it is necessary to discuss the objectives of financial accounting first, and agreement on this may not be reached. However, if the objective is to provide useful information to large numbers of outside investors in a fast-changing world, there seem to be good arguments for private-sector standard setting. This may fit better in a common law context. Nevertheless, an enforcement mechanism is of great importance, and some government involvement is probably needed here. However, a government regulatory agency (e.g. the SEC in the United States) is compatible with a common law system.

4.2  Here again, opinions may differ. Essentially, arguments for private-sector standards would include factors such as expertise, professionalism, speed and flexibility. Arguments for legal rules would include factors such as precision, and control by the state, which is supposed to democratically represent the people as a whole.

## Chapter 5

5.1  The basic thesis is this:

1. In all countries, the government will be interested in the calculation of profit in order to calculate taxable income and prudently distributable profit.
2. Financial reporting rules in a country tend to be driven by large companies because they exercise the greatest influence over the rule-makers.
3. In countries with large numbers of listed companies that have large numbers of non-director shareholders, there will be a demand for large quantities of published, audited financial information used for making financial decisions.
4. In these countries, the government's accounting/tax rules will be unsuitable for financial reporting, and so accounting calculations will have to be done twice.
5. In other countries, a few large 'international' companies may volunteer to use non-tax rules for group accounts.

If, for example, the United Kingdom and the United States are countries as described in point (3) above, whereas Germany and Italy are not, the financial reporting will differ.

5.2  The users are addressed in Chapter 1. The beneficiaries from harmonization might be split into (a) users and (b) preparers. Governments might be seen to be users for the purposes of tax collection, but they also might wish to help users and preparers. The same applies to intergovernmental organizations, such as the European Union.

Users include investors and lenders who operate across national borders. These would include institutions, such as banks. Companies, in their capacity as purchasers of shares in other companies or as analysts of suppliers or customers, would also gain from harmonization.

Preparers of multinational financial statements would gain from simplifications, and they would also benefit as users of their own accounting information from various parts of the group. Accountancy firms are sometimes seen as beneficiaries, but at present they gain work as auditors and consultants from the existence of international differences.

In terms of who is doing what to bring about harmonization, the picture is initially confusing, because the greater beneficiaries are seen to be doing little; that is, users are not sufficiently aware or sufficiently organized to address the problem. Preparers are too busy to act because they are trying to cope with – or to take advantage of – all the differences. However, some senior businessmen put public and private pressure on accountants to reduce differences. This is most notable in the case of companies such as the oil company Shell, which is listed on several exchanges and tries to produce one annual report for all purposes.

Governments are nevertheless taking action. For example, the harmonization programme in the EU was active in the 1970s and 1980s. Also, the International Organization of Securities Commissions (IOSCO) is a committee of government agencies that has put considerable backing behind the IASB.

Perhaps the harmonizing body with the highest profile is the IASB, whose predecessor (the IASC) was committee of accountancy bodies that is largely controlled by the auditing professions. Of course, the international differences severely complicate the work of some auditors. However, there is an element of paradox in the fact that auditors are the most active in trying to remove lucrative international differences.

The influence of the IASB is increasing rapidly, as outlined in Section 5.6, but many difficulties lie ahead.

## Chapter 6

6.1  The structure of an answer here requires, first, a discussion of what the needs of financial statement users are, as outlined in Chapter 1, and, second, an outline of aspects of disclosure as in Chapter 6. An argued opinion should follow. Note that your views on the adequacy of disclosure requirements may be influenced by your ranking of user needs, and that your views may change as your studies develop.

Assuming that sophisticated investors are seen as the main users, it is relevant that the old IASC board contained representatives of the financial analysis profession for many years. From 2001, three of the fourteen board members are selected from this background. This suggests that serious note is taken of their professed needs.

Perhaps, for unsophisticated shareholders, IFRS statements provide an unnecessary amount of data.

6.2  In essence, the two formats highlight different subtotals, total assets for the horizontal format and net assets for the vertical format, and you should consider the differing importance and usefulness of these. Note that it is possible to conclude that the choice of format does not matter much, because users can rearrange the numbers. Note also that, in practice, local law or custom may make the decision for you.

## Chapter 7

7.1 The five required ratios for each company are set out in the table below:

|  | P | Q |
|---|---|---|
| $\dfrac{\text{gross profit}}{\text{turnover}}$ | $\dfrac{9{,}000}{45{,}000} = 20\%$ | $\dfrac{8{,}182}{40{,}909} = 20\%$ |
| $\dfrac{\text{net operating profit}}{\text{turnover}}$ | $\dfrac{5{,}000}{45{,}000} = 11\%$ | $\dfrac{4{,}091}{40{,}909} = 10\%$ |
| $\dfrac{\text{net profit}}{\text{owners' equity}}$ | $\dfrac{4{,}000}{34{,}000} = 12\%$ | $\dfrac{3{,}901}{28{,}250} = 14\%$ |
| ROCE | $\dfrac{5{,}000}{44{,}000} = 11\%$ | $\dfrac{4{,}901}{38{,}250} = 13\%$ |
| gearing | $\dfrac{10{,}000}{34{,}000} = 29\%$ | $\dfrac{10{,}000}{28{,}250} = 35\%$ |

Although P and Q appear somewhat similar in overall profile, Q shows itself to be more efficient in its operations and use of resources through the third and fourth ratios. On the other hand, Q has a higher gearing ratio which would tend to make potential future lenders slightly more wary of Q than of P, other things being equal.

7.2

|  | 20X2 (€000) | 20X3 (€000) |
|---|---|---|
| **Workings:** |  |  |
| Turnover (T) | 541 | 675 |
| *less* Cost of sales | 369 | 481 |
| Gross profit (GP) | 172 (derived) | 194 (derived) |
| GP/T | (172 × 100)/541 = 31.8% | (194 × 100)/675 = 28.7% |
| Closing reserves | 53 | 82 |
| Dividends proposed | 20 | 30 |
|  | 73 | 112 |
| *less* Opening reserves | 21 | 53 |
| Net profit (NP) | 52 (derived) | 59 (derived) |
| NP/T | (52 × 100)/541 = 9.6% | (59 × 100)/675 = 8.7% |
| T/NAE | 541/303 = 1.8 × | 675/432 = 1.6 × |
| NP/NAE | (52 × 100)/303 = 17.2% | (59 × 100)/432 = 13.7% |
| CA/CL | 188/92 : 1 = 2.0 : 1 | 269/162 : 1 = 1.7 : 1 |
| QA/CL | 102/92 : 1 = 1.1 : 1 | 92/162 : 1 = 0.6 : 1 |

GP/T   The deterioration could be due to a rise in purchase prices not passed on in increased selling prices and/or a change in sales mix, etc.

NP/T   Roughly in line with the decline in GP/T, it could also be caused by high administration and/or sales expenses.

T/NAE   The full-year effect of the increased investment has not yet materialized. In addition, year-end inventories have doubled, possibly indicating a build-up for a promotional drive.

NP/NAE   The decline is attributable to the combined effects of the two preceding ratios.

CA/CL   Working capital has increased, notably due to inventory and debtors. The inventory build-up, partly financed by an increase in creditors, has been noted above and this may be coupled with a planned (or lax) credit control.

QA/CL   The increased investment has produced a liquidity problem.

## Chapter 8

8.1   See text (Sections 2.2 and 8.1), but avoid the unthinking use of technical phrases and formal definitions. Remember that it would be possible to define the terms differently from the IASB's definitions. Also, remember that not all elements meet the criteria for recognition in financial statements.

8.2   (a) No, traditional financial accounting based on the historical cost convention does not make the going concern convention unnecessary. Indeed, traditional and current practice rely heavily on the going concern convention. Inventory is evaluated on the assumption that it will eventually be sold in the ordinary course of business. Fixed assets are depreciated over their estimated useful lives to the business, and this requires the assumption that the business will continue to operate over the period of those lives. Prepayments assume that the firm will operate and use the service acquired, for the whole basis of the accruals convention is that the business is a continuing operation. The going concern convention is, therefore, crucial to current accounting practice even though that practice is based on the historical cost convention.

(b) The reason why a shareholder needs a report at all is to use the report to influence some future action or decision. If this is not so, then the shareholder has no important use for the report, whatever its contents. However, the above does not strictly answer the question. The shareholder may well find a report on past events extremely useful as a guide to predicting future outcomes and future trends. Equally, however, the shareholder may find management's estimate of future events to be directly useful. Perhaps the short answer to the question is 'both'!

## Chapter 9

9.1   A (non-current) fixed asset may be distinguished from other types of asset insofar as it has all of the following characteristics:

■ it is intended to be held by an entity for use in the production or supply of goods and services on a continuing basis;
■ it is intended to have a life of more than one accounting period;
■ it is not intended for sale in the ordinary course of business.

In a full answer, all these points could be illustrated.

9.2   The proposition as stated is certainly defensible. On the other hand, it could be suggested that:

(a) past information can be relevant if it improves the quality of estimates about the future;

(b) management cannot be allowed to produce its own estimates because they might introduce biases, and accountants must therefore seek to confine themselves as far as possible to 'facts'.

Of course, even conventional accounting has large amounts of 'future' in it. For example, the definitions of 'asset' and 'liability' involve expectations. Also, estimates of the future are needed in order to measure change in, for example:

- receivables (expected receipts);
- depreciation (expected lives of assets);
- pension liabilities (expected lives and future pay levels of employees – see Chapter 11).

## Chapter 10

10.1 The inventory figure for production cost of manufactured items can certainly never be reliable in the sense that it involves no estimates. However, it can be precisely determined and precisely calculated, once the necessary arbitrary assumptions about overhead behaviour have been made. Such precision could be seen as improving comparability, and therefore relevance.

10.2 (a) **Violas.** Since the inventory is reduced to nil by 30 September, profits under all historical cost assumptions will be the same, as differences in calculated profit arise only because of different assumptions about usage. Thus we have a unified result for requirements (i)–(iii):

|  | € |
| --- | --- |
| Sales | 2,700 |
| Cost of sales | 1,750 |
| Gross profit | 950 |
| Value of closing inventory | 250 |

(iv) However, under replacement cost:

|  |  | € | € |
| --- | --- | --- | --- |
| Sales |  |  | 2,700 |
| Cost of sales | 31 March | 400 |  |
|  | 30 June | 350 |  |
|  | 30 September | 900 |  |
|  |  |  | 1,650 |
| Operating profit |  |  | 1,050 |
| Holding loss realized | 1 April | 50 |  |
|  | 30 November | 50 |  |
|  |  |  | 100 |
| Gross profit |  |  | 950 |

**Cellos**

(i) FIFO

|  | € | € |
|---|---|---|
| Sales |  | 3,200 |
| Purchases | 3,600 |  |
| Closing inventory |  |  |
| (1 @ 800) |  |  |
| (1 @ 900) | 1,700 | 1,900 |
| Gross profit |  | 1,300 |

(ii) LIFO

|  | € | € |
|---|---|---|
| Sales |  | 3,200 |
| Purchases | 3,600 |  |
| Closing inventory |  |  |
| (1 @ 600) |  |  |
| (1 @ 900) | 1,500 | 2,100 |
| Gross Profit |  | 1,100 |

(iii) Weighted average calculation:

| Inventory to 30 June: | |
|---|---|
| 2 @ 600 | = 1,200 |
| 1 @ 700 | = 700 |
| 3 | 1,900 |

30 June weighted average = 633 (i.e. 1,900 ÷ 3)

| 2 @ 633 | = 1,266 |
|---|---|
| 1 @ 800 | = 800 |
| 3 | 2,066 |

30 September weighted average = 689 (i.e. 2,066 ÷ 3)

| 1 @ 689 | = 689 | |
|---|---|---|
| 1 @ 900 | = 900 | |
| 2 | 1,589 | (closing inventory) |

|  | € |
|---|---|
| Sales | 3,200 |
| Cost of sales |  |
| 1 @ 633 |  |
| 2 @ 689 | 2,011 |
| Gross profit | 1,189 |

(iv) Replacement cost calculation:

| | | | |
|---|---|---|---|
| As at 30 June: replacement cost of inventory | = 3 × 700 | = | 2,100 |
| Profit on sale | | = | 300 |
| Holding gains | | = | 200 |
| As at 30 September: replacement cost of inventory | = 3 × 800 | = | 2,400 |
| Profit on sale | | = | 600 |
| Holding gains | | = | 200 |
| As at 30 November: replacement cost of inventory | = 2 × 900 | = | 1,800 |
| Holding gain | | = | 100 |
| Total operating profit | | = | 900 |
| Total holding gains | | = | 500 |

(b) In relation to the various methods:

  (i) FIFO seems to produce more up-to-date costs in the balance sheet;
  (ii) LIFO seems to produce more up-to-date expense figures in the income calculation;
  (iii) the weighted average method achieves neither of the above, or a bit of both, depending on your attitude;
  (iv) the use of replacement cost achieves both, at the cost of more complexity and more subjectivity if actual replacement costs are used (rather than the price of the most recent purchase).

## Chapter 11

11.1 This should cause a bit of thought. What about depreciation provisions and provisions for possible bad debts? These are likely to be shown as deductions on the asset side of the balance sheet, because they might better be described as 'allowances' or 'value adjustments'. The proper word in IFRS for the bad debts is 'impairments'. However, what about receipts for sales already received where the sale has not yet been made? Presumably, these could be seen as amounts owing to customers. Furthermore, a problem occurs with the treatment of government grants received in relation to assets. These are often shown as 'deferred income', which is presented outside equity. This treatment seems doubtful, but the topic is beyond the scope of this book.

11.2 The point is that, if provisions are overstated, then expenses and liabilities are too large. This makes profit (and therefore reserves) too small. This can be called the creation of secret reserves. The point is almost certainly overstated in the question, but the general direction of the argument is surely correct. Human attitude will always be a factor, but 'whim' can be influenced and perhaps controlled by the creation of professional norms and practices. Some would argue that legal or centrally inspired accounting plans can remove the human element, but others might reply that such plans are purely arbitrary and are indeed themselves created by human whim. There is scope for debate here!

# Chapter 12

12.1 Of course, tax regulations in any country are likely to affect the economic behaviour of managers. This would be reflected in the accounts. However, let us assume that the question refers to a more direct effect of tax on accounting practices.

One would expect major influence in countries where accounting rules must follow tax rules or where they tend to follow tax rules (because of the absence of accounting rules on a particular issue or because of the need to establish deductibility for tax purposes or to avoid taxable gains). This issue is addressed in Chapter 5 of the text.

It is clear that the effect of tax on asset valuation provisions and depreciation is larger in Germany than it is in the United Kingdom, for example. In general, in many continental European countries, because tax calculations are based closely on accounting numbers, tax minimization involves avoiding upward valuations, maximizing depreciation within the tax limits, seeking ways of writing down assets, and increasing provisions. To a large extent, such activities would have little effect on tax liabilities in the United Kingdom or the United States. Furthermore, companies in capital-market countries would be wary of the potential commercial disadvantages of making their financial statements look less attractive.

In principle, it ought to be possible to relieve the group accounts from some of these pressures, because such statements are not relevant for tax purposes in most countries. The EU Seventh Directive allows group accounts to use different rules from parent accounts. In 1998, laws were passed in Germany and several other countries enabling the use of international standards in consolidated statements, and this became compulsory for EU listed companies for 2005 onwards.

12.2

| Year | 1 | 2 | 3 | 4 |
|---|---|---|---|---|
| *Tax balances* | | | | |
| Asset balance 1 January | 7,000 | 9,600 | 12,480 | 15,584 |
| Additions | 5,000 | 6,000 | 7,000 | — |
| Depreciation (20%) | 2,400 | 3,120 | 3,896 | 3,117 |
| Balance 31 December | 9,600 | 12,480 | 15,584 | 12,467 |
| *Accounting balance* | | | | |
| 31 December (as question) | 13,500 | 17,550 | 22,095 | 19,885 |
| Temporary difference | 3,900 | 5,070 | 6,511 | 7,418 |
| Deferred tax liability | 1,170 | 1,521 | 1,302 | 1,484 |
| Effect on income statement | | −351 | +219 | −182 |

## Chapter 13

13.1  The statement that expenses and revenues are subjective is in general correct, although there can be very large variations in degree of subjectivity. For example, the wages expense is not very subjective but the depreciation expense is. Whilst past cash flows are facts in the sense that they have demonstrably happened, their timing – and, indeed, their existence – can be manipulated by management. For example, management could make cash flow look good by:

(a) postponing the purchase of necessary fixed assets;
(b) selling fixed assets that are needed;
(c) selling valuable investments that had originally been intended to be held for the long term;
(d) borrowing money just before the year end and paying it back just after;
(e) postponing all payments in the last month of the year until the first day of next year.

The implications for trend considerations of such manipulation could be considerable.

13.2  The first major figure to look at is the net cash flow provided by operating activities, of 3,608 millions, which is larger than the operating earnings, mainly because of the depreciation charges which have no cash effect. An amount of almost equal size has been used in net investing activities, which can be expected to lead to future profits and positive cash flows. The interest and dividends paid are both sizable but the creation of new debt exceeds the retirement of old debt by some 1,500 millions. The net effect of all this is that the cash and cash equivalents figures between the start and the end of the year have fallen by some 450 millions. They also still seem large. Perhaps a key issue is what Bayer intends to do with all this money.

## Chapter 14

14.1  See text, but briefly:

(a) a subsidiary implies control through shareholding or dominant influence;
(b) a joint venture implies joint control by two or more parties;
(c) an associate implies significant influence, without control or dominant influence;
(d) an investment in shares implies a relatively passive role, with no significant influence.

With a subsidiary, the usual approach is consolidation, including complete combination of individual enterprise accounting statements, with the necessary recognition of minority interests. With an associate, the usual approach is equity accounting, where the investment figure is increased by the appropriate proportion of the success of the associate, i.e. in effect a one-line proportional consolidation. With a joint venture, equity accounting is common, but so is line-by-line proportional consolidation. With an investment in shares, no benefits are taken in the consolidated accounts except for dividends.

Note that there may be practical difficulties of differentiation that underlie the above apparently straightforward distinctions.

14.2    **Consolidated balance sheet as at 30.6.X8**

|  | €000 |
|---|---|
| *Assets* | |
| Goodwill (Note 1) | 50 |
| Land and plant | 1,200 |
| Inventory (1,000 − 10) | 990 |
| Debtors (240 − 2) | 238 |
|  | 2,478 |
| *Liabilities* | |
| Creditors (46 − 2) | 44 |
|  | 2,434 |
| *Represented by* | |
| Ordinary €1 shares | 1,000 |
| Reserves (Note 2) | 1,280.5 |
|  | 2,280.5 |
| Non-controlling interest (Note 3) | 153.5 |
|  | 2,434 |

| **Note 1** | € | € |
|---|---|---|
| Cost of investment in B | | 275 |
| *less* ordinary shares acquired | 75 | |
| reserves acquired 75% × 200 | 150 | 225 |
| Goodwill on acquisition | | 50 |

| **Note 2** | | |
|---|---|---|
| Reserves A | | 1,045 |
| Reserves since acquisition of B | | |
| 75% (524 − 10 − 200) | | 235.5 |
|  | | 1,280.5 |

| **Note 3** | | |
|---|---|---|
| Non-controlling interest | | |
| 25% ordinary shares | | 25 |
| 25% reserves = 25% × 514 | | 128.5 |
|  | | 153.5 |

# Chapter 15

15.1  (a)                                    **Loan–Debtor**

| | € | | € |
|---|---|---|---|
| Year 1 | 10,000 | Loss on loan | 500 |
|  | | Balance carried down | 9,500 |
|  | 10,000 | | 10,000 |
| Year 2 balance brought down | 9,500 | | |
| Gain | 1,000 | Balance carried down | 10,500 |
|  | 10,500 | | 10,500 |
| Year 3 balance brought down | 10,500 | Cash | 10,600 |
| Gain | 100 | | |
|  | 10,600 | | 10,600 |

(b) The transactions would be handled thus:

- Year 1, loss of €500 taken to profit and loss.
- Year 2, gain of €1,000 taken to profit and loss.
- Year 3, gain of €100 taken to profit and loss.

The year 1 treatment is supported by both matching and prudence.

The year 2 treatment proposed here is much more debatable. It is supported by the matching convention and also by the consistency convention, but it clearly goes against prudence. A middle approach would be to take €500 of the year 2 gain to the income statement (to reverse the loss in year 1) and to take the remaining €500 to reserves. Different approaches are allowed in different countries, and they can all be both defended and criticized. The IASB would require the treatment suggested in the bullet points above.

The year 3 treatment is surely generally acceptable, because the whole thing is now history. The gain is fully realized under any criteria.

15.2 (a) *Closing rate method*

**Income statement for year to 31 December 20X0**

|  | Rate of exchange | FC |
|---|---|---|
| Net profit | 2 | 150 |
| Taxation | 2 | 75 |
|  |  | 75 |
| Dividend | 2 | 30 |
|  |  | 45 |

**Balance sheet as at 31 December 20X0**

|  | Rate of exchange | FC | FC |
|---|---|---|---|
| Fixed assets | 2 |  | 165 |
| Inventory | 2 | 180 |  |
| Debtors | 2 | 120 |  |
|  |  | 300 |  |
| Creditors | 2 | 120 | 180 |
|  |  |  | 345 |
| Ordinary share capital | 3 |  | 200 |
| Retained profits (from above) |  |  | 45 |
| Reserves – exchange difference |  |  | 100 |
|  |  |  | 345 |

(b) *Temporal rate method*

### Income statement for year 31 December 20X0

|  | Rate of exchange | FC | FC |
|---|---|---|---|
| Sales | 2.5 |  | 600 |
| Opening inventory | 3 | 80 |  |
| Purchases | 2.5 | 480 |  |
|  |  | 560 |  |
| Closing inventory | 2 | 180 | 380 |
|  |  |  | 220 |
| Depreciation | 3 |  | 40 |
|  |  |  | 180 |
| Taxation | 2 |  | 75 |
|  |  |  | 105 |
| Dividends | 2 |  | 30 |
|  |  |  | 75 |
| Gain on exchange (from balance sheet) |  |  | 15 |
|  |  |  | 90 |

### Balance sheet as at 31 December 20X0

|  | Rate of exchange | FC | FC |
|---|---|---|---|
| Fixed assets | 3 |  | 110 |
| Inventory | 2 | 180 |  |
| Debtors | 2 | 120 |  |
|  |  | 300 |  |
| Creditors | 2 | 120 | 180 |
|  |  |  | 290 |
| Ordinary share capital | 3 |  | 200 |
| Retained profits (75 + balance 15) |  |  | 90 |
|  |  |  | 290 |

# Chapter 16

16.1 (a) *Historical cost accounting*

| Income statements for the years: | 20X0 | 20X1 |
|---|---|---|
|  | € | € |
| Sales | 3,000 | 3,600 |
| Cost of sales | (2,000) | (2,000) |
| Gross profit | 1,000 | 1,600 |
| Expenses (rent) | (600) | (700) |
| Net profit | 400 | 900 |
| Tax | (200) | (450) |
| Retained profit | 200 | 450 |

| Balance sheets at year ends: | 20X0 | | 20X1 |
|---|---|---|---|
| Inventory | € | | € |
| @ 1,000 (4) | 4,000 | (2) | 2,000 |
| @ 1,200 (2) | 2,400 | (2) | 2,400 |
| @ 1,400 (0) | 0 | (2) | 2,800 |
| | 6,400 | | 7,200 |
| Cash | 3,800 | | 3,450 |
| | 10,200 | | 10,650 |
| Capital | 10,000 | | 10,000 |
| Retained profits | 200 | | 650 |
| | 10,200 | | 10,650 |

(b) *Replacement cost accounting*

| Income statements for the years: | 20X0 | | 20X1 |
|---|---|---|---|
| | € | | € |
| Sales | 3,000 | | 3,600 |
| Cost of sales | (2,200) | | (2,600) |
| Gross profit | 800 | | 1,000 |
| Expenses (rent) | (600) | | (700) |
| Operating profit | 200 | | 300 |
| Tax paid | (200) | | (450) |
| Current cost profit/(loss) | 0 | | (150) |
| Realized holding gain (2 × 100) | 200 | (2 × 300) | 600 |
| Historical cost profit | 200 | | 450 |

| Balance sheets at year ends: | 20X0 | | 20X1 |
|---|---|---|---|
| Inventory | € | | € |
| @ 1,300 (6) | 7,800 | (0) | 0 |
| @ 1,400 (0) | 0 | (6) | 8,400 |
| | | | |
| Cash | 3,800 | | 3,450 |
| | 11,600 | | 11,850 |
| Capital | 10,000 | | 10,000 |
| Realized holding gain | 200 | | 800 |
| Distributable profits | 0 | | (150) |
| Unrealized holding gain | 1,400 | | 1,200 |
| | 11,600 | | 11,850 |

(c) The figures show that, given an intention to continue the operations of the business at the current level, the historical cost profit figure is misleading. Indeed, in the second year the business has an operating loss on the replacement cost basis.

16.2

**Duck Co. balance sheet as at 31 December 20X0**

|  | € |  | € |
|---|---|---|---|
| Fixed assets: | 12,600 | Shareholders' interest: | |
| *less* Depreciation | 1,260 | Shares | 10,000 |
| | 11,340 | | |
| Current assets: | | Profit | (20) |
| Inventory | 4,000 | Holding gains | 3,600 |
| Cash | 10,000 | | 950   4,550 |
| | 8,000 | | 14,530 |
| | 47,900 | Loan | 8,000 |
| | (9,000) | Current liabilities: | |
| | (35,550) | Creditors | 960 |
| | (13,200)   8,150   12,150 | | |
| | 23,490 | | 23,490 |

**Income statement for the year to 31 December 20X1**

|  | € |  | € |
|---|---|---|---|
| Purchases | 8,000 | Sales | 7,200 |
| | 8,250 | | 10,800 |
| | 8,500 | | 15,600 |
| | 10,800   35,550 | | 14,300   47,900 |
| Holding gains | 950 | | |
| | 36,500 | | |
| Closing inventory (40 × 100) | 4,000 | | |
| | 32,500 | | |
| Gross profit carried down | 15,400 | | |
| | 47,900 | | 47,900 |
| General expenses | 13,200 | Gross profit brought down | 15,400 |
| Loan interest | 960 | | |
| Depreciation | 1,260 | Net loss carried down | 20 |
| | 15,420 | | 15,420 |

Inventory holding gains are calculated as follows:

| | | |
|---|---|---|
| 1 March | $100 - 60 = 40 \times (-5) =$ | (200) |
| 1 June | $210 - 150 = 60 \times 10 \ =$ | 600 |
| 1 September | $310 - 280 = 30 \times 5 \ \ \ =$ | 150 |
| 1 December | $430 - 390 = 40 \times 10 \ =$ | 400 |
| | | 950 |

Holding gains are those gains, or credit balances, caused by increases in the recorded figures of resources over the period during which they are held by a business. They cause an increase in the ownership claims on the business, but have not arisen as the result of a transaction.

Whether or not any particular holding gains are to be regarded as distributable is a function of the capital maintenance assumption adopted. As discussed in the text of the chapter, the numerical increase in resources represented by the holding gain will need to be used in the replacement of the original resources once they have been used. If, therefore, the capital maintenance concept being used is the maintenance of the current operating capability of the business, then the holding gains are not available for distribution as dividend. Note that this logic follows whether or not the holding gains are 'realized' through the sale of the original resource.

## Chapter 17

17.1  (a)  Nine ratios are readily available:

|  | A | B |
|---|---|---|
| Gearing | $\dfrac{100}{200} = 50\%$ | $\dfrac{130}{650} = 20\%$ |
| Working capital | $\dfrac{180}{160} = 9{:}8$ | $\dfrac{200}{120} = 5{:}3$ |
| Quick assets | $\dfrac{100}{160} = 62\%$ | $\dfrac{100}{120} = 83\%$ |
| ROE | $\dfrac{30}{100} = 30\%$ | $\dfrac{100}{520} = 19\%$ |
| ROCE | $\dfrac{30 + 10}{200} = 20\%$ | $\dfrac{100 + 13}{650} = 17\%$ |
| $\dfrac{\text{Gross profit}}{\text{sales}}$ | $\dfrac{600}{1{,}000} = 60\%$ | $\dfrac{1{,}000}{3{,}000} = 33\%$ |
| $\dfrac{\text{Net profit}}{\text{sales}}$ | $\dfrac{30}{1{,}000} = 3\%$ | $\dfrac{100}{3{,}000} = 3\%$ |
| $\dfrac{\text{Debtors} \times 365}{\text{sales}}$ | $\dfrac{100 \times 365}{1{,}000} = 36 \text{ days}$ | $\dfrac{90 \times 365}{3{,}000} = 11 \text{ days}$ |
| $\dfrac{\text{Creditors} \times 365}{\text{Cost of sales}}$ | $\dfrac{110 \times 365}{400} = 100 \text{ days}$ | $\dfrac{120 \times 365}{2{,}000} = 22 \text{ days}$ |

(b)  Although A and B have very similar net profit to sales percentages, they reach this point in different ways. A has a high gross profit percentage (lower turnover, higher margin) and a higher ROCE. Its materially higher gearing ratio turns this slightly higher ROCE into a considerably higher ROE. From a shareholder viewpoint, most of this makes A sound preferable to B. But it should be remembered that B has more 'slack' in its structure. A lender might well feel happier granting further loans to B, because it has a lower gearing ratio and better liquidity ratios. A's debtors' payback and – particularly, and, worryingly – creditors' payback periods are much higher.

It must be noted that B's balance sheet includes a large revaluation of its land. This is a major inconsistency and distorts the figures considerably. In terms of return on original investments, ROE and ROCE for B are considerably understated. Perhaps more usefully in terms of return on current value invested, ROE and ROCE for A are overstated.

## Chapter 18

18.1  Now you are on your own. It isn't easy, but it is what real-life international accounting is all about!

# Glossary of terms

*This glossary is primarily written in English as used by the International Accounting Standards Board. This is largely British English, although we include many cross-references to US English. Many continental European companies translate their financial statements into a form of mid-Atlantic English.*

*Terms used in an entry that are themselves defined elsewhere in the glossary are shown in small capitals.*

**accelerated depreciation** DEPRECIATION that is either at a faster rate than would be suggested by an asset's expected life or using methods that charge proportionately more depreciation in earlier years. This is most commonly found in the context of tax concessions designed to encourage investment. For the calculation of taxable income in such cases, businesses would be allowed to depreciate certain assets (such as energy-saving devices or assets in depressed regions) more quickly than accountants otherwise would. This occurs in many countries.

**account** A record of all the bookkeeping entries relating to a particular item. For example, the wages account would record all the payments of wages. An account in the double-entry system has a debit side (left) and a credit side (right). Often accounts are referred to as T-accounts because of the rulings on the page that divide the left from the right and underline the title. Of course, pages have now generally been replaced by spaces on a computer disk. A business may have thousands of accounts, including one for each DEBTOR and CREDITOR.

In the early days of accounting, there were only personal accounts (for people who owed and were owed money). Later, there were 'real' accounts for property of various sorts; and 'nominal' accounts for impersonal, unreal items like wages and electricity. Accounts may be collected together in groups in ledgers, or books of account.

'Accounts' may also mean financial statements, such as BALANCE SHEETS and INCOME STATEMENTS.

**accountability** The major original purpose of accounting; so that the owners of resources (now shareholders, for example) can check up on the managers or stewards of those resources (now boards of directors, for example).

**accountancy and accounting** Terms used interchangeably by many people. However, in the United Kingdom it tends to be, for example, the *accountancy* profession, but management *accounting*. That is, accountancy tends to be associated with the profession, and accounting with the subject matter, particularly in the context of education or theory. In the United States, the word 'accountancy' is rarer.

**accounting policies** The detailed methods of valuation and measurement that a particular company has chosen from those generally accepted by law, accounting standards or commercial practice. These policies must be used consistently from item to similar item and, generally, from year to year.

**accounting principles** In the United States, conventions of practice, but in the United Kingdom something more fundamental and theoretical. Thus, the American GENERALLY ACCEPTED ACCOUNTING PRINCIPLES encompasses a wide range of broad and detailed accounting rules of practice. In the United Kingdom, the detailed rules are often called practices, policies or bases; and broader matters ACCRUALS or CONSERVATISM were traditionally referred to as concepts or conventions. So, in the United Kingdom, GAAP may mean 'generally accepted accounting practices'.

**accounting standards** Technical accounting rules of RECOGNITION, MEASUREMENT and disclosure set by committees of accountants. The exact title of accounting standards varies from country to country. The practical use of the words seems to originate officially with the Accounting Standards Steering Committee (later the Accounting Standards Committee) in the United Kingdom in 1970.

**accounts payable** US (and sometimes IASB) expression for CREDITORS. These are amounts owed by the business, usually as a result of purchases in the normal course of trade from suppliers who allow the business to pay at some point after purchase. Discounts will often be allowed for early payment of such accounts. The total of accounts payable at the period end form part of CURRENT LIABILITIES on a BALANCE SHEET.

**accounts receivable** US (and sometimes IASB) expression for DEBTORS. These are the amounts to be paid to the business by outsiders, normally as a result of sales to customers who have not yet settled their bills. Accounts receivable are valued at the amount of the accounts, less an allowance or IMPAIRMENT (PROVISION in UK terminology) for any amounts thought likely to be uncollectable. Those that are fairly certain to be uncollectable are bad debts; and there may also be allowances for specific amounts expected to be uncollectable, and general allowances against the total of accounts receivable. The general allowances would be calculated in the light of experience with bad debts. In certain countries, the size of allowances is, in effect, controlled by the amounts allowed for tax purposes. All these allowances reflect the perceived need for CONSERVATISM, particularly in the valuation of such CURRENT ASSETS. After taking into account these provisions, the total of accounts receivable will be part of CURRENT ASSETS on a BALANCE SHEET.

**accruals basis of accounting** The standard practice of concentrating on the period to which an expense or revenue relates rather than on the period in which cash is paid or received. Part of it is the MATCHING principle. More details are given under that heading.

**accrued expenses (or accruals)** Expenses that relate to a year but for which a bill will not be received until the following year. RECOGNITION of accrued expenses results from the need regularly to draw up financial statements at a fixed time (for example, at the end of a company's year).

During a year, electricity will be used or properties will be rented, yet at the year end the related bills may not have been received. Thus, at the year end, 'accrued' expenses are charged against income by accountants even though cash has not been paid nor the bills even received. The double entry for this is the creation of a CURRENT LIABILITY on the balance sheets. This practice may apply also to wages and salaries, taxes, and so on. An allocation of amounts to 'this year' and 'next year' may be necessary where a supplier's account straddles two accounting years. The practice is an example of the use of the MATCHING concept.

Similarly, some accounts of suppliers that are paid in any year may be wholly or partly paid on behalf of the activities of the next year. In this case, the relevant expenses for the year will have to be adjusted downwards by the accountant, and a CURRENT ASSET called 'prepayments' recorded on the balance sheet. Thus, payments of property taxes and insurance premiums may be partly prepayments.

**accumulated depreciation** The total amount by which the accounting value of a FIXED ASSET has so far been reduced to take account of the fact that it is wearing out or becoming obsolete (see DEPRECIATION).

**acid test** Name sometimes given to a ratio of some of a business's liquid assets to some of its short-term debts. It is thus one test of the likelihood of liquidity problems. It is also called the quick ratio.

**activity-based costing (ABC)** The practice of relating as many expenses as possible, often previously regarded as overheads, to particular production activities.

**allowances** US expression for amounts charged against profit for reductions in value (or IMPAIRMENTS) of assets.

**amortization** DEPRECIATION of INTANGIBLE ASSETS.

**annual general meeting (AGM)** The meeting at which shareholders may question directors on the contents of a company's annual report and financial statements; vote on the directors' recommendation for dividends; vote on replacement for retiring members of the board; and conduct other business within the company's rules.

**asset** According to the IASB's CONCEPTUAL FRAMEWORK: a resource controlled by an entity, as a result of past events, from which future economic benefits are expected to flow to the entity.

**Associate (or associated company)** IASB or British term for an entity over which another has SIGNIFICANT INFLUENCE. The term is not so well known in the United States. According to IAS 28 and the EU Seventh DIRECTIVE, a company will be presumed to be an associated company if it is owned to the extent of 20 per cent or more and is not a subsidiary or joint venture (see CONSOLIDATED FINANCIAL STATEMENTS).

**auditing standards** Rules for the practice of auditors, formalized in a similar way to the technical rules of ACCOUNTING STANDARDS. The rules contain ethical guidelines as well as detailing the work to be covered by an audit and the standard practice for the audit report.

**authorized share capital** The maximum amount of a particular type of share in a particular company that may be issued. It may be interesting information to shareholders as it puts a limit on the number of co-owners.

**average cost (AVCO)** In the context of INVENTORY valuation, a method of determining the historical cost of a particular type of inventory. As its name suggests, the cost of any unit of inventory or material used is deemed to be the average of the unit costs at which the inventory was bought. The average can be worked out at set intervals or each time there is a further purchase. AVCO is allowed by IAS 2 and by the EU Fourth Directive and is a minority practice in some countries. See FIFO and LIFO.

**balance sheet** A snapshot of the accounting records of ASSETS, LIABILITIES and equity of a business at a particular moment, most obviously the accounting year end. The balance sheet is the longest established of the main financial statements produced by a business. As its name suggests, it is a sheet of the balances from the double-entry system at a particular time. It is important to note that it is probably neither a snapshot of what the business is *worth* nor of what the separate assets are worth. This is because not all the business's items of value are recognized by accountants as ASSETS, and because the asset valuation methods used are normally based on past costs rather than on present market values. As part of an attempt to give the balance sheet more meaning, the IASB proposes to adopt the term 'statement of financial position' instead.

**Big Four (formerly Big Eight, then the Big Six, then Big Five)** An expression used to describe the world's largest accounting firms, which have offices virtually throughout the world. In alphabetical order these are:

- Deloitte Touche Tohmatsu
- Ernst & Young
- KPMG (Klynveld Peat Marwick Goerdeler)
- PricewaterhouseCoopers

**business combinations** Acquisitions or mergers involving two or more business entities.

**capital allowances** A system of DEPRECIATION used in the determination of taxable income in the UK and Ireland. This tends to be more generous than the depreciation that accountants charge for financial accounting purposes.

**capital employed** The aggregate finance used by a business. Sometimes the expression is used to refer to the total of all LIABILITIES and capital; sometimes it means 'net capital employed'; that is, it excludes current liabilities.

**capital lease** US term for FINANCE LEASE.

**capitalization** The inclusion of an item in a BALANCE SHEET. See, also, RECOGNITION.

**cash flow** Sometimes used to refer very loosely to the amount of cash coming into or out of a business in a particular period. However, it can be used as a more precise accounting term, particularly in North America, to refer to NET INCOME with DEPRECIATION charges added back. The latter will have been deducted in the calculation of the former but is not of course a cash payment of the period in question. Thus, profit plus depreciation gives an impression of cash generated by trading operations. This is not very exact, particularly because of changes in INVENTORY (stocks) and because of outstanding credit sales and purchases that have been included in the calculation of profit but will not yet have led to cash movements. However, as a quick measure it may have its uses.

**cash flow statements** Financial statements that concentrate on the movement of cash in the year, rather than using the ACCRUALS BASIS.

**closing rate method** UK term for the method of foreign currency translation, whereby the BALANCE SHEET items of a subsidiary are translated at the balance sheet rate, and the INCOME STATEMENT items translated at that rate or at the average for the period.

**common stock** US term for the ordinary shares in a corporation. Normally a majority of the ownership capital will comprise issues of common stock, though PREFERENCE/PREFERRED SHARES are also issued.

comprehensive income All the gains and losses recorded for a period, not just those realized.

conceptual framework A theoretical structure to underlie the technical rules in accounting. Several standard setting bodies have published such frameworks since the mid-1970s, beginning in the USA. The IASC published a framework in 1989.

conservatism The fundamental and ancient accounting concept that accountants should, when in doubt, show the worse picture rather than the better. Conservatism requires that assets should be shown at the lowest of all reasonable values; that all foreseeable losses should be accounted for immediately, but that profits should never be recorded until they become REALIZED. The IASB uses the word 'prudence' and does not give the concept a high status.

consistency The concept that a company should use the same rules of measurement and valuation from item to item and from year to year in its financial statements. This is now well established in most developed countries. A company may be allowed to change in special circumstances, such as an alteration in ACCOUNTING STANDARDS, but the change should always be disclosed in the annual report. The purpose of consistency is to enable a better comparison of a year's profits and values with those of previous years. The concept that different *companies* should use the same rules to assist intercompany comparisons might be called UNIFORMITY.

consolidated financial statements A means of presenting the position and results of a parent and its subsidiary companies as if they were a single entity. Consolidation ignores the separation of parents and subsidiaries due to legal and geographical factors; it accounts for the group of companies as if they were a single entity. Approximately, the financial statements of all the companies in a group are added together, with adjustments to extract intra-group trading and indebtedness.

contingent liabilities Possible future obligations or present obligations that are remote or unquantifiable. They are not accounted for, in the sense of adjusting the financial statements, but are explained in the notes to the BALANCE SHEET.

creditor A 'truster', i.e. someone to whom a business owes money. The US expression is ACCOUNTS PAYABLE. Creditors are generally created by purchases 'on credit' but would include tax bills. Short-term creditors are included under 'current liabilities' on a BALANCE SHEET; they are expected to be paid within the year. If credit purchases are the cause, the title used might be 'trade creditors'.

'Long-term' creditors are those who are not expected to be paid within the year. These might be trade creditors but would more likely be holders of bonds or debentures. The latter would normally be entitled to receive interest, whereas trade creditors are generally not. However, trade creditors often offer discounts for prompt payment, which is an implied way of charging interest.

current asset An ASSET on a BALANCE SHEET that is not intended for continuing use in the business, or that is expected to turn into cash within one year. Such assets include INVENTORIES, ACCOUNTS RECEIVABLE (US)/DEBTORS (UK), and cash. Also, a balance sheet may include current asset investments.

current cost accounting (CCA) One of many possible systems designed to adjust accounting for changing prices. It is often included under the generic heading INFLATION ACCOUNTING, although its normal form does not involve adjustments for inflation but for specific price changes relating to the business's assets.

current liabilities Generally, those amounts on a BALANCE SHEET that are expected to be paid by the business within a year. Thus they will include trade CREDITORS (UK)/ACCOUNTS PAYABLE (US), certain tax liabilities, and declared DIVIDENDS. Bank overdrafts are included on the grounds that they fluctuate in size and are technically recallable at short notice.

current purchasing power accounting (CPP) A UK term for the method of adjusting HISTORICAL COST ACCOUNTING financial statements to take account of inflation. The US equivalent is GENERAL PRICE LEVEL ADJUSTED or constant dollar.

current rate method The US term for a method of foreign currency translation. The UK term is CLOSING RATE METHOD, although this implies some greater flexibility in the choice of rates.

current ratio The CURRENT ASSETS divided by the CURRENT LIABILITIES of an entity at a particular date.


debtors In a BALANCE SHEET, debtors are usually mostly trade debtors, i.e. customers who have not yet paid cash. The US terminology is ACCOUNTS RECEIVABLE. Such amounts are shown as CURRENT ASSETS because they are generally expected to be paid within a year.

In a balance sheet, debtors are valued at what they are expected to pay to the business, bearing in mind the principle of CONSERVATISM. Thus, bad debts are written off, and PROVISIONS (ALLOWANCES in US terminology or IMPAIRMENTS) are made for doubtful debts. The allowances can be both specific (against suspected debts) and general (based on the average experience of bad debts).

deferred tax Under IASB or US rules, the tax related to temporary differences between the financial reporting value of an ASSET or LIABILITY and its tax basis.

depreciation A charge against the revenues of a period to represent the wearing out, usage or consumption of NON-CURRENT (FIXED) ASSETS in that period. So, machinery and equipment, vehicles and buildings are generally depreciated, although land normally is not. The technique of depreciation means that accountants do not charge the whole cost of a fixed asset against the revenues of the year of purchase, but they charge it gradually over the years of the use and wearing out of the asset.

deprival value The amount by which a business would be worse off if it were deprived of a particular asset. This is sometimes referred to as its 'value to the business' or 'value to the owner'.

Directives of the EU on company law Blueprints for laws that must be enacted as laws throughout the European Union. This is part of the process of harmonization of company law and accountancy. The European Commission drafts Directives, which are then adopted by the Council of Ministers and implemented into national laws. The most important Directives for accounting are the Fourth and the Seventh.

discounted cash flow (DCF) Future cash flows, adjusted to take account of their timing. Such 'discounted' cash flows are used when making investment choices between competing projects. The most reliable method of deciding which project is best and whether any particular one is worth doing is to work out each project's net present value (NPV) by adding up all the discounted expected net cash flows. The NPV calculation will include the outflow of the initial investment. A project with a positive NPV is worth doing; the project with the highest NPV is the best.

**dividend**  A payment by a company to its shareholders out of the profits made by the company.

**earnings**  A technical accounting term, meaning the amount of profit (normally for a year) available to the ordinary shareholders (UK)/common stockholders (US). That is, it is the profit after all operating expenses, interest charges, taxes and DIVIDENDS on PREFERRED/PREFERENCE stock.

**earnings per share (EPS)**  The most recent year's total EARNINGS divided by the average number of ordinary/common shares outstanding in the year.

**efficient market hypothesis**  An elegant and important theory, usually applied to the price of shares on large stock exchanges, that all publicly available information is immediately taken into account in the price of shares. In markets such as the New York or London stock exchanges there are many buyers and sellers of shares, the prices are well known, and much other information is freely available. In such cases, one would expect that new relevant information about a company would very rapidly affect its share price.

**equity**  An element of the balance sheet showing the owners' interests. It is equal to the total assets minus the total liabilities.

**equity method**  A method used, particularly as part of the preparation of CONSOLIDATED FINANCIAL STATEMENTS, for the inclusion of ASSOCIATES (those companies over which a group has 'significant influence' but not a controlling interest) and for some joint ventures.

**exceptional items**  A UK expression for those items in a profit and loss account that are within the ordinary activities of the business but are of unusual size. The treatment for these is to disclose them separately in the account or the notes to it. Such items are to be distinguished from EXTRAORDINARY ITEMS.

**exposure drafts**  Documents that precede the issue of ACCOUNTING STANDARDS. They are intended to attract response from companies, auditors, academics, investment analysts, financial institutions, etc.

**extraordinary items**  Gains or losses that are outside the ordinary activities of the business, are of material size, and are not expected to recur. The narrowness of interpretation of this expression differs greatly internationally. Under IASB rules, such a category is no longer shown.

**fair value**  The amount that willing buyers and sellers would exchange something for in a market at arm's length. For example, assets and liabilities of new subsidiaries are brought into consolidated accounts at fair values rather than book values. This is designed to be an estimate of their cost to the group at the date of acquisition of a subsidiary.

**FEE**  The Fédération des Experts Comptables Européens, a Brussels-based body of European professional accountancy institutes.

**FIFO (first-in, first-out)**  A common assumption for accounting purposes about the flow of items of raw materials or other INVENTORIES. It need not be expected to correspond with physical reality but may be used for accounting purposes. The assumption is that the first units to be received as part of inventories are the first ones to be used up or sold. This means that the most recent units are deemed to be those left at the period end. When prices are rising, and assuming a reasonably constant purchasing of materials, FIFO leads to a fairly up-to-date closing inventory value figure. However it gives an out-of-date and therefore low figure for the cost of sales. This leads to what many argue is an overstatement of profit figures, when prices are rising.

**finance lease** A contract that transfers the majority of risks and rewards of an ASSET to the lessee.

**financial instrument** A contract involving the creation of a financial ASSET of one entity and a financial LIABILITY or EQUITY instrument of another entity.

**fiscal year** US expression for the period for which companies prepare their annual financial statements. The majority of US companies use 31 December as the fiscal year end, which corresponds with the year end for tax purposes. In the United Kingdom, the expression 'fiscal year' means tax year.

**fixed assets** The assets that are to continue to be used in the business, such as land, buildings and machines, and certain intangible assets and investments. The complement is CURRENT ASSETS. An equivalent IASB or US expression is 'non-current assets'.

**gearing** A measurement of the degree to which a business is funded by loans rather than SHAREHOLDERS' EQUITY. The US expression is LEVERAGE.

**generally accepted accounting principles (GAAP)** A technical term, particularly used in the United States, to include the ACCOUNTING STANDARDS of the Financial Accounting Standards Board, and extant rules of predecessor bodies. Also included are the rules of the SECURITIES AND EXCHANGE COMMISSION (SEC).

**general price level adjusted accounting (GPLA)** A US term for a system of adjusting historical cost accounting by price indices to take account of inflation. It is also called constant dollar accounting or, in the United Kingdom, CURRENT PURCHASING POWER ACCOUNTING.

**going concern** An important underlying concept in accounting practice. The assumption for most businesses is that they will continue for the foreseeable future. This means that, for most purposes, the break-up or forced-sale value of the assets is not relevant.

**goodwill** The amount paid for a company in excess of the FAIR VALUE of its NET ASSETS at the date of acquisition. Goodwill exists because a GOING CONCERN business is usually worth more than the sum of the accounting values of its identifiable NET ASSETS. This may be looked upon as its ability to earn future profits above those of a similar newly formed company, or it may be seen as the 'goodwill' of customers, the established network of contacts, loyal staff, skilled management, and so on.

**group accounts** UK expression for CONSOLIDATED FINANCIAL STATEMENTS.

**historical cost accounting** The conventional system of accounting, widely established throughout the world except in some countries where inflation is endemic and high. Even in the latter countries, the GENERAL PRICE LEVEL ADJUSTED system is a set of simple adjustments carried out annually from historical cost records.

**holding company** A company that owns or controls others. In the narrow use of the expression, it implies that the company does not actively trade but operates through various subsidiaries.

**IFRS** When used collectively, all the extant accounting standards and interpretations issued by the IASB and its predecessor.

**impairment** The loss of value of an ASSET below its book value (i.e. generally its depreciated cost). Under IAS 36 this is measured by comparing the book value with the recoverable amount (usually the DISCOUNTED CASH FLOWS expected from the ASSET).

**income statement** The statement of revenues and expenses of a particular period, leading to the calculation of net income or net profit. The format of the income statement is either 'vertical'/'statement' form or 'horizontal'/'two-sided'/'account' form.

  The equivalent UK statement is the PROFIT AND LOSS ACCOUNT. However, not all revenues and expenses are shown: see STATEMENT OF RECOGNIZED INCOME AND EXPENSE.

**inflation accounting** Usually interpreted as encompassing all sorts of systems that might adjust or replace HISTORICAL COST ACCOUNTING to take account of changing prices. Many such systems are poorly described by the term, because they do not involve a recognition of general price level movements. Systems that do adjust for inflation are called CURRENT PURCHASING POWER ACCOUNTING (UK), GENERAL PRICE LEVEL ADJUSTED ACCOUNTING (US) or constant dollar accounting (US).

**intangible assets** ASSETS, such as goodwill or patents, that are not physical or tangible.

**interim dividend** DIVIDEND payment based on the profits of less than a full accounting period.

**interim report** A half-yearly or more frequent report generally from companies listed on a stock exchange.

**International Accounting Standards Board (IASB)** The standard setting body set up in 2001 by the International Accounting Standards Committee Foundation, a private sector trust.

**International Accounting Standards Committee (IASC)** An organization whose purpose was to devise and promulgate international standards in order to reduce the variation of practices in financial reporting throughout the world. It was founded in 1973 by accountancy bodies and replaced in 2001 by the IASB.

**International Federation of Accountants (IFAC)** A body comprising representatives from the accountancy professions of many nations. It was formed in 1977, and is based in New York. Its largest task is the organization of the four-yearly World Congresses of Accountants. It also has committees that promote international harmonization of auditing and management accounting. However, it leaves the area of accounting standards to the IASB.

**International Financial Reporting Interpretations Committee (IFRIC)** A subsidary committee of the IASB that issues interpretations of standards.

**inventories** Raw materials, work-in-progress and goods ready for sale. In the United Kingdom, the word 'stocks' is generally used instead.

**investment properties** Properties held by a business for investment or rental income, rather than for owner-occupation or as inventory.

**lease** A contract whereby one party (the lessor) agrees to give the use of an ASSET to another party (the lessee) in exchange for a rental payment.

**leverage** US term for the degree to which a business is funded by loans rather than by shareholders' equity. In a profitable highly levered company, a percentage increase in trading profit will be magnified by the time it reaches the stockholders, because the return to the lenders is a fixed amount of interest. The equivalent UK expression is GEARING.

**liabilities** Present obligations of an entity, arising from past events, the settlement of which is expected to result in an outflow of resources (usually cash). Most liabilities are of known amount and date. They include long-term loans, bank overdrafts and amounts owed to suppliers. There are current and non-current liabilities. The former are expected to be paid within a year from the date of the BALANCE SHEET on which they appear. Most measures of liquidity include knowing the total of current liabilities; NET CURRENT ASSETS is the difference between the current assets and the current liabilities.

Liabilities are valued at the amounts expected to be paid at the expected maturity date. In some cases, amounts that are not quite certain will be included as liabilities (PROVISIONS); they will be valued at the best estimate available.

**LIFO (last-in, first-out)** One of the methods available under US rules (but not under IAS 2) for the calculation of the cost of INVENTORIES, in those frequent cases where it is difficult or impossible to determine exactly which items remain or have been used. When prices are rising, LIFO will lead to more up-to-date values for the use of inventory in cost of sales and, thus, lower profits. Therefore, it is popular with many companies in Germany, Italy and the United States, where it is allowed for tax purposes.

However, an inventory value shown in a BALANCE SHEET may be seriously misleading as it can be based on very old prices.

**matching** A convention that the expenses and revenues measured in order to calculate the profit for a period should be those that can be related together for that period.

**materiality** A concept in IASB accounting that rules need not be strictly applied to unimportant amounts and that financial statements should not be swamped by unimportant items. For example, some companies may have very small amounts of a particular revenue, expense, ASSET or LIABILITY; if such an account would normally be shown in the financial statements, it nevertheless need not be if it is immaterial in size. This will help to make the statements clearer, by omission of trivial amounts. Materiality is also to be seen at work in the extensive rounding of numbers in financial statements.

Similarly, a strictly correct measurement or valuation method may be ignored for immaterial items. For example, the fitting of new and improved door locks on an office building is strictly an enhancement of the building and should lead to that ASSET being shown at a higher cost in the relevant BALANCE SHEET. However, the cost will be immaterial in the context of the building, and capitalization would complicate future depreciation charges. Thus, it would be normal to treat the new locks as an expense.

There is no precise definition of what is material. However, an item is immaterial if omission or mistreatment of it would not alter a reader's assessment of the financial statements. As a rule of thumb, this might be expressed as a few per cent of sales or profit.

**measurement** The calculation of the value of an item to be recorded in a financial statement.

**merger accounting** A method of accounting for a business combination. In the United States it was (until 2001) in fairly common use, under the name of POOLING OF INTERESTS, under which heading more details may be found.

**minority interests** The capital provided by group shareholders who are not parent company shareholders. Many subsidiary companies are not fully owned by the parent company. This means that they are partly owned by 'minority' shareholders outside the group. In the preparation of CONSOLIDATED FINANCIAL STATEMENTS, accountants bring in 100 per cent of all ASSETS, LIABILITIES, expenses and revenues of subsidiaries. This is because the group fully *controls* the subsidiary, even if it does not fully *own* it. In such financial statements, the subsidiary is subsumed into the rest of the group, and the capital provided by the minority shareholders is separately recognized as part of the capital of the group under the heading 'minority interests'. This amount grows each time the relevant subsidiary makes a profit that is not distributed.

In the consolidated INCOME STATEMENT, the share of the group profit owned by minorities is also shown separately.

In IFRS, these items are now referred to as non-controlling interests.

**net assets** The worth of a business in accounting terms as measured from its BALANCE SHEET. That is, it is the total of all the recorded ASSETS less the LIABILITIES that are owed to outsiders. Naturally, this total equals the SHAREHOLDERS' EQUITY.

However, in reality, a business is nearly always worth more than its net assets, because accountants will generally have been using HISTORICAL COST ACCOUNTING as a measurement basis, and because important assets such as the goodwill of customers will have been excluded due to the CONSERVATISM and money measurement conventions. Thus, the market capitalization of a company will nearly always be greater than its accounting 'net assets'.

**net current assets** The net current assets or WORKING CAPITAL of a business is the excess of the CURRENT ASSETS (such as cash, INVENTORIES and DEBTORS/ACCOUNTS RECEIVABLE) over the CURRENT LIABILITIES (such as trade creditors and overdrafts).

This is a measure of the extent to which a business is safe from liquidity problems. See also CURRENT RATIO.

**net income** Normal US expression for NET PROFIT in UK terminology.

**net profit** Normal UK expression for the excess of all the revenues over all the expenses of a business for a period. The PROFIT AND LOSS ACCOUNT of a business will show the net profit before tax and the net profit after tax. The profit is then available for distribution as DIVIDENDS (assuming there is sufficient cash) or for transfer to various RESERVES. After any DIVIDENDS on PREFERENCE SHARES have been deducted, the figure may be called EARNINGS.

**net realizable value (NRV)** The amount that could be raised by selling an ASSET, less the costs of the sale. Normally, NRV implies a sale in the normal course of trade; thus, there would also be a deduction for any costs to bring the ASSET into a saleable state.

**nominal value** Most shares have a nominal or par value. This is little more than a label to distinguish a share from any of a different value issued by the same company. Normally, the shares will be currently exchanged at above the nominal value, and the company will consequently issue any new shares at approximately the market rate.

DIVIDENDS may be expressed as a percentage of nominal value; and share capital is recorded at nominal value, any excess being recorded as SHARE PREMIUM.

**non-controlling interests** See MINORITY INTERESTS.

**non-current assets** See FIXED ASSETS.

**off-balance sheet finance** An entity's obligations that are not recorded on its balance sheet. One important example of off-balance sheet finance is the existence of LEASES that are not treated as ASSETS and LIABILITIES (capitalized). Suppose that a business decided to lease most of its plant and equipment rather than buying it. Suppose, too, that it does not capitalize its leases, because it or its leases fall outside the rules or because it is in a country where capitalization is not required. Now, let us compare this company with a similar one that has borrowed money and bought all its assets. The lessee has few assets and few loans, whereas the buying company has many assets and many loans. Thus, the lessee will appear to have a much better GEARING/LEVERAGE position and a better return on capital. This is despite the fact that it is using the same amount of ASSETS and has contracted to make LEASE payments for many future years.

In several countries, it is now necessary for FINANCE LEASES to be capitalized as though owned, and for an equal LIABILITY to be created. This adjusts for the otherwise misleading off-balance sheet finance. It expresses SUBSTANCE OVER FORM. There are many other ways of achieving off-balance sheet finance. In the context of CONSOLIDATED FINANCIAL STATEMENTS, it may be possible to exclude companies that are in substance subsidiaries.

**ordinary shares** The normal type of shares, called COMMON STOCK in the United States. They can be distinguished from PREFERENCE SHARES.

**own shares** Shares in a company bought back by the company from its shareholders. In the United States, own shares are called TREASURY STOCK.

**paid-in surplus** US expression for SHARE PREMIUM.

**par value** The normal US expression for NOMINAL VALUE.

**parent** An entity that controls another (the subsidiary).

**pay-back method** A popular technique for appraising the likely success of projects, or for choosing between projects. It involves the analysis of their expected future net cash inflows, followed by a calculation of how many years it will take for the original capital investment to be recovered. It seems to be popular because it is simple to use and, perhaps more importantly, simple to explain to non-financial managers.

**pooling of interests** A method of accounting for business combinations that was fairly common in the United States until 2001. It was then abolished in the US, and by IASB from 2005. The method has several attractions to companies and it was therefore necessary for there to be rules to control its use. In the United States, these rules were to be found in APB Opinion 16, and they included that the merger should be accomplished by the exchange of shares only, so that no cash leaves the group of companies. The UK equivalent term is 'merger accounting'.

The 'acquisition' or 'purchase' method of preparing CONSOLIDATED FINANCIAL STATEMENTS is now used for all combinations under IFRS or US rules.

**preferred stock (US)/preference shares (UK)** Shares normally having preference over ORDINARY SHARES/COMMON STOCK for DIVIDEND payments and for the return of capital if a company is wound up. That is, ordinary/common DIVIDENDS cannot be paid in a particular year until the preference/preferred DIVIDEND (generally including arrears), which is usually a fixed percentage, has been paid.

**present value** The value(s) of something reduced by a discount rate to allow for the time value of money.

**private limited company** A company that is not allowed to create a market in its securities. Such companies have special designatory letters after their names, such as Ltd, GmbH, Sarl, BV, Srl. They are to be distinguished from PUBLIC LIMITED COMPANIES. In most countries where this distinction exists, private companies are much more numerous than public companies. Rules of disclosure, audit, profit distribution, etc. may be less onerous for private companies.

**profit and loss account** The UK expression for the financial statement that summarizes the difference between the revenues and expenses of a period. Such statements may be drawn up frequently for the managers of a business, but a full audited statement is normally only published for each accounting year. The equivalent US expression is INCOME STATEMENT; and generally, the IASB also uses this term. See, also, STATEMENT OF TOTAL RECOGNIZED GAINS AND LOSSES.

**proportional (or proportionate) consolidation** A technique, used as part of the preparation of CONSOLIDATED FINANCIAL STATEMENTS for a group of companies, that brings into the CONSOLIDATED FINANCIAL STATEMENTS the group's share of all the ASSETS, LIABILITIES, revenues and expenses of the partly owned company. The method is virtually unknown in the United Kingdom and the United States, but is allowed under IASB rules and in several European countries for dealing with investments in companies that are held on a joint venture basis with one or more other investing companies.

**provision** A liability of uncertain timing or amount. However, the word is also used in the UK to mean an allowance against the value of an asset. A RESERVE, on the other hand, is an amount voluntarily or compulsorily set aside out of profit (after it has been calculated), often in order to demonstrate that the amount is not to be distributed as DIVIDENDS.

US usage of the words is also loose. For example, it is not unknown for accountants and others to talk about a 'bad debt RESERVE' or 'pension RESERVE'; and in some continental European countries there may be very large 'provisions for contingencies' that Anglo-Saxon practice would treat as RESERVES. In US terminology, 'allowance' is often used instead of 'provision', and an amount set aside to cover an expected liability would often be called a RESERVE.

**prudence** A concept found in the accounting practices of nearly all countries. It implies being cautious in the valuation of ASSETS or the measurement of profit. It means taking the lowest reasonable estimate of the value of ASSETS, anticipating losses but not profits.

In the United States, 'CONSERVATISM' is the word generally used for this concept.

**public limited company** A company whose securities (shares and loan stock) may legally be publicly traded. In the United Kingdom, the legal form of such a company is set out in the Companies Acts. The company must have 'public limited company' (or plc) as part of its name. There are equivalents to this form in other European countries (e.g. SA, AG, NV, SpA), but in the United States the nearest equivalent is a corporation that is registered with the SECURITIES AND EXCHANGE COMMISSION.

Often, the expression 'public company' is used loosely to mean companies that actually have traded shares.

**quarterly reporting** Abbreviated financial statements as, for example, published quarterly by companies registered with the SECURITIES AND EXCHANGE COMMISSION in the United States.

**realization convention** A well-established principle of conventional accounting, that gains or profits should only be recognized when they have been objectively realized by some transaction or event. This is consistent with the concept of CONSERVATISM, which anticipates losses but never profits. However, the convention is increasingly departed from under IFRS.

**receivables** The IASB and US expression for amounts of money due to a business; often known as ACCOUNTS RECEIVABLE. The UK term is DEBTORS.

**recognition** The process of incorporating an item in a financial statement.

**reducing balance depreciation** A technique of calculating the depreciation charge, usually for machines, whereby the annual charge reduces over the years of an asset's life. A fixed percentage DEPRECIATION is charged each year on the cost (first year) or the undepreciated cost (subsequent years).

**replacement cost accounting** A system of preparing financial statements in which all ASSETS (and expenses relating to them, such as DEPRECIATION) are valued at current replacement costs.

**reserves** UK term for undistributed gains. These include accumulated profits and revaluations. There is no equivalent US term. Reserves should be distinguished from PROVISIONS, which are charged in the calculation of profit, and represent LIABILITIES. Of course, neither reserves nor PROVISIONS are amounts of cash. Reserves belong to shareholders and are part of a total of shareholders' EQUITY, which also includes share capital. This total is represented by all the assets of the business, less the liabilities owed to outsiders.

It should be noted that this terminology is used somewhat loosely by some accountants. In the United States, 'reserve' is used to cover some of the meanings of PROVISION in the United Kingdom.

**restricted surplus** A US expression for amounts of past profit that are unavailable for distribution to shareholders. The UK equivalent would be 'undistributable reserves'.

**retained profit/earnings** Amounts of profit, earned in the preceding year and former years, that have not yet been paid out as DIVIDENDS. 'Retained earnings' is a typical US expression for such amounts, though it would also be understood in the United Kingdom. 'Retained profit' is a more usual UK expression.

**revaluation** HISTORICAL COST is the basis for the valuation of many ASSETS. However, under IASB and some other rules, it is acceptable to revalue fixed assets annually. These revaluations can be done on the basis of FAIR VALUE or NET REALIZABLE VALUE. It is quite normal for large companies in some European countries to show land and buildings at revalued amounts in their balance sheets. Clearly, one purpose of this is to avoid a seriously misleading impression of their worth, when prices have risen substantially.

**sale-and-leaseback** A method of raising funds by a company without immediately depleting resources or incurring LIABILITIES. If a company owns and uses FIXED ASSETS, it may find it advantageous, for tax or other reasons, to sell them to a financial institution (the lessor) who then leases them back to the company.

The assets do not physically move as part of this process; so the company's business is not interrupted. The company receives a lump sum, which it may need for various purposes, and agrees to make future LEASE payments. Legally, it no longer owns the ASSETS, nor does it have a legal liability. However, since the real substance of the situation is not well represented by the legal form, it has now become accounting practice for certain LEASES in several countries to be recorded as both an ASSET and a LIABILITY in the lessee's BALANCE SHEET.

**sales** The figure for sales recorded in the financial statements for a period, including all those sales agreed or delivered in the period, rather than those that are paid for in cash. The sales figure will be shown net of sales taxes (VAT, etc.).

In the United Kingdom, the word TURNOVER is used in the financial statements, although 'sales' is generally used in the books of account.

**secret reserves** Various means by which a company, particularly a financial institution, can make its true financial strength unclear in its financial statements. The purpose of this is to build up resources in case of future difficulty. If that future difficulty eventually emerges, it may be possible to hide it completely by merely absorbing it using the secret reserves. This may avoid a dangerous loss of confidence in the bank or other company concerned.

Secret reserves may be created by deliberately allowing FIXED ASSETS or INVENTORIES to be undervalued, or by creating unnecessary PROVISIONS.

The problem with such accounting practices is that they do indeed obscure the true financial position of a company from its shareholders and lenders. Thus, deliberate creation of secret reserves has gradually been outlawed in most countries.

**Securities and Exchange Commission (SEC)** The US government agency set up in 1934 after the Wall Street Crash of 1929. Its function is to control the issue and exchange of publicly traded shares. Companies with such shares must register with the SEC, and then obey a mass of detailed regulations about disclosure and audit of financial information. An SEC-registered company in the United States is the nearest equivalent to a PUBLIC LIMITED COMPANY in Europe. In both cases, not all such companies are listed on a stock exchange.

**segment reporting** The disclosure of SALES, profit or ASSETS by line of business or by geographical area.

**shareholders' equity** The total of the shareholders' interest in a company. This will include the original share capital, amounts contributed in excess of the PAR VALUE of shares (i.e. SHARE PREMIUM or paid-in surplus), and retained profits.

**share premium** Amounts paid into a company (by shareholders when they purchased shares from the company) in excess of the NOMINAL VALUE of the shares. Shares are recorded at NOMINAL VALUES. However, share premium may be treated for most purposes exactly as if it were share capital. Both are included in SHAREHOLDERS' EQUITY.

In the United States there are many equivalent expressions, e.g. 'paid-in surplus'.

**significant influence** The power to influence the financial and operating policies of an entity. Under IASB rules, this is presumed to exist once an investor has a 20 per cent or more holding in the voting shares of the entity.

SORIE See STATEMENT OF RECOGNIZED INCOME AND EXPENSE.

**Statement of financial position** A term sometimes used in the US, and proposed by the IASB, for BALANCE SHEET.

**Statement of recognized income and expense** An IFRS statement that starts with the net income and adds any other gains and losses, e.g. revaluations of assets not recorded in the income statement.

**Statement of total recognized gains and losses** A UK statement equivalent to the SORIE.

**stock** US term for securities of various kinds; for example, COMMON STOCK or PREFERRED STOCK (equivalent to ordinary and preference shares in UK terminology). However, the word 'share' is also understood in the United States, so that 'stockholder' and 'shareholder' are interchangeable. In the United Kingdom this meaning survives, particularly in the expressions 'Stock Exchange' and 'Loan Stock'.

A source of great confusion in Anglo-American conversation is the British use of the word 'stocks' for what are called INVENTORIES in the United States and under IFRS.

**straight-line depreciation** A system of calculating the annual DEPRECIATION expense of a FIXED ASSET. This method charges equal annual instalments against profit over the useful life of the ASSET. In total, the cost of the asset less any estimated residual scrap value is depreciated. This method is simple to use and thus very popular.

STRGL See STATEMENT OF TOTAL RECOGNIZED GAINS AND LOSSES.

**substance over form** The presentation in financial statements of the underlying economic substance of a particular transaction, rather than the superficial legal or technical form of it. This is a fundamental idea in accounting. For example, when plant is leased by a lessee from a lessor there is no transfer of legal ownership or creation of legal liabilities. However, in many cases, the transaction is very similar to a purchase of ASSETS and borrowing of money by the lessee. The plant will be at the lessee's premises, and the lessee will have contracted to pay a series of future LEASE payments. To concentrate on the legal form of the transaction would ignore the economic reality. However, of course, the economic substance depends on the exact legal form of the lease contract.

This method of thinking is taken the furthest in the United States. Another example there is the 'correction' of interest receipts or payments on loans that have a non-commercial rate of interest.

**tangible assets** ASSETS with physical existence, such as property, plant or equipment.

**temporal method** The principal method of foreign currency translation used in the United States between 1975 and 1981. It is now only to be used in particular circumstances in IASB rules, but is fairly common in Germany.

**temporary difference** The difference between the financial reporting value of an ASSET or LIABILITY and its basis for tax purposes.

**timing difference** A difference between the expenses and revenues recorded in the calculation of profit and the amounts treated as deductions or increases in the calculation of taxable income. For example, accelerated DEPRECIATION for tax purposes will allow plant and machinery to be charged for tax purposes over a shorter period than that used by accountants as the useful life for DEPRECIATION in financial statements.

**treasury stock** US expression for a company's shares that have been bought back by the company and not cancelled. The shares are held 'in the corporate treasury'. They receive no DIVIDENDS and carry no votes at company meetings.

The UK equivalent term is 'OWN SHARES'. The term 'treasury stock' is confusing to a UK reader because it might appear to refer to government bonds issued by the Treasury. The IASB term is 'treasury shares'.

**trial balance** Part of the process of producing financial statements from the records in a double-entry bookkeeping system. The trial balance marshals all the debit and credit balances on the various accounts on to one page. If this does not balance immediately, then errors must be investigated. Once balance is achieved then some of the individual items are used to prepare the INCOME STATEMENT, and the remaining items are shown on the BALANCE SHEET.

**true and fair view** The overriding legal requirement for the presentation of financial statements of companies in the United Kingdom, most of the (British) Commonwealth and the European Union. The nearest IASB or US equivalent is 'fair presentation'.

**turnover** The UK expression used in PROFIT AND LOSS ACCOUNTS for the SALES revenue of an accounting period. This is shown net of value added tax.

**undistributable reserves** Amounts, paid in by shareholders or notionally allocated out of profits, that are not available for distribution to the shareholders as DIVIDENDS. The US term is RESTRICTED SURPLUS.

Undistributable reserves would include SHARE PREMIUM and reserves on the REVALUATION of ASSETS.

**uniformity** The use of the same rules of accounting or financial statement presentation from one company to another. Improvements in uniformity are encouraged by the setting of ACCOUNTING STANDARDS. One reason for this is to improve comparability between the financial statements of different companies.

**uniting of interests** The former IASB term for POOLING OF INTERESTS.

**unusual items** US term for amounts that are not outside the ordinary course of the business but that are unusual in size or incidence. The approximate UK equivalent is EXCEPTIONAL ITEMS.

**window dressing** The manipulation of figures in financial statements in order to make them appear better (or perhaps worse) than they otherwise would be. A company might wish to do this in order to affect the actions of existing or potential shareholders or lenders, the government, or other readers of financial statements.

**working capital** The difference between CURRENT ASSETS and CURRENT LIABILITIES. This total is also known as NET CURRENT ASSETS, under which entry there are more details.

# Index

abridged accounts 99
accountancy profession 7–9, 76–8, 79
accounting equation 375
accounting periods 37
accounting policies 341–9, 421
accruals 38–40, 170, 222, 387–8
acid test 130
acquisition accounting 273, 279–80
activity-based costing (ABC) 198
AEG 357
African countries 79
agriculture 428
allocation methods 176–81
Amoco 279
amortization 181, 184
annual financial reports 94
assets
    balance sheet equation 28–9
    book value per share 133, 172, 173
    claims against 14
    classification 96
    cost capitalization 152
    current assets 96, 98, 100
    definition 14
    deprival value 316–19
    fixed assets 96, 98, 100, 164–5
    hierarchy of decisions 148–57
    primacy of definitions 146–8
    recognition 148–52, 165–7
    for sale (IFRS 5) 111–12, 429
    tangible assets 98, 100, 164, 167
    turnover ratios 123–4
    see also financial assets; intangible assets
associates 425
assumptions 38–40
Astra 279
audits 6–7, 8, 72, 76–8, 94
Australia 57

bad debts 390
balance sheet equation 27–9
balance sheets 14–21, 37, 94, 95–101,
        386–7
    abridged accounts 99
    accruals 38–40, 170, 222, 387–8
    consolidated statements 271–4
    Fourth Directive 96, 98–100, 151

interpretation 336–9
    layout 95, 96–7, 215
    liquidity analysis 96
    prepayments 387–8
    profits 18
    wages 19
banks 71
base inventory 201–3
BASF 148, 239
Bayer 97, 106, 245–6, 341
book value per share 133, 172, 173
bookkeeping see double-entry bookkeeping
borrowings
    and cash flow 260
    costs 424
    debenture loans 222, 233
    equity compared to debt 232–3
    and inflation 304
    interest cover 130–1
    lenders 5, 71–4, 116
    long-term borrowings 128
BP 279
brand names 165, 166
Brierley, J.E.C. 63
British Airways 63
business combinations 272–3, 429
business entities 37, 50–3
business licence tax 240
buy-backs of shares 227

capital 7, 15–17, 99, 101
    see also borrowings; equity
capital allowances 239
capital gains 239
capital leases 168–9, 422, 423
capital maintenance concept 306–9, 318
capitalization
    costs 152
    interest 152, 367
    leases 167–9, 245
cash 15–17, 18–19, 215–18
    cash ratio 130
    definition 216
    equivalents 251–2
cash flow and borrowings 260
cash flow statements 29–30, 94, 108–9,
        249–62, 421

cash flow statements (*continued*)
  depreciation 255
  direct method 253
  financing activities 251, 252–3
  indirect method 253–4
  industry differences 260
  inventory 255
  investing activities 251, 252
  layout 255–6
  operating activities 251, 252, 253–4
CEPSA 153, 154
Chambers, R.J. 313
chart of accounts 49, 54, 55
China 57
classifications
  assets 96
  international accounting 63–70
  legal systems 63
  liabilities 96–7
  Nobes' classification 65–7, 69–70
  survey data 65
  tax bases 238
codified law 49, 74
*commissaires aux comptes* 8
common law 49, 50–1
common size statements 117, 121–2
Companies Act (2006) 56
company names 51–2
comparability 40–1, 117
completeness 42
comprehensive income *see* income
  statements
computer software costs 370
concepts 35–45
  accounting periods 37
  accruals 38–40, 170, 222, 387–8
  assumptions 38–40
  business entity 37
  future development 44
  going concern 40, 43
  hierarchy 42–4
  objectives 38, 44
  relevance 40–1
  reliability 41–2, 44
  true and fair view 81, 82–5
conservatism 36, 42
consistency 40–1
consolidated statements 53, 54, 63
  balance sheets 271–4
  EU Directives 82
  income statements 276
  standard (IAS 27) 63, 87–8, 264–5,
    424–5
  *see also* group accounting
construction contracts 206–9, 421

contingent liabilities 225–6
continuously contemporary accounting
    (CoCoA) 313
corporation tax *see* taxation
cost accounting 197–211
  activity-based costing (ABC) 198
  base inventory 201–3
  capitalization of costs 152
  construction contracts 206–9, 421
  current replacement cost 156, 174–5,
    206, 302–4, 308, 313–16
  first in, first out (FIFO) 199, 202–3, 205
  historical cost 155, 157, 197–8, 304, 306
  inflation 299
  last in, first out (LIFO) 200, 203, 205, 320
  retail inventory method 203–4
  standard cost 203
  unit costs 198–9
  weighted averages 204–5
cost capitalization 152
Costa Crociere 148–50
counting inventory 196–7, 203–4
credit balances 376–7
creditors 18, 20, 99, 100–1, 221–3
  payment ratio 132
culture 359–60
currencies *see* foreign currency translation
current assets 96, 98, 100
  *see also* inventories
current investments 218
current liabilities 96
current purchasing power accounting 306,
    310
current ratio 130
current replacement cost 156, 174–5, 206,
    302–4, 308, 313–16
current value accounting 307, 309, 312–16
  economic value 156, 183, 313
  net realizable value 156, 204–5, 313
customers 5, 116

Daimler-Benz 62
DaimlerChrysler 279
David, R. 63
*de facto* harmonization 80
*de jure* harmonization 80
debenture loans 222, 233
debit balances 376–7
debt *see* borrowings
debtors (receivables) 18, 19, 98, 100,
    215–18
  collection ratio 131
  doubtful 217, 390
declining charge 176–8
deferred income 222

deferred tax 241–5
definitions of accounting 4
depreciation 40, 75, 155, 170–83, 194, 304
    allocation methods 176–81
    amortization 181, 184
    bookkeeping entry 390
    in cash flow statements 255
    declining charge 176–8
    disposals 182
    double-declining-balance 178
    in France 180
    in Germany 75, 180
    intangible assets 181, 185
    mid-year purchases 182
    net book value 173
    reducing balance method 176–8, 180
    replacement values 174–5
    residual values 182
    revaluation method 178–9
    of revalued assets 186
    straight-line 172, 179
    and taxation 175–6, 239, 242–3
    terminology 184–5
    usage method 178
    useful economic life 181–2
deprival value 316–19
derivative instruments 369–70
Deutsche Bank 232
Directives 80–2
    see also Fourth Directive
disclosure requirements 110–13, 215, 429
    interim financial reports 112–13
    related parties 424
    segment reporting 110–11, 429–30
discontinued operations 111–12, 331, 429
discounted cash flow (DCF) 339–40
disposals 182
distributable profits 228–9
dividends 226, 282, 370
    cover ratio 334
    taxation 237, 239–40
    yield 335
dominant influence 283
double-declining-balance 178
double-entry bookkeeping 7, 48, 376–96
    account set up 375–6
    accounting equation 375
    advantages 379–80
    bad debts 390
    credit balances 376–7
    debit balances 376–7
    depreciation 390
    doubtful debts 217, 390
    errors 394
    inventory account 385–6

rules of recording 375–80
    taxation 393
    trading accounts 381–5
    trial balance 380, 392–6
doubtful debts 217, 390

earnings per share (EPS) 112, 133–4,
    331–4, 426
economic double taxation 237
economic substance 41–2
economic value 156, 183, 313
employee benefits 423
employee representative groups 5, 116
Enron 265
entities 37, 50–3
equity 20, 28, 226–9
    compared to debt 232–3
    legal reserve 228
    profit and loss reserves 228–9
    revaluation reserve 228
    share premium account 227–8
    statement of changes in equity 108
    subscribed capital 152, 226–7
equity convention 308
equity method of group accounting 281–2
European Union
    accountancy profession 8
    company names 51–2
    Directives 80–2
        see also Fourth Directive
    expansion 85
    harmonization 80–5, 361–5
    IFRS 58
    legal system 49
    regulation 8, 49, 53–6, 58
    stock exchanges 72–3
    see also France; Germany
events after reporting date 421
expenses 19, 21, 25, 28–9, 105
    accruals 38–40, 170, 222, 387–8
    formation expenses 152
    matching revenue with 38–40, 43, 147
    prepayments 387–8
    primacy of definitions 146–8
    repairs and maintenance 147–8, 153, 155
    research and development 150, 368
    to sales ratio 120–2
experts comptables 8
extraordinary items 331

fair value 155, 156, 157, 320–1
fairness 73
faithful representation 41, 44
FASB (Financial Accounting Standards
    Board) 36, 44, 57

Fiat 63, 64
finance (capital) leases 168–9, 422, 423
financial accounting 5–6, 7
financial appraisal 329–53
  and accounting policies 341–9
  balance sheet interpretation 336–9
  discounted cash flow (DCF) 339–40
  dividend cover 334
  dividend yield 335
  earnings per share (EPS) 112, 133–4,
    331–4, 426
  non-recurring items 330–1
  PE ratios 112, 335–6
  valuation through expectations 339–40
  valuation through market values 340–1
  see also ratio analysis
financial assets 98, 100, 427
  cash and receivables 215–18
  disclosures (IFRS 7) 215, 429
  investments 98, 100, 218–21, 368–9
  presentation (IAS 32) 215, 425
  recognition and measurement (IAS 39)
    215, 218, 220–1, 427
  revaluation 220–1
  see also equity
financial culture 359–60
financial instruments (IFRS 9) 215, 430
financial management 7
financing activities, cash flow 251, 252–3
finished goods 195–6
first in, first out (FIFO) 199, 202–3, 205
first-time adoption (IFRS 1) 428
fixed assets 96, 98, 100, 164–5
fixed investments 218
foreign currency translation 288–97
  conversion 289
  current rate method 292
  financial statement translation 289,
    292–3
  in France 291
  functional currency 293
  in Germany 291
  mixed rate method 292–3
  share capital 295
  standard (IAS 21) 289, 293, 423–4
  temporal method 292–3
  transactions 289–91
  unsettled transactions 290–1
formation expenses 152
Fourth Directive 44, 80–4, 95, 431–2
  balance sheets 96, 98–100, 151
  construction contracts 209
  fixed assets 164–5
  goodwill 275
  inventories 205

liabilities 222
  provisions 223–4
  true and fair view 81, 82–5
Framework for Financial Statements 5–6,
    35–6, 38, 44
France
  asset revaluation 319
  currency translation 291
  depreciation 180
  regulation 54
  taxation 240
  see also European Union
Frank, W.G. 65
FRS 15 (depreciation) 171
functional currency 293
funds' management ratios 131–3
  creditors' payment ratio 132
  debtors' collection 131
  inventory turnover 132–3

GAAP 56–7, 57–8, 364, 367–71
gains as other comprehensive income 186
gains on sale 187
gearing 126–7, 359
General Motors 163
general price adjustments 305–9
general price-level adjusted systems
    310–12
Germany
  accountancy profession 76–8
  banks 71
  currency translation 291
  depreciation 75, 180
  gearing ratios 359
  inflation accounting 305
  regulation 53–4
  repair expenses 147–8
  taxation 236, 238, 240, 242
  see also European Union
GlaxoSmithKline 362–4, 367–71
going concern convention 40, 43
goodwill 165–6, 367–8
  group accounting 272, 274, 275
governments
  and asset revaluation 319
  grants 423
  as users of accounts 5, 116
grants 423
gross profit margin 119–20
group accounting 53, 263–87
  consolidated statements 53, 54, 63
    balance sheets 271–4
    EU Directives 82
    income statements 276
  dividends 282

dominant influence 283
equity method 281–2
goodwill 272, 274, 275
intercompany transactions 277–9
investments 267–70
non-controlling interests 269, 276–7
one-line consolidation 282
parent financial statements 270–1
proportional consolidation 280–1
significant influence 269, 283
uniting of interests 279–80
guarantor obligations 370

harmonization 80–5, 361–5
Directives 80–2
*see also* Fourth Directive
EU expansion 85
principles of valuation 82–3
Regulation (2002) 85
true and fair view 81, 82–5
hidden reserves 231
hierarchy of concepts 42–4
hierarchy of decisions 148–57
historical cost 155, 157, 197–8, 304, 306
hybrid securities 233
hyperinflation 305, 425

IASB (International Accounting Standards
Board) 8–9, 44, 85–9
concepts 35–45
*Framework for Financial Statements* 5–6,
35–6, 38, 44
influence 86–9
nature and purpose 85–6
IASC (International Accounting Standards
Committee) 8, 36, 85–6
IASC Foundation 8–9
IFAC (International Federation of
Accountants) 8
IFRSs (International Financial Reporting
Standards) 8, 35, 58, 420–30
adoption 86–9
IAS 1 (presentation) 58, 95–7, 101–2,
420
IAS 2 (inventories) 205, 420
IAS 7 (cash flow statements) 250–3, 421
IAS 8 (policies, estimates and errors) 421
IAS 10 (events after reporting date) 421
IAS 11 (construction contracts) 209, 421
IAS 12 (income taxes) 421–2
IAS 16 (property, plant and equipment)
164, 171, 181, 182, 188–9, 422
IAS 17 (leases) 422–3
IAS 18 (revenue) 423
IAS 19 (employee benefits) 423

IAS 20 (government grants) 423
IAS 21 (foreign exchange) 289, 293,
423–4
IAS 23 (borrowing costs) 424
IAS 24 (related party disclosure) 424
IAS 26 (retirement benefit plans) 424
IAS 27 (consolidated statements) 63,
87–8, 264–5, 424–5
IAS 28 (associates) 425
IAS 29 (hyperinflation) 305, 425
IAS 31 (joint ventures) 268, 283, 425
IAS 32 (financial instruments) 215, 425
IAS 33 (earnings per share) 112, 426
IAS 34 (interim reporting) 112–13, 426
IAS 36 (impairment) 183, 341, 426
IAS 37 (provisions and contingencies)
223, 224, 225, 427
IAS 38 (intangible assets) 150, 164, 165,
341, 427
IAS 39 (financial assets) 215, 218, 220–1,
427
IAS 40 (investment property) 188, 427–8
IAS 41 (agriculture) 428
IFRS 1 (first-time adoption) 428
IFRS 2 (share-based payments) 428
IFRS 3 (business combinations) 272–3,
429
IFRS 4 (insurance contracts) 429
IFRS 5 (assets for sale & discontinued
operation) 111–12, 429
IFRS 6 (mineral resources) 429
IFRS 7 (disclosures) 215, 429
IFRS 8 (segment reporting) 111, 429–30
IFRS 9 (financial instruments) 215, 430
Level A objective 43–4
small and medium-sized enterprises 58,
89
impairment 182–5, 341, 426
income recognition 157–60
income statements 21–7, 94, 101–8, 383–5
consolidated 276
Fourth Directive 102–5
layout 101, 102–3, 105
other comprehensive income 101,
104–8, 186
revenue 21, 24, 105
wages 21–2, 25
income taxes 421–2
inflation 299, 304–5, 309
and borrowings 304
hyperinflation 305, 425
and taxation 304
ING 185
input valuation 197–8, 206
institutional investors 71

insurance contracts 429
intangible assets 98, 100, 148, 164–7, 368
    brand names 165, 166
    depreciation 181, 184
    recognition 165–6
    standard (IAS 38) 150, 164, 165, 341,
        427
intercompany transactions 277–9
interest payments
    capitalization 152, 367
    cover ratio 130–1
    and taxation 239–40
interim financial reports 112–13, 426
international accounting 62–92, 360–1
    classifications 63–70
    differences 62–3
        influences on 70–9
        and taxation 236, 237–40
    EU harmonization 80–5
    groupings of major countries 66, 68
    history 62
    terminology 9, 355–8
inventories 17–18, 21, 24, 193–213, 205,
        420
    base inventory 201–3
    bookkeeping 385–6
    and cash flow statements 255
    construction contracts 206–9
    counting methods 196–7, 203–4
    finished goods 195–6
    Fourth Directive 205
    net realizable value 156, 204–5, 313
    overhead allocation 197–8
    and profit calculation 194–5, 203–4
    raw materials 195–6
    retail inventory 203–4
    turnover ratio 132–3
    valuation flow chart 210
    work-in-progress 195–6
    see also cost accounting
investing activities cash flow 251, 252
investment properties 160, 185, 188,
        427–8
investment ratios 133–4
investments 98, 100, 218–21, 368–9
    current investments 218
    fixed investments 218
    gains and losses 185, 186, 187, 220–1
    group accounting 267–70
    valuation 219–20
investors 5, 71, 116
Italy 319

Japan 7, 79
joint ventures 267–70, 283, 425

land and buildings
    effect of price changes 299–300
    investment properties 160, 185, 188,
        427–8
    property for own use 185
    standards (IAS 16 and 40) 164, 171, 181,
        188–9, 422, 427–8
    see also revaluation of assets
language 9, 184–5, 355–8
last in, first out (LIFO) 200, 203, 205, 320
leases 41–2, 167–70, 422–3
    capitalization 167–9, 245
    finance (capital) 168–9, 422, 423
    operating 168–9, 422
legal reserve 228
legal systems 48–50, 74, 78
    classification 63
lenders 5, 71–4, 116
liabilities 20, 221–6
    accruals 38–40, 170, 222, 387–8
    classification 96–7
    contingent 225–6
    creditors 18, 20, 99, 100–1, 221–3
    current 96
    debenture loans 222, 233
    deferred income 222
    definition 147, 148, 221
    Fourth Directive 222
    hierarchy of decisions 148–57
    measurement 152–7
    provisions 99, 101, 147–8, 217, 223–5,
        229–32
limited liability partnerships 51
liquidity analysis 96
liquidity ratios 129–30
long-term borrowings 128

macro/uniform system 67, 69
management accounting 5–6, 48
management decision-making 4–5, 35
market value per share 133
Marks and Spencer 159
matching revenue with expenses 38–40,
        43, 147
materiality 41
merger accounting 273, 279–80
micro/professional system 67, 69
Microsoft 163–4
mineral resources 429
minority interests 269, 276–7
mixed rate currency translation 292–3

Nair, R.D. 65
net book value 133, 172, 173
net operating profit 122

net profit margin 120
net realizable value 156, 204–5, 313
Netherlands 54, 56
neutrality 42, 43
Nobes' classification 65–7, 69–70
Nokia 150–1, 227
non-controlling interests 269, 276–7
non-financial resource ratios 124
non-recurring items 330–1
non-voting shares 226
Nordic countries 57
Norsk Hydro 362
notes to the financial statements 110

one-line consolidation 282
operating activities cash flow 251, 252, 253–4
operating leases 168–9, 422
options 369
ordinary shareholders 226
other comprehensive income 101, 104–8, 186
output valuation 197–8, 204
overhead allocation 197–8

par value of shares 227
parent financial statements 270–1
partnerships 50–1, 52
payables see creditors
payroll taxes 240
PE ratios 112, 335–6
pensions 223, 225, 369
periodic inventory counting 196, 197, 203–4
perpetual inventory 196–7
pooling of interests 279–80
preference shareholders 128–9, 226–7
prepayments 387–8
presentation
    balance sheets 96–7, 215
    cash flow statements 255–6
    financial assets (IAS 32) 215, 425
    income statements 102–3, 105
    standard (IAS 1) 58, 95–7, 101–2, 420
price changes 298–325
    capital maintenance concept 306–9, 318
    current purchasing power accounting 306, 310
    current value accounting 307, 309, 312–16
    and depreciation 304
    deprival value 316–19
    equity convention 308
    general adjustments 305–9

general price-level adjusted systems 310–12
    historical cost 155, 157, 197–8, 304, 306
    inflation 299, 304–5, 309, 425
    land and buildings 299–300
    profit measurement 300
    replacement costs 156, 174–5, 206, 302–4, 308, 313–16
    specific adjustments 305–9
primacy of definitions 146–8
private companies 51
profit and loss account see income statements
profit and loss reserves 228–9
profit ratios 119–22
    expenses to sales 120–2
    gross profit margin 119–20
    net operating profit 122
    net profit margin 120
profitability ratios 122–9
    asset turnover ratios 123–4
    gearing 126–7
    non-financial resource ratios 124
    return on capital employed (ROCE) 125–9
    return on equity (ROE) 124–5, 127–9
profits 18, 26–7
    accounting profit and taxable profit 237, 238
    calculation 62–3, 194–5, 203–4
    construction contracts 206–9, 421
    discontinued operations 331
    distributable profits 228–9
    earnings per share (EPS) 112, 133–4, 331–4, 426
    matching revenue with expenses 38–40, 43, 147
    measurement 300
    non-recurring items 330–1
property see land and buildings
proportional consolidation 280–1
provisions 99, 101, 147–8, 217, 223–5, 229–32, 427
    Fourth Directive 223–4
prudence 36, 42, 43
public companies 51, 52
public information 5, 116
pyramid of ratios 135–6

quick assets ratio 130

rates of tax 237, 240–1
ratio analysis 116–42
    deferred tax 245
    funds' management ratios 131–3

ratio analysis (*continued*)
  industry-specific considerations 135
  interest cover 130–1
  investment ratios 133–4
  liquidity ratios 129–30
  PE ratios 112, 335–6
  profit ratios 119–22
  profitability ratios 122–9
  pyramid of ratios 135–6
  *see also* financial appraisal
raw materials 195–6
realization convention 158
receivables 18, 19, 98, 100, 215–18
  doubtful 217, 390
  short-term 217
  valuation 218
recognition of assets 148–52
  financial 215, 218, 220–1, 427
  intangible 165–6
  tangible 167
recognition of income 157–60
reducing balance depreciation 176–8, 180
regional taxes 240
regulation 7–9, 48–60
  Australia 57
  business entities 37, 50–3
  China 57
  European Union 8, 49, 53–6, 58
  France 54
  GAAP 56–7, 57–8, 364, 367–71
  Germany 53–4
  international standards 58
  Netherlands 54, 56
  Nordic countries 57
  United Kingdom 56
  United States 56–7
  *see also* legal systems
related party disclosure 424
relevance 40–1
reliability 41–2, 44
remuneration schemes 359–60
repairs and maintenance 147–8, 153, 155
replacement cost 156, 174–5, 206, 302–4, 308, 313–16
research and development 150, 368
reserves 99, 101, 217, 229–32
  hidden 231
  legal 228
  revaluation 228
  secret 231
residual values 182
restructuring costs 368
retail inventory 203–4
retail prices index 299

retirement benefit plans 424
return on capital employed (ROCE) 125–9
return on equity (ROE) 124–5, 127–9
revaluation of assets 160, 185–8
  depreciation of revalued assets 186
  financial assets 220–1
  gains as other comprehensive income 186
  gains on sale 187
  government-controlled 319
  by management 319–20
revaluation method of depreciation 178–9
revaluation reserve 228
revenue 21, 24, 105, 423
  matching with expenses 38–40, 43, 147
roll-over relief 239
Roman codified law 49, 74
Royal Bank of Scotland 332, 333
rules of recording 375–80

sales costs *see* cost accounting
SAP 293
SEC (Securities and Exchange Commission) 56–7
secret reserves 231
segment reporting 110–11, 429–30
share capital 295
  buy-backs 227
  equity compared to debt 232–3
  non-voting shares 226
  par value 227
  preference shares 128–9, 226–7
  subscribed capital 152, 226–7
  subsidiary companies 273–4
  treasury shares 227
  voting shares 265–7
share options 369
share premium account 227–8
share-based payments 428
shareholders 71, 74
  classes 128–9, 226
  ordinary 226
short-term receivables 217
significant influence 269, 283
small and medium-sized enterprises 58, 89
social security taxes 240
sole traders 50, 236
Spain 319
specific price adjustments 305–9
standard cost 203
standardisation 80
standards
  FASB 36, 44, 57
  *Framework for Financial Statements* 5–6, 35–6, 38, 44

FRS 15 (depreciation) 171
GAAP 56–7, 57–8, 364, 367–71
IASB 8–9, 44, 85–9
    see also IFRSs
IASC 8–9, 36, 85–6
regulation 7–9, 48–60
statement of changes in equity 108
stock exchanges 52, 72–3
straight-line depreciation 172, 179
subscribed capital 152, 226–7
subsidiaries 53, 264–7
    share capital 273–4
    see also group accounting
substance over form 169
suppliers 5, 116
survey data 65

tangible assets 98, 100, 164
    recognition 167
taxation 48, 75–6, 78–9, 235–48
    accounting profit and taxable profit
        237, 238
    and asset values 236
    bookkeeping 393
    business licence tax 240
    capital gains 239
    classification of tax bases 238
    deferred tax 241–5
    and depreciation 175–6, 239, 242–3
    dividends 237, 239–40
    economic double taxation 237
    history of company tax 236–7
    IAS 12 (income taxes) 421–2
    and inflation 304
    interest payments 239–40
    international differences 236,
        237–40
        France 240
        Germany 236, 238, 240, 242
    payroll taxes 240
    rates of tax 237, 243–41
    regional taxes 240
    social security taxes 240

timing of payments 238
    and wars 237
temporal currency translation 292–3
terminology 9, 184–5, 355–8
timeliness 41
Total Oil 356–7
trading accounts 381–5
treasury shares 227
trial balance 380, 392–6
true and fair view 81, 82–5

understandability 41
unit costs 198–9
United Kingdom 56
United States 56–7
uniting of interests 279–80
usage method of depreciation 178
useful economic life 181–2
users of accounts 4–7, 35–6, 116

valuation 152–7, 188, 189
    through expectations 339–40
    harmonization of principles 82–3
    inventories 210
    investment properties 160, 185, 188–9
    investments 219–20
    market values 343–41
    provisions 225
    receivables 218
    see also revaluation of assets
value in use 156, 183
Variable Interest Entities 371
Volkswagen 150
voting shares 265–7

wages 19, 21–2, 25
wars 237
weighted average costing 204–5
work-in-progress 195–6
working capital ratio 130
written-down value 172

Zeneca 279